Readings in
Distributed Computing Systems

Readings in Distributed Computing Systems

Thomas L. Casavant
and
Mukesh Singhal

IEEE Computer Society Press
Los Alamitos, California

Washington • Brussels • Tokyo

Library of Congress Cataloging-in-Publication Data

Casavant, Thomas.
    Readings in Distributed Computing Systems / Thomas Casavant and Mukesh Singhal.
        p.   cm. — (A Computer Society Press tutorial)
    Includes bibliographical references.
    ISBN 0-8186-3032-9 (case). — ISBN 0-8186-3031-0 (fiche)
    1. Electronic data processing — Distributed processing.
I. Singhal, Mukesh.   II. Title.   III. Series: IEEE Computer Society Press tutorial.
QA76.9.D5C35   1994
004' .36 — dc20   92-40164
                                                       CIP

Published by the
IEEE Computer Society Press
10662 Los Vaqueros Circle
P.O. Box 3014
Los Alamitos, CA 90720-1264

IEEE Computer Society Press Order Number 3032
Library of Congress Number 92-40164
IEEE Catalog Number EH0359-0
ISBN 0-8186-3031-0 (microfiche)
ISBN 0-8186-3032-9 (case)

Additional copies can be ordered from

IEEE Computer Society Press	IEEE Service Center	IEEE Computer Society	IEEE Computer Society
Customer Service Center	445 Hoes Lane	13, avenue de l'Aquilon	Ooshima Building
10662 Los Vaqueros Circle	P.O. Box 1331	B-1200 Brussels	2-19-1 Minami-Aoyama
P.O. Box 3014	Piscataway, NJ 08855-1331	BELGIUM	Minato-ku, Tokyo 107
Los Alamitos, CA 90720-1264	Tel: (908) 981-1393	Tel: +32-2-770-2198	JAPAN
Tel: (714) 821-8380	Fax: (908) 981-9667	Fax: +32-2-770-8505	Tel: +81-3-3408-3118
Fax: (714) 821-4641			Fax: +81-3-3408-3553
Email: cs.books@computer.org			

Technical editors: Jon T. Butler and V. Rao Vemuri
Production editor/copy editor: Phyllis Walker
Book layout: Diamond Disc, Christopher Patterson
Cover design/book design: VB Designs, Toni Van Buskirk
Cover photography: The Stock Market/Tom Sanders © 1990
Printed in the United States of America by Braun-Brumfield, Inc.

The Institute of Electrical and Electronics Engineers, Inc.

Foreword

This is the third of our *Readings in* volumes, a series published by the IEEE Computer Society Press. Our intent is to provide, in one text, tutorial and intermediate material on developing areas in computer science and engineering. A unique aspect of this series is its origin. Each volume is developed from a special issue of *Computer* magazine, the IEEE Computer Society's flagship periodical. That is, the editors have chosen papers to produce both a special issue of *Computer* and, subsequently, a *Readings in* volume. The papers in *Computer* provide a tutorial introduction to the subject matter and target an audience with a broad background. The papers in our *Readings in* series provide a wider perspective of the subject and significantly greater coverage.

The *Readings in* series is appropriate for (1) students in senior- and graduate-level courses, (2) engineers seeking a convenient way to improve their knowledge, and (3) managers wishing to augment their technical expertise. The guiding principle motivating this series is the delivery of the most up-to-date information in emerging fields. Because computer scientists and engineers deal with rapidly changing technology, they need access to tutorial descriptions of new and promising developments. Our *Readings in* texts will satisfy that need.

Papers chosen for this volume were judged on their technical content, quality, and clarity of exposition. As with other Computer Society Press products, this text has undergone thorough review. In addition, all of the previously published papers had to pass *Computer* magazine's strict review process.

We wish to thank all who have contributed to this effort: the authors, who devoted substantial effort to produce the high quality required for their papers to be selected, and our referees, who donated their expertise and time to evaluate the manuscripts and provide feedback to the authors. A special acknowledgment is due the editors, Thomas L. Casavant and Mukesh Singhal, whose time and energies were required to read the papers, direct an extensive administrative effort, coordinate referee reports, select final papers, and secure timely and high-quality revisions.

Jon T. Butler and

V. Rao Vemuri

Preface

The major impetus for this text was the overwhelming response to our call for papers for the August 1991 special issue of *Computer* magazine on distributed computing systems. Over 117 authors, some very well known, submitted papers of excellent quality. Since *Computer* could publish only seven of these papers because of space limitations, we viewed this as an ideal opportunity to publish a tutorial text on the subject. As an introduction and foundation to the subject, we took the seven papers that *Computer* had selected, and then we added 24 other papers to provide significantly broader coverage for specialists and nonspecialists alike.

Distributed computing systems has emerged as an active research area, with both the number of researchers in the field and the number of distributed system prototypes increasing dramatically. This unprecedented interest can be judged from the increase in

Thomas L. Casavant and

Mukesh Singhal

- Professional meetings: There many international conferences, symposia, and workshops that focus totally on distributed computing systems, such as the International Conference on Distributed Computing Systems, the ACM Symposium on Principles of Distributed Computing, and the IEEE Workshop on Parallel and Distributed Systems. Other conferences, such as the International Conference on Parallel Processing and the Computer Software and Applications Conference (COMPSAC), now devote tracks solely to distributed computing systems.
- Journals: Journals dedicated to the topic of distributed computing systems include *Distributed Computing,* by Springer-Verlag; *IEEE Transactions on Parallel and Distributed Systems*; and the *Journal of Parallel and Distributed Computing*, by Academic Press. Other journals covering the topic as a regular subject include *IEEE Transactions on Software Engineering; ACM Transactions on Computer Systems;* and *Real-Time Systems*, by Kluwer Academic Publishers. Several journals have devoted special issues to distributed computing systems, including *IEEE*

Transactions on Software Engineering, January 1987; *IEEE Transactions on Computers*, December 1988 and August 1989; *Algorithmica*, 1988; and *Computer*, August 1991.
- Industrial push: Industries and universities have developed a number of prototype implementations of distributed systems, including Mach at Carnegie Mellon University; V-Kernel at Stanford University; Sprite at the University of California, Berkeley; Amoeba at Vrije University, Amsterdam; System R* at IBM; Locus at the University of California, Los Angeles; VAX-Cluster at Digital Equipment Corporation; and the Spring Project at the University of Massachusetts-Amherst.

The purpose of this text is twofold: to present new developments in the distributed computing systems field and to summarize the current state of the art. Our goal is to provide condensed information to new researchers, as well as a unified perspective to researchers currently active in the field.

Contents

Introduction

Most readers are already familiar with distributed computing systems, at least as users. Automated teller machine networks, airline reservation systems, and on-site validation of credit cards provide three examples of the pervasiveness of distributed systems in everyday life. The computer research community relies heavily on distributed systems for electronic mail, remote login, network file systems, page swapping, and remote file transfer. The Internet electronic mail system, for example, is one of the most useful pieces of scientific infrastructure developed in the past 10 years.

Basically, a distributed computing system consists of a collection of autonomous computers connected by a communication network. The sites typically do not share memory, and communication is solely by means of message passing.

Over the past two decades, the availability of fast, inexpensive processors and advances in communication technology have made distributed computing an attractive means of information processing.

As early as 1978, Enslow[1] specified five properties for defining a distributed computing system:

Thomas L. Casavant and

Mukesh Singhal

- *Multiplicity* of general-purpose resource components, both physical and logical, that can be dynamically assigned to specific tasks;
- *Physical distribution* of the physical and logical resources by means of a communications network;
- *High-level operating system* that unifies and integrates the control of the distributed components;
- *System transparency,* which allows services to be requested by name only; and
- *Cooperative autonomy,* characterizing the operation and interaction of both physical and logical resources.

The many practical motivations for distributed systems include higher performance or throughput, increased reliability, and improved access to data over a geographically dispersed area.[2] However, pursuing these potential advantages has exposed a broad set of new problems. Ironically, attempts to exploit a feature often degrade that very feature. For example, improving reliability through redundancy immediately requires recovery mechanisms, which can themselves become a serious source of potential failure and reduce overall system reliability. During the last two decades, a number of subfields have become well established. Cutting across the subfields are two camps of researchers who see their motivations differently: One camp views distribution as a means to an end; the other views it as imposed by the situation. In the first case, distribution of resources is seen as a way to achieve some goal, such as

- Massively parallel, general-purpose, high-speed computing;
- Fault tolerance, reliability, or availability; or
- Real-time response demands.

In the second case, distributed computation is forced on a designer because of some existing, overriding situation, such as

- Distributed database systems,
- Automated manufacturing,
- Remote sensing and control, or
- Coordinated decision making.

Challenges

The issues facing the distributed-computing community divide roughly into two categories: system design issues and application-oriented issues. System design issues can be subdivided into hardware-oriented and software-oriented issues. Applications issues, which take the perspective of a system user, can be thought of as system models and programming support.

System design issues

The hardware-oriented issues of system design include hardware measures for fault tolerance, physical networks and communications protocol design, and physical clock synchronization.

Fault-tolerance mechanisms generally demand redundancy in hardware resources. For example, in the Tandem system, which is designed to meet rigid reliability and availability requirements in a database environment, each hardware component is duplicated. This demands not only hardware but also software to "roll back" the system state to the last known consistent state before component failure.

The design of physical networks and communication protocols can have a direct impact on system efficiency and reliability. For example, in the case of a system distributed throughout one building, a carrie-sense protocol on an Ethernet media is sufficient. But a space-borne system, such as the space station, requires a radio, packet-switched network to function.

The software-oriented issues of system design include distributed algorithms, naming and resource location, resource allocation, distributed operating systems, system integration, reliability, tools and languages, real-time systems, and performance measurement.

Distributed algorithms encompass many fundamental, challenging problems in distributed-systems design, including distributed mutual exclusion, distributed consensus, Byzantine agreement, deadlock handling, logical clocks, distributed snapshots, load sharing/scheduling, and crash recovery. Distributed-algorithm design is complicated by the lack of both global memory and physically synchronized clocks.

Distributed snapshots and clock synchronization have recently attracted attention as ways to compensate for the lack of global memory. A distributed-snapshot algorithm collects a partial global state of a distributed system to help identify several interesting properties. Clock-synchronization schemes compensate for the lack of a physically synchronized global clock. Fault tolerance and crash recovery are gaining importance, because distributed systems are being commercialized.

Load-sharing and distributed-scheduling techniques improve performance and efficiency by effectively distributing the work load throughout the system. Researchers are investigating load-sharing policies that are stable, efficient, and easy to implement. Distributed scheduling decomposes a task into several subtasks and allocates them over a set of processors to hasten computation by overlapping subtask execution and minimizing communication. Since optimal solutions to this problem are NP hard (even if accurate system state information were available), researchers are looking into heuristic methods.

With performance measurement and modeling techniques, performance can be predicted and potential design flaws identified before an actual system is built. Performance analysis of distributed systems has been done, primarily with analytic modeling and simulation, but it can be difficult. Thus, empirical techniques are needed to study actual performance.

As design techniques approach maturity, many companies and universities have launched projects to construct real-life distributed systems, and a number of them now have prototype implementations — for example, Mach at Carnegie Mellon University; V-Kernel at Stanford University; Sprite at the University of California, Berkeley; Amoeba at Vrije University in Amsterdam; System R* at IBM; Locus at the University of California, Los Angeles; VAX-Cluster at Digital Equipment Corporation; and the Spring Project at the University of Massachusetts-Amherst.

Application-oriented issues

From the application designer's point of view, which includes algorithmic design, the first question is "What does my system look like?" Many models have been proposed and continue to be explored. The communicating sequential process (CSP) model is a very simple synchronous message-passing model. However, as the area has matured, the loose structure of the CSP has led to more restricted paradigms, such as the rendezvous mechanism of Ada and remote procedure call. Some models have been proposed to meet the needs of specific applications — for example, the transaction model as it relates to on-line transaction processing. Other modeling issues include virtual shared memory and decisions about processor granularity.

The application designer's second concern is the practical matter of programming support. Research in this area brings reality to the models described above. This reality comes in the form of languages, operating system interfaces, and higher level abstractions for building applications such as databases (for example, the general-purpose relational database Ingres [Interactive Graphics and Retrieval System]). In addition to a means of specifying computations and communications, automated and semiautomated tools are needed to help produce, debug, and verify distributed applications. In fact, the need for tools is becoming a pervasive problem that will require a great deal of attention.

The future of distributed computing

Although distributed computing has been an active research topic for at least two decades, several design issues still face researchers and system builders.

The first issue involves theoretical aspects, including global state, logical/physical clock synchronization, and algorithm verification. Global state is necessary to compensate for the lack of global memory. A distributed-snapshot algorithm collects a global state of a distributed system that helps identify interesting properties, but the lack of global memory makes verification of distributed algorithms tedious and error-prone. Verification techniques for shared memory systems are not directly applicable to distributed-memory systems. They require other techniques (probably snapshot-based or temporal-logic based).

Second, although fault tolerance and crash recovery have already received much attention, system reliability will become even more important as distributed systems become more and more commercialized. Instead of concentrating on hardware redundancy, future research efforts should also investigate software techniques for achieving fault tolerance.

Third, tools and languages are badly needed. This area includes tools for specifying, analyzing, transforming, debugging, creating, and verifying distributed software, as well as new languages, language extensions, operating system primitives, compilation techniques, debuggers, and software-creation methods. One of the greatest challenges to users of distributed systems is the creation of reliable, working distributed software. Advances in theory, practical tools, methods, and languages are essential for building reliable and efficient distributed software.

The fourth issue is high-performance systems. Constructing massively parallel systems (10^5 or more processors) will require physically distributed memory. Topological, as well as technological, issues will continue to be important in designing interconnection networks for these systems. Technological challenges will center on optical communications and the VLSI-related issues of module integration, multichip and board layout, and packaging.

Fifth, real-time distributed systems will become more important for automated manufacturing, remote sensing and control, and other time-critical missions. Past research in real-time distributed systems emphasized efficient task-scheduling algorithms to meet task deadlines under various constraints. Future research will focus on system structuring and total system design.

Finally, as design techniques approach perfection, we will see a proliferation of actual distributed systems with significantly improved fault tolerance, resource sharing, and communications. These systems will function as single, coherent, powerful virtual machines providing transparent user access to network-wide resources.

References

1. P.H. Enslow, Jr., "What is a 'Distributed' Data Processing System?," *Computer*, Vol. 11, No. 1, Jan. 1978, pp. 13–21.
2. J.A. Stankovic, "A Perspective on Distributed Computer Systems," *IEEE Trans. Computers*, Vol. C-33, No. 12, Dec. 1984, pp. 1102–1115.

Distributed Computing Systems: An Overview

Distributed Computing

A distributed computer system (DCS) is a collection of computers connected by a communications subnet and logically integrated in varying degrees by a distributed operating system and/or distributed database system. Each computer node may be a uniprocessor, a multiprocessor, or a multicomputer. The communications subnet may be a widely geographically dispersed collection of communication processors or a local area network. Typical applications that use distributed computing include e-mail, teleconferencing, electronic funds transfers, multimedia telecommunications, command and control systems, and support for general purpose computing in industrial and academic settings. The widespread use of distributed computer systems is due to the price-performance revolution in microelectronics, the development of cost effective and efficient communication subnets [4] (which is itself due to the merging of data communications and computer communications), the development of resource sharing software, and the increased user demands for communication, economical sharing of resources, and productivity.

A DCS potentially provides significant advantages, including good performance, good reliability, good resource sharing, and extensibility [35, 41]. Potential performance enhancement is due to multiple processors and an efficient subnet, as well as avoiding contention and bottlenecks that exist in uniprocessors and multiprocessors. Potential reliability improvements are due to the data and control redundancy possible, the geographical distribution of the system, and the ability for hosts and communication processors to perform mutual inspection. With the proper subnet, distributed operating system [46], and distributed database [85], it is possible to share hardware and software resources in a cost effective manner, increasing productivity and lowering costs. Possibly the most important potential advantage of a DCS is extensibility. Extensibility is the ability to easily adapt to both short- and long-term changes without significant disruption of the system. Short-term changes include varying work loads and host or subnet failures or additions. Long-term changes are associated with major modifications to the requirements or content of the system.

DCS research encompasses many areas, including local- and

John A. Stankovic

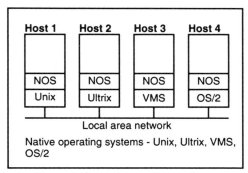

Figure 1. Network operating systems.

wide-area networks, distributed operating systems, distributed databases, distributed file servers, concurrent and distributed programming languages, specification languages for concurrent system, theory of parallel algorithms, theory of distributed computing, parallel architectures and interconnection structures, fault tolerant and ultrareliable systems, distributed real-time systems, cooperative problem solving techniques of artificial intelligence, distributed debugging, distributed simulation, distributed applications, and a methodology for the design, construction, and maintenance of large, complex distributed systems. Many prototype distributed computer systems have been built at university, industrial, commercial, and government research laboratories, and production systems of all sizes and types have proliferated. It is impossible to survey all distributed computing systems research. An extensive survey and bibliography would require hundreds of pages. Instead, this paper focuses on two important areas: distributed operating systems and distributed databases.

Distributed operating systems

Operating systems for distributed computing systems can be categorized into two broad categories: network operating systems and distributed operating systems [113].

(1)   Network operating systems. Consider the situation where each of the hosts of a computer network has a local operating system that is independent of the network. The sum total of all the operating system software added to each host in order to communicate and share resources is called a network operating system (NOS). The added software often includes modifications to the local operating system. NOSs are characterized by being built on top of existing operating systems, and they attempt to hide the differences between the underlying systems, as shown in Figure 1.

(2)   Distributed operating systems. Consider an integrated computer network where there is one native operating system for all the distributed hosts. This is called a distributed operating system (DOS). See Figure 2. Examples of DOSs include the V system [28], Eden [66], Amoeba [78], the Cambridge distributed computing system [79], Medusa [83], Locus [87], and Mach [93]. Examples of real-time distributed operating systems include MARS [59] and Spring [116]. A DOS is designed with the network requirements in mind from its inception and it tries to manage the resources of the network in a global fashion. Therefore, retrofitting a DOS to existing operating systems and other software is not a problem for DOSs. Since DOSs are used to satisfy a wide variety of requirements, their various implementations are quite different.

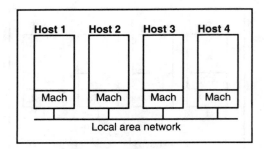

Figure 2. Distributed operating system — Mach.

Note that the boundary between NOSs and DOSs is not always clearly distinguishable. In this paper we primarily consider distributed operating systems issues divided into six categories: process structures, access control and communication, reliability, heterogeneity, efficiency, and real-time. In the section entitled "Distributed databases," we present a similar breakdown applied to distributed databases.

Process structures

The conventional notion of a process is an address space with a single execution trace through it. Because of the parallelism inherent in multiprocessing and distributed computing, we have seen that recent operating systems are supporting the separation of address space (sometimes called a task) and execution traces (called threads or lightweight processes) [93, 94]. In most systems the address space and threads are restricted to reside on a single node (a uni- or multiprocessor). However, some systems such as Ivy, the Apollo domain, and Clouds [33] support a distributed address space (sometimes called a distributed shared memory—see [82] for a summary of issues involved with distributed shared memory), and distributed threads executing on that address space. Regardless of whether the address space is local or distributed [42], there has been significant work done on the following topics: supporting very large, but sparse address spaces, efficiently copying information between address spaces using a technique called *copy on write* where only the data actually used gets copied [43], and supporting efficient file management by mapping files into the address space and then using virtual memory techniques to access the file.

At a higher level, distributed operating systems use tasks and threads to support either a procedure or an object-based paradigm [29]. If objects are used, there are two variations: the passive and active object models. Because the object-based paradigm is so important and well-suited to distributed computing, we will present some basic information about objects and then discuss the active and passive object paradigms.

A data abstraction is a collection of information and a set of operations defined on that information. An object is an instantiation of a data abstraction. The concept of an object is usually supported by a kernel that may also define a primitive set of objects. Higher level objects are then constructed from more primitive objects in some structured fashion. All hardware and software resources of a DCS can be regarded as objects. The concept of an object and its implications form an elegant basis for a DCS [83, 113]. For example, distributed systems' functions such as allocation of objects to a host, moving objects, remote access to objects, sharing objects across the network, and providing interfaces between disparate objects are all "conceptually" simple, because they are all handled by yet other objects. The object concept is powerful and can easily support the popular client-server model of distributed computing.

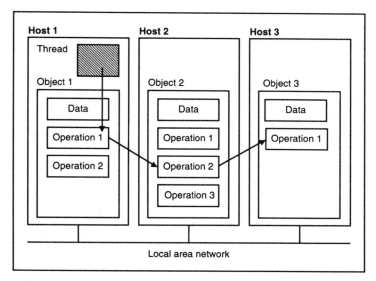

Figure 3. Distributed computation (thread through passive objects).

Objects also serve as the primitive entity supporting more complicated distributed computational structures. One type of distributed computation is a process (thread) that executes as a sequential trace through passive objects, but does so across multiple hosts, as shown in Figure 3. The objects are permanent but the execution properties are supplied by an external process (thread) executing in the address space of the object.

Another form of a distributed computation is to have clusters of objects, each with internal, active threads, running in parallel and communicating with each other based on the various types of interprocess communication (IPC) used. This is known as the active object model (see Figure 4). The cluster of processes may be colocated, or distributed in some fashion. Other notions of what constitutes a distributed program are possible; for example, object invocations can support additional semantics (such as found in database transactions).

The major problem with object-based systems has been poor execution time performance. However, this is not really a problem with the object abstraction itself, but with inefficient implementation of access to objects. The most common reason given for poor execution time is that current architectures are ill-suited for object-based systems. Another problem is choosing the right granularity for an object. If every integer or character and their associated operations are treated as objects, then the overhead is too high. If the granularity of an object is too large, then the benefits of the object-based system are lost.

Access control and communications

A distributed system consists of a collection of resources managed by the distributed operating system. Accessing the resources must be controlled in two ways. First, the manner used to access the resource must be suitable to the resource and requirements under consideration. For example, a printer must be shared serially, local data of an object should not be shareable, and a read-only file can be accessed simultaneously by any number of users. In an object-based system, access can be controlled on an operation-by-operation basis. For example, a given user may be restricted to only using the insert operation on a queue object, while another user may be able to access the queue using both insert and remove operations. Second, access to a resource must be restricted to a set

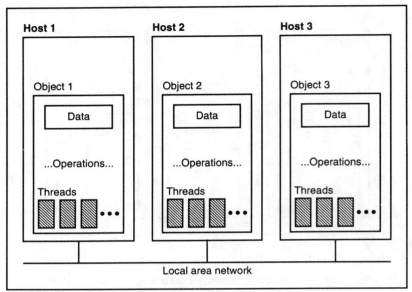

Figure 4. Local area network — Active objects.

of allowable users. In many systems this is done by an access control list, an access control matrix, or capabilities. The MIT Athena project developed an authentication server called Kerberos based on a third party authentication model [80] that uses private key encryption.

Communication has been the focus of much of the work in distributed operating systems, providing the glue that binds logically and physically separated processes [54, 92]. Remote procedure calls (RPCs) extend the semantics of programming language's procedure calls to communication across nodes of a DCS. Lightweight RPCs [18] have been developed to make such calls as efficient as possible. Many systems also support general synchronous and asynchronous send and receive primitives whose semantics are different and more general than RPC semantics. Broadcasting and multicasting are also common primitives found in DOSs and they provide useful services in achieving consensus and other forms of global coordination. For systems with high reliability requirements, reliable broadcast facilities might be provided [55].

Implementing communication facilities is done either directly in the kernels of the operating systems (as in the V system [28]), or as user-level services (as in MACH [93]). This is a classical trade-off between performance and flexibility. Intermediate between these approaches lies the x-kernel [54] where basic primitives required for all communication primitives are provided at the kernel level and protocol-specific logic is programmable at a higher level.

Reliability

While reliability is a fundamental issue for any system, the redundancy found in DCSs makes them particularly well-suited for the implementation of reliability techniques. We begin the discussion on reliability with a few definitions.

A *fault* is a mechanical or algorithmic defect that may generate an error. A fault may be permanent, transient, or intermittent. An *error* is an item of information which, when processed by the normal algorithms of the system, will produce a failure. A *failure* is an event at which a system violates its specifications. *Reliability* can then be defined as the degree of tolerance against errors and faults. Increased reliability comes from fault avoidance and fault tolerance. *Fault avoidance* results from conservative design practices such as using high reliability components and nonambitious design. *Fault tolerance* employs error detection and redundancy to deal with faults and errors. Most of what we discuss here relates to the fault tolerance aspect of reliability.

Reliability is a complex, multidimensional activity that must simultaneously address some or all of the following: fault confinement, fault detection, fault masking, retries, fault diagnosis, reconfiguration, recovery, restart, repair, and reintegration. Further, distributed systems require more than reliability — they need to be dependable. Dependability is the trustworthiness of a computer system and it subsumes reliability, availability, safety, and security. System architectures such as Delta-4 [88] strive for dependability. We cannot do justice to all these issues in this short paper. Instead we will discuss several of the more important issues related to reliability in DOSs.

Reliable DOSs should support replicated files, exception handlers, testing procedures executed from remote hosts, and avoid single points of failure by a combination of replication, backup facilities, and distributed control. Distributed control could be used for file servers, name servers, scheduling algorithms, and other executive control functions. Process structure, how environment information is kept, the homogeneity of various hosts, and the scheduling algorithm may allow for relocatability of processes. Interprocess communication (IPC) might be supported as a reliable remote procedure call [81, 109] and also provide reliable atomic broadcasts as is done in Isis [19]. Reliable IPC would enforce "at least once" or "exactly once" semantics depending on the type of IPC being invoked, and atomic broadcasts guarantee that either all processes that are to receive the message will indeed receive it, or none will. Other DOS reliability solutions are required to avoid invoking processes that are not active, to avoid the situation where a process remains active but is not used, and to avoid attempts to communicate with terminated processes.

ARGUS [70], a distributed programming language, has incorporated reliability concerns into the programming language explicitly. It does this by supporting the idea of an atomic object, transactions, nested actions, reliable remote procedure calls, stable variables, guardians (which are modules that service node failures and synchronize concurrent access to data), exception handlers, periodic and background testing procedures, and recovery of a committed update given the present update does not complete. A distributed program written in ARGUS may potentially experience deadlock. Currently, deadlocks are broken by timing out and aborting actions.

Distributed databases make use of many reliability features such as stable storage, transactions, nested transactions [76], commit and recovery protocols [103], nonblocking commit protocols [102], termination protocols [104], checkpointing, replication, primary/backups, logs/audit trails, differential files [99], and time-outs to detect failures. Operating system support is required to make these mechanisms more efficient [47, 87, 119, 131] .

One aspect of reliability not stressed enough in DCS research is the need for robust solutions, that is, the solutions must explicitly assume an unreliable network, tolerate host failures, network partitionings, and lost, duplicate, out-of-order, or noisy data. Robust algorithms must sometimes make decisions after reaching only approximate agreement or by using statistical properties of the system (assumed known or dynamically calculated). A related question is, at what level should the robust algorithms, and reliability in general, be supported? Most systems attempt to have the subnet ensure reliable, error-free data transmission between processes. However, according to the end-to-end argument [97], such functions placed at the lower levels of the system are often redundant and unnecessary. The rationale for this argument is that since the application has to take into account errors introduced not only by the subnet, many of the error detection and recovery functions can be correctly and completely provided only at the application level.

The relationship of reliability to the other issues discussed in this paper is very strong. For example, object-based systems confine errors to a large degree, define a consistent system state to support rollback and restart, and limit propagation of rollback activities. However, if objects are supported on a distributed shared memory, special problems arise [134]. Since objects can represent unreliable resources (such as processors and disks), and since higher level objects can be built using lower level objects, the goal of reliable system design is to create "reliable" objects out of unreliable objects. For example, a stable storage can be created out of several disk objects and the proper logic. Then a physical processor, a checkpointing capability, a stable storage, and logic can be used to create a stable processor. One can proceed in this fashion to create a very reliable system. The main drawback is potential loss of execution time efficiency. For many systems, it is just too costly to incorporate an extensive number of reliability mechanisms. Reliability is also enhanced by proper access control and judicial use of distributed control. The major challenge is to integrate solutions to all these issues in a cost effective manner and produce an extremely reliable system.

Heterogeneity

Incompatibility problems arise in heterogeneous DCSs in a number of ways [10], and at all levels. First, incompatibility is due to the different internal formatting schemes that exist in a collection of different communication and host processors. Second, incompatibility also arises from the differences in communication protocols and topology when networks are connected to other networks via gateways. Third, major incompatibilities arise due to different operating systems, file servers, and database systems that might exist on a network or a set of networks.

The easiest solution to this general problem for a single DCS is to avoid the issue by using a homogeneous collection of machines and software. If this is not practical, then some form of translation is necessary. Some earlier systems left this translation to the user. This is no longer acceptable.

Translation done by the DCS system can be done at the receiver host or at the source host. If it is done at the receiver host, then the data traverse the network in their original form. The data usually are supplemented with extra information to guide the translation. The problem with this approach is that at every host there must be a translator to convert each format in the system to the format used on the receiving host. When there exist n different formats, this requires the support of $(n - 1)$ translators at each host. Performing the translation at the source host before transmitting the data is subject to all the same problems.

There are two better solutions, each applicable under different situations: an intermediate translator, or an intermediate standard data format.

An intermediate translator accepts data from the source and produces the acceptable format for the destination. This is usually used when the number of different types of necessary conversions is small. For example, a gateway linking two different networks acts as an intermediate translator.

For a given conversion problem, if the number of different types to be dealt with grows large, then a single intermediate translator becomes unmanageable. In this case, an intermediate standard data format (interface) is declared, hosts convert to the standard, data are moved in the format of the standard, and another conversion is performed at the destination. By choosing the standard to be the most common format in the system, the number of conversions can be reduced.

At a high level of abstraction the heterogeneity problem and the necessary translations are well understood. At the implementation level a number of complications exist. The issues are precision loss, format incompatibilities (minus zero value in sign magnitude, and 1's complement cannot be represented in 2's complement), data type incompatibilities (mapping of an upper- or lower-case terminal to an upper-case-only terminal is a loss of information), efficiency concerns, the number and locations of the translators, and what constitutes a good intermediate data format for a given incompatibility problem.

As DCSs become more integrated, one can expect that both programs and complicated forms of data might be moved to heterogeneous hosts. How will a program run on this host, given that the host has different word lengths, different machine code, and different operating system primitives? How will database relations stored as part of a CODASYL database be converted to a relational model and its associated storage scheme? Moving a data-structure object requires knowledge about the semantics of the structure (for example, that some of the fields are pointers and these have to be updated upon a move). How should this information be imparted to the translators, what are the limitations, if any, and what are the benefits and costs of having this kind of flexibility? In general, the problem of providing translation for movement of data and programs between heterogeneous hosts and networks has not been solved. The main problem is ensuring that such programs and data are interpreted correctly at the destination host. In fact, the more difficult problems in this area have been largely ignored.

The Open Systems Foundation (OSF) distributed computing environment (DCE) is attempting to address the problem of programming and managing heterogeneous distributed-computer systems by establishing a set of standards for the major components of such systems. This includes standards for RPCs, distributed file servers, and distributed management.

Efficiency

Distributed computer systems are meant to be efficient in a multitude of ways. Resources (files, compilers, debuggers, and other software products) developed at one host can be shared by users on other hosts, limiting duplicate efforts. Expensive hardware resources can also be shared, minimizing costs. Communication facilities, such as the remote procedure call, electronic mail, and file transfer protocols, also improve efficiency by enabling better and faster transfer of information. The multiplicity of processing elements might also be exploited to improve response time and throughput of user processes. While efficiency concerns exist at every level in the system, they must also be treated as an integrated "system" level issue. For example, a good design, the proper trade-offs between levels, and the pairing down of over-ambitious features usually improves efficiency. Here we will concentrate on discussing efficiency as it relates to the execution time of processes (threads).

Once the system is operational, improving response time and throughput of user processes (threads) is largely the responsibility of scheduling and resource management algorithms [6, 30, 32, 39, 75, 111, 112, 126], and the mechanisms used to move processes and data [28, 33, 42, 127]. The scheduling algorithm is intimately related to the resource allocator because a process will not be scheduled for the CPU if it is waiting for a resource. If a DCS is to exploit the multiplicity of processors and resources in the network, it must contain more than simply n independent schedulers. The local schedulers must interact and cooperate, and the degree to which this occurs can vary widely. We suggest that a good scheduling algorithm for a DCS will be a heuristic that acts like an "expert system." This expert system's task is to effectively utilize the resources of the entire distributed system given a complex and dynamically changing environment. We hope to illustrate this in the following discussion.

In the remainder of this section when we refer to the scheduling algorithm, we are referring to the part of the scheduler (possibly an expert system) that is responsible for choosing the host of execution for a process. We assume that there is another part of the scheduler that assigns the local CPU to the highest priority-ready process.

We divide the characteristics of a DCS that influence response time and throughput into system characteristics and scheduling algorithm characteristics. System characteristics include the number, type, and speed of processors, caches, and memories; the allocation of data and programs; whether data and programs can be moved; the amount and location of replicated data and programs; how data are partitioned; partitioned functionality in the form of dedicated processors; any special-purpose hardware; characteristics of the communication subnet; and special problems of distribution such as no central clock and the inherent delays in the system. A good scheduling algorithm would take the system characteristics into account. Scheduling algorithm characteristics include the type and amount of state information used, how and when that information is transmitted, how the information is used (degree and type of cooperation between distributed scheduling entities), when the algorithm is invoked, adaptability of the algorithm, and the stability of the algorithm [24, 110].

The type of state information used by scheduling algorithms includes queue lengths, CPU utilization, amount of free memory, estimated average response time, or combinations of various information in making its scheduling decision. The type of information also refers to whether the information is local or networkwide information. For example, a scheduling algorithm on host 1 could use queue lengths of all the hosts in the network in making its decision. The amount of state information refers to the number of different types of information used by the scheduler.

Information used by a scheduler can be transmitted periodically or asynchronously. If asynchronously, it may be sent only when requested (as in bidding), it may be piggybacked on other messages between hosts, or it may be sent only when conditions change by some amount. The information may be broadcast to all hosts, sent to neighbors only, or to some specific set of hosts.

The information is used to estimate the loads on other hosts of the network in order to make an informed global scheduling decision. However, the data received are out of date and even the ordering of events might not be known [63]. It is necessary to manipulate the data in some way to obtain better estimates. Several examples are very old data can be discarded (given that state information is time stamped, a linear estimation of the state extrapolated to the current time might be feasible); conditional probabilities on the accuracy of the state information might be calculated in parallel with the scheduler by some monitor nodes and applied to the received state information; the estimates can be some function of the age of the state information; or some form of (iterative) message interchange might be feasible.

Before a process is actually moved, the cost of moving it must be accounted for in determining the estimated benefit of the move. This cost is different if the process has not yet begun execution than if it is already in progress. In both cases, the resources required must also be considered. If a process is in execution, then environment information (like the process control block) probably should be moved with the process. It is expected that in many cases the decision will be not to move the process.

Schedulers invoked too often will produce excessive overhead. If they are not invoked often enough, they will not be able to react fast enough to changing conditions. There will be undue start-up delay for processes. There must be some ideal invocation schedule that is a function of the load.

In a complicated DCS environment, it can be expected that the scheduler will have to be quite adaptive [74, 110]. A scheduler might make minor adjustments in weighing the importance of various factors as the network state changes in an attempt to track a slowly changing environment. Major changes in the network state might require major adjustments in the scheduling algorithms. For example, under very light loads, there does not seem to be much justification for networkwide scheduling, so the algorithm might be turned off — except the part that can recognize a change in the load. At moderate loads, the full-blown scheduling algorithm might be employed. This might include an individual host refusing all requests for information, and refusing to accept any process because it is too busy. Under heavy loads on all hosts, it again seems unnecessary to use networkwide scheduling. A bidding scheme might use both source and server directed bidding [112]. An overloaded hosts asks for bids and is the source of work for some other hosts in the network. Similarly, a lightly loaded host may make a reverse bid (ask the rest of the network for some work). The two types of bidding might coexist. Schedulers could be designed in a multilevel fashion with decisions being made at different rates — local decisions and state information updates occur frequently, but more global exchange of decisions and state information might proceed at a slower rate because of the inherent cost of these global actions.

A classic efficiency question in any system is what should be supported by the kernel, or more generally by the operating system, and what should be left to the user? The trend in DCS is to provide minimal support at the kernel level — for example, supporting objects, primitive IPC mechanisms, and processes (threads). Then other operating system functions are supported as higher level processes. On the other hand, because of efficiency concerns some researchers advocate putting more in the kernel, including communication protocols, real-time systems support, or even supporting the concept of a transaction in the kernel. This argument will never be settled conclusively since it is a function of the requirements and types of processes running.

Of course, many other efficiency questions remain. These include the efficiency of the object model, the end-to-end argument, locking granularity, performance of remote operations, improvements due to distributed control, the cost effectiveness of various reliability mechanisms, efficiently dealing with heterogeneity, hardware support for operating system functions [7], and handling the I/0 bottleneck via disk arrays of various types called RAID 1 through 6 [56, 86] (redundant arrays of inexpensive disks). Efficiency is not a separate issue, but must be addressed for each issue in order to result in an efficient, reliable, and extensible DCS. A difficult question to answer is exactly what is acceptable performance, given that multiple decisions are being made at all levels and that these decisions are being made in the presence of missing and inaccurate information.

Real-time applications

Real-time applications such as nuclear power plants and process control are inherently distributed and have severe real-time and reliability requirements. These requirements add considerable complication to a DCS. Examples of demanding real-time systems include ESS [13], REBUS [9], and SIFT [132]. ESS is a software-controlled electronic switching system developed by the Bell System for placing telephone calls. The system meets severe real-time and reliability requirements. REBUS is a fault-tolerant distributed system for industrial real-time control, and SIFT is a fault-tolerant flight control system. Generally, these systems are built with technology that is tailored to these applications, because many of the concepts and ideas used in general purpose distributed computing are not applicable when deadlines must be guaranteed. For example, remote procedure calls, creating tasks and threads, and requesting operating system services are all done in a manner that ignores deadlines, causes processes to block at any time, and only provides reasonable average case performance. None of these things are reasonable when it is critical that deadlines be met. In fact, many misconceptions [115] exist when dealing with distributed, real-time systems. However, significant new research efforts are now being conducted to combat these misconceptions and to provide a science of real-time computing in the areas of formal verification, scheduling theory and algorithms [72, 91], communications protocols [8, 135], and operating systems [98, 116, 125]. The goal of this new research in real-time systems is to develop predictable systems even when the systems are highly complex, distributed, and operate in nondeterministic environments [117].

Other distributed real-time applications such as airline reservation and banking applicants have less severe real-time constraints and are easier to build. These systems can utilize most of the general- purpose distributed computing technology described in this paper, and generally approach the problem as if real-time computing were equivalent to fast computing, which is false. While this seems to be common practice, some additions are required to deal with real-time constraints; for example, scheduling algorithms may give preference to processes with earlier deadlines or processes holding a resource may be aborted if a process with a more urgent deadline requires the resource. Results from the more demanding real-time systems may also be applicable to these *soft* real-time systems.

Distributed databases

Database systems have existed for many years providing significant benefits in high availability and reliability, reduced costs, good performance, and ease of sharing information. Most are built using what can be called a database architecture [34, 85] (see Figure 5). The architecture includes a query language for users, a data model that describes the information content of the database as seen by the users, a schema (the definition of the structure, semantics and constraints on the use of the database), a mapping that describes the physical storage structure used to implement the data model, a description of how the physical data will be accessed, and, of course, the data (database) itself. All these components are then integrated into a collection of software that handles all accesses to the database. This software is called the database management system (DBMS). The DBMS usually supports a transaction model. In this section, we discuss various transaction structures, access and concurrency control, reliability, heterogeneity, efficiency techniques, and real-time distributed databases.

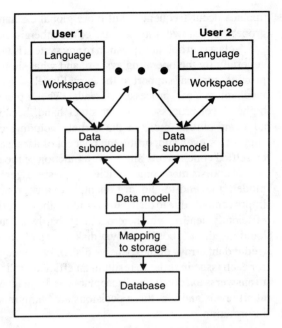

Figure 5. Database architecture.

Transaction structures

A transaction is an abstraction that allows programmers to group a sequence of actions on the database into a logical execution unit [17, 58, 65, 107]. Transactions either commit or abort. If the transaction successfully completes all its work, the transaction commits. A transaction that aborts does so without completing its operations, and any effect of executed actions must be undone. Transactions have four properties, known as the ACID properties: atomicity, consistency, isolation, and durability. *Atomicity* means that either the entire transaction completes, or it is as if the transaction never executed. *Consistency* means that the transaction maintains the integrity constraints of the database. *Isolation* means that even if transactions execute concurrently, their results appear as if they were executed in some serial order. *Durability* means that all changes made by a committed transaction are permanent.

A distributed database is a *single* logical database, but it is physically distributed over many sites (nodes). A distributed database management system (DBMS) controls access to the distributed data supporting the ACID properties, but with the added complication imposed by the physical distribution. For example, a user may issue a transaction that updates various data that, transparent to the user, physically reside on many different nodes [118]. The software that supports the ACID properties of transactions must then interact with all these nodes in a manner that is consistent with the ACID properties. This usually requires supporting remote node slave transactions, distributed concurrency control, recovery, and commit protocols.

There have been many papers and books written about these basic aspects of distributed database management systems [15, 16, 17, 58, 85]. Rather than discussing these basic issues, we will discuss some of the extended transaction models that have been recently developed.

The traditional transaction model, while powerful because of its ability to mask the effects of failures and concurrency, has shortcomings when applied to complex applications such as computer-aided design, computer-aided software engineering, distributed operating systems, and multimedia databases. In these applications, there is a need for greater functionality and performance than can be achieved with traditional transactions. For example, two programmers working on a joint programming project may wish for their transactions to be cooperative and to see partial results of the other user, rather than being competitive and isolated, properties exhibited by the traditional transaction model. Also, traditional transactions only exploit very simple semantics (such as read-only and write-only semantics) of the transactions in order to achieve greater concurrency and performance.

Many extended transaction models have been proposed to support the greater functionality and performance required by complex applications. These include nested transactions [76, 89], multilevel transactions [77, 11], cooperative transactions [60], compensating transactions [61], recoverable communicating actions [128], split transactions [90], and sagas [44, 45]. Each of these transaction models has different semantics with respect to visibility, consistency, recovery and permanence in their attempt to be useful for various complex applications. As an example, a nested transaction is composed of subtransactions that may execute concurrently. Subtransactions are serializable with respect to siblings and other nonrelated transactions. Subtransactions are failure atomic with respect to their parent transaction. A subtransaction can abort without necessarily causing the parent to abort. The other extended models have features such as relaxing serializability or failure atomicity, may have structures other than hierarchical, and may exhibit different abort dependencies. The relationship and utility of these models is currently being explored. In this regard, a comprehensive and flexible framework called ACTA [31], has been developed to provide a formal description and a reasoning procedure for the properties of all these extended transaction models.

There is another dimension along which traditional transactions have changed for complex applications. Initially, traditional transactions were considered as performing simple read or write operations on the database. However, there has been a merger of ideas from object-based programming and database systems, resulting in object-based databases [14, 22, 73]. Here, transactions and extended transactions perform higher level operations on objects that reside in the database. Using object-based databases provides more support for complex applications than having to work with simple read and write operations.

Access and concurrency control

Most access control in distributed databases is supported by the underlying operating system. In particular, it is the operating system that verifies that a database user is who he claims to be and that controls which user is allowed to read or write various data. Users are typically grouped so that each group has the same rights. Maintaining and updating the various rights assigned to each group is nontrivial, and is exacerbated when heterogeneous databases are considered.

In a database system, multiple transactions will be executing in parallel and may conflict over the use of data. Protocols for resolving data access conflicts between transactions are called concurrency control protocols [5, 15, 62, 67, 123]. The correctness of a concurrency control protocol is usually based on the concept of serializability [16]. Serializability means that the effect of a set of executed transactions (permitted to run in parallel) must be the same as some serial execution of that set of transactions. In many cases — and at all levels — the strict condition of serializability is not required. Relaxing this requirement can usually result in access techniques that are more efficient in the sense of allowing more parallelism and faster execution times. Due to space limitations we will not discuss these extensions here. See [129, 130].

Three major classes of concurrency control protocols are: locking, time stamp ordering [95], and validation (also called the optimistic approach [62]). Locking is a well-known technique. In the database context the most common form of locking is called two-phase locking. See [16] for a description of this protocol.

Time stamp ordering is an approach where all accesses to data are time stamped, and then some common rule is followed by all transactions in such a way as to ensure serializability [123]. This technique can be useful at all levels of a system, especially if time stamps are already being generated for other reasons, such as to detect lost messages or failed hosts. A variation of the time-stamp-ordering approach is the multiversion approach. This approach is interesting because it integrates concurrency control with recovery. In this scheme, each change to the database results in a new version. Concurrency control is enforced on a version basis, and old versions serve as checkpoints. Handling multiple versions efficiently is accomplished by differential files [99].

Validation is a technique that permits unrestricted access to data items (resulting in no blocking and hence fast access to data), but then checks for potential conflicts at the commit point. The commit point is the time at which a transaction is sure that it will complete. This approach is useful when few conflicts are expected, because access is very fast; if most transactions are validated (due to the few conflicts), then there is also little overhead due to aborting any nonvalidated transactions. Most validation protocols assume a particular recovery scheme, and can also be considered to integrate concurrency control and recovery.

Reliability

Recovery management in distributed databases is a complex process [58, 102, 103]. Recovery is initiated due to problems such as invalid inputs, integrity violations, deadlocks, and node and media failures. All of these faults, except node failures, are addressed by simple transaction rollback. Node failures require much more complicated solutions. All solutions are based on data redundancy and make use of stable storage where past information concerning the database has been saved and can survive failures.

It is the recovery manager component of database systems that is responsible for recovery. Generally, the recovery manager must operate under six scenarios.

(1)   Under normal operation the recovery manager logs each transaction and its work, and at transaction commit time checks transaction consistency, records the commit operation on the log, and forces the log to stable storage.

(2)   If a transaction must be rolled back, the recovery manager performs the rollback to a specific checkpoint, or completely aborts the transaction (essentially a rollback to the beginning of the transaction).

(3)   If any database resource manager crashes, the recovery manager must obtain the proper log records and restore the resource manager to the most recent committed state.

(4)   After a node crash, the recovery manager must restore the state of all the resource managers at that node and resolve any outstanding distributed transactions that were using that node at the time of the crash and were not able to be resolved due to the crash.

(5)   The recovery manager is responsible for handling media recovery (such as a disk crash) by using an update log and archive copies or copies from other nodes if replicated data is supported by the system.

(6)   It is typical that distributed databases have recovery managers at each node that

cooperate to handle many of the previous scenarios. These recovery managers themselves may fail. Restart requires reintegrating a recovery manager into the set of active recovery managers in the distributed system.

Actually supporting all of the above scenarios is difficult and requires sophisticated strategies for what information is contained in a log, how and when to write the log, how to maintain the log over a long time period, how to undo transaction operations, how to redo transaction operations, how to utilize the archives, how and when to checkpoint, and how to interact with concurrency control and commit processing.

Many performance trade-offs arise when implementing recovery management: for example, how often and how to take checkpoints. If frequent checkpoints are taken, then recovery is faster and less work is lost. However, taking checkpoints too often significantly slows the "normal" operation of the system. Another question arises in how to efficiently log the information needed for recovery. For example, many systems perform a lazy commit, where at commit time, all the log records are created but only pushed to disk at a later time. This reduces the guarantees that the system can provide about the updates, but it improves performance.

Heterogeneity

As defined above, a distributed database is a single logical database, physically residing on multiple nodes. For a distributed database system there is a single query language, data model, schema and transaction management strategy. This is in contrast to a federated database system that is a collection of autonomous database systems integrated for cooperation. The autonomous systems may have identical query languages, data models, schemas and transaction management strategies, or they may be heterogeneous along any or all of these dimensions. The degree of integration varies from a single unified system constructed with new models for query languages and data models — for example, built on top of the autonomous components to those systems with minimal interaction and without any unified models. These latter systems are called multidatabase systems. Federated systems arise when databases are developed independently, then need to be highly integrated. Multidatabase systems arise when individual database management systems wish to retain a great degree of autonomy and only provide minimal interaction.

Heterogeneity in database systems also arises from differences in underlying operating systems or hardware, from differences in DBMSs, and from semantics of the data itself. Several examples of these forms of heterogeneity follow.

Operating systems on different machines may support different file systems, naming conventions and IPC. Hardware instruction sets, data formats, and processing components may also be different at various nodes. Each of these may give rise to differences that must be resolved for proper integration of the databases.

If DBMSs have different query languages, data models, or transaction strategies, then problems arise. For example, differences in query languages may mean that some requests become illegal when issued on data in the "other" database. Differences in data models arise from many sources, including what structures each supports (for example, relations versus record types) and from how constraints are specified. One transaction strategy might employ two-phase locking with after image logging, while another uses some form of optimistic concurrency control.

Other problems arise from semantics of the data. Semantic heterogeneity is not well understood and arises from differences in the meaning, definition, or interpretation of the related data in the various databases. For example, course grades may be defined on an [A, B, C, D, F] scale in one database and on a numerical scale in another database. How do we resolve the differences when a query fetches grades from *both* databases?

Solutions to the heterogeneity problem are usually difficult and costly both in development costs in dollars and in run-time execution costs. Differences in query languages are usually solved by mapping commands in one language to an equivalent set of commands in the other, and vice versa. If more than two query languages are involved, then an intermediate language is defined and mappings occur to and from this intermediate language. Mappings must be defined for the data model and schema integration. For example, an integrated schema would contain the description of the data described by all component schemas and the mappings between them. It is also possible to restrict what data in a given database can be seen by the federation of databases. This is sometimes called an export schema. Solutions must also be developed for query decomposition and optimization, and global transaction management in federated database systems. The complexities found here are beyond the scope of this paper. Interested readers should see [71, 101, 124].

Efficiency

Distributed database systems make use of many techniques for improving efficiency, including distributed and local query optimization, various forms of buffering, lazy evaluation, disk space allocation tailored to access requirements, the use of mapping caches, parallelism in subtransactions, and nonserializability. Parallelism in subtransactions and nonserializability have been mentioned before so these issues will not be discussed here. It is often necessary for operating systems that support databases to be specifically tailored for database functions, and if not, then the support provided by the operating system is usually inefficient. See [119] for a discussion on this issue.

To obtain good performance in distributed databases, query optimization is critical. Query optimization can be categorized as either heuristic where *ad hoc* rules transform the original query into an equivalent query that can be processed more quickly, or systematic where the estimated cost of various alternatives are computed using analytical cost models that reflect the details of the physical distributed database. In relational databases, Join, Selection, and Projection are the most time consuming and frequent operations in queries and hence most query optimizers deal with these operations. For example, a Join is one of the most time consuming relational operators because the resultant size can be equal to the product of the sizes of the original relations. The most common optimization is to first perform Projections and Selections to minimize intermediate relations to be Joined. In a distributed setting, minimizing the intermediate relations can also leave the effect of minimizing the amount of data that needs to be transferred across the network. Specialized query optimization techniques also exist for statistical databases [84] and memory resident databases [133].

Supporting a database buffer (sometimes called a database cache) is one of the most important efficiency techniques required [40, 96]. The database buffer manager acts to make pages accessible in main memory (reading from the disk) and to coordinate writes to the disk. In doing the reading and writing, it attempts to minimize I/0 and to do as much I/0 in a lazy fashion as possible. One example of the lazy I/0 would be that at transaction commit time only the log records are forced to the disk, the commit completes and the actual data records are written at a later time when the disk is idle, or if forced for other reasons, such as a need for more buffer space. Part of the buffer managers's task is to interact with one log manager by writing to the log and to cooperate with the recovery manager. If done poorly, disk I/0s for logging can become a bottleneck.

Disk space allocation is another important consideration in attaining good database performance. In general, the space allocation strategy should be such that fast address translation from logical block numbers to physical disk addresses can occur without any I/0, and the space allocation should be done to support both direct and sequential access.

The full mapping of relations through multiple intermediate levels of abstractions (for example, from relations, to segments, to OS files, to logical disks, to extents, and to disk blocks) down to the physical layer must be done efficiently. In fact, one should try to eliminate unnecessary intermediate layers (still retaining data independence), and use various forms of mapping caches to speed up the translations.

Real-time transaction systems

Real-time transaction systems are becoming increasingly important in a wide range of applications. One example of a real-time transaction system is a computer integrated manufacturing system where the system keeps track of the state of physical machines, manages various presses in the production line, and collects statistical data from manufacturing operations. Transactions executing on the database may have deadlines in order to reflect, in a timely manner, the state of manufacturing operations or to respond to the control messages from operators. For instance, the information describing the current state of an object may need to be updated before a team of robots can work on the object. The update transaction is considered successful only if the data (the information) is changed consistently (in the view of all the robots) and the update operation is done within the specified time period so that all the robots can begin working with a consistent view of the situation. Other applications of real-time database systems can be found in program trading in the stock market, radar tracking systems, command and control systems, and air traffic control systems.

Real-time transaction processing is complex because it requires an integrated set of protocols that must not only satisfy database consistency requirements, but also operate under timing constraints [36, 37, 50, 69]. The algorithms and protocols that must be integrated include CPU scheduling, concurrency control, conflict resolution, transaction restart, transaction wakeup, deadlock, buffer management, and disk I/0 scheduling [21, 23, 25, 26, 50, 100]. Each of these algorithms or protocols should directly address the real-time constraints. To date, work on real-time databases has investigated a centralized, secondary storage real-time database [1, 2, 3]. As is usually required in traditional database systems, work so far has required that all the real-time transaction operations maintain data consistency as defined by serializability. Serializability may be relaxed in some real-time database systems, depending on the application environment and data properties [105, 114, 69], but little actual work has been done in this area. Serializability is enforced by using a real-time version of either the two-phase locking protocol or optimistic concurrency control. Optimistic concurrency control has been shown to perform better than two-phase locking when integrated with priority-driven CPU scheduling in real-time database systems [48, 49, 53].

In addition to timing constraints, in many real-time database applications, each transaction imparts a value to the system that is related to its criticalness and to when it completes execution (relative to its deadline). In general, the selection of a value function depends on the application [72]. To date, the value of a transaction has been modeled as a function of its criticalness, start time, deadline, and the current system time. Here criticalness represents the importance of transactions, while deadlines constitute the time constraints of real-time transactions. Criticalness and deadline are two characteristics of real-time transactions and they are not necessarily related. A transaction that has a short deadline does not imply that it has high criticalness. Transactions with the same criticalness may have different deadlines and transactions with the same deadline may have different criticalness values. Basically, the higher the criticalness of a transaction, the larger its value to the system. It is important to note that the value of a transaction is time-variant. A transaction that has missed its deadline will not be as valuable to the system as it would be if it had completed before its deadline.

Other important issues and results for real-time distributed databases include:

- In a real-time system, I/0 scheduling is an important issue with respect to the system performance. In order to minimize transaction loss probability, a good disk scheduling algorithm should take into account not only the *time constraint* of a transaction, but also the *disk service time* [25].
- Used for I/O, the *earliest deadline* discipline ignores the characteristics of disk service time, and, therefore, does not perform well except when the I/0 load is low.
- Various conflict resolution protocols that directly address deadlines and criticalness can have a important impact on performance over protocols that ignore such information.
- How can priority inversion (this refers to the situation where a high priority transaction is blocked due to a low priority transaction holding a lock on a data item) be solved [52, 106]?
- How can soft real-time transaction systems be interfaced to hard real-time components?
- How can real-time transactions themselves be guaranteed to meet hard deadlines?
- How will real-time buffering algorithms impact real-time optimistic concurrency control [51]?
- How will semantics-based concurrency control techniques impact real-time performance?
- How will the algorithms and performance results be impacted when extended to a distributed real-time system?
- How can correctness criteria other than serializability be exploited in real-time transaction systems?

Summary

Distributed computer systems began in the early 1970s with a few experimental systems. Since that time tremendous progress has been made in many disciplines that support distributed computing. The progress has been so remarkable that DCSs are commonplace and quite large. For example, the Internet has over 500,000 nodes on it. This paper has discussed two of the areas that played a major role in this achievement: distributed operating systems and distributed databases. For more information on distributed computing, see the following books and surveys [4, 35, 41, 46, 58, 85, 113, 115, 121]. As mentioned in the introduction, many areas of distributed computing could not be covered in this paper. One important area omitted is distributed file servers such as NFS and Andrew. For more information on these and other distributed file servers, see the survey paper [68].

Acknowledgments

I enthusiastically thank Panos Chrysanthis and Krithi Ramamritham for their valuable comments on this work.

Glossary

Access control list. A model of protection where rights are maintained as a list associated with each object. See Capability list and Access control matrix.

Access control matrix. A model of protection where rows of the matrix represent domains of execution and columns represent the objects in the system. The entries in the matrix indicate the allowable operations each domain of execution can perform on each object.

Active object model. An object that has one or more execution activities (for example, threads) associated with it at all times. Operation invocations on the object use these resident threads for execution.

Asynchronous send. An interprocess communication primitive where the sending process does not wait for a reply before continuing to execute. See Synchronous send.

Atomic broadcast. A communication primitive that supports the result that either all hosts (or processes) receive the message, or none of them see the message. See Broadcasting.

Atomicity. A property of a transaction where either the entire transaction completes, or it is as if the transaction never executed. See Transaction.

Bidding. A distributed scheduling scheme that requests hosts to provide information in the form of a bid as to how well that host can accept new work.

Broadcasting. Sending a message to all hosts or processes in the system. See Multicasting.

Capability list. A model of protection where rights are maintained as a list associated with each execution domain. See Access control list and Access control matrix.

Client-server model. A software architecture that includes server processes that provide services and client processes that request services via well-defined interfaces. A particular process can be both a server and a client process.

Consistency. A property of a transaction which means that the transaction maintains the integrity of the database. See Transaction.

Copy-on-write. Data are delayed from being copied between address spaces until either the source or the destination actually performs a write operation.

Data abstraction. A collection of information (data) and a set of operations on that information.

Differential files. A representation of a collection of data as the difference from some point of reference. Used as a technique for storing large and volatile files.

Distributed computing environment (DCE). A computing environment that exploits the potential of computer networks without the need to understand the underlying complexity. This environment is to meet the needs of end users, system administrators, and application developers.

Distributed operating system (DOS). A native operating system that runs on and controls a network of computers.

Distributed shared memory. The abstraction of shared memory in a physically nonshared distributed system.

Durability. A property of a transaction which means that all changes made by a committed transaction are permanent. See Transaction.

Federated database system. A collection of autonomous database systems integrated for purposes of cooperation.

Hard real time. Tasks have deadlines or other timing constraints, and serious consequences could occur if a task misses a deadline. See Soft real time.

Isolation. A property of transactions which means that even if transactions execute concurrently, their results appear as if they were executed in some serial order. See Transaction and Serializability.

Lazy evaluation. A performance improvement technique that postpones taking an action or even a part of an action until the results of that action (subaction) are actually required.

Lightweight process. An efficiency technique that separates the address space and rights from the execution activity. Most useful for parallel programs and multiprocessors.

Lightweight remote procedure call. An efficiency technique to reduce the execution time cost of remote procedure calls when the processes happen to reside on the same host.

Multicasting. Sending a message to all members of a defined group. See Broadcasting.

Nested transaction. A transaction model that permits a transaction to be composed of subtransactions that can fail without necessarily aborting the parent transaction.

Network operating system (NOS). A layer of software added to local operating systems to enable a distributed collection of computers to cooperate.

Network partitioning. A failure situation where the communication network(s) connecting the hosts of a distributed system have failed in such a manner that two or more independent subnets are executing without being able to communicate with each other.

Object. An instantiation of a data abstraction. See Data abstraction.

Passive object. An object that has no execution activity assigned to it. The execution activity gets mapped into the object upon invocation of operations of the object.

Process. A program in execution including the address space, the current state of the computation, and various rights to which this program is entitled.

RAID. Redundant arrays of inexpensive disks to enhance I/0 throughput and fault tolerance.

Real-time applications. Applications where tasks have specific deadlines or other timing constraints such as periodic requirements.

Recoverable communicating actions. A complex transaction model to support long and cooperative nonhierarchical computations involving communicating processes.

Remote procedure call (RPC). A synchronous communication method that provides the same semantics as a procedure call, but it occurs across hosts in a distributed system.

Sagas. A complex transaction model for long lived activities consisting of a set of component transactions that can commit as soon as they complete. If the saga aborts, committed components are compensated.

Serializability. A correctness criterion which states that the effect of a set of executed transactions must be the same as some serial execution of that set of transactions.

Soft real time. In a soft real-time system tasks have deadlines or other timing constraints, but no serious complications occur if a deadline is missed. See Hard real time.

Split transactions. A complex transaction model where the splitting transaction delegates the responsibility for aborting or committing changes made to a subset of objects it has accessed to the split transaction.

Synchronous send. An interprocess communication primitive where the sending process waits for a reply before proceeding. See Asynchronous send.

Time stamp ordering. A concurrency control technique where all accesses to data are time stamped and then some common rule is followed to ensure serializability. See Serializability.

Thread. Represents the execution activity of a process. Multiple threads can exist in one process.

Transaction. An abstraction that groups a sequence of actions on a database into a logical execution unit. Traditional transactions have four properties. See Atomicity, Consistency, Isolation, and Durability.

Validation. A concurrency control technique that permits unrestricted access to data items, but then checks for potential conflicts at the transaction commit point.

References

[1] R. Abbott and H. Garcia-Molina, "Scheduling Real-Time Transactions," *ACM SIGMOD Record,* Mar. 1988.

[2] R. Abbott and H. Garcia-Molina, "Scheduling Real-Time Transactions: A Performance Evaluation," *Proc. 14th VLDB Conf.,* 1988.

[3] R. Abbott and H. Garcia-Molina, "Scheduling Real-Time Transactions with Disk Resident Data," *Proc. 15th VLDB Conf.,* 1989.

[4] B. Abeysundara and A. Kamal, "High Speed Local Area Networks and Their Performance: A Survey," *ACM Computing Surveys,* Vol. 23, No. 2, June 1991.

[5] R. Agrawal, M.J. Carey and M. Livny, "Concurrency Control Performance Modeling: Alternatives and Implications," *ACM Trans. Database Systems,* Vol. 12, No. 4, Dec. 1987.

[6] T. Anderson et al., "Scheduler Activations: Effective Kernel Support for the User-Level Management of Parallelism," Tech. Report TR 90-04-02, Univ. of Washington, Oct. 1990.

[7] T. Anderson et al., "Interaction of Architecture and OS Design," tech. report, Dept. of Computer Science, Univ. of Washington, Aug. 1990.

[8] K. Arvind, K. Ramamritham, and J. Stankovic, "A Local Area Network Architecture for Communication in Distributed Real-Time Systems," invited paper, *Real-Time Systems J.,* Vol. 3, No. 2, May 1991, pp. 113-147.

[9] J. Ayache, J. Courtiat, and M. Diaz, "REBUS, A Fault Tolerant Distributed System for Industrial Control," *IEEE Trans. Computers.,* Vol. C-31, July 1982.

[10] M. Bach, N. Coguen, and M. Kaplan, "The ADAPT System: A Generalized Approach towards Data Conversion," *Proc. VLDB,* 1979.

[11] B. Badrinath and K. Ramamritham, "Performance Evaluation of Semantics-Based Multilevel Concurrency Control Protocols," *Proc. ACM SIGMOD,* 1990, pp 163-172.

[12] J. Ball et al., "RIG, Rochester's Intelligent Gateway: System Overview," *IEEE Trans. Software Eng.,* Vol. SE-2, No. 4, Dec. 1980.

[13] D. Barclay, E. Byrne, and F. Ng, "A Real-Time Database Management System for No. 5 ESS," *Bell System Tech. J.,* Vol. 61, No. 9, Nov. 1982.

[14] D. Batory, "GENESIS: A Project to Develop an Extensible Database Management System," *Proc. Int'l Workshop Object-Oriented Database Sytems,* 1986, pp. 207-208.

[15] P.A. Bernstein, D.W. Shipman, and J.B. Rothnie, Jr., "Concurrency Control in a System for Distributed Databases (SDD-1)," *ACM Trans. Database Systems,* Vol. 5, No. 1, Mar. 1980, pp. 18-25.

[16] P. Bernstein and N. Goodman, "Concurrency Control in Distributed Database Systems," *ACM Computing Surveys,* Vol. 13, No. 2, June 1981.

[17] A. Bernstein, V. Hadzilacos, and N. Goodman, *Concurrency Control and Recovery in Database Systems,* Addison Wesley, Reading, Mass, 1987.

[18] B.N. Bershad, T.E. Anderson, and E.D. Lazowska, "Lightweight Remote Procedure Call," *ACM Trans. Computer Systems,* Vol. 8, No. 1, Feb. 1990, pp. 37-55.

[19] K. Birman, "Replication and Fault-Tolerance in the ISIS System," *ACM Symp. OS Principles,* Vol. 19, No. 5, Dec. 1985.

[20] A. Birrell et al., "Grapevine: An Exercise in Distributed Computing," *Comm. ACM,* Vol. 25, Apr. 1982, pp. 260-274.

[21] A. Buchmann et al., "Time-Critical Database Scheduling: A Framework for Integrating Real-Time Scheduling and Concurrency Control," *Proc. Data Eng. Conf.,* 1989.

[22] M. Carey et al., "The Architecture of the EXODUS Extensible DBMS," *Readings in Database Systems,* Morgan Kaufmann, 1988, pp. 488-501.

[23] M.J. Carey, R. Jauhari, and M. Livny, "Priority in DBMS Resource Scheduling," *Proc. 15th VLDB Conf.,* 1989.

[24] T. Casavant and J. Kuhl, "A Taxonomy of Scheduling in General Purpose Distributed Computing Systems," *Trans. Software Eng.,* Vol. 14, No. 2, Feb. 1988.

[25] S. Chen et al., "Performance Evaluation of Two New Disk Scheduling Algorithms for Real-Time Systems," *Real-Time Systems,* Vol. 3, No. 3, Sept. 1991.

[26] S. Chen and D. Towsley, "Performance of a Mirrored Disk in a Real-Time Transaction System," *Proc. 1991 ACM SIGMETRICS,* 1991.

[27] D. Cheriton, H. Goosen, and P. Boyle, "Paradigm: A Highly Scalable Shared Memory Multicomputer Architecture," *Computer,* Feb. 1991.

[28] D. Cheriton and W. Zwaenepoel, "Distributed Process Groups in the V Kernel," *ACM Trans. Computer Systems,* Vol. 3, No. 2, May 1985.

[29] R. Chin and S. Chanson, "Distributed Object Based Programming Systems," *ACM Computing Surveys,* Vol. 23, No. 1, Mar. 1991.

[30] T. Chou and J. Abraham, "Load Balancing in Distributed Systems," *IEEE Trans. Software Eng.,* Vol. SE-8, No. 4, July 1982.

[31] P. Chrysanthis and K. Ramamritham, "ACTA; A Framework for Specifying and Reasoning about Transaction Structure and Behavior," *Proc. ACM SIGMOD Int'l Conf. Management Data,* 1990, pp. 194-203.

[32] W. Chu et al., "Task Allocation in Distributed Data Processing," *Computer,* Vol. 13, Nov. 1980, pp. 57-69.

[33] P. Dasgupta et al., "The Clouds Distributed Operating System," *Computer,* Vol. 24, No. 11, Nov. 1991, pp. 34-44.

[34] C.J. Date, *An Introduction to Database Systems,* Addison Wesley, Reading, Mass., 1975.

[35] D.W. Davies et al., *Distributed Systems Architecture and Implementation,* Vol. 105, Lecture Notes in Computer Science, Springer-Verlag, Berlin, Germany, 1981.

[36] U. Dayal et al., "The HiPAC Project: Combining Active Database and Timing Constraints," *ACM SIGMOD Record,* Mar. 1988.

[37] U. Dayal, "Active Database Management Systems," *Proc. 3rd Int'l Conf. Data and Knowledge Management,* 1988.

[38] J. Dion, "The Cambridge File Server," *ACM Cperating Systems Rev.,* Oct. 1980.

[39] K. Efe, "Heuristic Models of Task Assignment Scheduling in Distributed Systems," *Computer,* Vol. 15, June 1982.

[40] W. Effelsberg and T. Haerder, "Principles of Database Buffer Management," *ACM Trans. Database Systems,* Vol. 9, No. 4, Dec. 1984.

[41] P. Enslow, "What is a Distributed Data Processing System," *Computer,* Vol. 11, Jan. 1978.

[42] E. Felten and J. Zahorjan, "Issues in the Implementation of a Remote Memory Paging System," Tech. Report TR 91-03-09, Univ. of Washington, Mar. 1991.

[43] R. Fitzgerald and R. Rashid, "Integration of Virtual Memory Management and Interprocess Communication in Accent, *ACM Trans. Computer Systems,* Vol. 4, No. 2, May 1986.

[44] H. Garcia-Molina et al., "Modeling Long-Running Activities as Nested Sagas," *IEEE Tech. Committee Data Eng.,* 14(1):14-18, Mar. 1991.

[45] H. Garcia-Molina and K. Salem, "SAGAS," *Proc. ACM SIGMOD Int'l Conf. Management Data,* 1987, pp. 249-259.

[46] A. Goscinski, *Distributed Operating Systems: The Logical Design,* Addison Wesley, Sydney, Australia, 1991.

[47] J. Gray, "Notes on Database Operating Systems," *Operating Systems: An Advanced Course,* Springer-Verlag, Berlin, Germany, 1979.

[48] J.R. Haritsa, M.J. Carey, and M. Livny, "On Being Optimistic about Real-Time Constraints," *Principles of Distributed Computing,* 1990.

[49] J.R. Haritsa, M.J. Carey, and M. Livny, "Dynamic Real-Time Optimistic Concurrency Control," *Proc. 11th Real-Time Systems Symp.,* 1990.

[50] J. Huang et al., "Experimental Evaluation of Real-Time Transaction Processing," *Proc. Real-Time System Symp.,* 1989.

[51] J. Huang and J. Stankovic, "Real-Time Buffer Management," COINS TR 90-65, Univ. of Massachusetts, Aug. 1990.

[52] J. Huang et al., "Priority Inheritance under Two-Phase Locking," *Proc. Real-Time Systems Symp.,* 1991.

[53] J. Huang et al., "Experimental Evaluation of Real-Time Optimistic Concurrency Control Schemes," *Proc. VLDB,* 1991.

[54] N. Hutchinson and L. Peterson, "The *x*-Kernel: An Architecture for Implementing Network Protocols," *IEEE Trans. Software Eng.,* Vol. 17, No. 1, Jan. 1991.

[55] T. Joseph and K. Birman, "Reliable Broadcast Protocols," Tech. Report TR 88-918, Cornell Univ., June 1988.

[56] R. Katz, G. Gibson, and D. Patterson, "Disk System Architectures for High Performance Computing," *Proc. IEEE,* Vol. 77, No. 12, Dec. 1989.

[57] J.P. Kearns and S. DeFazio, "Diversity in Database Reference Behavior," *Performance Evaluation Rev.,* Vol. 17, No. 1, May 1989.

[58] W. Kohler, "A Survey of Techniques for Synchronization and Recovery in Decentralized Computer Systems," *ACM Computing Surveys,* Vol. 13, No. 2, June 1981.

[59] H. Kopetz et al., "Distributed Fault Tolerant Real-Time Systems: The Mars Approach," *IEEE Micro,* Vol. 9, No. 1, Feb. 1989, pp. 25-40.

[60] H. Korth, W. Kim, and F. Bancilhon, "On Long-Duration CAD Transactions," *Information Sciences,* Vol. 46, No. 1-2, Oct.-Nov. 1988, pp. 73-107.

[61] H. Korth, E. Levy, and A. Silberschatz, "Compensating Transactions: A New Recovery Paradigm," *Proc. 16th VLDB Conf.,* 1990, pp. 95-106.

[62] H.T. Hung and J.T. Robinson, "On Optimistic Methods for Concurrency Control," *ACM Trans. Database Systems,* Vol. 6, No. 2, June 1981.

[63] L. Lamport, "Time, Clocks, and the Ordering of Events in a Distributed System," *Comm. ACM,* July 1978.

[64] L. Lamport, R. Shostak, and M. Pease, "The Byzantine Generals Problem," *ACM Trans. Programming Language and Systems,* Vol. 4, No. 3, July 1982.

[65] B. Lampson, "Atomic Transactions," *Lecture Notes in Computer Science,* Vol. 105, Springer-Verlag, Berlin, Germany, 1980, pp. 365-370.

[66] E. Lazowska et al., "The Architecture for the Eden System," *Proc. 8th Ann. Symp. Operating System Principles,* 1981.

[67] G. LeLann, "Algorithms for Distributed Data-Sharing Systems That Use Tickets," *Proc. 3rd Berkeley Workshop Distributed Databases and Computer Networks,* 1978.

[68] E. Levy and A. Silberschatz, "Distributed File Systems: Concepts and Examples," *ACM Computing Surveys,* Vol. 22, No. 4, Dec. 1990.

[69] K.J. Lin, "Consistency Issues in Real-Time Database Systems," *Proc. 22nd Hawaii Int'l Conf. System Sciences,* 1989.

[70] B. Liskov and R. Scheifler, "Guardians and Actions: Linguistic Support for Robust, Distributed Systems," *Proc. 9th Symp. Principles Programming Languages,* 1982, pp. 7-19.

[71] W. Litwin, L. Mark, and N. Roussopoulos, "Interoperability of Multiple Autonomous Databases," *ACM Computing Surveys,* Vol. 22, No. 3, Sept. 1990.

[72] C.D. Locke, *Best-Effort Decision Making for Real-Time Scheduling,* doctoral dissertation, Carnegie Mellon Univ., Pittsburgh, Pa., 1986.

[73] D. Maier et al., "Development of an Object-Oriented DBMS," *Proc. Object-Oriented Programming Systems, Languages, and Applications,* 1986, pp. 472-482.

[74] R. Mirchandaney, D. Towsley, and J. Stankovic, "Adaptive Load Sharing in Heterogeneous Distributed Systems," *J. Parallel and Distributed Computing,* Vol. 9, Sept. 1990, pp. 331-346.

[75] R. Mirchandaney, D. Towsley, and J. Stankovic, "Analysis of the Effects of Delays on Load Sharing," *IEEE Trans. Computers,* Vol. 38, No. 11, Nov. 1989, pp. 1513-1525.

[76] J.E.B. Moss, *Nested Transactions: An Approach to Reliable Distributed Computing,* doctoral thesis, Massachusetts Inst. of Technology, Cambridge, Mass., Apr. 1981.

[77] J.E.B. Moss, N. Griffeth, and M. Graham, "Abstraction in Recovery Management," *Proc. ACM SIGMOD Int'l Conf. Management Data,* 1986, pp. 72-83.

[78] S.J. Mullender et al., "Experiences with the Amoeba Distributed Operating System," *Comm. ACM,* Vol. 33, No. 12, Dec. 1990.

[79] K.M. Needham and A.J. Herbert, *The Cambridge Distributed Computing System,* Addison-Wesley, London, UK, 1982.

[80] R.M. Needham and M. Schroeder, "Using Encryption for Authentication in Large Networks of Computers," *Comm. ACM,* Vol. 21, No. 12, Dec. 1978, pp. 993-999.

[81] B.J. Nelson, "Remote Procedure Call," Tech. Report CSL-81-9, Xerox Corp., May 1981.

[82] B. Nitzberg and V. Lo, "Distributed Shared Memory: A Survey of Issues and Algorithms," *Computer,* Vol. 24, No. 8, Aug. 1991, pp. 52-60.

[83] J. Ousterhout, D. Scelza, and P. Sindhu, "Medusa: An Experiment in Distributed Operating System Structure," *Comm. ACM,* Vol. 23, Feb. 1980.

[84] G. Ozsoyoglu, V. Matos, and Z. Meral Ozsoyoglu, "Query Processing Techniques in the Summary-Table-by-Example Database Query Language," *ACM Trans. Database Systems,* Vol. 14, No. 4, 1989, pp. 526-573.

[85] M. Özsu and P. Valduriez, *Principles of Distributed Database Systems,* Prentice Hall, Englewood Cliffs, N.J., 1991.

[86] D. Patterson, G. Gibson, and R. Katz, "A Case for Redundant Arrays of Inexpensive Disks (RAID)," *Proc. ACM SIGMOD,* 1988.

[87] G. Popek et al., "LOCUS, A Network Transparent, High Reliability Distributed System," *Proc. 8th Symp. Operating System Principles,* 1981, pp. 14-16.

[88] D. Powell et. al. "The Delta-4 Distributed Fault Tolerant Architecture," Report No. 91055, Laboratoire d'Automatique et d'Analyse des Systemes, Feb. 1991.

[89] C. Pu, *Replication and Nested Transactions in the Eden Distributed System,* doctoral thesis, Univ. of Washington, 1986.

[90] C. Pu, G. Kaiser, and N. Hutchinson, "Split Transactions for Open-Ended Activities, *Proc. 11th Int'l Conf. VLDB,* 1988, pp. 26-37.

[91] K. Ramamritham, J. Stankovic, and P. Shiah, "Efficient Scheduling Algorithms For Real-Time Multiprocessor Systems," *IEEE Trans. Parallel and Distributed Computing,* Vol. 1, No. 2, Apr. 1990, pp. 184-194.

[92] R.F. Rashid and G.G. Robertson, "Accent: A Communication Oriented Network Operating System Kernel," *Proc. 8th Symp. Operating System Principles,* 1981.

[93] R. Rashid, "Threads of a New System, UNIX Review," Aug. 1986, pp 37-49.

[94] R. Rashid et al., "Machine Independent Virtual Memory Management for Paged Uniprocessor and Multiprocessor Architectures," *IEEE Trans. Computers,* Vol. 37, No 8, Aug. 1988.

[95] D.J. Rosenkrantz, R.E. Stearns, and P.M. Lewis, "System Level Concurrency Control for Distributed Database Systems," *ACM Trans. Database Systems,* Vol. 3, No. 2, June 1978.

[96] G.M. Sacco and M. Schkolnick, "Buffer Management in Relational Database Systems," *ACM Trans. Database Systems,* Vol. 11, No. 4, Dec. 1986.

[97] J.H. Saltzer, D.P. Reed, and D.D. Clark, "End-to-End Arguments in System Design," *Proc. 2nd Int'l Conf. Distributed Computing Systems,* 1981.

[98] K. Schwan, A. Geith, and H. Zhou, "From Chaos(Base) to Chaos(Arc): A Family of Real-Time Kernels," *Proc. Real-Time Systems Symp.,* 1990, pp. 82-91.

[99] D.G. Severance and G.M. Lohman, "Differential Files: Their Application to the Maintenance of Large-Databases," *ACM Trans. Database Systems,* Vol. 1, No. 3, Sept. 1976.

[100] L. Sha, R. Rajknmar, and J.P. Lehoczky, "Concurrency Control for Distributed Real-Time Databases," *ACM SIGMOD Record,* Mar. 1988.

[101] A. Sheth and J. Larson, "Federated Database Systems for Managing Distributed, Heterogeneous, and Autonomous Databases," *ACM Computing Surveys,* Vol. 22, No. 3, Sept. 1990.

[102] D. Skeen, "Nonblocking Commit Protocols," *Proc. ACM SIGMOD,* 1981.

[103] D. Skeen and M. Stonebraker, "A Formal Model of Crash Recovery in a Distributed System," *IEEE Trans. Software Eng.,* Vol. SE-9, No. 3, May 1983.

[104] D. Skeen, "A Decentralized Termination Protocol," *Proc. 1st IEEE Symp. Reliability Distributed Software Database Systems,* 1981.

[105] S.H. Son, "Using Replication for High Performance Database Support in Distributed Real-Time Systems," *Proc. 8th Real-Time Systems Symp.,* 1987.

[106] S.H. Son and C.H. Chang, "Priority-Based Scheduling in Real-Time Database Systems," *Proc. 15th VLDB Conf.,* 1989.

[107] A.Z. Spector and P.M. Schwarz, "Transactions: A Construct for Reliable Distributed Computing," *ACM Operating System Rev.,* Vol. 17, No. 2, Apr. 1983.

[108] S.K. Shrivastava, "On the Treatment of Orphans in a Distributed System," *Proc. 3rd Symp. Reliability Distributed Systems,* 1983.

[109] S.K. Shrivastava and F. Panzieri, "The Design of a Reliable Remote Procedure Call Mechanism," *Trans. Computers,* Vol. C-31, July 1982.

[110] J.A. Stankovic, "Simulations of Three Adaptive, Decentralized, Controlled Job Scheduling Algorithms," *Computer Networks,* Vol. 8, No. 3, June 1984, pp. 199-217.

[111] J.A. Stankovic, "Bayesian Decision Theory and Its Application to Decentralized Control of Job Scheduling," *IEEE Trans. Computers,* Vol. C-34, Jan. 1985.

[112] J.A. Stankovic and I.S. Sidhu, "An Adaptive Bidding Algorithm for Processes, Clusters and Distributed Groups," *Proc. 4th Int'l Conf. Distributed Computing,* 1984.

[113] J.A. Stankovic, "A Perspective on Distributed Computer Systems," *Trans. Computers,* Vol. C-33, No. 12, Dec. 1984, pp. 1102-1115.

[114] J.A. Stankovic and W. Zhao, "On Real-Time Transactions," *ACM SIGMOD Record,* Mar. 1988.

[115] J.A. Stankovic, "Misconceptions about Real-Time Computing: A Serious Problem For Next Generation Systems," *Computer,* Vol. 21, No. 10, Oct. 1988, pp. 10-19.

[116] J.A. Stankovic and K. Ramamritham, "The Spring Kernel: A New Paradigm for Real-Time Systems," *IEEE Software,* Vol. 8, No. 3, May 1991, pp. 62-72.

[117] J.A. Stankovic and K. Ramamritham, "What is Predictability for Real-Time Systems — An Editorial," *Real-Time Systems J.,* Vol. 2, Dec. 1990, pp. 247-254.

[118] M. Stonebraker and E. Neuhold, "A Distributed Database Version of INGRES," *Proc. Berkeley Workshop Distributed Data Management and Computer Networks,* 1977, pp. 19-36.

[119] M. Stonebraker, "Operating System Support for Database Management," *Comm. ACM,* Vol. 24, July 1981, pp. 412-418.

[120] H. Sturgess, J. Mitchell, and I. Isreal, "Issues in the Design and Use of Distributed File System," *ACM Operating System Rev.,* July 1980.

[121] A. Tanenbaum and R. van Renesse, "Distributed Operating Systems," *ACM Computing Surveys,* Vol. 17, No. 4, Dec. 1985, pp. 419-470.

[122] M. Theimer, K. Lantz, and D.R. Cheriton, "Preemptable Remote Execution Facility for the V-System," *Proc. 10th Symp. Operating Systems Principles,* 1985, pp. 2-12.

[123] R.H. Thomas, "A Majority Consensus Approach on Concurrency Control for Multiple Copy Databases," *ACM Trans. Database Systems.,* Vol. 4, No. 2, June 1979, pp. 180-209.

[124] G. Thomas et al., "Heterogeneous Distributed Database Systems for Production Use" *ACM Computing Surveys,* Vol. 22, No. 3, Sept. 1990.

[125] H. Tokuda and C. Mercer, "Arts: A Distributed Real-Time Kernel," *ACM Operating Systems Rev.,* July 1989, pp. 29-53.

[126] D. Towsley, G. Rommel, and J. Stankovic, "Analysis of Fork-Join Program Response Times on Multiprocessors," *IEEE Trans. Parallel and Distributed Systems,* Vol. 1, No. 3, July 1990, pp. 286-303.

[127] R. Vaswani and J. Zahorjan, "Implications of Cache Affinity on Processor Scheduling for Multiprogrammed, Shared Memory Multiprocessors," Tech. Report TR 91-03-03, Univ. of Washington, Mar. 1991.

[128] S. Vinter, K. Ramamritham, and D. Stemple, "Recoverable Actions in Gutenberg," *Proc. 6th Int'l Conf. Distributed Computing Systems,* 1986, pp. 242-249.

[129] W. Weihl, *Specification and Implementation of Atomic Data Types*, doctoral thesis, Massachusetts Inst. of Technology, Cambridge, Mass., Mar. 1984.

[130] W. Weihl, "Commutativity Based Concurrency Control for Abstract Data Types," *Trans. Computers,* Vol. 37, No. 12, Dec. 1988, pp. 1488-1505.

[131] M. Weinstein et al., "Transactions and Synchronization in a Distributed Operating System," *ACM Symp. Operating Systems Principles,* Vol. 19, No. 5, Dec. 1985.

[132] J. Wensley et al., "SIFT: Design and Analysis of a Fault-Tolerant Computer for Aircraft Control," *Proc. IEEE,* Oct. 1978, pp. 1240-1255.

[133] K. Whang and R. Krishnamurthy, "Query Optimization in a Memory-Resident Domain Relational Calculus Database System," *ACM Trans. Database Systems,* Vol. 15, No. 1, Mar. 1990, pp. 67-95.

[134] K. Wu and W. Fuchs, "Recoverable Distributed Shared Virtual Memory," *IEEE Trans. Computers,* Vol. 39, No. 4, Apr. 1990.

[135] W. Zhao, J. Stankovic, and K. Ramamritham, "A Window Protocol for Transmission of Time Constrained Messages," *IEEE Trans. Computers,* Vol. 39, No. 9, Sept. 1990, pp. 1186-1203.

A Taxonomy of Scheduling in General-Purpose Distributed Computing Systems

T he study of distributed computing has grown to include a large range of applications [16], [17], [31], [32], [37], [54], [55]. However, at the core of all the efforts to exploit the potential power of distributed computation are issues related to the management and allocation of system resources relative to the computational load of the system. This is particularly true of attempts to construct large, *general-purpose* multiprocessors [3], [8], [25], [26], [44], [45], [46], [50], [61], [67].

The notion that a loosely coupled collection of processors could function as a more powerful general-purpose computing facility has existed for quite some time. A large body of work has focused on the problem of managing the resources of a system in such a way as to effectively exploit this power. The result of this effort has been the proposal of a variety of widely differing techniques and methodologies for distributed-resource management. Along with these competing proposals has come the inevitable proliferation of inconsistent and even contradictory terminology, as well as a number of slightly differing problem formulations and assumptions. Thus, it is difficult to analyze the relative merits of alternative schemes in a meaningful fashion. It is also difficult to focus a common effort on approaches and areas of study that seem most likely to prove fruitful.

This paper attempts to tie the many facets of distributed scheduling together under a common, uniform set of terminology. We provide a taxonomy to classify distributed-scheduling algorithms according to a reasonably small set of salient features. This provides a convenient means to quickly describe the central aspects of a particular approach and offers a basis for comparison of commonly classified schemes.

Earlier works attempted to classify certain aspects of the scheduling problem. A paper by Casey [9] gives the basis of a hierarchical categorization. The taxonomy that we present here agrees with the nature of Casey's categorization. However, we include a large number of additional fundamental distinguishing features that differentiate among existing approaches. Hence, our taxonomy provides a more detailed and complete look at the basic issues addressed by Casey. This greater detail is necessary to allow meaningful comparisons of different approaches. Wang

Thomas L. Casavant and

Jon G. Kuhl

and Morris [65] provide a taxonomy of load-sharing schemes that contrast with the taxonomy presented by Casey. They succinctly describe the range of solutions to the load-sharing problem. They describe solutions as either *source initiative* or *server initiative*. In addition, they characterize solutions along a continuous range, according to the degree of information dependency involved. Our taxonomy takes a much broader view of the distributed-scheduling problem, in which load sharing is only one of several possible *basic* strategies available to a system designer. Thus, the Wang and Morris classifications describe only a narrow category within the taxonomy described here.

Among existing taxonomies, one can find examples of hierarchical and flat classification schemes. Our taxonomy proposes a hybrid of these two — hierarchical as long as possible in order to reduce the total number of classes and flat when the descriptors of the system may be chosen in an arbitrary order. The levels in the hierarchy — chosen in order to keep the description of the taxonomy itself small — do not necessarily reflect any ordering of importance among characteristics. In other words, the descriptors comprising the taxonomy do not attempt to hierarchically order the characteristics of scheduling systems from more to less general. This point should be stressed especially with respect to the positioning of the flat portion of the taxonomy near the bottom of the hierarchy. For example, load balancing is a characteristic that pervades a large number of distributed-scheduling systems, but for the sake of reducing the size of the description of the taxonomy, it has been placed in the flat portion of the taxonomy, and for the sake of brevity, the flat portion has been placed near the bottom of the hierarchy.

This paper is organized into four sections following this introduction. The first section, "The scheduling problem — Describing its solutions," defines the scheduling problem as it applies to distributed-resource management. It contains a taxonomy that allows *qualitative* description and comparison of distributed-scheduling systems. The next section, "Examples," presents examples from the literature to demonstrate the use of the taxonomy in qualitatively describing and comparing existing systems. The last two sections, "Discussion" and "Conclusions," present ideas raised by the taxonomy and also suggest areas in need of additional work.

The scheduling problem — Describing its solutions

The *general scheduling problem* has been described a number of times and in many different ways [12], [22], [63] and is usually a restatement of the classical notions of job sequencing [13] in the study of production management [7]. For the purposes of distributed-process scheduling, we take a broader view of the scheduling function: as a resource management resource. This management resource is basically a mechanism or policy used to efficiently and effectively manage the access to and use of a resource by its various consumers. Hence, we may view every instance of the scheduling problem as consisting of three main components:

- Policy,
- Consumer(s), and
- Resource(s).

Like other management or control problems, understanding the functioning of a scheduler is best done by observing the effect it has on its environment. Then one can observe the behavior of the scheduler in terms of how *policy* affects *consumers* and *resources*. Note that although there is only one policy, the scheduler may be viewed in terms of how it affects either or both consumers and resources. This relationship between the scheduler, the policy, consumers, and resources is shown in Figure 1.

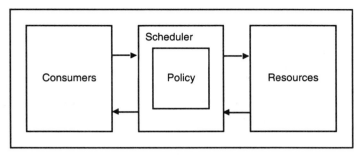

Figure 1. Scheduling system.

In light of this description of the scheduling problem, the following two properties must be considered when any scheduling system is being evaluated:

- Performance: The satisfaction of the consumers with how well the scheduler manages the resource in question.
- Efficiency: The satisfaction the consumers feel about how difficult or costly it is to access the management resource itself.

In other words, consumers want to be able to quickly and efficiently access the actual resource in question but do not desire to be hindered by overhead problems associated with using the management function itself.

One by-product of this statement of the general scheduling problem is the unification of two terms in common use in the literature. There is often an implicit distinction between the terms *allocation* and *scheduling*. However, it can be argued that these are merely alternative formulations of the same problem, with allocation posed in terms of *resource allocation* from the resources' point of view and *scheduling* viewed from the consumers' point of view. In this sense, allocation and scheduling are merely two terms describing the same general mechanism from two different viewpoints.

The classification scheme

The usefulness of the four-category taxonomy of computer architecture presented by Flynn [20] has been well demonstrated by its ability to compare systems through their relation to that taxonomy. The goal of our taxonomy is to provide a commonly accepted set of terms and to provide a mechanism to allow comparison of past work in the area of distributed scheduling in a qualitative way. In addition, it is hoped that the categories and their relationships to each other have been chosen carefully enough to indicate areas in need of future work and to help classify future work.

We tried to keep the taxonomy small by ordering it hierarchically when possible, but some choices of characteristics can be made independent of previous design choices and thus are specified as a set of descriptors from which a subset may be chosen. The taxonomy, discussed here in terms of distributed-process scheduling, is also applicable to a larger set of resources. In fact, the taxonomy could be employed to classify any set of resource-management systems. However, we will focus our attention on the area of process management, since it is in this area that we hope to derive relationships useful in determining potential areas for future work.

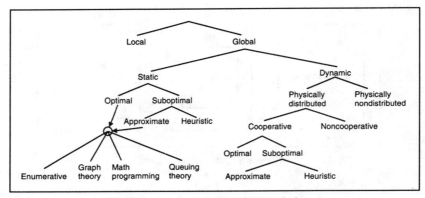

Figure 2. Task-scheduling characteristics.

Hierarchical classification. The structure of the *hierarchical* portion of the taxonomy is shown in Figure 2. A discussion of the hierarchical portion follows.

Local versus global. We may distinguish between *local* and *global* scheduling at the highest level. Local scheduling involves the assignment of processes to the time-slices of a single processor. Since scheduling on single-processor systems [12], [62], as well as sequencing or job-shop processing [13], [18], has been actively studied for many years, our taxonomy focuses on global scheduling. Global scheduling involves deciding *where* to execute a process, and the job of local scheduling is left to the operating system of the processor to which the process is ultimately allocated. This allows the processors in a multiprocessor increased autonomy, while it reduces the responsibility (and consequently the overhead) of the global-scheduling mechanism. Note that this does not imply that global scheduling must be done by a single central authority, but rather that we view the problems of local and global scheduling as separate issues (at least logically), with separate mechanisms at work to solve each.

Static versus dynamic. The next level in the hierarchy (beneath global scheduling) is a choice between *static* and *dynamic* scheduling. This choice indicates the time at which scheduling or assignment decisions are made. In the case of static scheduling, information regarding the total mix of processes in the system, as well as all the independent subtasks involved in a job or task force [26], [44] is assumed to be available by the time the program object modules are linked into load modules. Hence, each executable image in a system has a static assignment to a particular processor, and each time that process image is submitted for execution, it is assigned to that processor. A more relaxed definition of static scheduling may include algorithms that schedule task forces for a particular hardware configuration. Over a period of time, the topology of the system may change, but characteristics describing the task force remain the same. Hence, the scheduler may generate a new assignment of processes to processors to serve as the schedule until the topology changes again.

Note that the term *static scheduling* used here has the same meaning as *deterministic scheduling* in [22] and *task scheduling* in [56]. In our attempt to develop a consistent set of terms and taxonomy, we will not use these alternative terms here.

Optimal versus suboptimal. In a case where all the information regarding the state of the system and the resource needs of a process are known, an *optimal* assignment can be made based on some criterion function [5], [14], [21], [35], [40], [48]. Examples of optimization measures are minimizing total process-completion time, maximizing utilization of resources in the system, and maximizing system throughput. In the event that these problems are computationally infeasible, *suboptimal* solutions may be tried [2], [34], [47]. Within the realm of suboptimal solutions to the scheduling problem, we may think of two general categories: approximate and heuristic.

Approximate versus heuristic. The first branch beneath the suboptimal solutions is labeled *approximate.* A solution in this branch uses the same formal computational model for the algorithm, but instead of searching the entire solution space for an optimal solution, it is satisfied when it finds a "good" one. This solution is categorized as *suboptimal-approximate.* The assumption that a "good" solution can be recognized may not be so insignificant, but in cases where a metric is available for evaluating a solution, this technique can be used to decrease the time taken to find an acceptable solution schedule. Factors that determine whether this approach is worthy of pursuit include

- The availability of a function to evaluate a solution,
- The time required to evaluate a solution,
- The ability to judge according to some metric the value of an optimal solution, and
- The availability of a mechanism for intelligently pruning the solution space.

The second branch beneath the suboptimal solutions is labeled *heuristic* [15], [30], [66]. This branch represents the category of static algorithms that make the most realistic assumptions about a priori knowledge concerning process and system-loading characteristics. It also represents the solutions to the static-scheduling problem that require the most reasonable amount of time and other system resources to perform their function. The most distinguishing feature of heuristic schedulers is that they make use of special parameters that affect the system in indirect ways. Often, the parameter being monitored is correlated to system performance in an indirect, instead of a direct, way. This alternate parameter is much simpler to monitor or to calculate. For example, clustering groups of processes that communicate heavily on the same processor and physically separating processes that would benefit from parallelism [52] directly decrease the overhead involved in passing information between processors, while reducing the interference among processes that may run without synchronization with one another. This result has an impact on the overall service that users receive but cannot be *directly* related (in a quantitative way) to system performance as the user sees it. Hence, our intuition, if nothing else, leads us to believe that taking the aforementioned actions when possible will improve system performance. However, we may not be able to *prove* that a first-order relationship between the mechanism employed and the desired result exists.

Optimal and suboptimal-approximate techniques. Regardless of whether a static solution is *optimal* or *suboptimal-approximate,* there are four basic categories of task-allocation algorithms that can be used to arrive at an assignment of processes to processors:

- Solution space enumeration and search [48];
- Graph theoretic [4], [57], [58];
- Mathematical programming [5], [14], [21], [35], [40]; and
- Queuing theoretic [10], [28], [29].

Dynamic solutions. In dynamic scheduling, the more realistic assumption is made that very little a priori knowledge is available about the resource needs of a process. In static scheduling, a decision is made for a process image before the process is ever executed, while in dynamic scheduling, no decision is made until a process begins its life in the dynamic environment of the system. Since it is the responsibility of the running system to decide where a process is to execute, it is only natural to next ask where the decision itself is to be made.

Physically distributed versus physically nondistributed. The next level in the hierarchy involves whether the work involved in making decisions should be *physically distributed* among the processors [17] or the responsibility for the task of global dynamic scheduling should physically reside in a single processor [44] (*physically nondistributed*). At this level, the concern is with the logical authority of the decision-making process.

Cooperative versus noncooperative. Within the realm of distributed global, dynamic scheduling, we may also distinguish between those mechanisms that involve cooperation between the distributed components (*cooperative*) and those in which the individual processors make decisions independent of the actions of the other processors (*noncooperative*). The question here is one of the degree of *autonomy* that each processor has in determining how its own resources should be used. In the cooperative case, each processor has the responsibility to carry out its own portion of the scheduling task, but all processors are working toward a common, system-wide goal, instead of making decisions based on the way in which the decision will affect local performance only. In the noncooperative case, individual processors act alone as autonomous entities and arrive at decisions regarding the use of their resources independent of the effect of their decision on the rest of the system.

As in the static scheduling case, the taxonomy tree has reached a point where we may consider optimal, suboptimal-approximate, and suboptimal-heuristic solutions. The discussion presented for the static case also applies here.

Flat classification. In addition to the hierarchical portion of the taxonomy already discussed, there are a number of other distinguishing characteristics that scheduling systems may have. Here, we deal with characteristics that do not fit uniquely under any particular branch of the tree-structured taxonomy given thus far but are still important in the way in which they describe the behavior of a scheduler. In other words, the following could be branches beneath several of the leaves shown in Figure 2. In the interest of clarity, these characteristics are not repeated under each leaf but are presented here as a *flat* extension to the scheme presented thus far. It should be noted that these attributes represent a *set* of characteristics, and any particular scheduling subsystem may possess some subset of this set. Finally, the placement of these characteristics near the bottom of the tree is not intended to be an indication of their relative importance or of any relationship to other categories of the hierarchical portion. Rather, this position was determined primarily to reduce the size of the description of the taxonomy.

Adaptive versus nonadaptive. An *adaptive* solution to the scheduling problem is one in which the algorithms and parameters used to implement the scheduling policy change dynamically according to the previous and current behavior of the system in response to previous decisions made by the scheduling system. An example of such an adaptive scheduler would be one that takes many parameters into consideration in making its decisions [52]. In response to the behavior of the system, the scheduler may start to ignore one parameter or reduce the importance of that parameter if it believes that parameter is either providing information that is inconsistent with the rest of the inputs or not providing any information regarding the change in system state in relation to the values of the other parameters being observed. A second example of adaptive scheduling would be one that is based on the stochastic learning automata model [39]. An analogy may be drawn here between the notion of an adaptive scheduler and adaptive control [38], although the usefulness of such an analogy for purposes of performance analysis and implementation is questionable [51]. In contrast to an adaptive scheduler, a *nonadaptive* scheduler would be one that does not necessarily modify its basic control mechanism on the basis of the history of system activity. An example would be a scheduler that always weighs its inputs in the same way regardless of the history of the system's behavior.

Load balancing. This category of policies, which has received a great deal of attention in the literature [10], [11], [36], [40], [41], [42], [46], [53], approaches the problem with the philosophy that being fair to the hardware resources of the system is good for the users of that system. The basic idea is to attempt to balance (in some sense) the load on all processors in such a way that allows progress by all processes on all nodes to proceed at approximately the same rate. This solution is most effective when the nodes of a system are homogeneous, since this allows all nodes to know a great deal about the structure of the other nodes. Normally, information would be passed about the network periodically or on demand [1], [60] in order to allow all nodes to obtain a local estimate concerning the global state of the system. Then the nodes act together in order to remove work from heavily loaded nodes and place it at lightly loaded nodes. This is a class of load-balancing solutions that relies heavily on the assumption that the information at each node is quite accurate in order to prevent processes from endlessly being circulated about the system without making much progress. Another concern here is deciding on the basic unit used to measure the load on individual notes.

As was pointed out in the introduction, the placement of this characteristic near the bottom of the hierarchy in the flat portion of the taxonomy is not related to its relative importance or generality compared with characteristics at higher levels. In fact, it might be observed that — at the point at which a choice is made between optimal and suboptimal characteristics — a specific objective or cost function must have already been made. However, the purpose of the hierarchy is not so much to describe relationships between classes of the taxonomy but rather to reduce the size of the overall description of the taxonomy so as to make it more useful in comparing different approaches to solving the scheduling problem.

Bidding. In this class of policy mechanisms, a basic protocol framework exists that describes the way in which processes are assigned to processors. The resulting scheduler is one that is usually cooperative in the sense that enough information is exchanged (between nodes with tasks to execute and nodes that may be able to execute tasks) so that an assignment of tasks to processors can be made that is beneficial to all nodes in the system as a whole.

To illustrate the basic mechanism of *bidding*, the framework and terminology of [49] will be used. Each node in the network is responsible for two roles with respect to the bidding process: *manager* and *contractor*. The manager represents the task in need of a location to execute and the contractor represents a node that is able to do work for other nodes. Note that a single node takes on both of these roles and there are no nodes that are strictly managers or strictly contractors. The manager announces the existence of a task in need of execution by a *task announcement* and then receives *bids* from the other nodes (contractors). A wide variety of possibilities exists concerning the type and amount of information exchanged in order to make decisions [53], [59]. The type and amount of information exchanged are the major factors in determining the effectiveness and performance of a scheduler employing the notion of bidding. A very important feature of this class of schedulers is that all nodes generally have full autonomy in the sense that the manager ultimately has the power to decide where to send a task from among those nodes that respond with bids. In addition, the contractors are also autonomous, since they are never forced to accept work if they do not choose to do so.

Probabilistic. This classification has existed in scheduling systems for some time [13]. The basic idea for this scheme is motivated by the fact that in many assignment problems, the number of permutations of the available work and the number of mappings to processors is so large that to analytically examine the entire solution space would require a prohibitive amount of time. Instead, the idea of randomly (according to some known distribution) choosing some process as the next to assign is used. By this method being used repeatedly, a number of different schedules may be generated, and then this set is analyzed to choose the best from among those randomly generated. The fact that an important attribute is used to bias the random choosing process would lead one to expect that the schedule would be better than one chosen entirely at random. The argument that this method actually produces a good selection is based on the expectation that enough variation is introduced by the random choosing to allow a "good" solution to get into the randomly chosen set.

In an alternative view of probabilistic schedulers are those that employ the principles of decision theory in the form of team theory [24]. These would be classified as probabilistic, since suboptimal decisions are influenced by prior probabilities derived from *best-guesses* to the actual states of nature. In addition, these prior probabilities are used to determine (utilizing some random experiment) the next action (or scheduling decision).

One-time assignment versus dynamic reassignment. In this classification, we consider the entities to be scheduled. If the entities are jobs in the traditional batch-processing sense of the term [19], [23], then we consider the single point in time in which a decision is made as to where and when the job is to execute. While this technique technically corresponds to a dynamic approach, it is static in the sense that once a decision has been made to place and execute a job, no further decisions are made concerning the job. We would characterize this class as *one-time assignment*. Notice that in this mechanism, the only information usable by the scheduler to make its decision is the information given it by the user or submitter of the job. This information might include estimated execution time or other system resource demands. One critical point here is the fact that once users of a system understand the underlying scheduling mechanism, they may present false information to the system in order to receive better response. This point fringes on the area of psychological behavior, but human interaction is an important design factor to consider in this case, since the behavior of the scheduler itself is trying to mimic a general philosophy. Hence, the interaction of this philosophy with the system's users must be considered.

In contrast, solutions in the *dynamic-reassignment* class try to improve on earlier decisions by using information on smaller computation units — the executing subtasks of jobs or task forces. This category represents the set of systems that do not trust their users to provide accurate descriptive information and use dynamically created information to adapt to changing demands of user processes. This adaptation takes the form of migrating processes (including current process state information). There is clearly a price to be paid in terms of overhead, and this price must be carefully weighed against possible benefits.

An interesting analogy exists between the differentiation made here and the question of preemption versus nonpreemption in uniprocessor scheduling systems. Here, the difference lies in whether or not to move a process from one place to another once an assignment has been made, while in the uniprocessor case the question is whether or not to remove the running process from the processor once a decision has been made to let it run.

Examples

In this section, examples will be taken from the published literature to demonstrate their relationships to one another with respect to the taxonomy detailed in the preceding section. The purpose of this section is twofold. The first is to show that many different scheduling algorithms can fit into the taxonomy. The second is to show that the categories of the taxonomy actually correspond, in most cases, to methods that have been examined.

Global static

In [48], we see an example of an optimal, enumerative approach to the task-assignment problem. The criterion function is defined in terms of optimizing the amount of time a task will require for all interprocess communication and execution, where the tasks submitted by users are assumed to be broken into suitable modules before execution. The cost function is called a *minimax criterion*, since it is intended to minimize the maximum execution and communication time required by any single processor involved in the assignment. Graphs are then used to represent the module-to-processor assignments, and the assignments are then transformed to a type of graph matching known as *weak homomorphisms*. The optimal search of this solution space can then be done using the A* algorithm from artificial intelligence [43]. The solution also achieves a certain degree of processor load balancing as well.

Reference [4] gives a good demonstration of the usefulness of the taxonomy in that the paper describes the algorithm given as a solution to the optimal dynamic assignment problem for a two-processor system. However, in attempting to make an objective comparison of the system in this paper with other dynamic systems, we see that the algorithm proposed is actually a static one. In terms of the taxonomy that we present here, we would categorize this as a static, optimal, graph-theoretical approach in which the a priori assumptions are expanded to include more information about the set of tasks to be executed. The way in which reassignment of tasks is performed during process execution is decided upon before any of the program modules begin execution. Instead of reassignment decisions being made during execution, the stronger assumption is simply made that all information about the dynamic needs of a collection of program modules is available a priori. This assumption says that if a collection of modules possesses a certain communication pattern at the beginning of its execution and this pattern is completely predictable, then this pattern may change over the course of execution and these variations are predictable as well. Costs of relocation are also assumed to be available, and this assumption appears to be quite reasonable.

The model presented in [35] represents an example of an optimal, mathematical-programming formulation employing a branch-and-bound technique to search the solution space. The goals of the solution are to minimize interprocessor communications, balance the utilization of all processors, and satisfy all other engineering application requirements. The model given defines a cost function that includes interprocessor-communication costs and processor-execution costs. The assignment is then represented by a set of zero-one variables, and the total execution cost is then represented by a summation of all costs incurred in the assignment. In addition to the above, the problem is subject to constraints that allow the solution to satisfy the load-balancing and engineering-application requirements. The algorithm then used to search the solution space (consisting of all potential assignments) is derived from the basic branch-and-bound technique.

Again, in [10], we see an example of the use of the taxonomy in comparing the proposed system to other approaches. The title of the paper, "Load Balancing in Distributed Systems," indicates that the goal of the solution is to balance the load among the processors in the system in some way. However, the solution actually fits into the static, optimal, queueing-theoretical class. The goal of the solution is to minimize the execution time of the entire program to maximize performance, and the algorithm is derived from results in Markov decision theory. In contrast to the definition of load balancing given earlier, where the goal was to even the load and utilization of system resources, the approach in this paper is consumer oriented.

An interesting approximate, mathematical-programming solution, motivated from the viewpoint of fault-tolerance, is presented in [2]. The algorithm is suggested by the computational complexity of the optimal solution to the same problem. In the basic solution to a mathematical-programming problem, the state space is either implicitly or explicitly enumerated and searched. One approximation method mentioned in this paper [64] involves first removing the integer constraint, solving the continuous-optimization problem, discretizing the continuous solution, and obtaining a bound on the discretization error. Whereas this bound is with respect to the continuous optimum, the algorithm proposed in this paper directly uses an approximation to solve the discrete problem and bound its performance with respect to the discrete optimum.

The last static example to be given here appears in [66]. This paper gives a heuristic-based approach to the problem by using extractable data and synchronization requirements of the different subtasks. The three primary heuristics used are

- Loss of parallelism,
- Synchronization, and
- Data sources.

The way in which loss of parallelism is used is to assign tasks to nodes one at a time in order to effect the least loss of parallelism based on the number of units required for execution by the task currently under consideration. The synchronization constraints are phrased in terms of *firing conditions* that are used to describe precedence relationships between subtasks. Finally, data source information is used in much the same way that a functional program uses precedence relationships between parallel portions of a computation that take the roles of varying classes of suppliers of variables to other subtasks. The final heuristic algorithm involves weighing each of the previous heuristics and combining them. A distinguishing feature of the algorithm is its use of a greedy approach to find a solution, when at the time decisions are made, there can be no guarantee that a decision is optimal. Hence, an optimal solution would more carefully search the solution space using a backtrack or branch-and-bound method, as well as using an exact optimization criterion instead of the heuristics suggested.

Global dynamic

Among the dynamic solutions presented in the literature, the majority fit into the general category of physically distributed, cooperative, suboptimal, and heuristic. There are, however, examples for some of the other classes.

First, in the category of physically nondistributed, one of the best examples is the experimental system developed for the Cm* architecture — Medusa [44]. In this system, the functions of the operating system (for example, file system and scheduler) are physically partitioned and placed at different places in the system. Hence, the scheduling function is placed at a particular place and is accessed by all users at that location.

Another rare example exists in the physically distributed, noncooperative class. In this example [27], random-level order scheduling is employed at all nodes independently in a tightly coupled MIMD machine. Hence, the overhead involved in this algorithm is minimized, since no information need be exchanged to make random decisions. The mechanism suggested is thought to work best in moderate to heavily loaded systems, since in these cases, a random policy is thought to give a reasonably balanced load on all processors. In contrast to a cooperative solution, this algorithm does not detect or try to avoid system overloading by sharing loading information among processors but makes the assumption that it will be under heavy load most of the time and bases all of its decisions on that assumption. Clearly, here the processors are not necessarily concerned with the utilization of their own resources, but neither are they concerned with the effect their individual decisions will have on the other processors in the system.

It should be pointed out that although the above two algorithms (and many others) are given in terms relating to general-purpose distributed-processing systems, they do not strictly adhere to the definition of a distributed-data-processing system as given in [17].

In [57], another rare example exists in the form of a physically distributed, cooperative, *optimal* solution in a dynamic environment. The solution is given for the two-processor case in which critical load factors are calculated prior to program execution. The method employed is to use a graph-theoretical approach to solving for load factors for each process on each processor. These load factors are then used at runtime to determine when a task could run better if placed on the other processor.

The final class (and largest in terms of amount of existing work) is the class of physically distributed, cooperative, suboptimal, and heuristic solutions.

In [53], a solution is given that is adaptive, load-balancing, and makes one-time assignments of jobs to processors. No a priori assumptions are made about the characteristics of the jobs to be scheduled. One major restriction of these algorithms is that they only consider assignment of jobs to processors, and once a job becomes an active process, no reassignment of processes is considered, regardless of the possible benefit. This is very defensible, though, if the overhead involved in moving a process is very high (which may be the case in many circumstances). Whereas this solution cannot exactly be considered as a bidding approach, exchange of information occurs between processes in order for the algorithms to function. The first algorithm (a copy of which resides at each host) compares its own "busyness" with its estimate of the "busyness" of the least busy host. If the difference exceeds the bins (or threshold) designated at the current time, one job is moved from the job queue of the busier host to the less busy one. The second algorithm allows each host to compare itself with all other hosts and involves two biases. If the difference exceeds bias1 but not bias2, then one job is moved. If the difference exceeds bias2, then two jobs are moved. Also, there is an upper limit set on the number of jobs that can move at once in the entire system. The third algorithm is the same as algorithm one, except that an antithrashing mechanism is added to account for the fact that a delay is present between the time a decision is made to move a job and the time it arrives at the destination. All three algorithms had an adaptive feature added that would turn off all parts of the respective algorithm (except the monitoring of load) when system load was below a particular minimum threshold. This had the effect of stopping *processor thrashing* whenever it was practically impossible to balance the system load due to lack of work to balance. In the high-load case, the algorithm was turned off to reduce extraneous overhead when the algorithm could not effect any improvement in the system under any redistribution of jobs. This last feature also supports the notion in the noncooperative example given earlier, in that the load is usually automatically balanced as a side effect of heavy loading. The remainder of the paper focuses on simulation results to reveal the impact of modifying the biasing parameters.

The work reported in [6] is an example of an algorithm that employs the heuristic of load balancing and probabilistically estimates the remaining processing times of processes in the system. The remaining processing time for a process was estimated by one of the following methods:

- Memoryless: $Re(t) = E\{S\}$
- Pastrepeats: $Re(t) = t$

- Distribution: $\quad Re(t) = E\{S - t \mid S > t\}$
- Optimal: $\qquad Re(t) = R(t)$

where $R(t)$ is the remaining time needed, given that t seconds have already elapsed; S is the service time random variable; and $Re(t)$ is the scheduler's estimate of $R(t)$. The algorithm then basically uses the first three methods to predict response times in order to obtain an expected-delay measure, which in turn is used by pairs of processors to balance their load on a pairwise basis. This mechanism is adopted by all pairs on a dynamic basis to balance the system load.

Another adaptive algorithm is discussed in [52] and is based on the bidding concept. The heuristic mentioned here utilizes prior information concerning the known characteristics of processes such as resource requirements, process priority, special resource needs, precedence constraints, and the need for clustering and distributed groups. The basic algorithm periodically evaluates each process at a current node to decide whether or not to transmit bid requests for a particular process. The bid requests include information needed for contractor nodes to make decisions regarding how well they may be able to execute the process in question. The manager receives bids, compares them to the local evaluation, and will transfer the process if the difference between the best bid and the local estimate is above a certain threshold. The key to the algorithm is the formulation of a function to be used in a modified McCulloch-Pitts neuron. The neuron (implemented as a subroutine) evaluates the current performance of individual processes. Several different functions were proposed, simulated, and discussed in this paper. The adaptive nature of this algorithm is in the fact that it dynamically modifies the number of hops that a bid request is allowed to travel, depending on current conditions. The most significant result is that the information regarding process clustering and distributed groups seems to have had little impact on the overall performance of the system.

The final example to be discussed here [55] is based on a heuristic derived from the area of Bayesian decision theory [33]. The algorithm uses no a priori knowledge regarding task characteristics and is dynamic in the sense that the probability distributions that allow maximizing decisions to be made based on the most likely current state of nature are updated dynamically. Monitor nodes make observations every f seconds and update probabilities. Every d seconds, the scheduler itself is invoked to approximate the current state of nature and make the appropriate maximizing action. It was found that the parameters f and d could be tuned to obtain maximum performance for a minimum cost.

Discussion

In this section, we will attempt to demonstrate the application of the qualitative description tool presented earlier to a role beyond that of classifying existing systems. In particular, we will utilize two behavior characteristics — *performance* and *efficiency* — in conjunction with the classification mechanism presented in the taxonomy to identify general qualities of scheduling systems that will lend themselves to managing large numbers of processors. In addition, the uniform terminology presented will be employed to show that some earlier-thought-to-be-synonymous notions are actually distinct and that the distinctions are valuable. Also, in at least one case, two earlier-thought-to-be-different notions will be shown to be much the same.

Decentralized versus distributed scheduling

When considering the decision-making policy of a scheduling system, there are two fundamental components — *authority* and *responsibility*. When authority is distributed to the entities of a resource management system, we call this *decentralized*. When responsibility for making and carrying out policy decisions is shared among the entities in a distributed system, we say that the scheduler is *distributed*. This differentiation exists in many other organizational structures. Any system that possesses decentralized authority must have distributed responsibility, but it is possible to allocate responsibility for gathering information and carrying out policy decisions without giving the authority to change past or make future decisions.

Dynamic versus adaptive scheduling

The terms *dynamic scheduling* and *adaptive scheduling* are quite often attached to various proposed algorithms in the literature, but there appears to be some confusion as to the actual difference between these two concepts. The more common property to find in a scheduler (or resource management subsystem) is the dynamic property. In a dynamic situation, the scheduler takes into account the current state of affairs as it perceives them in the system. This is done during the normal operation of the system under a dynamic and unpredictable load. In an adaptive system, the scheduling policy itself reflects changes in its environment — the running system. Notice that the difference here is one of level in the hierarchical solution to the scheduling problem. Whereas a dynamic solution takes environmental inputs into account when making its decisions, an adaptive solution takes environmental stimuli into account to modify the scheduling policy itself.

The resource/consumer dichotomy in performance analysis

As is the case in describing the actions or qualitative behavior of a resource management subsystem, the performance of the scheduling mechanisms employed may be viewed from either the resource or consumer point of view. When considering performance from the consumer (or user) point of view, the metric involved is often one of minimizing individual program completion times: *response*. Alternately, the resource point of view also considers the rate of process execution in evaluating performance, but from the view of total system *throughput*. In contrast to response, throughput is concerned with seeing that *all* users are treated fairly and that *all* are making progress. Notice that the resource view of maximizing resource utilization is compatible with the desire for maximum system throughput. Another way of stating this, however, is that all users, when considered as a single collective user, are treated best in this environment of maximizing system throughput or maximizing resource utilization. This is the basic philosophy of load-balancing mechanisms. There is an inherent conflict, though, in trying to optimize both response and throughput.

Focusing on future directions

In this section, the earlier-presented taxonomy, in conjunction with two terms used to quantitatively describe system behavior, will be used to discuss possibilities for distributed scheduling in the environment of a large system of loosely coupled processors. In previous work related to the scheduling problem, the basic notion of performance has been concerned with evaluating the way in which users' individual needs are being satisfied. The metrics most commonly applied are response and throughput [23]. While these terms accurately characterize the goals of the system in terms of how well users are served, they are difficult to measure during the normal operation of a system. In addition to this problem, the metrics do not lend themselves well to direct interpretation as to the action to be performed to increase performance when it is not at an acceptable level.

These metrics are also difficult to apply when analysis or simulation of such systems is attempted. The reason for this is that two important aspects of scheduling are necessarily intertwined. These two aspects are performance and efficiency. Performance is the part of a system's behavior that encompasses how well the resource to be managed is being used to the benefit of all users of the system. Efficiency, though, is concerned with the added cost (or overhead) associated with the resource management facility itself. In terms of these two criteria, we may think of desirable system behavior as that having the highest level of performance possible, while incurring the least overhead in doing it. Clearly, the exact combination of these two that brings about the most desirable behavior is dependent on many factors and in many ways resembles the space/time trade-off present in common algorithm design. The point to be made here is that simultaneous evaluation of performance and efficiency is very difficult because of this inherent entanglement. What we suggest is a methodology for designing scheduling systems in which performance and efficiency are separately observable.

Current and future investigations will involve studies to better understand the relationships between performance, efficiency, and their components as they affect quantitative behavior. It is hoped that a much better understanding can be gained regarding the costs and benefits of alternative distributed-scheduling strategies.

Conclusions

This paper has sought to bring together the ideas and work in the area of resource management generated in the last 15 to 20 years. The intention was to provide a suitable framework for comparing past work in the area of resource management, while providing a tool for classifying and discussing future work. This has been done through the presentation of common terminology and a taxonomy on the mechanisms employed in computer system resource management. While the taxonomy could be used to discuss many different types of resource management, the attention of the paper and included examples has been on the application of the taxonomy to the processing resource. Finally, recommendations regarding possible fruitful areas for future research in the area of scheduling in large-scale, general-purpose distributed computer systems have been discussed.

As is the case in any survey, there are many pieces of work to be considered. It is hoped that the examples presented fairly represent the true state of research in this area, while it is acknowledged that not all such examples have been discussed. In addition to the references at the end of this paper, an annotated bibliography is included. It lists work that — although not explicitly mentioned in the text — has aided in the construction of this taxonomy through the support of additional examples. The exclusion of any particular result was not intentional nor should it be construed as a judgment of the merit of that work. Decisions as to which papers to use as examples were made purely on the basis of their applicability to the context of the discussion in which they appear.

References

[1] A.K. Agrawala, S.K. Tripathi, and G. Ricart, "Adaptive Routing Using a Virtual Waiting Time Technique," *IEEE Trans. Software Eng.*, Vol. SE-8, No. 1, Jan. 1982, pp. 76–81.

[2] J.A. Bannister and K.S. Trivedi, "Task Allocation in Fault-Tolerant Distributed Systems," *Acta Informatica,* Vol. 20, 1983, pp. 261–281.

[3] J.F. Bartlett, "A Nonstop Kernel," *Proc. Eighth ACM Symp. Operating Systems Principles*, ACM Press, New York, N.Y., 1981, pp. 22–29.

[4] S.H. Bokhari, "Dual Processor Scheduling with Dynamic Reassignment," *IEEE Trans. Software Eng.*, Vol. SE-5, No. 4, July 1979, pp. 326–334.

[5] S.H. Bokhari, "A Shortest Tree Algorithm for Optimal Assignments across Space and Time in a Distributed Processor System, IEEE *Trans. Software Eng.*, Vol. SE-7, No. 6, Nov. 1981, pp. 335–341.

[6] R.M. Bryant and R.A. Finkel, "A Stable Distributed Scheduling Algorithm," *Proc. Second Int'l Conf. Distributed Computing Systems*, IEEE Computer Soc. Press, Los Alamitos, Calif., 1981, pp. 314–323.

[7] E.S. Buffa, *Modern Production Management*, fifth ed., Wiley, New York, N.Y., 1977.

[8] T.L. Casavant and J.G. Kuhl, "Design of a Loosely-Coupled Distributed Multiprocessing Network," *Proc. 1984 Int'l Conf. Parallel Processing*, IEEE Computer Soc. Press, Los Alamitos, Calif., 1984, pp. 42–45.

[9] L.M. Casey, "Decentralized Scheduling," *Australian Computer J.*, Vol. 13, May 1981, pp. 58–63.

[10] T.C.K. Chou and J.A. Abraham, "Load Balancing in Distributed Systems," *IEEE Trans. Software Eng.*, Vol. SE-8, No. 4, July 1982, pp. 401–412.

[11] Y.C. Chow and W.H. Kohler, "Models for Dynamic Load Balancing in a Heterogeneous Multiple Processor System," *IEEE Trans. Computers*, Vol. C-28, No. 5, May 1979, pp. 354–361.

[12] E.G. Coffman and P.J. Denning, *Operating Systems Theory*, Prentice-Hall, Inc., Englewood Cliffs, N.J., 1973.

[13] R.W. Conway, W.L. Maxwell, and L.W. Miller, *Theory of Scheduling*, Addison-Wesley Pub. Co., Reading, Mass., 1967.

[14] K.W. Doty, P.L. McEntire, and J.G. O'Reilly, "Task Allocation in a Distributed Computer System," *Proc. INFOCOM '82*, IEEE Computer Soc. Press, Los Alamitos, Calif., 1982, pp. 33–38.

[15] K. Efe, "Heuristic Models of Task Assignment Scheduling in Distributed Systems," *Computer*, Vol. 15, No. 6, June 1982, pp. 50–56.

[16] C.S. Ellis, J.A. Feldman, and J.E. Heliotis, "Language Constructs and Support Systems for Distributed Computing," *Proc. ACM SIGACT-SIGOPS Symp. Principles Distributed Computing*, ACM Press, New York, N.Y., 1982, pp. 1–9.

[17] P.H. Enslow, Jr., "What Is a 'Distributed' Data Processing System?," *Computer*, Vol. 11, No. 1, Jan. 1978, pp. 13–21.

[18] J.R. Evans et al., *Applied Production and Operations Management*, West Pub. Co., St. Paul, Minn., 1984.

[19] I. Flores, *OSMVT*, Allyn and Bacon, Inc., Rockleigh, N.J., 1973.

[20] M.J. Flynn, "Very High-Speed Computing Systems," *Proc. IEEE*, Vol. 54, Dec. 1966, pp. 1901–1909.

[21] A. Gabrielian and D.B. Tyler, "Optimal Object Allocation in Distributed Computer Systems," *Proc. Fourth Int'l Conf. Distributed Computing Systems*, IEEE Computer Soc. Press, Los Alamitos, Calif., 1984, pp. 84–95.

[22] M.J. Gonzalez, "Deterministic Processor Scheduling," *ACM Computing Surveys*, Vol. 9, No. 3, Sept. 1977, pp. 173–204.

[23] H. Hellerman and T.F. Conroy, *Computer System Performance*, McGraw-Hill, Inc., New York, N.Y., 1975.

[24] Y. Ho, "Team Decision Theory and Information Structures," *Proc. IEEE*, Vol. 68, No. 6, June 1980, pp. 644–654.

[25] E.D. Jensen, "The Honeywell Experimental Distributed Processor — An Overview," *Computer*, Vol. 11, No. 1, Jan. 1978, pp. 28–38.

[26] A.K. Jones et al., "StarOS, a Multiprocessor Operating System for the Support of Task Forces," *Proc. Seventh ACM Symp. Operating Systems Principles*, ACM Press, New York, N.Y., 1979, pp. 117–127.

[27] D. Klappholz and H.C. Park, "Parallelized Process Scheduling for a Tightly-Coupled MIMD Machine," *Proc. 1984 Int'l Conf. Parallel Processing*, IEEE Computer Soc. Press, Los Alamitos, Calif., 1984, pp. 315–321.

[28] L. Kleinrock, *Queuing Systems, Vol. 2: Computer Applications*, Wiley, New York, N.Y., 1976.

[29] L. Kleinrock and A. Nilsson, "On Optimal Scheduling Algorithms for Time-Shared Systems," *J. ACM*, Vol. 28, No. 3, July 1981, pp. 477–486.

[30] C.P. Kruskal and A. Weiss, "Allocating Independent Subtasks on Parallel Processor — Extended

Abstract," *Proc. 1984 Int'l Conf. Parallel Processing*, IEEE Computer Soc. Press, Los Alamitos, Calif., 1984, pp. 236–240.

[31] R.E. Larson, *Tutorial: Distributed Control*, IEEE Computer Soc. Press, Los Alamitos, Calif., 1979.

[32] G. Le Lann, *Motivations, Objectives and Characterizations of Distributed Systems* (*Lecture Notes in Computer Science, Vol. 105*), Springer-Verlag Pub., New York, N.Y., 1981, pp. 1–9.

[33] B.W. Lindgren, *Elements of Decision Theory*, The MacMillan Pub. Co., New York, N.Y., 1971.

[34] V.M. Lo, "Heuristic Algorithms for Task Assignment in Distributed Systems," *Proc. Fourth Int'l Conf. Distributed Computing Systems*, IEEE Computer Soc. Press, Los Alamitos, Calif., 1984, pp. 30–39.

[35] P.Y.R. Ma, E.Y.S. Lee, and J. Tsuchiya, "A Task Allocation Model for Distributed Computing Systems," *IEEE Trans. Computers*, Vol. C-31, No. 1, Jan. 1982, pp. 41–47.

[36] R. Manner, "Hardware Task/Processor Scheduling in a Polyprocessor Environment," *IEEE Trans. Computers*, Vol. C-33, No. 7, July 1984, pp. 626–636.

[37] P.L. McEntire, J.G. O'Reilly, and R.E. Larson, *Distributed Computing: Concepts and Implementations*, IEEE Press, New York, N.Y., 1984.

[38] E. Mishkin and L. Braun, Jr., *Adaptive Control Systems*, McGraw-Hill, Inc., New York, N.Y., 1961.

[39] K. Narendra, "Learning Automata —A Survey," *IEEE Trans. Systems, Man, and Cybernetics*, Vol. SMC-4, No. 4, July 1974, pp. 323–334.

[40] L.M. Ni and K. Hwang, "Optimal Load Balancing Strategies for a Multiple Processor System," *Proc. Int'l Conf. Parallel Processing*, IEEE Computer Soc. Press, Los Alamitos, Calif., 1981, pp. 352–357.

[41] L.M. Ni and K. Abani, "Nonpreemptive Load Balancing in a Class of Local Area Networks," *Proc. Computer Networking Symp.*, IEEE Computer Soc. Press, Los Alamitos, Calif., 1981, pp. 113–118.

[42] L.M. Ni and K. Hwang, "Optimal Load Balancing in a Multiple Processor System with Many Job Classes," *IEEE Trans. Software Eng.*, Vol. SE-11, No. 5, May 1985, pp. 491–496.

[43] N.J. Nilsson, *Principles of Artificial Intelligence*, Tioga, Palo Alto, Calif., 1980.

[44] J. Ousterhout, D. Scelza, and P. Sindhu, "Medusa: An Experiment in Distributed Operating System Structure," *Comm. ACM*, Vol. 23, No. 2, Feb. 1980, pp. 92–105.

[45] G. Popek et al., "LOCUS: A Network Transparent, High Reliability Distributed System," *Proc. Eighth ACM Symp. Operating Systems Principles*, ACM Press, New York, N.Y., 1981, pp. 169–177.

[46] M.L. Powell and B.P. Miller, "Process Migration in DEMOS/MP," *Proc. Ninth ACM Symp. Operating Systems Principles (OS Review)*, Vol. 17, No. 5, Oct. 1983, pp. 110–119.

[47] C.C. Price and S. Krishnaprasad, "Software Allocation Models for Distributed Computing Systems," *Proc. Fourth Int'l Conf. Distributed Computing Systems*, IEEE Computer Soc. Press, Los Alamitos, Calif., 1984, pp. 40–48.

[48] C. Shen and W. Tsai, "A Graph Matching Approach to Optimal Task Assignment in Distributed Computing Systems Using a Minimax Criterion," *IEEE Trans. Computers*, Vol. C-34, No. 3, Mar. 1985, pp. 197–203.

[49] R.G. Smith, "The Contract Net Protocol: High-Level Communication and Control in a Distributed Problem Solver," *IEEE Trans. Computers*, Vol. C-29, No. 12, Dec. 1980, pp. 1104–1113.

[50] M.H. Solomon and R.A. Finkel, "The ROSCOE Distributed Operating System," *Proc. Seventh ACM Symp. Operating Systems Principles*, ACM Press, New York, N.Y., 1979, pp. 108–114.

[51] J.A. Stankovic, "Simulations of Three Adaptive, Decentralized, Controlled Job Scheduling Algorithms," *Computer Networks*, Vol. 8, No. 3, June 1984, pp. 199–217.

[52] J.A. Stankovic, "A Perspective on Distributed Computer Systems," *IEEE Trans. Computers*, Vol. C-33, No. 12, Dec. 1984, pp. 1102–1115.

[53] J.A. Stankovic, "An Application of Bayesian Decision Theory to Decentralized Control of Job Scheduling," *IEEE Trans. Computers*, Vol. C-34, No. 2, Feb. 1985, pp. 117–130.

[54] J.A. Stankovic et al., "An Evaluation of the Applicability of Different Mathematical Approaches to

the Analysis of Decentralized Control Algorithms," *Proc. COMPSAC '82,* IEEE Computer Soc. Press, Los Alamitos, Calif., 1982, pp. 62–69.

[55] J.A. Stankovic and I.S. Sidhu, "An Adaptive Bidding Algorithm for Processes, Clusters and Distributed Groups," *Proc. Fourth Int'l Conf. Distributed Computing Systems,* IEEE Computer Soc. Press, Los Alamitos, Calif., 1984, pp. 49–59.

[56] J.A. Stankovic et al., "A Review of Current Research and Critical Issues in Distributed System Software," *IEEE Computer Soc. Distributed Processing Technical Committee Newsletter,* Vol. 7, No. 1, Mar. 1985, pp. 14–47.

[57] H.S. Stone, "Critical Load Factors in Two-Processor Distributed Systems," *IEEE Trans. Software Eng.,* Vol. SE-4, No. 3, May 1978, pp. 254–258.

[58] H.S. Stone and S.H. Bokhari, "Control of Distributed Processes," *Computer,* Vol. 11, No. 7, July 1978, pp. 97–106.

[59] H. Sullivan and T. Bashkow, "A Large-Scale Homogeneous, Fully Distributed Machine —II," *Proc. Fourth Symp. Computer Architecture,* IEEE Computer Soc. Press, Los Alamitos, Calif., 1977, pp. 118–124.

[60] A.S. Tanenbaum, *Computer Networks,* Prentice-Hall, Inc., Englewood Cliffs, N.J., 1981.

[61] D.P. Tsay and M.T. Liu, "MIKE: A Network Operating System for the Distributed Double-Loop Computer Network," *IEEE Trans. Software Eng.,* Vol. SE-9, No. 2, Mar. 1983, pp. 143–154.

[62] D.C. Tsichritzis and P.A. Bernstein, *Operating Systems,* Academic Press, Inc., New York, N.Y., 1974.

[63] K. Vairavan and R.A. DeMillo, "On the Computational Complexity of a Generalized Scheduling Problem," *IEEE Trans. Computers,* Vol. C-25, No. 11, Nov. 1976, pp. 1067–1073.

[64] R.A. Wagner and K.S. Trivedi, "Hardware Configuration Selection through Discretizing a Continuous Variable Solution," *Proc. Seventh IFIP Symp. Computer Performance Modeling, Measurement and Evaluation,* 1980, pp. 127–142.

[65] Y.T. Wang and R.J.T. Morris, "Load Sharing in Distributed Systems," *IEEE Trans. Computers,* Vol. C-34, No. 3, Mar. 1985, pp. 204–217.

[66] M.O. Ward and D.J. Romero, "Assigning Parallel-Executable, Intercommunicating Subtasks to Processors," *Proc. 1984 Int'l Conf. Parallel Processing,* IEEE Computer Soc. Press, Los Alamitos, Calif., 1984, pp. 392–394.

[67] L.D. Wittie and A.M. Van Tilborg, "MICROS, a Distributed Operating System for MICRONET, a Reconfigurable Network Computer," *IEEE Trans. Computers,* Vol. C-29, No. 12, Dec. 1980, pp. 1133–1144.

Annotated bibliography

Application of taxonomy to examples from literature

References on this list contain additional examples not discussed in the section of the text entitled "Examples," as well as abbreviated descriptions of examples that are discussed there. The purpose of this list is to demonstrate the use of the taxonomy described in the section entitled "The scheduling problem — Describing its solutions" to classify large numbers of examples from the literature.

1. G.R. Andrews, D.P. Dobkin, and P.J. Downey, "Distributed Allocation with Pools of Servers," *Proc. ACM SIGACT-SIGOPS Symp. Principles Distributed Computing,* ACM Press, New York, N.Y., 1982, pp. 73–83.

Global, dynamic, distributed (however, in a limited sense), cooperative, suboptimal, heuristic, bidding, nonadaptive, dynamic reassignment.

2. J.A. Bannister and K.S. Trivedi, "Task Allocation in Fault-Tolerant Distributed Systems," *Acta Informatica,* Vol. 20, 1983, pp. 261–281.

Global, static, suboptimal, approximate, mathematical-programming.

3. F. Berman and L. Snyder, "On Mapping Parallel Algorithms into Parallel Architectures," *Proc. 1984 Int'l Conf. Parallel Processing*, IEEE Computer Soc. Press, Los Alamitos, Calif., 1984, pp. 307–309.

Global, static, optimal, graph-theoretical.

4. S.H. Bokhari, "Dual Processor Scheduling with Dynamic Reassignment," *IEEE Trans. Software Eng.*, Vol. SE-5, No. 4, July 1979, pp. 326–334.

Global, static, optimal, graph-theoretical.

5. S.H. Bokhari, "A Shortest Tree Algorithm for Optimal Assignments across Space and Time in a Distributed Processor System," *IEEE Trans. Software Eng.*, Vol. SE-7, No. 6, Nov. 1981, pp. 335–341.

Global, static, optimal, mathematical-programming, intended for tree-structured applications.

6. R.M. Bryant and R.A. Finkel, "A Stable Distributed Scheduling Algorithm," *Proc. Second Int'l Conf. Distributed Computing Systems*, IEEE Computer Soc. Press, Los Alamitos, Calif., 1981, pp. 314–323.

Global, dynamic, physically distributed, cooperative, suboptimal, heuristic, probabilistic, load-balancing.

7. T.L. Casavant and J.G. Kuhl, "Design of a Loosely-Coupled Distributed Multiprocessing Network," *Proc. 1984 Int'l Conf. Parallel Processing*, IEEE Computer Soc. Press, Los Alamitos, Calif., 1984, pp. 42–45.

Global, dynamic, physically distributed, cooperative, suboptimal, heuristic, load-balancing, bidding, dynamic reassignment.

8. L.M. Casey, "Decentralized Scheduling," *Australian Computer J.*, Vol. 13, May 1981, pp. 58–63.

Global, dynamic, physically distributed, cooperative, suboptimal, heuristic, load-balancing.

9. T.C.K. Chou and J. A. Abraham, "Load Balancing in Distributed Systems," *IEEE Trans. Software Eng.*, Vol. SE-8, No. 4, July 1982, pp. 401–412.

Global, static, optimal, queuing-theoretical.

10. T.C.K. Chou and J.A. Abraham, "Load Redistribution under Failure in Distributed Systems," *IEEE Trans. Computers,* Vol. C-32, No. 9, Sept. 1983, pp. 799–808.

Global, dynamic (but with static pairings of supporting and supported processors), distributed, cooperative, suboptimal, provides three separate heuristic mechanisms, motivated from fault-recovery aspect.

11. Y.C. Chow and W.H. Kohler, "Models for Dynamic Load Balancing in a Heterogeneous Multiple Processor System," *IEEE Trans. Computers*, Vol. C-28, No. 5, May 1979, pp. 354–361.

Global, dynamic, physically distributed, cooperative, suboptimal, heuristic, load-balancing, (part of the heuristic approach is based on results from queuing theory).

12. W.W. Chu et al., " Task Allocation in Distributed Data Processing," *Computer*, Vol. 13, No. 11, Nov. 1980, pp. 57–69.

Global, static, optimal, suboptimal, heuristic, heuristic approached based on graph theory and mathematical programming are discussed.

13. K.W. Doty, P.L. McEntire, and J.G. O'Reilly, "Task Allocation in a Distributed Computer System," *Proc. INFOCOM '82*, IEEE Computer Soc. Press, Los Alamitos, Calif., 1982, pp. 33–38.

Global, static, optimal, mathematical-programming (nonlinear spatial dynamic programming).

14. K. Efe, "Heuristic Models of Task Assignment Scheduling in Distributed Systems," *Computer*, Vol. 15, No. 6, June 1982, pp. 50–56.

Global, static, suboptimal, heuristic, load-balancing.

15. J.A.B. Fortes and F. Parisi-Presicce, "Optimal Linear Schedules for the Parallel Execution of Algorithms," *Proc. 1984 Int'l Conf. Parallel Processing*, IEEE Computer Soc. Press, Los Alamitos, Calif., 1984, pp. 322–329.

Global, static, optimal, uses results from mathematical programming for a large class of data-dependency-driven applications.

16. A. Gabrielian and D.B. Tyler, "Optimal Object Allocation in Distributed Computer Systems," *Proc. Fourth Int'l Conf. Distributed Computing Systems*, IEEE Computer Soc. Press, Los Alamitos, Calif., 1984, pp. 84–95.

Global, static, optimal, mathematical-programming, uses a heuristic to obtain a solution close to optimal, employs backtracking to find optimal one from that.

17. C. Gao, J.W.S. Liu, and M. Railey, "Load Balancing Algorithms in Homogeneous Distributed Systems," *Proc. 1984 Int'l Conf. Parallel Processing*, IEEE Computer Soc. Press, Los Alamitos, Calif., 1984, pp. 302–306.

Global, dynamic, distributed, cooperative, suboptimal, heuristic, probabilistic.

18. W. Huen et al., "TECHNEC, a Network Computer for Distributed Task Control," *Proc. First Rocky Mountain Symp. Microcomputers*, IEEE Computer Soc. Press, Los Alamitos, Calif., 1977, pp. 233–237.

Global, static, suboptimal, heuristic.

19. K. Hwang et al., "A Unix-Based Local Computer Network with Load Balancing," *Computer*, Vol. 15, No. 4, Apr. 1982, pp. 55–65.

Global, dynamic, physically distributed, cooperative, suboptimal, heuristic, load-balancing.

20. D. Klappholz and H.C. Park, "Parallelized Process Scheduling for a Tightly-Coupled MIMD Machine," *Proc. 1984 Int'l Conf. Parallel Processing*, IEEE Computer Soc. Press, Los Alamitos, Calif., 1984, pp. 315–321.

Global, dynamic, physically distributed, noncooperative.

21. C.P. Kruskal and A. Weiss, "Allocating Independent Subtasks on Parallel Processors — Extended Abstract," *Proc. 1984 Int'l Conf. Parallel Processing*, IEEE Computer Soc. Press, Los Alamitos, Calif., 1984, pp. 236–240.

Global, static, suboptimal, but optimal for a set of optimistic assumptions, heuristic, problem stated in terms of queuing theory.

22. V.M. Lo, "Heuristic Algorithms for Task Assignment in Distributed Systems," *Proc. Fourth Int'l Conf. Distributed Computing Systems*, IEEE Computer Soc. Press, Los Alamitos, Calif., 1984, pp. 30–39.

Global, static, suboptimal, approximate, graph-theoretical.

23. V.M. Lo, "Task Assignment to Minimize Completion Time," *Proc. Fifth Int'l Conf. Distributed Computing Systems*, IEEE Computer Soc. Press, Los Alamitos, Calif., 1985, pp. 329–336.

Global, static, optimal, mathematical-programming for some special cases, but in general is suboptimal, heuristic using the LPT algorithm.

24. P.Y.R. Ma, E.Y.S. Lee, and J. Tsuchiya, "A Task Allocation Model for Distributed Computing Systems," *IEEE Trans. Computers*, Vol. C-31, No. 1, Jan. 1982, pp. 41–47.

Global, static, optimal, mathematical-programming (branch-and-bound).

25. S. Majumdar and M.L. Green, "A Distributed Real Time Resource Manager," *Proc. Distributed Data Acquisition, Computing, and Control Symp.*, IEEE Computer Soc. Press, Los Alamitos, Calif., 1980, pp. 185–193.

Global, dynamic, distributed, cooperative, suboptimal, heuristic, load-balancing, nonadaptive.

26. R. Manner, "Hardware Task/Processor Scheduling in a Polyprocessor Environment," *IEEE Trans. Computers*, Vol. C-33, No. 7, July 1984, pp. 626–636.

Global, dynamic, distributed control and responsibility, but centralized information in hardware on bus lines; cooperative, optimal, (priority) load-balancing.

27. L.M. Ni and K. Hwang, "Optimal Load Balancing Strategies for a Multiple Processor System," *Proc. Int'l Conf. Parallel Processing*, IEEE Computer Soc. Press, Los Alamitos, Calif., 1981, pp. 352–357.

Global, static, optimal, mathematical-programming.

28. L.M. Ni and K. Abani, "Nonpreemptive Load Balancing in a Class of Local Area Networks," *Proc. Computer Networking Symp.*, IEEE Computer Soc. Press, Los Alamitos, Calif., 1981, pp. 113–118.

Global, dynamic, distributed, cooperative, optimal and suboptimal solutions given — mathematical-programming and adaptive load-balancing, respectively.

29. J. Ousterhout, D. Scelza, and P. Sindhu, "Medusa: An Experiment in Distributed Operating System Structure," *Comm. ACM*, Vol. 23, No. 2, Feb. 1980, pp. 92–105.

Global, dynamic, physically nondistributed.

30. M.L. Powell and B.P. Miller, "Process Migration in DEMOS/MP," *Proc. Ninth ACM Symp. Operating Systems Principles (OS Review)*, Vol. 17, No. 5, Oct. 1983, pp. 110–119.

Global, dynamic, distributed, cooperative, suboptimal, heuristic, load-balancing, but no specific decision rule given.

31. C.C. Price and S. Krishnaprasad, "Software Allocation Models for Distributed Computing Systems," *Proc. Fourth Int'l Conf. Distributed Computing Systems*, IEEE Computer Soc. Press, Los Alamitos, Calif., 1984, pp. 40–48.

Global, static, optimal, mathematical-programming, but also suggest heuristics.

32. C.V. Ramamoorthy et al., "Optimal Scheduling Strategies in a Multiprocessor System," *IEEE Trans. Computers*, Vol. C-21, No. 2, Feb. 1972, pp. 137–146.

Global, static, optimal solution presented for comparison with the heuristic one also presented; graph theory is employed in the sense that it uses task-precedence graphs.

33. K. Ramamritham and J.A. Stankovic, "Dynamic Task Scheduling in Distributed Hard Real-Time Systems," *Proc. Fourth Int'l Conf. Distributed Computing Systems*, IEEE Computer Soc. Press, Los Alamitos, Calif., 1984, pp. 96–107.

Global, dynamic, distributed, cooperative, suboptimal, heuristic, bidding, one-time assignments (a real-time guarantee is applied before migration).

34. J. Reif and P. Spirakis, "Real-Time Resource Allocation in a Distributed System," *Proc. ACM SIGACT-SIGOPS Symp. Principles Distributed Computing*, ACM Press, New York, N.Y., 1982, pp. 84–94.

Global, dynamic, distributed, noncooperative, probabilistic.

35. S. Sahni, "Scheduling Multipipeline and Multiprocessor Computers," *Proc. 1984 Int'l Conf. Parallel Processing*, 1984, pp. 333–337.

Global, static, suboptimal, heuristic.

36. T.G. Saponis and P.L. Crews, "A Model for Decentralized Control in a Fully Distributed Processing System," *Proc. COMPCON Fall '80*, IEEE Computer Soc. Press, Los Alamitos, Calif., 1980, pp. 307–312.

Global, static, suboptimal, heuristic based on load balancing; also intended for applications of the nature of coupled recurrence systems.

37. C. Shen and W. Tsai, "A Graph Matching Approach to Optimal Task Assignment in Distributed Computing Systems Using a Minimax Criterion," *IEEE Trans. Computers*, Vol. C-34, No. 3, Mar. 1985, pp. 197–203.

Global, static, optimal, enumerative.

38. J.A. Stankovic, "The Analysis of a Decentralized Control Algorithm for Job Scheduling Utilizing Bayesian Decision Theory," *Proc. Int'l Conf. Parallel Processing*, IEEE Computer Soc. Press, Los Alamitos, Calif., 1981, pp. 333–337.

Global, dynamic, distributed, cooperative, suboptimal, heuristic, one-time assignment, probabilistic.

39. J.A. Stankovic, "A Heuristic for Cooperation among Decentralized Controllers," *Proc. INFOCOM '83*, IEEE Computer Soc. Press, Los Alamitos, Calif., 1983, pp. 331–339.

Global, dynamic, distributed, cooperative, suboptimal, heuristic, one-time assignment, probabilistic.

40. J.A. Stankovic, "Simulations of Three Adaptive, Decentralized, Controlled, Job Scheduling Algorithms," *Computer Networks*, Vol. 8, No. 3, June 1984, pp. 199–217.

Global, dynamic, physically distributed, cooperative, suboptimal, heuristic, adaptive, load-balancing, one-time assignment; three variants of this basic approach given.

41. J.A. Stankovic, "An Application of Bayesian Decision Theory to Decentralized Control of Job Scheduling," *IEEE Trans. Computers*, Vol. C-34, No. 2, Feb. 1985, pp. 117–130.

Global, dynamic, physically distributed, cooperative, suboptimal, heuristic based on results from Bayesian decision theory.

42. J.A. Stankovic, "Stability and Distributed Scheduling Algorithms," *Proc. ACM Nat'l Conf.*, ACM Press, New York, N.Y., 1985.

Here, there are two separate algorithms specified. The first is global, dynamic, physically distributed, cooperative, heuristic, adaptive, dynamic reassignment based on stochastic learning automata. The second is global, dynamic, physically distributed, cooperative, heuristic, bidding, one-time assignment.

43. J.A. Stankovic and I.S. Sidhu, "An Adaptive Bidding Algorithm for Processes, Clusters and Distributed Groups," *Proc. Fourth Int'l Conf. Distributed Computing Systems*, IEEE Computer Soc. Press, Los Alamitos, Calif., 1984, pp. 49–59.

Global, dynamic, physically distributed, cooperative, suboptimal, heuristic, adaptive, bidding, additional heuristics regarding clusters and distributed groups.

44. H.S. Stone, "Critical Load Factors in Two-Processor Distributed Systems," *IEEE Trans. Software Eng.*, Vol. SE-4, No. 3, May 1978, pp. 254–258.

Global, dynamic, physically distributed, cooperative, optimal, (graph theory based).

45. H.S. Stone and S.H. Bokhari, "Control of Distributed Processes," *Computer*, Vol. 11, No. 7, July 1978, pp. 97–106.

Global, static, optimal, graph-theoretical.

46. H. Sullivan and T. Bashkow, "A Large-Scale Homogeneous, Fully Distributed Machine — I," *Proc. Fourth Symp. Computer Architecture*, IEEE Computer Soc. Press, Los Alamitos, Calif., 1977, pp. 105–117.

Global, dynamic, physically distributed, cooperative, suboptimal, heuristic, bidding.

47. A.M. Van Tilborg and L.D. Wittie, "Wave Scheduling — Decentralized Scheduling of Task Forces in Multicomputers," *IEEE Trans. Computers*, Vol. C-33, No. 9, Sept. 1984, pp. 835–844.

Global, dynamic, distributed, cooperative, suboptimal, heuristic, probabilistic, adaptive; assumes tree-structured (logically) task forces.

48. R.A. Wagner and K.S. Trivedi, "Hardware Configuration Selection through Discretizing a Continuous Variable Solution," *Proc. Seventh IFIP Symp. Computer Performance Modeling, Measurement and Evaluation*, 1980, pp. 127–142.

Global, static, suboptimal, approximate, mathematical-programming.

49. Y.T. Wang and R.J.T. Morris, "Load Sharing in Distributed Systems," *IEEE Trans. Computers*, Vol. C-34, No. 3, Mar. 1985, pp. 204–217.

Global, dynamic, physically distributed, cooperative, suboptimal, heuristic, one-time assignment, load-balancing.

50. M.O. Ward and D.J. Romero, "Assigning Parallel-Executable, Intercommunicating Subtasks to Processors," *Proc. 1984 Int'l Conf. Parallel Processing*, IEEE Computer Soc. Press, Los Alamitos, Calif., 1984, pp. 392–394.

Global, static, suboptimal, heuristic.

51. L.D. Wittie and A.M. Van Tilborg, "MICROS, a Distributed Operating System for MICRONET, a Reconfigurable Network Computer," *IEEE Trans. Computers*, Vol. C-29, No. 12, Dec. 1980, pp. 1133–1144.

Global, dynamic, physically distributed, cooperative, suboptimal, heuristic, load-balancing (also with respect to message traffic).

Deadlock Detection in Distributed Systems

A distributed system is a network of sites that exchange information with each other by message passing. A site consists of computing and storage facilities and an interface to local users and to a communication network. A primary motivation for using distributed systems is the possibility of resource sharing — a process can request and release resources (local or remote) in an order not known a priori; a process can request some resources while holding others. In such an environment, if the sequence of resource allocation to processes is not controlled, a deadlock may occur.

A deadlock occurs when processes holding some resources request access to resources held by other processes in the same set. The simplest illustration of a deadlock consists of two processes, each holding a different resource in exclusive mode and each requesting an access to resources held by other processes. Unless the deadlock is resolved, all the processes involved are blocked indefinitely. Therefore, a deadlock requires the attention of a process outside those involved in the deadlock for its detection and resolution.

A deadlock is resolved by aborting one or more processes involved in the deadlock and granting the released resources to other processes involved in the deadlock. A process is aborted by withdrawing all its resource requests, restoring its state to an appropriate previous state, relinquishing all the resources it acquired after that state, and restoring all the relinquished resources to their original states. In the simplest case, a process is aborted by starting it afresh and relinquishing all the resources it held.

Mukesh Singhal

Resource versus communication deadlock

Two types of deadlock have been discussed in the literature: resource deadlock and communication deadlock. In resource deadlocks, processes make access to resources (for example, data objects in database systems, buffers in store-and-forward communication networks). A process acquires a resource before accessing it and relinquishes it after using it. A process that requires resources for execution cannot proceed until it has acquired all those resources. A set of processes is resource-deadlocked if each process in the set requests a resource held by another process in the set.

In communication deadlocks, messages are the resources for which processes wait.[1] Reception of a message takes a process out of wait — that is, unblocks it. A set of processes is communication-deadlocked if each process in the set is waiting for a message from another process in the set and no process in the set ever sends a message. In this paper we limit our discussion to resource deadlocks in distributed systems.

To present the state of the art of deadlock detection in distributed systems, this paper describes a series of deadlock detection techniques based on centralized, hierarchical, and distributed

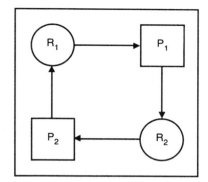

Figure 1. Resource allocation graph.

control organizations. The paper complements one by Knapp, which discusses deadlock detection in distributed database systems.[2] Knapp emphasizes the underlying theoretical principles of deadlock detection and gives an example of each principle. In contrast, this paper examines deadlock detection in distributed systems more from the point of view of its practical implications. It presents an up-to-date and comprehensive survey of deadlock detection algorithms, discusses their merits and drawbacks, and compares their performance (delays as well as message complexity). Moreover, this paper examines related issues, such as correctness of the algorithms, performance of the algorithms, and deadlock resolution, which require further research.

Graph-theoretic model of deadlocks

The state of a system is in general dynamic; that is, system processes continuously acquire and release resources. Characterization of deadlocks requires a representation of the state of process-resource interactions. The state of process-resource interactions is modeled by a bipartite directed graph called a resource allocation graph. Nodes of this graph are processes and resources of a system, and edges of the graph depict assignments or pending requests. A pending request is represented by a request edge directed from the node of a requesting process to the node of the requested resource. A resource assignment is represented by an assignment edge directed from the node of an assigned resource to the node of the process assigned. For example, Figure 1 shows the resource allocation graph for two processes P_1 and P_2 and two resources R_1 and R_2, where edges $R_1 \rightarrow P_1$ and $R_2 \rightarrow P_2$ are assignment edges and edges $P_2 \rightarrow R_1$ and $P_1 \rightarrow R_2$ are request edges.

A system is deadlocked if its resource allocation graph contains a directed cycle in which each request edge is followed by an assignment edge. Since the resource allocation graph of Figure 1 contains a directed cycle, processes P_1 and P_2 are deadlocked. A deadlock can be detected by constructing the resource allocation graph and searching it for cycles.

In a distributed database system (DDBS), the user accesses the data objects of the database by executing transactions. A transaction can be viewed as a process that performs a sequence of reads and writes on data objects. The data objects of a database can be viewed as resources that are acquired (by locking) and released (by unlocking) by transactions. In DDBS literature the resource allocation graph is referred to as a transaction-wait-for (TWF) graph.[3] In a TWF graph, nodes are transactions and there is a directed edge from node T_1 to node T_2 if T_1 is blocked and must wait for T_2 to release some data object. A system is deadlocked if and only if there is a directed cycle in its TWF graph. Since both graphs denote the state of process-resource interaction, we will collectively refer to them as state graphs.

Deadlock-handling strategies

The three strategies for handling deadlocks are deadlock prevention, deadlock avoidance, and deadlock detection. In deadlock prevention, resources are granted to requesting processes in such a way that a request for a resource never leads to a deadlock. The simplest way to prevent a deadlock is to acquire all the needed resources before a process starts executing. In another method of deadlock prevention, a blocked process releases the resources requested by an active process.

In deadlock avoidance strategy, a resource is granted to a process only if the resulting state is safe. (A state is safe if there is at least one execution sequence that allows all processes to run to completion.) Finally, in deadlock detection strategy, resources are granted to a process without any check. Periodically (or whenever a request for a resource has to wait) the status of resource allocation and pending requests is examined to determine if a set of processes is deadlocked. This examination is performed by a deadlock detection algorithm.

If a deadlock is discovered, the system recovers from it by aborting one or more deadlocked processes. The suitability of a deadlock-handling strategy greatly depends on the application. Both deadlock prevention and deadlock avoidance are conservative, overly cautious strategies. They are preferred if deadlocks are frequent or if the occurrence of a deadlock is highly undesirable. In contrast, deadlock detection is a lazy, optimistic strategy, which grants a resource to a request if the resource is available, hoping that this will not lead to a deadlock. Deadlock handling is complicated in distributed systems because no site has accurate knowledge of the current state of the system and because every intersite communication involves a finite and unpredictable delay. Next, we examine the complexity and practicality of the three deadlock-handling approaches in distributed systems.

Deadlock prevention

Deadlock prevention is commonly achieved either by having a process acquire all the needed resources simultaneously before it begins executing or by preempting a process that holds the needed resource. In the former method, a process requests (or releases) a remote resource by sending a request message (or release message) to the site where the resource is located. This method has the following drawbacks:

(1)   It is inefficient because it decreases system concurrency.

(2)   A set of processes may get deadlocked in the resource-acquiring phase. For example, suppose process P_1 at site S_1 and process P_2 at site S_2 simultaneously request two resources R_3 and R_4 located at sites S3 and S_4, respectively. It may happen that S_3 grants R_3 to P_1 and S_4 grants R_4 to P_2, resulting in a deadlock. This problem can be handled by forcing processes to acquire needed resources one by one, but that approach is highly inefficient and impractical.

(3)   In many systems future resource requirements are unpredictable (not known a priori).

In the latter method, an active process forces a blocked process, which holds the needed resource, to abort. This method is inefficient because several processes may be aborted without any deadlock.

Deadlock avoidance

For deadlock avoidance in distributed systems, a resource is granted to a process if the resulting global system state is safe (the global state includes all the processes and resources of the distributed system). The following problems make deadlock avoidance impractical in distributed systems:

(1)   Because every site has to keep track of the global state of the system, huge storage capacity and extensive communication ability are necessary.

(2)   The process of checking for a safe global state must be mutually exclusive. Otherwise, if several sites concurrently perform checks for a safe global state (each site for a different resource request), they may all find the state safe but the net global state may not be safe. This restriction severely limits the concurrency and throughput of the system.

(3)   Due to the large numbers of processes and resources, checking for safe states is computationally expensive.

Deadlock detection

Deadlock detection requires examination of process-resource interactions for the presence of cyclic wait. In distributed systems deadlock detection has two advantages:

- Once a cycle is formed in the state graph, it persists until it is detected and broken.
- Cycle detection can proceed concurrently with the normal activities of a system; therefore, it does not have a serious effect on system throughput.

For these reasons, the literature on deadlock handling in distributed systems is highly biased toward deadlock detection.

Issues in deadlock detection

Deadlock detection involves two basic tasks: maintenance of the state graph and search of the state graph for the presence of cycles. Because in distributed systems a cycle may involve several sites, the search for cycles greatly depends on how the system state graph is represented across the system.

Classified according to the way state graph information is maintained and the search for cycles is carried out, the three types of algorithms for deadlock detection in distributed systems are centralized, distributed, and hierarchical algorithms. In centralized algorithms the state graph is maintained at a single designated site, which has the sole responsibility of updating it and searching it for cycles. In distributed algorithms the state graph is distributed over many sites of the system, and a cycle may span state graphs located at several sites, making distributed processing necessary to detect it. In centralized algorithms the global state of the system is known and deadlock detection is simple. In distributed algorithms the problem of deadlock detection is more complex because no site may have accurate knowledge of the system state.[4] In hierarchical algorithms sites are arranged in a hierarchy, and a site detects deadlocks involving only its descendant sites. Hierarchical algorithms exploit access patterns local to a cluster of sites to efficiently detect deadlocks.

Correctness of deadlock detection algorithms

To be correct, a deadlock detection algorithm must satisfy two criteria:

- No undetected deadlocks: the algorithm must detect all existing deadlocks in finite time.
- No false deadlocks: the algorithm should not report nonexistent deadlocks.

In distributed systems where there is no global memory and communication occurs solely by messages, it is difficult to design a correct deadlock detection algorithm because sites may receive out-of-date and inconsistent state graphs of the system. As a result, sites may detect a cycle that never existed but whose different segments existed in the system at different times. That is why many deadlock detection algorithms reported in the literature are incorrect.

Strengths and weaknesses of centralized algorithms

In centralized deadlock detection algorithms, a designated site, often called the control site, has the responsibility of constructing the global state graph and searching it for cycles. The control site may maintain the global state graph all the time, or it may build it whenever deadlock detection is to be carried out by soliciting the local state graph from every site. Centralized algorithms are conceptually simple and are easy to implement. Deadlock resolution is simple in these algorithms — the control site has the complete information about the deadlock cycle, and it can optimally resolve the deadlock.

However, because control is centralized at a single site, centralized deadlock detection algorithms have a single point of failure. Communication links near the control site are likely to be congested because the control site receives state graph information from all the other sites. Also, the message traffic generated by deadlock detection activity is independent of the rate of deadlock formation and the structure of deadlock cycles.

Strengths and weaknesses of distributed algorithms

In distributed deadlock detection algorithms, the responsibility of detecting a global deadlock is shared equally among the sites. The global state graph is spread over many sites, and several sites participate in the detection of a global cycle. Unlike centralized algorithms, distributed algorithms are not vulnerable to a single point of failure, and no site is swamped with deadlock detection activity. Deadlock detection is initiated only if a waiting process is suspected to be part of a deadlock cycle.

But deadlock resolution is often cumbersome in distributed deadlock detection algorithms because several sites may detect the same deadlock and may not be aware of other sites and/or processes involved in the deadlock. Distributed algorithms are difficult to design because sites may collectively report the existence of a global cycle after seeing its segments at different instants (though all the segments never existed simultaneously) due to the system's lack of globally shared memory. Also, proof of correctness is difficult for these algorithms.

Strengths and weaknesses of hierarchical algorithms

In hierarchical deadlock detection algorithms, sites are arranged hierarchically, and a site detects deadlocks involving only its descendant sites. To efficiently detect deadlocks, hierarchical algorithms exploit access patterns local to a cluster of sites. They tend to get the best of both worlds: they have no single point of failure (as centralized algorithms have), and a site is not bogged down by deadlock detection activities that it is not concerned with (as sometimes happens in distributed algorithms). For efficiency, most deadlocks should be localized to as few clusters as possible; the objective of hierarchical algorithms will be defeated if most deadlocks span several clusters.

Next, we describe a series of centralized, distributed, and hierarchical deadlock detection algorithms. We discuss the basic idea behind their operations, compare them with each other, and discuss their pros and cons. We also summarize the performance of these algorithms in terms of message traffic, message size, and delay in detecting a deadlock (see Table 1). It is not possible to enumerate these performance measures with high accuracy for many deadlock detection algorithms for the following reasons: the random nature of the TWF graph topology, the invocation of deadlock detection activities even though there is no deadlock, and the initiation of deadlock detection by several processes in a deadlock cycle. Therefore, for most algorithms we have given performance bounds rather than exact numbers (for example, the maximum number of messages transferred to detect a global cycle).

Centralized deadlock detection algorithms

In the simplest centralized deadlock detection algorithm, a designated site called the control site maintains the state graph of the entire system and checks it for the existence of deadlock cycles.

Table 1. Performance comparison of distributed deadlock detection algorithms.

Algorithm	Number of messages	Delay	Message size
Goldman	$<m, n$	$t + nT$	Variable (medium)
Isloor-Marsland	$r(N - 1)$	0	Constant (small)
Menasce-Muntz	$m(n - 1)$	nT	Variable (small)
Obermarck	$m(n - 1)/2$	nT	Variable (medium)
Chandy et al.	$<m, n$	$t + nT$	Constant (small)
Haas-Mohan	$m(n - 1)$	$t + (n - 1)T$	Variable (medium)
Sugihara et al.	$<m, n$	$(n - 1)T$	Constant (small)
Sinha-Natarajan	best confi. $2(n - 1)$ worst confi. $m(n - 1)$	$2(n - 1)T$	Constant (small)
Mitchell-Merritt	$m(n - 1)$	$(n - 1)T$	Constant (small)
Bracha-Toueg	$4m(N - 1)$	$4dT$	Variable (medium)

N = number of sites
n = number of sites in deadlock cycle
m = number of processes involved in deadlock
T = intersite communication delays
t = deadlock initiation delay
r = TWF graph update rate
d = diameter of TWF graph

All sites request or release resources (even local resources) by sending "request resource" or "release resource" messages to the control site. When the control site receives such a message, it correspondingly updates its state graph. This algorithm is conceptually simple and easy to implement. However, it is highly inefficient because all the resource acquisition and release requests must go through the control site, causing large delays in response to user requests, large communication overhead, and congestion of communication links near the control site. Also, the algorithm's reliability is poor because if the control site fails, not only does deadlock detection stop, but also the entire system comes to a halt. This is because all the status information resides at the control site.

Some problems of this algorithm (such as long response time and congested communication links near the control site) can be mitigated by having each site maintain its resource status (state graph) locally and by having every site send its resource status to a designated site periodically for construction of the global state graph (and detection of deadlocks). However, due to the inherent communication delay and the lack of perfectly synchronized clocks in distributed systems, the designated site may get an inconsistent view of the system and detect false deadlocks.[5] For example, suppose two resources R_1 and R2 are stored at sites S_1 and S_2, respectively. Suppose the following two transactions T_1 and T_2 are started almost simultaneously at sites S_3 and S_4, respectively:

T_1	T_2
Lock R_1	Lock R_1
Unlock R_1	Unlock R_1
Lock R_2	Lock R_2
Unlock R_2	Unlock R_2

Suppose the Lock R_1 request of T_1 arrives at S_1 and locks R_1, followed by the Lock R_1 request of T_2, which waits at S_1. At this point S_1 reports its status, $T_2 \rightarrow T_1$, to the designated site. Suppose the Lock R_2 request of T_2 arrives at S_2 and locks R_2, followed by the Lock R_2 request of T_1, which waits at S_2. At this point S_2 reports its status, $T_1 \rightarrow T_2$, to the designated site, which, after constructing the global state graph, reports a false deadlock $T_1 \rightarrow T_2 \rightarrow T_1$.

Ho-Ramamoorthy algorithm

In an attempt to solve the problem of the above algorithm, Ho and Ramamoorthy have presented two centralized deadlock detection algorithms called the two-phase and one-phase algorithms.[5] These algorithms, respectively, collect two consecutive status reports and keep two status tables at each site to ensure that the control site gets a consistent view of the system.

Two phase algorithm. Every site maintains a status table, which contains the status of all processes initiated at that site. The status of a process includes all resources locked and all resources being waited for. Periodically, a designated site requests the status table from all sites, constructs a state graph from the received information, and searches it for cycles. If there is no cycle, then the system is not deadlocked. Otherwise, the designated site again requests status tables from all the sites and again constructs a state graph, using only the transactions common to both reports. If the same cycle is detected again, the system is declared deadlocked.

Ho and Ramamoorthy claimed that by selecting the transactions common to two consecutive reports, the designated site gets a consistent view of the system (a view that correctly reflects the state of the system) because if a deadlock exists, the same wait-for condition must exist in both reports. However, this claim is incorrect — a cycle in the wait-for conditions of the transactions common to two consecutive reports does not imply a deadlock — and the two-phase algorithm can report false deadlocks. By getting two consecutive reports, the designated site reduces but does not eliminate the probability of getting an inconsistent view.

One-phase algorithm. The one-phase algorithm requires only one phase of status reports from sites, but each site maintains two status tables: a resource status table and a process status table. The resource status table keeps track of the transactions that have locked or are waiting for resources stored at that site. The process status table keeps track of the resources locked by or waited for by all the transactions at that site. Periodically, a designated site requests both tables from all other sites, constructs a state graph using only the transactions for which the resource table matches the process table, and searches it for cycles. If no cycle is found, then the system is not deadlocked; otherwise, a deadlock has been detected.

The algorithm does not detect false deadlocks because it eliminates inconsistency in state information by using only the information common to both tables. For example, if the resource table at S_1 indicates that resource R_1 is being waited for by a process P_2 (that is, $R_1 \rightarrow P_2$) and the process table at S_2 indicates that process P_2 is waiting for resource R_1 (that is, $P_2 \rightarrow R_1$), then edge $P_2 \rightarrow R_1$ in the constructed state graph correctly reflects the system state. If either of these entries is missing from the resource or process table, then a request message or release message from S_2 to S_1 is in transit and $P_2 \rightarrow R_1$ cannot be ascertained. The one-phase algorithm is faster and requires fewer messages than the two-phase algorithm. But it requires more storage because every site maintains and exchanges two status tables.

Distributed deadlock detection algorithms

In distributed algorithms all sites cooperate to detect a cycle in the state graph, which is distributed over several sites of the system. Deadlock detection can be initiated whenever a process is forced to wait, and it can be initiated either by the local site of the process or by the

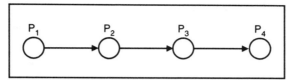

Figure 2. Example of OBPL (ordered blocked process list).

site where the process waits. Information about the state graph can be maintained and circulated in various forms (for example, table,[5] list,[6] string,[7,8] and probe[1,9]) during the deadlock detection phase.

Goldman's algorithm

Goldman's algorithm[6] exchanges deadlock-related information in the form of an ordered blocked process list (OBPL), in which each process (except the last) is blocked by its successor. The last process in an OBPL may either be waiting to access a resource or be running. For example, OBPL P_1, P_2, P_3, P_4 represents the state graph in Figure 2.

The algorithm detects a deadlock by repeatedly expanding the OBPL, appending the process that holds the resource needed by the last process in the list until either a deadlock is discovered (that is, the last process is blocked by a process in the list) or the OBPL is discarded (the last process is running). As an example, suppose in the system shown in Figure 3 process P_1 initiates deadlock detection and sends OBPL P_1, P_2 to process P_2. When process P_2 receives the OBPL, it appends P_3 to the OBPL and sends the new OBPL P_1, P_2, P_3 to P_3. Likewise, P_3 sends OBPL P_1, P_2, P_3, P_4 to P_4 and P_4 sends OBPL P_1, P_2, P_3, P_4, P_5 to P_5. When P_5 receives the OBPL, it discards the OBPL because it is not blocked. Had P_5 been blocked by $P_1, P_2, P_3,$ or P_4, a deadlock would have been detected by P_5.

An advantage of Goldman's algorithm is that it does not require continuous maintenance of TWF graphs. It constructs an OBPL whenever deadlock detection is to be carried out. However, it requires that every process have at most one outstanding resource request.

Isloor-Marsland algorithm

The "on-line" deadlock detection algorithm of Isloor and Marsland[10] detects deadlocks at the earliest possible instant — that is, at the time of making decisions about data allocation at the concerned site. It is based on the concept of reachable set. The reachable set of a node in the state graph is the set of all the nodes that can be reached from it. A process is deadlocked if the reachable set of the corresponding node contains the node itself.

The algorithm detects deadlocks by constructing reachable sets and checking whether any node belongs to its own reachable set. To do this, every site maintains the system state graph and reachable sets for each node in the state graph; the reachable sets are continually updated whenever edges are added to or deleted from the state graph. Whenever a resource is allocated, whenever a process is made to wait for a resource, or whenever a process releases a resource, the corresponding information is broadcast to all other sites. Therefore, if r changes per second occur in the state graph, then the algorithm requires $r(N-1)$ messages per second for deadlock detection. However, the messages are short because they contain only an update to the state graph resulting from the execution of a request.

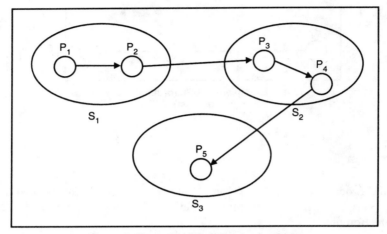

Figure 3. Example of Goldman's algorithm.

Menasce-Muntz algorithm

The deadlock detection algorithm of Menasce and Muntz[3] propagates only the two end points of a directed path (called a blocking pair), rather than the whole path, to detect deadlocks. The blockingset(T) of a transaction T is the set of all nonblocked transactions that can be reached from T by following all directed paths in the TWF graph. This is the set of transactions responsible for blocking the transaction T. When a transaction T gets blocked, then for each transaction T_i in the blockingset(T), the algorithm sends the blocking pair (T, T_i) to the home sites of T and T_i. (In other words, information about the condensed TWF graph is sent along the paths of the global TWF graph.)

Figure 4 illustrates the algorithm for a deadlock involving three transactions T_1, T_2, and T_3. Initially T_1 is blocked by T_2 and T_2 by T_3, and the home sites of T_1 and T_2 have the knowledge of the TWF graph $T_1 \rightarrow T_2$ and $T_2 \rightarrow T_3$, respectively. Now, when T_3 makes a request and is blocked by T_1, the blocking pair (T_3, T_2) is sent to the home site of T_2. This causes an edge from T_3 to T_2 to be added in the TWF of the home site of T_2, resulting in a cycle $T_3 \rightarrow T_2 \rightarrow T_3$ and detection of a deadlock at the home site of T_2.

Gligor and Shattuck[4] have shown that this algorithm fails to detect some deadlocks for two reasons: First, in the case of a nonlocal request, the determination of whether a transaction is blocked or not is incorrect because that determination cannot be made until the response arrives from a remote site. Second, even if this response arrives to determine correctly whether a transaction is blocked or not, the algorithm does not make use of it. Gligor and Shattuck have fixed this algorithm by precisely defining the status of all the transactions, whether active, blocked, or waiting for the outcome of a nonlocal resource request, and by having the algorithm propagate appropriate blocking pairs when it becomes certain that a waiting transaction is blocked.

Obermarck's algorithm

In Obermarck's algorithm,[8] the nonlocal portion of the global TWF graph at a site is abstracted by a distinct node, called "external" or Ex, which helps determine potential multisite deadlocks without requiring a huge global TWF graph to be stored at each site. Deadlock

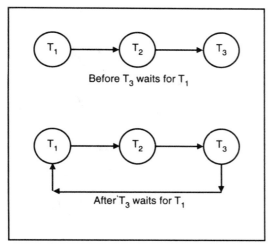

Before T_3 waits for T_1

After T_3 waits for T_1

Figure 4. Example of Menasce-Muntz algorithm.

detection at a site follows the following iterative process:

(1)   A site waits for deadlock-related information (produced in the previous deadlock detection iteration) from other sites.

(2)   The site combines the received information with its local TWF graph, detects all cycles, and breaks only cycles that do not contain the node Ex.

(3)   For all cycles Ex $\rightarrow T_1 \rightarrow T_2 \rightarrow$ Ex that contain the node Ex (these cycles are potential candidates for global deadlocks), the site transmits them in string form Ex, T_1, T_2, Ex to all other sites.

The algorithm reduces message traffic by lexically ordering the nodes (transactions) and sending a string Ex, T_1, T_2, T_3, Ex to other sites only if T_1 is higher than T_3 in the lexical ordering.

Chandy-Misra-Haas algorithm

Chandy, Misra, and Haas's algorithm[1] uses a special message called a probe. A probe is a triplet (i, j, k) denoting that it belongs to a deadlock detection initiated for process P_i and is being sent by the home site of P_j to the home site of P_k. A probe message travels along the edges of the global TWF graph, and a deadlock is discovered when a probe message returns to its initiating process. As an example, consider the system shown in Figure 5. If process P_1 initiates deadlock detection, it sends probe $(1, 3, 4)$ to the controller C_2 at site S_2. Since P_6 is waiting for P_8 and P_7 is waiting for P_{10}, C_2 sends probes $(1, 6, 8)$ and $(1, 7, 10)$ to C_3, which in turn sends probe $(1, 9, 1)$ to C_1. On receipt of probe $(1, 9, 1)$, C_1 declares that P_1 is deadlocked.

In Haas and Mohan's algorithm,[7] a variation of Chandy, Misra, and Haas's algorithm, a process comes to know (besides detecting that it is deadlocked) all the deadlock cycles in which it is involved. The algorithm achieves this by passing more information about the potential cycles in a probe message. In this algorithm a message consists of not only the information about the initiator of the deadlock, but also all the paths to it.

Mitchell-Merritt algorithm

In the deadlock detection algorithm of Mitchell and Merritt,[11] each node of the TWF graph has two labels: private and public. The private label of each node is unique to that node, and initially both labels have the same value. The algorithm detects a deadlock by propagating the public labels of nodes in a backward direction in the TWF graph. When a transaction gets blocked, the public and private labels of its node in the TWF graph are changed to a value greater than their previous values and greater than the public labels of the blocking transaction. (Blocked transactions update their labels in this manner periodically.) A deadlock is detected when a transaction receives its own public label. In essence, the largest public label propagates in a backward direction in a deadlock cycle. Deadlock resolution is simple in this algorithm because only one process detects a deadlock (that process can resolve the deadlock by aborting itself).

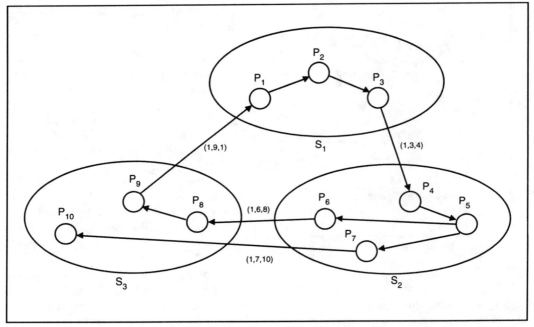

Figure 5. Example of Chandy-Misra-Haas algorithm.

Sugihara et al.'s algorithm

As in Obermarck's algorithm, in Sugihara et al.'s algorithm[12] every site maintains only a local TWF graph. A wait for a remote resource is reflected by adding a global edge to the local TWF graphs of the site of the requesting process and the site of the process holding the requested resource. In a global edge the nodes corresponding to the requesting process and the process holding the requested resource are referred to as the O-node and the I-node, respectively (Figure 6).

A site initiates deadlock detection by sending a message, similar to the probe message of Chandy, Misra, and Haas, whenever the addition of an edge (due to a resource wait) in its TWF graph creates a new path between any of its I-nodes and O-nodes. Note that a site can be involved in a global deadlock only when there is a path between some of its I-nodes and O-nodes. The algorithm has a unique resolver for every deadlock, and deadlock resolution does not cause detection of false deadlocks. An advantage of the algorithm is that a site maintains minimal information about the global TWF graph.

Sinha-Natarajan algorithm

Sinha and Natarajan's algorithm[9] does not construct the TWF graph, but it follows the edges of the graph to search for cycles. Transactions are prioritized, and an antagonistic conflict is said to occur when a transaction waits for a data object that is locked by a lower-priority transaction. The algorithm initiates deadlock detection only when an antagonistic conflict occurs, rather than whenever a transaction begins to wait for another transaction. Therefore, it requires fewer messages to detect deadlocks and generates fewer messages during normal conditions.

The algorithm detects a deadlock by circulating a probe message through a cycle in the global TWF graph. A probe message is a 2-tuple (i, j) where i is the transaction that faced the antagonistic conflict and initiated deadlock detection and j is the transaction of the lowest priority among all the transactions (nodes of the TWF graph) the probe has traversed so far. When a waiting transaction receives a probe initiated by a lower-priority transaction, the probe is discarded. (Thus, the algorithm filters out redundant messages).

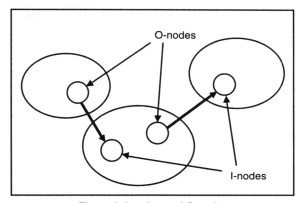

Figure 6. I-nodes and O-nodes.

An interesting property of this algorithm is that a deadlock is detected when the probe issued by the highest-priority process in the cycle returns to that process. (There is only one detector of every deadlock.) Deadlock resolution is simple; the detector of a deadlock can resolve the deadlock by aborting the lowest-priority transaction of the cycle. Choudhary et al. have shown that this algorithm detects false deadlocks and fails to report all deadlocks because it overlooks the possibility of a transaction waiting transitively on a deadlock cycle and because probes of aborted transactions are not deleted properly.[13]

Badal's algorithm

Badal's algorithm[14] exploits the fact that deadlocks can be divided into several categories based on the complexity of their topology; the frequency of deadlock occurrence and the costs of deadlock detection differ among categories. There is no point in detecting simple deadlocks with an algorithm designed to detect complex deadlocks. Badal optimizes performance by using three levels of deadlock detection; activity at each level is more complex (and expensive) than at the preceding level. Deadlock detection starts at the first level algorithm and is delegated to the next higher level if the current-level algorithm fails to report a deadlock. The third-level algorithm is designed to detect global deadlocks that escape the first two levels, and it closely resembles Obermarck's algorithm.

The most attractive feature of Badal's algorithm is that it detects the most frequent deadlocks with minimum overhead (first- and second-level algorithms) and switches to an expensive algorithm (third level) only when really needed. However, it has a fixed overhead due to information kept in lock tables, frequent checking of deadlocks of length two, and longer messages. Consequently, it is most suitable in environments where deadlocks occur frequently, justifying the fixed overhead.

Bracha-Toueg algorithm

In Bracha and Toueg's deadlock detection algorithm for generalized environments, called the r-out-of-s request model,[15] a process can request any r resources from a pool of s resources. After issuing an r-out-of-s request, a process remains blocked until it gets any r out of the s resources. The algorithm consists of two phases: notify and grant. In the first phase, notify messages are propagated downward in forestlike patterns of the TWF graph; in the second phase, grant messages are echoed back from all active processes, simulating the granting of resources to requests. At the end of the second phase, all the processes that are not made active are deadlocked.

Because the system state is dynamic, the TWF graph may change during the execution of the algorithm. The algorithm overcomes such changes by propagating special Freeze messages throughout the system. When a process receives a Freeze message, it saves a snapshot of its state. Deadlocks are detected by running the deadlock detection algorithm on the collection of snapshots thus obtained.

Hierarchical deadlock detection algorithms

In hierarchical algorithms sites are (logically) arranged in hierarchical fashion, and a site is responsible for detecting deadlocks involving only its children sites. To optimize performance, these algorithms take advantage of access patterns localized to a cluster of sites.

Menasce-Muntz algorithm

In the hierarchical deadlock detection algorithm of Menasce and Muntz,[3] all the resource controllers are arranged in tree fashion. The controllers at the bottommost level, called leaf controllers, manage resources; the others, called nonleaf controllers, are responsible for deadlock detection. A leaf controller maintains the part of the global TWF graph that is concerned with the allocation of the resources at that leaf controller. A nonleaf controller maintains the TWF graph spanning its children controllers and is responsible for detecting only deadlocks involving its own leaf controllers. Whenever a change occurs in a controller's TWF graph due to a resource allocation, wait, or release, the change is propagated to its parent controller. The parent controller makes the changes in its TWF graph, searches for cycles, and propagates the changes upward if necessary. A nonleaf controller can be kept up to date about the TWF graphs of its children continuously (that is, whenever a change occurs) or periodically.

Ho-Ramamoorthy algorithm

In the hierarchical algorithm of Ho and Ramamoorthy,[5] sites are grouped into several disjoint clusters. Periodically, a site is chosen as the central control site, which dynamically chooses a control site for each cluster (Figure 7). The central site requests every control site for its intercluster transaction status information and wait-for relations. As a result, a control site collects status tables from all the sites in its cluster and applies the one-phase deadlock detection algorithm to detect all deadlocks involving only intracluster transactions. Then it sends intercluster transaction status information and wait-for relations (derived from the information thus collected) to the central site. The central site splices the intercluster information thus received, constructs a system state graph, and searches it for cycles. Thus, a control site detects all deadlocks located in its cluster, and the central site detects all intercluster deadlocks.

Future research directions

Several issues related to deadlock detection in distributed systems have not been adequately studied and require further research.

Algorithm correctness

There is a dearth of sophisticated formal methods to prove the correctness of deadlock detection algorithms for distributed systems. Most researchers have used informal, intuitive

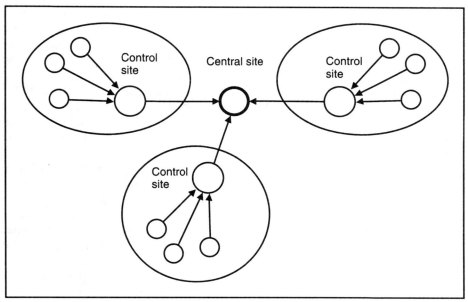

Figure 7. Example of Ho-Ramamoorthy algorithm.

arguments to show the correctness of their algorithms. But intuition has proved to be highly unreliable, and more than half the algorithms have been found incorrect. A formal proof of the correctness of deadlock detection algorithms is difficult for several reasons:

- The TWF graph and deadlock cycles can form in innumerable ways, making it difficult to imagine and exhaustively study all conceivable situations.
- Deadlock is very sensitive to the timing of requests.
- In distributed systems, message delays are unpredictable and there is no global memory.

Time-dependent proof techniques are particularly necessary.

Algorithm performance

Although many deadlock detection algorithms have been proposed for distributed systems, their performance analysis has not received sufficient attention. Most authors (for example, Obermarck and Sinha and Natarajan) have evaluated their algorithms on the basis of the number of messages exchanged to detect an existing cycle in the TWF graph. This performance criterion is deceptive because deadlock detection algorithms also exchange messages during normal conditions (when there is no deadlock). The number of messages exchanged may not be a true indicator of communication overhead because some algorithms[7,8,10] exchange long messages whereas others[1,3] exchange short messages. Therefore, we require a different criterion for computing communication overhead, which should take into account the number as well as the size of messages exchanged, not only in deadlocked conditions but also in normal conditions.

The persistence of deadlocks results in wasteful utilization of resources and increased response time to user requests. Therefore, an important performance measure of deadlock detection algorithms is the average deadlock persistence time. There is often a trade-off between message traffic and deadlock persistence time. For example, although the on-line deadlock detection algorithm of Isloor and Marsland detects a deadlock at the earliest instant, it has high message traffic. On the other hand, Obermarck's algorithm has less message traffic, but its deadlock persistence time is proportional to the size of the cycle. This trade-off is intuitive — quick detection of deadlock requires fast dissemination of information about the state graph, which implies high message traffic.

There is another dimension to the trade-off between message traffic and deadlock persistence time. For example, Chandy, Misra, and Haas's algorithm requires short messages, but when it detects a deadlock, it takes a while to resolve it. In contrast, Haas and Mohan's algorithm exchanges longer messages; however, when a process detects a deadlock, it knows all the processes involved in it, and therefore the deadlock can be resolved quickly.

Besides communication overhead and deadlock persistence time, any evaluation of deadlock detection algorithms should consider measures such as storage overhead for deadlock detection information, processing overhead to search for cycles, and additional processing overhead to optimally resolve deadlocks. Among the factors that influence these measures are the techniques used for deadlock detection, the data access behavior of processes, the request-release pattern of processes, and resource holding time. How these factors influence performance and how the performance characteristics of different detection algorithms compare with each other are not well understood. A complete performance study of deadlock detection algorithms calls for the development of performance models, the measurement of performance using analytic or simulation techniques, and a performance comparison of existing algorithms.

Deadlock resolution

Persistence of a deadlock has two major disadvantages: First, all the resources held by deadlocked processes are not available to any other process. Second, the deadlock persistence time gets added to the response time of each process involved in the deadlock. Therefore, the problem of promptly and efficiently resolving a detected deadlock is as important as the problem of deadlock detection itself. Unfortunately, most deadlock detection algorithms for distributed systems do not address the problem of deadlock resolution.

A deadlock is resolved by aborting at least one process involved in the deadlock and granting the released resources to other processes involved in the deadlock. Efficient resolution of a deadlock requires knowledge of all the processes involved in the deadlock and all resources held by these processes. When a deadlock is detected, the speed of its resolution depends on how much information about it is available, which in turn depends on how much information is passed around during the deadlock detection phase. In existing distributed deadlock detection algorithms, deadlock resolution is complicated by at least one of the following problems:

(1) A process that detects a deadlock does not know all the processes (and resources held by them) involved in the deadlock — for example, the algorithms of Chandy, Misra, and Haas and Menasce and Muntz.

(2) Two or more processes may independently detect the same deadlock — for example, the Chandry-Misra-Haas and Goldman algorithms. If every process that detects a deadlock resolves it, then deadlock resolution will be inefficient because several processes will be aborted to resolve a deadlock (different processes may choose to abort different processes). Therefore, we need some postdetection processing to select a process to be responsible for resolving the deadlock.

Many deadlock detection algorithms require an additional round of message exchanges to select a deadlock resolver and/or to gather the information needed to efficiently resolve a deadlock. The Sinha-Natarajan algorithm is one of the exceptions where each deadlock is detected only by the highest-priority process that (upon deadlock detection) knows the lowest-priority processes in the deadlock cycle. There is often a trade-off between the volume of information exchanged during the deadlock detection phase and the amount of time needed to resolve a deadlock once it is detected. For example, Haas and Mohan's algorithm exchanges long messages, but when a deadlock is detected, its resolution is quick. On the other hand, in Menasce and Muntz's algorithm the messages exchanged are short, but when a deadlock is detected, its resolution is tedious and time consuming.

Whether it is better to exchange long messages during the deadlock detection phase and resolve a detected deadlock quickly or to exchange short messages during the deadlock detection phase and do extra computation to resolve a detected deadlock depends on how frequently deadlocks occur in a system. If deadlocks are frequent, then the former approach should perform better and vice versa. Even after all the information necessary to resolve a deadlock is available, resolution involves the following nontrivial steps:

- Select a victim (the process to be aborted) for the optimal resolution of a deadlock (this step may be computationally tedious).
- Abort the victim, release all the resources held by it, restore all the released resources to their previous states, and grant the released resources to deadlocked processes.
- Delete all the deadlock detection information concerning the victim at all sites.

Execution of the second step is complicated in environments where a process can simultaneously wait for multiple resources because the allocation of a released resource to another process can cause a deadlock. The third step is even more critical because if the information about the victim is not deleted quickly and properly, it may be counted in several other (false) cycles, causing detection of false deadlocks. As Choudhary et al. point out, the failure to delete probe messages in the Sinha-Natarajan algorithm causes the detection of false deadlocks. To be safe, during the execution of the second and third steps, the deadlock detection process (at least in potential deadlocks that include the victim) must be halted to avoid detection of false deadlocks. In the Sugihara et al. algorithm, a control token serializes global deadlock resolution to eliminate its side effects on the deadlock detection process.

False deadlocks. In environments where a process can simultaneously wait for multiple resources, deadlock resolution is even more complex because an edge may be shared by two or more cycles, and deleting that edge will break all those deadlocks. However, since the search for each cycle is carried out independently, deadlock detection initiated for some cycles may not be aware of the deleted edge, resulting in detection of false deadlocks. Figure 8 illustrates such a scenario. Two deadlocks share an edge (T_4, T_5). Suppose the top cycle has been detected by process T_3, which is breaking it by deleting the edge (T_4, T_5). Concurrently process T_8 may initiate a deadlock detection message, and it may happen that T_3 breaks the edge (T_4, T_5) after the deadlock detection message initiated by T_8 has crossed (or traversed) it. In this case, T_8 will detect a (false) deadlock involving processes $T_4, T_5, T_7, T_8,$ and $T_9,$ which has already been broken by T_3.

In brief, deadlock detection involves detecting a static condition — once a deadlock cycle is formed, it persists until it is detected and broken. On the other hand, deadlock resolution is a dynamic process — it changes the state graph by deleting its edges and nodes. Two forces are working in opposite directions: the wait for resources adds edges and nodes to the state graph, while deadlock resolution removes them from the state graph. Therefore, if deadlock resolution is not carefully incorporated into deadlock detection, false deadlocks are likely to be detected.

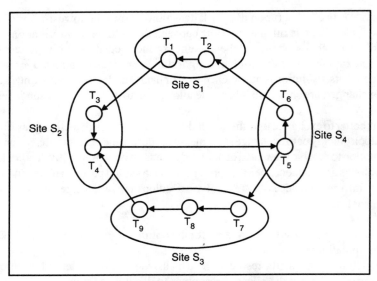

Figure 8. Detection of a false deadlock.

Deadlock probability. The frequency of deadlocks is a crucial factor in the design of distributed systems. If deadlocks are infrequent, then a time-out mechanism is the best approach to handling deadlocks because it has very low overhead. In a time-out mechanism a transaction or a process is aborted after it has waited for more than a specified period, called the time-out interval, after issuing a resource request. The most critical issue in a time-out mechanism is to choose an appropriate time-out interval; if the time-out interval is short, then many transactions may be aborted unnecessarily (that is, without being deadlocked), and if the time-out interval is long, then deadlocks will persist for a long time. The time-out mechanism is also susceptible to cyclic restarts, in which transactions are repeatedly aborted and restarted.

The probability of deadlocks depends on factors such as process mix, resource request and release patterns, resource holding time, and the average number of data objects held (locked) by processes. The probability of deadlocks is difficult to analyze because deadlock occurrence is highly sensitive to the timing and order in which resource requests are made. Gray et al.[16] have done an approximate analysis of deadlock probability and found that

- Transaction waits and deadlocks are rare, but they both increase linearly with the degree of multiprogramming;
- Most deadlocks are of length (size) two;
- Deadlocks rise as the fourth power of transaction size; and
- Waits rise as the second power of transaction size.

The probability of deadlock is an important parameter, and any further work in this direction will be a worthwhile contribution.

To sum up, of the three types of algorithms for detecting global deadlocks, distributed are the most prominent and most thoroughly investigated. All distributed deadlock detection algorithms have a common goal — to detect cycles that span several sites in a distributed manner — yet they differ in the ways they achieve this goal. The following are the most salient characteristics of these algorithms:

(1) The form in which the algorithm maintains and passes around information about the process-resource interaction. Goldman's algorithm uses *lists,* Haas-Mohan's and Obermarck's use *strings,* Isloor-Marsland's uses *sets,* and Menasce-Muntz's uses the *condensed TWF graph.*

(2) The way the algorithm conducts the search for cycles. Obermarck's algorithm sends lists of the edges of a directed path in the state graph; Chandy et al.'s and Sinha-Natarajan's circulate a probe message along the edges of the state graph; Menasce-Muntz's passes the condensed TWF graph; Mitchell-Merritt's passes a label.

(3) The amount of information available about a deadlock when it is detected. In the algorithms of Chandy et al., Menasce-Muntz, Sinha-Natarajan, and Sugihara et al., a process that detects a deadlock knows that it is deadlocked but does not know all the other processes involved in the deadlock; in Goldman's and Haas-Mohan's algorithms, a process that detects a deadlock knows all the other processes involved in that deadlock.

Although several deadlock detection algorithms have been proposed for distributed systems, a number of issues remain to be addressed. Future research should focus on efficient resolution of deadlocks, correctness of distributed deadlock detection, modeling and performance analysis of deadlock detection algorithms, and the probability of deadlocks in distributed systems.

Acknowledgments

The author is deeply indebted to Virgil Gligor of the University of Maryland, T.V. Lakshman of Bellcore, and seven anonymous referees whose comments on an earlier version were instrumental in improving the quality of presentation and enhancing the technical content of this paper. The author is also thankful to Bruce Shriver, editor-in-chief of *Computer*, for his encouragement and valuable suggestions for revising the paper.

References

1. K.M. Chandy, J. Misra, and L.M. Haas, "Distributed Deadlock Detection," *ACM Trans. Computer Systems,* May 1983, pp. 144-156.

2. E. Knapp, "Deadlock Detection in Distributed Database Systems," *ACM Computing Surveys,* Dec. 1987, pp. 303-328.

3. D.E. Menasce and R.R. Muntz, "Locking and Deadlock Detection in Distributed Databases," *IEEE Trans. Software Eng.,* May 1979, pp. 195-202.

4. V.D. Gligor and S.H. Shattuck, "On Deadlock Detection in Distributed Systems," *IEEE Trans. Software Eng.,* Sept. 1980, pp. 435-440.

5. G.S. Ho and C.V. Ramamoorthy, "Protocols for Deadlock Detection in Distributed Database Systems," *IEEE Trans. Software Eng.,* Nov. 1982, pp. 554-557.

6. B. Goldman, "Deadlock Detection in Computer Networks," Tech. Report MIT/LCS/TR-185, Massachusetts Inst. of Technology, Cambridge, Mass., Sept. 1977.

7. L.M. Haas and C. Mohan, "A Distributed Detection Algorithm for a Resource-Based System," research report, IBM Research Laboratory, San Jose, Calif., 1983.

8. R. Obermarck, "Distributed Deadlock Detection Algorithm," *ACM Trans. Database Systems,* June 1982, pp. 187-210.

9. M.K. Sinha and N. Natarajan, "A Priority-Based Distributed Deadlock Detection Algorithm," *IEEE Trans. Software Eng.,* Jan. 1985, pp. 67-80.

10. S.S. Isloor and T.A. Marsland, "An Effective On-line Deadlock Detection Technique for Distributed Database Management Systems," *Proc. Compsac '78,* 1978, pp. 283-288.

11 . D.P. Mitchell and M.J. Merritt, "A Distributed Algorithm for Deadlock Detection and Resolution," *Proc. ACM Conf. Principles Distributed Computing,* 1984, pp. 282-284.

12. K. Sugihara et al., "A Distributed Algorithm for Deadlock Detection and Resolution," *Proc. Fourth Symp. Reliability Distributed Software and Database Systems,* 1984, pp. 169-176.

13. A.L. Choudhary et al., "A Modified Priority-Based Probe Algorithm for Distributed Deadlock Detection and Resolution," *IEEE Trans. Software Eng.,* Jan. 1989, pp. 10-17.

14. D.J. Badal, "The Distributed Deadlock Detection Algorithm," *ACM Trans. Computer Systems,* Nov. 1986, pp. 320-337.

15. G. Bracha and S. Toueg, "A Distributed Algorithm for Generalized Deadlock Detection," *Proc. ACM Symp. Principles Distributed Computing,* 1984, pp. 285-301.

16. J. Gray et al., "A Straw-Man Analysis of the Probability of Waiting and Deadlocks in a Database System," IBM Research Report, 1981.

Additional reading

Theory

E.G. Coffman et al., "System Deadlocks," *ACM Computing Surveys,* June 1971, pp. 66-78.

R.C. Holt, "Some Deadlock Properties of Computer Systems," *ACM Computing Surveys,* Dec. 1972, pp. 179-195.

O. Wolfson and M. Yannakakis, "Deadlock Freedom (and Safety) of Transactions in a Distributed Database," *Proc. Fourth ACM SIGACT/SIGMOD Symp. Principles Database Systems,* 1985.

Algorithms

A.N. Chandra et al., "Communication Protocol for Deadlock Detection in Computer Networks," *IBM Tech. Disclosure Bull.,* Vol. 16, No. 10, Mar. 1974, pp. 3471-3481.

L.M. Haas, *Two Approaches to Deadlock Detection in Distributed Systems*, doctoral dissertation, Dept. of Computer Science, Univ. of Texas at Austin, Texas, 1981.

W. Tasi and G. Belford, "Detecting Deadlocks in Distributed Systems," *Proc. IEEE Infocom,* 1982, pp. 89-95.

A.K. Elmagarmid, *Deadlock Detection and Resolution in Distributed Processing Systems*, doctoral dissertation, Dept. of Computer and Information Science, Ohio State Univ., Columbus, Ohio, 1985.

A.N. Choudhary, *Two Distributed Deadlock Detection Algorithms and Their Performance*, master's thesis, Dept. of Electrical and Computer Eng., Univ. of Massachusetts, Mass., 1986.

N. Natarajan, "A Distributed Scheme for Detecting Communication Deadlocks," *IEEE Trans. Software Eng.,* Apr. 1986, pp. 531-537.

I. Cidon et al., "Local Distributed Deadlock Detection by Cycle Detection and Clustering," *IEEE Trans. Software Eng.,* Jan. 1987, pp. 3-14.

B. Awerbuch and S. Micali, "Dynamic Deadlock Resolution Protocols," *Proc. 27th Ann. Symp. Foundations Computer Science,* 1987, pp. 196-207.

M. Roesler and W.A. Burkhard, "Resolution of Deadlocks in Object-Oriented Distributed Systems," *IEEE Trans. Computers,* Aug. 1989, pp. 1212-1224.

B.A. Sanders and P.A. Heuberger, "Distributed Deadlock Detection and Resolution with Probes," *Proc. Third Int'l Workshop Distributed Algorithms*, 1989.

Survey

S.S. Isloor and T.A. Marsland, "The Deadlock Problem: An Overview," *Computer,* Sept. 1980, pp. 58-77.

M. Singhal, "Deadlock Detection in Distributed Systems: Status and Perspective," Tech. Report No. OSU-CISRC-TR-86-10, Dept. of Computer and Information Science, Ohio State Univ., Columbus, Ohio, June 1986.

A.K. Elmagarmid, "A Survey of Distributed Deadlock Detection Algorithms," *ACM SIGMOD Records,* Sept. 1986.

Correctness

J.R. Jagannathan and R. Vasudevan, "Comments on Protocols for Deadlock Detection in Distributed Database Systems: Corrigenda," *Trans. Software Eng.,* May 1983, p. 271.

G. Wuu and A. Bernstein, "False Deadlock Detection in Distributed Systems," *IEEE Trans. Software Eng.,* Aug. 1985, pp. 820-821.

A.K. Elmagarmid et al., "A Distributed Deadlock Detection and Resolution Algorithm and Its Correctness," *IEEE Trans. Software Eng.,* Oct. 1988, pp. 1443-1452.

K. Shafer and M. Singhal, "A Correct Priority-Based Probe Algorithm for Distributed Deadlock Detection and Resolution and Proof of Its Correctness," Tech. Report No. OSU-CISRC-4/89-TR16, Dept. of Computer and Information Science, Ohio State Univ., Columbus, Ohio, Apr. 1989.

Performance

J.R. Jagannathan and R. Vasudevan, "A Distributed Deadlock Detection and Resolution Scheme: Performance Study," *Proc. Third Int'l Conf. Distributed Computing Systems,* 1982, pp. 496-501.

Probability of deadlocks

C.A. Ellis, "On the Probability of Deadlocks in Computer Systems," *Proc. Fourth Symp. Operating Systems Principles,* 1973, pp. 88-95.

A.W. Shum and P.G. Spirakis, "Performance Analysis of Concurrency Control Methods in Database Systems," *Performance '81,* 1981, pp. 1-19.

W. Massey, "A Probabilistic Analysis of a Database," *Performance Evaluation Rev.,* Vol. 14, No. 1, May 1986, pp. 141-146.

Theoretical Aspects

Logical Time in Distributed Computing Systems

Unlike conventional sequential programs, the computations performed by distributed computing systems do not yield a linear sequence of events. The interrelationships between the events performed in a distributed system inherently define a partial ordering — genuinely concurrent events have no influence on one another.

In the past, designers have typically used a simplified view of distributed computations, imposing an interleaved total ordering on the events performed. However, new computing concepts now let us use the full partial ordering of events as defined by their causal relationships — that is, the ability of one event to directly, or transitively, affect another. In this paper, I define this partial ordering, describe its generalized and practical implementations in terms of partially ordered logical clocks, and summarize some current applications of the new technology.

Definitions

Colin Fidge

For a system using both asynchronous and synchronous message-passing and process-nesting, the causal relationships between events in a distributed computation are captured as follows.

The relation "happened before," denoted "$\rightarrow$," is the smallest relation satisfying the six conditions listed below. It is an irreflexive, transitive relation among the *events* performed during a given *computation*. An event is a uniquely identified runtime instance of an atomic action of interest, and a computation is a particular run or execution of the distributed computing system. A computation consists of one or more possibly nested *process instances*, which are uniquely identified runtime instantiations of a particular process definition.

- *Condition 1: Sequential behavior.* If events e and f occur in the same process instance p, and f occurs after e, then $e \rightarrow f$.
- *Condition 2: Process creation.* If event e and process instance q occur in process instance p, event f occurs in q, and q begins after e, then $e \rightarrow f$.
- *Condition 3: Process termination.* If event e and process

instance q occur in process instance p, event f occurs in q, and e occurs after q terminates, then $f \rightarrow e$.

- *Condition 4: Synchronous (unbuffered) message-passing.* If event e is a synchronous input (output) and event f is the corresponding output (input), and there is an event g such that $e \rightarrow g$, then $f \rightarrow g$. If there is an event h such that $h \rightarrow e$, then $h \rightarrow f$.
- *Condition 5: Asynchronous (buffered) message-passing.* If event e is an asynchronous send, and event f is the corresponding receive, then $e \rightarrow f$.
- *Condition 6: Transitivity.* If $e \rightarrow f$ and $f \rightarrow g$, then $e \rightarrow g$.

An event e "occurs in" a process instance p if p executes e. A process instance q occurs in a process instance p if q is a subprocess of p. "After" is used only when referring to actions that occur within a single process instance. Each process consists of a *sequence* of actions.[1]

Partially ordered logical clocks

Figure 1 shows a computation performed by a distributed program P. Shortly after it starts executing, P spawns two process instances Q and R. All three processes perform a number of events. Some are actions internal to a process, such as E, or are communication actions such as G. (For clarity I treat process creation and termination as special cases, although it is possible to consider these actions as synchronizing events.) After performing event H, process R creates two processes S and T, and suspends itself during the lifetime of its offspring. Processes P and S communicate via synchronous message-passing; event F outputs a message that is simultaneously input by event I. Processes P and Q communicate via asynchronous message-passing; event G denotes the sending of a message later received by event C.

After processes S and T terminate, process R resumes execution and performs event L. After processes Q and R terminate, the main program, process P, performs a final event M, and the computation ends.

Partially ordered logical clocks characterize all interrelationships between these events. In Figure 1, the annotation at each event shows the partially ordered time at that point in the computation. I explain the maintenance and use of this information below.

Notation

Because the time readings must be partially ordered, a single integer or real value is inadequate as a data structure. Assume that p_i denotes a process instance uniquely identified by i. We can represent a partially ordered time reading made by p_i with a set of pairs

$$\{(i,n_i),...,(l,n_l)\}$$

Here each pair consists of a process instance identifier j and a numerical "counter" value n_j representing the value of the counter in p_j as perceived by p_i. Each process thus maintains knowledge of the counters in all other processes of which it has heard. Process instances not represented in the set have the default counter value 0.

Assume that e_i represents a unique event e performed by process instance p_i, and t_{e_i} is the time stamp attached to some permanent record of the execution of this event. Then $t_{e_i}(j)$ is the value of the counter for p_j in this time stamp. For example, in Figure 1,

$$t_G = \{(P,4), (R,1), (S,1)\}$$

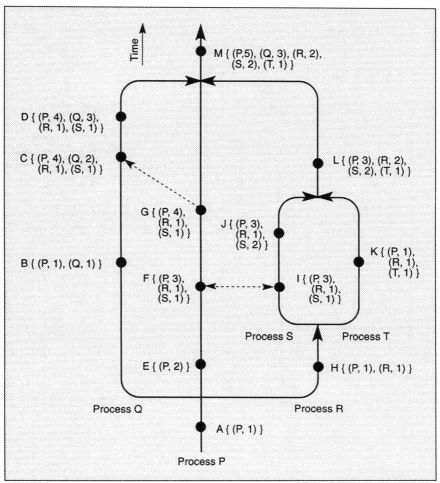

Figure 1. A distributed computation. Expressions in braces show the partially ordered time at each event. Solid arrows represent flow control; dotted arrows show interprocess communication.

is the time when process P performed event G. (Because event names are unique in Figure 1, I omit the process identifier subscripts: G is equivalent to G_p.) From this we can determine the "local" counter value for process P at that time,

$$t_G(P) = 4$$

and the last known value for process S,

$$t_G(S) = 1$$

When it performed event G, process P had received no information from process Q, hence

$$t_G(Q) = 0$$

A handy function in the following definitions is *max*. Given one or more partially ordered time readings, *max* returns a time reading in which every counter is set to the maximum of all corresponding values in the arguments presented to it, for example,

$$max(\{(i,2), (j,1), (k,3)\}, \{(i,4), (k,1)\}) = \{(i,4), (j,1), (k,3)\}$$

The counter for p_j has the default value 0 in the second argument to *max* above.

Rules

A computation can maintain a partially ordered logical clock using nine rules.[2] For the rules below to apply, each process instance p_i created during the lifetime of the computation (including the outer-level main program) must maintain an auxiliary variable c_i to hold the current partially ordered time as perceived by p_i.

- *Rule A: Initialization.* When the program begins execution, the time is initialized to the empty set; that is, $c_m := \{\}$, where m is the process instance identifier associated with the main program.

Since zero-valued counters are implicit, $\{\}$ is equivalent to the infinite set $\{(i,0), (j,0),...\}$ for every possible process identifier.

- *Rule B: Ticking.* Whenever a process instance p_i performs an event, it increments $c_i(i)$ at least once.

For instance, in performing event D, process Q increments its own counter from 2 to 3.

In Figure 1 each counter has been incremented exactly once for each event performed. However, the rules are valid for any number of "ticks," as long as the counters never decrease.

- *Rule C: Monotonically increasing counters.* No counter in any c_i is ever decremented.

- *Rule D: Process creation.* Whenever a process instance p_i creates a set of process instances $p_j,...,p_l$, they each inherit the current time from p_i; that is, $\forall x:\{j...l\} \cdot c_x := c_i$.

Thus, when process R spawns processes S and T, they both learn that the counters for P and R have value 1. They also create pairs for themselves the first time they each perform an event (K and I).

- *Rule E: Process termination.* Whenever a set of process instances $p_j,...,p_l$ terminates, the parent process instance p_i merges all the children's logical clocks by maximizing the counter values; that is, $c_i := max(c_i,c_j,...,c_l)$.

In this way process R learns of all activity known to its offspring S and T when they terminate (including updated knowledge of process P). The main program P (which cannot terminate until all processes it has created have terminated) similarly learns from the demise of Q and R.

- *Rule F: Synchronous events.* During a synchronizing event, all process instances involved $(p_j,...,p_l)$ maximize their local clocks using the counters from every other participating process instance; that is, $\forall x:\{j...l\} \cdot c_x := max(c_j,...,c_l)$. A computation applies this rule only after any increments required by rule B.

Thus, during the synchronous message-passing action represented by events F and I, process S learns of the time in process P and vice versa: Logical time information is exchanged in both directions (hence the double-headed arrow in Figure 1). This happens because the synchronization resulting from unbuffered message-passing is symmetric: both sender and receiver block. Figure 1 shows only a biparty interaction, but rule F allows for any number of synchronizing processes.

Asynchronous communication is asymmetric (only receivers block) and hence requires two rules:

- *Rule G: Sending.* Whenever a process instance p_i sends a message, that message carries the current value of c_i. A process applies this rule only after any increments required by rule B.

- *Rule H: Receiving.* Upon receiving a message, the receiving process instance p_j maximizes its counter values using those received in the piggybacked time stamp $c_{received}$; that is, $c_j := max(c_j, c_{received})$.

Thus event C allows process Q to learn of those events known to process P when event G was performed. Although Figure 1 shows only a biparty communication, these rules also apply to broadcast messages.

The logical clock information is always piggybacked onto *existing* communication pathways and thus must reflect the structure of the computation.

- *Rule I: Time-stamping.* The time stamp t_{e_i}, associated with the execution of event e_i by process instance p_i, is the value of c_i immediately following the application of rules B through H.

Finally, with these rules in place, we can determine the "happened before" relations using the comparison property of such time stamps:

- *Comparison property.* Given two time stamps t_{e_i} and t_{f_j}, event e_i happened before event f_j if and only if t_{f_j} has knowledge of process p_i as recent as the execution of e_i, but not vice versa; that is,

$$e_i \rightarrow f_j \iff (t_{e_i}(i) \le t_{f_j}(i)) \wedge (t_{e_i}(j) < t_{f_j}(j))$$

We need to compare only two pairs from the sets to establish whether there is a causal relationship between the two events. The first comparison is true if and only if e_i can causally affect f_j. The second comparison precludes reflexivity because it would be nonsensical to say that an event happened before itself.[1] (Because synchronously communicating processes may independently time-stamp their part of a shared event, as do F and I in Figure 1, it may not always be easy to directly test $e_i \ne f_j$.)

Elsewhere I have formally shown that these rules are sufficient to implement the "happened before" relation.[2] The rules are robust enough for asynchronous message "overtaking" (that is, non-FIFO queuing of messages destined for a particular process instance). The rules also preserve the equivalence between asynchronous message-passing and synchronous message-passing with an intervening buffer process, and between synchronous message-passing and a single event shared among the communicating processes.

As Figure 2 shows, substituting the appropriate counter values from the time stamps into the formula from the comparison property establishes the relationships defined by the computation in Figure 1. The final category in Figure 2 shows the principal advantage of partially ordered logical clocks over previous time-stamping methods.[1] Where no causal relationship exists between events, no arbitrary ordering is imposed on them. Thus we can tell, for instance, that events K and J could occur in either order, or at exactly the same time. Even though Figure 1 suggests that K occurred before J in real time (taking a line drawn horizontally through the diagram to represent an instant in global real time), the logical behavior of the computation does not enforce this temporal ordering. A slightly

Tests for $e \rightarrow f$ where

- e and f are the same event:
$$(2 \leq 2) \wedge (2 \not< 2) \Rightarrow \neg(C \rightarrow C)$$

- e and f are different events in the same process:
$$(1 \leq 3) \wedge (1 < 3) \Rightarrow B \rightarrow D$$
$$(2 \not\leq 1) \wedge (2 \not< 1) \Rightarrow \neg(C \rightarrow B)$$

- e and f are in different processes with an intervening communication action:
$$(2 \leq 4) \wedge (0 < 3) \Rightarrow E \rightarrow D$$
$$(2 \not\leq 0) \wedge (3 \not< 2) \Rightarrow \neg(J \rightarrow E)$$

- e is in a subprocess of the process containing f or vice versa:
$$(1 \leq 1) \wedge (0 < 2) \Rightarrow H \rightarrow J$$
$$(5 \not\leq 3) \wedge (2 \not< 1) \Rightarrow \neg(M \rightarrow I)$$

- e and f are different parts of a synchronous communication event:
$$(3 \leq 3) \wedge (1 \not< 1) \Rightarrow \neg(F \rightarrow I)$$
$$(1 \leq 1) \wedge (3 \not< 3) \Rightarrow \neg(I \rightarrow F)$$

- e and f are "potentially concurrent"; that is, there is no causal relationship between them:
$$(2 \not\leq 0) \wedge (1 < 2) \Rightarrow \neg(C \rightarrow J)$$
$$(2 \not\leq 1) \wedge (0 < 2) \Rightarrow \neg(J \rightarrow C)$$
$$(1 \not\leq 0) \wedge (0 < 2) \Rightarrow \neg(K \rightarrow J)$$
$$(2 \not\leq 0) \wedge (0 < 1) \Rightarrow \neg(J \rightarrow K)$$

Figure 2. Some "happened before" relationships defined between two arbitrary events e and f by the time stamps in Figure 1.

different interleaving of the same computation may result in J occurring before K. (Think of the dots in Figure 1 as beads free to slide up and down the time lines, as long as they do not violate causality by, for example, causing communication arrows to point backward.)

Optimizations

In their full generality, as described in the previous section, partially ordered logical clocks may be impractically expensive for long-lived computations. For instance, the rules placed no upper bound on the size of the set of pairs, and their number was limited only by the number of process instances created at runtime. Nevertheless, several optimizations are possible, depending on the application environment in which the clocks will be used.

Static number of processes

Where there is no process-nesting, and the system knows the number of processes to be created at compile time, the "set of pairs" data structure is unnecessary. Instead, each process can use an array of counters, with one element reserved per process.[3]

This frequently used optimization is known as "vector time"[3] because each clock reading is a vector (array) of counter values. It has the obvious advantage of placing an upper bound on the storage requirements for the auxiliary clock variables. In a formal proof, Charron-Bost demonstrated that a vector of length n is minimal for n static processes.[4]

The vector-time optimization can be applied to languages with nested concurrency if they do not allow recursive process definitions.[2] This restriction means that only one instance of each static process definition can execute at any given time. The system can determine from the source code the maximum number of runtime process instances simultaneously executing and reserve only one vector element for each. Every time a particular process definition is instantiated, it uses the same element in the logical clock vector, because no other copies of itself are currently running.

Comparisons known a priori

So far we have assumed that the computation maintains counters for every process instance. However, if we know in advance the processes that contain the events we wish to study, then we need to keep counter values only for those processes.[5] Nevertheless, other "uninteresting" processes must still maintain an auxiliary clock variable and transfer information at communication events. Otherwise, the partial ordering may fail to correctly reflect transitive interprocess dependences. All processes and all synchronizing actions in a computation must actively participate.[1]

Only new values piggybacked

When the number of processes in the vector-time model is large, the transmission of the clock arrays during message-passing represents a significant overhead. In such cases each process can maintain, via two further auxiliary arrays, the value of the "local" counter when a vector was last sent to each other process, and when each counter for other processes was last updated. Using this information, the process can piggyback on an outgoing message only those counter values that have been modified since the last communication with the target process, assuming message overtaking is precluded.[6]

Implementations and applications

Partially ordered logical clocks have been used in a number of practical and theoretical areas.

Languages

Inmos's Occam has only one interprocess communication mechanism, synchronous message-passing, and nested concurrency without recursion. Thus, programmers can easily add partially ordered clocks. I have experimentally introduced "logical timers" in a way consistent with Occam's existing real-time timer.[2]

So far we have assumed that message-passing is the only interprocess communication medium. Languages that allow interprocess synchronization in other ways — for example, through access to shared memory, monitors, and semaphores — must also incorporate rules for such synchronization.

Bryan has defined partially ordered time for Ada.[7] In Ada, there are several unusual ways that tasks (processes) define causal relationships between events. The Ada rendezvous causes two tasks to synchronize while the "accept" code is executed, after which independent execution continues. One task can unconditionally "abort" another. Unhandled exceptions may propagate to another task. When shared variables are used, the Ada standard guarantees synchronization only at certain points in the computation. Bryan has formally defined the causal relationships for all of these activities.

Debugging distributed systems

Programmers trying to debug distributed computing systems are faced with a frustrating inability to see what is happening in the network of processes.[2] To detect the occurrence of events in geographically distant processes, an observer must receive a "notification" message. Because of unpredictable propagation delays, the arrival times of these notifications may bear no resemblance to the order in which the events originally occurred. Time-stamping the notifications at their source with the current real time is also unhelpful, even when the local real-time clocks are closely synchronized, because the real-time ordering of events may be affected by CPU loads unrelated to the computation of interest. The perceived ordering of events based on these time stamps may be merely an artifact of relative processor speeds, with no significance for the computation itself, and may be different each time the same computation is performed.

In the past, a popular approach to this problem was to time-stamp events using so-called Lamport clocks (totally ordered logical clocks).[1] Unfortunately, these time stamps impose on unrelated concurrent events an arbitrary ordering that the observer cannot distinguish from genuine causal relationships.

Time-stamping the event notifications with partially ordered time readings resolves all the debugging problems. The observer receives an accurate representation of the event orderings, can see all causal relationships, and can derive all possible totally ordered interleavings. Most importantly, the technique greatly reduces the number of tests required. It is never necessary to perform the same computation more than once to see whether different event orderings (interleavings) are possible.[2]

Partially ordered logical clocks have been used experimentally for the detection of global conditions in a homogeneous network of processors,[8] for two prototype implementations of a monitor for Ada programs,[5] and for a prototype temporal assertion checker for Occam.[2]

Definition of global states

The "happened before" relation provides for straightforward definitions of normally subtle concepts. For instance, a "cut" of a distributed computation partitions the events performed into two sets: "past" and "future." In a consistent cut, the set of past events C does not violate causality; for example, it does not contain the reception of a message without its transmission. This concept has a very simple definition in terms of partially ordered time.[3] Assume that E represents the set of all events performed during a computation using only asynchronous message-passing. Then a consistent cut C is a finite subset $C \subseteq E$ such that

$$\forall e: E; c: C \cdot (e \rightarrow c) \Rightarrow (e \ \text{Œ} \ C)$$

In other words, if any event e "happened before" an event c in the cut set C, then e must also be in the cut set.

This is an important concept in the theory of distributed error recovery and rollback. Consider a distributed system consisting of a static number of nonnested processes, each of which periodically stores a "snapshot" of its local state (including the contents of message queues). If a set of snapshot events $S \subseteq C$, one from each process, forms the leading edge of a consistent cut C — that is,

$$\forall s: S; c: C \cdot \neg(s \rightarrow c)$$

then these local states form a valid global state from which an erroneous computation may be restarted.

Partially ordered time has also been used in the analysis of other global state problems, for instance, characterization of distributed deadlocks.[9]

Concurrency measures

A concurrency measure is a software metric that objectively assesses how concurrent a computation is. It measures the structure of the computation graph, rather than elapsed execution time. Partially ordered logical clocks have proved important in the definition and proposed implementations of such measures.

One of the simplest such measures, known as ω, counts the number of concurrent pairs of events that occurred during the computation and divides this by the total number of pairs of events between processes.[10] For a given computation C, consisting of two or more nonnested processes, the measure is defined as

$$\omega(C) = \frac{\left|\left\{(e_i, f_j) : e_i \operatorname{co} f_{ij}\right\}\right|}{\left|\left\{(e_i, f_i) : i \neq j\right\}\right|}$$

where the relation "co" is true between two distinct events if and only if they cannot causally affect one another; that is,

$$e_i \operatorname{co} f_j \iff \neg(e_i \to f_j) \wedge \neg(f_j \to e_i)$$

Charron-Bost[10] has defined a more discerning measure, m, using consistent cuts:

$$m(C) = \frac{\mu - \mu^s}{\mu^c - \mu^s}$$

The value μ represents the number of consistent cuts that occurred during the computation, μ^s is the number of consistent cuts that would be possible if the computation consisted of only one process, and μ^c is the number of consistent cuts possible if causal relationships due to interprocess communication are ignored.

Because both ω and m are defined in terms of the "happened before" relation, they can both be implemented by time-stamping all events with partially ordered time readings for postmortem analysis. Elsewhere I have investigated measures that allow for process-nesting or can be evaluated efficiently at runtime.[11]

Enforcement of causal ordering

The "causal ordering" abstraction, which prevents asynchronous message overtaking, has applications in several areas.[12] For management of replicated data in distributed databases, it can be used with a "write-enabling" token model to ensure that updates are applied in the same order at all sites. When monitoring activity in distributed systems, it ensures that all observers receive notification of events in the same order. Also, in the allocation of shared resources, causal ordering guarantees that servers honor requests in the order that they were made, rather than received.

The rule required for enforcement of causal ordering is easily defined in terms of "happened before."[12] For two send events e_i and f_j, where both messages are received by process p_k as events g_k and h_k, respectively, we need to guarantee that

$$(e_i \to f_j) \Rightarrow (g_k \to h_k)$$

A possible implementation of this rule using vector time (for computations without process-nesting) involves piggybacking control information on each outgoing message m, so the destination process knows whether there are other messages in transit that it must receive before it can accept m.[12] The piggybacked information consists of a bounded number of destination-site/vector-time pairs representing messages known to be in transit to the destination process. A destination process must not accept a message until all the message's time stamps "happened before" the current local time.

Conclusions

Partially ordered logical clocks are a fundamental new approach to the analysis and control of computations performed by distributed computing systems. They accurately reflect causality and are unperturbed by the random influences of system load, relative processor speeds, and different system configurations. In testing and debugging, they greatly reduce the number of tests required by simultaneously presenting any observer with all possible interleavings of events. Both their theory and practical application are now well established, but we will see further progress in both areas in the near future.

Acknowledgments

Thanks to Friedemann Mattern, Michel Raynal, Bernadette Charron-Bost, Doug Bryan, Dieter Haban, Sigurd Meldal, and Mukesh Singhal for keeping me abreast of their work on partially ordered clocks. Special thanks to Doug Bryan, Andrew Lister, and the anonymous referees for their numerous helpful comments on drafts of this paper.

This work was supported by an Australian postdoctoral research fellowship and an Australian Telecommunications and Electronics Research Board project grant.

References

1. L. Lamport, "Time, Clocks, and the Ordering of Events in a Distributed System," *Comm. ACM*, Vol. 21, No. 7, July 1978, pp. 558-565.

2. C.J. Fidge, *Dynamic Analysis of Event Orderings in Message-Passing Systems*, doctoral dissertation, Australian Nat'l Univ., Australia, 1989.

3. F. Mattern, "Virtual Time and Global States of Distributed Systems," in *Parallel and Distributed Algorithms*, M. Cosnard and P. Quinton, eds., North-Holland, Amsterdam, The Netherlands, 1989, pp. 215-226.

4. B. Charron-Bost, "Concerning the Size of Clocks," Tech. Report 569, Laboratory of Research in Information Science, Univ. of Paris-South, Paris, France, 1990.

5. S. Meldal, "Supporting Architecture Mappings in Concurrent Systems Design," *Proc. Fifth Australian Software Eng. Conf.*, IREE, Sydney, Australia, 1990, pp. 207-212.

6. M. Singhal and A. Kshemkalyani, "An Efficient Implementation of Vector Clocks," tech. report, Dept. of Computer and Information Science, Ohio State Univ., Columbus, Ohio, 1990.

7. D. Bryan, "An Algebraic Specification of the Partial Orders Generated by Concurrent Ada Computations," *Proc. Tri-Ada*, ACM Press, New York, N.Y., 1989, pp. 225-241.

8. D. Haban and W. Weigel, "Global Events and Global Breakpoints in Distributed Systems," *Proc. 21st Hawaii Int'l Conf. System Sciences, Vol. II*, IEEE Computer Soc. Press, Los Alamitos, Calif., 1989, pp. 166-175 (microfiche only).

9. A.D. Kshemkalyani and M. Singhal, "Characterization of Distributed Deadlocks," Tech. Report OSU-CISRC-6/90-TR15, Computer and Information Science Research Center, Ohio State Univ., Columbus, Ohio, 1990.

10. B. Charron-Bost, "Combinatorics and Geometry of Consistent Cuts: Application to Concurrency Theory," in *Distributed Algorithms*, J.-C. Bermond and M. Raynal, eds., *Lecture Notes in Computer Science*, Vol. 392, Springer-Verlag, Berlin, 1989.

11. C.J. Fidge, "A Simple Run-Time Concurrency Measure," in *The Transputer in Australasia (ATOUG-3)*, T. Bossomaier, T. Hintz, and J. Hulskamp, eds., IOS Press, Amsterdam, The Netherlands, 1990, pp. 92-101.

12. M. Raynal and A. Schiper, "The Causal Ordering Abstraction and a Simple Way to Implement It," Tech. Report 1132, INRIA, Paris, France, 1989.

The Many Faces of Consensus in Distributed Systems

Bob and Alice have discovered that they have many interests in common. On a cold winter day, Alice sends Bob electronic mail at 10:00 a.m. saying, "Let's meet at noon in front of La Tryste." As it happens, the e-mail connection between our two protagonists is known to lose messages and the two prefer not to use the telephone. But today they are lucky and Alice's message arrives at Bob's workstation at 10:20 a.m. Bob looks at his calendar and sees that he is free for lunch. So, he sends an acknowledgment.

Alice receives the acknowledgment at 10:45 a.m. and prepares to go out, when a thought occurs to her: "If Bob doesn't know that I received his acknowledgment, he will think that I won't wait for him. I'd better send an acknowledgment to his acknowledgment."

And so it goes. One can show that neither Bob nor Alice will make it to La Tryste, unless at least one is willing to risk waiting outside in the cold without ever meeting the other.

The parable of La Tryste

The above parable of human consensus holds many lessons for designers of distributed systems.

John Turek and

Dennis Shasha

Lessons from Bob and Alice

(1)   *Easier problem lesson:* If Alice were trying to send the first message to Bob and wanted to be sure it arrived, then the first acknowledgment would have sufficed. The issue is that Bob is not sure that Alice knows that the first message arrived, so he might not go to La Tryste. Thus, the problem of transmission is easier than the problem of agreement.

(2)   *Reliable network lesson:* A phone call appears to solve the problem:

> Alice: "Let's meet at noon."
> Bob: "Sure, see you then."

The phone connection solves the problem under the assumption that whatever one party says, the other party will hear within a bounded delay or the speaker will be aware of a problem within a bounded delay. If the assumption breaks down, either Bob or Alice may get stuck waiting outside in the cold.

(3)   *Probability lesson:* Imagine that Alice and Bob each send a flurry of duplicate messages instead of a single message each time. They might act on the assumption that at least one will arrive. If they were right with probability p for each flurry, then a two-message protocol would succeed with probability p^2. Here, success means that neither would wait outside in the cold and they would lunch together at La Tryste.

The price of failure may be higher in many applications. If the computers used by air traffic controllers were subject to these kinds of faults, then we would be much more reluctant to use the airlines. For this reason, the probabilistic approaches cited in the literature eschew such risks. Instead, they insist that if a decision is taken, it will be right. These approaches ensure that a decision will be made within a bounded amount of time with high probability.

Consenting adults

In the consensus problem, a set of agents must all agree on a decision based on their initial states. Typically, only two decisions are allowed: 0 and 1. (Once a protocol for two decisions is available, it can be extended to allow any number of decisions.) The numbers may represent actions; for example, the 1 may represent "commit" and the 0 may represent "abort" in a distributed database system. The agents must all output the same value and there must be some initial state in which 0 is the outcome and one in which 1 is the output.

Formally, a consensus protocol is correct if the following conditions are met:

- *Consistency:* All agents agree on the same value and all decisions are final.
- *Validity:* The value agreed upon by the agents must have been some agent's input.
- *Termination:* Each agent decides on a value within a finite number of steps.

In our parable, the *consistency* condition would be violated if it were possible for either Bob or Alice to wait outside in the cold alone. The *validity* condition would be violated if both Bob and Alice wanted to meet at La Tryste, but neither of them went. (This condition rules out the consistent but uninteresting solution where everyone always decides the same thing: for example, "don't meet.") The *termination* condition would be violated if they were never to agree.

A prominent application of consensus is in distributed database commit protocols. In such protocols, all server sites must agree whether to "commit" or "abort," and if any site wants to abort, then they must all abort. Because mixed inputs must lead all sites to abort, the commit problem is strictly harder than consensus, implying that any impossibility result for consensus translates to an impossibility result for the commit problem.

Ordered atomic broadcast protocols constitute a second important application of consensus. Such protocols try to guarantee the following: If two messages m and m' are sent, then either m will be received first at every working site or m' will be received first at every working site. As we will see, any system that can implement ordered atomic broadcast can also achieve consensus. So, whenever consensus is impossible, so is ordered atomic broadcast.

Similarly, any distributed system that embodies coordinated activity — from the synchronization of clocks in a distributed system, to the election of leaders, to the coordination of rocket firings — embodies consensus [Bir89].

Moreover, consensus is closely related to fault tolerance. A system is *synchronous* if all processors proceed at predictable speeds. Otherwise, the system is *asynchronous*. A protocol is *wait-free* if no processor can indefinitely block the progress of any other processor. Herlihy [Her88], among others, showed that in an environment where n processors operate asynchronously, the ability to reach consensus among all the processors is a necessary condition for achieving wait-free implementations of many shared data structures and is sufficient for achieving wait-free implementations of any shared data structure. In other words, any asynchronous distributed system for which data sharing is important must be able to achieve consensus in order to be resilient to certain failures.

Consensus can be easy or difficult to achieve, depending on the kind of computer system that one is using (synchronous or asynchronous) and on one's failure assumptions. In their famous paper, Fischer, Lynch, and Paterson [FLP85] showed that deterministic consensus among two or more processors in an asynchronous distributed system was impossible. Since then, many other papers have examined the problem under different failure and synchrony assumptions. For example, Fischer, Lynch, and Merritt [FLM86] showed that consensus cannot be achieved in a synchronous environment if even just one third of the processors are maliciously faulty. Given the role of consensus as a building block, these assumptions have a large impact on what can be achieved in practice.

This paper presents a survey of these results, relating them to practice, and explaining the small collection of elegant ideas embodied in their proofs. The goal is to give the practitioner some intuition about what guarantees the hardware and software in a system must make in order to achieve a given level of reliability and performance.

Guide to the rest of the paper

This survey focuses on two categories of failures: *fail-stop and Byzantine*. Fail-stop failures are failures where processors fail by stopping. While this is not a problem when processors are synchronous, the combination of asynchrony and fail-stop failures can make consensus impossible. Byzantine failures are failures where processors fail by acting maliciously (that is, try to make the other processors make inconsistent decisions). This is a useful, though pessimistic, model of software failures. Depending on the number of failures in the system, consensus may be impossible under Byzantine failures, even when the system is synchronous.

The section entitled "Slowness leads to indecision" focuses on fail-stop failures in asynchronous message passing systems under a variety of time-bound assumptions. The subsection entitled "Agreeing on shared memory" extends these results to shared memory systems, giving a hierarchy of primitives that allow an increasing number of agents to achieve consensus. The techniques used to prove the impossibility results are given in the subsection entitled "Proving the impossible." The next subsection, entitled "Sharing messages," shows that the message passing and shared memory models are of equivalent power. We conclude our discussion of asynchronous systems in the subsection entitled "Foiling your adversary" by showing how randomization can be used to overcome the impossibility results and to achieve consensus within a finite expected time.

The section entitled "Plotting out a Byzantine agreement" focuses on Byzantine failures in a synchronous message passing system and shows how the number of failures and connectivity of the network affect our ability to achieve consensus. The subsection entitled "The masquerade" illustrates the techniques that are used to prove the impossibility results for Byzantine failures. We conclude our discussion of Byzantine failures in the subsection entitled "Sign on the dotted line" by showing how encryption can be used to overcome the impossibility results, allowing consensus to be reached.

Slowness leads to indecision

A distributed system is made up of processors communicating through a shared communications medium, as illustrated in Figure 1. Sometimes, the communications media can be assumed to be reliable (for example, in backplane networks). Sometimes, processors can be assumed to be reliable (for example, in quadruple redundant hardware configurations). Suppose a given distributed system must solve problems at least as difficult as the consensus problem (for example, the system includes a distributed database). The designer should know how reliable the components must be for the consensus problem to be solvable. This section looks at how synchrony affects the spectrum of possibilities.

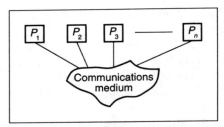

Figure 1. A distributed system.

A world of (im)possibilities

Let us return to our original scenario where Bob and Alice are sending each other messages across a computer network. The difficulty they encounter is that there are no bounds on the network delay and messages may get lost. We observed that consensus was impossible under these constraints. Let us strengthen the network so that messages are never lost, though they can be delayed, but add the condition that either Bob or Alice could be fired at any time. Since the network never fails, Alice could send Bob a message and then wait for his response. But if Bob gets fired before he receives Alice's message, Alice may end up waiting indefinitely. Under these conditions, is consensus possible?

Fischer, Lynch, and Paterson showed the surprising result that in a distributed system with an unbounded but finite message delay, there exists no protocol to guarantee consensus within a finite amount of time when at most a single processor can fail by stopping. We discuss the reasoning behind their theorem in the subsection entitled "Proving the impossible." Their result implies a negative answer to Bob and Alice.

While the Fischer, Lynch, and Paterson impossibility result showed that consensus cannot be guaranteed in a completely asynchronous system, it does not give much intuition on what can be achieved in practice. More optimistic assumptions on the timing constraints within the network and among processors can yield consensus protocols, even in the presence of multiple failures. Dolev, Dwork, and Stockmeyer [DDS87] addressed this issue by identifying a set of system parameters by which asynchronous systems can be classified. We consider a subset of these parameters below.

(1)   *Processors* can be either *synchronous* or *asynchronous.* Processors are said to be synchronous if they proceed at predictable speeds. Otherwise, processors are said to be asynchronous. Formally, processors are synchronous if and only if there exists a constant $s \geq 1$ such that for every $s + 1$ steps taken by any processor, every other processor will have taken at least one step.

(2)   *Communication delay can be either bounded or unbounded.* As discussed above, communication delay is said to be bounded when messages arrive within some maximum predictable delay. Otherwise, communication delay is said to be unbounded. Formally, communication delay is bounded if and only if every message sent by a processor arrives at its destination within t real-time steps, for some predetermined t.

(3)   *Messages can be either ordered or unordered.* Messages are ordered when the order in which messages arrive depends on the time in which they were sent. Otherwise, messages are said to be unordered. Formally, messages are ordered if and only if, when processor P_1 sends message m_1 to processor P_r at real time t_1, processor P_2 sends message m_2 to processor P_r at real time t_2, and $t_1 < t_2$, then P_r receives m_1 before it receives m_2.

(4)   *Transmission mechanism can be either point-to-point or broadcast.* The transmission mechanism is point-to-point if in an atomic step, a processor can send a message to at most one other processor. The transmission mechanism is broadcast if in an atomic step, a processor can send a message to all the processors.

When messages are unordered, communication is unbounded, and processors are asynchronous, the system is the one studied by Fischer, Lynch, and Paterson. An overview of the landscape given by Dolev, Dwork, and Stockmeyer can be seen in Table 1. The table shows that there are three minimal

Table 1. Conditions under which consensus is possible.

Processors	Message Order				Communication
	Unordered		Ordered		
Asynchronous	No	No	Yes	No	Unbounded
	No	No	Yes	No	
					Bounded
Synchronous	Yes	Yes	Yes	Yes	
	No	No	Yes	Yes	Unbounded
	Point-to-point	Broadcast		Point-to-point	
	Transmission mechanism				

cases for which consensus can be achieved, as follows:

- Case 1: Processors synchronous and communication bounded.
- Case 2: Messages ordered and transmission mechanism broadcast.
- Case 3: Processors synchronous and messages ordered.

We have included the third minimality case for completeness; however, the best known algorithm for achieving consensus in this case requires an exponential number of messages and appears to be of little practical interest.

Case 1 describes the situation in which processors can tell if another has failed by using time-outs. Standard commit protocols that work under the fail-stop assumption, such as three-phase commit [BHG87], can be used.

Case 2 describes the situation in which processors can be asynchronous and it is even possible that some of them will fail. However, they have an ordered atomic broadcast primitive (perhaps because they share a reliable bus). To solve consensus, each processor broadcasts its initial value to all other processors. They then read messages from the network deciding on the first value received. Since messages are ordered, all the processors will agree about which is the first value on the network.

A variation of Case 2 is to assume that the transmission mechanism allows broadcast to at most k other processors, or k-casting. Dolev, Dwork, and Stockmeyer showed that if k-casting is possible and messages are ordered, the system can achieve deterministic consensus in the presence of up to $k - 1$ failures.

Another variation assumes that processors are "nearly" synchronous. If a processor can read, process, and write to the network in one atomic step, the addition of bounded communication delay and broadcast transmission will be sufficient for achieving consensus. The idea is that if processors can execute a critical section of code within a predictable amount of time, then the problems associated with processor asynchrony can be overcome. This often can be achieved in practice by having processors disable interrupts during the critical section.

Agreeing on shared memory

In the previous subsection, we discussed impossibility results in networked systems. Does consensus become easier to implement in a system having a reliable shared memory? A superficial intuition might suggest that the inherent broadcast capabilities and reliability of the shared memory might suffice for consensus. While this is true for the Byzantine failures in synchronous systems that we discuss in the section entitled "Plotting out a Byzantine agreement," it is not the case for the asynchronous systems we are studying in this subsection. Herlihy showed that in a distributed system with asynchronous processors and a shared memory that supports only reads and writes, one cannot achieve consensus. Achieving consensus requires the addition of synchronization primitives to the shared memory. In fact, Herlihy showed that there exists a hierarchy of increasingly more powerful synchronization primitives allowing processors to achieve consensus in the presence of increasingly many faults.

To understand why shared memory is not enough, recall the minimum conditions presented by Dolev, Dwork, and Stockmeyer. Shared memory with read and write provides the equivalent of a broadcast mechanism, but does not offer the equivalent of ordered messages. Once two processors have written their messages to the shared memory, there is no way for a third processor to determine which processor wrote its message first. Actually, because of the asynchronous nature of the processors, even two writing processors cannot even agree on who wrote its message first.

Given an asynchronous shared memory system prone to fail-stop failures, Herlihy defined the consensus number of a synchronization primitive. A primitive having a consensus number of n can achieve consensus among an arbitrary number of processors, even if up to $n-1$ processors stop. By definition, a primitive with consensus number $n-1$, but not n, cannot simulate a primitive having consensus number n (otherwise, it too would have consensus number n). Conversely, a primitive with consensus number n can simulate a primitive with consensus number $n-1$.

For example, atomic read and write operations have a consensus number of 1, but not 2. Therefore, in a shared memory allowing only reads and writes, no deterministic algorithm can achieve consensus among two or more processors, even if only one of the processors is allowed to fail.

Fetch&add, shown in Figure 2, reads and increments a location from memory in one atomic step. *Fetch&add* has a consensus number of 2, but not 3. Therefore, by adding *fetch&add*, or a variant, to the shared memory, one cannot achieve consensus in three or more processors in the presence of two or more failures.

An important notion is that of a universal primitive, which has a consensus number of n for arbitrary n; that is, any number of processors can stop and consensus can still be reached. One such primitive is the *compare&swap*, shown in Figure 3. Compare&swap replaces the value in memory location m with *new* if and only if the old value in memory is equal to *old*. It is not difficult to see that the compare&swap is universal. Assume that a specified memory location, m, has an initial value of $\perp$. Each processor, P_i, proceeds as follows:

(1) Write initial value to location $a[i]$.
(2) Compare&swap($v, \perp, i$). Attempt to replace the $\perp$ in location v with the processor ID.
(3) Decide $a[v]$.

Only one processor, P, will succeed with the compare&swap. The value that P places in v will be the value decided on by all the processors.

```
fetch&add(m, v)
    begin /*Atomic action*/
        oldm ← m
        m ← m + v;
        return(oldm);
    end; /*Atomic action*/
```

Figure 2. *Fetch&add* (consensus number = 2).

```
compare&swap(m, new, old)
    begin /*Atomic action*/
        if (m = old) then
        begin
            m ← new;
            return (true)
        end
        else return (false);
    end; /*Atomic action*/
```

Figure 3. *Compare&swap* (consensus number = n).

A consequence of Herlihy's work is that the compare&swap is a more powerful synchronization primitive for the purpose of achieving consensus than test&set and fetch&add, thereby dispelling a popular myth on the relative power of these primitives. Of course, this does not preclude the usefulness of these primitives, as combining can make them more efficient than the compare&swap. It just turns out that there are certain things that they cannot do.

A *wait-free* protocol is one in which no processor can be held up indefinitely by the actions, or failures, of the other processors. Since consensus in the presence of an arbitrary number of failures cannot be achieved without the use of a universal primitive, it follows that there exist computations that cannot be performed in a wait-free manner in a distributed system without a universal primitive. Herlihy showed that in the presence of a universal primitive, any computation can be performed in a wait-free fashion. Thus, the ability to achieve consensus is necessary for any general-purpose distributed system that purports to be resilient to failures.

Proving the impossible

Recall that Bob and Alice can send one another messages. The problem is that the network can lose messages, so that when Bob sends Alice a message, he cannot be sure that she receives it. Intuitively, it seems clear that Bob and Alice cannot guarantee that one of them will not wait outside in the cold. After Bob receives the first message, we get the following scenario:

Bob: "I know that Alice wants to go out with me, but does she know that I know?" So, Bob sends Alice a message, which she receives . . .

Alice: "I know that Bob knows that I want to go out with him, but does he know that I know that he knows?" So, Alice sends Bob a message, which he receives. . .

Bob: "I know that Alice knows that I know that she wants to go out with me, but does she know that I know that she knows that I know?" So, Bob sends Alice a message, which she receives . . . And so on . . . .

This idea is captured by a simple proof. Agents can decide either yes or no. We define an event, *e,* to be the receipt of a message, *m,* by one of the two agents. For the sake of generality, *m* may be an empty message.

Since our protocol is deterministic, decisions made by the two agents can be said to occur only when an event occurs. Let *e* be the event that made Bob decide whether or not to join Alice at La Tryste. Since it is possible that none of Bob's subsequent messages will reach Alice, we can assume that once Bob has decided, Alice also must have decided the same thing.

However, it is also possible that Bob never received the message, *m,* returned by event, *e.* Of course, to Alice, the situation looks the same whether or not Bob received message *m,* so she will have decided regardless. This implies that Bob also must have decided and, in fact, message *m* cannot have been the deciding message, yielding a contradiction.

The one way around the above contradiction is to assume that Bob decides before he ever receives the first message. For the consensus problem, this trivial solution, where a decision is reached before the protocol even begins, is disallowed by the validity requirement; namely, there exists an initial state where a yes decision will be reached if there are no failures and an initial state where a no decision will be reached if there are no failures.

Bald men don't tell lies. Here, we describe the proof of the impossibility result given by Fischer, Lynch, and Paterson. Namely, in a completely asynchronous message passing system (that is, one whose messages have unbounded but finite transit times), no deterministic consensus protocol can tolerate even a single processor failure.

Processor	Inputs to processors					
P_1 $\Leftarrow$	0	1	1	...	1	1
P_2 $\Leftarrow$	0	0	1	...	1	1
P_3 $\Leftarrow$	0	0	0	...	1	1
P_{m-1} $\Leftarrow$	0	0	0	...	1	1
P_m $\Leftarrow$	0	0	0	...	0	1
Decides	0	?	?	...	?	1

Figure 4. Initial inputs to processors and the resulting decisions.

The state of a system, denoted a *configuration*, is defined by the messages that have not yet been delivered to their destinations and the individual states (that is, program counter and internal memory) of the individual processors. If, at some point in the computation, either 0 or 1 can still be reached, the system is said to be in a *bivalent* state. Otherwise, the system is said to be in a *univalent* state. We say the system is *0-valent* if 0 has been decided and *1-valent* if 1 has been decided.

An event, *e*, is defined to be the receipt of a message, *m*, by a processor. For the sake of generality, *m* may be an empty message. Since the protocol is assumed to be deterministic, decisions made by the processors can be said to occur only when an event occurs. A sequence, or subsequence, of events is called a *schedule*. The proof of the Fischer, Lynch, and Paterson result proceeds by showing that an adversary can keep the protocol going forever by slowing processors down or killing a single processor. Specifically, the following two lemmas prove the theorem:

- Lemma 1: There exists an initial configuration that is bivalent.
- Lemma 2: Given a bivalent configuration, there exists a nonempty schedule leading to another bivalent configuration.

Lemma 1 is best described by a variation on the bald man's paradox. A man with a full head of hair is not bald. A man with no hair is bald. A man can be either bald or not bald. For example, one could say that if a man has 1000 or more hairs he is not bald and that otherwise he is bald. If one were to remove each hair one at a time from a man with a full head of hair, then there would come a point when pulling one more hair would cause us to change our description of the man. However, if the man were wearing a hat, and only 999 strands of his hair were showing, it would be impossible to determine whether or not he were bald!

If all processors start with an initial value of 0, then the system must decide 0 to satisfy the validity condition on consensus. Likewise, if all processors start with an initial value of 1, then the system should decide 1. It is possible, as shown in Figure 4, to go from a configuration where all processors start with an input value of 0 to a configuration where all processors start with an input value of 1 by flipping one processor's input value at a time. Assume that there is no initial bivalent state. As with the bald man's paradox, there must be a single processor whereby flipping that input bit shifts the decision from a 0 to a 1. If an adversary were to cause the processor corresponding to that bit to fail before the protocol even began, then the two configurations would be impossible to distinguish from one another and would reach the same decision. This yields a contradiction, since by assumption one configuration would have yielded a 0 and the other a 1.

In order to prove Lemma 2, assume that the system is currently in a bivalent configuration, *C*. If there exists a schedule taking the system to another bivalent configuration, then we are done. Otherwise, since the system was in a bivalent configuration, there exist (see Figure 5) at least two events, *e* and *e'*, where e takes the system to a 0-valent configuration, *D,* and *e'* takes the system to a 1-valent configuration, *D',* and no events lead to another bivalent state. Call *e* and *e'* the deciding events. There are two cases, as follows:

(1)   The deciding events *e* and *e'* occur on different processors. Since events denote message

receptions, applying e and e' in either order yields the same configuration, F. By assumption, if e is applied first, then F is 0-valent. If e' is applied first, then F is 1-valent. This is clearly absurd. Hence, in a deterministic consensus protocol, any pair of deciding events yielding different valences must occur on the same processor.

(2)   Suppose deciding events e and e' both occur on some processor, P. If e occurs first and then P fails, the resulting configuration should be 0-valent. If e' occurs first and then P fails, the resulting configuration should be 1-valent. But there is no difference between these configurations. Again, we get a contradiction.

Since there exists an initial bivalent state, and the adversary can keep the system in a bivalent state for an arbitrary period of time, there is no way of guaranteeing consensus in an asynchronous distributed system where one processor can fail.

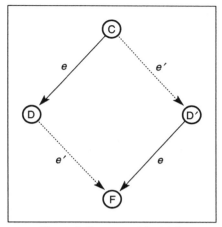

Figure 5. From one bivalent state to another.

A different approach to understanding the issues and difficulties of the consensus problem uses a formalism called *knowledge logic*. We haven't used that formalism, in order to keep the present paper short and self-contained, but much of the present research in consensus uses that formalism.

Sharing messages

Herlihy proved that asynchronous processors, communicating via a shared memory, cannot achieve deterministic consensus in the presence of one faulty processor. He used a technique similar to the one used by Fischer, Lynch, and Paterson. In this subsection, we choose to relate the two results using a different kind of glue.

Even though consensus cannot be achieved in an asynchronous message-passing environment with faults or in an asynchronous shared-memory environment with faults, it would still seem that shared memory provides a more powerful primitive than message passing. In one sense, this is true since it can be shown that some problems can be solved on shared memory, even if a majority of the processors fail. The same problem cannot be solved in a message passing environment under the same conditions. But what if fewer than half the processors are allowed to fail? Attiya, Bar-Noy, and Dolev [ABD90] showed that under these circumstances, the message passing system of Fischer, Lynch, and Paterson can reliably emulate a shared memory environment.

This result immediately enables us to apply results from the message-passing model of Fischer, Lynch, and Paterson to the read-write shared-memory model. As a result, the Fischer, Lynch, and Paterson impossibility result implies Herlihy's result, thus showing that in the presence of even one fault, consensus cannot be achieved in an asynchronous, read-write, shared-memory system.

Also, this result provides us with an easier framework in which to implement protocols for asynchronous message passing systems. In the subsection entitled "Foiling your adversary," we present a randomized algorithm for achieving consensus in an asynchronous shared-memory system. Because of the emulation result, that protocol can be mapped in a straightforward fashion to a message passing environment.

One failure too many. Before showing how to implement a shared memory, we will briefly discuss what we expect from a shared memory and why we cannot reliably emulate shared memory in a message passing system where a majority of the processors are allowed to fail.

In order to tolerate k failures, we need to maintain at least one copy of an object at $k + 1$ different processors. Otherwise, the k failures could occur at the processors containing the copies of the object and the value of the object would be lost. However, maintaining at least one copy does not solve all our problems. Since the processors holding the copies may be slow to respond, when two processors (or even the same processor) read a copy of an object, they may not read the same copy. The fact that a writer may not have completed its write operation means that the later of two read operations may actually get an "earlier" version of the object. This leads to inconsistent executions.

The correctness criterion that we expect from a shared memory is the ability to implement *shared atomic registers*. An atomic register satisfies the following property: If processor P_1 finishes accessing the register before processor P_2 begins accessing the register and one of the accesses is a write; then P_2 reads or writes a "later" version than P_1. Specifically, assume that each value written into the register has a unique version number; then P_2 will see (write) a version number that is equal to or greater than that seen (written) by P_1.

In order to see why no algorithm could tolerate even half the processors failing, consider a scenario in which the processors are partitioned into two groups of exactly equal size. Messages from one group to the other are "slow," while messages within each of the groups proceed at predictable rates. Given this scenario, processors in one group cannot distinguish between the situations in which all the processors in the other group are being slow or have failed. If the protocol assumes that the processors are slow, an adversary could cause the processors in the other group to fail. The protocol would not terminate and, therefore, would not be correct. If the protocol assumes that the processors in the other group have failed, then the two groups could come to different decisions violating consistency.

Two majorities always intersect. The critical problem in the preceding discussion is that if the network can partition the set of processors, then two independent components of the system can proceed independently. This observation was captured in 1979 by Gifford [Gif79] when he presented the idea of a *quorum* consensus. His algorithm shows how to reliably maintain several replicas of a data item in a synchronous distributed system prone only to fail-stop failures. The idea is to make m copies of a data object X, $\{X_1, X_2, \ldots, X_m\}$. Writing proceeds by writing $w > k$ copies of X, where k is the number of failures that can be tolerated. This set of writes is called a *write quorum*. Reading proceeds by reading r copies of X. This set of reads is called a *read quorum*. The sum of the write and read quorums, $w + r$, must be greater than m in order to ensure that an intersection exists between every pair of writes and reads.

Attiya, Bar-Noy, and Dolev used this idea to show how to emulate a reliable shared memory in an asynchronous message passing system where less than half the processors can fail. To illustrate the algorithm, we first give an algorithm to emulate shared memory in a synchronous message passing system. Associated with each copy is a *version number*. At any point in time, the copy (or copies) with the largest version number defines the current version. A read is executed as follows:

(1)   Retrieve a read quorum of X.
(2)   Select the copy with the largest version number.

A write is executed as follows:

(1)   Retrieve the currently largest version number using the read procedure above.
(2)   Increment the version number.
(3)   Send the new value along with the new version number to a write quorum.

The processors receiving the new value will replace the "old" value in their local memory if and only if the version number of the new value is larger than the version number of the old value. Some

Time step	Processor 1 (W₁)	Processor 2 (R₁)	Processor 3 (R₂)
1	Write X_1		
2		Read X_1	
3		Read X_3	
4			Read X_2
5	Write X_2		Read X_3

Figure 6. Example showing how quorums can fail in asynchronous environments.

care needs to be taken if multiple writers are allowed. In that case, we must guarantee that the writers all write unique version numbers (in order to avoid confusion). One can do this by concatenating the version number with the writing processor's ID.

While the above algorithm works well in a synchronous system, it will not work in an asynchronous system. The primary difficulty is that one cannot guarantee that the copies will be read in the correct order. One such situation can be seen in Figure 6. There are three replicas, X_1, X_2, X_3, of an object, X. A writer, W_1, could succeed in writing to X_1 before slowing down. A subsequent reader, R_1, may read a quorum containing X_1 and X_3, thereby getting the new version of X written by W_1. Later, another reader, R_2, reads a quorum consisting of X_2 and X_3. This quorum does not contain the new version of X written by W_1. Therefore, R_2 gets an earlier version than R_1, violating the conditions required for atomic registers.

Attiya, Bar-Noy, and Dolev got around this problem using a technique that has turned out to be quite powerful in designing protocols for asynchronous distributed systems: *altruism*. Rather than being greedy and having each process trying to complete its own operation as quickly as possible, each process acts altruistically. If it sees that some other process may not have completed its operation, it takes time out to help the process complete. In this case, the readers will help the writer. When a reader reads a quorum and realizes that the writer did not finish its job, it helps out by playing the role of the writer and writing a quorum with the current value and version number. For this approach to tolerate k failures, the read and write quorums must each be at least $k + 1$ in size. In addition, the system can have no less than $2k + 1$ processors.

Foiling your adversary

We have already seen that deterministic consensus cannot be achieved in an asynchronous system where even one processor is allowed to fail. Here, we show that probability provides a powerful tool in this context. Each processor is allowed to flip a coin. The result of this random coin toss cannot be affected by the adversary. In all other ways, the adversary remains unaffected; it can still slow down processors at will. The algorithm we present guarantees both validity and consistency upon termination. Therefore, the adversary can affect only when the final decision is reached and not the correctness of the final decision.

In order to simplify presentation, we show an algorithm given by Aspnes [Asp90] that works in shared memory. We know from the subsection entitled "Sharing messages," that any such algorithm can be converted into an algorithm that will function in a message passing system. The algorithm takes its inspiration from a one-dimensional random walk.

Being unable to agree with Alice on a meeting time, Bob—to console himself—goes out drinking and becomes intoxicated. At the end of the road on which the bar is located lies his house. At about the same distance from the bar, in the other direction, lies Alice's house. He is undecided whether to go home and sleep or to go to Alice's house and chat. Assume that every time he takes a step, he will stagger in the direction of either his house or Alice's house, with equal probability. If both houses

```
randcon(in)
   begin
      if in = 1
         globalcount ← globalcount + 1;
      else
         globalcount ← globalcount - 1;
      while -n < globalcount < n
      begin
         if globalcount < 0
            globalcount ← globalcount - 1;
         else if globalcount > 0
            globalcount ← globalcount + 1;
         else
         begin /*Atomic action*/
            if flip() = 1
               globalcount ← globalcount + 1;
            else
               globalcount ← globalcount - 1;
         end; /*Atomic action*/
      end;
      if globalcount > 0 decide(1);
      else decide(0);
   end;
```

Figure 7. Simplified algorithm for randomized consensus.

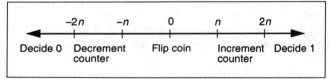

Figure 8. Regions for coin tosses in randomized consensus.

lie n steps away from the bar, how many steps will Bob take before reaching one of the two possible destinations?

The answer to the above question is $O(n^2)$ expected steps. The walk provides us with the basis of the randomized consensus algorithm. Assume, if or simplicity, that processors can flip a coin and then either add or subtract 1 from a global counter in one atomic step. Under this condition, the basic algorithm for randomized consensus on n processors can be seen in Figure 7.

Because the adversary has no control over the coin flips (or the order in which they are added to the global counter) the time required to hit one of the absorbing boundaries at either n or $-n$ corresponds to Bob's random walk. Once one of the boundaries has been reached, the remaining processors will eventually make the same decision.

To make the algorithm work even when one cannot flip a coin and increment the counter in one atomic step requires extending the region in which one can flip a coin. These regions are shown in Figure 8.

The adversary that has been proposed is more powerful than what one would encounter in practice. In fact, the adversary will not maliciously adjust the speeds of the processors; rather, the speed of the processors will be affected randomly. Aspnes and Herlihy [AH90] gave an algorithm with the same running time as that of the above algorithm that uses a weakly biased coin that will land on the same side at all the processors with high probability. Since the correctness of that algorithm is not particularly intuitive, we omit the details concerning it. In practice, the biased coin can be replaced by a shared table of "random" coin flips that the processors read in order to get the ith coin flip. With a failure model in which delays occur randomly, this modification to their consensus protocol yields an $O(n)$ algorithm.

Plotting out a Byzantine agreement

Bob, Alice, and Joan are trying to get together for lunch. To simplify things, they have decided to use the telephone so that the communication medium can be assumed to be reliable. Conference calling is not available, so at any one time Bob can talk with either Alice or Joan, but not both. Mistrust and insincerity abound; however, at most one of the members of the trio is truly malicious (we do not know which one) and is trying to make one of the other two wait outside in the snow. Is there some protocol that the three can adopt such that (1) the two honest individuals will agree on whether or not to meet; (2) if all honest ones want to meet, then they will meet; and (3) if no honest ones want to meet, then they won't meet?

This problem is equivalent to the Byzantine generals problem studied by Lamport, Shostak, and Pease [LSP82]. In their parable, several divisions of the Byzantine army are posted outside an enemy camp. Each division, headed by its own general, is trying to decide whether or not to attack the enemy camp. However, some of the generals are traitors and will try to keep the honest generals from reaching an agreement. A Byzantine failure is one in which a processor becomes traitorous and acts maliciously. The problem of reaching consensus in a distributed system prone to Byzantine failures is known as *Byzantine agreement.*

Byzantine failures were originally used to model hardware failures (or inherent flakiness) in avionics sensors. Aside from hardware failures, Byzantine failures can also be used to model software failures. If the software fails, we have no idea what it might do. Since it could do anything, the only fully general assumption that one can make is that it will do the worst thing possible. For it to do that, we assume that it is omniscient with respect to the state of the other (honest) processors.

This section discusses under what conditions Byzantine failures can be tolerated in a synchronous distributed system.

Avoiding traitors

Given a synchronous message passing system, is it possible to reach consensus in the presence of Byzantine failures? In order to answer this question, we need to be more specific regarding what the processors can do.

If Bob, Alice, and Joan were to make a conference call, then Bob would hear the same message that the others heard, and it would be impossible for the traitor to lie. Thus, under a communications medium that "broadcasts" messages to all the processors, Byzantine failures are no longer a problem. Therefore, because of the inherent broadcast capabilities of shared memory, Byzantine failures do not constitute a serious problem in that environment. As we show in the subsection entitled "Sign on the dotted line . . . ," the ability to verify the *authenticity* of messages partially simulates this broadcast ability.

Lamport, Shostak, and Pease [LSP82] showed that when authentication is not available, Byzantine agreement is possible if and only if there are at least $3k + 1$ processors when k of the processors can fail. In other words, if one third or more of the processors are malicious, no deterministic algorithm guarantees consensus among the honest processors. We give their proof of this result in the subsection entitled "The masquerade."

When fewer than one third of the processors in a complete network are traitorous, deterministic agreement without authentication is possible. The solution given by Lamport, Shostak, and Pease requires a number of messages that is exponential in the number of individuals. Other researchers later showed that a polynomial number of messages will suffice for solving the problem under the same constraints. The subsection entitled "Sign on the dotted line . . . " gives an efficient solution that uses authentication.

Fischer, Lynch, and Merritt extended the Lamport, Shostak, and Pease result to show that additional problems arise when the communication network is not complete. The connectivity of a graph is defined as the minimum number of nodes whose removal partitions the graph into two separate components. For example, Figure 9 shows a graph having connectivity two. For the purposes of our discussion, the nodes represent the processors and an edge indicates that the two connected processors can communicate with one another. Fischer, Lynch, and Merritt showed that Byzantine

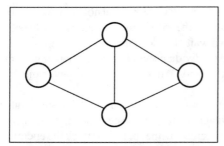

Figure 9. Graph with connectivity two.

agreement is possible if and only if the graph representing the communications network between the processors has connectivity greater than $2k + 1$, where k is the number of Byzantine failures that can occur. In other words, if removing half the individuals can partition the remaining individuals into two or more noncommunicating groups, then Byzantine agreement will not be possible.

The masquerade

When Joan decided to join Bob and Alice for lunch, nobody could be sure who was honest. We first show that with three agents and at most one possibly faulty agent, the other two agents cannot agree on whether or not to meet. Intuitively, the difficulty is that Bob, assuming he is honest, cannot distinguish between the case where Alice is lying and the case where Joan is lying.

Fischer, Lynch, and Merritt gave a simple proof of this idea. Suppose there was an algorithm that solved the problem at hand. Figure 10 gives three scenarios leading to the failure of any Byzantine agreement protocol that does not use authentication. In these scenarios, there are three agents, A, B, and C.

In Scenario 1, A is faulty. B and C start with the same input value, 0. B sees A starting with a value of 0 and C sees A starting with a value of 1. By the validity condition, the algorithm should ensure that B and C both decide 0.

In Scenario 2, B is faulty. A starts with a 1 and C starts with a 0. If B sends the same messages to C as it did in Scenario 1, C will see the same situation as in Scenario 1. (We assume that in Scenario 1 A, the traitor, sends the same messages to C as in this scenario.) Therefore, the algorithm must once again decide 0.

In Scenario 3, C is faulty. A starts with a 1 and B starts with a 1. If C sends the same messages to A as it did in Scenario 2, then A will see the same situation as in Scenario 2. (We assume that in the second scenario, B, the traitor, sends the same messages to A as in this scenario.) Again, the algorithm must decide 0. However, the two nonfaulty processors both have an input value of 1, so the decision of 0 violates validity. This proves that consensus is impossible.

This result can be extended to an arbitrary number of processors by dividing the processors into three equally sized groups. If one of the groups is allowed to contain all the faulty processors, the scenarios above can be simulated. The simulation proves the general result that Byzantine agreement is not possible if one third of the processors are faulty.

Sign on the dotted line . . .

As we see in the above subsection, if Joan, Bob, or Alice is malicious, then the malicious one can send conflicting messages to the other two. Suppose Joan is the malicious one. Even if Alice forwarded Joan's message to Bob, Bob would not know if Alice were forging Joan's message or if Joan was being insincere; therefore, he does not know with whom to agree.

However, if Alice forwards a photocopy of Joan's message, Bob can see that the writing is truly Joan's and will become immediately aware of the fact that it is Joan who must be the malicious individual. So he agrees with Alice. Joan is foiled.

The reason that this approach avoids the above problems is that the traitorous agent can no longer send any message he wishes, since he cannot forge a signature. In computer systems, algorithms that use the guarantee that signatures are not corrupted are called *authentication algorithms*. Encryption provides the basis for authentication. Lamport, Shostak, and Pease give a simple authentication algorithm.

For the sake of simplicity, we assume the existence of a unique coordinator, C. When the coordinator is honest, all honest agents will output the initial input of the coordinator. When the coordinator is dishonest, all honest agents will output a 0. The algorithm proceeds in $t + 1$ phases. Each message sent by a processor carries the signatures of all processors that have seen and transmitted the message. In phase i, there should be i signatures (in addition to the coordinator's) and no duplicates. That makes the message *legitimate*.

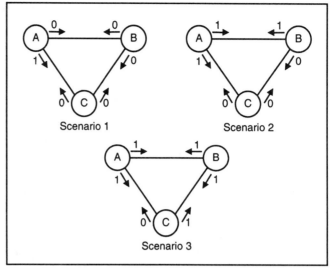

Figure 10. Scenarios leading to failure of Byzantine agreement.

- Phase 1: The coordinator signs and sends an initial value to all agents. This constitutes their input. Note that the coordinator may send different initial values to different processors or may fail before sending messages to all processors.
- Phases 2 through $t + 1$: Each agent first signs and sends all legitimate messages received in the previous phase to all the processors. If the message is legitimate, then the agent records the value contained in the message.
- At the end of Phase $t + 1$, an agent decides v if v is the only legitimate value it received. Otherwise, it decides 0.

The algorithm satisfies *termination*: It ends after $t + 1$ phases. The algorithm satisfies *validity*: If all processors function correctly and they all have the same input, then they will agree on their initial input. The algorithm satisfies *consistency:* All correctly functioning processors will see the same values as all other correctly functioning processors and, therefore, will all reach the same decision. With less than $t + 1$ phases, it is possible for an adversary to force different processors to reach different decisions.

Dolev and Strong [DS83] improved this exponential algorithm by noticing that one does not have to resend old messages. Their algorithm sends a number of messages that is quadratic in the number of processors.

Summary

In order for a group of processors to arrive at a common decision, the processors must solve the consensus problem. Since agreement is fundamental for many operations (for example, transaction commit and ordered atomic broadcast), consensus provides a fundamental building block for distributed systems. To avoid wasting time when designing these systems, designers should be aware of situations in which no algorithm is possible and in which algorithms already have been discovered.

The fine line between impossibility and possibility trades off processor reliability against network reliability. The more reliable the processors are, the less reliable the network is required to be.

Table 2. Conditions required for consensus.

	Networks			
	Ordered reliable time-bounded broadcast	Reliable time-bounded	Reliable unbounded	Unreliable
Processors never fail	Yes	Yes	Yes	No
Site failures Diagnostic time-out	Yes	Yes	No	No
Site failures No diagnostic time-out	Yes	No	No	No

(1) In a synchronous distributed system with reliable message delivery where processors can fail by acting maliciously (Byzantine failures), consensus is possible, as long as fewer than one third of the processors fail.

(2) In an asynchronous distributed system with reliable message delivery where processors can fail by stopping, consensus is not possible, even if only one process can fail. (We summarize the capabilities of different asynchronous systems in Table 2, where we indicate by "Yes" the conditions under which consensus is possible.)

(3) In a synchronous distributed system where messages can be dropped, consensus is not possible, even if none of the processors fail.

Shared memory has the effect of increasing the reliability of the communications medium. It is essentially equivalent to adding a broadcast capability to a network. This allows one to avoid many of the problems created by Byzantine failures, but not the problems created by asynchrony. In an asynchronous distributed system with a reliable read-write shared memory, consensus is not possible, even if only one process can fail. On the other hand, by adding synchronization primitives such as compare&swap, consensus becomes possible. The power of shared memory depends on the primitives it supports.

One way to overcome many of the impossibility results is through the use of techniques such as *randomization and authentication*. By adding randomization, asynchronous processors utilizing a read-write shared memory can achieve consensus, with high probability, in the presence of any number of stopping failures. By adding authentication, processors in a synchronous message passing system with reliable message delivery can achieve consensus in the presence of any number of Byzantine failures. These techniques not only overcome impossibility, but often yield efficient algorithms.

Besides being useful, the consensus problem has yielded many elegant impossibility proofs. These proofs teach the following simple moral that we should all take to heart: Global knowledge is much stronger than local knowledge.

Or, to put it in terms of our parable: Bob and Alice should ask to share an office.

Acknowledgments

We thank Rajat Datta, Maurice Herlihy, and Farnam Jahanian for helpful discussions and the anonymous referees for their helpful comments. We also thank Bob and Alice for their help in the preparation (and the presentation) of this paper. This research was partially supported by the National Science Foundation under grants IRI-89-01699 and CCR-91-03953 and by the Office of Naval Research under grants N00014-90-J-1110 and N00014-91-J-1472.

References

[Asp90]   J. Aspnes, "Time- and Space-Efficient Randomized Consensus," *Proc. Ninth Ann. ACM Symp. Principles Distributed Computing,* ACM Press, New York, N.Y., 1990, pp. 325-331.

[AH90]   J. Aspnes and M. Herlihy, "Fast Randomized Consensus Using Shared Memory," *J. Algorithms,* Vol. 11, No. 3, Sept. 1990, pp. 441-461.

[ABD90]   H. Attiya, A. Bar-Noy, and D. Dolev, "Sharing Memory Robustly in Message Passing Systems," *Proc. Ninth Ann. ACM Symp. Principles Distributed Computing,* ACM Press, New York, N.Y., 1990, pp. 363-382.

[BHG87]   P. Bernstein, V. Hadzilacos, and N. Goodman, *Concurrency Control and Recovery in Database Systems,* Addison-Wesley, Reading, Mass., 1987.

[Bir89]   K. Birman, "How Robust Are Distributed Systems?," Tech. Report TR 89-1014, Dept. of Computer Science, Cornell Univ., Ithaca, N.Y., June 1989.

[DS83]   D. Dolev and H. Strong, "Authenticated Algorithms for Byzantine Agreement," *SIAM J. Computing,* Vol. 12, No. 4, Nov. 1983, pp. 656-666.

[DDS87]   D. Dolev, C. Dwork, and L. Stockmeyer, "On the Minimal Synchronism Needed for Distributed Consensus," *J. ACM,* Vol. 34, No. 1, Jan. 1987, pp. 77-97.

[FLP85]   M. Fischer, N. Lynch, and M. Paterson, "Impossibility of Distributed Consensus with One Faulty Process," *J. ACM,* Vol. 32, No. 2, Apr. 1985, pp. 374-382.

[FLM86]   M. Fischer, N. Lynch, and M. Merritt, "Easy Impossibility Proofs for Distributed Consensus Problems," *Distributed Computing,* Vol. 1, Jan. 1986, pp. 26-39.

[Gif79]   D. Gifford, "Weighted Voting for Replicated Data," *Proc. Seventh ACM Symp. Operating System Principles,* ACM Press, New York, N.Y., 1979, pp. 150-159.

[Her88]   M. Herlihy, "Impossibility and Universality Results for Wait-Free Synchronization," *Proc. Seventh Ann. ACM Symp. Principles Distributed Computing,* ACM Press, New York, N.Y., 1988, pp. 276-290.

[LSP82]   L. Lamport, R. Shostak, and M. Pease, "The Byzantine Generals Problem," *ACM Trans. Programming Languages and Systems,* Vol. 4, No. 3, July 1982, pp. 382-401.

Self-Stabilization in Distributed Systems

A distributed system consists of a set of loosely connected machines that do not share a global memory. Depending on the way the machines are connected in the network and the time it takes for two machines to communicate with each other, each machine gets a partial view of the global state.

A fundamental criterion in the design of robust distributed systems is to embed the capability of recovery from unforeseen perturbances. While most existing systems cater to permanent failures by introducing redundant components, the issue of transient failures is often ignored or inadequately addressed. Considering the computation in a distributed system to be a totally or partially ordered sequence of states in the state space, it is conceivable to encounter a transient malfunction due to message corruption, sensor malfunction, or incorrect read/write memory operation that transforms the global state of the system into an illegal state from which recovery is not guaranteed.

Examples are token-ring networks in which the token is lost or duplicate tokens are generated, or sliding window protocols in which the window alignment is lost due to transient errors. The essence of these examples is that if the set of possible global states of a distributed system is partitioned into legal and illegal states, then transient failures can potentially put the system into an illegal state; this can continue indefinitely, unless it is externally detected and suitable corrective measures are taken.

A self-stabilizing system guarantees that regardless of the current state, the system is guaranteed to recover to a legal configuration in a finite number of steps and remain in a legal configuration until a subsequent malfunction occurs. This property makes the system more robust. No start-up or initialization procedure needs to be used because the system stabilizes by itself. If one machine fails and restarts, its local state may cause an illegal

Mitchell Flatebo,

Ajoy Kumar Datta, and

Sukumar Ghosh

global state, but the system will correct itself in a finite amount of time. The ability of the system to correct certain errors without outside intervention makes a self-stabilizing system more reliable and more desirable than systems that are not self-stabilizing.

The notion of self-stabilization has been prevalent in the field of mathematics and control theory for many years. Consider for example the Newton-Raphson method of finding the square root of a number where, regardless of what estimate is made about the initial value of the square root, the solution converges to the desired value in a finite number of steps. Similar notions have been used in feedback control systems for many decades. In the field of distributed systems, the study of self-stabilization was pioneered by Dijkstra [1], and has received considerable attention in recent years.

This paper presents state-of-the-art design of self-stabilizing distributed systems. To avoid a lengthy description of the various systems that have been studied to date, we focus our presentation on a few classical paradigms in distributed systems. These include (1) mutual exclusion, which is at the heart of any distributed computation, (2) communication protocols, and (3) some specific applications. Within each of these areas, we discuss the issues of design and analysis, along with impossibility results, wherever applicable.

The design of self-stabilizing systems

In 1974, Dijkstra introduced the property of self-stabilization in distributed systems [1]. His system consisted of a set of n finite state machines connected in the form of a ring. He defines a *privilege* of a machine to be the ability to change its current state. This ability is based on a boolean predicate that consists of its current state and the states of its neighbors. When a machine has a privilege, it is able to change its current state, which is referred to as a *move*.

A system is called self-stabilizing when, regardless of the initial state and regardless of the privilege selected each time, it always converges to a legal configuration in a finite number of steps. Furthermore, when multiple machines enjoy a privilege at the same time, the choice of the machine that is entitled to make a move is made by a central demon, which arbitrarily decides which privileged machine will make the next move.

The legal states must satisfy the following properties:

- [P1] There must be at least one privilege in the system (no deadlock).
- [P2] Every move from a legal state must again put the system into a legal state (closure).
- [P3] During an infinite execution, each machine should enjoy a privilege an infinite number of times (no starvation).
- [P4] Given any two legal states, there is a series of moves that change one legal state to the other (reachability).

Dijkstra considered a legal state as one in which exactly one machine enjoys a privilege. This corresponds to a form of mutual exclusion, because the privileged process is the only process that is allowed in its critical section. Once the process leaves the critical section, it passes the privilege to one of its neighbors. This characterization of legal states has been used in many of the early papers on self-stabilization and will be used here also. The remainder of this section discusses several issues in the design of self-stabilizing mutual exclusion algorithms.

Number of states per machine
An interesting issue in self-stabilizing systems is the number of states that each machine is required to have. Dijkstra [1] offered three solutions for a directed ring with n machines $(0, 1, ..., n - 1)$ each having K-states (1) $K \geq n$, (2) $K = 4$, and (3) $K = 3$. It was later proven that a minimum of three states

Table 1. Dijkstra's three-state algorithm.

State of machine 0	State of machine 1	State of machine 2	State of machine 3	Privileged machines	Machine to make move
0	1	0	2	0,2,3	0
2	1	0	2	1,2	1
2	2	0	2	1	1
2	0	0	2	0	0
1	0	0	2	1	1
1	1	0	2	2	2
1	1	1	2	2	2
1	1	2	2	1	1
1	2	2	2	0	0
0	2	2	2	1	1
0	0	2	2	2	2
0	0	0	2	3	3
0	0	0	1	2	2

are required in a self-stabilizing ring [2]. In all of his algorithms, Dijkstra had at least one exceptional machine that behaved differently from the others. His first solution ($K \geq n$) is described below. For any machine, we use the symbols S, L, and R to denote its state and the states of its left and right neighbors, respectively.

{the exceptional machine}
if $L = S$ then $S := (S + 1) \bmod K$ fi;
{the other machines}
if $L \neq S$ then $S := L$ fi;

This is a simple algorithm, but it requires a number of states that depends on the size of the ring. This may be awkward for some applications. The second solution uses only three-state machines and is presented below. The state of each machine is in {0,1,2}.

{the bottom machine, machine 0}
if $(S + 1) \bmod 3 = R$ then $S := (S - 1) \bmod 3$
{the top machine, machine $n - 1$}
if $L = R$ and $(L + 1) \bmod 3 \neq S$ then $S := (L + 1) \bmod 3$
{the other machines}
if $(S + 1) \bmod 3 = L$ then $S := L$
if $(S + 1) \bmod 3 = R$ then $S := R$

A sample execution of Dijkstra's three-state algorithm is shown in Table 1. The example is for a ring of four processes (0,1,2,3). Machine 0 is the bottom machine and machine 3 is the top machine. The last column in the table gives the number of the machine chosen to make the next move. Initially, three privileges exist in the system. The number of privileges decreases until there is only one privilege in the system. One can see from the table that the privilege eventually travels through the system in the sequence 0, 1, 2, 3, 2, 1, 0, ... All four properties P1, P2, P3, and P4 are satisfied, so the system is stabilized.

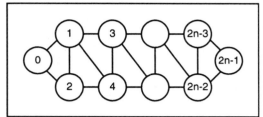

Figure 1. Special network needing only binary-state machines

There are special networks where the number of states required by each processor is two. In [3], a network organized like the one in Figure 1 needs only two states per machine. The algorithm uses information from all of its neighbors. The following algorithm uses s[i] to denote the state of machine i and there are two possible states for each machine, 0 and 1. In the algorithm, b is used to denote an arbitrary state (0 or 1) and b̃ is used as the complementary state of b.

For machine 0:
if (s[0],s[1])=(b̃, b) then s[0]:=b
For machine 2n–1:
if (s[2n–1],s[2n–2])=(b,b) then s[2n–1]:= b̃
For even numbered machines:
if (s[2i–2],s[2i–1],s[2i],s[2i+1]) = (b,b,b̃,b) then s[2i] : = b
For odd numbered machines:
if (s[2i–2],s[2i–1],s[2i],s[2i+1]) = (b,b,b,b̃) then s[2i-1] : = b̃

In this algorithm, each machine must examine the states of all its neighbors. Thus, a large atomicity is assumed because each machine must be able to examine the states of all its neighbors in one atomic step. The algorithm also requires an even number of machines (at least six). However, the algorithm shows that self-stabilizing algorithms requiring a small number of states can be designed.

In [4], a solution is presented with an odd number of machines in a ring. Each node has two states, 0 and 1. Given a global state, the nodes make moves according to the following:

- If the local state is different from its left neighbor's state, then the state is changed to be the same as its left neighbor.
- If the local state is the same as its left neighbor's state, the state is chosen randomly from 0 and 1.

At each step, the nodes make their moves in synchronization. A node has a privilege if its state is the same as its left neighbor's state. It is shown, using probability theory, that eventually only one privilege exists in the system. This algorithm requires that the nodes operate synchronously, but it shows that the number of states required for each node may be reduced using a probabilistic algorithm.

Besides these algorithms designed for specific networks, algorithms for arbitrary networks have been developed. However, the number of states required depends on the number of machines in the network, which can be large. These algorithms are difficult to develop. A feasible way is to find a minimum spanning tree of the graph, and treat the root and leaves as exceptional nodes for the algorithm. This idea of creating a minimal spanning tree can be combined with the algorithm for tree-structured systems [5].

Another approach is to split the graph into several cycles. Once this is done, an algorithm can be applied that will guarantee that only one privilege will exist in each cycle. There will be more than one privilege in the system if there is more than one cycle. This violates the mutual exclusion properties, but for some applications, one privilege in each cycle may be an acceptable criterion for a legal configuration.

The intuitive way of designing a self-stabilizing algorithm for an arbitrary network is to use the idea of propagating privileges. In an arbitrary network, a node with a privilege will pass the privilege on to one of its neighbors. If the choice is made randomly, each node will eventually enjoy the privilege, and the system will satisfy properties P2, P3, and P4 given earlier in this section. The only other property that needs to be satisfied is P1. Randomization can also help in reducing the number of privileges. The difficulty arises when one tries to analyze the efficiency of the algorithm. Probability theory can be used to verify the correctness of the algorithm, and can be used to establish some expected time for the system to stabilize. The privileges move around the system in a random fashion, however, so there is no absolute boundary on the convergence time. Randomization can be useful, but the analysis of the algorithm may be difficult.

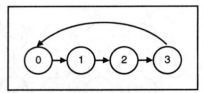

Figure 2. Ring of four machines.

In general, developing algorithms that work on arbitrary networks is more difficult and requires more states. The number of states required is normally of the order of n, where n is the number of machines in the network.

Uniform versus nonuniform networks

Another issue in this area is that of the processes being uniform. In a network, it is desirable to have each machine use the same algorithm. In the preceding section, at least one of the machines had a privilege and move that was different from the rest of the machines. These machines are known as exceptional machines, and the algorithms are nonuniform.

Self-stabilization algorithms for distributed systems should be uniform, but this is usually not possible. As a simple example, consider the ring of four processors in Figure 2. Assume there is a uniform self-stabilizing algorithm for this ring. If all processors have the same state when started, all must have privileges because there must be at least one privilege in the system (property P1). Both 0 and 2 can make moves and change their states (one making a move does not affect the neighbors of the other,). Now, 0 and 2 are in the same state and so are 1 and 3. At least two machines must have a privilege, because 0 and 2 have the same states and their neighbors have the same states as do 1 and 3. Now two machines can again make moves and leave the network in a similar situation.

Even though uniformity is a desirable property, most algorithms that have been developed use at least one exceptional machine. However, uniformity is not always unattainable. In [6], a uniform self-stabilizing algorithm for a ring of n processors, where n is prime, is given. This paper also noted that for a ring of composite size, the algorithm failed only because of deadlocking, but if deadlock can be tolerated or can be corrected easily from outside the system, then the algorithm may still be useful. The probabilistic algorithm discussed earlier in the subsection entitled "Number of states per machine," is also uniform. These examples show that uniformity may be achieved depending on the network and specifications of the system.

Central versus distributed demon

Dijkstra originally assumed the presence of a central demon to decide which machine with a privilege would be the one to make the next move. The presence of a central demon is normally not practical. Therefore, many of the initial algorithms have been extended to use a distributed demon so that each privileged machine makes its own decision on whether or not to make a move. In a self-stabilizing system without a central demon, machines make decisions locally. These decisions will eventually force the system toward some global requirement (a legal state), and then this requirement of the system will be maintained.

It is interesting to note that although many early algorithms (Dijkstra's three-, four-, and K-state algorithms) were developed assuming the presence of a central demon (and did not deal with the possibility of having a distributed demon), the algorithms also worked with distributed demons.

Even though a central demon is not desirable, it is usually easier to verify a weak correctness criterion on an algorithm using this assumption. For this reason, self-stabilizing systems are often developed assuming the presence of a central demon. After the weak correctness is verified, the system is examined to see if the system is still self-stabilizing when the assumption of a central demon is removed. If it is not, the algorithm is extended so that a central demon is not necessary.

The extendability of algorithms is examined in [7]. The authors have shown that letting all machines operate simultaneously will not affect the correctness of some algorithms. This relaxing of what the authors call interleaving assumptions is very useful in the verification of self-stabilizing systems. As an example, the authors verified that Dijkstra's algorithms are correct even in the presence of a distributed demon. Originally, Dijkstra's algorithms were only proven to be correct in the presence of a central demon. But in the paper, the central demon assumption is shown to be unnecessary for both the three- and four-state algorithms. The K-state solution is shown to be valid for a distributed demon only if $K > n$ (n is the number of machines) because there is a cycle of illegal global states if $K = n$.

The authors [7] developed lemmas that can be used to show that an algorithm that is correct in the presence of a central demon is also correct when the central demon assumption is lifted. This is useful in the verification process because once the algorithm is verified in the presence of a central demon, the algorithm may be correct even when the central demon assumption is lifted without any modification to the algorithm. This of course may not be the case for all algorithms, but these lemmas can be helpful in the process of verification.

Shared memory models

Systems having shared memory between machines where processes communicate with each other by reading and writing to registers have also been used [8]. In this model, no processor has direct access to the state of its neighbors, and the only way to determine this is by passing information through shared registers. If two processors, p_i and p_j are neighbors, then there are two registers, i and j between the two nodes. To communicate, p_i writes to i and reads from j, and p_j writes to j and reads from i.

The algorithms work for an arbitrarily connected graph. They also work if the graph changed during execution (such as node failure). So, the system is allowed to be dynamic. In the algorithm, eventually only one process can change a register at any instance, and this is when the system is stabilized. The only assumption made is that all read/write operations performed on the registers are atomic.

The final algorithm given in [8] is a dynamic, self-stabilizing protocol for mutual exclusion. The algorithm only requires that all nodes be connected (the network should not be partitioned). Node failures may cause an illegal global state, but the protocol is dynamic and self-stabilizing. This means that even with a node failing, the system will again converge to a legal state. If a node is restarted, an illegal global state may again occur, but the system will automatically correct itself. The size of the registers are on the order of $\log(n)$, where n is the number of processors. The only assumption made is that the read/write operations on the registers are atomic. This weak assumption makes the implementation of the algorithm feasible.

Mutual exclusion

The previous sections discussed self-stabilizing systems in terms of only one action occurring after a finite amount of time. The action could be changing a state or changing the contents of a register.

In a mutual exclusion algorithm each process has a critical section of code. Only one process can enter its critical section, and every process that wants to enter its critical section must enter it in a finite amount of time. If a process has a privilege, it can enter its critical section; once it is finished, it can pass the privilege to a neighbor. If the process does not want to enter its critical section, it can simply pass the privilege along. Since the self-stabilizing algorithms mentioned adhere to the four properties (P1, P2, P3, and P4) described earlier, mutual exclusion is also satisfied. Since eventually, there is only one privilege in the system and each process enjoys a privilege an infinite number of times, a process is guaranteed to enter its critical section in a finite amount of time.

A self-stabilizing mutual exclusion system can also be described in terms of a token system. A token system has the processes circulating tokens. If a process has one of these tokens, it is allowed to enter its critical section. Brown, Gouda, and Wu used this system in [9] to describe self-stabilizing mutual exclusion systems. At first, there may be more than one token in the system, but after a finite amount of time, only one token exists in the system that is circulated among the processes. The authors mention that these systems are easier to implement in circuits, and they show how the implementation would be done with flip-flops.

All of the models, token systems, privileges, and shared memory are forms of mutual exclusion. The algorithms also tolerate nodes failing and restarting or bad initialization, so they are more tolerant of errors than other mutual exclusion algorithms.

Self-stabilizing protocols

When designing communication protocols, a protocol is self-stabilizing if and only if, starting from an illegal state, the protocol is guaranteed to converge to a safe or legal state in a finite number of steps. This property allows the processes in a distributed system to reestablish coordination between each other when an error occurs that causes the loss of coordination.

A communication protocol is described as being a collection of processes that exchange messages over communication links in a network. The protocol may be adversely affected for several reasons:

- Initialization to an illegal state.
- A change in the mode of operation (not all processes get the request for the change at the same time, so an illegal global state may occur.)
- Transmission errors because of message loss or corruption.
- Process failure and recovery.
- A local memory crash that changes the local state of a process.

Previously, these five types of errors have been treated separately, but if a protocol is self-stabilizing, they will all be corrected in a finite number of steps regardless of the reason for the loss of coordination [10]. The remainder of this section describes specific self-stabilizing protocols and also describes self-stabilizing extensions for message-passing systems.

Protocols

Many protocols have been developed for message-passing systems. These protocols work if the initial configuration of the system is legal and no errors occur that will corrupt the global state of the system. These assumptions are not always realistic. For this reason, self-stabilizing protocols are necessary in order to deal with these possible errors.

In [10], two protocols are extended to be self-stabilizing. These protocols are the sliding window protocol (the sender keeps a window of frames to be sent and the receiver has a window of frames that it can receive) and the two-way handshake (the sender asks to open a connection and the receiver either accepts or rejects the request, and once the connection is open, the sender can send messages to the receiver). The authors in [10] show that in order for a protocol to be self-stabilizing, three requirements must be satisfied:

- The protocol must be nonterminating (at least one machine must generate an infinite number of messages during a computation),
- The machines must be infinite state machines, and
- There must be a time-out mechanism in order to generate lost messages.

The reason they are infinite state machines is because the counter for the message number can grow without bound.

The original sliding window protocol works if everything is initialized properly, but if the local variables in the sender and receiver are initialized improperly, a legal state may never be reached. The extended protocol handles this by setting its local variables to match the message number when it receives a message if its local variable is less than the incoming message number. In this way, initial messages may be lost, but a legal state will eventually be reached and then the algorithm will act the same way that the old protocol did. The loss of messages is a bad side effect, but it is shown in [11] that a reliable data link protocol cannot be designed to tolerate node failures without the loss of at least one message.

In the two-way handshake protocol, the protocol can be seen as two machines, a sender and a receiver. The sender requests a connection, and the receiver accepts or rejects it. The protocol works fine if the machines are initialized properly. But if they are not, the system may never reach a legal state. When the receiver receives a request to either open or close the connection, it first sets its local status variable (to either open or closed) and then sends a reply. Once the sender gets the reply, it can change its local status variable. If the system starts in a legal configuration and both the sender and receiver have their variables set to closed, then the following statements are true:

- If the sender believes the connection is open, then the connection is open.
- If the sender believes the connection is closed, then the connection is closed.

This is one way in which the protocol may fail to work. If the system is initialized improperly, and the sender believes that the connection is open while the receiver thinks the connection is closed, the protocol does not work. The extended protocol combats this in a similar way to the extension of the sliding window protocol. Each message has a counter attached to it. This enables the sender and receiver to synchronize if the system is in an illegal state because they both know which connection is valid.

Both of these previous extensions require an unbounded counter in order to work as shown in [10]. This requirement is not realistic, and can be eliminated. The protocol discussed in [12] is an extension of the alternating-bit protocol. The extension is what has been called pseudo-stabilizing [13], (described in the subsection entitled "Pseudo-stabilization,") but the difference usually does not matter in most practical applications. The algorithm does not use an unbounded counter; instead it generates an aperiodic sequence in order to achieve self-stabilization. It is shown that the only way the algorithm cannot stabilize is if each new sequence number is the same as the next to last sequence number. But if this is the case, the sequence numbers that are generated would be periodic. Instead of using an aperiodic sequence, a random sequence can be used and the protocol will still work. Random sequences are better than aperiodic sequences because they are easy to generate.

Extensions of general protocols

In general, protocols can be extended to be stabilizing. In [14], Katz and Perry use snapshots to get a global picture of the system. In the beginning, the snapshots may not be accurate, but eventually the snapshots provide an accurate picture of the global state of the system, since the snapshot algorithm is also self-stabilizing. Once the snapshots are accurate, if the global state is illegal, the system is reset to some default state. The reset is done by passing reset tokens to the other processors. Once a process receives one of these tokens, the process stops normal execution and initializes to some default local state. Eventually the system will converge to some legal state, and the snapshots will be accurate. At this point no resets are necessary and the system returns to normal execution, with the succeeding snapshots not causing the system to reset. Initially, unnecessary resets may occur because of the inaccurate snapshots, but after the system converges to some legal configuration, no resets are done and the system is stabilized.

In [15], a distributed reset system is also described. The resets are again used to achieve self-stabilization of the distributed system. The method the authors describe is the same as the one mentioned above. A global snapshot is obtained, and if the global state is illegal, a distributed reset is initiated. The way the reset is done is described in waves. First, a spanning tree is constructed, where the root is considered the leader. When some process requests a reset, it forwards the request to the root or the leader. Other processes do the same if they want to request a reset. This is referred to as the *request wave*. After this, the root starts what is called a *reset wave* where each process resets its local state. Once the reset wave reaches the leaves of the tree, the leaves start a *completion wave*. When this last wave reaches the root, the reset is complete, and another request for a reset can be started. This procedure can be built into any system to make it fault-tolerant and self-stabilizing.

In [10], time-out mechanisms are used that examine the communication links along with the local variables of all processes. These time-out actions are difficult to implement, but they are necessary in these protocols. The reason they are necessary is because the sender, after time-out, examines the links to see if they are empty in order to decide if old messages should be resent. These requirements make the extensions of communication protocols expensive and difficult. On the other hand, the alternating-bit protocol [10] is very similar to the original protocol and uses a time-out action that is not as expensive to implement, so the algorithm is a practical stabilizing protocol.

Other areas

Besides mutual exclusion and communication protocols, there have been other areas that have used self-stabilization. Recently, an algorithm has been developed that can be used to synchronize clocks [16]. This algorithm can guarantee that all the clocks in the system will show the same time, and that the time is incremented at each step, no matter what initial times the clocks showed. This is useful because no matter what the clocks show on start-up, in a finite amount of time they will all show the same time. So, no synchronization program needs to be run.

Self-stabilization has proven to be useful in many other areas as well. Among these is load balancing. Self-stabilized load balancing [17] guarantees that after the system stabilizes, every task will be scheduled on at least one processor regardless of failures or recoveries of processors. Fault isolation [18] and graph theoretic problems [15] are also research areas using self-stabilization. Two other areas that are discussed in more depth in this section are distributed process control and fault tolerance, which have both theoretical and practical applications in distributed systems.

Distributed process control

A relatively new area that uses self-stabilizing systems is robotics. Self-stabilizing systems can be used in robot path planning or in the design of assembly line robots. This helps in design, because the robot can stabilize and complete its tasks if an error or power failure occurs. On-line modifications can also be made because the robot will be able to correct itself once the changes are made. A simple example of this is given in [18]. In this paper, the robot is a cart with wheels and a movable arm, and the goal of the system is to position the end of the arm, or hand, on some point. The robot can tolerate the temporary failure of any of the parts (arm, cart, or hand) because the system is self-stabilizing and inherently fault tolerant.

Similar to the robot example are general process control systems. These systems must be able to tolerate many errors. The traditional way of dealing with the errors is by examining all cases. This is very complicated, and a better alternative, as discussed in [18], is to have a self-stabilizing system that will be able to handle errors more easily. The errors may cause the system to be unreliable for a short time, but the system will converge to a legal state and continue working properly. This system is much simpler since all possible cases no longer have to be examined. Before, there was a possibility of missing cases that could cause complete system failure. But using self-stabilization, all the cases are automatically taken care of, which makes the system easier to design. The system is also easier to maintain, because on-line changes of the system can be made without fear of complete system failure.

Fault tolerance

Self-stabilization has also been useful in the design of fault-tolerant systems. Self-stabilizing systems are more robust and inherently fault tolerant, so the systems are easier to design. Transient errors are corrected automatically. Networks that change over time or nodes that fail are taken care of by dynamic self-stabilizing protocols [8]. If modifications to the system are made, the system does not have to be restarted. It will correct itself. All of these advantages make self-stabilizing algorithms inherently fault tolerant.

Related to fault tolerance is Byzantine agreement [19]. Self-stabilizing Byzantine agreement [20] is more restrictive, because instead of having to reach agreement every time, the self-stabilizing version has mostly Byzantine agreement, where the number of failures to reach Byzantine agreements is finite. The algorithm given is faster than other Byzantine agreement algorithms, although errors do occur initially. The authors [20] mention that this algorithm should not be used if each agreement is necessary or if only a few attempts to reach agreement will occur. On the other hand, if agreements are needed over and over, this algorithm may be useful because it is faster and has only a few failures in the beginning. The algorithm has the property that a disagreement in one attempt will reduce the probability of disagreement at the next step. Another property is that the number of initial disagreements is directly proportional to the number of faulty processors. This inherent fault tolerance of self-stabilizing systems is very important in distributed systems because it makes the systems more robust.

Limitations of self-stabilization

The obvious problem in self-stabilizing systems is the time it takes for a system to correct itself when started in an illegal state or when there is an error resulting in an illegal state. If a system cannot tolerate this initial unknown period, then self-stabilization does not help. Even if the initial unknown can be tolerated for a brief period of time, the system may not converge to a legal state quickly enough.

Another difficulty lies in the need for an exceptional machine. Almost all self-stabilizing algorithms rely on there being at least one exceptional machine. Again, this is not a major drawback in most distributed systems.

In [21], it is shown that when classes of systems are simulated by another class, self-stabilization is not preserved through the simulation. The authors give a compiler as an example of a simulator because it simulates the source code by object code. They mention that it is desirable that the compiler either preserve or force self-stabilization. If it could force self-stabilization, the designer would not have to worry about it because the compiler would take care of it. However, the authors show that for many classes of systems, there is no simulation that forces self-stabilization. More importantly, there is not even a simulation that preserves self-stabilization for many classes of systems. For this reason, the instability of self-stabilization across system classes should be considered when one system is modeled by another.

The rest of this section describes other limitations. There is convergence, where response trade-offs can make a system converge to a legal state quickly with many errors, or converge slowly with fewer errors. A system can be pseudo-stabilizing and not stabilizing, which may or may not matter, depending on the application. Finally, the difficulties in verifying that a system is self-stabilizing are briefly examined.

Convergence response trade-offs

In [22], the authors used *convergence span* to denote the maximum number of critical transitions made before the system is in a legal state, and *response span* to denote the maximum number of transitions made to get from some starting state to some goal state. Critical transitions are similar to errors occurring in the system due to a move. For example, in a mutual exclusion system, if one process is in its critical section and another process makes a move and enters its critical section, an error has occurred because more than one process has been allowed to enter its critical section.

The authors [22] develop several self-stabilizing termination detection algorithms. Each of the algorithms has different properties. For a ring of n processes, one has comparative convergence and response spans (both of the order of n), one has a fast convergent span (of the order of 1) and a slow response span (of the order of n^2), and the last one shows the relationship between the two spans. If the convergence span is decreased by a factor of k ($1 \leq k \leq n$), the response span is increased by this same factor. So, the convergence span is of the order of n/k while the response span is $n*k$. This relationship is only shown for the termination detection algorithm, but the authors believe that a similar relationship exists in other classes of self-stabilizing systems.

This relationship is reasonable because the more checks that are made, the longer it will take to converge, and fewer errors will be made. This relationship is extremely useful in the design of self-stabilizing systems because the system can be modified according to the goal of the system. Depending on the requirements of the system, one can have fast convergence with many errors, or slower convergence with fewer errors, or something in between the two extremes.

Pseudostabilization

It is sometimes expensive to design self-stabilizing systems. Some of the expense can be reduced by lessening the requirements of the system. In [13], a lesser requirement is defined that will work in most practical situations. Burns et al. [13] define stabilization in terms of computation, which is just a series of global states. A system is said to stabilize if and only if every computation has some state in it such that any computation starting from this state will be in the set of legal computations. On the other hand, in order for a system to pseudo-stabilize, every computation only needs to have some state such that the suffix of the computation beginning at this state is in the set of legal computations.

The property of pseudo-stabilization is obviously weaker than the requirement of stabilization, but the difference becomes clearer in the following example:

Let the set of global states be {0, 1, 2},
the state transitions be {(0,0),(0,1),(1,1),(1,2),(2,2)},
and the set of legal computations be {(0,0,...),(1,1,...),(2,2,...)}.

The system does not stabilize because the computation (1,1,1,...) does not have a state such that every computation beginning with that state will be in the set of legal computations. For example, the computation (1,1,2,2,...) is not in the set of legal computations. However, the system does pseudo-stabilize because every computation has one of the following forms:

(0,0,...) (1,1,...) (2,2,...)
(0,...,0,1,1,...) (1,...,1,2,2,...)
(0,...,0,1,...,1,2,2,...).

All of these forms have a suffix that is in the set of legal computations. So, the system is pseudo-stabilizing.

The difference between the two forms arises because of the way the set of legal configurations is defined. Previously, the legal configurations were defined in terms of legal states. If they are defined in terms of legal states (every computation converges to a legal state because the system is self-stabilizing and because of property P2), then every computation that starts from this state will be a computation of all legal states. On the other hand, if the legal configurations are defined in terms of computations, the states are not necessarily legal or illegal. This is where there is a difference between stabilization and pseudo-stabilization.

This difference can be used to a designer's advantage. In the section titled "Protocols," the sliding window and two-way handshake protocols [10] are described. Both of these algorithms need unbounded sequence numbers that cannot be implemented. The reason they need the unbounded sequence numbers is to achieve self-stabilization, and the authors show that any stabilizing protocol must have infinite state machines. On the other hand, the alternating bit protocol [12] did not need these unbounded sequence numbers. This is because the alternating bit protocol is pseudo-stabilizing [13], not stabilizing. This shows that the design of a pseudo-stabilizing system may be more practical, and it will also be sufficient in most practical applications.

Verification of self-stabilizing systems

When designing self-stabilizing systems, verifying the correctness of these algorithms may be difficult, but there has been some work done in this area. In [10], a convergence stair method is developed where the legal states are built up step by step. Proving that the algorithm stabilizes in each step verifies the correctness of the entire algorithm.

When using a shared memory model, it is usually assumed that there is read/write atomicity. In [7], it is shown that the interleaved assumptions can be relaxed, which will make it easier to verify the correctness of the algorithm.

In [13], Burns and Gouda say that it is sometimes too difficult and time consuming to find and implement the algorithm. This may not be necessary depending on the goal of the system. Algorithms that are pseudostabilizing are usually sufficient in a system, and are easier to implement and more efficient to run.

Advantages

There are many advantages in using self-stabilizing systems. Algorithms have been developed to withstand dynamic network changes or a change in the mode of operation in the system. In [23], an adaptive routing protocol is developed. This protocol changes operation slightly, depending on the characteristics of the network. This has been done before, but the authors [23] have combined two or more protocols in order to make the system even more adaptable. If the network changes so much that the current protocol is not as efficient as another protocol, the nodes in the network actually change the protocol being used. The composite protocol, as the authors call it, is self-stabilizing. So, all nodes will eventually change to the new protocol. Once they all change, the system once again operates correctly. These composite protocols work well if the network changes often and the changes are large enough to warrant a change of protocols.

Another advantage is that algorithms designed for systems that are not self-stabilizing can sometimes be easily extended to become self-stabilizing, so that programs do not have to be entirely rewritten. An example of this extension is given in the section titled "Extensions of Generic Protocol." Resets [14,15] can be used to force the system into a legal state. Once the system is in a legal state, resets are no longer necessary and the system operates normally. The clock synchronization algorithm [16] discussed earlier shows that self-stabilizing synchronization algorithms are possible to develop.

Since message passing is the normal way that nodes communicate with each other in a distributed system, self-stabilizing protocols can be designed that handle node failure or other errors while running, and no external programs need to be run to fix any malfunctions. These systems in general are fault-tolerant, and are preferable if the self-stabilization is easily added.

Future research problems

In all self-stabilizing algorithms, there is a finite amount of time on start-up (or after a node fails and starts up again) where the global state may be illegal. This needs to be corrected as quickly as possible. So, the amount of convergence time necessary needs to be as small as possible. Many algorithms are of the order of n^2 or worse where n is the number of nodes. In many situations this is not fast enough. For example, in [24], Dijkstra's K-state algorithm is analyzed. The number of moves each node makes is of the order of $n^{1.5}$ and the number of messages passed is of the order of n^2 where n is the number of machines. The convergence rate and the number of messages passed is relatively high. Thus, the implementation of self-stabilizing algorithms can be expensive.

Another area is the number of states required by each machine in order to achieve self-stabilization. There are some networks [3] where only two states are necessary, but more often, machines have k states where k is greater than the number of nodes in the network. Two algorithms [3,4] that only use two states were discussed in the section titled "Number of states per machine," but these work only for certain networks. The relationship between the network topology and the number of states required to achieve self-stabilization is still an open question.

Distributed process control systems, such as assembly-line robots, automatic flight control systems, or other real-time systems can be designed to be self-stabilizing. The self-stabilization aspect of the systems can usually be added to the existing system without too much difficulty, and these systems can correct certain errors. They are more robust than normal distributed process control systems because of their fault-tolerant nature. There has not been much research in this area, but it is increasing because of the simplicity of design and maintenance of the systems.

Conclusions

Self-stabilization has been used in many areas, and the areas of study continue to grow. Algorithms have been developed using central or distributed demons [1,7] and uniform and nonuniform networks [6]. The algorithms that assume a central demon can usually be easily extended to support distributed demons, so these algorithms are still useful when applied to distributed systems. A dynamic self-stabilizing protocol assuming only read-write atomicity has also been developed [8]. Extensions of communication protocols that are self-stabilizing have also been developed, such as the sliding window protocol, the two-way handshake, and the alternating-bit protocol [10,12]. General protocols can be extended to be self-stabilizing [14,15].

The major drawback of self-stabilizing systems is the initial illegal configurations. The system must converge quickly in order to make the illegal configurations less serious. Verification of the systems can be difficult, but there are ways to make it easier. Relaxing interleaving assumptions may help [7], and Multari [10] shows how a convergence stair can be used (the algorithm is verified at each step). Some of the assumptions made when designing the systems make it nearly impossible to implement the systems. For example, the protocols discussed in the section "Extensions of general protocol," require a time-out action that needs to examine the contents of the communication link and also needs to know the values of some nonlocal variables. Global time-out actions are usually avoided, which makes these algorithms difficult to implement [10]. Another requirement of these algorithms is that they need unbounded sequence numbers for the message counters [10]. This is also not possible when trying to implement the algorithm. However, the authors mention that using 64 bits for the sequence number is sufficient in most practical situations.

These requirements may not be necessary in some cases. The alternating-bit protocol [12], does not need unbounded sequence numbers, nor does it need expensive global time-out actions. Therefore, this protocol can be implemented relatively easily, and even though the algorithm is pseudostabilizing and not stabilizing, this does not affect the usefulness of the algorithm in most situations.

The most extensive work in self-stabilization has been done in the area of mutual exclusion [1,2,6,9]. The reason for this is mainly due to Dijkstra's original self-stabilizing model [1], where a legal state is defined to be a state in which only one privilege existed in the system. This definition is used in many of the self-stabilization papers, and it is a form of mutual exclusion since the existence of one privilege implies that the only process allowed in its critical section is the one that possesses the privilege. There has been a great deal of work in this area, but many other areas have begun to use self-stabilization in order to design more robust distributed systems. These other areas include synchronization [16], distributed process control [17,18], inherent fault tolerance [17,18] which also includes Byzantine agreement [20] (a group of functioning processes agree on some value even in the presence of faulty or malicious processes), graph theoretic problems, and also probabilistic self-stabilization [4]. These are some of the many areas of distributed systems that have used self-stabilization in order to design more robust distributed systems.

References

[1] E. Dijkstra, "Self-Stabilization in Spite of Distributed Control," *Comm. ACM* , Vol. 17, 1974, pp. 643–644.

[2] S. Ghosh, "Understanding Self-Stabilization in Distributed Systems," Tech. Report TR-90-02, Dept. of Computer Science, Univ. of Iowa, Iowa City, Iowa, Mar. 1990.

[3] S. Ghosh, "Self-Stabilizing Distributed Systems with Binary Machines," *Proc. 28th Allerton Conf. Communication, Control and Computing,* 1990.

[4] T. Herman, "Probabilistic Self-Stabilization," *Information Processing Letters,* Vol. 35, 1990, pp. 63–67.

[5] H. Kruijer, "Self-Stabilization (in Spite of Distributed Control) in Tree Structure Systems," *Information Processing Letters,* Vol. 8, No. 2, 1979, pp. 91–95.

[6] J. Burns and J. Pachl, "Uniform Self-Stabilizing Rings," *ACM Trans. Prog. Languages and Systems,* Vol. 11, No. 2, 1989, pp. 330–344.

[7] J. Burns, M. Gouda, and R. Miller, "On Relaxing Interleaving Assumptions," *Proc. MCC Workshop Self-Stabilization,* 1989.

[8] Dolev, Israeli, and Moran, "Self-Stabilization of Dynamic Systems Assuming Only Read/Write Atomicity," *Proc. 9th Ann. Symp. Principles Distributed Computing*, ACM Press, New York, N.Y., 1989.

[9] G. Brown, M. Gouda, and M. Wu, "Token Systems that Self Stabilize," *IEEE Trans. Computers,* Vol. 38, No. 6, June 1989, pp. 845–852.

[10] M. Gouda and N. Multari, "Self-Stabilizing Communication Protocols," *IEEE Trans. Computers,* Vol. 40, No. 4, Apr. 1991, pp. 448–458.

[11] A. Fekete, N. Lynch, and Y. Mansour, "The Data Link Layer: Two Impossibility Results," *Proc. ACM Symp. Principles Distributed Computing,* ACM Press, New York, N.Y., 1988.

[12] Y. Afek and G. Brown, "Alternating-Bit Protocol," *Proc. Eighth Symp. Reliable Distributed Systems,* IEEE Computer Soc. Press, Los Alamitos, Calif., 1989.

[13] J. Burns and M. Gouda, "Stabilization and Pseudostabilization," Tech. Report TR-90-13, Dept. of Computer Sciences, Univ. of Texas, Austin, Texas, May 1990.

[14] S. Katz and K. Perry, "Self-Stabilizing Extensions of Message-Passing Systems," *Proc. MCC Workshop Self-Stabilization,* 1989.

[15] A. Arora and M. Gouda, "Distributed Reset," *10th Conf. Foundations Software Technology and Theoretical Computer Science,* 1990.

[16] M. Gouda and T. Herman, "Stabilizing Unison," *Information Proc. Letters,* Vol. 35, 1990, pp. 171–175.

[17] F. Bastani and M. Kam, "A Self-Stabilizing Ring Protocol for Load Balancing in Distributed Real-Time Process Control Systems," Tech. Report No. UH-CS-87-8, Dept. of Computer Science, Univ. of Houston, Texas, Nov. 1987.

[18] F. Bastani, I. Yen, and I. Chen, "A Class of Inherently Fault-Tolerant Distributed Programs," *IEEE Trans. Software Eng.,* Vol. 14, No. 1, 1988, pp. 1432–1442.

[19] L. Lamport, R. Shostak, and M. Pease, "The Byzantine Generals Problem," *ACM Trans. Programming Languages and Systems,* Vol. 4, No. 3, July 1982, pp. 382–401.

[20] F. Bastani and Y. Zhao, "A Self-Adjusting Algorithm for Byzantine Agreement," Tech. Report No. UH-CS-87-6, Univ. of Houston, Texas, Oct. 1987.

[21] M. Gouda, R. Howell, and L. Rosier, "The Instability of Self-Stabilization," *Acta Informatica,* Vol. 27, 1990, pp. 697–724.

[22] M. Evangelist and M. Gouda, "Convergence/Response Tradeoffs," Tech. Report STP-124-89, MCC Software Technology Program, Mar. 1989; also appeared as *Proc. Second IEEE Symp. Parallel and Distributed Processing,* IEEE Computer Soc. Press, Los Alamitos, Calif, 1990.

[23] A. Arora, M. Gouda, and T. Herman, "Composite Routing Protocols," *Proc. Second IEEE Symp. Parallel and Distributed Processing,* IEEE Computer Soc. Press, Los Alamitos, Calif., 1990.

[24] J. Chang, G. Gonnet, and D. Rotem, "On the Costs of Self-Stabilization," *Information Proc. Letters,* Vol. 24, 1987, pp. 311–316.

General

A Model for Executing Computations in a Distributed Environment

A s part of our research into transparent execution of computational services in a distributed environment, we developed a high-level model that identifies the essential steps necessary to execute a computation in a distributed environment. Using the steps identified by the model, we can distinguish properties of distributed execution systems by examining when, where, and in what order these steps are performed. Our reasons for postulating such a model are twofold:

(1)   The model provides a concrete basis for comparing and understanding existing distributed systems that allow remote computations to be invoked.

(2)   The model identifies the decisions that must be made in designing any new mechanism that executes actions in a distributed system.

Specifically for our work, we use the model as a design framework for a mechanism that provides transparent execution of user-level actions in a distributed environment.

Craig E. Wills

We use the term *action* to represent a named computation that can be specified for execution. Many types of actions are executed in a distributed environment. For example, using a command interpreter, a user specifies that a command be executed. This causes a process to be created with its binary image loaded from a file. In another example, a process on one machine executes a network service on another machine by contacting a process listening at a well-known communication port on that machine. In a third example, a computation on a client machine initiates a call to a process on a server machine through a remote procedure call mechanism.

The common denominator between the execution of these different types of actions is the underlying steps needed to transform an action name into the invocation of the computation named by the action. With the model we identify the essential steps, called *components*, necessary to cause an action such as a command, a network service, or a remote procedure call to be executed in a distributed environment. The components form an *action execution model*, which is an abstraction of the necessary steps that must be taken to execute an action in a distributed environment. The model is *complete* in that it captures all decisions that are necessary to execute an action at this level of abstraction. The model does not encompass details of how the action is carried out, such as how synchronization, communication, and machine failure are handled. These details are specified as part of the invocation protocol step of the model.

This paper explains the origin of the model, describes its components, analyzes how characteristics of distributed systems are captured by the model, and shows how the model applies to existing systems. The paper concludes with a brief description of how the model was applied to generate a framework for a new approach to executing computations in a distributed environment. This framework was used to implement a working prototype of a distributed execution mechanism.

Approach

In the development of an action execution model for a distributed environment, we define an action as a named computation. The *execution* of an action translates an action name into the invocation of the computation needed to carry out the action. As a first step in understanding the problem, we propose a set of questions that need to be answered about any action that is performed within a distributed system. How, when, and where these questions are answered in the course of executing an action both characterize a system and influence the interface presented to its users. For any action, the questions that must be answered are:

- When should this action be executed?
- What is the action to be executed?
- Where should the action be invoked for execution?
- How is the action going to be invoked for execution?

This list arises from applying a set of investigative questions to systems that execute actions in a distributed environment. The four questions of interest are similar to those raised by Shoch [11] concerning naming in computer networks. In his work, Shoch distinguishes between names, addresses, and routes as follows:

- The *name* of a resource indicates what we seek,
- An *address* indicates where it is, and
- A *route* tells us how to get there.

Shoch's model decomposes the steps of a name resolution system, which he applies to two examples: the telephone system and interconnected computer networks. In a similar fashion, our work decomposes the steps needed to execute an action in a distributed environment. Using similar notation as Shoch's we have

- The *specification* of an action indicates when to execute,
- The *name* of an action indicates what to execute,
- An *address* indicates where to invoke it, and
- A *means* tells us how to invoke it.

As seen, our notation is similar with two exceptions. First, we include the question *when*, given by a specification, as part of our model. The specification is a mapping between a condition and an action name to execute when the condition is true. Second, *how* is a means for invocation rather than a route. This distinction is analogous to traveling from one city to another. For the question, "How did you travel?" the answer could either be the means of transportation used or the physical route taken. The question must be answered in context — and for invoking an action the means is the appropriate answer.

Shoch's work was important to help define important terms in internetworking and how they relate to each other. Like Shoch's, our model is at a high level and attempts to show relations between important abstractions concerning execution mechanisms in a distributed environment. In looking at related work of models for remote execution, Spector provided early work on a communication model, giving a taxonomy of communication instructions for performing remote operations [13]. He went on to implement a communications subsystem based upon his model.

Other work in distributed execution mechanisms has not focused so much on abstract models, but rather on structures or frameworks that can be translated directly into executable code. The HCS project provides a structure for making remote computations available in a heterogeneous environment [7]. Other work has focused on combining a computational model along with a system for generating distributed applications from a set of templates based on remote procedure call [12].

Our work is not focused on a particular model that can be translated into executable code, but rather we try to abstract the concepts that must be present in any action execution mechanism and show how they are used in different computational models. The four questions we pose identify the decisions that must be made. The visibility of these decisions varies between systems. If only one means exists to invoke an action, then how an action is invoked is not an issue. But if many machines can invoke an action, then selection of a machine is an important component. What is important to realize is that whether the decision is explicit or implicit, each of these questions must be bound to an answer. The decisions may be made at system design time, at the time of specifying an action, or in the course of executing the action. The decisions themselves are made by the components of the action execution model, which are identified and described in the following.

The initiation component

As the name implies, the initiation component, denoted as INITIATE, initiates an action for execution. In terms of the decisions that must be made, the initiation component determines *what* and *when* actions should be executed. A *specification* is a mapping between a condition and an action. For the specification, the initiation component causes the action to be executed if the condition is true. In general, a specification can contain compound conditions and actions that allow an action to be executed based on multiple conditions, and multiple actions to be executed based on a single condition.

Simple examples of specifications are an exception handling routine specified by a programmer to handle the occurrence of an exception in his program, or commands for execution specified by a user using a command interpreter. In the latter case, we view the command not just as an action, but as a specification with a nil condition so execution is immediate. The command interpreter is an example of a *user interface*, which allows the user to form specifications and initiate actions for execution.

More sophisticated tools allow specifications to be given with conditions that depend on system state. For example, actions may be specified to execute at a particular time, or be triggered when a file is modified or a system resource is in short supply. Execution of one action may also implicitly occur if the execution of another action fails.

The binding components

The initiation component introduces an action into the system for execution. The binding components then make the decisions concerning how and where the action will be invoked. In addition, the action name presented for execution may not be unique within the action name space, so an absolute name must be determined. The binding components are so named because they bind values to the decisions necessary to invoke an action once it has been initiated.

The components that perform the necessary bindings are *resolution*, *protocol*, *mapping*, *location*, and *selection*. They make the decisions about what unique action name to use, as well as how and where to invoke the action. The timing, location, and the order in which these bindings are made characterize a particular system. In this section we look at the details of each component and express fundamental ordering relations that must hold between the components.

Resolution

The name presented for execution by the initiation component identifies the action to execute, but does not necessarily identify a unique action name corresponding to a single action within the action name space. The use of partial, nonabsolute names arises in systems that allow shorthand forms for names, or multiple versions of an action. In such cases a *name resolution mechanism* is needed to translate a partial name into a complete name in the action name space. In our model, this translation is performed by the resolution component, denoted as RESOLVE.

The relationship between the initiation and resolution components determines an *ordering relation* between the two components if partial names are allowed. A partial ordering relation, denoted by the symbol "<," is defined between two components if one component must always precede the other. Thus for any system that allows partial names the ordering relation

$$INITIATE < RESOLVE$$

is defined. This relation indicates that if partial action names can be specified, then the resolution component must follow the initiation component to resolve the name into an absolute name.

Resolution of a partial name to a complete name is performed by applying *contexts* to the partial name. Two common types of resolution mechanisms in operating systems are a *current working directory* and a *search path*. A current working directory is a single context that is used to resolve file names in a hierarchical file system. A search path is used to produce an absolute command name from a partial command name and a set of directories that are searched until the command is found.

Protocol and mapping

The protocol and mapping components determine how an action is invoked. These components determine the *invocation protocol* needed to invoke the action and the *underlying name* to use for the action given this protocol.

An invocation protocol is a set of conventions for communicating with an existing process or creating a new process to carry out the computation defined by an action. For example, one invocation protocol is to create a new process with a binary image loaded from a file. Another example of a protocol is to contact a process on another machine using a network protocol and make a request for an action to be carried out. The protocol component, denoted as PROTOCOL, chooses the protocol to use for a particular action, although in many systems this decision is fixed because all actions are invoked in the same manner.

The underlying name is the name needed by the invocation protocol to invoke the action. The underlying name is dependent on the protocol. The underlying name for an action should not be confused with the specified action name. The underlying name is a low-level name that is used for invocation. The action name is a high-level name that is specified by the user. The notion of two name spaces is supported by Watson's [14] conjecture that naming systems should "support at least two levels of identifiers, one convenient for people and one convenient for machines." Our identification of an invocation protocol and an underlying name within this protocol for invoking an action is similar to ideas proposed by Lantz, Edighoffer, and Hitson [6]. They identify (*medium name, identifier-in-medium*) pairs for making requests to servers to access services.

High-level names are mapped into low-level names by the mapping component, denoted as MAP. The mapping component transforms a unique high-level action name to a low-level name. Confusion between the two names is possible because many systems use the same name space for high- and low-level names. For example, in the Unix operating system, a file name is both the name of a command, and the name of the file needed to load into memory to invoke the command. In such cases we view the mapping as a static identity function. If the two name spaces are not the same then

$$\text{RESOLVE} < \text{MAP}$$

because the mapping component uses an absolute name produced by the resolution component. The relationship between the mapping and protocol components also defines the obvious ordering relation

$$\text{PROTOCOL} < \text{MAP}$$

Many issues arise concerning the details of the invocation protocol. These include synchronization, communication, failure handling, authentication, and the execution environment. While not at the same level of abstraction as other model components, these details are important when considering actual implementation of an execution mechanism. Two of these issues on how an action is invoked also have bearing on the availability of an action for a user or from one machine to another. They are *authentication* and the invocation of an action within an *execution environment*.

Authentication

Authentication is the act of determining if the initiator, such as a user, of an action has permission to invoke the action. Although authentication is performed as part of invocation, it may also be performed by other components to ensure that invocation does not fail. For example, the resolution component may use authentication to not just resolve an absolute action name, but to resolve an absolute action name that the initiator has permission to use. Another example is the use of authentication in the location component. Rather than locate all server machines that can invoke an action, the component may locate all such machines that the initiator has permission to use.

This treatment of authentication is analogous to the end-to-end argument made by Saltzer, Reed, and Clark [10], concerning reliability in a distributed system. They argue that reliability for a transaction, such as file transfer, is the ultimate responsibility of the end points of the transaction. Consequently, any intermediate reliability guarantees cannot be used to guarantee the end-to-end reliability of the transaction, but can only be justified on efficiency grounds. In a similar manner, we argue that authentication of action invocation must ultimately be done by the servers that control the actions, but intermediate authentication checks may be valuable for increased efficiency.

Execution environment

The execution environment is the set of bindings between names and values used by an action once it has been invoked. At invocation, an execution environment is established for the newly created action. Many systems have the notion that the environment is *inherited* from the invoker of the action. Inheritance means that the execution environment of the process invoking the action is established for the process carrying out the invoked action.

The execution environment consists of three kinds of bindings between names and values:

- Parameters are names known to the invoked action and the values are bound by the invoker. For example, parameters are used to establish values for a procedure call or to give flags or options for a command.
- Local bindings are specific to an invoked action and initialized at invocation time. For example, each process in the Unix system has its own set of environment variables, which are local bindings between named strings and string values.
- Global bindings are the names and values shared between all actions in a system. For example, the same file name space is often shared by all processes in a system.

The principal question concerning the execution environment is how much of the environment can and needs to be shared between the process invoking an action and the process carrying out the action. If the action expects to manipulate named files, then the action can only be invoked on machines that share the same global bindings. In other cases, such as a procedure call paradigm with nonshared memory, all values are established with parameters so global bindings do not have to be shared.

Location and selection

The *location* and *selection* components determine where an action is invoked. These components locate the set of server machines that are available to invoke the action, and select a machine from this set to actually carry out the action.

The location component, denoted as LOCATE, finds the set of machines that are eligible to invoke the action. For example, if all of the server machines are identical, then the set of eligible machines may be all the server machines. In other systems, the set of eligible server machines may vary for each action, in which case a mechanism to locate eligible machines is needed. The set of eligible machines may be obtained by broadcasting a request, accessing a local store of information that has been distributed by the servers, or accessing well-known information servers.

The selection component, denoted as SELECT, selects an eligible machine to invoke the action. The component is trivial if only one machine is available. If multiple machines are available, the selection policy may still be trivial by randomly selecting a machine, or more complex by gathering state information about the server machines to select the best server in terms of response or some other performance criteria. Much work on the issue of *load sharing*, attempting to move computations from lightly loaded to heavily loaded machines, is applicable to this problem. Again, the relationship between the two components defines the ordering relation

$$LOCATE < SELECT$$

Characterization of the model

In the previous section we identified the binding components of our model and stated a set of ordering relations that must hold between the components. Once the binding components have determined how and where a particular action should be invoked, the invocation component, denoted as INVOKE, causes the action to be carried out. The binding and invocation components represent the *system interface*, which executes an action by translating an action name into an invoked action. To invoke an action, the invocation component uses three values that are supplied by the binding components: It uses

- The invocation protocol determined by the protocol component,
- The underlying name determined by the mapping component, and
- The server machine determined by the selection component.

In this section, we define possible binding times for the components and where each component can be performed. We define additional terminology based on the binding time and ordering relations of the components.

Component binding times

The binding time for a component is when that component is bound to the decision it makes. There are three strategies for when to bind a name to a value [8]. In the context of our model, for a given action, the decision made by each of the components is made at one of three binding times.

- Static binding is done at system generation time, which means the decision is the same for every action that is executed within the system.
- Early binding is done at session initialization or action specification time, which means the decision is made by the initiator of an action.
- Late binding is done at action execution time, which means the decision is made dynamically after the action has been initiated and execution has begun.

Figure 1 shows the components and the possible binding times for each. As shown, the binding time of the initiation and invocation components are fixed. As previously stated, the initiation component uses a specification to initiate execution with an action name. Invocation is always the last component because it uses the invocation protocol, underlying name, and server machine determined by the binding components to invoke the action.

The timing and the ordering of the binding components, however, does vary between systems and characterizes a system. In Figure 1 the dashed boxes represent positions for each of the five binding components (shown to the right in no particular order) to be placed within the model subject to the ordering constraints previously given. The dashed boxes are only a representation and do not fix the number of components at each binding time. Later we will use this representation to show the ordering and binding times for specific systems.

Static binding is used for components that have a fixed decision. For example, in the Unix system all commands are invoked in the same manner. Early binding is used when the initiator needs to make an explicit decision, such as requiring the user to select a particular server machine for invocation as part of the specification. Late binding is used when the decision can be put off until execution. For example, the resolution of a partial name to a unique command name is performed at execution time in the Unix system.

The binding time of a component is a trade-off between flexibility and performance. The later a component is bound to a value, the more easily the system can adapt to change. However each decision that is made at execution time incurs additional run-time costs, although some decisions made at execution time, such as where to invoke, may actually benefit the performance by finding a better machine to execute the action. The binding times also influence a user's perception of the system. Obviously, if the decisions are made statically, the decisions are fixed for the user. If the decision is made at specification time then the user must be explicitly aware of the decision. Only if the decision is made dynamically is it transparent to the user.

Component binding location

Where a component makes each decision also characterizes a system. For an action, each

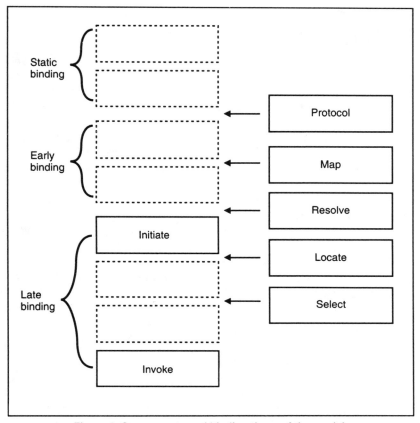

Figure 1. Components and binding times of the model.

component can be performed in one of three places:

- At a client machine, which initiates the action;
- At a server machine, which invokes the action; or
- At an intermediary machine, which neither initiates nor invokes the action.

The initiation component is always performed by the client machine, and the invocation component is always performed by the server machine. The other components may be performed by any of the three machines given above. For example, the client machine may also resolve the action to a complete name, but an intermediate machine may contain a central database that is consulted to locate which machines provide the action. The server machine may map the action name into its underlying name for invocation.

Where a component is performed is determined by where information needed to make the decision is available. Decisions made by the client machine do not require network overhead, but the necessary information may not be available. An intermediary machine allows information to be centralized, but adds communication with another machine to the task of executing an action. Decisions made by the server machine are transparent to the client, but these decisions can only be made once the server machine has been selected.

Transparency and the model components

Given the ordering relations and binding times of the model, we can define different forms of transparency as they relate to action execution for distributed systems.

Location transparency denotes a system in which the names for actions are independent of where the action is invoked. Systems that are location transparent exhibit the characteristics that RESOLVE < SELECT, and SELECT is bound at action execution time. The relation ensures the absolute name for the action is determined prior to the selection of a server machine. The binding time ensures the server machine is not fixed or selected by the initiator.

Access transparency denotes a system in which all actions are initiated in the same manner whether invoked on the client or a server machine. This condition is true if the choice of an invocation protocol for invoking an action is not made at specification time. The invocation protocol is either static or chosen after the action has been initiated.

In light of the model, another type of transparency that we introduce is protocol transparency . A system is protocol transparent if RESOLVE < PROTOCOL and the protocol is chosen at execution time. Similar to location transparency, the ordering relation and binding time requirement ensure that the name of the action is independent of how the action is invoked.

Finally, *network transparency* means that an invoked action executes in the same manner regardless of where it is invoked. This condition is met if the portions of the execution environment used by the action are the same irrespective of which server machine is selected to carry out the action. This situation requires that the global name bindings be shared between the client and server machines or the invoked action does not use names from the global bindings.

Application of the model to existing work

In this section we apply the action execution model to four existing systems and show how these systems are characterized by the ordering and binding time of the model components. These systems are representative of a wide range of systems that allow actions to be executed in a distributed environment. Two of the systems employ a command-oriented paradigm for execution of tasks, one uses a remote procedure call paradigm, and the other an object-oriented model. In each case the partial orderings given in the "Binding components" section hold between the components with the complete ordering dependent on the characteristics of each system.

Unix

Although not originally developed as a distributed system, the Unix operating system [9] exemplifies a system that is command-oriented, and one that has been used as a basis for much work in distributed systems. To characterize the system we apply our model. The Unix system was designed as a single machine system, but now includes explicit commands for accessing files and executing commands on remote machines. For our discussion we assume the user interface is a command interpreter, or *shell* in the Unix system, that allows users to specify commands for immediate execution. The model components and their binding times needed to execute the text-processing command *tex* are given in Figure 2.

As shown, most of the decisions are fixed for all commands. Because commands are invoked on the local machine the location and selection components are trivial. All commands are invoked by creating a process loaded with the contents of a binary file. Because commands are named the same as files, the name space presented to the user for specifying commands is the same as the underlying name space for invoking commands.

Resolution is performed at execution time by the shell. This function alleviates the user from having to specify a complete file name for each command. Resolution uses a search path, maintained

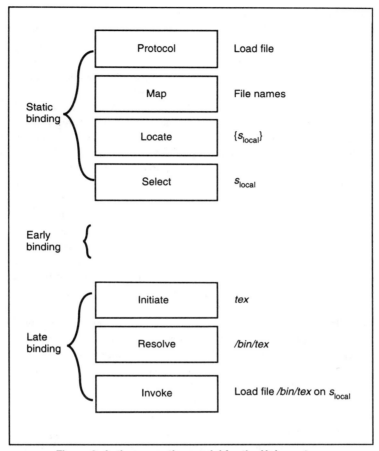

Figure 2. Action execution model for the Unix system.

as a local binding for each process, which specifies an ordered list of directories to search when a partially specified command name is given. The search path is iterated over until a valid directory/ name pair is found. A pair is valid if the file is executable and the user is authorized to execute the file. In the example, *tex* has been resolved to the complete file name*/bin/tex*.

For invocation, the newly created process inherits the execution environment and the user identification from the parent process (in this case, the shell). This environment includes the current working directory, a context in the file name space, and a set of environment variables, which are local bindings between named strings and string values. The new process also inherits a set of parameters that include textual arguments to the command and a set of standard byte stream descriptors used by the command to read input, and write output and error data. In a single machine environment the global bindings, such as file names, are implicitly inherited.

Of interest to our work is how command-oriented systems have been extended to a distributed environment. In the case of the Unix system, a local command *rsh* is used to invoke commands on remote Unix system machines. This command requires the user to specify the remote machine as a parameter to the command, and authenticates that the user has an account on this machine. Resolution is performed on the remote machine using the search path environment variable from the execution environment that is established on the remote machine from a start-up file. Thus, remote command execution in the Unix system is neither access, location, nor network transparent for the user.

Locus

In contrast to the Unix system, the Locus distributed operating system was designed and built specifically to provide its users a network transparent Unix operating system [5]. The system provides a network-wide file system and distributed process execution over a set of machines with heterogeneous architecture. Each machine runs the Locus operating system. Commands are specified by the user in the same fashion as a single machine Unix system, but their execution is carried out in an access transparent manner. A description of the Locus system in terms of our action execution model, again executing the command *tex* specified from a shell, is shown in Figure 3.

Commands are invoked identical to Unix commands, except the newly created process may be on a remote machine. Resolution and authentication are also identical to the Unix system. The key differences from the Unix system are locating and selecting a machine for invocation and accommodating heterogeneous architectures.

Location of eligible machines to invoke a command is made by examining a set of preferred execution sites specified by the system call setxsites() (also available as a shell command). This primitive is usually invoked by the user as part of session initialization to specify the set of available machines. Selection of a machine for invocation involves keeping track of the load on each machine and selecting the least loaded eligible machine.

To accommodate heterogeneous architectures, Locus uses a hidden directory, which is a special directory that contains binary files for specific machine architectures. A command is resolved to a complete name (actually a hidden directory), a machine is then selected for invocation, and the command name is mapped to a machine-specific binary file located in the underlying hidden directory. In the example of Figure 3, a VAX architecture machine has been selected for invocation so the associated binary file is mapped for invocation.

In summary, Locus uses a two-level name space where the high-level names appear to the user as normal Unix system file names, and the hidden low-level names include a "tag" that is architecture specific. In the case where all machines in the distributed system are of the same type, a two-level name space is not needed and the same executable file is used by all machines. The Locus distributed system provides its users access-transparent command execution over a homogeneous operating system environment. Although not location transparent (because the user must specify the set of eligible server machines), the specification of this set is often hidden at session initialization.

Remote procedure call

The remote procedure call (RPC) is a mechanism for one process to request that a procedure be executed by another process, most commonly on another machine. Remote procedures are invoked by suspending the calling environment, packaging the list of procedure parameters and sending them across the network to a server process that invokes the remote procedure. When the remote procedure finishes execution, the results are passed back to the calling procedure and execution resumes as if a normal procedure call had been made.

A full-scale implementation of an RPC mechanism was made by Birrell and Nelson [4] at Xerox PARC as part of the Cedar programming environment. A model of their mechanism is shown in Figure 4 for the remote procedure *F* that is part of the interface *FileAccess.Alpine*.

Procedures are organized into *interface modules*. Each interface is a list of procedure names, together with the types of their arguments and results. An RPC interface is described by a *type* and an *instance*. A type is the absolute name for the interface (thus resolution is not needed), while an instance corresponds to a server machine that exports the interface. In the example, the interface type

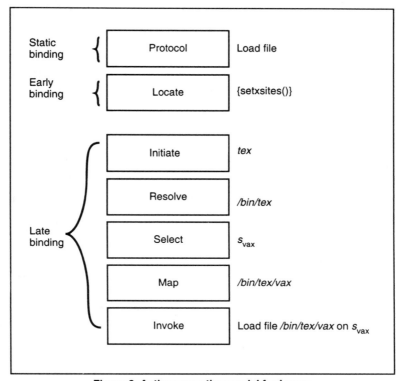

Figure 3. Action execution model for Locus.

FileAccess. Alpine has been specified, and a machine must be selected that exports an instance of the interface. The Grapevine distributed database [3] is used to locate all instances of the interface and the closest (most responsive) server machine is selected for RPC binding. Binding is completed by performing any required authentication on the caller, and then mapping the exported interface to a unique identifier and an index for the procedure within the interface. A *stub* routine, which is a local procedure that handles the RPC communications protocol, invokes the procedure using the unique identifier of the interface and the procedure index. In the example, *F* is mapped to the third procedure in the interface.

The RPC mechanism is access and location transparent—the programmer specifies all procedures (remote and local) in the same manner and the specific server machine for each interface does not need to be given. Another characteristic of RPC mechanisms is that communication between the client and server is through the parameters. Unlike a programming language where procedures can share data through global data structures in the invoker's address space, the remote procedure does not have access to the same address space. Data must be shared through parameters or through shared global data objects such as files.

Object-oriented systems

Just as procedure-oriented languages have motivated research into distributed computing in the form of remote procedure calls, object-oriented languages have motivated research into object-oriented distributed systems. Because procedures share many characteristics with data abstraction languages, it is not surprising that the execution of actions in object-oriented distributed systems share

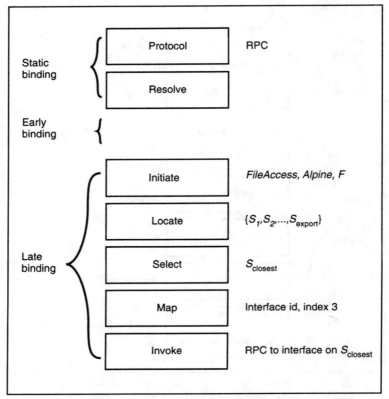

Figure 4. Action execution model for Birrell and Nelson's RPC.

many characteristics with remote procedure mechanisms. Rather than associating procedures with an interface, procedures are associated with an object. This similarity is evident when comparing the action execution model for the object-based system Eden [1] shown in Figure 5, with the model for Birrell and Nelson's RPC shown in Figure 4.

The Eden system is composed of objects called *Eden objects*, or *Ejects*. Each Eject has a data part and a set of invocation procedures that can be invoked by other Ejects (all computations are done by one Eject procedure invoking another Eject procedure). Ejects are relatively large, compared to objects in Smalltalk, on the granularity of directories or mailboxes. In the example taken from the mail system Edmas [2], *MailBox. Deliver* is a specification of the *Deliver* procedure for a *MailBox* Eject that allows a mail message Eject to deliver itself to a mailbox. At execution time the Eden kernel locates the server machine that contains the target *MailBox* Eject. In Eden each Eject resides at one machine, although Ejects are mobile and may move between machines over time. Once the target Eject has been located, the Eden kernel authenticates that the message Eject has the capability to use this mailbox and the *MailBox* Eject maps *Deliver* to its underlying invocation procedure within the Eject. Capabilities for mailboxes are established through invocation of a lookup procedure in a central directory Eject.

The distinguishing characteristic of an object-based system such as Eden is data abstraction and restricting access to the underlying object through a well-defined set of procedures. The user of an object must hold a capability for an object to invoke a procedure defined by the object.

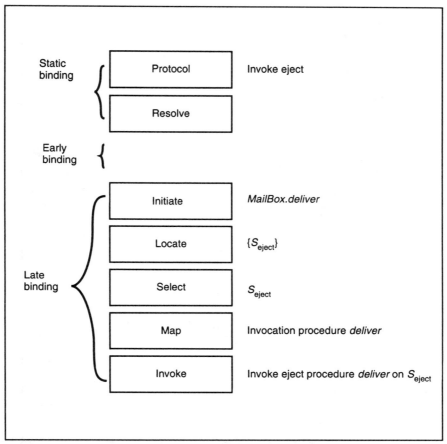

Figure 5. Action execution model for Eden.

Distributed object-oriented systems are location-, access-, and network-transparent for the invoker of an object procedure.

A new approach

In addition to examining existing systems the model can be used as a framework for designing new systems [15]. We propose the following set of design principles for the transparent execution of user-level actions. We call these actions *services*. The design principles and the component orderings implied by these principles for a *service execution mechanism* are given as follows:

(1)   The user should only need to specify what service he would like to perform. He does not need to be concerned with where or how it is invoked (RESOLVE < SELECT   and RESOLVE < PROTOCOL).

(2)   The user should be able to specify partial names for services. The appropriate absolute service name should be resolved. In addition, the user should be able to easily identify and switch use between different versions of a service (INITIATE < RESOLVE).

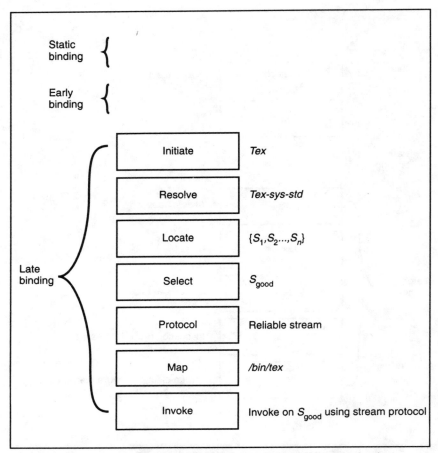

Figure 6. Action execution model for the service execution mechanism.

(3)   A service may have multiple instances, each offered by a different server machine. Each server machine has control over what services it offers. The addition or deletion (except if it is the last) of a service instance should be transparent to the user (RESOLVE < LOCATE).

(4)   The implementation of a service instance is machine specific. A service is defined by what it does, not how it is done. Thus the implementation of a service does not have to be the same for each machine offering an instance of a service (SELECT < PROTOCOL).

The application of these principles and the component orderings they define, along with the required orderings previously defined, lead to the following total ordering for the components of the service execution mechanism derived in [15].

INITIATE < RESOLVE < LOCATE < SELECT
< PROTOCOL < MAP < INVOKE

Figure 6 shows an example of the model applied to our design for the execution of the service *tex*, which invokes the TeX text processor. Resolution of the partial service name *tex* is performed using a service set that results in a standard system version of the service being resolved. The number of server machines located that offer the service is dependent on the service, and we use heuristics that select a good, but not necessarily optimal, machine to invoke the service. A client process on the user's client machine contacts a cycle server on the selected machine using a reliable, stream protocol and passes authentication and execution environment information as needed. The cycle server maps the service name to an underlying file name that is used to start execution of the process to perform the service.

The service mechanism exhibits a number of transparency characteristics.

(1)   The mechanism provides *network transparency* by limiting the use of a service to the machines that share the necessary execution environment of the service. Thus, many services can be shared between machines in homogeneous portions of the computing engine while fewer services are offered between machines in different global execution environments.

(2)   The mechanism is *location transparent* because the user does not need to be aware of which machines offer a service. Services from newly added server machines are transparently added to the set of services available to the user.

(3)   The mechanism is both *access* and *protocol transparent* because all services are initiated in the same manner, and the protocol used for invocation is transparent to the user. New services that use a common protocol for invocation are available to users at client machines without any additional work at the client machine.

Summary

In this paper, we presented a model for the execution of actions in a distributed environment. We identified the set of components necessary to execute an action within a system, defined the functionality of each component, and showed different types of transparency based upon the ordering and binding time of these components.

The existence of the model provided us with a common basis on which to compare a variety of mechanisms that execute actions within a distributed system, such as command execution, remote procedure calls, and object-oriented systems. The model also provided a framework for the components that our service execution mechanism must provide. The straightforward "generation" of the framework for a mechanism from a set of design principles is an appealing idea in distributed systems design. Not only is the model useful for our mechanism, but it provides a framework for the design of any execution mechanism in a distributed environment.

An interesting approach for future work is to extend the model to abstract the details of carrying out an action once it has been invoked. Some of these details that could be modeled are communication paradigms, failure recovery, and authentication mechanisms. Inclusion of these aspects would allow more depth of comparison between systems.

References

[1] G. Almes et al., "The Eden System: A Technical Review," *IEEE Trans. Software Eng.*, Vol. SE-11, No. 1, Jan. 1985, pp. 43-59.

[2] G.T. Almes and C.L. Holman, "Edmas: An Object-Oriented, Locally Distributed Mail System," *IEEE Trans. Software Eng.*, Vol. SE-13, No. 9, Sept. 1987, pp. 1001-1009.

[3] A. Birrell et al., "Grapevine: An Exercise in Distributed Computing," *Comm. ACM*, Vol. 25, No. 4, Apr. 1982, pp. 260-274.

[4] A.D. Birrell and B.J. Nelson, "Implementing Remote Procedure Calls," *ACM Trans. Computer Systems*, Vol. 2, No. 1, Feb. 1984, pp. 39-59.

[5] D.A. Butterfield and G.J. Popek, "Network Tasking in the Locus Distributed Unix System," *Proc. Summer USENIX Conf.*, USENIX Assoc., Berkeley, Calif., 1984, pp. 62-71.

[6] K.A. Lantz, J.L. Edighoffer, and B.L. Hitson, "Towards a Universal Directory Service," *Proc. Fourth ACM Symp. Principles Distributed Computing*, ACM Press, New York, N.Y., 1985, pp. 250-260.

[7] D. Notkin et al., "Interconnecting Heterogeneous Computer Systems," *Comm. ACM*, Vol. 31, No. 3, Mar. 1988, pp. 258-273.

[8] D.C. Oppen and Y.K. Dalal, "The Clearinghouse: A Decentralized Agent for Locating Named Objects in a Distributed Environment," *ACM Trans. Office Information Systems*, Vol. 1, No. 3, July 1983, pp. 230-253; earlier, expanded version published as Tech. Report OPD-T8103, Xerox Office Products Division, Systems Development Dept., Oct. 1981.

[9] D.M. Ritchie and K. Thompson. "The Unix Time-Sharing System," *Comm. ACM*, Vol. 17, No. 7, July 1974, pp. 365-375.

[10] J.H. Saltzer, D.P. Reed, and D.D. Clark, "End-to-End Arguments in Systems Design," *ACM Trans. Computer Systems*, Vol. 2, No. 4, Nov. 1984, pp. 277-288.

[11] J.F. Shoch, "Internetwork Naming, Addressing, and Routing," *Proc. IEEE COMPCON*, Fall 1978, pp. 72-79.

[12] A. Singh, J. Schaeffer, and M. Green, "A Template-Based Approach to the Generation of Distributed Applications Using a Network of Workstations," *IEEE Trans. Parallel and Distributed Systems*, Vol. 2, No. 1, Jan. 1991, pp. 52-67.

[13] A.Z. Spector, "Performing Remote Operations Efficiently on a Local Computer Network," *Comm. ACM*, Vol. 25, No. 4, Apr. 1982, pp. 246-260.

[14] R.W. Watson, "Identifiers (Naming) in Distributed Systems," *Distributed Systems — Architecture and Implementation, An Advanced Course*, Vol. 105, Springer-Verlag, New York, N.Y., 1981, pp. 191-210.

[15] C.E. Wills, "A Service Execution Mechanism for a Distributed Environment." *Proc. Ninth Int'l Conf. Distributed Computing Systems*, IEEE Computer Soc. Press, Los Alamitos, Calif., 1989, pp. 326-334.

Relaxed Consistency of Shared State in Distributed Servers

I n a distributed-server architecture, a service is often provided by one or more servers running on different machines in a network with the service functions distributed or replicated primarily for increased availability and performance [1], [2]. The servers may be organized as members of a *server group* that exports the service through a generic runtime interface, with the distribution and the replication of the functions hidden from clients. An application is then implemented as one or more clients communicating with the server group. An example is a distributed file server group where each member of the group manages a subset of the name space of all files. Client requests on disjoint subsets of the name space may be handled concurrently, increasing performance. If any of the members fails, only the files managed by the failed member are unavailable to clients. The runtime interface allows *group communication*, whereby group members may communicate with one another or with clients by exchanging messages (see Figure 1).

A direct consequence of the distributed-server architecture is the implementation of shared state in a decentralized fashion across the members of a server group. The state typically characterizes resources and is updated by the group messages exchanged. Examples of shared state include name-binding information, processing load at various members, and leadership in the group. The sharing requires members to coordinate with one another and to provide a consistent view of the state to clients. Viewing the access to server state as a multicopy update problem, one can adapt existing approaches for consistent updating of multiple data copies [3], [4] to enforce server state consistency. However, these approaches are inappropriate, since their generality may introduce unnecessary complexity and inflexibility in the access operations. Instead, the consistency requirements can be uniformly specified in terms of the order in which messages are exchanged between clients and group members in the access operations [5].

Absolute consistency of shared state requires every member of the group to have the same view of the state. It may be enforced by imposing a total order on group messages; that is, messages would

K. Ravindran and

Samuel T. Chanson

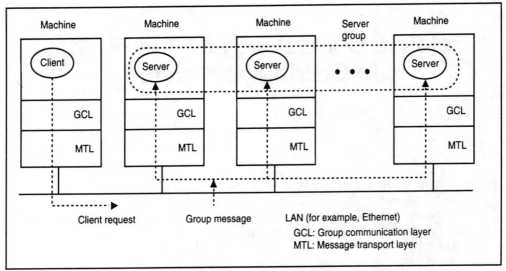

Figure 1. Layers of functions in a distributed application.

be delivered to all members in the same sequence. An example of such a constraint is that a message m_1 be delivered after a message m_2, which itself must be delivered after a message m_3. Absolute consistency is often enforced to avoid any inconsistency from affecting applications. For example, inconsistency in the contents of a database affects the correctness of applications that use the database.

However, it is often not necessary to enforce absolute consistency for many distributed applications, since they have an inherent ability to *tolerate* inconsistency without correctness being affected. In some cases, an inconsistency may not be perceivable. Consider, for example, a processor pool service that manages a pool of processors to execute programs dispatched by clients. In selecting a processor to execute a program, it does not matter if the program executes on one processor or the other [6]. In some other cases, an inconsistency may be detected and corrected transparently to the application. For example, inconsistency in name-binding information for a server may be detected when the information is used to access the server and may be corrected by a customized protocol. Such a *relaxed* consistency of shared state often has the following advantages:

(1)   A strict coordination among the server group members is not required. Consider, for example, a server group that provides the processor pool service. An update by a member to the list of available processors in the pool — say, adding a new processor to the list—need not be sent to other members immediately.

(2)   The relaxation may subsume handling machine and communication failures by virtue of enforcing state consistency to the extent required. In the previous example, a communication failure when an update is being sent to the processor list may not affect the pool service. So the failure need not be observed by the sender.

Thus, the ordering constraints on group messages can be weaker than a total order on the messages. This provides the potential for a higher degree of concurrency in access to server state without correctness being compromised. For example, a weaker constraint that m_1 and m_2 be delivered after m_3 allows the delivery of m_1 and m_2 to occur concurrently, possibly in different sequences, at various members.

The approach of relaxing consistency requirements and using application-specific protocols to deal with inconsistency forms the backbone of this paper. This approach differs from existing approaches used in distributed-agreement protocols, because they do not systematically exploit application characteristics [7], [8], [9]. To incorporate this approach in a generic framework, this paper formulates a model of distributed servers that allows elegant encapsulation of application-specific protocols into the access operations. In many cases, the operations need not be executed as atomic actions. This paper also describes sample applications to illustrate the use of this approach in designing distributed servers.

Model of a distributed server

The various servers providing a service form a server group with a unique group identifier *Srvr_Gid* and export the service under a unique, well-known service name *Srvc_Nm*. Client interactions with the group and interactions of the members among themselves (that is, intraserver communications) require exchanging messages with members of *Srvr_Gid*. Thus, the server group is specified by the pair (*Srvc_Nm, Srvr_Gid*). For example, a print spooler group *Prnt_Gid* provides print spooling service *Spool*, with each member of the group serving a subset of the clients. The spooler group is identified by (*Spool, Prnt_Gid*). The runtime interface specifies, in addition to the above, how client-server communications may take place — such as how many leaders are in the group, how a client may establish contact with a leader, and how the leader may arrange for the client to communicate with a member that will provide the service. Such an interface may be generic across various services in the system.

Shared state

The state of a server group — both service-generic and service-specific — is distributed across members of the group. Examples of service-generic state are lists containing information about membership in a group, locks on the underlying resource, and information about the leadership within the group. Examples of service-specific state are information on processor load and availability status maintained by a processor pool server and name-binding information maintained by a name server.

Let V represent a shared state of server group S_G (see Figure 2). V may assume a set of values depending on an attribute of the function it characterizes. Let $v_1, v_2, ..., v_N$ be the instances of V maintained by members $S_{g1}, S_{g2} ..., S_{gN}$, respectively. Then, the pair (*attribute, value* (v_i)) constitutes the *local view* of S_{gi} ($i = 1, 2, ..., N$). To illustrate, let V refer to the leader in S_G, as specified by the attribute Who_is_ldr. The view of S_{gi} (or simply S_g) on who the leader is may contain the process ID of the leader.

Group communication is used to coordinate among the S_g's and to realize access operations on V. A client accesses V by sending a group message to S_G. Since the local views may be different, it is often necessary to filter them and agree on the value of V. In one case, every S_g may respond with its view. The client may then apply a criterion, based on the attribute of V, to identify the S_g's that satisfy the criterion. In another case, the client may specify the attribute in the message to S_G. Only those S_g's whose views satisfy the criterion may respond. In either case, the client may establish a quorum on the responses [10]. For example, a client may specify the attribute Who_is_ldr in a group message to identify the leader in S_G. Either every S_g responds with its view of who the leader is or only those S_g's that project themselves as the leader respond. The client may then identify the leader from the responses.

Operations on shared state

The basic operations allow reading, writing, and locking and unlocking V. In the underlying

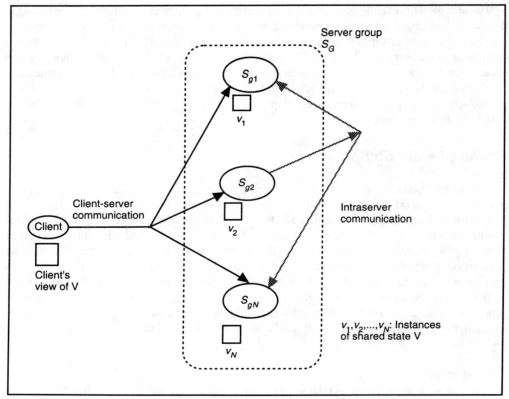

Figure 2. Model of a distributed server.

implementation, the "address" that "points" to V is the (*Srvr_Gid, attribute*) pair. Arbitration mechanisms to resolve contention among members are required in the lock and unlock operations. The applications may specify the required arbitration in the form of ordering constraints on the underlying group messages (say, for serializing access to a resource). For example, an application may specify that two lock operations for read be executed in any order at members. An application may integrate the lock and unlock functions into the read/write operations rather than using two distinct sets of protocols.

Extrinsic and intrinsic states

The state of server group S_G may be partitioned into two subsets — *intrinsic state* and *extrinsic state*. Whether a state is intrinsic or extrinsic influences the protocols to manage it.

A state is intrinsic if a write operation on the state may occur without any relationship to client requests or failures. An example is the ranking that may be maintained among the S_g's and used, say, in quorum consensus protocols. The ranking may change due to failure of an S_g or to a policy internal to S_G but is unrelated to client requests. Thus, the protocols to manage intrinsic state do not interact with the client protocols and, hence, can be asynchronous. In other words, the ordering on intraserver messages to manage intrinsic state is not related to that on client messages. Service-generic state is typically intrinsic and is used in the implementation of server groups.

A state is extrinsic if a write on the state may be caused by requests from a client. An example is a printer managed by a spooler group. The printer changes its state when clients access the printer for printouts and release it later. The protocols to manage extrinsic state thus interact with the client protocols (for example, handling client failures).

Based on the application-driven characterization of shared state described in this section, we now discuss consistency requirements on shared state.

Consistency requirements on shared state

In this section, we first characterize absolute consistency of shared state in distributed servers. We then make a case for relaxed consistency, which allows operations to be nonatomically executed, thereby increasing concurrency and efficiency.

Absolute consistency

Consider the state V shared among members of S_G. Absolute consistency of V means that the local views of the member S_g's should be the same at every tick in logical time, where a tick represents the receipt of a message.

A view change includes receiving a message (that is, an event) and a local computation on the message. Assuming that the views are identical prior to the occurrence of an event e^m, absolute consistency of V requires that e^m should occur at every member (we assume deterministic applications, so e^m causes the same computation at every member). The condition requires that if e^m is interspersed in an ordered sequence of events seen by an S_g as

$$EV\_SEQ = [e^1 \succ e^2 \succ ... \succ e^m \succ ... \succ e^k] \tag{1}$$

(where $e^1 \succ e^2$ specifies the order "e^2 occurs after e^{1}"), then each of the S_g's should also see EV_SEQ. Since the events are communicated in group messages, the condition for absolute consistency translates to the following: A message sent by S_g or a client should be received by all S_g's and in the same order with respect to other related messages [5], [11], [12], [13].

Let us see how consistency is enforced within S_G in light of simultaneous access to V by the S_g's — that is, *collisions*. The above condition ensures that the access messages sent by each of the colliding S_g's are received by every other S_g in the same order in relation to its own message (the sending of a message completes when the sender receives a copy of the message). The arbitration among colliding S_g's may be based on some policy, such as an S_g choosing the sender of the first message it received [14] or the S_g's agreeing on a ranking among them. The arbitration policy requires a total ordering of events that affect S_G, including failures of members and their joining or leaving S_G [5], [11], [15].

The total ordering on messages limits the communication-level concurrency possible in the application, particularly when S_G is large, since the ordering needs to be agreed upon identically across all the S_g's [9].

Relaxed consistency

A premise that has become prevalent in distributed operating systems is that the applications implemented by clients and servers often have an inherent ability to tolerate inconsistency in the shared state [16], [17]. This premise is based on the characteristics of many newer applications developed to exploit the distribution of service functions across clients and servers. Typically, the functions hitherto hardwired into a user program are provided by servers, and clients bind to the functions dynamically at runtime. Examples are locating a printer with certain features (laser printer) and selecting a least-loaded processor to execute a program.

The premise manifests in allowing applications to specify weak ordering constraints on group messages [5], [11]. In some cases, a message need not even be seen by every member; so, the group communications can be efficient [18]. Issues such as collisions may be handled by additional mechanisms (for example, back-off-based arbitration) in the access protocols. An inconsistency in V, say due to persistent message loss, either may not be perceivable to applications or may be detected upon use of V and corrected (transparently to applications) by customized protocols.

We now describe certain properties that enable applications to tolerate inconsistency.

Idempotent events. An event TR^m is *idempotent* if it does not cause a change in V. Typically, read operations on V are idempotent. Certain commutative properties hold for idempotent events. Consider the event sequence EV_SEQ given in Equation (1). Given that EV_SEQ and $[e^{m'}]$ are idempotent sequences, that is, contain only idempotent events, $EV\_SEQ \succ [e^{m'}]$ is an idempotent sequence; so is $[e^{m'}] \succ EV\_SEQ$. Also, $EV\_SEQ \succ EV\_SEQ' \succ [e^{m'}]$ is an idempotent sequence if EV_SEQ' is an idempotent sequence. These properties indicate that the nonexecution, reexecution, and misordering of idempotent operations at some members may not introduce inconsistency in V (see Figure 3). Thus the misordering of group messages used in such operations may be tolerated.

Suppose, for example, a client sends a group message to S_G to search for a file or to get time information from S_G. In both cases, the message need not be seen by every S_g, because the operations are idempotent. For file search, it suffices if the client gets a response from the S_g that manages the file. For time request, response from any of the S_g's will do. Thus, a communication failure that results in some S_G's not seeing the message may not affect successful completion of the operations.

However, nonidempotent events should be observed in the same order at every member. For example, if a leader S_g relinquishes leadership but some members do not receive the relinquishment message, their local views still project S_g as the leader. The inconsistency should be detected and corrected transparently to the applications.

Tolerable inconsistency. In some cases, a client may employ a protocol to detect an inconsistency in V when using the view returned from a member S_g and advise S_G to correct the inconsistency. In other cases, an inconsistency may simply be ignored. The following examples illustrate this:

(1)   Example 1: Suppose S_G exports name service. Then V is the name-to-address binding information that maps a service name to a server address. An inconsistency in V, say due to server migration to a different address, may result in a client either not reaching the server or reaching an incorrect server. In either case, the inconsistency may be detected by a protocol: in the former case by a lack of response and in the latter case by a negative response from the incorrect server. The client may then advise S_G to correct the information. Such a protocol may be transparently embedded in the client-server interface of an application (for example, a file manager).

(2)   Example 2: Consider a processor pool service provided by S_G. Each S_g maintains a local view of the computation load on the various processors in the pool. A change in the load on a processor may result in an inconsistency in the view, if the change is not executed by S_G as an atomic action. When a client specifies, say, an attribute Least-load to select a least-loaded processor, the inconsistency may result in selecting a processor that is not the least loaded. However, the processor may still be able to execute a program dispatched by the client, possibly at a lower performance. If the lower performance can be tolerated (for example, off-line computations), it is not necessary for the client to use the least-loaded processor. Otherwise, the client may confirm that the selected processor is in fact the least loaded. Such a protocol may be embedded in the client-server interface of the processor selection application, as described in the "Processor pool service" section.

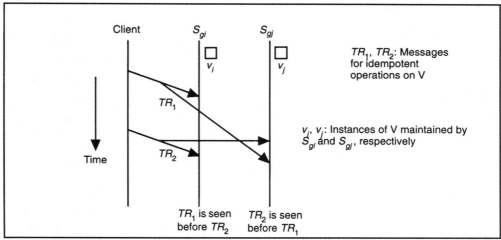

Figure 3. Scenario to illustrate acceptable weak ordering of messages.

The properties of applications described so far substantiate the premise that it is not necessary to enforce absolute consistency of shared state in many cases.

Implementation framework of access operations

The relaxed consistency leads one to a variety of decision components regarding design of server groups, as described in this section.

Complexity and efficiency trade-offs

Relaxing consistency requirements manifests in using a weak form of group communication as a vehicle for access operations. This will result in efficient execution of the operations, particularly when state inconsistencies arise infrequently. If an inconsistency does arise, it may be either ignored or detected upon using the state and corrected transparently to applications. Thus, relaxed consistency may be sufficient in many applications, as long as correct operation of S_G is not compromised. Applications that cannot tolerate inconsistency (such as distributed databases) may use strong message ordering.[1] The application-specific protocols are efficient in normal cases when the network does not lose or misorder messages; however, the protocols incorporate additional mechanisms to deal with the occasional inconsistencies [19].

Choice of group-communication primitive

Given a pair of messages x and y, the communication layer should provide a primitive that (1) allows applications to specify an ordering relation on the pair x and y (for example, message x is delivered after message y) and (2) atomically multicasts x and y for delivery at all members in *Srvr_Gid*. In the earlier example, the delivery of messages m_1 and m_2 after m_3 may be realized by specifying the ordering relations on the message pairs $m_3 \succ m_1$ and $m_3 \succ m_2$ and atomically

---

[1]The notion of *consistency* in distributed servers is different from that in distributed databases. The techniques to enforce consistency of user data in databases may not always be suitable or necessary for distributed servers, because the techniques are specific to the database service whose clients are usually intolerant to inconsistency in data (such as customers of a banking database) [16, 17].

multicasting them. With their concurrent delivery, m_1 and m_2 occur in the same computation step in logical time, with no perceivable inconsistency in the application.

Currently available communication primitives are Cbcast in Isis [5], Psync in x-Kernel [20], and the 0_send in our system [11]. The commonality in these primitives is the integration of causal ordering and group communication. However, they differ in the way the ordering relationships can be specified (the differences in the implementation of these primitives are not relevant to our discussion). For example, the Psync primitive derives the causal order on messages (that is, message dependencies) from the physical time order in which messages are sent and received, while the 0_send primitive allows a declarative specification of ordering constraints. The user may infer these constraints based on the knowledge of application or from the messages received. In contrast, the Group_send primitive in the V-Kernel [18] and its extended form in one of our earlier works [21] do not provide such features except for a basic multicast facility, thereby requiring the application to build the necessary communication features.

The computation based on a received message x causes the member to change its local view of the distributed state. So, a set of messages and the ordering on them specify the final state. If message ordering can be completely specified by members in the communication primitives, it is often sufficient for a member to process messages in the order in which they are received and guarantee state consistency at every step in logical time (assuming that members process a message deterministically — that is, processing the same at every member).

Supporting dynamic groups

Suppose a server entity S_g joins the group. A message $join(S_g)$, indicating the join, should be delivered at all group members before the first message m sent by the entity. Suppose the entity leaves the group (or fails). A message $leave(S_g)$, indicating the leave, should be delivered at members after the last message m' from the entity. The *join* and *leave* events of various members should be consistently ordered with respect to message activities in the group. The *join* and *leave* messages are used by applications to deal with the effects of membership changes on the shared state.

In summary, application-level state changes may be captured by message ordering and group membership changes, with the state consistency requirements reflected on the interspersing of these events.

Lock and unlock operations

We now describe a generic realization of the lock and unlock operations and how the communication primitives play a role in the realization. Since access to a shared state by server group members is distributed, the following issues are to be tackled:

- Failures of a member that has locked (or is in the process of locking) a resource may result in a permanent loss of the resource.
- Collisions among members may result in inconsistent access to the resource.

The mechanisms to handle failures and collisions should be integrated into the lock-acquisition protocol, as described below.

Protection of shared resources against failures

See Figure 4. Suppose a member S_g of the server group S_G has acquired a lock on a shared resource (Lock_acquired). The lock on the resource should be released when S_g unlocks the resource or when S_g fails. In the latter case, the event $leave(S_g)$ should cause a surviving member of S_G to infer that

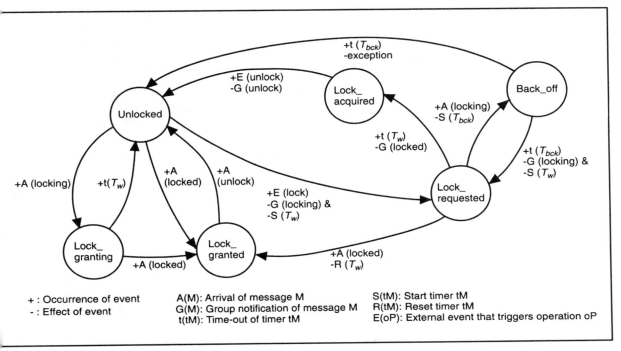

Figure 4. Finite state machine diagram of the lock acquisition protocol.

the lock has been released. Under guarantee from the communication layer that the *leave* event occurs in a bounded interval of time, the resource will not be perceived as lost.

Collision arbitration by time-out

The idea behind the arbitration is that a member intending to access a shared resource communicates its intention to other members of the group and waits for a certain time interval to see if the resource is available. If so, it locks the resource; otherwise, it backs off for a random interval of time and tries again [22]. Details are as follows:

Refer to Figure 4. Suppose a member S_g wishes to access V. If the local view indicates that V is locked or in the process of being locked (Lock_granted or Lock_granting), S_g queues up its lock request. If V is not locked (Unlocked), S_g updates its view to Lock_requested and sends an intraserver message Locking(V) requesting a lock. Since members may independently generate Locking messages, the ordering on the messages may not be deducible to the protocol. So, an additional mechanism is needed for arbitration. Accordingly, S_g waits for a time interval T_w, given by

$$T_w \geq 2 * T_{msg} \tag{2}$$

before accessing V; T_{msg} should be sufficiently large to allow intermachine message transfer (≈ 10 milliseconds in an Ethernet network). On receipt of this message, other S_g's update their views to Lock_granting and withhold any subsequent attempt to lock the resource during a time-out period T_w. The use of time-out at the requesting S_g guards against delays in message propagation and, hence, enables S_g to detect colliding lock requests. Should the requesting S_g fail during the lock-acquisition phase, the occurrence of either the *leave*(S_g) event or the time-out at other S_g's enables the latter to restore the resource to Unlocked and process the queued lock requests, if any.

The receipt of a Locking message by S_g from some other member during the interval T_w indicates a collision. The members involved in the collision may execute a collision-resolution protocol (see below). If no collision is detected during T_w, S_g sends a Locked intraserver message and updates its view to Lock_acquired. It may then access V. On receiving the Locked message, other S_g's update their views to Lock_granted.

If S_g detects a collision, it backs off for a random interval of time before trying the access again. If it again detects a collision, it backs off for a longer interval. After a certain number (Max_bckoff) of retries, it gives up and returns an exception to the application for appropriate handling.[2]

If the upper bound on T_{msg} is known (as in synchronous networks [13]), the protocol ensures correctness. Otherwise, the protocol should use an arbitration policy or incorporate an additional mechanism to deal with inconsistencies.

The lock operation requires two group messages in the normal case when there is no contention. The unlock operation can be realized with one group message.

The use of the arbitration protocol in distributed servers is illustrated in the "Distributed name server" and "Processor pool service" sections.

Arbitration by total ordering of messages

When ordering information across the entire group (that is, global) is not completely specifiable without additional knowledge about member activities, the time-out-based arbitration protocol may be used. However, the protocol executes nonatomically in the absence of the knowledge on T_{msg}. For applications that can deal with inconsistency, the protocol is sufficient. When contention is low, the frequency of inconsistent access is low, which results in good normal-case performance.

For total ordering, one requires some form of ranking among members that is maintained consistently in the presence of joining and leaving of members in *Srvr_Gid*. With ranking, the time-out-based preemption and collision handling are not required in the protocol. Other total-ordering protocols, such as Abcast in Isis [5] and the *Trans/Total* [9], may be used for the purpose. A ranking-based arbitration scheme using a coordinator that is described in one of our works requires six group messages to be sent for the locking protocol [23].

State updates during join and leave of members

A merge protocol is required that allows a server to join a server group, take part in the group's activities, and, subsequently, leave the group. The merge requires a new member to acquire a local view of V from other members.

State-acquisition phase

Suppose a server S_g wishes to merge with server group S_G. It first joins the group S_G, which allows S_g to receive messages destined for S_G.

Since S_g is not yet part of the group, its local instance of V should be initialized. Suppose S_g is a name server joining a name server group. After joining the group, S_g should acquire valid name bindings from other members of the group — using a customized protocol — to merge into the group's activities [17]. The merge protocol may use the group-communication primitives to exchange state information.

---

[2]The protocol is similar to the CSMA/CD protocol used in Ethernet — an S_g "listens" for an ongoing access to a shared resource; if no access is "sensed," S_g accesses the resource or backs off for a random interval before "listening" again.

Though the merge protocols and the ordering of join events are application-dependent, it is possible to outline the following simple generic techniques:

(1) *Immediate probe and merge.* After the join, S_g may probe the rest of the group with an intraserver message to solicit from the group members their views of V. S_g may then apply a quorum on the views. This technique is especially appropriate when V represents an intrinsic resource. For example, a new member may find out who the leader of the group is by specifying the attribute Who_is_ldr in a group message and filtering the responses from various members. This technique normally requires one group message and N responses.

(2) *Client-driven probe and merge.* The acquisition of V is triggered by a client request to S_g to access V. S_g may then probe the rest of the group to acquire V, using the protocol described above. This technique is appropriate when V represents an extrinsic resource. An example is the service-name-binding information maintained by a name server. When the server joins the name server group, it may not possess the binding information for a given service. It acquires the binding information from the group on a client request to access the service. The technique requires one group message and N responses.

(3) *Merge on the fly.* S_g may contend for access to V without the local view of V initialized. The protocols to acquire V are integrated into the protocols to access V. In other words, unlike the client-driven technique described above, there is no explicit state-acquisition phase. This technique may be used for both intrinsic and extrinsic resources. For example, a print spooler S_g may contend with other members of the spooler group to use a shared printer without prior knowledge of the printer state. The contention mechanism used for access also allows S_g to acquire the printer state. In the normal case, the technique does not require any additional messages.

Depending on the application, all of the above techniques may be supplemented by a passive *listen-and-merge* technique. Since the join allows S_g to receive messages destined for the group, S_g may acquire V based on such messages.

Detecting first member to join

Whether or not S_g should explicitly check if it is the first member of the group during the merge phase is application-dependent. For example, if S_g is merging with a group that advertises a service, S_g should detect that it is the first member, whereby it may initialize the local view and advertise the service on behalf of the group.

If the probe-and-merge techniques are used for state acquisition, S_g may detect that it is the first member by the lack of response to its probe messages. In the merge-on-the-fly technique, the detection is implicit in the protocols used to acquire V.

Leaving a group

The leaving of a member from a group should not introduce inconsistency. Typically, the member releases all the shared resources that it holds. This requires the member to notify other members of its leave if it is holding any shared resource. The *leave* event is useful for this purpose.

We now describe sample applications to illustrate how they specify ordering constraints on various protocol messages.

Distributed name server

A name service manages the name space of all services in a system. The name service is provided by a name server group NS that binds a unique and well-known service name to a server group

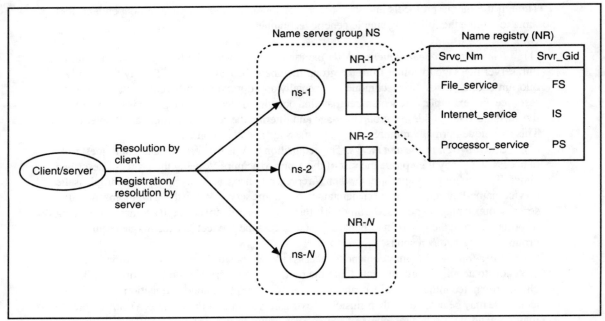

Figure 5. A model of a distributed name server.

providing the service. Clients locate a server by contacting the name server. To increase availability, each member of NS typically resides on a different machine in the system.

In Figure 5, the name server maintains a *name registry* that contains entries in the form (*Srvc_Nm, Srvr_Gid*) to bind service names to server groups. It supports two primitives: *name registration* and *name resolution*. The former allows a server group *Srvr_Gid* to make known the availability of its service to its clientele, while the latter allows a client to locate the service. The binding information (*Srvc_Nm, Srvr_Gid*) constitutes the shared state, with name registration being a write operation and name resolution being a read. A client performs only name resolution while a server performs both registration and resolution. Thus, the name-binding information is an extrinsic resource.

An inconsistency in the binding information may result in more than one group being registered as providing the same service. The inconsistency may be due to weak ordering of resolution and registration messages that may be generated spontaneously — that is, generated independently by name server/client entities. This can happen, for example, if a name server receives a resolution request from a client before a registration request under a different *Srvr_Gid*. The name server then returns the stale binding information — namely, the old *Srvr_Gid* — to the client. The mechanisms to detect and correct such inconsistencies should be integrated into the protocols for registration and resolution.

Name registration

The protocol used by a server for registration encapsulates the collision-handling mechanism described in the "Collision arbitration by time-out" subsection.

When a server S_i requests registration, its local name server ns_i checks its name registry to determine if the binding pertaining to *Srvc_Nm* already exists. If so, and if *Srvc_Nm* is bound to a different group *Srvr_Gid'*, ns_i fails the registration with a Registry_clash (*Srvc_Nm, Srvr_Gid'*) exception. Otherwise, ns_i sends an intraserver message Locking($Srvc\_Nm, Srvr\_Gid$) and awaits any objection for a time-out interval T_w. Upon receiving the Locking, each of the other name servers (that is, members in NS) searches its local name registry for inconsistencies. If a member finds $Srvc\_Nm$ bound to a different group $Srvr\_Gid'$, it raises an objection with a Locking($Srvc\_Nm, Srvr\_Gid'$) message to NS. Upon receiving objection within T_w, ns_i returns an exception Registry-collision($Srvc\_Nm$). If no objection to the registration is raised, ns_i completes the registration by updating its registry with the information ($Srvc\_Nm, Srvr\_Gid$) and sending an intraserver message Locked($Srvc\_Nm, Srvr\_Gid$). Upon receiving the Locked message, a member updates its registry. The various exceptions allow S_i to recover appropriately.

Name resolution

Inconsistencies in the binding information are still possible because of weak ordering of the registration messages. So, inconsistency detection is needed in the resolution operation as well.

Suppose a client sends a resolution request to its local name server ns_i. The resolution succeeds immediately if a binding can be established from the local name registry. Otherwise, ns_i sends an intraserver message to resolve $Srvc\_Nm$. Each of the members in NS searches its local registry and responds with the binding information, if found. The ns_i then checks for consistency of the information contained in the responses (ns_i may specify a quorum for this purpose). If an inconsistency is detected — that is, if more than one group claims to offer $Srvc\_Nm$ — ns_i returns an exception Inconsistent_binding to the client. If no binding can be established locally or remotely, ns_i returns an Unknown_binding exception.

These exceptions allow recovery by clients and servers during service access and service setup, respectively.

Name server recovery. If an inconsistency in $Srvc\_Nm$ is detected, ns_i creates a new group New_Srvr_Gid and sends an intraserver message Re_register($Srvc\_Nm, New\_Srvr\_Gid$) to NS. On receiving the Re_register message, each member ns_j that has an entry for $Srvc\_Nm$ in its registry removes the entry and delivers an asynchronous exception Re_register_service ($Srvc\_Nm, New\_Srvr\_Gid$) to the local server S_j that has registered $Srvc\_Nm$. The exception forces S_j to join New_Srvr_Gid and reregister $Srvc\_Nm$ under New_Srvr_Gid.

Service access by client

Service access is handled in the client interface with the name server (see Figure 6). It requires two levels of binding. In the first level, the client contacts the name server to resolve the service name $Srvc\_Nm$ to a server group $Srvr\_Gid$; in the second level, the client contacts $Srvr\_Gid$ for the required service.

The client handles the exceptions returned by the name server as follows:

- Unknown_binding: Aborts the access operation.
- Inconsistent_binding: Waits for a predetermined time (based on T_w) for the servers to recover and then retries. Aborts the access operation after a fixed number of retries.

If the client uses stale binding information that refers to a nonexistent group, the group-communication layer returns an appropriate exception, upon which the client recovers by resolving $Srvc\_Nm$ again.

Service setup by server

Service setup is handled in the server interface to the name server (see Figure 6). When a server, say S_i, wishes to set up the service $Srvc\_Nm$, it first resolves $Srvc\_Nm$. The resolution allows S_i to locate a server group providing the service if it already exists. If the resolution is successful — that is, if $Srvc\_Nm$ is already registered under a group $Srvr\_Gid$ — S_i merely has to join $Srvr\_Gid$. S_i may

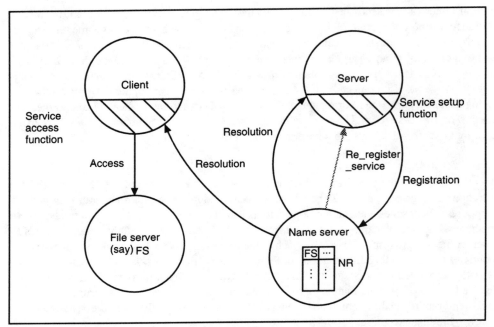

Figure 6. Client and server interfaces to the name server. (NR = name registry.)

acquire its local name registry from other members in NS using the immediate or client-driven probe-and-merge techniques.

S_i handles resolution exceptions as follows:

- Unknown_binding: The service does not yet exist; that is, S_i is the first member of its group. S_i forms a new group *New_Srvr_Gid* and registers it as providing the service.
- Inconsistent_binding: S_i may wait for other servers to recover and retry later to form the service.

S_i handles registration exceptions as follows:

- Registry_collision: S_i may back off for a random interval of time (typically $> T_w$) and try again to register the binding. S_i may give up registration after Max_bckoff retries.
- Registry_clash: S_i may merge with the existing server group *Srvr-Gid'*.

Processor pool service

A processor pool server manages a number of processors and allocates a processor to a client for executing a program. The allocation is based on some criterion, such as the least-loaded processor in a pool. A model of the pool server is shown in Figure 7. P_j is a pool server and C_j is a client that arranges the dispatch and execution of programs on an allocated processor. The P_j's are members of a server group PS.

Each P_j maintains a list of available processors in the pool. The processors may be listed according to some criterion, such as computational load. Also, each of the processors is marked either Up or

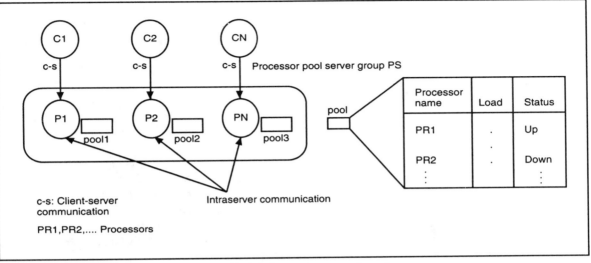

Figure 7. Model of a processor pool service.

Down, indicating whether the processor is available. The list, referred to as a *pool*, constitutes the shared state of PS. The *pool* is an extrinsic resource, since the allocation requests originate from the clients.

We now describe the operations on *pool* and how inconsistencies can be handled.

Write operation on *pool*

A leader in PS may periodically sample the load and the Up/Down status of processors and propagate an update to the instances of *pool* across PS. There is no need for guaranteed delivery of the update to each P_j, since a missed update may be corrected by the next sample update. So the update messages can be weakly ordered.

Selecting a processor

The client C_j requests P_j to select a processor for executing a program. If the selection is based on an attribute Accomm whereby any processor that can accommodate the program will do (for example, off-line computation), P_j simply uses its local view of *pool* for the selection. If *pool* is uninitialized — that is, if P_j has not yet merged with PS — P_j may resort to the client-driven merge protocol to acquire its view of *pool* (refer to "Client-driven probe and merge" in the "State-acquisition phase" subsection).

If the selection is based on more than one attribute, say a processor that not only can accommodate the program but is also the least loaded (for example, real-time computations), P_j may need to apply a quorum to ensure its view of *pool* is more current. For this purpose, P_j may send an intraserver message to PS, specifying the attributes Least_load and Accomm to solicit the local views of *pool* from other P_j's.

Since the read operation by P_j on *pool* is idempotent, multiple P_j's operating on *pool* constitutes an idempotent sequence, and the operations may be interspersed as nonatomic actions.

Acquiring a lock on PR

P_j should now acquire a lock on PR using the protocols described in the "Lock and unlock operations" section.

If a collision is detected during lock acquisition on PR, P_j backs off for a random interval of time and tries to acquire the lock again. If collision persists for Max_bckoff retries, P_j returns an exception to C_j. If the lock is acquired successfully, P_j updates PR to Lock_acquired and advises C_j to dispatch the program to the selected PR.

Lock recovery consists of delivering an Unlock message to the group PS in the event that P_j, which has locked PR, fails. Since PR is an extrinsic resource, the lock should be recovered if C_j fails. The failure of any of the P_k's that have not locked a processor does not introduce any inconsistency (namely, tolerable inconsistency).

Handling inconsistencies

An inconsistency in the lock on PR may result in more than one client dispatching programs to PR. This is a nonproblem though, since the programs are dispatched to different address spaces in PR. However, the criteria on which PR is selected may no longer hold. The effects of this inconsistency are application-dependent. Off-line computations may not be affected by the inconsistency. On the other hand, real-time computations may require another processor to be selected.

Another inconsistency is that the PR marked Up in *pool* may have subsequently failed. C_j detects the inconsistency when it tries to dispatch programs to PR, whereupon C_j sends a group message to PS to mark PR as Down. The update does not interfere with the periodic sample updates. C_j may then repeat the processor selection. The inconsistency in which a processor is marked Down in *pool* but is available results in the processor not being utilized until it is marked Up by the sample-update-based write operation. However, the inconsistency is not perceivable to the application.

Conclusions

We have presented a model of distributed servers. In this model, various servers providing a service are organized as members of a server group that exports the service through a generic runtime interface. The shared state of the group is implemented in a decentralized fashion across the group members. Examples of the state are the information on name bindings, the member list, the processing load at various members, and leadership in the group. The sharing of state manifests in the form of group communications for members to coordinate among themselves and provide a consistent view of the state to clients.

The model does not enforce absolute consistency of the state. This is based on the premise that many distributed applications have an inherent ability to tolerate state inconsistency, because the implications of the inconsistency are usually transparent to the application:

- In some cases, an inconsistency may not be perceivable.
- In other cases, an inconsistency may be detected and corrected transparently to the application.

The relaxation of the consistency constraints often has the advantage that strict coordination among the server group members is not required. This allows efficient access to the server state with a weak form of message ordering in group communications.

Since access operations need not be atomic, a high degree of concurrency and efficiency is possible without correctness being compromised. Where the consistency constraints cannot be relaxed (as in database applications), the model allows enforcing strong coordination among the members. This approach encourages the use of application-specific protocols — that is, protocols that deal with inconsistencies in an application-dependent manner.

To incorporate the relaxed-consistency approach as a generic framework, this paper describes how the application-specific protocols may be encapsulated into the access operations. Also, it presents sample applications to illustrate the use of the approach in designing distributed servers.

The application-specific aspect of shared state is somewhat similar to Cheriton's problem-oriented shared memory model [16]. However, the latter does not address the communication and coordination requirements in access to shared memory. Also, there is little discussion of how the access operations on the shared memory are procedurally realized.

We have been studying the distributed-server model on top of a message-oriented broadcast-communication platform that has been developed at Kansas State University. The platform allows a declarative specification of message-ordering constraints by applications and is being implemented on a network of Sun workstations interconnected by Ethernet. Our study involves both structuring of distributed servers and prototype implementations. The results of our study so far confirm the feasibility of the relaxed-consistency approach.

References

[1] F.C.M. Lau and E.G. Manning, "Cluster-Based Addressing for Reliable Distributed Systems," *Proc. Fourth Symp. Reliability Distributed Software and Database Systems*, IEEE Computer Soc. Press, Los Alamitos, Calif., 1984, pp. 146-154.

[2] A.S. Tanenbaum and R. van Renesse, "Reliability Issues in Distributed Operating Systems," *Proc. Seventh Symp. Reliability Distributed Software and Database Systems*, IEEE Computer Soc. Press, Los Alamitos, Calif., 1988, pp. 3-11.

[3] A.E. Abbadi, D. Sheen, and F. Cristian, "An Efficient Fault-Tolerant Protocol for Replicated Data Management," *Proc. Fourth Conf. Principles Database Systems*, ACM Press, New York, N.Y., 1985.

[4] D.P. Reed, "Implementing Atomic Actions on Decentralised Data," *ACM Trans. Computer Systems*, Vol. 1, No. 1, Feb. 1983, pp. 3-23.

[5] K.P. Birman and T.A. Joseph, "Reliable Communication in the Presence of Failures," *ACM Trans. Computer Systems*, Vol. 5, No. 1, Feb. 1987, pp. 47-76.

[6] M.M. Theimer and K.A. Lantz, "Finding Idle Machines in a Workstation-Based Distributed System," *Proc. Eighth Int'l Conf. Distributed Computing Systems*, IEEE Computer Soc. Press, Los Alamitos, Calif., 1988, pp. 112-122.

[7] K.J. Perry and S. Toueg, "Distributed Agreement in the Presence of Processor and Communication Faults," *IEEE Trans. Software Eng.*, Vol. SE-12, No. 3, Mar. 1986, pp. 477-482.

[8] S.W. Luan and V.D. Gligor, "A Fault-Tolerant Protocol for Atomic Broadcast," *IEEE Trans. Parallel and Distributed Systems*, Vol. 1, No. 3, July 1990, pp. 271-285.

[9] P.M. Melliar-Smith, L.E. Moser, and Y. Agrawala, "Broadcast Protocols for Distributed Systems," *IEEE Trans. Parallel and Distributed Systems*, Vol. 1, No. 1, Jan. 1990, pp. 17-25.

[10] M. Herlihy, "Quorum Consensus Replication Method for Abstract Data Types," *ACM Trans. Computer Systems*, Vol. 4, No. 1, Feb. 1986, pp. 32-53.

[11] K. Ravindran and S. Samdarshi, "A Flexible Causal Broadcast Communication Interface for Distributed Applications," *J. Parallel and Distributed Computing*, Vol. 16, No. 2, Oct. 1992, pp. 134-157.

[12] F. Schneider, D. Gries, and R. Schlicting, "Reliable Broadcast Protocols," *Science Computer Programming*, Vol. 3, No. 2, Mar. 1984.

[13] F. Cristian et al., "Atomic Broadcast: From Simple Diffusion to Byzantine Agreement," Tech. Report RJ4540(48668), IBM Research Lab., San Jose, Calif., Dec. 1984.

[14] L. Lamport, "Time, Clocks, and Ordering of Events in a Distributed System," *Comm. ACM*, Vol. 21, No. 7, July 1978, pp. 558-565.

[15] E.C. Cooper, "Replicated Distributed Programs," *Proc. 10th Symp. Operating System Principles*, ACM Press, New York, N.Y., 1985, pp. 63-78.

[16] D.R. Cheriton, "Problem-Oriented Shared Memory: A Decentralised Approach to Distributed System

Design," *Proc. Sixth Int'l Conf. Distributed Computing Systems*, IEEE Computer Soc. Press, Los Alamitos, Calif., 1986, pp. 190-197.

[17] B.W. Lampson, "Designing a Global Name Service," *Proc. Fifth Symp. Principles Distributed Computing*, ACM Press, New York, N.Y., 1986, pp. 1-10.

[18] D.R. Cheriton and W. Zwaenepoel, "Distributed Process Groups in the V-Kernel," *ACM Trans. Computer Systems*, Vol. 3, No. 2, May 1985, pp. 77-107.

[19] K. Ravindran and X.T. Lin, "Structural Complexity and Execution Efficiency of Distributed Application Protocols," to appear in *Proc. Conf. Comm. Architectures and Protocols, ACM SIGCOMM '93*, ACM Press, New York, N.Y., 1993.

[20] L.L. Peterson, N.C. Buchholz, and R.D. Schlichting, "Preserving and Using Context Information in Interprocess Communication," *ACM Trans. Computer Systems*, Vol. 7, No. 3, Aug. 1989, pp. 217-246.

[21] S.T. Chanson and K. Ravindran, "A Distributed Kernel Model for Reliable Group Communication," *Proc. Sixth Symp. Real-Time Systems*, IEEE Computer Soc. Press, Los Alamitos, Calif., 1986, pp. 138-146.

[22] R. Gusella and S. Zatti, "An Election Algorithm for a Distributed Clock Synchronization Program," *Proc. Sixth Int'l Conf. Distributed Computing Systems*, IEEE Computer Soc. Press, Los Alamitos, Calif., 1986, pp. 364-371.

[23] K. Ravindran and B. Prasad, "Communication Structures and Paradigms for Distributed Conferencing Applications," *Proc. 12th Int'l Conf. Distributed Computing Systems,* IEEE Computer Soc. Press, Los Alamitos, Calif., 1992, pp. 598-605.

Object-Oriented Systems

An Object-Based Taxonomy for Distributed Computing Systems

A taxonomy is a classification tool that allows different examples of some generic type to be described. The taxonomy presented here is a hierarchy of questions and answers about the features of distributed computing systems (DCSs). To describe a specific DCS, a taxonomy user traces paths through the hierarchy.

System descriptions produced from the taxonomy can be used as broad summaries. Alternatively, since the descriptions are derived from the same taxonomy, they can be used to compare systems with each other or with requirements. At Hewlett-Packard Laboratories we have used this taxonomy to describe and compare several distributed computing systems.[1-7] We have selectively used examples from these systems throughout the article.

Aside from system description, the taxonomy identifies a set of fundamental system features and provides terminology that can be used in the general discussion of a DCS. The taxonomy can also serve as the basis for designing a DCS that offers novel combinations of features.

The taxonomy uses terminology from an object-based model of distributed computing systems that we present in the section "Modeling distributed computing systems." For this reason we describe the taxonomy as being object based, though it doesn't matter whether the DCS is actually object based or not. A DCS is any loosely coupled computing system that provides services to support the execution and interaction of its components.

In this taxonomy we emphasize the runtime services the DCS provides to applications. Nevertheless, the scope of the taxonomy is not rigidly defined. There is no sudden cut-off point where we cease to address issues; rather, as we move further outside our main areas of interest, the taxonomy becomes sparser and questions become broader.

Bruce E. Martin,

Claus H. Pedersen, and

James Bedford-Roberts

Using the taxonomy

Before applying the taxonomy, users should first define the DCS to be described. The definition may be arbitrary, but the main point is to establish what constitutes the system before trying to classify it. The user must establish (1) the services the system provides to the applications built over it and (2) the services it relies on any underlying platform to provide.

Once the system has been defined, the user can start tracing through the taxonomy. Starting at the root of the hierarchy, the taxonomy presents a number of basic divisions. These divisions do not require any action from the user; they merely set the scene for the questions that follow.

Eventually, the divisions lead to questions about the system. For each question, the taxonomy will provide a set of possible answers. The user must select the answers that apply to the system. All the answers for a given question will be distinct from each other; generally they are not mutually exclusive, so many answers may apply. For each applicable answer, the taxonomy may lead to a further set of questions. At some point users will reach a leaf in the taxonomy; this can be either a question or an answer. Since we have emphasized breadth rather than depth, the user may very well be able to think of further questions and answers that could be added to the leaves of the taxonomy.

Taken together, the results — the answers selected by the user — provide a brief, overall description of the distributed computing system.

The taxonomy is presented using both figures and text. Each division, question, and answer is given a short heading. The figures arrange these headings graphically to show how they are related to each other. In the text, question headings appear in brackets and answer headings in parentheses. In the figures, division headings are printed in hexagons, question headings in rectangles, and answer headings in ovals.

The text expands on the headings, providing explanations and examples to help taxonomy users understand the questions and answers.

Modeling distributed computing systems

We use objects and threads to model DCSs. By forcing the taxonomy user to model systems in this way, the descriptions obtained are more succinct and easier to compare.

Objects are simple and unifying. Traditional terminology differs for similar concepts pursued in different areas of computer science. We use object notions to unify different terminology for similar concepts. For instance, computer security researchers traditionally discuss *protected resources*. We rephrase such abstractions using object terminology.

We assume a general definition of an object. The definition is such that diverse components of distributed computing systems can be modeled in terms of objects, even components that are not implemented or originally described in this way. For instance, a file can be viewed as an object with operations read, write, and seek.

Modeling with objects

An object comprises a set of defined states, a current state, and a set of operations. The current state is always one of the defined states. The only way to observe or change the object's current state is to invoke one of the operations. An operation is a parameterized transformation of an object's current state. An operation may yield a result. An algorithm implementing an operation is called a method. A method may access the representation of the object's state and may invoke operations on other objects.

Modeling with threads

The definition of object contains no temporal notions. Therefore, we define threads of control to introduce a partial ordering of events in the DCS. A thread of control is a totally ordered set of events defined by a programmer. The ordered events of a thread ultimately result from the execution of a

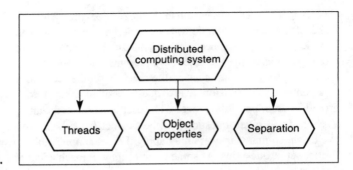

Figure 1. The top-level division.

program written in some programming language. In general, no order is assumed for the events of different threads.

In this model of a DCS based on objects and threads, the interesting events are thread creation, thread termination, operation invocation, and operation return.

A thread is global to the DCS; it can span several objects. A *synchronous* operation invocation causes the thread to migrate to the object executing the corresponding method. When the method completes, the thread migrates back to the object that invoked the operation. An *asynchronous* operation invocation, on the other hand, causes a new thread to be created. No order is assumed between the events of the original thread and those of the created thread.

A thread is executing in an object if the object has started executing the method but has not yet completed. If a thread that is executing in an object invokes another operation on another object, the thread is executing in multiple objects.

If, at a given time, there is more than one thread in the DCS, the threads are called *concurrent* threads.

Modeling nonuniform components

Each taxonomy question is really many questions rolled into one. The taxonomy user should answer a given question for each type of component modeled as an object.

Example: SOS (an object-oriented operating system) provides elementary objects that execute within a single virtual address space. Elementary objects from different virtual address spaces can be grouped into fragmented objects. Both elementary and fragmented objects fit the taxonomy's basic definition of an object. In describing SOS, the taxonomy user should traverse the taxonomy twice, once for elementary objects and once for fragmented objects.

The taxonomy

As Figure 1 shows, we divide the issues of DCSs into three distinct categories: threads, object properties, and separation. The threads subtree explores the creation, the number, and the control of threads in the DCS. The object properties subtree explores DCS features that are defined for objects in isolation. The separation subtree explores issues that arise because there are many objects in the DCS.

Threads

We examine how threads are created, how many threads can exist, and how they are controlled (see Figure 2).

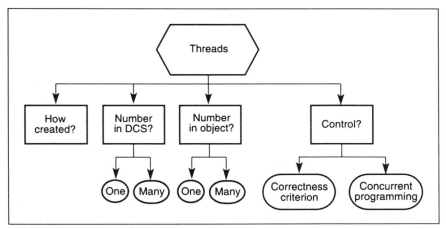

Figure 2. Threads.

[How created?] Describe how programs create threads. For instance, threads can be statically declared, dynamically created, or created as a result of an asynchronous operation invocation.

[Number in the DCS?] How many threads can execute concurrently in the DCS?

(One) The DCS does not support concurrent threads. Only one thread may exist in the DCS.

Example: MS-DOS allows only a single thread to execute.

(Many) Multiple threads may execute concurrently in the DCS.

Example: Unix allows multiple threads of control to execute.

[Number in object?] How many threads can execute concurrently in an object? Remember to answer this question for each kind of object in the DCS. Thus, if the DCS group objects in some fashion, it may also be appropriate to answer the question for the group.

(One) Only a single thread may execute in the object. Also, state whether the DCS allows the single executing thread in the object to invoke an operation of the same object. For instance, if *foo* and *bar* are operations defined on the same object, state whether the DCS allows the following thread: invoke foo; invoke bar; return bar; return foo.

(Many) The DCS allows multiple threads to execute concurrently within a single object.

[Control?] Haphazard interleavings of concurrent threads may result in semantic inconsistencies. A DCS may produce interleavings according to some correctness criterion. Such policies are typical of schedulers in database management systems. Alternatively, the DCS may leave management of concurrent threads to the programmer. How are concurrent threads managed?

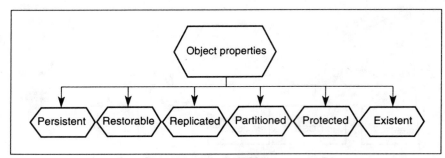

Figure 3. Object properties.

(Correctness criterion) The DCS schedules concurrent access to objects according to some correctness criterion. State the correctness criterion. For instance, a two-phase locking scheduler ensures serializability. That is, it schedules a set of a concurrent threads such that their effects are the same as some serial execution of the threads. State if and how the object programmer is aware of the scheduler. Perhaps it is completely hidden. Perhaps the program dynamically acquires locks according to a system-defined protocol. Maybe the programmer specifies acceptable interleavings based on the semantics of the object.

Example: In Arjuna[6] (a prototype object-oriented programming system), concurrent threads are serialized. The program acquires locks dynamically and the system releases them atomically. Programmers can provide scheduling information about acceptable interleavings by specializing the lock class.

(Concurrent programming) If a thread is programmed to interact with other concurrent threads, the interacting threads form a *concurrent program*. The process of describing how concurrent threads interact is called *concurrent programming*. Concurrent threads synchronize themselves using primitives provided by the DCS. The application programmer is aware of and responsible for the correctness of the concurrent execution in the DCS. The DCS provides basic tools, such as semaphores or monitors, for the programmer to use.

Example: Network Computing System (a remote procedure call system) provides mutual-exclusion primitives for concurrent programming.

Object properties

Object properties are DCS features defined for objects in isolation. As Figure 3 shows, we characterize the object properties supported by the DCS. Because the DCS may have several kinds of objects, remember to explore this subtree for each kind of object in the system.

Persistent. A persistent object does not depend on a thread in the DCS for its existence. We rejected the informal notion that a persistent object "persists by living on a disk." Just as RAM may lose its contents when turned off, a disk loses its contents when it is reformatted or corrupted. Such ideas of persistence are too technology dependent. We also rejected the notion that a persistent object is one that survives failures. Survival of failures is an orthogonal issue covered in a subsequent section. The subtree given in Figure 4 characterizes the level of support the DCS provides for persistent objects.

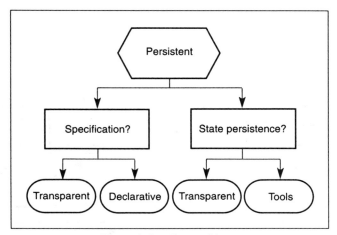

Figure 4. Persistent objects.

[Specification?] How does the programmer specify that an object is to be persistent?

(Transparent) All objects are persistent.

(Declarative) The programmer declares in some way that an object is persistent. The declarations can be either static or processed at runtime.

[State persistence?] How does the DCS support the persistent state for persistent objects?

(Transparent) The persistent state is automatically achieved without any programmer involvement.

(Tools) The programmer must provide code to support the DCS to obtain the persistent state.

 Example: Arjuna requires application programmers to provide save_state and restore_state methods for persistent objects.

Restorable. With a restorable object, prior states of the object can be restored under programmer control. Note that prior states of an object can be recovered automatically by a DCS in the event of a failure. Such activities are characterized in a later section concerning partial failures and the execution guarantees a DCS makes. This subtree, shown in Figure 5, is concerned with the model of state restoration presented to, and under control of, the programmer.

[Granularity?] What is the granularity of a restorable state? State whether a single object is restorable. State whether a group of objects can be restored to mutually consistent states.

 Example: A program may explicitly abort a computation in Arjuna. The set of accessed objects are restored to their original states.

[Decision to save?] Describe whether (and how) the programmer or the system decides to save the current state of an object. For example, the state of an object might be saved every n updates,

---

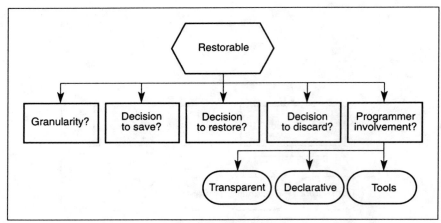

Figure 5. Restorable objects.

every *t* seconds, when some relation between two objects holds, or when a *commit* or *savestate* statement executes.

[Decision to restore?] Describe whether (and how) the programmer or the system indicates that a prior state of an object should be restored. For example, the programmer might indicate it with an *abort* or an *undo* statement.

[Decision to discard?] Describe whether (and how) the programmer or the system decides to discard prior states of an object. For instance, memory may be reclaimed if no more is available or if the programmer requests it.

[Programmer involvement?] How is the programmer involved in supporting restorable objects.

(Transparent) All objects are restorable. The programmer uses the constructs to save and restore states directly.

(Declarative) The programmer declares that an object is to be restorable.

(Tools) The programmer is involved in implementing this property. For instance, the programmer might provide code that the DCS executes.

Replicated. An object is replicated if the DCS maintains multiple copies of the object that a client object can identify as a single object. Objects may be replicated to enhance performance or to increase availability. Ideally, the replicas always exhibit the same behavior, but a DCS may trade consistency for performance. An application programmer may be involved in replicating the components. (See Figure 6.)

[How?] How does the DCS support replication?

(Hardware) The object's state and methods are replicated at different sites to improve performance or availability.

(Software) The DCS supports execution of replicated operations; that is, the DCS executes

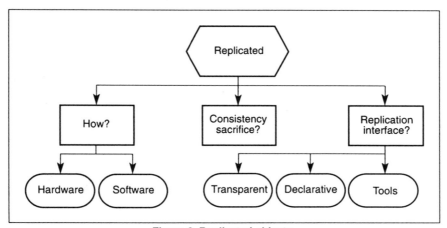

Figure 6. Replicated objects.

multiple implementations of the same operation. The probability that the same software fault will appear in all implementations is low, so the object remains highly available in spite of software faults.

[Consistency sacrifice?] Describe circumstances under which the DCS sacrifices the consistency of the replicated object. For instance, if the system updates all available replicas, consistency might be sacrificed if the network partitions into two subnets that cannot communicate.

[Replication interface?] How must the programmer consider replication in the DCS?

(Transparent) The programmer never considers the replication of objects. All objects are replicated, or the DCS decides which objects to replicate.

(Declarative) The programmer declares which objects should be replicated.

(Tools) The programmer is involved in replication by, for example, specifying where the replicas should exist or assigning weights to the replicas for weighted-voting consistency schemes.

Partitioned. An object is partitioned if the object's state and methods are fragmented on different nodes in the DCS. (See Figure 7.)

[Split?] How can an object be partitioned?

(State) An object's state can be partitioned into pieces that reside on different nodes.

[Granularity?] What are the minimal state components that can be partitioned?

Example: The state of an SOS fragmented object may reside on different nodes. An instance variable of the fragmented object cannot be partitioned; it resides on a single node.

(State/code) The object's state may be on a different node from where its code executes.

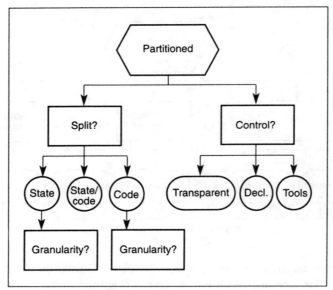

Figure 7. Partitioned objects.

(Code) The object's code may be partitioned into pieces that execute on different nodes.

[Granularity?] What are the minimal code components that can be partitioned? Perhaps each method of an object can execute on a different node, or maybe all methods implemented in a specific language must execute on a specific node.

Example: The methods of an SOS fragmented object may exist on different nodes.

[Control?] How is the partitioning of an object determined?

(Transparent) The DCS decides how an object is partitioned. For instance, it may have algorithms that change the way an object is partitioned for performance reasons.

(Declarative) The programmer can statically declare how an object is to be partitioned.

(Tools) The DCS provides tools the programmer can use at runtime to affect the way objects are partitioned. For instance, there may be some primitives that allow the programmer to move an object's method to another node.

Protected. The DCS may provide services that allow owners to selectively protect their objects from other users. (See Figure 8.)

[What is protected?] What objects does the DCS protect? Possible answers include machines, applications, methods, data, and groups of objects.

[What is trusted?] The question of what is trusted may apply to both objects and communication paths between objects. Also, state what things are trusted *for* and how trust is propagated. For instance, a

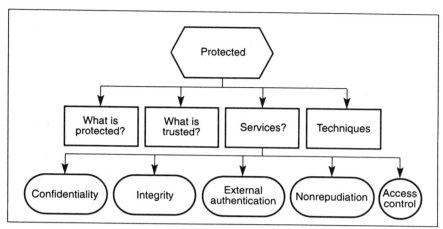

Figure 8. Protected objects.

name server may be trusted to keep names confidential. Clients may trust it because they trust the communication path to it and because they received the name server's address from a trusted source.

[Services?] What protection services does the DCS offer?

(Confidentiality) Information is not made available or disclosed without authorization.

(Integrity) Information cannot be altered or destroyed without authorization.

(External authentication) The identity of users outside the DCS is verified.

(Nonrepudiation) A user cannot later falsely establish that he has or has not interacted with an object.

(Access control) Users cannot interact with objects in specific ways without authorization. Describe the mechanisms used to support access control. For instance, are they based on capabilities, labels, or access control lists?

[Techniques?] Describe any visible underlying techniques by which the DCS supports protection services — for example, data encryption or key management techniques.

Existent. This subtree, shown in Figure 9, explores the creation and destruction of objects.

[How created?] Describe the programmer's view of an object's creation.

[How destroyed?] What can cause the destruction of an object?

(Programmer) The programmer can write code that deletes an object.

(Related objects) The object's existence depends on other related objects.

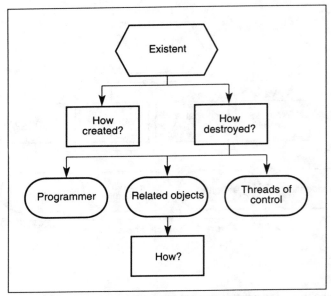

Figure 9. Creation and destruction of objects.

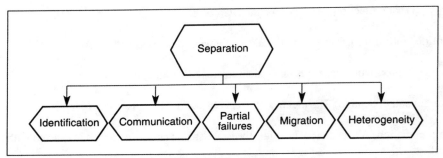

Figure 10. Separation.

[How?] How does the object depend on these relationships? By garbage collection, for example, whereby an object may be deleted automatically once there are no references to it. Perhaps an object is deleted when its container object is deleted.

(Threads of control) The DCS may delete an object when no threads of control are associated with it.

Separation

The object properties considered in the previous section could all be associated with a single object. In this section we consider issues that arise because we model a DCS as a collection of interacting objects. The goal of DCS design is to achieve an optimum degree of integration of these objects without sacrificing the flexibility and resilience obtained through separation. Thus, in this part of the taxonomy, we consider issues of both managing separation and achieving integration. (See Figure 10.)

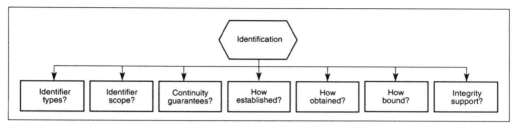

Figure 11. Identification.

Identification. Identification is the process by which the DCS and the application programmer distinguish objects. An identifier (ID) is a value used to distinguish an object. The DCS associates the identifier's value with the identified object. (See Figure 11.)

[Identifier types?] What are the types of identifier? The system may support many different types. These types may each address different objects, or they may overlap such that a given object can be distinguished by many types of identifier. Verify that the identifier is passed across the interface between the application and the system as a distinct parameter.

Example: Unix files can be identified by Unix path names, file descriptors, or i-numbers.

Answer the remaining question for each type of visible identifier.

[Identifier scope?] What is the identifier's scope; that is, what is the domain in which the identifier can be applied? Often, the scope of one identifier is defined by another object.

Example: The scope of a Unix file descriptor is a process and its descendants.

[Continuity guarantees?] What continuity is guaranteed about the referenced object each time a particular application uses an identifier? For instance, what can you say about the object's type, successive states, location, owner, and access rights each time the identifier is applied?

Example: A Unix file descriptor guarantees type continuity; it always identifies a file.

Example: A Network Computing System UUID (universally unique identifier) does not guarantee location continuity. The identified object's location may change.

[How established?] How is the identifier established in the first place? This is a broad question that leads to many others. For instance, who establishes the identifier and when? If it is the application, what constraints are there on the value that may be assigned to the identifier? If it is the DCS, what algorithm is used to establish the value?

[How obtained?] How is the identifier obtained once it exists?

[How bound?] How is the identifier bound to an object? If it is visible to the programmer, describe how the DCS locates an object.

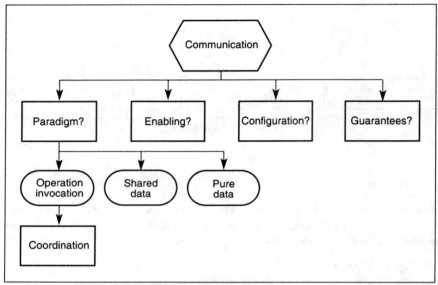

Figure 12. Communication.

[Integrity support?] How rigorously does the system support the identification scheme's integrity? For instance, what happens if the programmer tries to use an identifier when the associated object no longer exists? Also, can identifier values be reused for different objects within the system's lifetime? Finally, what happens if identifier values are used outside their scope? For instance, what happens if an identifier value was intended only to distinguish objects on machine A and a programmer tries to apply it on machine B?

Communication. Communication is the process by which different objects interact. (See Figure 12.) Here we distinguish between the object that instigates communication, referred to as the source object, and the object(s) the source is trying to communicate with, referred to as the target object(s).

[Paradigm?] What communication paradigms does the DCS support?

(Operation invocation) The source object can invoke operations on the target object.

[Coordination?] How are the source and target objects coordinated during the operation invocation? For instance, do they operate synchronously or asynchronously? In the asynchronous case describe what happens to the return parameters from the invocation.

(Shared state) The communication is based on the changing state shared among the communicating objects. The shared state can be either global variables or the "public" state of an object. The shared state can be read and written by all objects that share it, without invoking operations.

(Pure data) A pure-data transmission mechanism is supported. The DCS does not guarantee how the

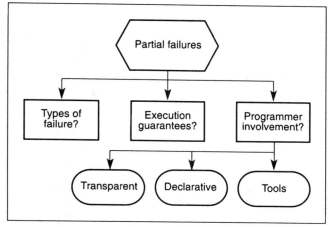

Figure 13. Partial failures.

receiving object processes the data that it receives; it only supports delivery of the data. Describe what kind of buffering policies are used for the sending as well as the receiving end. State whether the data is typed or untyped.

[Enabling?] What information or actions are required to enable communication between objects? Information may include things such as the identifier, type, or location of the target object. If the target object's location must be supplied, how is it specified and where does the programmer get this information? Actions may include the programmer's setting up a connection before trying to communicate. If so, describe how the programmer sets up a connection.

[Configuration?] What source-object to target-object configurations are possible? These can be broadcast, multicast, or point to point. In broadcast mode, communication is from one source object to an unspecified number of target objects. The sending object has no way of controlling which objects receive the message. In multicast mode, communication is from one source object to a specified set of target objects. In this case, state whether there may be replies associated with the multicast. Finally, in point-to-point mode, communication is from one source object to one target object.

[Guarantees?] What guarantees are made about the communication service? For instance, the communication may be guaranteed to be real-time preserving (isochronous). In this case, time intervals between each successive submission of information will be preserved such that the same intervals will apply at the receiving end. Another possible guarantee is "at most once," when the information is guaranteed to arrive no more than once at the target object(s). The communication service may guarantee that the order of information sent by one thread of control will be preserved upon arrival at the target object, or it may guarantee that no data will be lost in the communication process. There are many possible answers.

Partial failures. A significant difference between distributed and centralized systems is the possibility of partial failure of a computation. The interactions between two or more objects may be interrupted by processor, storage, or communication failures, and some or all of the objects may remain active. This subtree, shown in Figure 13, deals with whether and how a DCS supports the programmer in handling partial failures.

[Types of failure?] List the types of failures for which the DCS provides some kind of execution guarantee. For each type of failure, answer the remaining questions.

[Execution guarantees?] A DCS may make certain guarantees about execution to help the programmer in dealing with partial failures. What are those guarantees? For instance, the DCS may guarantee fail-stop behavior, or it may ensure that a group of operations are failure atomic; that is, that the effects of *all* operations are seen or none of them are seen.

Example: Arjuna ensures failure atomicity for a group of operations.

[Programmer involvement?] State whether the programmer is involved in handling partial failures, and if so how.

(Transparent) The programmer is not involved. Partial failures for all applications are handled equivalently.

(Declarative) The programmer must declare something about the code. For instance, the programmer declares that execution guarantees should be provided for a block of code.

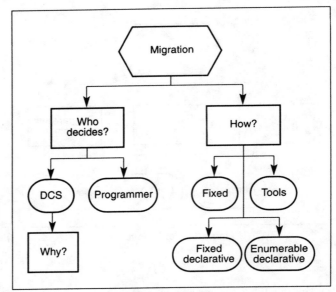

Figure 14. Migration.

(Tools) The programmer is involved in handling partial failures. For instance, the programmer might have to provide a method to undo the effects of an operation.

Migration. In the DCS, objects can move from one location to another. (See Figure 14.)

[Who decides?] Who decides to move an object?

(DCS) The DCS can move objects without a specific instruction from the programmer.

[Why?] Why does the DCS move objects? It may be to reduce communication or storage costs, or to balance its processing load.

Example: The Emerald system moves objects to reduce communication costs.

(Programmer) The programmer can issue "move" commands in the application program, causing the DCS to move objects.

Example: The Emerald system provides programmers with a *call-by-move* parameter-passing mode. Call-by-move provides a hint to the Emerald compiler to move an object passed as an argument to a remote site.

[How?] How is an object moved?

(Fixed) The DCS does it in one specific way.

(Fixed declarative) The programmer's declarations indicate one of a fixed number of alternatives.

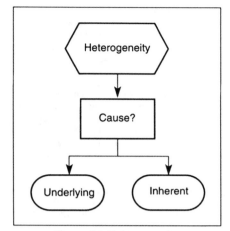

Figure 15. Heterogeneity.

For example, the programmer may declare that referenced objects are not to be moved when the referencing object is moved.

(Enumerable declarative) By combining declarations, the programmer can define new kinds of behavior to be associated with the moving of an object.

(Tools) The programmer writes executable code to support the DCS in moving an object.

Heterogeneity. A *homogeneous* DCS offers the same service and interface at every node. This means that a program written on one node can execute on any other node in the system. A *heterogeneous* DCS provides different services or interfaces at different nodes; consequently, the portability of programs is reduced. Heterogeneity can be explicitly introduced in the DCS design by enumerating different options for different nodes, or it can fail to be excluded by an incompletely defined design. (See Figure 15.)

[Cause?] What causes the heterogeneity observed by the programmer?

(Underlying) The underlying platform on top of which the DCS executes is both visible to the programmer and heterogeneous.

Example: The Network Computing System lets an object on an Intel 80386-based machine running MS-DOS invoke an object on a Motorola 68000-based machine running Unix. The underlying hardware and operating system architectures are visible to the programmers of both objects.

(Inherent) The DCS itself may offer a different service or interface at some nodes than at others.

Example: NCS supports both C and Pascal programming languages. Interfaces to the NCS services vary, depending on the programming language.

Inevitably, we spent much time discussing the completeness and orthogonality of the system features by which we structured our taxonomy of distributed computing systems. However, space limitations prevent us from including those discussions here. Readers with different backgrounds are likely to favor different structures. We also had difficulty designing questions that addressed qualitative issues; we preferred to ask about the services the DCS provides. In particular, we decided not to address performance issues, since we felt these might overwhelm other issues.

Our experience using the taxonomy was reassuring. First, we were able to produce short, comparable system descriptions. Furthermore, we found that our minimal model of objects and threads and the associated terminology was sufficient to describe real systems. In particular, we found the taxonomy useful for leading a user through the DCS in a systematic way.

The taxonomy emphasizes breadth rather than depth. It touches many areas of computer science, including security, naming, concurrency, and fault tolerance. Surveys exist that probe each area in more detail.[8-10]

Glossary

Access control list — A list of an object's authorized users, including their rights to invoke operations. Access control lists are held by the object.

Application — A set of objects that cooperate to provide some common benefit.

Asynchronous operation invocation — An operation invocation for which a new thread of control is created to execute the method. Subsequent events of the invoking thread are not ordered with respect to the events of the method execution.

Broadcast — Communication from one source object to an unspecified set of target objects. The sending object has no way of controlling which objects receive the message.

Capability — A token that identifies an object such that possession of the token confers access rights to the object. Capabilities are held by the user of the object.

Concurrent program — A program that specifies the interaction of concurrent threads. The process of specifying how concurrent threads interact is called concurrent programming.

Concurrent threads — A set of executing threads of control with more than one member.

Correctness criterion — The criterion used to state whether a schedule of concurrent threads is correct.

Distributed computing system (DCS) — A loosely coupled computing system that provides services to support the execution and interaction of its components.

Event — An action that can be considered to happen instantaneously. The events of interest are thread creation, thread termination, operation invocation, and operation return. Execution of method X is given by a pair of events — invoke X, return from X. If execution of method X causes operation Y to be invoked and its corresponding method to be executed, then the events caused by executing method X are invoke X, invoke Y, return from Y, return from X.

Failure atomicity — A guarantee made by a DCS that the effects of a group of operations are seen entirely or not at all.

Heterogeneous DCS — A DCS that offers a different service or interface at some nodes than at others.

Homogeneous DCS — A DCS that offers the same service and interface at every node.

Identifier — A value used to distinguish an object.

Label — A value associated with an object in a label-based security scheme. There are two types of labels held by objects — classification labels and clearance labels. Classification labels indicate the level of clearance required to access an object. Clearance labels indicate the level of clearance an object has been assigned.

Lock — A construct used to control concurrent access to objects. Locks may have protocols and notions of compatibility associated with them. An exclusive lock lets only a single thread access an object. Compatible locks allow multiple threads to access an object. See *two-phase locking*, below, for an example of a locking protocol.

Method — An algorithm that implements an operation.

Multicast — Communication from a single object to a specified set of objects.

Object — See "Modeling with objects" subhead on page 153.

Operation — See "Modeling with objects" subhead on page 153.

Partitioned object — An object whose state or methods are distributed on different nodes of the DCS.

Persistent object — An object whose existence does not depend on any given thread of control in the DCS.

Point-to-point — Communication from a source object to a single, specified target object.

Replicated object — An object with part or all of its state or methods replicated in the DCS.

Restorable object — An object for which prior states may be restored under programmer control.

Serializability — A correctness criterion for scheduling concurrent threads that defines the schedule as correct if it is equivalent to some serial (nonconcurrent) execution of the threads.

Synchronous operation invocation — An operation invocation in which no new thread of control is created. The thread migrates to the object on which the operation was invoked.

Taxonomy — A classification tool that allows different examples of some generic type to be described.

Thread of control — See "Modeling with threads" subhead on page 153.

Two-phase locking — A concurrency control protocol that ensures serializability. The protocol has two phases — the lock acquisition phase and the lock release phase. The protocol dictates that once a thread of control has released a lock, it cannot acquire additional locks.

Acknowledgments

We thank the following for comments that proved most useful in developing the taxonomy: Rod Bark, Harry Barman, Mike Cannon, Robert Cole, Nigel Derrett, Roger Fleming, Jussi Ketonen, Alan Snyder, Joe Sventek, Vijay Varadharajan, and Peter Williams. We are also grateful to the reviewers for making substantive comments that improved the taxonomy.

References

1. A. Black et al., "Distribution and Abstract Types in Emerald," *IEEE Trans. Software Eng.*, Vol. 13, No. 1, Jan. 1987, pp. 65-76.

2. M. Kong et al., *Network Computing System Reference Manual*, Prentice Hall, Englewood Cliffs, N.J., 1990.

3. A.S. Tanenbaum et al., "Experiences with the Amoeba Distributed Operating System," *Comm. ACM*, Vol. 33, No. 12, Dec. 1990, pp. 46-63.

4. C.H. Pedersen et al., "The Atlas Class Hierarchy," Tech. Report HPL-90-192, Hewlett-Packard Laboratories, Bristol, England, Nov. 1990.

5. M. Shapiro et al., "SOS: An Object-Oriented Operating System — Assessment and Perspectives," *Computing Systems*, Vol. 2, No. 4, Dec. 1989, pp. 287-337.

6. S.K. Shrivastava, G.N. Dixon, and G.D. Parrington, "An Overview of the Arjuna Distributed Programming System," *IEEE Software*, Vol. 8, No. 1, Jan. 1991, pp. 66-73.

7. A.Z. Spector, R.F. Pausch, and G. Bruell, "Camelot: A Flexible Distributed Transaction Processing System," *Proc. COMPCON Spring*, IEEE Computer Soc. Press, Los Alamitos, Calif., 1988, pp. 432-439.

8. S. Mullender and A.S. Tanenbaum, "Protection and Resource Control in Distributed Operating Systems," *Computer Networks*, Nov. 1984, pp. 421-432.

9. D.E. Comer and L.L. Peterson, "Understanding Naming in Distributed Systems," *Distributed Computing*, May 1989, pp. 51-60.

10. P. Bernstein and N. Goodman, "Concurrency Control in Distributed Database Systems," *ACM Computing Surveys*, Vol. 13, No. 2, June 1981, pp. 185-221.

Fragmented Objects for Distributed Abstractions

Fragmented objects (FOs) extend the object concept to a distributed environment. The abstract view of an FO is a single, shared object, of which the distribution is hidden to clients. In the concrete view, the FO designer controls (if wished) the distribution of data and function and of the communication between fragments.

Fragmented-object programming is supported by the FOG language, an extension of C++, and by a toolbox of predefined FOs. The FOG compiler ensures distributed type-safety of both the external and internal interfaces, verifies the encapsulation of FO instances, and automatically generates whatever coercions are necessary for marshaling or unmarshaling between layers. Currently, the toolbox contains mainly classes of primitive FOs, such as remote procedure call (RPC) and multicast communication channels.

The object-oriented-programming methodology is increasingly recognized as being of primary interest for structuring large, extensible, flexible, long-life software. It is natural to try to extend it to distributed applications. Some proposed extensions include support either for client/server remote invocation (as in Ansa [1]) or for the shared-object model (as in Orca [2] or Comandos [11]). Both models permit an application object to transparently access another shared, possibly remote, object. The network is transparent both for the clients and for the designer of a shared object.

Such distribution transparency simplifies the use and the implementation of a shared object. However, it prevents knowledgeable designers from taking advantage of distribution. For performance, availability, protection, or load balancing, there may be a need to *fragment* the data and/or the code of an object over several locations. The fragments together constitute a single logical entity, shared by the several client objects. Fragments cooperate to maintain a consistent view of this single logical entity. We propose the uniform concept of a *fragmented object* for designing and building distributed abstractions.

As is common in the object-oriented approach, an FO has two aspects: external (or "abstract") and internal (or "concrete"). Abstractly (to its clients), an FO appears as a single entity. It is

Mesaac Makpangou,

Yvon Gourhant,

Jean-Pierre Le Narzul, and

Marc Shapiro

accessed via a programmer-defined interface. Its components, and in particular their locations, are not visible (unless of course the designer chooses to let them show through the public interface). Concretely (internally), the FO encapsulates a set of cooperating fragments. Each fragment is an elementary object (that is, with a centralized representation). The fragments cooperate using lower level FOs, such as communication channels. The designer of an FO has full control over its distribution and can make good use of knowledge of the object's characteristics by, for instance, placing some particular data element or processing, choosing the most appropriate communication protocol, or handling failures according to the FO's semantics. The link between the external and the internal view is the public interface exported by the FO. One critical observation is that for a particular client, the interface is obtained through a particular *proxy* fragment.

The FO concept encompasses several abstractions: the grouping of fragments, the specification of cooperation between fragments, the specification of internal and external interfaces, and a mechanism for binding its clients to an FO.

Like the client/server and the shared-object models, the FO model supports distribution transparency for the clients of an FO. However, unlike the traditional models, FOs do not impose distribution transparency on FO designers. We specify distribution mechanisms, not policies; specific policies are programmer-defined. However, to facilitate their job, designers may choose existing policies from a toolkit of predefined FOs, implementing various distributed abstractions: for example, communication protocols, synchronization facilities, and sharing policies.

The fragmented-object concept and tools were first implemented as part of SOS, a distributed object-support operating system [14], which we do not present here. We are currently in the process of porting them to Unix.

This paper has two goals: to present the FO concept and tools to support it and to identify the benefits of structuring distributed applications as fragmented objects.

Fragmented objects

A fragmented object can be viewed at two different levels of abstraction: a level that corresponds to a client's (external, abstract) point of view and one that corresponds to its designer's (internal, concrete) point of view. For clients, an FO is a single, shared object (see Figure 1). It is shared by several client objects, localized in different address spaces, possibly on several sites. An FO can offer distinct, strongly typed interfaces to different clients. For the designer, an FO is an object with a fragmented representation (see Figure 2). It is composed of the following:

- A set of elementary objects — that is, its fragments. Each fragment is mapped within only one of the many address spaces overlapped by the FO.
- A client interface. The FO's interface is presented to each client via the public interface of a local fragment.
- An interface between fragments, called its *group interface*.
- Lower level shared FOs for communication between fragments, called *connective objects*.

In addition, a *binding* interface allows clients to bind to the FO. The rest of this section defines more precisely the construction of an FO.

Client access to an FO

The abstract interface of an FO is provided to some clients by a local interface fragment or proxy [13] of that FO. A fragment is an ordinary local object. Its public interface may be invoked locally. The client cannot distinguish between the interface of the fragment and that of the FO itself. An

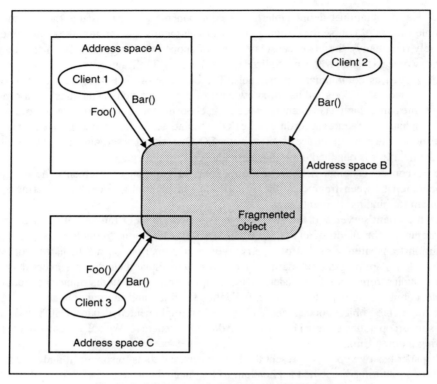

Figure 1. A fragmented object as seen by a client.

interface fragment is called a *proxy*. A fragment may hold local data, and process computations locally or forward them for processing to remote fragments. Remote communication entails *marshaling/unmarshaling* invocation parameters into/from a communication message. A *stub* is special case of a proxy, performing no local processing and reduced to the communication function [4].

For instance, a mailbox object, implemented by a central mail server, can be made accessible by proxies exported to users. A mail user with no special knowledge will bind to a particular mailbox, then call the drop(letter) or pickup(letter) methods of his local proxy. (Note that a *method* is a procedure associated with an object. In C++, methods are also called *member functions*.)

The interface provided to a client of an FO is defined by a contract, ensuring that every method it will invoke is effectively implemented by the FO. The client expects a specific interface; the FO provides that client with a proxy possessing this interface. (We allow different clients to see different interfaces to the same FO.). It is up to the compiler and the runtime to verify (as described in the subsection entitled "FOG compiler") that the actual interface conforms to the one expected by the client. For instance, a fragmented mailbox will export, to the user who owns it exclusively, a proxy allowing him to pickup messages. Other users will get a drop-only proxy. It is up to the fragmented mailbox to check the identity of the user. Accordingly, it provides the user with an appropriate interface and implementation of that interface.

The interface of the fragment offers transparency of the distribution to a client. A method of the fragment interface can be entirely implemented by the fragment itself or it can trigger invocations to other fragments.

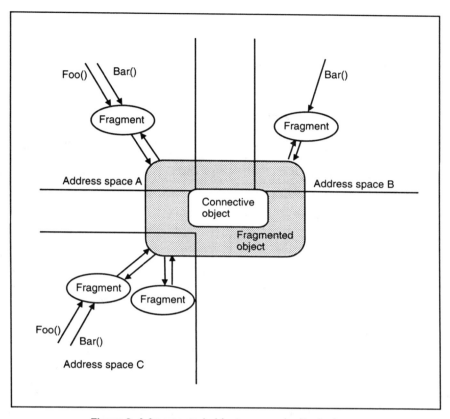

Figure 2. A fragmented object as seen by its designer.

Fragments

The concrete representation of an FO is fragmented onto several address spaces. The designer considers criteria such as protection, efficiency, and availability to decide the distribution of data among fragments. A fragment's interface is divided in three distinct parts, as follows:

- The *public* (or client) interface, which contains methods accessible by clients;
- The *private* interface, which is composed of internal methods accessible only from within the fragment; and
- The *group* interface, which comprises those methods that are internal to the FO as a whole (that is, those that can be invoked remotely from other fragments).

For instance, consider the implementation of a replicated file file as an FO. Each replica constitutes a fragment (see Figure 3). The client interface to file is record based: read(**out** record r), write(**in** record r), seek(**in int** position). (The meaning of the preceding is as follows: read is a method taking no input parameter and returning a result of type record; write takes an input parameter of type record and returns no result; and seek takes an integer parameter called position.) The group interface is different, being block based: put(**in** int blkno, **in** block blk). (Note that there is no need for a get() operation if file is fully replicated.)

In the file example, the set of all the put methods of the replicas constitutes the group interface.

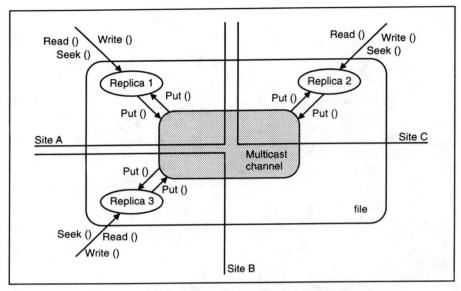

Figure 3. The fragmented representation of a replicated file.

The type-checking of the group interface ensures strongly typed communications between fragments. Communication between fragments is carried out by *connective objects*.

Connective objects

A connective object is just another FO at a lower level of abstraction. The most primitive connective objects are the communication objects, implemented by the system, with a fixed, predefined interface. At instantiation time, a primitive communication object checks that the connected ends are indeed allowed to communicate directly — that is, that they are fragments of a same FO. Communication objects implement the basic communication facilities, such as communication protocols (for example, remote procedure call, asynchronous remote procedure call, parallel remote procedure call, and functional remote procedure call).

The types of parameters in the group interface of an FO may be totally unrelated to the interface of its connective object. This necessitates type coercions for marshaling/unmarshaling. We return to the example of the replicated file; Figure 4 illustrates this issue. The group interface of the file FO is the put method. Each invocation of put maps onto a send(message) at one end of the transport communication channel and a receive(message) at the other end. The (int, block) parameter list must be coerced into the message datatype. Conversely, a receive(message) is mapped onto an upcall to put(**in int** blkno, **in block** blk). Our type-safe treatment of interprotocol-layer coercion is further detailed in the subsection entitled "FOG compiler."

Binding to an FO

Just as in the traditional client/server model, a client must bind to an FO before invoking it. There are three ways to perform a binding:

- Via local binding,
- Via a system-defined *binder*, or
- Via an FO-specific *provider*.

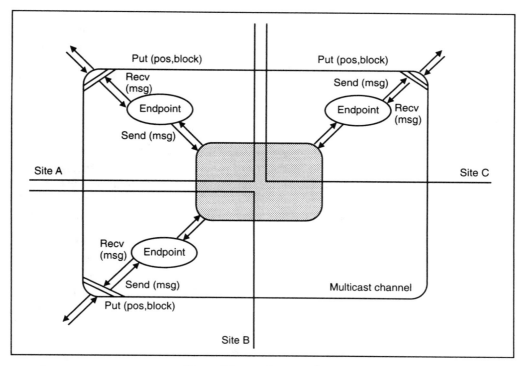

Figure 4. Invocation coercions.

The simplest case is local binding. When access is needed to an FO, its proxy is instantiated locally, which then uses internal knowledge to connect to its other fragments. This is appropriate for statically configured services (for example, the SOS Naming Service presented in the section entitled "Structuring a Name Service as FOs").

For added flexibility, one would use a system-defined binder, such as an Ansa Trader [1], that maintains mappings of interface descriptions to servers; an Ansa client interfaces to a distributed service using a stub. At binding time, the stub contacts the Trader with an interface description; this returns a server connection. Thereafter, the stub encapsulates that connection. This approach fits well for many services that do not require a dynamic selection of the specific implementation of the interface requested by a client.

In SOS, we generally use a more involved binding procedure, giving the FO designer more control. A binding has three steps. In the first step, a name lookup (similar to Ansa's Trader lookup) yields a provider object for the named interface. In the second step, the binding request is forwarded, by the distributed object manager [8],[14], to a particular method of the provider. In the third step, this method may dynamically instantiate a proxy implementation, based on, for instance, the user's identity, the binding request arguments (for example, type of access required), the type of the underlying system or architecture, or the load of the client's host.

These three binding approaches are each appropriate for certain classes of applications. An FO designer uses the one that best fits its needs.

The local binding consists of a simple instantiation of a proxy in the client's address space, followed by the establishment of connections between this proxy and other fragments of its FO. For the other two approaches, an FO designer first declares the type of the binder to use; then, for each client interface, an associated binding procedure is generated. A binding procedure relies on the declared binder to perform the binding. When invoked, any binding procedure returns a proxy fragment implementing its associated interface.

Tools for fragmented objects

The fragmented-object concept encompasses the specification of (1) a group of fragments, (2) internal cooperation, (3) the different interfaces, and (4) a mechanism for binding fragments to clients. A specialized language is helpful in writing these specifications. Its compiler will check the correctness of the specification (for example, the type-compatibility of the group interface) and will automatically generate code for common cases (such as marshaling/unmarshaling parameters). The language is complemented by a toolkit of low-level FO types.

Toolkit of predefined fragmented-object types

To assist programmers in structuring their applications as FOs, we provide a toolkit of predefined FO types, implementing some basic distribution mechanisms. These predefined FOs can be used as connective objects.

Communication channels

Currently, the toolkit contains mainly communication channels [10]. A channel object offers to the designer of its associated FO (that is, the FO using it as connective object) a well-defined interface for fragments to communicate with one another, through their group interface.

We distinguish point-to-point (between two fragments) and multipoint (between more than two fragments) communication channels.

Point-to-point channels

The root point-to-point channel type, rpcChannel, supports RPC. An rpcChannel has two kinds of fragment types: channel and channelStub, associated with a client and a server, respectively. The public interface of this FO is presented in Figure 5.

An FO of type rpcChannel implements both blocking and nonblocking remote procedure calls. All calls and replies are eventually delivered to their destinations.

Another point-to-point communication channel is fifoChannel. It has the same public interface as rpcChannel. In addition, invocations are delivered in FIFO order.

Multipoint channels

The root multipoint channel is multicastChannel. An FO of type multicastChannel has two kinds of fragments: multiChannel and multiChannelStub. The class multiChannel inherits from channel and the class multiChannelStub inherits from channelStub. The public interface of this FO, provided by multiChannel, is presented in Figure 5.

A multicastChannel supports both 1-to-N (one caller, many parallel callees) and 1-to-1-out-of-N (functional) invocations. The invoked objects may be a subset of the server fragments. Messages eventually reach their destinations, but no ordering is guaranteed.

Other available multipoint channels are fifoMulticastChannel and atomicMulticastChannel. They have the same client interface as the multicastChannel type. The fifoMulticastChannel guarantees FIFO delivery. The atomicMulticastChannel guarantees that invocations are delivered to all destinations in the same order.

```
// point-to-point communication
class channel {
public:
        // remote procedural call
        rpc (in message, out result);
        // deferred remote procedure call
        send (in message, out result);
};

// group communication
class multiChannel : channel
{       // in addition to the interface inherited from channel
public:
        // parallel remote procedure call
        prpc (in message, out, multiResult);
        // deferred parallel remote procedure call
        psend (in message, out multiResult);
};
```

Figure 5. FOG declarations of communication channels.

Ongoing work

Ultimately, our goal is for the toolkit to support most commonly used distributed abstractions. Our initial focus has been on communication protocols. Several new protocols (for example, causal broadcast) will eventually be integrated to the toolkit. We are actively investigating two other domains: (1) concurrency control and synchronization (2) and replication. FO types implementing semaphores, locks, and rendezvous are already specified and will be implemented.

The initial investigation concerning the specification of general FO types for replication is encouraging. Such an FO type should offer a generic interface for concurrency control and for accessing replicated data. Different implementations will offer different consistency policies (for example, causal consistency and strong consistency). Other important distributed abstractions, such as caching and distributed shared memory, will also be added.

FOG language

We have defined a language extension to C++ [15] called FOG (fragmented-object generator) [7]. It provides features for the designer to specify class groups, group interfaces, client interfaces, accesses to connective objects, and how a client binds to an FO. It is essentially a declarative interface language. The designer of an FO specifies interfaces and connections. (Note that for simplicity, the declarations presented in this paper take some liberties with the exact FOG syntax.)

Class group

Just as an elementary object is an instance of a *class*, an FO is an instance of a *class group*. The class group defines the behavior and representation of the FO by listing the classes of the fragments. These in turn specify the public, private, and group interfaces, as well as the component objects (fragments and connections). Just as there can be several instances of a class, several fragmented instances can be instantiated from the same class group.

To explain the FOG language, we return to the replicated file example. Figure 6 shows the declarations of this example in the FOG language. More details can be found in reference [7] and the "Structuring a name service as FOs" section.

The file class group is composed of one fragment class replica, which can be instantiated several times in several sites. All the replicas of some file together constitute a single fragmented instance.

Interfaces

A client invokes file via the public interface of its local instance of replica, the client interface of file for this client.

The put method of the group interface is invoked by the forwarding method update, signaled by the "!" syntax. A forwarding method, like the traditional RPC stub, forwards the invocation to its corresponding method[s] of the group interface. This syntax means that an invocation of update invokes the psend method of the connective object chan that upcalls the put method of the group interface. We present only the code for updates. To ensure consistency between replicas, each one has to obtain a token before accessing the data.

Consider, for instance, that a client wants to write a record. First, it invokes the write method of the client interface of a replica. The write method, after executing some code locally (computing the block number and possibly splitting the record across blocks), invokes the private update forwarding method for every block. The update method forwards the invocation, through the multicast channel chan, to the remote put method of all replicas (including the calling replica).

```
// A class group defining the FO type file
group file { replica;}

// the class of file fragments
class replica
{
public:             // the public interface
        read (out record r);
        write (in record r);
        seek (in int position)
private             // the private interface
        update (in int blkno, in block blk)
        ! chan.psend ! replica::put (blkno, blk);
                    // atomic multicast channel
        // multicastChannel chan;
group:              // the group interface
        put (in int blkno, in block blk):
};
```

Figure 6. Declaration of file in the FOG language.

Binding

The FOG compiler help supports the local binding to FOs. There is only one single client interface within a simple FO. The FOG compiler generates a default import procedure that performs the local binding. The reference of this FO is passed as argument to this procedure. It instantiates a proxy implementing the client interface and connects it to other fragments of its FO.

For the time being, the FOG compiler provides no support for the binding using a system-defined binder. The main reason for this is that SOS, our supporting system, has no global binder.

To help support the FO-specific binding approach, the FOG language provides a feature for exporting client interfaces. This is done as follows: The FO designer specifies a *provider* class. For each client interface, this class has a particular method, qualified by the key word **export** and returning a fragment implementing this interface. For each export method, the compiler will generate its associated import procedure, with the same arguments, plus a reference that will designate a provider object. (Note that there can be several providers for one FO.)

When a client wants to bind to an FO, it invokes the import procedure corresponding to the expected client interface; the reference of a provider is passed as argument. The import procedure initiates a migration request to the designated provider. The effect is an upcall to the export method of the provider, which returns a fragment. Upon completion, the reference of the fragment is returned to the client by the import procedure.

FOG compiler

From the interface declarations, the FOG compiler generates C++ interfaces and code, so that clients see FOs as ordinary C++ objects. Also, it verifies the correctness of the group interface declarations to ensure the encapsulation of the fragmentation.

First, for each method of the group interface, there must exist at least one forwarding method implemented by a member of the class group. Also, for each forwarding method, there must exist a corresponding method in the group interface. Their signatures must match. Second, it checks the type-safety of the interconnection between fragments of the same FO. Fragments are located in different address spaces, compiled separately, and instantiated at different times. Therefore, in addition to the compile-time checks, runtime checks are needed. At binding time, communication privileges are checked. (Fragment instances belong to a common FO instance; fragment classes belong to a common class group.) The code generated by the compiler also checks the correctness of the connection establishment to a connective object by fragments; these fragments have to verify the first condition on the group interface.

The FOG compiler generates the code and structures necessary to marshal/unmarshal parameters of group interface invocations. It also generalizes the traditional stub generation to handle parallel and/or deferred invocations, handling of exceptions, and so forth. Unlike a traditional stub generator (based on a predefined communication primitive), the FOG compiler can generate marshaling/ unmarshaling coercion methods based on different interfaces of communication objects: It automatically provides a glue between forwarding methods of an FO and the client interface offered by its connective object. For instance, the **in** parameters (int, block) of the update method of replica (see Figure 6) are coerced into a message. The compiler looks up the declaration of the field chan of the class replica: multiChannel. Then, it looks up the declaration of the method psend of this class (see Figure 5). Finally, it generates a class putMessage inheriting from message, containing two fields of types **int** and **block**.

An instance of this putMessage is allocated by the generated update method and is passed to the psend method of the connective object chan, which in turn, invokes all the replicas. At the receiving side, the putMessage is coerced into the types expected by the put method of replica, also (int, block). There are no **out** parameters. If there were, they would be coerced into a result, when returning.

Currently, coercions are done according to a hardwired external representation of data. As an extension, we plan to replace this with programmer-defined coercions. These are guaranteed to be type-safe, because the compiler has checked the group interface.

Structuring a Name Service as FOs

The SOS system includes a naming facility, implemented by a distributed Name Service, allowing applications to associate symbolic names with objects that they manage. In this paper, for the sake of brevity, we describe only one aspect of the SOS Name Service. The actual Name Service is more advanced, as it is layered, user-centered, and configurable on a per-user basis. The SOS Name Space, described here, corresponds to its bottom layer.

The SOS Name Service (NS) is implemented by server objects instantiated at boot time in separate "naming contexts" and by Name Service proxies located in the client's contexts. These objects cooperate to process the clients' requests and to ensure the consistency of the distributed Name Space. They constitute an FO, called NameService. The NameService FO uses two connective objects. The first is a multicastChannel between clients and servers. The second, of type Tree, actually manages the distributed Name Space.

The Tree FO

The tree is decomposed into multiple partitions according a per-server partitioning similar to the one of V-System [6], in which each part is a vertical slice, starting at the root of the tree. Each partition, managed by a treeFragment, is made of nodes and leaves associated with info data. The set of treeFragments constitutes the Tree FO (see Figure 7). The main role of Tree is to manage the distribution of the tree and to ensure its consistency.

Interfaces

The public interface includes three operations, shown in Figure 8. The lookUp function has local scope, as it looks up the path p in the local partition of the distributed tree (returning its associated info). The addLeaf function has global scope; it creates a leaf somewhere in the distributed tree; this leaf is associated with info i. The addNode function also has global scope; it creates a node somewhere in the distributed tree, associated with info i.

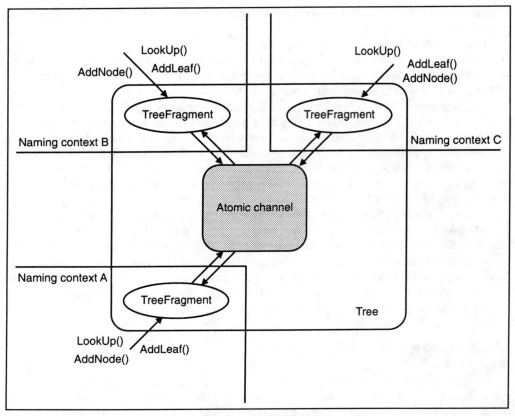

Figure 7. The Tree FO.

A treeFragment object also implements a group interface, consisting of two kinds of functions. First, there are functions, corresponding to those of the public interface, that have a global scope, namely groupAddNode and groupAddLeaf. Second, there are groupVerify, groupLock, and groupUnLock to ensure consistency of the distributed tree despite concurrent requests addressed to different treeFragments.

For instance, an addNode request is processed as follows. First, groupLock locks the father node of p in all treeFragment partitions managing the father. Then, groupVerify checks that the path doesn't already exist in any partition; groupAddNode adds the node in the selected part. Finally, groupUnLock unlocks the father node.

Connective object

The Tree fragments are connected by a communication channel of type atomicChannel. The groupLock and groupUnLock functions use a protocol on the atomicChannel, ensuring that all requests are delivered to all fragments in the same order. The groupVerify, groupAddNode, and groupAddLeaf functions use a cheaper protocol (on the same atomicChannel) ensuring that all requests are delivered to all fragments (but not necessarily in the same order).

The NameService FO

The NameService FO is composed of two types of fragments: nsServer and nsProxy (see

```
class tree Fragment
{
public:
        lookUp (in path p, out info i);
        addLeaf (in path p, in info i);
        addNode (in path p, in info i);
};
```

Figure 8. Client Interface of the Tree FO.

Figure 9). The role of an nsServer fragment is to resolve symbolic names and to map the Name Service requests onto operations on Tree. An nsProxy fragment represents the Name Service for a particular client. Each nsProxy fragment manages a local cache of name prefixes; each entry of this cache associates a name prefix with the group of nsServer fragments handling the names with this same prefix.

Interfaces

A client of the SOS Name Service uses the public interface of the associated nsProxy fragment to create a directory (createDir), to associate a symbolic name to an object (addName), and to look up a symbolic name (lookUp). Each of these functions performs the following operations:

(1)   It searches for the longest prefix matching the argument of the request in the local cache; this step determines the reference of the group of nsServer fragments expected to handle the subtree containing this name.

(2)   It invokes the following nsServer fragments to continue the processing of the client request via their corresponding group interface: groupAddName, groupCreateDir, and groupLookUp functions.

Figure 10 represents the declaration of the NameService FO in the FOG language.

Connective objects

As mentioned earlier, the NameService uses two connective objects: multicastChannel and Tree. The multicastChannel (taken from the toolkit) connects each nsProxy to all nsServer fragments. It provides the invocation protocols that the nsProxy fragments need to invoke their nsServer counterparts. As stated earlier, binding of nsServer to Tree uses "local binding"; that is, it uses static configuration data. The second connective object, Tree, encapsulates the SOS distributed tree of names, as explained in the subsection entitled "The Tree FO." It is shared by all nsServer fragments. Unlike multicastChannel, this connective object type is not offered by the toolkit of low-level FOs; it is programmer defined.

Binding

Each nsServer binds locally (that is, using static configuration data) to the two connective objects: the Tree and the multicastChannel. A client binds to the NameService via an NS-specific provider. The export method of nsServer (acting as a provider) instantiates an nsProxy, initializes it, establishes connections with all nsServer fragments, and returns it.

Currently, only one single implementation of the nsProxy interface is supported; we plan several in the future (for example, different caching policies). The provider will decide which one should be exported to any specific client.

Discussion and comparison

We now discuss the advantages of our approach, then compare it to some related work.

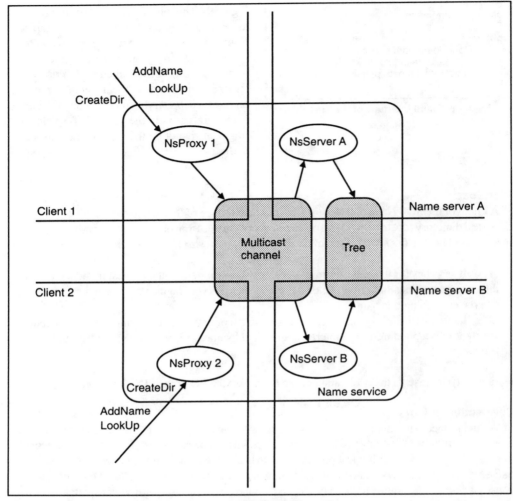

Figure 9. The NameService FO.

Benefits of the FO approach

The FO approach extends object-oriented programming to the distributed case. It retains the well-known advantages of object orientation, while additionally taking into account features specific to distribution: for example, interaction between separate, independently designed applications; existence of separate address spaces; consideration of geographical distribution of data and function; and interworking of different layers of protocol.

We now list the benefits we claim for FO programming, based on specific examples. First, the benefits of object-oriented programming, especially in a distributed setting, are: separation of interface from implementation, safer programming, and reuse. These are discussed below.

(1)   Separation of interface from implementation. An interface specification is called a *type*. An object of some type may be replaced by another object of a compatible type. A type may have many implementations (*classes*). As a result,

• The abstract view of an object is separate from the object designer's concrete view,

```
// The class group NameService FO type
group NameService {nsProxy, nsServer;}

// The fragment classes
class nsServer
{
group:                            // group interface
      groupLookUp (in String name, out reference obj);
      groupAddName (in String name, in reference obj);
      groupCreateDir (in String name);
};


class nsProxy
{
public:                           // public interface
      lookUp (in String name, out reference obj);
      addName (in String name, in reference obj);
      createDir (in String name);
private;
      cache tableOfPrefixes;           // the prefix cache
      multiChannel mchan;              // a multicast channel

      // multicast to a group of servers
      forwardLookUp (in String name, future out reference obj[ ].
            in reference callees)
          ! mchan.prpc (callees)! nsServer::groupLookUp (name, nr);

      // functional rpc towards a group of servers
      forwardaddName (in String name, in reference obj, in reference callees)
            ! mchan.rpc (callees) ! nsServer::groupAddName (name,obj);
      // functional rpc towards a group of servers
      forwardCreateDir (in String name, in reference callees)
            ! mchan.rpc (callees) ! nsServer::groupCreateDir (name);
};
```

Figure 10. Declaration of the NameService FO.

- It is easy to switch between different *policies* for the same *mechanism*, and
- Components can evolve independently.

To illustrate this point, consider the Name Service example. The Tree designer may decide to replicate certain partitions or, on the contrary, to maintain a centralized image of the tree; these changes would not affect the NameService FO. Conversely, the Name Service designer could change the distribution of service between nsServer and nsProxy (for example, to a different caching policy); such a change would affect only the cooperation between the clients and servers.

(2)   Safer programming. An object is *encapsulated*, meaning that access is allowed only through its public interface. Strongly typed language compilers such as C++ ensure that the use of an object is compatible with its declared type. However, such safety traditionally is checked only within a single address space. The FOG compiler extends these checks to separate address spaces. Type checks extend to checking (both statically and dynamically) that binding to an FO returns an interface conforming to what the client requested, and that its usage conforms to its type. Encapsulation checks extend to verify that the group interface of a fragment is accessible only to fragment classes of the same fragmented type and that fragment instances only invoke other fragments of the same FO instance.

In the Name Service example, the FOG compiler not only checks (like any standard C++ compiler) that clients access **NameService** and **Tree** via their public interface only and that the actual arguments conform to declaration, but it also checks that the fragments of two separate Name Service instances do not interfere and that only Name Service fragments do access — for example, **groupLookUp**.

(3)   Reuse. The above characteristics encourage the development of libraries of generic types and classes, to be reused in different applications. In our case, this is illustrated by the toolkit of predefined FOs. The **Tree** FO could now be added to the toolkit, for reuse by other distributed applications manipulating a tree structure.

We now examine the solutions to some specific problems of distributed programming addressed by the FO approach, by FOG, and by our toolkit: support for different levels of transparency, separation of interfaces, high-level communication abstractions, and support for layered protocols and:

(1)   Appropriate transparency for both clients and designers. Distribution is transparent for clients. Yet, the designer has full control of distribution of data items, their respective locations, and all aspects of communication between them. For instance, the **Tree** fragments are connected by a channel of type **atomicChannel**, supporting atomic parallel invocations, whereas the **NameService** fragments are connected by a **multicastChannel** only. Each FO may use what it actually needs and no more; switching to a different policy is easy, accomplished by just replacing a connective object.

It is sometimes useful to allow clients to control some aspect of distribution, by exporting an appropriate interface from the FO. For instance, in the actual implementation of Tree, each method has an extra partID parameter, controlling the location of directory data. Conversely, some FO designers would rather have network transparency *inside* their FO also. This is done easily, either by using FOG as a pure stub generator — see Item (4) below — or by using a connective FO class that handles distribution internally, such as Tree.

(2)   High-level communication abstractions. Communication occurs via shared fragmented objects. In most existing systems, only primitive, untyped communication objects are available, such as a **send(bytestream)/receive(bytestream)** channel. Our approach instead encourages the use of high-level communication abstractions. For instance, Name Service **nsProxys** and **nsServers** communicate through a shared **Tree**. This is consistent with the object-oriented approach.

(3)   Multiple layers of protocol. Multiple levels of abstraction (layers of protocol) are present together in the same framework. In the case of the Name Service, these are **NameService, Tree,** and the channel level (**atomicChannel, multicastChannel**). Coercions (marshaling/unmarshaling) between these multiple layers are handled automatically and in a type-safe manner.

(4)   Separation of interfaces. FOG separates the public interface of an FO from the internal (group) one and supports both downcalls and upcalls ("!" notation). The compiler automatically generates any necessary forwarding between interfaces. Thus, it includes and supersedes the functionality of a traditional stub generator. The use of public versus group interfaces is shown in the Name Service example; for instance, the public **addName** looks up data and sets locks before using the internal **groupAddName**; it would be dangerous to expose the latter in the public interface. Forwarding is explicit.

Related work

Several projects have proposed distributed extensions of the object paradigm: client/server-type remote object invocation, as in Ansa; shared objects, as in Orca or Comandos; and approaches found in models such as Gothic and Topologies that are more closely related to our FOs.

The client/server model

The better known model is the client/server remote invocation, where the server is seen as a remote object accessed via a stub at the client's location. Thus, the computation model of the Ansa architecture [1] supports remote object invocation. A client interfaces to a distributed service using a stub, a placeholder object for a remote server, automatically generated from an interface description. It has no useful local data or processing capability; its only function is to marshal/unmarshal arguments and forward invocations to the server. A stub remotely extends access to the server object, but is not as flexible as a fragmented object. Stub generation is one of the functions of the FOG compiler; FOs are a superset of the client/server model.

The shared-object model

Orca [2] and Comandos [11] support distributed shared objects, giving the illusion of a single global object space. In Orca, shared objects are dynamically replicated under the control of the Orca runtime. All the replicas of a shared object form a single object. Orca ensures transparent access to the replicas and executes a consistency-preservation protocol among them. The decision of whether to create new replicas or to migrate the object on to the sites where the object is frequently used is made automatically by the Orca runtime, based on statistics of recent access. The Comandos approach is opposite to ours: In Comandos, shared objects are not fragmented; instead, address spaces are fragmented across sites. When an activity requests access to a remote shared object, its address space "diffuses" over to the site of this object.

Orca and Comandos hide distribution to both the clients and the designers of a shared object. While simple, this automatic approach has drawbacks. First, replication, migration, or diffusion of activities are just specific sharing policies. Second, no single consistency policy is suitable for all applications. In our model, the designer has a choice of levels of transparency and of policies. It is possible to choose an Orca-like automatic replication by appropriate choice of connective objects. But, it is also possible for knowledgeable designers to exercise more fine control, based on protection, efficiency, or fault-tolerance criteria, deciding how and where to place data and function.

Other systems supporting a similar model are Emerald [9] and Amber [5].

Other FO approaches

Gothic's fragmented objects [3] are based on "multifunctions" a parallelized generalization of procedures to N callers and P callees. Although we use the same name, our FO model differs from Gothic in three ways. First, we focus on distributed, rather than parallel, computations. Second, we give the designer full control over the distribution, whereas the Gothic system provides only automatic mechanisms. Third, we support multiple client interfaces, whereas Gothic enforces a single global interface to a fragmented object.

Topologies [12] bear some similarities to our FOs. They allow programmers to define distributed shared objects on a message-passing multicomputer. Topologies bear a close resemblance to the primitive communication objects of our FO toolkit. Reference [12] describes only communication-oriented Topologies and seems to lack our general concept of fragmented objects. The implementation described concentrates on high-performance communication on a hypercube, based on kernel-level Topologies. Consequently, Topology interfaces are restricted to send and receive operations, whereas we allow high-level, programmer-defined interfaces.

Conclusions

This paper defines the fragmented-object concept, an extension of objects to the distributed environment. Its main strength is that it provides the appropriate level of distribution visibility to the implementer of a distributed service, while hiding the distribution of fragments from its clients. Some tools available to the fragmented-object programmer are listed: a library of predefined fragmented objects, the FOG language, and the FOG compiler. The design of FOG draws upon the experience of the SOS Distributed Object-Oriented System and other distributed applications written for SOS. (Note that the SOS Distributed Object Manager, the SOS Naming Service, and communication protocols are structured as FOs.)

From our experience with SOS, we strongly believe that the FO approach is well suited for structuring many different kinds of distributed abstractions, such as synchronization abstractions, distributed shared memory, cache and replication managers, and protocols. The toolkit of predefined FO types implementing these distributed abstractions is of primary interest in encouraging programmers to write distributed applications. It will progressively accumulate abstractions needed by a large number of applications.

Acknowledgments

We are grateful to Willy Zwaenepoel, from Rice University, Houston, Texas, for his many comments on the draft of this paper.

References

[1] Architecture Projects Management Limited, "An Engineer's Introduction to the Architecture," Tech. Report TR.03.02, Ansa, Cambridge, United Kingdom, 1989.

[2] H.E. Bal and A.S. Tanenbaum, "Distributed Programming with Shared Data," *Proc. ICCL*, IEEE Computer Soc. Press, Los Alamitos, Calif., 1988, pp. 82-91.

[3] J.-P. Banâtre, Michel Banâtre, and F. Ployette, "An Overview of the Gothic Distributed Operating System," Rapport de Recherche 504, INRIA, France, 1986.

[4] A.D. Birrell and B.J. Nelson, "Implementing Remote Procedure Calls," *ACM Trans. Computer Systems*, Vol. 2, No. 1, Feb. 1984, pp. 39-59.

[5] J.S. Chase et al., "The Amber System: Parallel Programming on a Network of Multiprocessors," *Proc. 12th ACM Symp. Operating Systems Principles*, ACM Press, New York, N.Y., 1989, pp. 147-158.

[6] D.R. Cheriton and T.P. Mann, "Decentralizing a Global Naming Service for Improved Performance and Fault Tolerance," *ACM Trans. Computer Systems*, Vol. 7, No. 2, May 1989, pp. 147-183.

[7] Y. Gourhant and M. Shapiro, "FOG/C++: A Fragmented-Object Generator," *Proc. C++ Conf.*, Usenix Assoc., Berkeley, Calif., 1990, pp. 63-74.

[8] S. Habert, *Gestion d'Objets et Migration dans les Systèmes Répartis,* doctoral thesis, Université Paris-6, Pierre-et-Marie-Curie, Paris, France, 1989.

[9] N.C. Hutchinson, "Emerald: An Object-Based Language for Distributed Programming," Tech. Report 87-01-01, Dept. of Computer Science, Univ. of Washington, Seattle, Wash., 1987.

[10] M.M. Makpangou, *Protocoles de Communication et Programmation par Objets: L'Exemple de SOS*, doctoral thesis, Université Paris VI, Paris, France, 1989.

[11] J. Alves Marques et al., "Implementing the Commandos Architecture," *Proc. 5th Ann. ESPRIT Conf.*, 1985, pp. 1140-1157.

[12] K. Schwan and W. Bo, "Topologies — Distributed Objects on Multicomputers," *ACM Trans. Computer Systems*, Vol. 8, No. 2, May 1990, pp. 111-157.

[13] M. Shapiro, "Structure and Encapsulation in Distributed Systems: The Proxy Principle," *Proc. Sixth Int'l Conf. Distributed Computer Systems*, IEEE Computer Soc. Press, Los Alamitos, Calif., 1986, pp. 198-204.

[14] M. Shapiro et al., "SOS: An Object-Oriented Operating System — Assessment and Perspectives," *Computing Systems*, Vol. 2, No. 4, Dec. 1989, pp. 287-338.

[15] B. Stroustrup, *The C++ Programming Language*, Addison-Wesley, Reading, Mass., 1985.

Configuring Object-Based Distributed Programs in REX

A ssessment of the impact of object-oriented programming varies considerably. On the one hand OOP is hailed as a major revolution in programming paradigms, and on the other, it is considered to be merely an extension to the use of abstract data types. Reality is somewhere in between. There is no doubt that OOP has taken a number of sound and useful concepts and combined them in a form that captures popular imagination [Wegner 90]:

(1) *Encapsulation* permits the association of state and behavior to form an *object*. This provides the benefit of abstraction during design and simplifies independent construction. This is essentially the concept of abstract data types.

(2) *Classes* serve as templates from which object instances are created. Classes thereby permit the use of a single behavior specification for the set of all object instances created from that class.

(3) *Inheritance* provides a mechanism for the reuse of the behavior of one class in the definition of a new class. It establishes a class hierarchy that represents a generalization/ specialization relationship between parent/child classes.

Jeff Kramer,

Jeff Magee,

Morris Sloman, and

Naranker Dulay

The object-oriented-design (OOD) approach is essentially one of modeling, with real-world entities being modeled as objects. The class hierarchy describes the relationship between the behaviors of the required objects. The underlying execution model is that of objects manipulating their local state and affecting others by sending messages that invoke methods (operations) in a client-server relationship. Those methods available for invocation are made visible at the object interface (Figure 1). All these are very appealing notions.

However, there are some weaknesses that seem to emanate from the lack of an *explicit description of the program structure* in OOP. Based on previous experience with Conic [Kramer 85, 89, 90a, 90b, Magee 89], we argue that a separate and explicit description of program structure in terms of object instances and their interactions facilitates program description, construction, and modification, and complements the object-oriented concepts. This is missing from most other approaches.

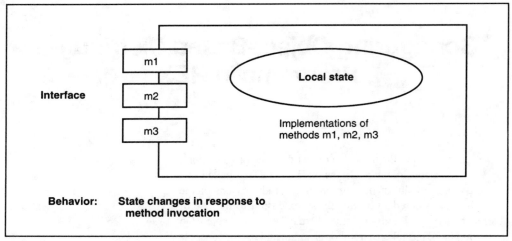

Figure 1. An object in OOP.

OOD methods generally emphasize the definition of classes in an inheritance hierarchy. This defines the relation between *classes*, but ignores the actual structure of the required program. It seems more sensible to consider class inheritance *after* the designer has established what objects are required. Explicit program structure, in terms of object *instances* and the interconnections or bindings between them, is a natural outcome of traditional design techniques such as the system structure diagram of JSD ([Jackson 83], data flow diagrams and structure charts of SASD [Page-Jones 80]). This resulting design structure of objects instances can be used to determine the classes required to perform the application processing [Kramer 90a], and *then* organized into an inheritance hierarchy to try to maximize software reuse.

To some extent, this lack of an explicit structural description in OOP is excused by the use of dynamic object creation and dynamic binding between objects. However, it is very difficult to determine the current overall structure of a program because it is embedded in the object code as parameters, instructions for instances to be created, and references to objects to which bindings are required. This paper will show that even such dynamic programs can benefit by making the possible object instance structures more explicit.

OOP is also offered as one of the prime technologies expected to cope with large-scale applications and the issues of "megaprogramming" [Wegner 90]. Megaprogramming is programming in the large, with multiple personnel and multiple computers, where the programs are expected to have a long lifetime. Structural descriptions are ideally suited to programming in the large [DeRemer 76], as they provide a clear and useful reference abstraction for the personnel involved in the distributed development process, including program construction, evolution (modification), and software management.

What of concurrency and distribution? The success of OOP has encouraged researchers and language developers to examine its application to parallel and distributed programming. The model seems ideal: concurrent, distributable objects that send messages to invoke one anothers' methods. But there are a number of key issues that impact its use in a distributed environment. For instance, at what granularity level should concurrency be provided? Should objects become active entities like processes, or have the ability to create threads of execution within objects? We believe that the combination of OOP concepts and structural descriptions has much to offer. Others have also recognized the importance of highlighting the structural configuration view in a distributed environment [Barbacci 88, Goguen 86, Kaplan 88, Kramer 85, Leblanc 82, LeBlanc 85, Lee 86, Nehmer 87, Purtilo 88].

In the "Concurrency and distribution" section of this paper, we examine the major issues that impact the use of OOP in a parallel and distributed environment: concurrency control, object interaction, interfaces, binding, and inheritance. We discuss the relative merits of current solutions to these issues. We describe and justify an approach based on the use of active objects with essentially explicit interfaces and bindings, and the use of composition as a pragmatic alternative to inheritance. An explicit configuration language is used to define program structure as a set of objects and their bindings. This configuration language is separate from that used for programming objects as context-independent types (like classes) with well-defined interfaces.

Since a key feature of the approach is its explicit and separate expression of software structure, it is termed *configuration oriented programming*. This emphasis on software architecture leads to clear designs, and produces flexible object-based[1] systems. In addition, the approach supports dynamic change, expressible at the configuration level as changes to the configuration of object instances and/or their bindings. The utility and versatility of the approach is explained and illustrated in the "Configuration oriented programming in REX" section using a number of examples. We conclude by summarizing the approach and giving the current status of the work.

Concurrency and distribution issues

In this section, we discuss some of the main issues in the use of object-oriented concepts in a parallel and distributed environment. We make no attempt to present a survey; instead we describe the main concepts and their relative merits.

Object concurrency and interaction

There are two main approaches to the provision of concurrency in object-based languages: the *thread model of concurrency* (multiple threads of execution within an object) or the *active object model of concurrency* (the objects themselves are considered as active but sequential (compare processes)).

Thread model of concurrency. Concurrency can be introduced by permitting objects to create new threads of execution using statements such as **cobegin...coend** [Nierstrasz 87]. This can be used in a client object to create multiple threads. Each thread can in turn send messages to invoke methods on other server objects, which could themselves introduce further concurrency — thereby forming a "tree" of execution threads through objects (Figure 2). At a particular server object, concurrency can occur through multiple invocation of its methods by different execution threads. This thread model thus provides a grain of concurrency finer than that of an object, and requires additional concurrency control primitives (such as semaphores) for synchronization and to control access to shared data [Steigerwald 90]. Use of such synchronization primitives is generally difficult and error-prone. Although some improvement has been made by permitting separate expression of this synchronization in systems such as Guide [Decouchant 91], they can still require highly complex expressions.

A variation of this approach is the use of asynchronous method invocation. This permits the client

---

[1] [Wegner 87] makes a distinction between object-based, class-based, and object-oriented languages. Object-based languages support encapsulation in the form of objects, class-based extend this to include classes, and object-oriented further extend this to include inheritance. Strictly speaking, our language can be classified as class based.

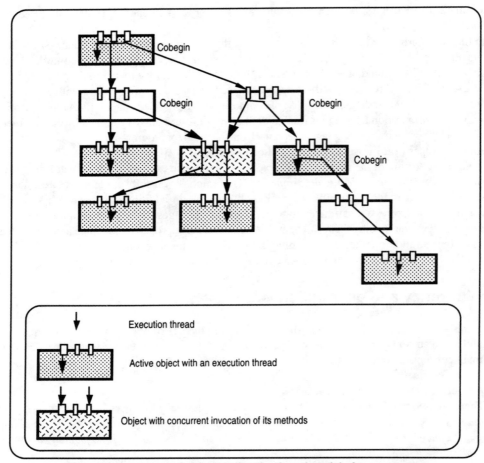

Figure 2. A program of objects using the thread model of concurrency.

to continue execution, and creates another thread of execution at the invoked server object. Although this appears to be attractive for distribution in providing an asynchronous form of communication, it is rather too primitive (low-level). For the common case of invocation with results, the programmer is left with the task of matching replies [Agha 86, Yonezawa 86].

So, although these approaches provide a fine grain of concurrency, they can be referred to as the "assembler level" of concurrent OOP.

Active object model of concurrency. In order to make the concurrency control clearer, the grain of active concurrency can be made coarser and restricted to coincide with an object. Objects thus support only one active thread. A program would consist of sequential active objects (compare processes) that communicate and synchronize via passive objects (compare monitors). Concurrency is then controlled by queuing invocations at monitor objects, combined with the ability to suspend a thread of execution through the use of synchronization variables such as condition variables. Although this approach to concurrency is easier for the programmer, it suffers from being nonuniform in its use of two forms of objects, and its restriction to a form of indirect interaction via monitor objects.

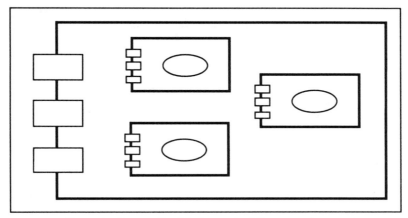

Figure 3. Composite object encapsulating concurrency.

Furthermore, monitors are more suited to interaction through shared memory than in a distributed environment.

This leads us to seek a more uniform form of concurrency that is clear and well-suited to distribution. Such an approach is the use of sequential active objects (compare processes) that communicate directly with one another by remote method invocation. A distributed program then consists of a number of distributed communicating objects that can handle one invocation at a time. This sacrifices the fine-grain concurrency of the concurrent threads approach, and adopts the object as the grain of concurrency and distribution. In so doing, the need for additional synchronization primitives within an object are obviated, and all that is necessary is the ability of an object to wait on a selection of possible invocations/messages.

The use of active sequential process objects is our preferred approach. The interface for interaction with an object is discussed in the next section. How can more complex objects be constructed that encapsulate inherently parallel activities? We propose a simple approach that permits the definition of a composite object as a composition of primitive, active sequential objects (Figure 3). Composition is discussed in the "Program structure: object creation and binding" section.

Object interfaces

Modularization is a necessary facility — not only for distribution, but also for sound software engineering. One of its recommended principles is that the interface to a module should explicitly define all the means of affecting its behavior and state. We now examine and assess object interfaces in this light.

Objects interact by method invocation. An object interface is usually described by the methods that it offers (Figure 1). However, its use of the methods of other objects is not described explicitly at the object interface but embedded internally in the object code. This is analogous to publishing offered service interfaces in distributed systems, but hiding service requirements. We believe that both the "services" *provided* and *required* are necessary for the description of object behavior, and ought to be explicitly defined at the object interface. The interface can thus clearly and explicitly identify the methods offered and used, the types of data associated with each, and even the form of interaction (such as uni- or bidirectional information flow).

This form of interface definition can be extended to object naming. In the same way that (from the point of view of the invoked object), an invocation is from an anonymous (unnamed) object, so

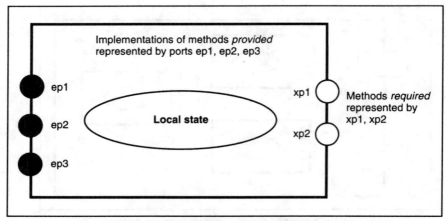

Figure 4. An object with explicit interfaces.

calls on other objects can be anonymous by making them indirect. Object code need never refer directly to other objects, but can rather refer indirectly via remote references declared at its interface. Object binding can be performed separately; in this way, an object achieves context independence. This facilitates its use and reuse in different contexts. In practice we define an object interface in terms of

- The set of typed ports representing the methods that the object *provides* and
- The set of typed remote port references representing the methods *required* from other objects (Figure 4).

Program structure: Object creation and binding

The structure of a program can be thought of as consisting of a number of object instances bound together according to their ability to communicate; that is, interconnections are bindings between required and provided interfaces. In a distributed environment, the objects can reside on different machines and communication can be remote. In addition it is necessary to allocate objects to physical nodes in the network either explicitly by the programmer or implicitly by the system.

The most common object-oriented approach is dynamic object instantiation and binding. The distributed configuration starts as a single object that dynamically creates other objects locally or remotely. The binding between object interfaces is direct, by reference. These references can be obtained as instantiation parameters from the parent object that created it, as parameters in methods invoked on the object, or by querying some form of name server or trader to locate a suitable server instance. Object creation, binding, and allocation are embedded in the object programming language.

On the other hand, program structure can be thought of as essentially static. It can be elaborated initially as the distributed program configuration, which is unchanged during program execution. Object creation, binding, and allocation can be specified either within the object programming language or specified separately in a configuration language (compare Module Interconnection Language).

Whereas the dynamic approach is undoubtedly more flexible in expressing computations in which the structure changes over time, it has problems in the creation of the initial program structure and in managing long running programs (such as embedded systems) where explicit structure is beneficial. Conversely, the static approach causes difficulties in programming systems that change in response to user demands (such as transaction systems).

The approach advocated in this paper is a synthesis of these two approaches. The structure of object instances can be explicitly and separately described. However, this description includes the description of structural changes (object creation/deletion and binding) that can be invoked by objects to perform dynamic change. The structure is thus available explicitly for management purposes, but can change in response to the demands of the application computation. Furthermore, in order to retain the flexibility of dynamic binding where appropriate, traditional communication is enhanced by the ability to send port references in messages. This is discussed and illustrated in the "Configuration-oriented programming in REX section."

Inheritance and composition

Inheritance in object-oriented programming languages permits objects to share both behavior and data with their parent superclasses. An example of the use of shared behavior is objects instantiated from subclasses of a parent superclass Queue that supported methods for queue insertion and deletion. These objects could then share the ability to be inserted and removed. However, while it is easy to see the utility of this mechanism in constructing complex sequential object behavior, it is less simple in relation to parallel and distributed systems, as object encapsulation can be violated. For instance, a subclass may refer to variables or local private operations in its superclass, or even to superclasses further up the inheritance hierarchy. Such use of shared class variables and procedures cannot be efficiently supported in distributed systems. Wegner [Wegner 87] has gone so far as to state "... distribution is inconsistent with inheritance."

On the other hand, composition seems to offer a viable alternative to inheritance. Composition is a technique for *constructing* systems, and its inverse, decomposition, is a means of *designing* systems. Composition provides a powerful means of abstraction in that it permits a collection of components to be treated as a single component. We therefore support the view that composition provides a sensible and efficient alternative to inheritance for distributed programming [Raj 89]. We present an example to support this view in "Configuration-oriented programming in REX."

Summary

We have discussed the relative merits of the main approaches to the issues of object concurrency and interaction, object interfaces and binding, and to inheritance, particularly as applied to a parallel and distributed environment. We have argued for the use of active objects and explicit interfaces and bindings. In particular, we argue that an explicit configuration language is required to define program structure as a set of objects and their bindings. This configuration language should be separate from that used for programming objects as context-independent types (classes). This language should also support hierarchic composition, as this is more flexible and powerful than inheritance for constructing distributed applications. In the following section, we describe our configuration-oriented, object-based approach using a number of simple examples to illustrate its utility and versatility.

Configuration-oriented programming in REX

The main concepts of configuration-oriented programming discussed in the previous section, namely those of explicit structure and hierarchic composition, are illustrated by examples from the REX environment for the development of distributed programs [REX 89]. We concentrate on the configuration facilities provided by Darwin, the REX configuration language. Darwin includes facilities for hierarchic definition of composite objects, for parameterization of objects, for multiple instantiation of both objects and interface interaction points, for dynamic binding and instance

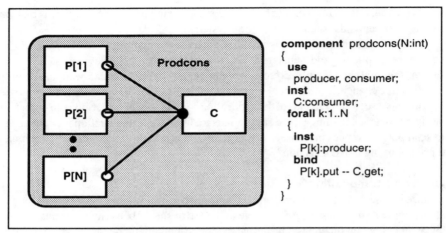

Figure 5. Darwin producer-consumer program.

creation, for conditional configurations with evaluation of guards at object instantiation, and even for recursive definition of objects. This work owes much to earlier experience using the Conic configuration language [Magee 89].

Producer-consumer

Figure 5 depicts the structure of a simple producer-consumer system together with the description of that structure in Darwin. The basic structuring entity in Darwin is the component. Components may be parameterized with the basic types int, real and string. Components are composed from other component types. The specific types used to construct a component are declared by:

> **use** *<list of component types>* .

In the example, the component prodcons is constructed from the component types consumer and producer. Instances of these component types are declared by:

> **inst** *<instance name>* : *<component type>* (*<parameters>*).

or sometimes to avoid inventing an unnecessary name for a single instance:

> **inst** *<component type>* (*<parameters>*)

Instance declaration is analogous to the declaration of variables in conventional sequential programming languages. The example declares one instance C of the consumer component type and using the replicator **forall**, a set of instances P[k] of producer where k ranges from 1 to N. These component types do not require actual parameters. Connections between instances are declared by:

> **bind** *<instance>.<service required>* — *<instance>.<service provided>*.

```
process producer;              process consumer;
require put;                   provide get;
var                            var
  put: @port(integer,real);      get: port(integer,real);
  i:integer;                     i:integer; r:real;
begin                          begin
  for i:=1 to 100 do             loop
    put ! (i, sqrt(i));            get ? (i, r);
end.                               writeln(i,r);
                                 end;
                               end.
```

Figure 6. Producer and consumer process programs.

In the example, a connection is made from each producer instance P[k].put to the consumer instance C.get.

Components in Darwin may be constructed from other component types, as above, or they may be process types programmed in a sequential programming language augmented with message passing operations. In the following we use Pascal to program process types. Figure 6 gives the programs for the producer and consumer process types of Figure 5.

Services in REX are provided via ports, which are queues of messages. For example, the consumer process of Figure 6 queues messages consisting of an integer value and a real value. Messages are transferred from the port into the local variables of the processes via the receive operation. In this case the operation is get?(i,r). The compiler or preprocessor ensures that the types of variables mentioned in a receive operation are compatible with the port on which the operation is performed. Ports are accessed remotely by remote references. A remote reference type is declared by prefixing the port declaration with an @ symbol. In the example, the variable put holds a reference value that refers to a port to which messages consisting of an integer and a real value can be sent. Messages are sent to a remote port by performing a send operation on a remote port reference. In the example, the send operation is put!(i,sqrt(i). The send operation is synchronous in that it blocks until the message has been received. Again, the compiler checks that the values sent are compatible with the declared port reference type.

It should now be clear that the effect of a bind declaration in Darwin is to assign the port reference value *provided* by one process into the port reference value *required* by another process. These bindings are typed checked using structural type descriptions supplied by process compilers to the Darwin compiler. Port references may also be sent in messages to allow more complex communication protocols than the simple unidirectional protocol of Figure 6. For example, the client and server processes of Figure 7 interact by means of a remote rendezvous protocol.

Client-server

The client process sends a message to the server consisting of a real value and a reference to its local port crep. The reference to crep is computed by the @ operator. The server process receives the real value into the variable angle and the reference value into the variable srep. Srep is used to send the computed sine value back to the client. Note that the protocol works for any number of clients connected to the server. However, the syntax for declaring port reference types requires simplification to enhance the readability of programs. With no change to the semantics of the underlying operations, an alternative syntax for declaring port references is provided such that ->type_list is equivalent to @port(type_list). Furthermore, since rendezvous interaction is very common, the compiler provides

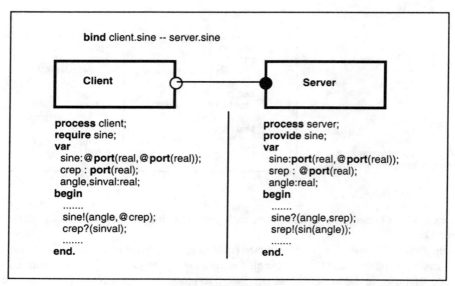

Figure 7. Client-server.

```
process client;               process server;
require sine;                  provide sine;
var                           var
  sine:->real->real;            sine:port(real->real);
  angle,sinval:real;            angle:real;
begin                         begin
  .......                        .......
  sine!(angle->sinval);         sine?(angle->sin(angle));
  .......                        .......
end.                          end.
```

Figure 8. Client-server (alternative syntax).

an implicit reply port for the caller together with an implicit port reference variable for the callee of a remote rendezvous. The program of Figure 7 now becomes the program of Figure 8. Note that the "->" notation aptly describes the particular process view of the message sequences; for the client this is sending a real and receiving a real. Rex also provides an extended rendezvous and selective receive statements [Magee 90].

General practitioners' group practice

This example program models the workings of a general medical practitioner's group practice. The practice consists of a surgery and a set of patients. When they become sick, patients visit the doctors' surgery. At the receptionist's desk they wait for one of the doctors to become free. When a doctor is free he examines the patient, diagnoses his or her illness, and sends the patient off with a prescription. The doctor then returns to the receptionist to collect another patient. The example is a modified version of that specified in [Potts 89].

Figure 9 gives the top-level decomposition in which the practice is divided into two components, the surgery and the patients. The component is parameterized with the number of doctors in the practice ndoc and the number of patients to be treated npat before the program terminates. The Darwin program is annotated with information on how the practice component is to be executed in a distributed environment. The component surgery is to be instantiated on the machine named skid and patients on bench. By default, if a location for an instance is not specified with the @loc annotation, the instance is located with its enclosing component. The surgery is constructed from

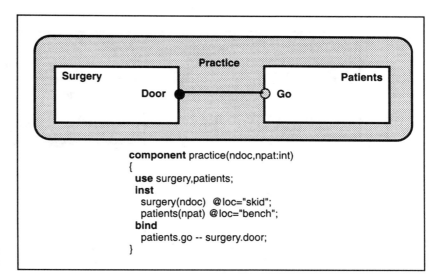

```
component practice(ndoc,npat:int)
{
  use surgery,patients;
  inst
    surgery(ndoc)  @loc="skid";
    patients(npat) @loc="bench";
  bind
    patients.go -- surgery.door;
}
```

Figure 9. GP's group practice.

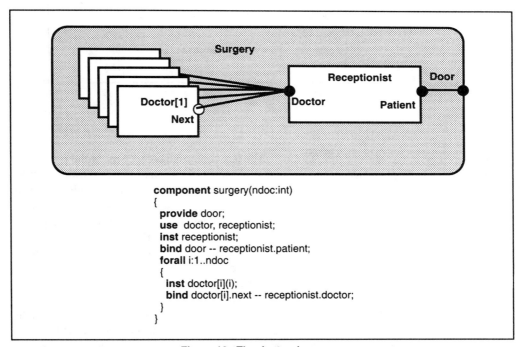

```
component surgery(ndoc:int)
{
  provide door;
  use  doctor, receptionist;
  inst receptionist;
  bind door -- receptionist.patient;
  forall i:1..ndoc
  {
    inst doctor[i](i);
    bind doctor[i].next -- receptionist.doctor;
  }
}
```

Figure 10. The doctors' surgery.

the process types doctor and receptionist as shown in Figure 10. The receptionist process provides two ports (doctor and patient) on which are queued respectively, free doctor processes and sick patient processes that have "entered" through the door of the surgery. Note that interfaces to Darwin composite components are specified using **provide** and **require** in precisely the same way that process interfaces are specified. Composite component interfaces are implemented by binding them to a process instance port. For example in Figure 10 door is bound to receptionist.patient.

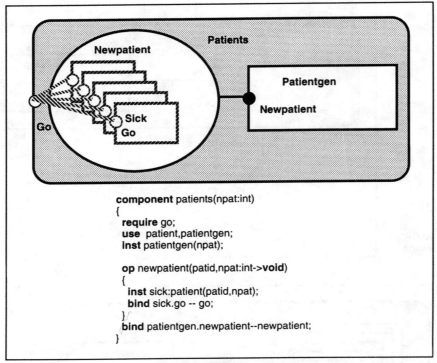

```
component patients(npat:int)
{
  require go;
  use  patient,patientgen;
  inst patientgen(npat);

  op newpatient(patid,npat:int->void)
  {
    inst sick:patient(patid,npat);
    bind sick.go -- go;
  }
  bind patientgen.newpatient--newpatient;
}
```

Figure 11. The patients.

```
process patientgen(npat:integer);
require newpatient;
var
  newpatient: ->integer,integer->void;
  i:integer;
begin
  for i:= 1 to npat do
  begin
    delay(1 * seconds);
    newpatient!(i,npat->void);
  end;
end.
```

Figure 12. Patient generator process.

The last composite component in the program is the set of patients. This component can be implemented in two different ways. We could statically declare an array of patient processes that delay for some period of time and then become sick, or we can use a patient generator task to dynamically create sick patients. We will choose the latter technique, since in addition to showing dynamic structure creation in Darwin it uses memory more efficiently. The patients component is described in Figure 11.

The patientgen process instance periodically invokes the configuration operation newpatient to create a new sick patient. Each new patient process has its requirement for a reference value (sick.go) associated with the interface requirement (go) of the patients composite component. At runtime, the required value will be a reference to the receptionist's port receptionist.patient. Configuration operations are invoked by the normal Rex message passing operation as shown (see Figure 12) in the code for the patient generator process. Void indicates that a message is returned from the configuration operation for synchronization purposes; however, it contains no information. The newpatient reference variable type of Figure 12 is thus used to send a message consisting of two integers and a reference to a port used only for synchronization. The

```
process patient(id:name; npat:integer);
require go;
var
    go: ->name,illness->prescription;
    I:illness; P:prescription;
begin
    writeln("patient ",id:1," Sick");
    I:=id*id;              {illness is arbitrarily denoted  by id² }
    go!(id,I->P);
    writeln("patient ",id:1," got Prescription ",P:1);
    If id=npat then halt;
end.
```

Figure 13. Patient process.

synchronization port in the example is not declared explicitly. It is provided by the compiler for the operation:

newpatient!(i,npat->**void**).

An alternative but semantically identical declaration for newpatient would be:

newpatient: @**port**(integer,integer,@**port**()).

The remaining three process types share the following type definitions:

```
type
    name        = integer;
    illness     = integer;
    prescription = integer;
```

The **patient** process of Figure 13 simply sends a message consisting of the name of the patient and his/her illness and then waits for the prescription. The last patient process created by the patient generator terminates the distributed program when id = npat.

The **doctor** process of Figure 14, contains the most complex port type description we have yet introduced. This may be easily understood with the aid of the message sequence chart of Figure 14, which is really just an alternative way of laying out the type declaration. The doctor process sends a synchronization message to the receptionist consisting of a reference to its own implicit port. The receptionist replies with the details of a patient, such as name, illness, and a prescription port reference. The doctor returns a prescription directly to the patient using the prescription reference. The alternative syntax for the port reference variable next would be:

next: @**port**(@**port**(name,illness, @**port**(prescription)))

The remaining **receptionist** process acts as a mailbox (Figure 15). On one side there is a queue of sick patients and on the other, a queue of free doctors. The **receptionist** repeatedly gets a patient and forwards it to a doctor for diagnosis. The *General practitioner's group practice* is an example of a multiserver system, with the patients as clients and the doctors as servers. The server processes could just as easily return a reference to a record of ports representing a file access interface, for

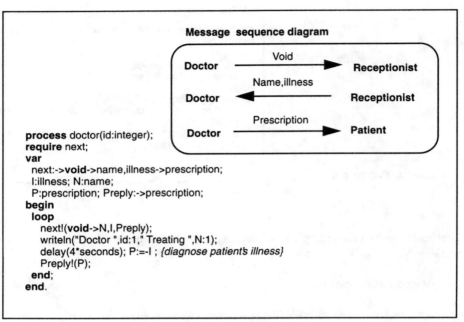

```
                        Message sequence diagram

                                    Void
            Doctor    ────────────────────►   Receptionist

                               Name,illness
            Doctor    ◄────────────────────    Receptionist

                              Prescription
            Doctor    ────────────────────►   Patient


process doctor(id:integer);
require next;
var
  next:->void->name,illness->prescription;
  I:illness; N:name;
  P:prescription; Preply:->prescription;
begin
 loop
   next!(void->N,I,Preply);
   writeln("Doctor ",id:1," Treating ",N:1);
   delay(4*seconds); P:=-I ; {diagnose patient's illness}
   Preply!(P);
 end;
end.
```

Figure 14. Doctor process.

```
process receptionist;
provide doctor,patient;
var
  doctor: port(void->name,illness->prescription);
  patient:port(name,illness->prescription);
  I:illness; N:integer; Preply:->prescription;
begin
 loop
   patient?(N,I,Preply);
   doctor?(void->N,I,Preply);
 end;
```

Figure 15. Receptionist process.

example. The reader who has attempted to program a multiserver in a language such as Ada [DoD 83] or Occam [Inmos 88] (or even REX's predecessor CONIC [Magee 89]) will appreciate the elegance of the program.

Composition as an alternative to inheritance

The modularity of the previous example means that it would be trivial to replace the doctors' surgery with a single doctor process. However, this doctor process would not have precisely the same form as the program of Figure 14 since it would not require the receptionist access protocol. The single or lone doctor program is described in Figure 16.

Suppose we had started with the lonedoctor process and then wished to reuse its functionality in the multidoctor surgery. In a sequential, object-oriented system such as Smalltalk, we would make groupdoctor a subclass of lonedoctor and thus let it inherit the functionality of lonedoctor, that is, lonedoctor **class** groupdoctor {.....}. In Darwin, the same effect is achieved by composition as shown in Figure 17. The process raccess provides the additional receptionist access protocol necessary to let lonedoctor work in the surgery environment. Note that groupdoctor has precisely the same functionality as the doctor process of Figure 14. Admittedly, this is less elegant than the inheritance mechanism. However, it is difficult to see how the inheritance mechanism would deal with the composition of synchronization in other than simple

```
process lonedoctor(id:integer);
require next;
var
  patient:port(name,illness->prescription);
  I:illness; N:name;
  P:prescription; Preply:->prescription;
begin
  loop
    patient?(N,I,Preply);
    writeln("Doctor ",id:1," Treating ",N:1);
            delay(4*seconds); P:=-I ; {diagnose patient's illness}
    Preply!(P);
  end;
end.
```

Figure 16. Lonedoctor process.

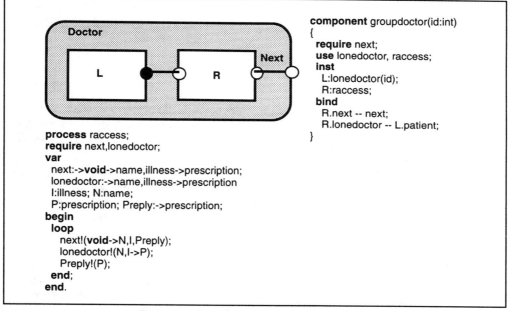

```
process raccess;
require next,lonedoctor;
var
  next:->void->name,illness->prescription;
  lonedoctor:->name,illness->prescription
  I:illness; N:name;
  P:prescription; Preply:->prescription;
begin
  loop
    next!(void->N,I,Preply);
    lonedoctor!(N,I->P);
    Preply!(P);
  end;
end.
```

```
component groupdoctor(id:int)
{
  require next;
  use lonedoctor, raccess;
  inst
    L:lonedoctor(id);
    R:raccess;
  bind
    R.next -- next;
    R.lonedoctor -- L.patient;
}
```

Figure 17. Constructed groupdoctor program.

cases. For instance, the Guide language [Decouchant 91] supports inheritance by replacing synchronization constraints rather than composing them.

Guarded configuration programs

Now that we have the lone doctor process of Figure 16, it would be sensible to use it, rather than the surgery component when the parameter of the practice program ndoc=1. This avoids the overhead of the receptionist in a single doctor surgery. This can be accomplished using the Darwin **when** construct as shown in Figure 18.

Recursive configuration programs

Guards are also required to terminate recursive configuration programs. Recursive configurations

```
component practice(ndoc,npat:int)
{
  use surgery,patients,lonedoctor;
  inst patients(npat) @loc="bench";
  when ndoc==1 {
    inst lonedoctor(1) @loc="skid";
    bind patients.go — lonedoctor.patient;
  }
  when ndoc>1 {
    inst surgery(ndoc) @loc="skid";
    bind patients.go — surgery.door;
  }
}
```

Figure 18. Guarded practice program.

are commonly used to describe regular structures such as trees. Figure 19 is the Darwin description of a binary tree of component instances of type node. RightTree and LeftTree are both instances of the enclosing type BinTree giving the recursive structure definition.

Synchronous message-passing primitives (where the sending process blocks until the message has been received) have been used in the above examples. Where possible, the process component compiler optimizes communication by indicating where interprocessor acknowledgments are not required, like in the case of remote rendezvous (request reply) communication. REX also provides an asynchronous-send primitive, and mechanisms to enable reliable message passing transactions to be programmed where these are not supported by the underlying communication transport system. The examples presented in this section have been executed on both a parallel, transputer-based machine and on a network of Sun 4 workstations.

Conclusions

Object-oriented programming has lead to a proliferation of literature, languages, tools, and unfortunately, hyperbole comparable only with that of structured programming. A reasoned and careful evaluation is necessary to extract the real benefits that OOP offers, especially if one seeks to extend it to cater for concurrency and distribution as well.

In this paper we have briefly discussed conventional OOP and found it wanting in its support for describing program configuration or structure. We have discussed the key issues that impact its use in a distributed environment — concurrency control, object interfaces, binding and inheritance — pointing out the relative merits of current solutions to these issues. For instance, most object-oriented languages do not support explicit interfaces of services *required* by an object, only those services offered. We believe that both are often needed for management purposes and to fully identify object functionality.

We have introduced and illustrated the utility of our configuration-oriented programming approach, based on the use of a separate and explicit configuration language to define program structure as a set of active objects (components) with explicit interfaces and bindings, together with the ability to compose them hierarchically to build up more complex components. This provides an alternative to inheritance for reuse of behavior in distributed systems.

In the discussion of object concurrency and interaction, we made the distinction between the threads and active (process) object models, and indicated our preference for the latter. Conventional OOP with inheritance does not scale for large, distributed applications, but is still appropriate as a programming technique for individual sequential components. Furthermore it seems appropriate that it should be possible to pass simple objects (with their state and behavior) in messages and as invocation parameters. This provides a powerful yet practical means of communication, even in a distributed environment. Since the port interface specifies the types of object that it can accept or produce, it can ensure that the behavior for communicated objects is also available and need not be sent.

The REX work is heavily based on Conic, which we have had extensive experience with for a number of years. This has provided us with convincing evidence of the utility of the configuration approach for distributed program design [Kramer 90a], construction [Magee 89], evolution

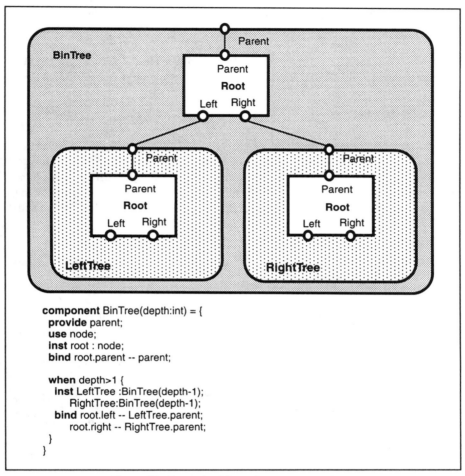

```
component BinTree(depth:int) = {
  provide parent;
  use node;
  inst root : node;
  bind root.parent -- parent;

  when depth>1 {
    inst LeftTree :BinTree(depth-1);
        RightTree:BinTree(depth-1);
    bind root.left -- LeftTree.parent;
        root.right -- RightTree.parent;
  }
}
```

Figure 19. Recursive binary tree component.

[Kramer 90b], and management using graphic tools such as ConicDraw [Kramer 89]. However, a number of limitations to Conic and its implementation have also been recognized. It provided support for *post hoc* evolutionary change, but no linguistic support for dynamic programmed change where the configuration changes are embedded in the configuration description (as illustrated in the patients component). Component interfaces in Conic are simpler, and do not support grouping ports as interfaces. The communications primitives in Conic were tailored for asynchronous and rendezvous communication, but were not sufficiently flexible in dealing with more complex interactions such as those illustrated in the receptionist component. Finally, there is no integrated support for components written in different programming languages. These limitations are being addressed in REX and its configuration language, Darwin.

The current status of the work is that a compiler that translates Darwin into C has been implemented and the communication primitives have been embedded in components written in C, C++, and Pascal. Colleagues in the REX project are embedding the primitives in other languages such as Modula 2.

Some particular aspects of megaprogramming have been neglected. For instance, persistence and atomicity of objects and actions is beyond the scope of this paper, but there is promising research in this area (see Arjuna [Shrivastava 89]). Nevertheless, we believe that configuring object-based distributable programs offers a realistic framework to provide the necessary support for large distributed systems.

Acknowledgments

Acknowledgment is made to our colleagues at Imperial College (Steve Crane, Essie Cheung, Anthony Finkelstein, Keng Ng, and Kevin Twidle) and also to our partners in the REX project (at T.U. Berlin, GMD Karlsruhe, Siemens, Stollman, Karlsruhe University and 2i in Germany, Intracom and Intrasoft in Greece, Tecsi in France, and PRG Oxford in the UK) for their contribution to the work described in this paper. We gratefully acknowledge the SERC under grant GE/F/04605 and the CEC in the REX Project (2080) for their financial support.

References

[Agha 86]   G. Agha, *Actors: A Model of Concurrent Computation in Distributed Systems*, MIT Press, Cambridge, Mass., 1986.

[Barbacci 88] M.R. Barbacci, C.B. Weinstock, and J.M. Wing, "Programming at the Processor-Memory Switch Level," *Proc. 10th IEEE Int'l Conf. Software Eng.*, IEEE Computer Soc. Press, Los Alamitos, Calif., 1988.

[DeRemer 76]   F. DeRemer and H.H. Kron. "Programming-in-the-Large versus Programming-in-the-Small," *IEEE Trans. Software Eng.*, Vol. SE-2, No. 2, June 1976.

[Decouchant 91] D. Decouchant et al., "A Synchronisation Mechanism for an Object-Oriented Distributed System," *Bull-IMAG*, Rapport Technique 9-9, Mar. 1991.

[DoD 83]   Department of Defense, U.S., *Reference Manual for the Ada Programming Language*, ANSI/MIL-STD-1815A, DoD, Washington, D.C., Jan. 1983.

[Goguen 86]   J.A. Goguen. "Reusing and Interconnecting Software Components," *Computer*, Vol. 19, No. 2, Feb. 1986.

[Inmos 88]]   Inmos Ltd., *OCCAM 2 Reference Manual*, Prentice Hall, Englewood Cliffs, N.J., 1988.

[Jackson 83]   M.A. Jackson, *System Development*, Prentice Hall, Englewood Cliffs, N.J., 1983.

[Kaplan 88]   S. Kaplan and G. Kaiser, "Garp: Graph Abstractions for Concurrent Programming," *ESOP '88*, Springer-Verlag, New York, 1988, pp. 191-205.

[Kramer 85]   J. Kramer and J. Magee, "Dynamic Configuration for Distributed Systems," *IEEE Trans. Software Eng.*, Vol. SE-11, No. 4, Apr. 1985, pp. 424-436.

[Kramer 89]   J. Kramer, J. Magee, and K. Ng, "Graphical Configuration Programming," *Computer*, Vol. 22, No. 10, Oct. 1989, pp. 53-65.

[Kramer 90a]   J. Kramer, J. Magee, and A. Finkelstein, "A Constructive Approach to the Design of Distributed Systems," *Proc. 10th Int'l Conf. Distributed Computing Systems*, IEEE Computer Soc. Press, Los Alamitos, Calif., 1990, pp. 580-587.

[Kramer 90b]   J. Kramer and J. Magee, "The Evolving Philosopher's Problem: Dynamic Change Management," *IEEE Trans. Software Eng.*, Vol. SE-16, No. 11, Nov. 1990, pp. 1293-1306.

[Leblanc 82]   R.J. Leblanc and A.B. MacCabe, "The Design of a Programming Language Based on a Connectivity Network," *Proc. Third Int'l Conf. Distributed Computing Systems*, IEEE Computer Soc. Press, Los Alamitos, Calif., 1992.

[LeBlanc 85]   T. LeBlanc and S. Friedberg, "HPC: A Model of Structure and Change in Distributed Systems," *IEEE Trans. Computers*, Vol. C-34, No. 12, Dec. 1985.

[Lee 86]   I. Lee, N. Prywes, and B. Szymanski, "Partitioning of Massive/Real-Time Programs for Parallel Processing," *Advances in Computers*, M.C. Yovits, ed., Academic Press, San Diego, Calif., 1986.

[Magee 89]   J. Magee, J. Kramer, and M. Sloman, "Constructing Distributed Systems in Conic," *IEEE Trans. Software Eng.* Vol. SE-15, No. 6, June 1989.

[Magee 90]   J. Magee et al., "An Overview of the REX Software Architecture," *Proc. Second IEEE Computer Soc. Workshop Future Trends Distributed Computer Systems*, IEEE Computer Soc. Press, Los Alamitos, Calif., 1990.

[Nehmer 87]   J. Nehmer et al., "Key Concepts of the INCAS Multicomputer Project," *IEEE Trans. Software Eng.*, Vol. SE-13, No. 8, Aug. 1987.

[Nierstrasz 87] O.M. Nierstrasz, "Active Objects in Hybrid," *Proc. OOPSLA*, ACM Press, New York, N.Y., 1987.

[Page-Jones 88] M. Page-Jones, *Practical Guide to Structured Systems Design*, Prentice Hall Int'l Eds., Englewood Cliffs, N.J., 1988.

[Potts 89]   C. Potts, "Succeedings of the 5th International Workshop on Specification and Design," *ACM SIGSoft, Software Eng. Notes*, Vol. 14, No. 5, July 1989, pp 35-42.

[Purtilo 88]   J. Purtilo, "A Software Interconnection Technology," Tech. Report-2139, Computer Science Dept., Univ. of Maryland, Md., 1988.

[Raj 89]   R.K. Raj and H.M. Levy, "A Compositional Model for Software Reuse," *The Computer J.*, Vol. 32, No. 4, 1989, pp. 312-322.

[REX 89]   REX Technical Annexe, *ESPRIT Project 2080*, European Economic Commission, Mar. 1989.

[Steigerwald 90] R. Steigerwald, "Concurrent Programming in Smalltalk-80," *ACM SIGPlan Notices*, Vol. 25, No. 8, Aug. 1990, pp. 27-36.

[Shrivastava 89] S.K. Shrivastava, G.N. Dixon, and G.D. Partington, "An Overview of Arjuna, A Programming System for Reliable Distributed Computing," Tech. Report 298, Computing Laboratory, Univ. of Newcastle-upon-Tyne, United Kingdom, Nov. 1989.

[Wegner 87]   P. Wegner, "Dimensions of Object-Based Language Design," *Proc. OOPSLA*, ACM Press, New York, N.Y., 1987.

[Wegner 90]   P. Wegner, "Concepts and Paradigms of Object-Oriented Programming," *OOPS Messenger (ACM SIGPlan)*, Vol. 1, No. 1, Aug. 1990, pp. 7-87.

[Yonezawa 86]   A. Yonezawa, J.P. Briot, and E. Shibayama, "Object-Oriented Programming in ABCL/1," *ACM SIGPlan Notices*, Vol. 21, No. 11, Nov. 1986, pp. 258-268.

CHAPTER 5

Fault Tolerance and Crash Recovery

Probabilistic Diagnosis of
Multiprocessor Systems

Sunggu Lee and

Kang G. Shin

T he progress made in the development of powerful single-chip processors (and even single-chip multiprocessors) has led to the construction of increasingly sophisticated multiprocessor systems with tens of thousands of processing elements (PEs). Suppose that the mean-time-to-failure (MTTF) of a PE is 10 years and that the distribution of failure interarrival times is Poisson. Then, a system with 10,000 PEs can expect to have 952 faulty PEs after one year. An example of a modern multiprocessor with a large number of PEs is the Connection Machine — built by Thinking Machines Corporation — which has 64K PEs. With this many PEs, we can expect to have 6,090 faulty PEs after one year.

Thus, it is imperative that multiprocessor systems with large numbers of PEs be provided with good fault-tolerance capabilities. In addition, in order to maintain a highly reliable system, faulty PEs must be diagnosed and periodically removed (either physically or by reconfiguration) from the system. In large systems with more than about 1,000 PEs, the fault diagnosis and reconfiguration tasks should be automated for efficient operation. However, the problem of identifying the faulty PEs in large systems is an extremely difficult task, especially since faulty PEs can accuse nonfaulty PEs of being faulty, PEs can be intermittently faulty, and tests to detect faulty PEs can be incomplete. Because of the difficulty of this task, methods for the diagnosis of large multiprocessor systems have traditionally relied on several restrictive assumptions about the number and type of faulty PEs and the behavior of faulty and nonfaulty PEs. In recent years, these assumptions have been removed or relaxed to produce more general and practical self-diagnosis algorithms.

Because of the large size of the systems being considered and the degree of difficulty of the problem of producing general self-diagnosis algorithms, we will consider diagnosis only at the level of a PE. This type of diagnosis is referred to as *system-level diagnosis*. A fundamental model for system-level diagnosis was developed by Preparata, Metze, and Chien [21] in 1967. In their model, referred to as the *PMC model*, it is assumed that PEs can test each other to arrive at separate conclusions about the fault status of other PEs. The system is modeled by a directed graph in which the vertices correspond to PEs and the edges correspond to inter-PE testing assignments. A *fault syndrome* is defined as a binary labeling of the directed edges, with each label representing the result of the corresponding inter-PE test. (For brevity's sake, we shorten "fault syndrome" to "syndrome" in the remainder of this paper.) As can be imagined, use of this model can lead to an extremely large number of syndromes being identified. The diagnosis subsystem is faced with the task of analyzing a syndrome to identify the set of faulty PEs. However, because of the arbitrary manner in which faulty — and even nonfaulty — PEs can evaluate other PEs, there are myriad syndromes that can result for every set of faulty PEs. Nonfaulty PEs may exhibit arbitrary behavior because of other intermittently faulty PEs or because of the use of tests that are not able to catch all faulty PEs.

The currently available methods for system-level diagnosis can be broadly categorized into *deterministic* methods and *probabilistic* methods. (Note that our use of the term *probabilistic* is different from that referred to by Maheswari and Hakimi [19]; if our categorization is used, their diagnosis model would be deterministic.) In the deterministic methods, a restriction is imposed on the set of faulty nodes (such as an upper bound on the size of the fault set) and it is guaranteed that all faulty nodes (or a well-specified subset of the fault set) are caught by the diagnosis procedure. The important issues in deterministic methods are the characterization of testing graphs in which a given type of fault set can be diagnosed; the procedures for determining the number or type of faulty nodes that can be diagnosed, given a testing graph; and the procedures for identifying the fault set. In the probabilistic methods, no restrictions (other than perhaps allowing only permanently faulty nodes) are placed on the fault set. Instead, a probability model is used to model the behavior of faulty and nonfaulty nodes; based on this model, a procedure — which may be heuristic — is used to identify a set of nodes as faulty based on the syndrome observed. The important issues in probabilistic methods are the complexity of the diagnosis procedure and the "quality" of the diagnoses obtained. These methods frequently use probability parameters to describe the probabilistic behavior of nonfaulty and faulty nodes and to evaluate the quality of the diagnoses produced. Because deterministic system-level diagnosis methods have been studied extensively (several good survey papers on this subject already exist [9], [11], [15]), this paper surveys and analyzes the currently available methods for probabilistic system-level diagnosis.

Preliminaries

In this section, we introduce the notation and definitions used in this paper, discuss methods for conducting the inter-PE tests required by system-level diagnosis, and describe the diagnosis classification scheme proposed in this paper.

Notation and definitions

A system S is composed of N *nodes* (processing elements), denoted by the set $V = \{u_1, ..., u_N\}$, where each node $u_i \in V$ is assigned a particular subset of the nodes in V to test. The set of testing assignments in S is represented by a directed graph $G = (V, E)$, called the *testing graph*, where vertex $u_i \in V$ represents a node (processing element) and edge $(u_i, u_j) \in E$ represents the fact that u_i tests u_j. The *fault coverage* of a test is defined as the probability that the test can detect a fault in the tested node, given that there is a fault present. Test outcomes are represented by binary variables a_{ij} such that $a_{ij} = 1$ if u_j fails u_i's test and $a_{ij} = 0$ if u_j passes u_i's test. a_{ij} is undefined if u_i does not test u_j. A syndrome SD is a function from E to $\{0, 1\}$. The function SD is defined such that for all $(u_i, u_j) \in E$, $SD((u_i, u_j)) \equiv a_{ij}$.

Figure 1 shows an example of a testing graph and a syndrome. We assume that the testing graph is a subgraph of the graph representing the interconnection structure of the system. Although it is not adopted by everyone, this assumption makes the task of testing nodes substantially easier. Thus, if the system has a point-to-point interconnection structure, then a node can test only those nodes to which it is directly connected. The testing graph of Figure 1, for example, can map directly onto a two-dimensional, torus-wrapped, mesh-interconnection topology.

On the basis of a syndrome SD, a *diagnosis* is performed when a set of nodes is identified as being faulty. The diagnosis is said to be *correct* if there are no nonfaulty nodes mistakenly identified as faulty. Otherwise, the diagnosis is said to be *incorrect*. Similarly, the diagnosis is said to be *complete* if all faulty nodes are identified as such. Otherwise, the diagnosis is said to be *incomplete*. If a diagnosis identifies the exact set of faulty nodes, then it is a *correct and complete* diagnosis. The *diagnostic accuracy* of a diagnosis algorithm refers to the percentage of diagnoses

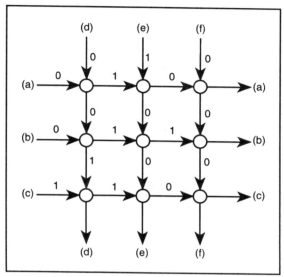

Figure 1. An example of a testing graph and a syndrome.

produced that are both correct and complete. A diagnosis algorithm is said to be *optimal* if it results in the highest possible level of diagnostic accuracy. The set of nodes that a given node u_i tests will be denoted by (u_i). Likewise, the set of nodes that test u_i will be denoted by $\Gamma^{-1}(u_i)$, where $\Gamma^{-1}(u_i) = \Gamma_1^{-1}(u_i) \cup \Gamma_0^{-1}(u_i)$ and $\Gamma_k^{-1}(u_i) = \{u_j \in \Gamma^{-1}(u_i) : a_{ji} = k\}$, $k = 0, 1$.

Testing

One of the most generally accepted methods for system-level testing is *comparison testing*. In comparison testing, in order for node u_i to test another node u_j, identical application tasks are executed on the two nodes. The test result is a 1 if and only if u_i and u_j produce different results. Likewise, the test result is a 1 if and only if u_i and u_j produce different results when u_j tests u_i. Thus, comparison testing requires only an undirected testing graph model.

Another practical method of system-level testing is *on-line processor monitoring*. In the on-line processor-monitoring method of Blough and Masson [4], a simple hardware device was used to repeatedly capture a block of data from the tested node; then, the data were analyzed on the testing node for the presence of an error. Indications of abnormal behavior in the captured data block signaled a faulty processor. Alternatively, one can consider creating a system task that snoops on the packets coming in and going out of a node. The task examines the packet formats and checks whether or not they conform to the standard. The error rates detected in the packets and the traffic volume can be monitored to decide whether or not the node from which the packets originated is faulty. Also, to detect communication link failures and node crashes, a status monitor task can be established on each node to periodically exchange data with neighboring nodes.

Finally, a low-level self-testing method can be used. In this method, each node performs a self-test and stores the result of the self-test in a special fault status register. When a node wishes to test a neighboring node, it simply reads the special fault status register of the node to be tested. Note that in the use of this testing method, a separate diagnosis procedure is not even necessary if there is a method of reliably distributing the results of the self-tests to all of the nodes. Note also that this method simply relegates the testing problem to a lower level.

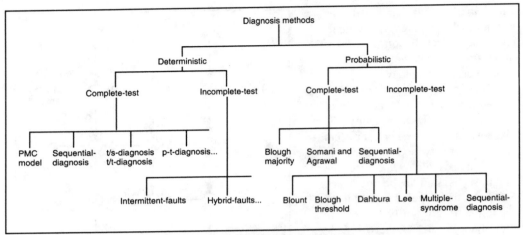

Figure 2. Classification of diagnosis methods.

This paper uses a directed testing graph model so that all system-level testing methods can be included in the testing model. Note that in the presence of intermittently faulty nodes, none of the testing methods described can achieve close to 100-percent fault coverage.

Classification of system-level diagnosis methods

Figure 2 shows the classification of diagnosis methods proposed in this paper. Deterministic-diagnosis methods can be classified into *complete-test* methods and *incomplete-test* methods. In the complete-test methods, it is assumed that the system-level tests conducted by one node on another node have complete (100-percent) fault coverage. This restriction is removed in the incomplete-test methods. The complete-test methods include the PMC model and diagnosis method [21], sequential-diagnosis methods based on the PMC model [14], [21], and several methods using generalizations of the PMC model. The incomplete-test methods include methods for handling intermittent-fault and hybrid-fault situations, which are explicitly bounded combinations of intermittently and permanently faulty nodes [20]. (The interested reader is referred to Dahbura [9], Friedman and Simoncini [11], and Kime [15] for authoritative surveys on deterministic-diagnosis methods.)

Probabilistic-diagnosis methods are also classified into *complete-test* methods and *incomplete-test* methods. The complete-test methods assume inter-PE tests with 100-percent fault coverage, while the incomplete-test methods assume that inter-PE tests can have less than 100-percent fault coverage. Assuming possibly incomplete inter-PE tests is equivalent to permitting intermittent faults from a system-level-diagnosis viewpoint [3]. This is because if a node u_j is intermittently faulty, then any nonfaulty node u_i that tests u_j may evaluate u_j to be faulty or nonfaulty, depending on the status of u_j during the test. Additionally, u_j can arbitrarily evaluate any nodes that it tests, since it is faulty. The same statement can be made if u_j is assumed to be permanently faulty, but the tests performed upon u_j are incomplete.

Preliminary discussion of probabilistic diagnosis

Probabilistic-diagnosis methods do not make any prior assumptions about the set of faulty nodes and, in general, can be used with arbitrary testing graphs. As a consequence, probabilistic methods cannot guarantee that a correct and complete diagnosis is made. Thus, the quality of the diagnosis methods must be substantiated by other means.

Three arguments used to support probabilistic-diagnosis algorithms are

(1)   Using analysis to show that high diagnostic accuracy is achieved in certain situations;
(2)   Guaranteeing that the set of nodes most likely to be faulty, given the syndrome, is found; and
(3)   Showing that as the number of nodes in the system grows to infinity, diagnostic accuracy approaches 100 percent.

While (2)—guaranteeing the most probable diagnosis—is the most appealing, it has been shown that finding the most probable diagnosis, given the global syndrome information, is an NP-hard problem [3], [17]. From a practical perspective, (3) is insufficient, as good diagnostic accuracy is desired for finite systems. However, since automated diagnosis is particularly important for large systems, asymptotically correct and complete diagnosis is certainly a desirable property of any probabilistic-diagnosis algorithm. All three arguments have been used to support the probabilistic-diagnosis methods surveyed in this paper.

Probabilistic-diagnosis methods have two serious limitations that must be understood before one attempts to use the methods. First, probabilistic methods usually require the use of probability parameters to model the behavior of faulty and nonfaulty nodes and to evaluate the quality of the diagnoses produced. The issue of obtaining these probability parameter values in real computer systems is an important, unsolved problem that needs to be investigated. However, some of the diagnosis methods described in this paper can be implemented without one knowing the probability parameter values or with one having imprecise, estimated values; in these diagnosis methods, the probability parameters are used primarily for analyzing the diagnosis algorithms. A second limitation of all of the incomplete-test probabilistic-diagnosis methods described in this paper is that they assume that the results of inter-PE tests performed by different nodes are statistically independent. However, since most of the diagnosis methods described here permit arbitrary behavior of the faulty nodes, statistically dependent test results of faulty nodes do not negate the usefulness of the diagnosis methods, although such results may lower the level of diagnostic accuracy produced.

Probabilistic methods differ in the types of probability parameters used and in the probability model used to define the probability of occurrence of particular syndromes. Below, we discuss the different ways in which probability parameters and models are used in probabilistic-diagnosis methods.

Testing models

A *testing model* describes the test outcomes that are possible, given that the testing and tested nodes are faulty and nonfaulty. Friedman and Simoncini [11] presented a complete tabulation of all of the nonequivalent testing models. The most general testing model, referred to as the *0-information tester*, is one in which all test outcomes are possible, regardless of the fault statuses of the testing and tested nodes. This testing model was actually used by Blount [8] to produce a diagnosis method that guaranteed the most probable diagnosis but had exponential computational complexity.

For the 0-information tester model, the probability parameters that describe the possible values of a_{ij}, given different fault statuses of u_i and u_j, are given in Table 1. The fault status of u_k ($k = i$ or j) is denoted by δ_k (for u_k is faulty) and δ'_k (for u_k is nonfaulty). Let $fs_i \in \{\delta_i, \delta'_i\}$ and $fs_j \in \{\delta_j, \delta'_j\}$. All possible combinations of fs_i, fs_j, and $a_{ij} = m$ values are shown along with $P(a_{ij} = m \mid fs_i, fs_j)$ in each of these combinations, where $m = 0$ or 1. Thus, p_{ij} is the probability that a nonfaulty node u_i will correctly diagnose a faulty node u_j. Hence, under a permanent fault model and assuming that all possible faults within a node are equally likely, p_{ij} is the fault coverage of the test applied by u_i on u_j. For ease of notation, p_{ij} will be referred to as fault coverage, even when intermittent faults are permitted. r_{ij} and s_{ij} are the probabilities of a faulty node correctly diagnosing a nonfaulty node and a faulty node, respectively. As explained by Blount [8], r_{ij} and s_{ij} can model the extent to which a faulty node u_i can

Table 1. Probability parameters for the 0-information tester model.

fs_i	fs_j	m	$P\,(a_{ij} = m \mid fs_i, fs_j)$
δ'_i	δ'_j	0	q_{ij}
δ'_i	δ'_j	1	$1 - q_{ij}$
δ'_i	δ_j	1	p_{ij}
δ'_i	δ_j	0	$1 - p_{ij}$
δ_i	δ'_j	0	r_{ij}
δ_i	δ'_j	1	$1 - r_{ij}$
δ_i	δ_j	1	s_{ij}
δ_i	δ_j	0	$1 - s_{ij}$

pass judgment on u_j. The two parameters r_{ij} and s_{ij} are useful in modeling the behavior of faulty nodes. Finally, the parameter q_{ij} is meant to model the possibility of a faulty link between two nonfaulty nodes u_i and u_j corrupting the test a_{ij}.

Most probabilistic-diagnosis methods use a testing model that is more restrictive than the 0-information tester model. In the commonly used *partial-test model*, the restriction $q_{ij} = 1$ is used. This implies that a nonfaulty node must always evaluate another nonfaulty node that it tests to be nonfaulty. Since the only way for $q_{ij} < 1$ is with a faulty testing link, the use of the partial-test model is justified if the testing link (u_i, u_j) is assumed to be part of the node u_j. Another restriction that is sometimes used is $p_{ij} = 1$; this results in a complete-test model.

Let f_i denote the prior fault probability of u_i. In many of the diagnosis algorithms, all nodes and all tests are treated identically; when this is the case, fixed values are assumed for the prior fault probability of a node, test fault coverage, and other parameters. Fixed probability parameter values are denoted by the corresponding letters, without subscripts. Thus, for example, f and p refer to the average f_i and p_{ij} values, respectively.

Probability models

A probability model is characterized by defining a *probability space*, which is a triple (Ω, Θ, P), where Ω is the *sample space*, Θ is the *event space*, and P is a *probability measure*. The probability model that is most often used, implicitly or explicitly, in most probabilistic methods, is referred to as the *common probability model*. In this model, the sample space Ω is defined as the set of all possible syndrome and fault set pairs, given a testing graph $G = (V, E)$. Formally,

$$\Omega = \{(SD, F) : F \subseteq V \text{ and where } SD \text{ is a function from } E \text{ to } \{0, 1\}\}$$

Then, the event space Θ is taken to be the set of all possible subsets of Ω. The probability measure P is easily defined using the probability parameters defined above by assuming that all nodes in the set F are faulty and all nodes in the set $V - F$ are nonfaulty. If the 0-information tester is used, all possible syndrome and fault set pairs can have a finite probability value. However, if the partial-test or complete-test model is used, then certain syndrome and fault set pairs will have a zero probability value. As an example—under both testing models—consider a situation in which $u_i, u_j \in V - F$ and $SD((u_i, u_j)) \equiv a_{ij} = 1$ can never occur; in this example, the probability of such a syndrome and fault set pair is zero.

Blough [3] introduced a probability model that is more general than the common probability model. Blough modeled the behavior of faulty nodes not by the parameters r_{ij} and s_{ij} defined above,

Table 2. Pros and cons of three probability models.

Probability model	Pros	Cons
Common	• Exact analysis and optimal diagnosis possible	• Requires estimates of how faulty nodes behave • Exponential computational complexity for optimal diagnosis
Lee [17]	• Exact analysis and optimal diagnosis possible, given partial syndrome information	• Requires estimates of how faulty nodes behave • Limits syndrome information used
Blough [3]	• No parameterization of behavior of faulty nodes	• Exact analysis not possible • Many indistinguishable algorithms • Optimal diagnosis not possible

but rather by assuming that faulty nodes behave in the manner most detrimental to the diagnosis algorithm. In Blough's model, the sample space Ω is the same as that for the common model. However, the basic events of the model are defined to consist of all sets of syndrome and fault set pairs whose syndromes are identical (except for the edges out of faulty nodes) and whose fault sets are the same. Thus, a syndrome and fault set pair (SD', F') is contained in a basic event B, where B is defined as

$$B = \{(SD, F) : F = F' \text{ and } \forall (u_i, u_j) \in E \text{ with } u_i \in V - F, SD((u_i, u_j)) = SD'((u_i, u_j))\}$$

B_{set} is defined as the set of all sets B such that B is a basic event of the testing graph G. The event space is the set of all subsets of B_{set}. In Blough's model, the probability of correct and complete diagnosis by an algorithm A is defined as the minimum of the probabilities of the syndrome and fault set pairs in the event B such that the event B contains the actual syndrome observed and the fault set F is the set of nodes diagnosed to be faulty.

Lee [17] introduced another generalization of the common probability model. He noted that most probabilistic-diagnosis methods use less than the global syndrome information in diagnosing the fault status of each node. He assumed a distributed self-diagnosis method in which each node diagnoses itself as faulty or nonfaulty based on a limited form of the global syndrome information referred to as *partial* syndrome information. A different probability space is used for the diagnosis of each node. For a given node u_i, let the partial syndrome used in the diagnosis of u_i be denoted by SD_i and let SD_i^{all} denote the set of all such partial syndromes. Then, for u_i, the sample space is defined as

$$\Omega_i = \{(SD_i, fs_i) : SD_i \in SD_i^{all}, fs_i \in \{\delta_i, \delta'_i\}\}$$

The event space Θ_i is the set of all possible subsets of Ω_i. Finally, the definition used for the probability measure P_i is dependent on the partial syndrome information used.

There are pros and cons to all of the probability models introduced. Table 2 summarizes the pros and cons of the three probability models discussed above: the common probability model, Lee's probability model, and Blough's probability model.

With the use of the common probability model, an exact evaluation can be made of the posterior fault probability of each fault set, given a syndrome. Thus, it is possible to come up with a diagnosis algorithm that guarantees that the most probable diagnosis is made. Such a diagnosis algorithm can be shown to be optimal in diagnostic accuracy [3]. However, since finding the most probable diagnosis is NP-hard, this diagnosis algorithm has exponential computational complexity.

With the use of Lee's probability model [17], it is possible to produce the most probable diagnosis, given partial syndrome information, using a polynomial-time algorithm. Also, it can be shown that such a diagnosis algorithm is optimal in diagnostic accuracy among all diagnosis algorithms that use the same type of partial syndrome information. However, a limitation of both the common probability model and Lee's probability model is the requirement that the behavior of both nonfaulty and faulty nodes must be known or estimated, in terms of the probability parameters, before any probability analysis can be done.

The main advantage of Blough's probability model [3] is that the behavior of faulty nodes does not have to be parameterized before the model can be used. However, this results in many diagnosis algorithms that produce different diagnosis results all being evaluated as equal. Thus, Blough's model cannot distinguish between two diagnosis algorithms, one of which may perform significantly better than the other in terms of diagnostic accuracy. It follows that with Blough's model, exact probability analysis and optimal diagnosis are not possible. With his probability model, Blough makes statements regarding only the *asymptotic* (or upper-bound) behavior of various diagnosis algorithms.

General asymptotic results

Blough [3] presented several important results concerning the asymptotic behavior of diagnosis algorithms. *Asymptotic diagnostic accuracy* refers to the limiting value of the diagnostic accuracy of an algorithm, given that the number of nodes in the system is increased to infinity while the original testing graph structure is retained. While Blough used his own probability model, his asymptotic results extend to the other probability models discussed above.

The first set of his results addressed conditions under which no diagnosis algorithm is able to produce asymptotically correct and complete diagnosis. Blough [3] proved that if the number of edges in the testing graph grows slower than the number of nodes N, then the diagnostic accuracy of all diagnosis algorithms approaches zero. This is intuitively obvious, because isolated nodes must exist if the number of edges grows slower than N. A *regular* graph is a graph in which the number of edges adjacent to a vertex is the same for all vertices in the graph. Blough [3] proved that for regular testing graphs, the diagnostic accuracy of any diagnosis algorithm approaches zero as $N \rightarrow \infty$, if the number of testing edges grows slower than $N \log N$. Recently, Berman and Pelc [1] showed that this same result holds true for general testing graphs.

In addition, other investigators have obtained findings regarding conditions under which diagnosis algorithms can produce 100-percent-accurate diagnosis [3], [7], [23]. Their findings are given in the description of the various probabilistic-diagnosis methods in the next section.

Description of probabilistic-diagnosis methods

In this section, we give an overview of the methods available in the literature for probabilistic system-level diagnosis. A running example based on the testing graph and the syndrome shown in Figure 1 is used to illustrate some of the concepts and algorithms.

Complete-test probabilistic methods

If system-level testing is assumed to have 100-percent fault coverage, then several good deterministic methods exist that can guarantee that the unique set of faulty nodes is identified, provided the number of faulty nodes is less than an upper bound t. The reason that probabilistic methods have been introduced for this problem is to permit diagnosis in situations with more than t faulty nodes and for general testing graph structures.

Scheinerman [23] presented a probabilistic-diagnosis method for the complete-test model with desirable asymptotic properties. In this algorithm, a core group of nonfaulty nodes is identified by finding a strongly connected subgraph of G in which all links are labeled with a 0 and in which more than half of the total nodes are present. Every node with a path of 0-links from this core group is then added to this group of nonfaulty nodes. All other nodes are identified as faulty. Scheinerman [23] showed that his algorithm produces asymptotically correct and complete diagnosis in random graphs in which a node is connected to another node with probability $(c \log N)/N$, where $c > [1/(1 - f)]$. Scheinerman's algorithm [23] does not work for the testing graph and the syndrome shown in Figure 1. This is because if all 1-links are removed, the remaining graph does not contain a strongly connected subgraph of more than four nodes.

Blough, Sullivan, and Masson [6] presented another probabilistic-diagnosis method for the complete-test model. In their method, each node u_i simply diagnoses itself to be faulty or nonfaulty based on the majority opinion of its testers $\Gamma^{-1}(u_i)$. Thus, u_i diagnoses itself to be faulty if and only if $|\{u_j : a_{ji} = 1 \text{ and } u_j \in \Gamma^{-1}(u_i)\}| > |\Gamma^{-1}(u_i)|/2$. Blough, Sullivan, and Masson [6] showed that asymptotically, as the side of the system grows to infinity, 100-percent-accurate diagnoses can be obtained for testing graphs in the form of hypercubes if $f < 0.0835$. In addition, they showed that asymptotically correct and complete diagnosis can be obtained for a special class of testing graphs with $N \times \omega(N)$ testing links, where $\omega(N)$ is any function that approaches infinity, albeit arbitrarily slowly.

Example 1: Let us use Blough, Sullivan, and Masson's algorithm [6] on the testing graph and the syndrome shown in Figure 1. Since u_2 and u_7 are the only nodes tested to be faulty by more than $|\Gamma^{-1}(u_i)|/2 = 1$ other node, the set of nodes diagnosed to be faulty is $F = \{u_2, u_7\}$. It is noted that this diagnosis is incomplete, because either u_5 or u_6 must be faulty since u_5 accuses u_6 of being faulty.

Somani and Agarwal [24] introduced three additional complex probabilistic-diagnosis algorithms. Each of these three algorithms is based on three steps: (1) initially identifying all nodes as being *potentially* faulty or nonfaulty, (2) using the potentially nonfaulty nodes to identify *definitely* nonfaulty nodes, and (3) using the definitely nonfaulty nodes to identify other definitely nonfaulty and faulty nodes.

In the first algorithm, majority voting is used in the first step to identify each node as potentially faulty or nonfaulty. In the second step, an iteration is used in which majority voting among the potentially nonfaulty nodes is used to identify certain nodes as definitely nonfaulty; the test results of the nodes identified as definitely nonfaulty are then used directly to identify other nodes as definitely nonfaulty or faulty. In the third step, any remaining potentially faulty and nonfaulty nodes are identified as definitely faulty and nonfaulty, respectively. The second algorithm differs from the first algorithm only in that unanimous voting among the potentially nonfaulty nodes is used to identify definitely nonfaulty nodes. The third algorithm differs from the first algorithm in that unanimous voting is used in both the first and second steps. The second and third algorithms are meant to be successively simpler algorithms than the first algorithm. Somani and Agarwal [24] used several lemmas and theorems to describe the conditions under which their algorithms can guarantee to produce correct or correct and complete diagnosis. They also used examples to show that good diagnostic accuracy is obtained for several $\sqrt{N} \times \sqrt{N}$ meshes.

Example 2: To illustrate Somani and Agarwal's algorithms [24], let us again use Figure 1 as an example. The first algorithm uses majority voting in the first step to identify $\{u_2, u_7\}$ as potentially faulty and the rest of the nodes as potentially nonfaulty. Then, using majority voting among the nodes in $V - \{u_2, u_7\}$, we obtain the set of definitely nonfaulty nodes $NF = \{u_1, u_3, u_4, u_8, u_9\}$. Using the test results of the nodes in NF, we obtain the set of definitely nonfaulty nodes $NF = NF \cup \{u_6\}$ and the set of definitely faulty nodes $F = \{u_2, u_5, u_7\}$. Using the second and third algorithms, we obtain the same diagnosis as that obtained using the first algorithm, since majority voting among one or two incoming links is the same as unanimous voting among the incoming links.

Incomplete-test probabilistic methods

Probabilistic-diagnosis methods are most useful in those situations in which nodes can be intermittently faulty and system-level tests have significantly less than 100-percent fault coverage. However, even the best probabilistic-diagnosis method is not able to produce accurate diagnosis when the percentage of faulty nodes is too large and/or the fault coverage of system-level tests is too low.

The best possible probabilistic-diagnosis method, in terms of diagnostic accuracy, is the one that guarantees that the most probable diagnosis, given the syndrome, is found. Blount [8] described an early diagnosis method for solving the problem of finding the most probable diagnosis. Blount [8] used the 0-information tester model and the common probability model to define a mapping from syndromes to fault patterns. Blount's algorithm [8] finds the syndrome SD for which $P(SD, F)$ is the maximum for each possible fault set F. This information is encoded into a lookup table. Whenever a diagnosis needs to be made from an observed syndrome, the lookup table is accessed to find the most probable diagnosis F. Given $|E|$ edges and N nodes, there are $2^{|E|}$ possible syndromes and 2^N possible fault sets. Thus, to create the lookup table, $O(2^{N+|E|})$ calculations and $O(2^{|E|})$ memory locations are required. Lee [17] used the partial-test model and the common probability model to produce a method that was more efficient than Blount's [8] in searching for the most probable diagnosis, given a syndrome. Lee [17] introduced several heuristics that made the search more efficient by bounding the search tree as early as possible. Although the average behavior of Lee's diagnosis algorithm [17] is fairly good, the worst-case computational complexity of the method is $O(2^{|F|})$, where F is the set of faulty nodes found.

Realizing the limitations of finding the most probable diagnosis, Blough, Sullivan, and Masson [5] presented an $O(|E|)$ algorithm that produces asymptotically correct and complete diagnosis, provided that the number of testing links incident on each node is greater than $\log N$. In their algorithm [5], the number of 1-links directed toward a given node u_i is compared with a threshold value. Every node in which the threshold value is exceeded is included in the fault set F. Next, all outgoing links from nodes in the set F are changed to be 1-links. Any nodes that then exceed the threshold value are included in F. This process is repeated until none of the nodes in $V - F$ exceed their respective threshold values. The property of asymptotically correct and complete diagnosis is proven with threshold values chosen as follows:

$$\forall u_i \in V, \kappa_i = (1/2) \, |\Gamma^{-1}(u_i)| \, [f + p(1 - f)]$$

Blough, Sullivan, and Masson [5] gave examples to show that this algorithm performs well for testing graphs with 100 and 1,000 nodes and several sets of probability parameter values.

Example 3: To illustrate Blough, Sullivan, and Masson's algorithm [5], we need to add the parameters f_i and p_{ij} to the testing graph and the syndrome shown in Figure 1. Let us use the fixed values $f = 0.01$ and $p = 0.9$. Then, we obtain $k_i = 0.901$ for all $u_i \in V$. Every node with one or more incoming 1-link exceeds this threshold. Thus, the set $F = \{u_2, u_5, u_7, u_8\}$ is the initial set of faulty nodes. However, after changing all of the outgoing links from F to be 1-links, every node has at least one incoming 1-link. Thus, the final fault set is $F = V$.

Dahbura, Sabnani, and King [10] gave an $O(N^2)$ probabilistic-diagnosis algorithm that is based on comparison testing. In their algorithm, they repeatedly select and remove from the testing graph a node that is incident on the largest number of 1-links, until no 1-links remain in the testing graph. Using an assumed upper bound on the number of faulty nodes, Dahbura, Sabnani, and King [10] showed that for a completely connected testing graph, the probability of misdiagnosis is extremely small. Later, upon a reanalysis of Dahbura, Sabnani, and King's algorithm [10], Lee [17] showed that this algorithm has the same desirable asymptotic properties as Blough, Sullivan, and Masson's algorithm [5]. Also, simulations showed that Dahbura, Sabnani, and King's algorithm [10] performed significantly better than Blough, Sullivan, and Masson's algorithm [5], with the threshold given above, for several different topologies and sets of probability parameter values. This demonstrates that asymptotic accuracy is not a *sufficient* measure of the goodness of a probabilistic-diagnosis algorithms.

Example 4: Applying Dahbura, Sabnani, and King's algorithm [10] to Figure 1, with $f = 0.01$ and $p = 0.9$, we find that nodes u_2 and u_7, with two incoming 1-links each, have the largest number of incoming 1-links. Arbitrarily choosing u_2 from among these nodes, the initial fault set is $F = \{u_2\}$. u_2 and its incoming and outgoing links are removed from the graph G. Next, in $G - F$, u_7 has the largest number of incoming 1-links; thus, $F = F \cup \{u_7\}$. After u_2 and u_7 have been removed from the graph G, u_5 and u_6 each have one incoming 1-link and the rest of the nodes have no incoming 1-links. Arbitrarily choosing u_5 from the set $\{u_5, u_6\}$, we obtain $F = F \cup \{u_5\} = \{u_2, u_5, u_7\}$. Finally, in the graph $G - F$, there are no 1-links, and the algorithm terminates.

Lee [17] presented another set of diagnosis algorithms. It was first noted that many of the previous probabilistic-diagnosis algorithms used only partial syndrome information in diagnosing the fault status of each node. Several categories of diagnosis were defined, based on the type of partial syndrome information used in the diagnosis of each node. Then, for each category of diagnosis, Lee's probability model was used to calculate posterior fault probability values for each node. Faulty nodes were identified based on these posterior fault probability calculations. All algorithms developed were shown to have the same desirable asymptotic properties as those of Blough's algorithm [3]. The main advantage of Lee's diagnosis algorithms is that they produce the most probable diagnosis (thus, an optimal diagnosis), given a particular type of syndrome information. The main limitation of this type of method is that the diagnosis method is dependent on the use of probability parameter values.

Two of Lee's diagnosis algorithms [17] are described here: Algorithms OPT3A and OPT2A. (His other algorithms are of similar character to these two.) In Algorithm OPT3A, each node u_i compares the number of 1-links incident on it with a threshold z_{th_i}. z_{th_i} is obtained by the following equation:

$$z_{th_i} = \frac{\log\left[\dfrac{1-f_i}{f_i}\right]}{\log\left[\dfrac{A(1-B)}{(1-A)B}\right]} + \left|\Gamma^{-1}(u_i)\right| \frac{\log\left[\dfrac{1-B}{1-A}\right]}{\log\left[\dfrac{A(1-B)}{(1-A)B}\right]}$$

where $A = (1 - f)p + fs$ and $B = f(1 - r)$. All nodes in which the threshold is exceeded are diagnosed to be faulty. In Algorithm OPT2A, each node u_i calculates its posterior fault probability assuming partial syndrome information. The fault set F is initialized to $\emptyset$. The node u_j with the highest posterior fault probability is added to F. The posterior fault probabilities of all neighbors of u_j are updated, given the knowledge that u_j is faulty. Again, the node with the highest posterior fault probability in $V - F$ is added to F. This process is repeated until all 1-links in G originate from or terminate on nodes in F.

Example 5: We again use Figure 1, with the added parameters $f = 0.01$, $p = 0.9$, and $r = s = 0.5$. Using the equation shown above, we get $A = 0.896$, $B = 0.005$, and $z_{th_i} = 1.224$. Thus, using Algorithm OPT3A, we obtain the fault set $F = \{u_2, u_7\}$. For Algorithm OPT2A, we will use intuitive calculations rather than the complex equations given by Lee [17]. Initially, nodes u_2 and u_7 will have the highest posterior fault probabilities, because u_2 and u_7 have the largest number of incident 1-links. Starting with the fault set $F = \emptyset$, first one and then the other of u_2 and u_7 are added to F. Next, we note that the nodes u_5, u_6, and u_8 each have one 1-link incident on them. However, the 1-link incident on u_8 comes from $u_7 \in F$. Thus, u_5 and u_6 are more likely to be faulty than u_8. Next, the 0-link incident on u_5 comes from the known faulty node $u_2 \in F$, while u_6's incident 0-link comes from $u_3 \in V - F$. Thus, u_5 is the node with the highest updated posterior fault probability. The final fault set is $F = \{u_2, u_5, u_7\}$, since all 1-links are accounted for by the nodes in F.

Fussell and Rangarajan [12] introduced an entirely different type of diagnosis method. Given that the testing graph is a subgraph of the graph representing the interconnection structure, the previously described incomplete-test diagnosis methods require each node to be tested by at least $\log N$ other nodes for asymptotically correct and complete diagnosis. Fussell and Rangarajan [12] improved upon previous methods by showing that the same asymptotic result can be obtained for systems with lower connectivity (for example, meshes or rings) if each pair of nodes conducts multiple tests and the number of *these* tests on each node grows faster than $\log N$. Fussell and Rangarajan's algorithm [12] uses R stages of comparison testing. In testing stage i, all nodes are assumed to execute the same test task. After a testing stage, each node compares its results with the results of all adjacent nodes. The testing link between two nodes is labeled with a 1 for that testing stage if the two nodes have different results for the test task. In this manner, R independent syndromes are obtained. Two thresholds kv_i and sv_i are used. A node u_i is identified as faulty if and only if the number of testing stages in which it had greater than kv_i 1-links incident on it is greater than the second threshold sv_i. For all nodes, $u_i \in V$, kv_i is chosen to be $|\Gamma^{-1}(u_i)| - 1$ and a range of values is indicated as being acceptable for sv_i.

Example 6: To demonstrate Fussell and Rangarajan's algorithm [12], we need several syndromes of the form shown in Figure 1. Let us assume $R = 10$ testing stages, with the first two syndromes identical to the syndrome shown in Figure 1. In the third through the tenth syndromes, suppose that $a_{25} = 1$ and that all other link labels remain unchanged. Let us choose the threshold values $kv_i = 1$ and $sv_i = 7.5$. u_2 and u_7 have $2 > kv_i$ 1-links incident on them in $10 > sv_i$ syndromes. u_5 also has $2 > kv_i$ 1-links incident on it in $8 > sv_i$ syndromes. No other nodes have two 1-links incident on them in greater than $sv_i = 7.5$ syndromes. Thus, the fault set is $F = \{u_2, u_5, u_7\}$.

Using Lee's probability model [17], Lee and Shin [18] modified Fussell and Rangarajan's algorithm [12]. Referring to the use of multiple testing stages and multiple syndromes as a *multiple-syndrome diagnosis* method, Lee and Shin [18] derived an optimal multiple-syndrome diagnosis algorithm. The only change they introduced was in the way that the thresholds kv_i and sv_i are chosen. Lee and Shin's multiple-syndrome diagnosis algorithm [18] is the same as Fussell and Rangarajan's algorithm [12], except for the choice of the kv_i and sv_i thresholds. Posterior fault probability calculations are used to derive optimal values for kv_i and sv_i. Lee and Shin's algorithm [18] shares the same desirable asymptotic properties as Fussell and Rangarajan's algorithm [12].

Similar to a multiple-syndrome diagnosis strategy is a *sequential-diagnosis strategy* for probabilistic diagnosis. In sequential diagnosis, diagnosis is conducted in stages, with nodes identified as faulty in the ith stage replaced with spares before commencing with the $(i + 1)$th stage of diagnosis. From a diagnosis viewpoint, the only difference between multiple-syndrome diagnosis and sequential diagnosis is the replacement of nodes identified as faulty in the sequential-diagnosis strategy. Blough and Pelc [7] presented four algorithms for sequential diagnosis, given the four possible combinations of complete and incomplete system-level tests and perfect and imperfect spares. With the use of their algorithms, the total number of tests required to produce asymptotically correct and complete diagnosis is $O(N)$ in the complete-test, perfect-spare model, $O(N \log N)$ in both of the intermediate models, and $O(N \log^2 N)$ in the incomplete-test, imperfect-spare model. The basic diagnosis strategy takes place in two phases. In the first phase, a core set of nonfaulty nodes NF is identified. This is followed by the second phase, in which the nonfaulty nodes are used to determine the fault status of other nodes. The nodes found to be nonfaulty are added to NF and the nodes found to be faulty are replaced by spares and tested. Multiple tests and multiple replacements of spares are used in the cases of incomplete-tests and imperfect-spares, respectively. Blough and Pelc's sequential-diagnosis algorithms [7] permit asymptotically correct and complete diagnosis using testing graphs in the form of rings and meshes.

Distributed self-diagnosis

Three general types of approaches can be identified for performing distributed self-diagnosis using a probabilistic-diagnosis model. In the first type of approach, the communication of test results is mixed in with the actual testing and diagnosis. Deterministic methods such as those in Hosseini, Kuhl, and Reddy [13] and Kuhl and Reddy [16] cannot be used in this type of model, because tests to detect faulty nodes can be incomplete. Thus, redundant copies of test results and/or partial diagnosis results must be communicated over multiple paths. The diagnosis is made by taking into account the redundant copies received. In the second type of approach, a reliable broadcast procedure is used to distribute every node's test results to every other node. After this has been done, every nonfaulty node can then execute the appropriate diagnosis algorithm to arrive at its diagnosis of the overall system. In the third type of approach, each node diagnoses the fault status of its immediate neighbors only. This requires much less communication overhead than do the alternative methods.

Berman and Pelc's diagnosis method [1] is an example of the first type of approach to distributed self-diagnosis. It is designed for a special class of testing graphs with $O(N \log N)$ edges. These graphs are built such that the nodes can be partitioned into subsets of completely connected nodes. In the first stage, diagnosis is performed within a subset of the nodes forming a complete graph. A maximum clique of nodes connected by 0-links is found and labeled as nonfaulty; all other nodes in the subset are labeled as faulty. In the second stage, all nodes in each subset of completely connected nodes receive the diagnosis results of all other nodes. The final diagnosis for a given node u_i is the majority value of the received messages on u_i. The computational complexity of this algorithm is $O(N^c)$, where c is a constant that depends on the probability parameters f and p. Berman and Pelc [1] showed that their algorithm has a diagnostic accuracy of at least $(1 - N^{-1})(100$ percent).

The second type of approach to distributed self-diagnosis is very general but requires high communication overhead. Each node must initiate a reliable broadcast procedure to broadcast its test results. This reliable broadcast procedure was described in general terms by Yang and Masson [25]. Algorithms designed for specific architectures, such as hypercubes [22], are also available. After testing has been completed, suppose that the test evaluation results of each node are combined into a single message. Up to t faulty nodes can be tolerated by having each node send $2t + 1$ copies of its message to every other node along node-disjoint paths [25]. Since there are $N(N-1)$ possible sender-receiver pairs, there are $(2t + 1)N(N - 1)$ such message transmissions. After this reliable broadcast procedure, each node can use majority voting to determine the test evaluation results of all other nodes.

The third type of approach to distributed self-diagnosis applies to those diagnosis methods that identify each node as faulty or nonfaulty based on the test evaluations of only those nodes directly connected to it. In these diagnosis methods, each node u_i must reliably receive the tests results of nodes $u_j \in \Gamma^{-1}(u_i)$. If comparison testing is being used, then no extra communication is required for diagnosis, because each node knows the results of its comparison tests with its neighbors after the testing phase. With other inter-PE testing methods, it may be necessary to execute a reliable multicast procedure in which each node sends a message reliably to all of its adjacent nodes. Although this method has extremely low communication overhead compared to the previously described methods, the diagnosis result is dispersed throughout the system. To obtain a global diagnosis, the result of the individual diagnoses must be combined.

Comparison

A large number of probabilistic-diagnosis methods have been discussed in this paper. Table 3 shows a comparison of the various diagnosis methods on the basis of several factors important to probabilistic diagnosis. The various diagnosis algorithms or sets of diagnosis algorithms are denoted in the table by acronyms based on the respective last name(s) of the author(s) and the associated reference number. The computational complexities of the FR [12] algorithm and the LS [18] algorithm are dependent on R, the number of testing stages used, and $|\Gamma^{-1}(u_i)|$, the number of nodes testing a given node u_i. The computational complexity of the BEP [1] algorithm is $O(N^c)$, where c is a constant dependent on the probability parameters f and p. The notation $Pseudo$ under the "Optimal diagnosis" column refers to the fact that these algorithms (that is, LEE2 [17] and LS [18]) produce the optimal diagnosis within a subset of the set of all possible diagnosis algorithms. All of the diagnosis algorithms shown, except for the SA [24] algorithm, have been proven to produce asymptotically correct and complete diagnosis, provided certain prespecified conditions have been met. The number of testing links necessary for the asymptotic guarantee are shown in the fourth column. Finally, the fifth column shows the number of probability parameters used in the respective diagnosis algorithms. While probability parameters are necessary in analyzing the probabilistic-diagnosis algorithms, the diagnosis algorithm itself need not necessarily use all, or even any, of the parameters.

From Table 3, several patterns are apparent concerning the probabilistic-diagnosis algorithms. The algorithms that guarantee the optimal diagnosis all have exponential computational complexity. Polynomial-time algorithms can guarantee only "pseudo-optimal" diagnosis. Either $O(N)$ or $O(N \log N)$ testing links are required to guarantee asymptotically correct and complete diagnosis. The incomplete-test algorithms requiring $O(N)$ testing links are either multiple-syndrome or sequential-diagnosis algorithms. Although the BSM1 [6] algorithm also requires only $O(N)$ testing links, it is a complete-test algorithm that uses a special type of testing graph not normally used for computational purposes. Several of the probabilistic-diagnosis algorithms do not require any probability parameters. However, these algorithms are not necessarily better than the algorithms that require one or more probability parameters: The latter algorithms, with rough estimates of the necessary parameters, may produce better diagnosis results than the former algorithms.

Besides the factors listed in Table 3, another factor that is important in evaluating a probabilistic-diagnosis algorithm is diagnostic accuracy. However, it is difficult to quantify and compare this parameter, because different probability and diagnosis models are used by the probabilistic-diagnosis algorithms. Analyses of diagnostic accuracy can be found in some of the references listed on the table, and Lee [17] presented comparisons of diagnostic accuracy of several of the algorithms shown in the table.

Conclusions

In recent years, probabilistic-diagnosis methods have shown much promise of bridging the gap between theory and the practical application of system-level diagnosis ideas. While significant progress has been made toward the development of diagnosis algorithms that are suitable for the diagnosis of large multiprocessor systems, their practicality and usefulness have yet to be demonstrated with physical experimental systems. Toward this end, Bianchini, Goodwin, and Nydick [2] recently presented the first application of theoretical diagnosability results to a real distributed network

Table 3. Comparison of probabilistic-diagnosis methods.

	Computational complexity	Optimal diagnosis	Asymptotic guarantee	Number of links required	Number of probability parameters
Complete-test					
SCH [23]	$O(N^2)$	No	Yes	$O(N \log N)$	None
BSM1 [6]	$O(N)$	No	Yes	$O(N)$	None
SA [24]	$O(N^2)$	No	No	N/A	None
Incomplete-test					
BLO [8]	$O(2^{N+|E|})$	Yes	Yes	$O(N \log N)$	All
LEE1 [17]	$O(2^{|F|})$	Yes	Yes	$O(N \log N)$	4
BSM2 [5]	$O(|E|)$	No	Yes	$O(N \log N)$	2
DSK [10]	$O(N^2)$	No	Yes	$O(N \log N)$	None
LEE2 [17]	$O(N^2)$	Pseudo	Yes	$O(N \log N)$	4
FR [12]	$O(R \, |^{-1}(u_i)|)$	No	Yes	$O(N)$	1
LS [18]	$O(R \, |^{-1}(u_i)|)$	Pseudo	Yes	$O(N)$	2
BLP [7]	$O(N \log^2 N)$	No	Yes	$O(N)$	2
BEP[1]	$O(N^c)$	No	Yes	$O(N \log N)$	None

N/A = not applicable

environment. Their results are limited to the original PMC model of diagnosis [21], in which a tight fault bound is required and intermittently faulty nodes are not permitted. More general experimental work of this nature needs to be conducted in the future to determine if the newly proposed probabilistic-diagnosis methods can be practical and useful.

Acknowledgments

This work was supported in part by the National Science Foundation under grant MIP-9012549 and in part by the National Aeronautics and Space Administration under grants NAG-1-296 and NAG-1-492.

References

[1] P. Berman and A. Pelc, "Distributed Probabilistic Fault Diagnosis in Multiprocessor Systems," *Proc. Fault-Tolerant Computing: 20th Int'l Symp. (FTCS-20),* IEEE Computer Soc. Press, Los Alamitos, Calif., 1990, pp. 340-346.

[2] R. Bianchini, Jr., K. Goodwin, and D.S. Nydick, "Practical Application and Implementation of Distributed System-Level Diagnosis Theory," *Proc. Fault-Tolerant Computing: 20th Int'l Symp. (FTCS-20),* IEEE Computer Soc. Press, Los Alamitos, Calif., 1990, pp. 332-339.

[3] D.M. Blough, *Fault Detection and Diagnosis in Multiprocessor Systems*, doctoral dissertation, The Johns Hopkins Univ., Baltimore, Md., 1988.

[4] D.M. Blough and G.M. Masson, "Performance Analysis of a Generalized Upset Detection Procedure," *Proc. 17th Int'l Symp. Fault-Tolerant Computing (FTCS-17),* IEEE Computer Soc. Press, Los Alamitos, Calif., 1987, pp. 218-223.

[5] D.M. Blough, G.F. Sullivan, and G.M. Masson, "Almost Certain Diagnosis for Intermittently Faulty Systems," *Proc. 18th Int'l Symp. Fault-Tolerant Computing (FTCS-18)*, IEEE Computer Soc. Press, Los Alamitos, Calif., 1988, pp. 260-265.

[6] D.M. Blough, G.F. Sullivan, and G.M. Masson, "Fault Diagnosis for Sparsely Interconnected Multiprocessor Systems," *Proc. 19th Int'l Symp. Fault-Tolerant Computing (FTCS-19)*, IEEE Computer Soc. Press, Los Alamitos, Calif., 1989, pp. 62-69.

[7] D.M. Blough and A. Pelc, "Reliable Diagnosis and Repair in Constant-Degree Multiprocessor Systems," *Proc. Fault-Tolerant Computing: 20th Int'l Symp. (FTCS-20)*, IEEE Computer Soc. Press, Los Alamitos, Calif., 1990, pp. 316-323.

[8] M.L. Blount, "Probabilistic Treatment of Diagnosis in Digital Systems," *Proc. Seventh Ann. Int'l Conf. Fault-Tolerant Computing (FTCS-7)*, IEEE Computer Soc. Press, Los Alamitos, Calif., 1977, pp. 72-77.

[9] A.T. Dahbura, "System-Level Diagnosis: A Perspective for the Third Decade," in *Concurrent Computation: Algorithms, Architectures, Technologies*, S.K. Tewksbury, B.W. Dickinson, and S.C. Schwartz, eds., Plenum Pub. Corp., New York, N.Y., 1988.

[10] A.T. Dahbura, K.K. Sabnani, and L.L. King, "The Comparison Approach to Multiprocessor Fault Diagnosis," *IEEE Trans. Computers*, Vol. C-36, No. 3, Mar. 1987, pp. 373-378.

[11] A.D. Friedman and L. Simoncini, "System-Level Fault Diagnosis," *Computer*, Vol. 13, No. 3, Mar. 1980, pp. 47-53.

[12] D. Fussell and S. Rangarajan, "Probabilistic Diagnosis of Multiprocessor Systems with Arbitrary Connectivity," *Proc. 19th Int'l Symp. Fault-Tolerant Computing (FTCS-19)*, IEEE Computer Soc. Press, Los Alamitos, Calif., 1989, pp. 560-565.

[13] S.H. Hosseini, J.G. Kuhl, and S.M. Reddy, "On Self-Fault Diagnosis of the Distributed Systems," *IEEE Trans. Computers*, Vol. 37, No. 2, Feb. 1988, pp. 248-251.

[14] S. Huang, J. Xu, and T. Chen, "Characterization and Design of Sequentially t-Diagnosable Systems," *Proc. 19th Int'l Symp. Fault-Tolerant Computing (FTCS-19)*, IEEE Computer Soc. Press, Los Alamitos, Calif., 1989, pp. 554-559.

[15] C. Kime, "System Diagnosis," in *Fault-Tolerant Computing Theory and Techniques*, Vol. 2, D.K. Pradhan, ed., Prentice-Hall, Inc., Englewood Cliffs, N.J., 1986.

[16] J.G. Kuhl and S.M. Reddy, "Distributed Fault-Tolerance for Large Multiprocessor Systems," *Proc. Seventh Ann. Symp. Computer Architecture*, IEEE Computer Soc. Press, Los Alamitos, Calif., 1980, pp. 23-30.

[17] S. Lee, *Probabilistic Multiprocessor and Multicomputer Diagnosis*, doctoral dissertation, Univ. of Michigan, Ann Arbor, Mich., 1990.

[18] S. Lee and K.G. Shin, "Optimal Multiple Syndrome Probabilistic Diagnosis," *Proc. Fault-Tolerant Computing: 20th Int'l Symp. (FTCS-20)*, IEEE Computer Soc. Press, Los Alamitos, Calif., 1990, pp. 324-331.

[19] S.H. Maheswari and S.L. Hakimi, "On Models for Diagnosable Systems and Probabilistic Fault Diagnosis," *IEEE Trans. Computers*, Vol. C-25, No. 3, Mar. 1976, pp. 228-236.

[20] S. Mallela and G.M. Masson, "Diagnosis without Repair for Hybrid Fault Situations," *IEEE Trans. Computers*, Vol. C-29, No. 6, June 1980, pp. 461-470.

[21] F.P. Preparata, G. Metze, and R.T. Chien, "On the Connection Assignment Problem of Diagnosable Systems," *IEEE Trans. Electronic Computing*, Vol. EC-16, No. 6, Dec. 1967, pp. 848-854.

[22] P. Ramanathan and K.G. Shin, "Reliable Broadcast in Hypercube Multicomputers," *IEEE Trans. Computers*, Vol. 37, No. 12, Dec. 1988, pp. 1654-1657.

[23] E. Scheinerman, "Almost Sure Fault Tolerance in Random Graphs," *SIAM J. Computing*, Vol. 10, No. 6, Dec. 1987, pp. 1124-1134.

[24] A.K. Somani and V.K. Agarwal, "Distributed Syndrome Decoding for Regular Interconnected Structures," *Proc. 19th Int'l Symp. Fault-Tolerant Computing (FTCS-19)*, IEEE Computer Soc. Press, Los Alamitos, Calif., 1989, pp. 70-77.

[25] C.-L. Yang and G.M. Masson, "A Distributed Algorithm for Fault Diagnosis in Systems with Soft Failures," *IEEE Trans. Computers*, Vol. 37, No. 11, Nov. 1988, pp. 1476-1480.

The Delta-4 Distributed Fault-Tolerant Architecture

C omputer technology has entered almost every facet of modern society. Computers are pervasive, from home offices and small businesses to such major industries as banking, manufacturing, transportation, communication, and weapon systems. We rely so heavily on computers that any computer malfunction or misuse could have very severe consequences — for instance, when we entrust computers with our lives (in defense and medicine), our money, or our personal, confidential information. In many such cases, it is important that the computing systems that we rely on be truly *dependable* — that is, that they justify our confidence in the service that they deliver [1].

Despite the enormous improvements in the quality of computer technology that have been made during the last few decades, failures of computer system components cannot be ruled out completely. Some application areas therefore need computer systems that continue to provide their specified service despite component failures. Such computer systems are said to be *fault-tolerant*. Distributed computing systems — in which multiple computers interact by means of an underlying communication network to achieve some common purpose — offer attractive opportunities for providing fault tolerance, since their multiplicity of interconnected resources can be exploited to implement the redundancy that is necessary to survive failures.

Delta-4's[1] distributed fault-tolerant architecture aims to support incremental growth of functionality, dependability, and performance of distributed applications. The Delta-4 architecture features

(1)   A standard local area network technology, with minimum specialized hardware, to achieve fault tolerance using off-the-shelf host computers;

(2)   A distributed-application support environment to allow object-oriented description and programming of distributed applications;

(3)   Extensive use of multicast or group communication protocols to facilitate replicated processing; and

David Powell,

Peter Barrett,

Gottfried Bonn,

Marc Chérèque,

Douglas Seaton, and

Paulo Veríssimo

---

[1]The Delta-4 project gets its name from the four Ds in the full title of the project: "Definition and Design of an Open Dependable Distributed Architecture."

(4)   Built-in error processing and fault-treatment procedures to provide user-transparent fault tolerance.

The Delta-4 project has been investigating the links between fault tolerance and distribution to provide a computational and communication infrastructure for application domains that require distributed system solutions with various dependability and real-time constraints (for example, computer-integrated manufacturing, process control, and office systems). The scale of distribution in the targeted application domains is commensurate with the distances that can be covered by local area networks (from a few meters to several kilometers).

Dependability and real-time concepts

This section introduces some basic concepts and terminology regarding dependable and real-time computing.

Dependability

Dependability can be defined as the "trustworthiness of a computer system such that reliance can justifiably be placed on the service it delivers" [2]. Dependability is thus a global concept that subsumes the usual attributes of reliability (continuity of service), availability (readiness for usage), safety (avoidance of catastrophes), and security (prevention of unauthorized handling of information).

When one designs a dependable computing system, it is important to have very precise definitions of the notions of *failures, errors, faults,* and other related concepts (see [1] for a detailed exposition of dependability concepts and terminology). A system failure is said to occur when the service delivered by the system no longer complies with its *specification,* the latter being an agreed description of the system's expected function or service. An error is that part of the system state that is liable to lead to failure: An error affecting the service (that is, becoming visible to the user) is an indication that a failure occurs or has occurred. A fault is the adjudged or hypothesized cause of an error. An error is thus the manifestation of a fault *in the system,* and a failure is the effect of an error *on the service.*

Faults are thus the potential source of system undependability. Faults may be either due to some physical phenomenon inside or outside the system or caused accidentally or intentionally by human beings. They may either occur during the operational life of the system or be created during the design process. *Fault tolerance* — the ability to provide service complying with the specification in spite of faults — may be seen as complementary to fault-prevention techniques aimed at improving the quality of components and procedures to decrease the frequency at which faults occur or are introduced into the system. Fault tolerance is achieved by *error processing* and by *fault treatment* [3]. Error processing is aimed at removing errors from the computational state — before a failure occurs, if possible. Fault treatment is aimed at preventing faults from being activated again.[2]

Error processing may be carried out either by *error detection and recovery* or by *error compensation.* In error detection and recovery, the fact that the system is in an erroneous state must first be (urgently) ascertained. An error-free state is then substituted for the erroneous one. This error-free state may be some past state of the system (backward recovery) or some entirely new state (forward recovery). In error compensation, the erroneous state contains enough redundancy

---

[2]In anthropomorphic terms, *error processing* can be viewed as "symptom relief" and fault treatment as "curing the illness."

for the system to be able to deliver an error-free service from the erroneous (internal) state. Classic examples of error detection and recovery and error compensation are provided by atomic transactions [4] and triple-modular redundancy or voting techniques [5], respectively.

Fault treatment is a sequel to error processing: Whereas error processing is aimed at preventing errors from becoming visible to the user, fault treatment is necessary to prevent faults from causing further errors. Fault treatment entails fault diagnosis (determination of the cause of observed errors), fault passivation (preventing diagnosed faults from being activated again), and — if possible — system reconfiguration to restore the level of redundancy so that the system is able to tolerate further faults.

When one designs a fault-tolerant system, it is important to define clearly what types of faults the system is intended to tolerate and the assumed behavior (or failure modes) of faulty components. If the behavior of faulty components is different from that with which the system's error-processing and fault-treatment facilities can cope, the system will fail. In distributed systems, the behavior of a node is defined in terms of the messages that it sends over the network. The assumed failure modes of nodes are thus defined in terms of the messages that faulty nodes send or do not send. The simplest and most common assumption about node failures is that nodes are *fail-silent* [6]; that is, that they function correctly until the point of failure, when they "crash" and then remain forever silent (until they are repaired). (Note that fail silence is a subset of the properties of fail-stop processors [7] — that is, of "halt-on-failure.") The most severe failure mode that can be imagined is that of fail-uncontrolled nodes that fail in quite arbitrary or "Byzantine" ways [8]. Such nodes can fail by producing messages with erroneous content, messages that arrive too early or too late, or indeed "impromptu" messages that should never have been sent at all. In between these two extremes, it is possible to define failure modes of intermediate severity [9], [10]. Generally, when the assumed failure modes of system components become more severe, then more redundancy (and complexity) must be introduced into the system to tolerate a given number of simultaneously active faults.

Real time

Real-time systems are those that are able to offer an assurance of *timeliness* of service provision. The very notion of timeliness of service provision results from the fact that real-time services have associated with them not only a functional specification of "what" needs to be done but also a timing specification of "when" it should be done. Failure to meet the timing specification of a real-time service can be as severe as failure to meet its functional specification. According to the application and to the particular service being considered, the assurance of timeliness provided by a real-time system may range from a high expectation to a firm guarantee of service provision within a defined time interval.[3]

At least three sorts of times can enter into the timing specification of a real-time service. These are

(1)   A *liveline* indicating the beginning of the time interval in which service must be provided if the service is to be considered timely,

(2)   A *deadline* indicating the end of this time interval, and

(3)   A *targetline* (or "soft" deadline) specifying the time at which it would somehow be "best" for the service to be delivered — that is, the point at which maximum benefit or minimum cost is accrued.

The essential difference between a service deadline and a service targetline is that the former must be met if the service is to be timely, whereas missing a targetline, although undesirable, is

---

[3]Note that this view of real-time systems means more than just "high performance" or the ability to react "quickly" in response to asynchronous external events.

```
If (elapsed_time<10 s)          then (execute schedule A)
                                else (execute shcedule B)

If (alarm_A before alarm_B)     then (emergency shut-down)
                                else (normal shut-down)
```

Figure 1. Examples of time-dependent decisions.

not considered a failure. An alternative way to specify the timing constraints of real-time services is that of value-time or worth-time functions that indicate the benefit of service delivery as a function of the time of service delivery [11], [12].

In systems that are "real-time" in the sense defined above, the available resources (finite in any practical system) must be allocated to computation and communication activities. Then, as long as specified "worst-case" environmental constraints (like event-occurrence rate < specified maximum) are satisfied, it is guaranteed that all critical deadlines are met or that the cost of not meeting targetlines are minimized In some applications, even if the "worst-case" conditions are exceeded, it may be required that the system make a best effort to ensure that the number and cost of missed deadlines and targetlines are minimized.

Scheduling concerns the allocation of resources that must be time shared; the resources in question could be processing power, memory, and communication bandwidth. In real-time systems, scheduling algorithms are concerned more with the respect of livelines, deadlines, and targetlines than with ensuring fairness of resource usage. Consequently, most scheduling decisions need to take account of time explicitly when determining what activity should be scheduled next on a particular resource. Schedules can be calculated off line (during the system design phase). This is often the case when it must be guaranteed that all critical deadlines be met under specified worst-case conditions. A set of such precalculated static schedules may be necessary if the system is to operate in several different modes (start-up, production, normal shutdown, and emergency shutdown). The performance penalties incurred by such a static approach can be partially mitigated if it can be arranged for noncritical computation or communication to make use of the "holes" that are left in the precalculated schedules. In complex real-time applications, on-line (dynamic) scheduling may be preferable to off-line (static) scheduling, since the complexity of the application may be such that no a priori "worst case" can in fact be defined. Even if the "worst case" is known, it may be desired that the system degrade gracefully whenever the "worst case" is exceeded (consider a radar-tracking system designed to track, at most, 100 aircraft — if 101 aircraft happen to be within range, it may be better to track as many as possible rather than none at all).

Consistent time-dependent decisions (see Figure 1) must be made by different nodes of a distributed real-time system. Then, if the expense of an agreement protocol is not to be incurred for every such time-dependent decision, each node must have a consistent view of time. Consequently, the local clocks of each node in a distributed real-time system must be synchronized to a specified precision so that all (nonfaulty) nodes agree on an *approximate global time*. Furthermore, many applications require this global time to be synchronized to a known accuracy of some external standard of physical time. The precision and accuracy of clock synchronization determine the granularity at which different nodes can make consistent time-dependent decisions.

Dependability and real time in Delta-4

The Delta-4 architecture is a distributed architecture that seeks to be both open and dependable, as well as capable of supporting real-time applications. To be able to satisfy a large range of application requirements in a cost-effective manner, the Delta-4 architecture can provide various degrees of dependability and performance. By "open," it is meant that the architecture can use off-the-shelf computers, accommodate heterogeneity of the underlying hardware and system software, and provide portability of application software. However, in those application domains where real-time response is paramount, the heterogeneity and openness may need to be sacrificed to provide the appropriate assurance of timeliness. To this end, the Delta-4 architecture offers the following two variants, both based on subsystems that present a high degree of commonality:

- The Delta-4 Open System Architecture (D4-OSA), which — as its name suggests — is an open architecture able to accommodate heterogeneity, and
- The Delta-4 Extra Performance Architecture (D4-XPA), which provides explicit support for assuring timeliness.

This section outlines the dependability and real-time features of the architecture and compares the Delta-4 approach with related work.

Dependability in Delta-4

The Delta-4 architecture provides mechanisms for achieving dependability on a service-by-service basis in "money-critical" applications for which the relevant dependability attributes are reliability, availability, and security. The architecture is not aimed at life-critical applications in which safety is the major concern.[4] Delta-4 is concerned essentially with accidental physical faults (faults in the hardware components) and, to a lesser extent, with accidental design faults in software.

The basic paradigm for tolerating hardware faults in Delta-4 is that of replicated computations executed by distinct nodes of a distributed system. The units of replication are software components — logical runtime units of computation and data encapsulation that communicate with each other by means of messages (only). Software components may be replicated to different degrees according to their degree of criticality and the assumptions made about the failure modes of the underlying node hardware. For a given service, if a fail-silence assumption for the underlying hardware can be justified to a degree commensurate with the dependability objectives of that service, then the service can be made single-fault-tolerant by duplication. Indeed, duplication of the software components providing the service is sufficient to allow recovery from a fault that causes a node to stop sending messages over the communication system. However, if the fail-silence assumption cannot be justified to a sufficient degree for a particular service, then triplication becomes necessary so that errors due to fail-uncontrolled behavior can be masked by voting techniques.

It is of course assumed that hardware faults will occur independently in different nodes. In fact, any faults (of hardware or software origin) that manifest themselves independently in different nodes can be tolerated by straightforward replication techniques. Some design faults in system software at each node and, to a lesser degree, design faults in application software can be expected to have such independence in their manifestations, since the execution environments of replicas on distinct nodes are essentially different (due to loose synchronization and differing work loads). Such faults are commonly called *Heisenbugs* [13]. In addition to this possibility of tolerating certain software design faults, distributed fault-tolerance techniques have the following advantages over tightly coupled "stand-alone" fault-tolerance techniques:

(1)   Specialized hardware is kept to a minimum, since distributed fault tolerance is implemented primarily in software; the cost of specialized hardware design — or redesign when a technology update is required — is therefore minimized.

---

[4]However, note that reliability, availability, and security are of very real interest in safety-*related* sytems, such as systems that, if they fail, cause emergency shutdown and thus induce not only unavailability but also wear out of the primary, safety-*critical* protection system.

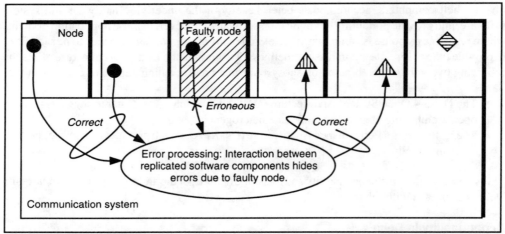

Figure 2. Illustration of the principle of error processing in the context of replicated computation.

(2)   Geographical separation of resources does not have to be "added on" if disaster recovery is to be provided; the same distributed fault-tolerance techniques can be used regardless of whether the replicas are close to or distant from each other.

(3)   Loose synchronization of replicas (through message passing) leads to improved tolerance of transient faults that could otherwise simultaneously affect all redundant computations at the same point of execution [14].

Software design faults that do not manifest themselves in the independent "Heisenbug" fashion cannot be tolerated by replication. Diverse designs must be used to define multiple variants. These multiple variants may be encapsulated within a software component (that can then be replicated for hardware fault tolerance) or constitute a distributed component made up of multiple variants executed on distinct nodes to be able to simultaneously tolerate both hardware and software faults. The latter approach has been investigated in Delta-4, although it has not yet been implemented [15].

In some multiuser application domains where data of a sensitive nature are manipulated, human faults of an intentional nature become a concern of considerable importance. There are two varieties of intentional faults: *malicious logic* and *intrusions*. Malicious logic refers to faults that are purposely introduced into a system at design time or at runtime to allow future illicit actions to be perpetrated (such as sabotage and access to confidential data). Malicious logic has not been addressed in Delta-4. However, intrusions have been explicitly addressed through the use of "intrusion-tolerance" methods aimed at supplementing conventional intrusion-prevention schemes. Replication is of little help when one is trying to tolerate intrusions. In fact, from the confidentiality viewpoint, replication is detrimental to security, since the number of different places where sensitive information can be found is greater in a system with replication than in one without replication. This therefore leads to more potential loopholes for an intruder to penetrate. The project has therefore investigated techniques based on *fragmentation scattering*; in these techniques, sensitive information is split into fragments and scattered over different nodes so that intrusions lead only to access to partial information (see [15], [16], [17]).

The remainder of this subsection is devoted to Delta-4 replication techniques for tolerating hardware faults and Heisenbug software faults.

Error processing. In the context of replicated computation, error processing consists of those techniques for coordinating replicated computation that allow communication and computation to proceed despite the fact that some of the replicas may reside on faulty nodes (see Figure 2). Delta-4 provides the following three different — but complementary — techniques for coordinating replicated computation: *active replication, passive replication,* and *semiactive replication.* These techniques are discussed below.

(1)   Active replication is a technique in which all replicas process all input messages concurrently so that their internal states are closely synchronized — in the absence of faults, outputs can be taken from any replica. The active-replication approach allows quasi-simultaneous recovery from a node failure. Furthermore, it is adapted to both the fail-silent- and fail-uncontrolled-node assumptions, since messages produced by different (active) replicas can be cross-checked (in value and time) [18]. However, active replication requires that all replicas can be guaranteed to be *deterministic* in the absence of faults; that is, it must be guaranteed that if nonfaulty replicas process identical input message streams, they will produce identical output message streams.

(2)   Passive replication is a technique in which only one of the replicas (the primary replica) processes the input messages and provides output messages. In the absence of faults, the other replicas (the standby replicas) do not process input messages and do not produce output messages; their internal states are regularly updated by means of checkpoints from the primary replica. Passive replication can be envisaged only if it is assumed that nodes are fail-silent. Unlike active replication, this technique does not require computation to be deterministic [19]. However, the performance overheads of transferring checkpoints and rolling back for recovery may not be acceptable in certain applications — especially in real-time applications.

(3)   Semiactive replication can be viewed as a hybrid of active replication and passive replication. Only one of the replicas (the leader replica) processes all input messages and provides output messages. In the absence of faults, the other replicas (the follower replicas) do not produce output messages; their internal state is updated either by direct processing of input messages or, where appropriate, by means of "minicheckpoints" from the leader replica. Semiactive replication seeks to achieve the low recovery overheads of active replication while relaxing the constraints on computation determinism. A minicheckpoint can be used to force the followers to obey all nondeterministic decisions made by the leader replica [20]. This possibility is particularly relevant for allowing replica-consistent preemption decisions. Like passive replication, this technique resides on the assumption that nodes are fail-silent. This technique is particularly suitable for replicating large "off-the-shelf" software components about which no assumption can be made on replica determinism and internal states (for example, commercially available database management software).

Figure 3 summarizes the relative merits of each of the above techniques.

Fault treatment. In the context of replicated computation, fault treatment consists essentially of the following three activities:

- Diagnosing the cause of error — that is, finding out what entity (node or replica) is at fault;
- If necessary, "passivating" the entity that is judged to be faulty (so that it will not cause further errors; and

Replication technique	Recovery overhead	Non-determinism	Accommodates fail-uncontrolled behavior
Active	Lowest	Forbidden	Yes
Passive	Highest	Allowed	No
Semiactive	Low	Resolved	No[5]

Figure 3. Comparison of replication techniques.

- If possible, creating new replicas on fault-free nodes to restore the level of redundancy and thus be able to tolerate further faults.

The set of sites on which replicas of a given software component can be located is termed the component's *replication domain*. The creation of a new replica on a fault-free node is called *cloning*. A new replica may be cloned

(1) At the same site at which the original replica was located; this could be the case either because the fault was considered to a be soft fault (like a Heisenbug), so that reinitialization of the state of the failed replica is sufficient to bring it back on line, or when corrective maintenance of the faulty node has been carried out, or

(2) At any other site in the component's replication domain, thus allowing corrective maintenance to be deferred (see Figure 4).

Real time in Delta-4

Support for heterogeneity and openness, and support for real time, are antagonistic aims: In heterogeneous distributed systems, the local schedulers at each node may not even be the same, let alone time-dependent. This is one of the motivations for the homogeneous XPA variant of the Delta-4 architecture [20], [21], in which heterogeneity and openness are sacrificed to provide assurance of timeliness. The XPA real-time variant of the Delta-4 architecture differs from the OSA variant by the following features of D4-XPA:

(1) Nodes are homogeneous. This eliminates the need, and therefore the performance penalties, of the translation of data representations during node interactions.

(2) Nodes are fail-silent. Since openness has been sacrificed in order to achieve real-time performance, nodes are purpose designed with built-in self-checking to support the fail-silent assumption. This eliminates the need for and the performance penalties of voting on the contents of transmitted messages.

(3) It uses semiactive replication for fault tolerance. The semiactive-replication technique was pioneered during the development of XPA, since it allows the potential nondeterminism of process preemption to be resolved. Explicit preemption points are inserted into the application code; whenever a follower replica reaches a preemption point, it awaits a "continue" or "preempt by message #n" instruction from the leader replica.

(4) A synchronized clock service is provided. For performance reasons, the clock service is built into the communication subsystem. Local clocks are synchronized with an internal precision of a few milliseconds and an external accuracy of less than a second.

(5) All nodes use a common real-time local executive. This executive allows real-time

---

[5] An extension of the semiactive-replication technique to accommodate fail-uncontrolled behavior is presently being investigated.

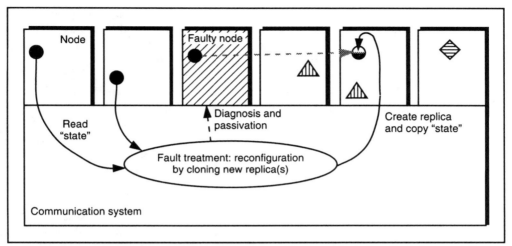

Figure 4. Illustration of the principle of fault treatment in the context of replicated computation.

processes to be scheduled dynamically according to a discipline of "most critical process first" and processes of the same criticality to be scheduled according to "earliest targetline first." Various techniques for deriving individual process targetlines from the overall targetline/ deadline of a distributed service are being investigated, as is the possibility of mapping an off-line precalculated schedule onto the dynamic runtime scheduling infrastructure.

(6)   The communication system is optimized for real-time performance. In particular, a collapsed-layering philosophy is followed based on an atomic multicast protocol providing multiple "qualities of service" (see the "D4-XPA collapsed-layered communications" subsubsection).

Note, however, that not all the Delta-4 target application domains require real-time response. As long as "sufficient" performance is attainable, the heterogeneity and openness criteria may be more important; in this case, the OSA variant of the architecture is preferred.

Related work

Message-passing replicated computation is used in a number of other distributed fault-tolerant systems, many of which are also aimed at supporting real-time applications [5], [22]-[30]. Here, some of these are described briefly and compared to Delta-4.

One of the first distributed fault-tolerant architectures was the Software Implemented Fault Tolerance (SIFT) multicomputer machine developed for critical flight-control applications [5], [31]. The Multicomputer Architecture for Fault Tolerance (MAFT) system is a more recent example of the same type of architecture [27], [32]. The SIFT architecture is based on general-purpose processors or nodes interconnected by a set of broadcast serial buses. Due to the criticality of the intended application domain (civil aircraft flight control), no restrictive assumption is made about node failure modes; that is, nodes may be fail-uncontrolled. To mask the arbitrary behavior of such nodes, each node is connected to every other node by its own private broadcast bus, and single-source data is broadcast to all nodes by means of a clock-synchronous, phased Byzantine agreement protocol [31]. Such an interconnection structure was feasible in SIFT, since the architecture was designed to accommodate at most eight nodes geographically located in the same equipment bay. It was required that the Delta-4 architecture be able to accommodate several tens of nodes spread out over quite considerable distances (as in a factory or several large neighboring buildings), so such an interconnection structure is not economically viable. Error processing in SIFT is based on majority voting of the results of tasks that are replicated across several nodes. Tasks are executed according to a static frame-based cyclic schedule (calculated off line). Delta-4 is intended to be an open architecture designed to accommodate heterogeneous nodes and local operating systems and serve a wider range of applications; systematic use of such synchronous frame-based scheduling was thus precluded. Finally, system reconfiguration after node failure is relatively simple in SIFT. Copies of the data necessary for the execution of all tasks can be maintained in every node of the system, since the elements of computation (tasks) contain little or no internal state (persistent data). In Delta-4, the elements of computation may be as large as a complete database system. The reconfiguration mechanism must be able to create (or *clone*) new replicas whose internal state is initialized by copying the state of existing replicas on nonfaulty nodes and transferring it across the network to the nodes on which new replicas are created.

Maintainable Real-Time Systems (MARS) [26], [33] is an example of a distributed fault-tolerant system for real-time applications in which the geographical distance between nodes goes beyond that of a single equipment bay. The nodes in MARS are assumed to be fail-silent (nodes are designed to be self-checking) and are interconnected by a serial baseband bus. The local clocks of each node are closely synchronized by means of a specially designed clock synchronization chip [34] that achieves such a tight synchronization (less than 10 milliseconds) that it can be used to control access to the serial bus by means of time-division multiplexing. Similarly to SIFT and MAFT, MARS uses cyclic scheduling of tasks based on a static (off-line) schedule, taking into account the worst-case or peak-load application scenario. However, MARS does not need to resort to majority voting, since nodes are assumed to be fail-silent; node failure results only in the absence of messages (detected in the time domain). Since all computation and all communication in MARS are statically scheduled, the times at which communication occurs and the quantity of transferred data are preestablished; therefore, the communication system does not have to worry about flow control to prevent buffer overflow. Furthermore, due to the fail-silent-node assumption and the static communication schedule, reliable broadcasting can be achieved by systematic $k + 1$ repetition of messages to mask k transmission errors. Like MARS, the real-time variant of the Delta-4 architecture (the XPA architecture) also adopts a fail-silent- node assumption to avoid the overheads of voting. However, unlike the static time-triggered approach of MARS, the XPA architecture adopts a dynamic event-triggered approach. This allows a more economical use of computation and communication resources for dynamic applications in which the load imposed on the system may suddenly vary due to the occurrence of asynchronous events. In many applications (such as the radar-tracking example mentioned in the "Real time" subsection), no a priori worst-case-load scenario can be determined; in such cases, the dynamic scheduling philosophy of XPA allows a best-effort approach to meeting application deadlines. As in MARS, the clocks of nodes in XPA are globally synchronized; however, for commercial reasons, clocks are synchronized without resorting to special-purpose hardware.

Isis [25], [35], [36] presents many similarities to Delta-4. Like Delta-4's open system architecture, the Isis system is aimed at providing user-transparent fault tolerance in a general-purpose distributed computing environment (as opposed to the SIFT and MARS systems, which are tailored to clock-synchronous, real-time applications). The Isis system provides a flexible toolkit of basic primitives that allows an application programmer to build a distributed application that is made fault-tolerant by replication of code and data. Isis assumes that nodes or processes fail only by crashing (that is, that they are fail-silent) and provides a single mechanism for process fault tolerance based on a coordinator-cohort scheme. This scheme is similar in some respects to Delta-4's semiactive-replication technique (the Isis coordinator-cohort scheme does not, however, address the issue of resolving replica nondeterminism). The tools provided by Isis could also allow implementation — by the application programmer — of actively replicated processes (restricted to a fail-silence assumption) and passively replicated processes (by making coordinators systematically transfer their state to cohorts when a service request is completed). In Delta-4, many applications can be designed as if they were to run on a system that never fails; since fault tolerance is managed by built-in system facilities, the issues of replication can be entirely hidden from the application programmer and specified only at configuration time. Isis also provides the basic state transfer mechanism [36] necessary to ensure the cloning of replicas for system reconfiguration during fault treatment. However, since Isis assumes fail silence, the state transfer tool does not provide a facility for error detection during state transfer by cross-checking states copied from multiple source replicas. Like Delta-4, Isis makes use of special communication facilities supporting multicast protocols based on a clock-asynchronous approach rather than the clock-synchronous techniques of SIFT and MARS. However, the Isis multicast protocol suite is implemented on top of the transmission-control protocol/Internet protocol (TCP/IP) such that each multicast results in a number of point-to-point TCP/IP messages. In Delta-4, the basic atomic multicast protocol is implemented on top of — or as an extension of — the medium access control protocol of selected local area networks (see the "Communications" subsection). This allows hardware broadcasting opportunities to be exploited for increased performance.

A system that resembles Delta-4 quite closely is IBM's Advanced Automation System (AAS) for the US Air Traffic Control Network [30]. The AAS concept of "server groups" is equivalent to that of the "replicated software component" developed here. In AAS, both active- and passive-replication techniques are available[6] but only for the case of server replicas that fail by responding late, not responding at all, or crashing. In our approach, the case of fail-uncontrolled (active) replicas — ones that can fail in quite arbitrary fashion — is also accommodated by means of a built-in voting mechanism. The Delta-4 atomic multicast protocol allows replicated entities to be logically addressed such that messages are delivered (with low overhead) to all replicas. This results in somewhat simpler management of active replicas than that in AAS. Processors in AAS are organized into distinct processor groups that each can support replicas of a given set of servers. There is a group service availability manager (gSAM) for each processor group, with replicas on all processors of that group, that is responsible for ensuring that the number of replicas of all servers supported by the processor group is maintained according to the server group's replication policy (specifying the minimum number of required replicas). If a server group can no longer execute according to its replication policy, then in some cases it may be moved to another processor group under the control of a global service availability manager (GSAM). Each processor group supports a group membership service and a group broadcast service that enables gSAM replicas to maintain a consistent view of the processor group's global state. A routed multicast facility for communication between server groups residing in the same or different processor groups is also provided. In Delta-4, management is based on the open distributed system concepts of "managed objects" and "management domains." The nearest equivalent to the AAS processor group and gSAM is a software component replication domain and its corresponding replication domain manager (see the "System administration" and "Cloning" subsections); however, since nodes in Delta-4 are not split into groups a priori, replication domains for different software components may overlap. Indeed, some software components may have a replication domain that spans all nodes in the system. A global processor membership service is provided over all nodes in a Delta-4 system and is built into the Delta-4 atomic multicast protocol.

---

[6]Referred to in AAS as *close* and *loose* synchronization of replicas.

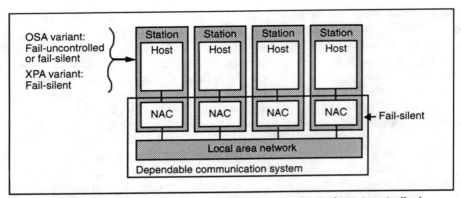

Figure 5. Delta-4 hardware architecture. (NAC = network attachment controller.)

Hardware architecture and communication issues

This section identifies the main hardware components of the Delta-4 architecture and outlines the communication facilities provided in the OSA and XPA variants of the architecture.

Hardware

The Delta-4 distributed system architecture has been designed so that it is capable of accommodating arbitrary fail-uncontrolled behavior by means of active-replication techniques. To be able to use standard local area networks instead of resorting to the costly interconnection topologies normally required to accommodate arbitrary failures [31], each node consists of two distinct parts: a host computer and a network attachment controller (NAC) (shown in Figure 5).

Host computers (on which replicas are executed) may be fail-uncontrolled or fail-silent; however, NACs are assumed to be fail-silent. This assumption for the NAC is substantiated by the use of hardware self-checking techniques. The important consequence of this split in failure mode assumptions between host and NAC is that even when a (fail-uncontrolled) host forwards erroneous data to its NAC, the latter will either process these data in a consistent manner or simply remain silent. The possibility of forwarding the data inconsistently to multiple destinations is effectively removed.

Active replication has the potential disadvantage of requiring computation to be deterministic. Therefore, when either the passive- or semiactive-replication techniques are preferred, it is necessary to assume that hosts are fail-silent. This is possible when the coverage of the host self-checking mechanisms[7] is commensurate with the dependability objectives of the supported application. In the XPA variant of the architecture, where openness and heterogeneity are sacrificed to support real-time applications, all hosts are purpose designed with built-in self-checking and are therefore assumed to be fail-silent.

To summarize, the OSA variant of the architecture can accommodate both fail-silent hosts and fail-uncontrolled hosts, whereas the XPA variant accommodates only fail-silent hosts. Fail-silent NACs are used in both variants.

As for the local area network itself, implementations exist for both the token bus (ISO8802/4) and the token ring (ISO8802/5). (ISO stands for International Standards Organization.) For performance reasons in the XPA real-time variant of the architecture, FDDI (ISO9314) has also been considered (but not yet implemented). FDDI is also of very real interest in the OSA

---

[7]Or, equivalently, the conditional probability that when a host fails, it fails by going silent.

context, since it is able to accommodate a high number of interconnected sites spread out over quite long distances (up to 200 kilometers). Since the local area network must also be dependable if the complete architecture is to be dependable, dual communication media can be employed in all local area network (LAN) implementations.

Communications

An essential feature of Delta-4 communications is the provision of multipoint services. Multipoint communication is necessary in some form or another as soon as replicated computation is considered for providing fault tolerance. In both variants of the architecture, multipoint communication is based on a low-level atomic multicast protocol (AMp) implemented either on top of, or as an extension to, the medium access control layer of a standard local area network.

In D4-OSA, the atomic service offered by this protocol is extended by further protocol layers to form the multipoint communication protocol (MCP) stack. MCP and the associated network management facilities of D4-OSA system administration collectively form the multipoint communication system (MCS).

In D4-XPA, the same basic protocol is used as the basis of a multiple-service protocol — the extended AMp (xAMp) — to build a collapsed-layered communication (CLC) stack that provides flexible and high-performance group communication facilities.

In both variants of the architecture, the communication software is executed by the NAC hardware (compare Figure 5), which — being fail-silent — greatly simplifies the design and the verification of the communication protocols.

Atomic multicast protocol. The Delta-4 AMp [37], [38] allows data frames to be delivered to a group of logically designated gates. The protocol ensures, for each frame, that either all addressed gates on nonfaulty nodes receive the frame or none do.[8] The protocol also ensures that frames are delivered to all addressed gates in a consistent order and that any changes in the membership of a gate group (due to node failure/reinsertion) are notified consistently to all members of that group.

The protocol is based on a centralized, two-phase accept protocol. In the first phase, the data frame is transmitted to all members of the group. The latter then inform the sender whether or not they are able to receive that frame. If all intended recipients can accept the data frame, the sender transmits an accept frame (if a participant perceives the data frame, but cannot accept it because of buffer limitations, a reject frame is sent). The protocol tolerates faults of both the sending and receiving nodes as well as transmission faults; it has been implemented in such a way that it can be ported to different underlying networks. It has been successfully implemented at present on top of the medium access control layer of the token bus (ISO8802/4) and the token ring (ISO8802/5).

Another protocol, providing the same service, has been implemented as a modification of the medium access control layer of the 8802/5 token ring [39]. This extension decreases the number of frames that need to be exchanged by making use of the "on-the-fly" bit flipping possibility of the token ring and is implemented partially in hardware.

D4-OSA multipoint communication protocol stack. The D4-OSA MCP stack has two major innovative features, as follows:

- The ability to coordinate communication to and from replicated endpoints and
- The provision of multipoint associations for connection-oriented communication between groups of peer entities.

---

[8]This occurs, for example, if any recipient cannot accept a frame because of lack of receive credit.

Quality of service	Agreement	Total order	Causal order per clabel	Rx queue reordering
BestEffortN	Best effort to *N*	No	FIFO	No
BestEffortTo	Best effort to list	No	FIFO	No
AtLeastN	Assured to *N*	No	FIFO	No
AtLeastTo	Assured to list	No	FIFO	No
Reliable	All	No	FIFO	No
Atomic	All or none	Yes (same gate)	Yes	No
Tight	All or none	Yes (same gate)	Yes	Yes

Figure 6. xAMp qualities of service.

The replicated-endpoint paradigm is used to implement the error processing associated with the active model. Replicated endpoints are provided by an interreplica protocol (IRp) situated at the bottom of the session layer [18]. This protocol coordinates the flow of information sent and received by the different replicas of a replicated software component. The information sent by each replica can be cross-checked for validity (in both the value and time domains) with that sent by the other replicas in the set. This is carried out in the (fail-silent) NACs before the actual information is sent over the network. The cross-check itself is based on the exchange of checksums of the data to be sent (for value-domain errors) and on the comparison of interreplica desynchronization (for time-domain errors). The flow of information to a replicated software component is also controlled by this protocol; a buffer-status voting mechanism is used to ensure that flow control toward a replicated destination is ensured despite the fact that a faulty replica could choose to refuse messages from the network. The protocol can be configured for either fail-uncontrolled hosts or fail-silent hosts.

Whereas the replicated endpoint facility provides for the transparent (or invisible) multicasting of information to a replicated destination, the MCP multipoint association facility allows visible multicasting between groups of peer software components (which may or may not be individually replicated). This service is delivered by the MCP multipoint session-layer protocol. Facilities are provided that allow software components to join and leave multipoint associations and for information to be multicasted to all or some members of the association. A sending entity may choose to include or exclude itself from the set of destinations for a particular message. All information transferred over such a multipoint association is delivered in a consistent order to all overlapping destinations.

The MCP stack also provides a fully conforming ISO session-layer service so that applications conforming to ISO standards can be used. The replicated-endpoint facility is offered both for the multipoint session-layer service and for the ISO-compatible bipoint service.

D4-XPA collapsed-layered communications. The D4-XPA communication subsystem provides the high performance that is a necessary (but not sufficient) condition for stringent real-time applications. To this end, a collapsed-layering philosophy is followed. Of course, removing layers also implies removing services, so the functionality of the remaining layers needs to be increased to palliate this. In D4-XPA, only four layers are defined: From the top down, these are the group management layer, the group communication layer, and the (standard) LAN medium access control and physical layers.

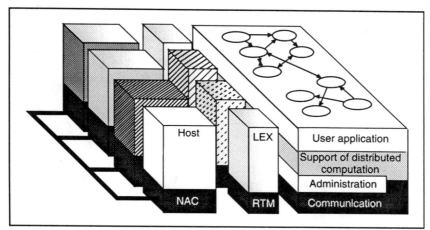

Figure 7. Abstract view of the Delta-4 architecture. (LEX = local executive, NAC = network attachment controller, and RTM = real-time monitor.)

The group management layer is responsible for choosing the group communication "quality of service" (see below) that is appropriate for the model of replication that is used within a particular group. It also implements an appropriate interreplica protocol to ensure replica consistency and error processing (in the semiactive-replication or leader-follower model).

The group communication layer is based on an extension of the basic AMp (that is, the xAMp) that provides multiple qualities of service (QOS) that can be selected according to the specific group communication requirements (see Figure 6).

The *BestEffortN* and *BestEffortTo* services ensure that the frame is received by a number *N* or by a specified list of the addressed recipients if the sender does not fail. The *Reliable* service ensures that if any recipient received the frame, all addressed recipients receive it, even if the sender fails. In all of these first three services, there is no guarantee of order at the receivers and no control of receive credit — frames are forwarded directly to the service users as soon as they are received. The *Atomic* service is the same as that provided by the basic AMp: It guarantees that even if the sender fails, all recipients, or none of them, receive the frame. This service ensures both consistent ordering (across multiple receive queues) and causal ordering (within a receive queue). The *Tight* service extends on the *Atomic* service by providing the possibility of allowing more urgent frames to overtake less urgent ones in the receive queues. Of course, this can only be done if the resulting frame deliveries to users are still consistently and causally ordered.

Software environment and management issues

Figure 7 provides an abstract view of the overall Delta-4 architecture. The left-hand "slice" of the diagram recapitulates the hardware architecture discussed in the previous section.

The middle slice of the figure represents the local executives residing on the host and NAC hardware. The local executives (LEXs) resident on the hosts are shown shaded differently (like the hosts) in order to underline that in the OSA variant of the architecture, heterogeneous host hardware and executive software may be accommodated. In practice, the present implementations all use different flavors of Unix.[9] In principle, however, the design philosophy of the OSA variant

---

[9]Unix is a registered trademark of Unix Systems Laboratories.

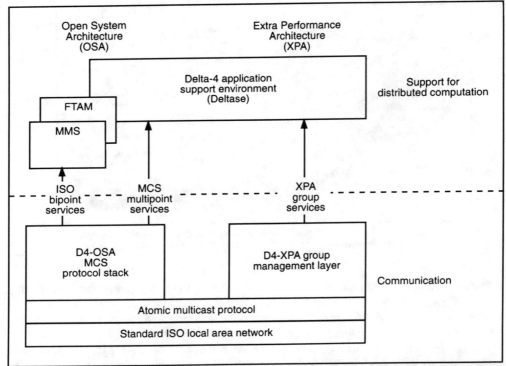

Figure 8. Computation and communication support in D4-OSA and D4-XPA. (FTAM = file transfer access method, MMS = manufacturing message service, ISO = International Standards Organization, and MCS = multipoint communication system.)

of the architecture would allow an implementation in which both Unix and non-Unix systems could coexist. In the XPA variant of the architecture, LEXs (and hosts) are homogeneous; currently, a specially developed real-time version of Unix (RT-Unix [40]) is used, but future implementations may adopt some other real-time operating system. In both variants of the architecture, the NACs use a real-time monitor (RTM) that is homogeneous across all NACs (although of course this is not mandatory).

The right-hand slice of the figure represents the distributed Delta-4 software, which can be represented in the following four parts:

- The distributed user application software, represented as a set of "software components" (logical units of distribution) that communicate by messages (only);
- The host-resident infrastructure for support of distributed computation;
- The computation and communication administration software (executing partly on the host computers and partly on the NACs); and
- The communication protocol software (executing on the NACs).

A particular host-resident infrastructure for supporting open object-oriented distributed computation has been developed for the Delta-4 architecture: the Delta-4 application support environment (Deltase). According to the philosophy of "open" distributed processing, Deltase facilitates the use of heterogeneous languages for implementing the various objects of a distributed application and allows the differences in underlying LEXs to be hidden. Deltase provides the means for generating software components called "capsules" (executable representations of objects). Capsules are coordinated by the Deltase execution support system that also provides support for error processing and fault treatment by means of replicated capsules. Deltase is mandatory in D4-XPA and is optional in D4-OSA.

Other host-resident infrastructures can be considered in the OSA variant of the architecture. In particular, since the communication system in D4-OSA provides a fully ISO-compatible (bipoint) presentation service (as well as innovative multipoint services), standard application-layer protocols — such as the manufacturing message service (MMS) (ISO9506) of the manufacturing automation protocol (MAP) and the ISO file transfer and access method (FTAM) (ISO8571) — can be used (see Figure 8).

In addition to the communication software already outlined in the previous section, a further important subsystem in the distributed software slice of Figure 7 is that of system administration. Delta-4 system administration provides the mechanisms for managing a Delta-4 system: It consists of both support for network management in the classic sense and support for managing the computation system.

In conjunction with Deltase/XEQ (see below), the Delta-4 administration system carries out the automatic fault-treatment functions mentioned previously.

Application support environment

The purpose of Deltase is to provide a single virtual machine for the support of modular applications on Delta-4 systems. This single virtual machine conceals the (possibly heterogeneous) underlying hardware and software, consisting of computers, local operating systems, language systems, and the communication system.

The computational model provides the model to be used for application programs that are to be supported by Deltase. This model has its origins in work on open distributed processing (ODP) within the ANSA (later ISA) project [41] and related work on standardization of a support environment for ODP (SE-ODP) within ECMA [42]. ODP is concerned with the definition of a generic architecture for distributed processing systems. The current implementation of Deltase is a prototype support environment for open distributed processing extended to include the Delta-4 approach to fault tolerance and real time.

The decomposition of an application into a number of language-level program modules, which interact with one another by means of procedure calls, is a widely used method for applications that are implemented as a single program and executed on a single machine. Deltase enables this application structure to be supported on Delta-4 systems — that is, to extend to distributed fault-tolerant systems a widely used application structure.

Since fault tolerance and distribution are made transparent to the application programmer, an application written for use with Deltase can be used, without change to the application code, on a small-scale system consisting of a single host machine with a suitable implementation of Deltase.

Deltase supports this computational model through a combination of

- Generation support — referred to as *Deltase/GEN* and
- Runtime support — referred to as *Deltase/XEQ*.

The language-level program modules are independent of the underlying computing environment and can be ported between different computing environments where that language is supported. Thus, Deltase provides vendors and users with a natural and economic way to migrate their software investment to new technology.

Concepts. The key concepts of the Delta-4 application support environment are summarized below.

Computational objects and services. For use with Deltase, the program modules (which together constitute an application) must be the program modules (which together constitute an application) must be computational objects. Each one encapsulates a private state and provides one (or more) clearly defined service interface(s) for operations on that state; each service interface offers a set of services. These services provide the only way for one computational object (the one invoking the service) to read or modify the private state of another computational object (the one offering the service). The specification of a service interface is independent of its many possible implementations; each service is defined by its parameters, results, effects, and constraints.

Remote procedure call. In distributed systems, the remote procedure call (RPC) mechanism is a direct extension of the widely used procedure call mechanism provided by many conventional programming languages. RPC provides a means of programming the interactions between objects, using existing language constructs, with each service treated as a separate procedure. The same language construct is therefore used both for the invocation of a service that is provided internally (by a local procedure) and for the invocation of a service that is provided externally (by another object). RPC is an abstraction away from messages, offering a familiar language-level construct for programming the interactions between computational objects. With language-based type-checking mechanisms at both the calling and the called objects, the use of RPC provides an assurance that code at both ends conforms to the same interface specification.

Interface trading. Before two computational objects can interact by way of RPC, a logical path between them must be established, through interface trading. An object (service provider) may offer its services for use by other objects by exporting that service interface; this offer will be added to a catalog of such offers. An object requiring the use of a particular set of services (service user) may find a service provider by invoking a search of that catalog for offers of service based on the specified interface type name. The effect of importing a service interface is to establish a logical interaction path. Such a path would enable the service user to invoke the services provided by the service provider through that particular interface.

Threads. To allow a service provider to process a number of service requests concurrently, Deltase supports the use of multiple threads of control within an object. Each thread handles one service request at a time; such threads — called *server threads* — are managed by Deltase. Server threads are not directly visible to the applications programmer, but the mutual exclusion of access to shared internal data remains the responsibility of the application programmer. Within an object, a server thread may create distinct subsidiary (forked) threads that disappear when their activity is complete. Typically, such forked threads are used to allow local processing to continue in parallel with service requests invoked by RPC (whose threads are blocked); computational progress may then occur on several hosts on behalf of a single original service request.

Transformers. To interact with alien computational worlds, Deltase uses the concept of a transformer. This is a "half-object"; it appears from one side as a conventional Deltase object but from the other side interacts according to the rules and the conventions of some other computational world. A transformer object can be used to provide access from the Deltase world to an existing (non-Deltase) software package. Typically, the software accessed in this way would be proprietary and commercially important. Conversely, a transformer object may provide access from the non-Deltase world to a service provided in the Deltase world (with the consequent benefits in terms of representational transparency and Delta-4 dependability) while preserving non-Deltase interface conventions and standards. More generally, transformer objects provide a means of interworking with other proprietary or standard computational worlds, presenting these to the Deltase world in a consistent, and preferably generic, manner. An important use for transformer objects is in interfacing to input-output devices, either directly or by way of existing drivers.

Implementation. Deltase/GEN is used to generate executable software components from the language-level computational objects; the term *capsule* is used for a software component that is generated from a computational object using Deltase/GEN. A capsule is directly executable on a particular type of host and under the chosen local operating system; for example, for operation under Unix, a capsule would be generated (and then handled) as a Unix process. A capsule consists of the compiled source code of one or more computational objects, together with additional code that provides the environment to map the computational object(s) onto the local operating system. This additional software is referred to as the *envelope*; each capsule contains one envelope, which represents all the code necessary to support all the computational objects within that capsule. The envelope is generated automatically by Deltase/GEN and includes the following:

- Interface modules corresponding to the services exported or imported by the computational objects (these modules are generated automatically from the service interface specifications);
- A set of environment-dependent library procedures;
- A thread scheduler for scheduling of threads local to that capsule; and
- Object-dependent support for error processing and fault treatment (see below).

Impact of fault tolerance. Deltase combines ODP concepts with the Delta-4 approach to fault tolerance based on user-transparent replicated computation. From the application programmer's viewpoint, fault tolerance is transparent. Deltase/GEN can automatically generate capsules and provide them with the additional runtime code necessary to support the Delta-4 replication models.

The error processing associated with the active replication model is carried out by the underlying communication system. However, this model requires that the observed behavior of each replica be identical in the absence of faults. From the viewpoint of Deltase/XEQ, this means that each replica of a capsule must process requests deterministically despite any possible internal parallelism. One means of ensuring this determinism is to structure each capsule as a state machine [43] so that capsule replicas process requests and supply responses in a strictly identical order. Adherence to the state machine model means that the object envelope must schedule threads in the same sequence and that the transfer of control from one thread to another must be at the same point in computation at all replicas.

In the case of the passive-replication model, Deltase/GEN generates an object envelope that allows a capsule replica to act either as the primary replica or as a backup replica. It is this special software in the object envelope that is responsible for sending and receiving checkpoints at appropriate times and updating the state of passive replicas. In the semiactive-replication model, Deltase/GEN must again generate an object envelope that allows a capsule replica to act either in leader mode or follower mode.

Deltase also provides support for the cloning mechanism associated with fault treatment (see the "Cloning" subsection).

System administration

System administration provides the mechanisms for managing a Delta-4 system: It consists of both support for network management in the classic sense and support for computation management.

Management functions. The term *administration* covers the set of management functions concerned with planning, organizing, supervising, and controlling a Delta-4 system. In particular, these management functions are concerned with maintaining a specified level of service and enabling the system to evolve by providing the means to add new facilities. Management of distributed systems is a complex and often ill-defined topic, for the following reasons [44]:

(1)   Distributed systems are large and complex;
(2)   Their components — very diverse in nature — all need to interact and be managed;
(3)   There are many different facets to management, since it has to deal not only with configuration, designation, performance, faults, security, and accounting but also with people and computers; and
(4)   There is a floating boundary between management and the normal functionality of the system.

The management of distributed systems is currently under intense discussion in the academic field as well as in the immense ISO standardization work, international multivendor initiatives (MAP, CNMA, and Open Systems Interconnection [OSI]/Network Management Forum), and network management product developments (IBM's Netview, Hewlett-Packard's Open View, and Digital Equipment Corporation's EMA). An important consequence of the sophisticated Delta-4 fault-tolerance facilities is that system administration must cover not only the management of communication resources but also those resources necessary for computation. Presently, as is the case in MAP [45], the following three categories of management functions are supported:

- Management of system configuration and naming,
- Performance management, and
- Fault and maintenance management.

The latter category of functions is particularly important in Delta-4, because it includes all aspects of fault treatment mentioned earlier. A further category of management functions concerned with security is also being investigated [17].

Management model and design principles. Delta-4 management is based on the ISO/OSI concept of "managed objects," which has been consistently extended so that it can be applied to objects outside the OSI scope — for instance, hardware and software components. Apart from their normal functionality, managed objects are characterized by

(1)   *Attributes* such as their version identification, their state and their operational parameters, information relative to their error and performance statistics, and their dependencies with respect to other managed objects;
(2)   Specially defined management *operations* to allow access to, and manipulation of, object attributes such as *create, clone, delete, reinitialize, set_value*, and *get_value*; and
(3)   *Events,* which are a means by which a managed object delivers management information asynchronously (events are a special form of attributes).

In accordance with the current state of the art in distributed systems management [41], [46], management specific to a set of managed objects is termed *domain management* and the set of objects is termed a *domain*. Examples of domains are sets of nodes, sets of replicas, and sets of software components. Since replicas of a given software component may be located only on certain nodes (those possessing the resources necessary for their execution), the set of such nodes is termed the software component *replication domain*.

Each management domain in Delta-4 is assigned an architectural component called a *domain manager*. A domain manager may consist of a single domain manager process (that may be replicated) or a set of *peer domain manager processes* that cooperate within the domain boundary to carry out domain-specific management tasks. Domain managers of different domains cooperate to fulfill common management policies.

Domain managers make use of two sorts of management information: management information about managed objects that is integrated within the domain manager and management information integrated within these managed objects that is closely related to their normal functionality. Both kinds of management information are conceptually summarized under the term *management information base (MIB)*, which therefore is, by its very principle, distributed.

The Delta-4 implementation presently comprises the following three types of domain managers:

(1)   A manager of communication objects within a communication domain — termed, in accordance with the MAP terminology, a *systems management application process (SMAP)* (a domain manager process of the communication domain manager);

(2)   Managers of application objects within replication domains, termed *replication domain managers*; and

(3)   A manager of a particular object within a replication domain that contains management information, termed a *global-MIB* or an *MIB domain manager*.

Communication domain managers in Delta-4 manage types of communication objects beyond those defined in present ISO, MAP, and IEEE standards. Furthermore, these communication objects may be replicated. By essence, the SMAPs cannot be replicated themselves. Consequently, SMAPs are executed by self-checking hardware — the fail-silent network attachment controllers. A special protocol (multipoint-common management information protocol [M-CMIP]) is used for the exchange of information between SMAPs. To manage replicated communication objects, SMAPs on different Delta-4 nodes must have a consistent view of the nonlocal features of such objects. To achieve this, the corresponding communication management information is stored in a separate global management database, the global-MIB. As this is critical information, the global-MIB is replicated and thus managed by a (replication) domain manager of its own (the MIB domain manager).

The architectural approach has also been applied to objects on the application level, as follows:

- *Processes*: These form the basis on which (existing) applications are built. In the present Delta-4 implementation, a Deltase capsule is represented by a Unix process.
- *Files*: In certain applications, the use of replicated global files may be useful.

These kernel management components, which support the Delta-4 fault-tolerance approach, are supplemented by a set of management application tools with graphical human interfaces to allow the control and the visualization of the Delta-4 system behavior. Among these are a configuration toolbox for the global-MIB and various status, utilization, and performance monitoring tools.

Cloning

Cloning techniques have been investigated and implemented for both Deltase capsules [47] and files. Cloning of higher level objects — for instance, file servers and databases — may be based on the cloning mechanisms of these basic managed objects.

The implemented cloning machinery for both capsules and files comprises the following:

(1) A replication domain manager (RDM).[10] The RDM applies a reconfiguration strategy to a set of replicated processes/files that have the same replication domain. The reconfiguration strategy defines when and where new replicas are to be instantiated — for instance, restoration of the replication degree of objects that have lost a replica due to node failure (by cloning them to nodes offering spare redundancy) and migration of all objects from a node (such as those due for maintenance).

(2) Object manager entities (OMEs). Local to the managed-application objects, OMEs perform the cloning protocol on request of the replication domain manager.

The cloning of Deltase capsules is carried out by three generic components: a capsule RDM, capsule OMEs, and *factories*. A factory exists on each node and is responsible for instantiation of capsule replicas on that node. To instantiate a capsule replica at a particular node, the replication domain manager makes use of the services offered by the factory resident at that node. Each capsule includes an OME as part of its envelope that is responsible for carrying out those operations that can be done only from within the capsule. The capsule OME consists of a set of library procedures, which are included in the envelope as part of the capsule generation process.

The initial state of a new capsule replica is obtained from the file generated by the capsule generation process. The current state of the replicated capsule is obtained from the OMEs of the existing replica(s) by what is essentially the same activity as the checkpointing activity associated with the passive-replication model. Further local state information is handled locally by the OME at the node where the new replica is created. This information consists of data specific to the local environment of the new replica, such as references to local resources.

Validation

For an architecture to be designated "dependable," it is necessary that users of the architecture may justifiably place their confidence in the architecture. Consequently, such an architecture must undergo extensive validation from both the verification viewpoint (removal of faults in the specification, design, or implementation) and the evaluation viewpoint (quantification of the provided dependability and performance).

Validation can and should be carried out at each step in the process of producing a system. At the specification stage, validation consists essentially of verifying that the specifications of the architecture are mutually consistent with each other and with the requirements of the intended application domains. This "informal" verification is carried out in Delta-4 by a "peer review process" during scientific and technical committee meetings. More tangible validation activities are carried out during the design and implementation phases. Ideally, all components of a system should be extensively validated. However, for the money-critical (as opposed to life-critical) applications for which Delta-4 is intended, it was decided to restrict the validation to the most important (or the most critical) subsystems [48].

---

[10]For fault tolerance, replication domain managers are also replicated; replicas of a replication domain manager are called *domain management entities (DMEs)*.

Design validation

Design validation is centered on descriptions or models of the future implementation. Its purpose is twofold: to verify that these models are consistent with the specifications and to evaluate or predict characteristics such as performance and dependability of the future implementation. The following two design validation activities have been carried out:

(1) *Protocol verification,* aimed at removing faults in the protocol design, has been carried out on various versions of the essential atomic multicasting protocol, AMp. This work used temporal logic specifications of the required properties of AMp and verification that a formal description of the protocol, in Estelle/R, satisfied these properties [49]. Present protocol verification work is centered on the interreplica protocol of the session layer of the OSA variant of the architecture [18].

(2) *Dependability evaluation* work is being carried out with a view to quantifying the dependability actually achievable by the Delta-4 architecture. The work carried out to date has centered on the communications infrastructure; it has shown the importance of coverage of the network attachment controller self-checking mechanisms (to substantiate the fail-silent assumption) and has identified the conditions under which redundant communication media should be employed [50]. Present dependability evaluation work is aimed at evaluating the availability and reliability of applications making use of the various Delta-4 fault-tolerance models.

Implementation validation

Implementation validation is centered on testing actual prototype versions of the architecture instead of on models. Like design validation, its purpose is twofold: to verify that the implementation provides the specified functionality and to evaluate and measure some characteristics of the actual implementation. Implementation validation has centered on the following two aspects:

(1) *Fault injection* (into the prototype hardware) has been used as a means of validating the self-checking mechanisms of the Delta-4 NACs and the implementation, on these NACs, of the AMp [51]. This activity contributes to the verification of the absence of implementation faults and residual design faults. In particular, it verifies that the system works as intended in the presence of the very faults it is meant to tolerate. Fault injection also enables the measurement of the effectiveness of the built-in error detection and fault-tolerance mechanisms by means of coverage, dormancy, and latency estimations.

(2) *Software reliability* evaluation is being carried out on many of the major software subsystems of the architecture. Static testing tools are being used to identify important characteristics of the implemented software. In addition, failure data are being collected during the software-development-and-testing phase in order to predict the rate at which residual design and implementation faults are expected to cause the system to fail when in operational use.

Conclusions

This paper gives an overview of the fault-tolerant distributed architecture developed by the Delta-4 project. The project has demonstrated that — with suitable hardware and software support — the "inherent" redundancy of distributed systems can be usefully exploited to allow dependability to be conferred on distributed applications on a service-by-service basis.

Prototype implementations of both variants of the architecture have been developed and successfully demonstrated. Two pilot applications of the architecture are nearing completion: a credit card authorization server for the Crédit Agricole banking company and a computer-integrated manufacturing system for the Renault automobile company.

Acknowledgments

This paper (dated June 1991) describes the work of a 13-partner consortium, partially financed by the European Commission (ESPRIT project 2252, Delta-4: Definition and Design of an Open Dependable Distributed Architecture). The 13 partners are Bull SA (France), Crédit Agricole (France), Ferranti International (United Kingdom), IEI-CNR (Italy), IITB-Fraunhofer (Germany), INESC (Portugal), LAAS-CNRS (France), LGI-IMAG (France), MARI (United Kingdom), SRD-AEA Technology (United Kingdom), Renault (France), SEMA Group (France), and the University of Newcastle (United Kingdom).

The authors wish to thank the numerous persons who contributed to the success of the Delta-4 project.

References

[1] J.C. Laprie, "Dependability: A Unifying Concept for Reliable Computing and Fault Tolerance," in *Dependability of Resilient Systems,* T. Anderson, ed., Blackwell Scientific Pub., 1989, pp. 1-28.

[2] W.C. Carter, "A Time for Reflection," *Proc. FTCS 12th Ann. Int'l Symp. Fault-Tolerant Computing,* IEEE Computer Soc. Press, Los Alamitos, Calif., 1982, p. 41.

[3] T.A. Anderson and P.A. Lee, *Fault Tolerance — Principles and Practice,* Prentice-Hall, New York, N.Y., 1981.

[4] B.W. Lampson, "Atomic Transactions," in *Distributed Systems — Architecture and Implementation, Lecture Notes in Computer Science,* Vol. 11, Springer-Verlag, Berlin, Germany, 1981.

[5] J.H. Wensley et al., "SIFT: The Design and Analysis of a Fault-Tolerant Computer for Aircraft Control," *Proc. IEEE,* Vol. 66, No. 10, Oct. 1978, pp. 1240-1255.

[6] D. Powell et al., "The Delta-4 Approach to Dependability in Open Distributed Computing Systems," *Proc. 18th Int'l Symp. Fault-Tolerant Computing (FTCS-18),* IEEE Computer Soc. Press, Los Alamitos, Calif., 1988, pp. 246-251.

[7] R.D. Schlichting and F.B. Schneider, "Fail-Stop Processors: An Approach to Designing Fault-Tolerant Computing Systems." *ACM Trans. Computer Systems,* Vol. 1, No. 3, Aug. 1983, pp. 222-238.

[8] L. Lamport, R. Shostak, and M. Pease, "The Byzantine Generals Problem," *ACM Trans. Programming Languages and Systems,* Vol. 4, No. 3, July 1982, pp. 382-401.

[9] F. Cristian et al., "Atomic Broadcast: From Simple Message Diffusion to Byzantine Agreement," *Proc. 15th Ann. Int'l Symp. Fault-Tolerant Computing (FTCS-15),* IEEE Computer Soc. Press, Los Alamitos, Calif., 1985, pp. 200-206.

[10] D. Powell, "Fault Assumptions and Assumption Coverage," LAAS-CNRS, Report No. 90.074, Apr. 1990 (revised May 1991).

[11] E.D. Jensen, C.D. Locke, and H. Tokuda, "A Time-Driven Scheduling Model for Real-Time Operating Systems," *Proc. Real-Time Systems Symp.,* IEEE Computer Soc. Press, Los Alamitos, Calif., 1985, pp. 112-122.

[12] E.D. Jensen and J.D. Northcutt, "Alpha: A Non-Proprietary OS for Large, Complex, Distributed Real-Time Systems," *Proc. Workshop Experimental Distributed Systems,* IEEE Computer Soc. Press, Los Alamitos, Calif., 1990, pp. 35-41.

[13] J. Gray, "Why Do Computers Stop and What Can Be Done about It?," *Proc. Fifth Symp. Reliability Distributed Software and Database Systems,* IEEE Computer Soc. Press, Los Alamitos, Calif., 1986, pp. 3-12.

[14] H. Kopetz et al., "Tolerating Transient Faults in MARS," *Proc. Fault-Tolerant Computing: 20th Int'l Symp. (FTCS-20),* IEEE Computer Soc. Press, Los Alamitos, Calif., 1990, pp. 466-473.

[15] D. Powell, ed., "Delta-4: A Generic Architecture for Dependable Distributed Computing," Research Reports ESPRIT, Springer-Verlag, New York, N.Y., 1991.

[16] J.M. Fray, Y. Deswarte, and D. Powell, "Intrusion-Tolerance Using Fine-Grain Fragmentation-Scattering," *Proc. Symp. Security and Privacy,* IEEE Computer Soc. Press, Los Alamitos, Calif., 1986, pp. 194-201.

[17] L. Blain and Y. Deswarte, "Intrusion-Tolerant Security Servers for Delta-4," *Proc. ESPRIT '90 Conf.,* Kluwer Academic Publishers, Norwell, Mass., 1990.

[18] M. Chérèque et al., "Coordination of Active Replicas within the Delta-4 Open Systems Architecture: The Inter-Replica Protocol (IRp)," Delta-4 Document No. E91.055, Sept. 1991.

[19] N.A. Speirs and P.A. Barrett, "Using Passive Replicates in Delta-4 to Provide Dependable Distributed Computing," *Proc. 19th Int'l Symp. Fault-Tolerant Computing (FTCS-19),* IEEE Computer Soc. Press, Los Alamitos, Calif., 1989, pp. 184-190.

[20] P.A. Barrett et al., "The Delta-4 Extra Performance Architecture (XPA)," *Proc Fault-Tolerant Computing: 20th Int'l Symp. (FTCS-20),* IEEE Computer Soc. Press, Los Alamitos, Calif., 1990, pp. 481-488.

[21] D. Seaton et al., "The Delta-4 Extra Performance Architecture and Real Time," Delta-4 Document No. E91.054, Sept. 1991.

[22] A. Borg, J. Baumbach, and S. Glazer, "A Message System Supporting Fault Tolerance," *Proc. Ninth Symp. Operating System Principles,* ACM Press, New York, N.Y., 1983, pp. 90-99.

[23] P. Gunningberg, "Voting and Redundancy Management Implemented by Protocols in Distributed Systems," *Proc. FTCS 13th Int'l Symp. Fault-Tolerant Computing,* IEEE Computer Soc. Press, Los Alamitos, Calif., 1983, pp. 182-185.

[24] E.C. Cooper, "Circus: A Replicated Procedure Call Facility," *Proc. Fourth Symp. Reliability Distributed Software and Database Systems,* IEEE Computer Soc. Press, Los Alamitos, Calif., 1984, pp. 11-24.

[25] K.P. Birman, "Replication and Fault-Tolerance in the ISIS System," *Proc. 10th ACM Symp. Operating System Principles,* ACM Press, New York, N.Y., 1985.

[26] H. Kopetz and W. Merker, "The Architecture of MARS," *Proc. 15th Ann. Int'l Symp. Fault-Tolerant Computing (FTCS-15),* IEEE Computer Soc. Press, Los Alamitos, Calif., 1985, pp. 274-279.

[27] C.J. Walter, R.M. Kieckhafer, and A.M. Finn, "MAFT: A Multicomputer Architecture for Fault-Tolerance in Real-Time Control Systems," *Proc. Real-Time Systems Symp.,* IEEE Computer Soc. Press, Los Alamitos, Calif., 1985, pp. 133-140.

[28] S.K. Shrivastava et al., "A Technical Overview of Arjuna: A System for Reliable Distributed Computing," Tech. Report Series No. 262, Univ. of Newcastle upon Tyne, UK, July 1988.

[29] S. Mishra, L.L. Peterson, and R.D. Schlichting, "Implementing Fault-Tolerant Replicated Objects Using Psync," *Proc. Eighth Symp. Reliable Distributed Systems,* IEEE Computer Soc. Press, Los Alamitos, Calif., 1989, pp. 42-52.

[30] F. Cristian, B. Dancey, and J. Dehn, "Fault-Tolerance in the Advanced Automation System," *Proc. Fault-Tolerant Computing: 20th Int'l Symp. (FTCS-20),* IEEE Computer Soc. Press, Los Alamitos, Calif., 1990, pp. 6-17.

[31] P.M. Melliar-Smith and R. L. Schwartz, "Formal Specification and Mechanical Verification of SIFT: A Fault-Tolerant Flight Control System," *IEEE Trans. Computers,* Vol. C-31, No. 7, July 1982, pp. 616-630.

[32] R.M. Kieckhafer et al., "The MAFT Architecture for Distributed Fault Tolerance," *IEEE Trans. Computers,* Vol. 37, No. 4, April 1988, pp. 398-405.

[33] H. Kopetz et al., "Distributed Fault-Tolerant Real-Time Systems: The MARS Approach," *IEEE Micro,* Vol. 9, No. 1, Feb. 1988, pp. 25-40.

[34] H. Kopetz and W. Ochsenreiter, "Clock Synchronization in Distributed Real-Time Systems," *IEEE Trans. Computers,* Vol. C-36, No. 8, Aug. 1987, pp. 933-940.

[35] K.P. Birman and T.A. Joseph, "Reliable Communication in the Presence of Failures," *ACM Trans. Computer Systems,* Vol. 5, No. 1, Feb. 1987, pp. 47-76.

[36] K.P. Birman and T.A. Joseph, "Exploiting Virtual Synchrony in Distributed Systems," *Proc. 11th ACM Symp. Operating System Principles,* ACM Press, New York, N.Y., 1987, pp. 123-138.

[37] P. Veríssimo, L. Rodrigues, and M. Baptista, "AMp: A Highly Parallel Atomic Multicast Protocol," *Proc. SIGCOM '89 Symp.,* ACM Press, New York, N.Y., 1989, pp. 83-93.

[38] L. Rodrigues et al., "xAMp: The Delta-4 Group Communication Service," Delta-4 Document No. E91.069, Sept. 1991.

[39] C. Guérin, H. Raison, and P. Martin, "Procedure for Dependable Message Broadcasting in a Ring and Mechanism for Implementing the Procedure," French Patent No. 85.2.2, Jan. 1985 (in French).

[40] *User's Guide to Ferranti Real-Time System V,* (SVC200), Ferranti Int'l, Document No. U20410, Release 1, Issue 1a.

[41] *The ANSA Reference Manual — Advanced Network System Architecture,* Architecture Project Management Ltd., Cambridge, UK, Mar. 1989.

[42] "Support Environment for Open Distributed Processing (SE-ODP)," ECMA, Tech. Report No. 49, Jan. 1990.

[43] F.B. Schneider, "The State Machine Approach: A Tutorial," *Proc. Workshop Fault-Tolerant Distributed Computing, Lecture Notes in Computer Science,* Springer-Verlag, New York, N.Y., 1988, pp. 102-107.

[44] M. Sloman, "Distributed Systems Management," Research Report No. 87/6, Imperial College, 1987.

[45] *Network Management Requirements Specification — Manufacturing Automation Protocol Specification,* North American MAP/TOP Users Group, Ann Arbor, Mich., 1987.

[46] M. Sloman, "Domain Management for Distributed Systems," *Proc. IFIP TC6/WG6.6 Symp. Integrated Network Management,* Elsevier Science Pub. BV, North Holland, Boston, Mass., 1989.

[47] U. Bügel and B. Gilmore, "Process Cloning in Delta-4," Delta-4 Document No. E91.052, Sept. 1991.

[48] K. Kanoun et al., "Delta-4 Architecture Validation," *Proc. ESPRIT '91 Conf.,* Office for Official Pub. of the European Communities, 1991, pp. 234-252.

[49] M. Baptista et al., "Formal Specification and Verification of a Network Independent Atomic Multicast Protocol," *Proc. Third Int'l Conf. Formal Description Techniques (FORTE '90),* North Holland Pub., New York, N.Y., 1990.

[50] K. Kanoun and D. Powell, "Dependability Evaluation of Bus and Ring Communication Topologies for the Delta-4 Distributed Fault-Tolerant Architecture," *Proc. 10th Symp. Reliable Distributed Systems,* IEEE Computer Soc. Press, Los Alamitos, Calif., 1991, pp. 130-141.

[51] J. Arlat et al., "Experimental Evaluation of the Fault Tolerance of an Atomic Multicast Protocol," *IEEE Trans. Reliability,* Vol. 39, No. 4, Oct. 1990, pp. 455-467 (special issue on experimental evaluation of computer reliability).

Rollback Recovery in Concurrent Systems

I t is now recognized that most hardware faults in computing systems are soft [6]. In other words, the majority of faults in the hardware are of a transitory nature. Typically, transitory hardware faults include transient hardware problems, operational errors, erroneous input data, and timing problems resulting from an unusual combination of circumstances [7]. It is quite reasonable to assume that most temporary malfunctions, like power supply glitches, radiation effects, and thermal or mechanical vibrations, though basically hardware related, manifest themselves as software errors such as control flow and instruction errors in the underlying program. If these errors are detected immediately upon their occurrence, a successful recovery is possible by a rollback of the program. Rollback recovery is a backward error recovery technique to recover from temporary faults in computing systems.

Rollback recovery in a program involves saving the states of the system during the normal execution so that if an error is detected during runtime, the program can be restarted from one of the consistent states that have been saved. The activity of saving the states of a system is termed *rollback point insertion* (or *checkpointing*). Rollback recovery has been practiced in database systems as well as in process control systems [3],[4], [16],[18],[19],[20]. In either case, an objective is that rollback points be inserted such that the cost of rollback and recovery is minimized. In most process control systems, a constraint is that it is essential to be able to recover within a specified time. Therefore, the insertion of rollback points is commonly viewed as an optimization problem. It has been shown that in database systems, an optimal strategy is to insert rollback points at regular intervals [3],[5],[21]. Chandy and Ramamoorthy [4] developed an optimal rollback point insertion technique for checkpointing process control systems. This technique was generalized by Upadhyaya and Saluja [19] to multiple retries to take into consideration errors that may occur during the recovery process.

Shin, Lin, and Lee [14] studied the checkpointing of real-time tasks from a task-oriented view. (In a task-oriented view, a task is assigned to a processor; the task is allowed to continue until it is finished. A failure in a processor affects only the task running on that processor.) They gave two analytical models for real-time checkpointing based on the speed and correctness of the execution

Shambhu J. Upadhyaya and

Aravindan Ranganathan

of tasks. They showed that under certain assumptions on error detection, an optimal decision in real-time systems is to insert rollback points at regular intervals. Since the checkpointing instant is arbitrary, their strategy might create a rollback point between the time of a failure and its detection, in which case the saved state of the system might be incorrect and the subsequent rollback recovery would then be unsuccessful. Although either a *cold restart* or saving the system state at multiple checkpoints may alleviate this problem, they may not be acceptable in practice for the following reasons: (1) The recovery time constraints in real-time systems may be so stringent that a cold restart is unacceptable and (2) the state saving at multiple checkpoints might require considerable storage.

The techniques discussed above are applicable only to uniprocess systems or concurrent systems where processes do not communicate with one another. In the model of Shin, Lin, and Lee [14], the interprocess communications are assumed to take place at the initiation and termination of a process. Such an assumption is rather restrictive, since real-time concurrent processes may communicate during their execution for maximal cooperation.

In concurrent systems where processes are allowed to communicate, a fault in one process may propagate to another process. Hence, when an error is detected by a process, it may force other processes that received a communication from it to roll back to a point prior to the point at which it received that communication. Similarly, a process that received an erroneous communication from another may in turn force a rollback on some other processes. Detection of an error in one process can thus initiate in a program a disastrous avalanche of rollback, termed by Randell [12] as the *domino effect*.

A number of techniques have been proposed to overcome the domino effect in concurrent systems. These techniques are based on restricted communication [1],[8], synchronization of the rollback point establishment [13],[15], and judicious placement of rollback points to form a recovery line [12]. In most existing solutions to limit the domino effect, the overheads are quite high and, in some cases, process autonomy is sacrificed significantly [13]. In the next section, we review all the existing techniques used to avoid the domino effect.

The unification of the avoidance of the domino effect and the timely recovery of processes within a specified deadline are the main topics of this paper. The technique we propose here can be employed for recovery in distributed process control applications that are generally subject to stringent deadlines. We present a new approach to rollback point insertion that requires no more than a three-step rollback on any process. Our model is introduced in the section entitled "A new communication model." This model, which is based on a common memory, is used to eliminate the domino effect. No process autonomy is sacrificed and no additional rollback points are inserted, contrary to most existing schemes. Next, a new rollback model and its application to meeting the user-specified deadline are presented in the section entitled "Rollback recovery mechanism." A graph model is used for the program; in this graph model, nodes represent tasks and edges represent control flow. Rollback points are inserted only in the edges of the program graph, which guarantees that single state saving is sufficient for successful recovery in uniprocess systems. Although multiple state savings per process may be necessary in concurrent systems, there is no need for a cold restart of the program under any circumstances. In the section entitled "A rollback point insertion strategy," the optimal checkpointing strategy of Chandy and Ramamoorthy [4] is extended to concurrent processes. In the section entitled "Experimental study," we present a computer simulation to study the effectiveness of our technique. A discussion appears in the final section.

Review of existing schemes

Before reviewing the existing schemes used to avoid the domino effect, we describe the phenomenon of the domino effect by means of the diagram in Figure 1. We assume that a program is composed of several processes that execute concurrently to maximize the throughput. Each process can be looked upon as a sequence of tasks. The figure shows two processes P_1 and P_2 communicating with each other. The sequence of tasks that are executed in the processes during the program execution is indicated by straight lines drawn downward with respect to time. The process interactions (communications) are indicated by straight-line arrows numbered 1 through 4 for ease of identification. The insertion of a rollback point is indicated by a small, rectangular box. Process P_1 inserts a rollback point at, let's say, x_1 and continues processing the next task. Similarly, process P_2 inserts a rollback point at, let's say, y_1. The processes communicate as determined by the program and insert more rollback points as shown in the figure. Let process P_2 detect an error as indicated in the figure. Since the error has been detected in P_2, Communication 4 may be erroneous and P_1 has to roll back to x_3 and process P_2 to y_2. The error in P_2 might have been caused by an erroneous communication received via Communication 3. Therefore, P_1 should roll back to x_2 to

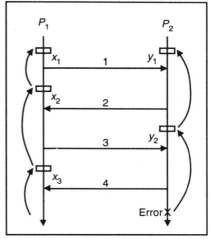

Figure 1. The domino effect.

retransmit Communication 3. Communication 2 can be suspected of being erroneous; subsequently, so can Communication 1. Finally, the processes roll back all the way to their respective origins before they can be restarted.

The domino effect can be avoided by the proper coordination of the communications and/or the rollback points. A number of strategies have been proposed to control the domino effect. The basic technique is to form a consistent set of active recovery points, called a *recovery line* [2], for the processes that communicated with each other, so that when any one of the processes involved detects an error, recovery is initiated from this recovery line.

The domino effect is a phenomenon found also in recovery block schemes [2]; Randell [12] introduced the idea of a conversation method to avoid the domino effect in recovery block schemes. In Randell's method, the domino effect is overcome by forcing the processes to leave their acceptance tests at the same instant. The whole program is divided into a number of tasks. Each process, after having completed its task, performs an acceptance (or validation) test to check the consistency of the results. Some typical validation tests are (1) a check for a divide-by-zero operation and (2) a range check on the values. If a process passes its acceptance test, then it waits for other processes to complete their acceptance tests. Upon completion of their acceptance tests, the states of the processes are saved and the next task is executed. If an error is detected by one of the processes, all the processes roll back to the previously saved state and resume execution. An advantage of this method is that multiple rollback is avoided; consequently, not much computation is undone during rollback. Rollback points are introduced in predefined positions, leading to the precise determination of the time spent in saving the states of the system during rollback point insertion. This method has a disadvantage in that processor time is wasted by waiting for other processes to complete their acceptance tests.

Kim [9] extended the idea of a conversation method to avoid the domino effect. He suggested the insertion of special rollback points, called *branch-RPs*, in addition to the regular rollback points inserted after the process has passed its acceptance tests. Branch-RPs are forced in a process prior to a communication being received from other processes. A monitor, consisting of a shared-data structure and all the operations that processes can perform on it, is used for interprocess communication. The advantage of this method is that processor time is not wasted (by waiting for other processes to complete their acceptance tests), thereby increasing the throughput of the processor. The disadvantages are that extra rollback points are introduced and that it is necessary to save the states of the previous rollback point, since a two-step rollback might result. Rollback point insertion due to communication cannot be predicted before the task execution and the time spent in saving states of the system cannot be determined precisely. Since additional rollback points are introduced, there is an increased overhead. This method requires a coordinating processor to save the states of the monitor at various instants of time in order to restore the monitors and maintain the rollback points. While this model is best suited for handling design faults, error recovery within a given deadline has not been addressed by this method.

Shin and Lee [13] discussed three methods for implementing recovery blocks used to recover from design faults. These are the *synchronous method*, the *asynchronous method*, and *pseudorecovery point implementation*. In the synchronous method, process autonomy is sacrificed and processes are forced to wait for commitments from other processes to establish a recovery line, leading to inefficient time utilization. In the asynchronous method, the establishment of rollback points in a process is made independent of other processes, and unbounded rollback propagation becomes a serious problem. As a compromise between asynchronous and synchronous rollback points, they proposed pseudorecovery point insertion so that unbounded rollback propagation is avoided. This method is best suited for handling design faults where an acceptance test is performed after the execution of a task. A recovery point is always established after the process has successfully performed an acceptance test. A pseudorecovery point is defined as a recovery point that is established without a preceding acceptance test.

Lee and Shin [11] discussed a quasi-synchronized method in which an external clock sends a state-save invocation signal at regular intervals that requests all the processes to establish a rollback point after completing their current instruction and to then execute a validation test. If the validation test succeeds, then the saved state would be regarded as a rollback point for the next interval. Each process has a record of its communication with other processes between rollback points. It is possible that a state-save invocation signal is given after a process sends a data item and before the other processes have received it. This results in an inconsistent state and may force further rollback. The instants at which rollback points are introduced cannot be determined beforehand and error recovery within a given period of time cannot be guaranteed.

Kant and Silberschatz [8] discussed the avoidance of the domino effect by the restriction of communication between the processes. They formulated a set of rules to restrict the communication in a least possible way so that multiple rollback could be avoided. Here, the insertion of rollback points again cannot be specified a priori and the error recovery within a given period of time was not discussed. They brought out the importance of *locally verifiable* and *not locally verifiable* variables, and they showed that conditions required for ensuring finite upper bounds on multiple rollback are more severe for not locally verifiable variables than for locally verifiable variables.

Ahamad and Lin [1] proposed a method to localize the effects of faults in a distributed system such that checkpointing and recovery in various processes are independent. They adopted pessimistic logging of messages for deterministic computation requiring a stable storage. Although no message logging is needed when system execution is nondeterministic, the locality principle demands the blocking of execution of processes by delaying the delivery of incoming messages until a checkpoint is taken by the sending process. This results in sacrificing process autonomy and may not be applicable to systems subject to stringent deadlines.

We propose a model for rollback recovery in concurrent systems in which the maximum time of recovery is specified and multiple rollback is limited to only three steps. We use a common memory similar to that in Kim's monitor [9] in order to support the interprocess communications. But the design of the common memory we use is much simpler compared to Kim's monitor. This common memory can be accessed by all the processes. No restriction is imposed on the communication;

however, certain conditions are placed on the data being sent and received. The method by which processes communicate is discussed in the next section.

A new communication model

The communication between processes plays a vital role in controlling the domino effect. Therefore, it is necessary to understand clearly how the processes communicate. We are developing a new communication model based on a common (shared) memory, where the communications can be stored and retransmitted. The main principle behind our model is to save the interprocess communications in a distributed manner so that the domino effect is alleviated. Since all the processes are allowed to communicate, a global record of active communications and saving at different instants would be difficult to implement and also would be time-consuming in a real-time setup. Therefore, the processes are allowed to handle their own communications. Each process has its share in the common memory through which it can transmit, and when rollback points are inserted, the state of the common memory relevant to the process will be saved. During the recovery, each process updates only its region in the common memory. The common memory can be implemented physically in a distributed manner. The implementation of the new communication model is explained below.

Let there be n processes $P_1, P_2, \ldots, P_n$ communicating with each other at a given time. Let the common memory CM be divided into N regions, CM_i, $1 \leq i \leq N$, where N is the maximum number of processes that can be scheduled in a system. Note that CM is used only for interprocess communication and not for internal operations within a process. Also, each process can read and write in its region in the common memory, but can only read from the regions of other processes. Standard memory-protection schemes can be established to accomplish this. Each process has its own local memory, for its exclusive use, which cannot be accessed by other processes. The regions in the common memory must be well organized so that transmitting and receiving a communication can be done easily. This is achieved by indexing each communication sent and received. The index field of each communication contains the name of the process sending it, the name of the process receiving it, and the sequence number of the communication. As an example, suppose that process P_j requires the kth communication from process P_i. Process P_j looks in the region CM_i for the index $PC(k, i, j)$, k representing the kth communication between process P_i (sender) and process P_j (receiver).

The organization of the common memory is as follows: At the starting address of each region in the common memory, a table is maintained that has the information about the messages available in that region. The first entry in the table contains the count of the messages. Following the count is the index of the communications available and a pointer to it. The number of indexes found in the table corresponds to the count. In Figure 2, which illustrates two processes P_i and P_j, the regions in the common memory and the tables associated with each region are shown. From the table, a process can find out the communications available for it. Therefore, if process P_j has to receive a communication from P_i, it reads the table from region CM_i of the common memory and finds index $PC(k, i, j)$ and the pointer to the message. If $PC(k, i, j)$ is missing in the table, then it means that process P_i has not yet computed the data and process P_j will have to wait.

Each process is associated with a number of pointers, as shown in Figure 2. The two processes P_i and P_j contain the starting addresses of their respective regions and the regions of other processes in the common memory. When a process needs data from another process, it finds its starting address in the common memory, accesses the first word in that region, and finds the length of the table; it then searches the table for the location of the data and reads the data. When a new communication arrives, it is written in the first available empty space within the corresponding region, until all the memory locations in that region are occupied. If a particular region in the common memory is full, then the message that was written earliest in that region is overwritten. This is based on the assumption that

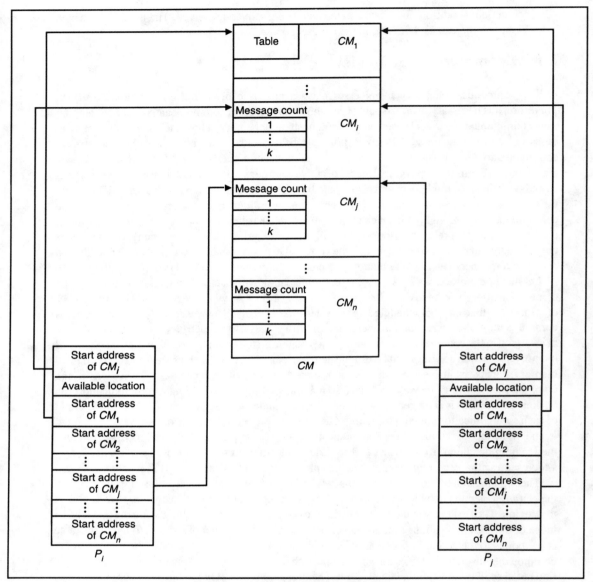

Figure 2. Layout of common memory.

communications are consumed as soon as they are transmitted. In reality, if there is a need for the communication that has been overwritten, it would be difficult to retrieve it and a deadlock would result. In order to avoid such deadlocks, the common-memory regions for the processes have to be increased; hence, determining the size of the common memory required for each process becomes a design problem. (This is an issue outside the scope of this paper.) The entries in the table have another field for data validation. A *true* validation field indicates that the message is error-free; a *false* validation field means that the message is not yet confirmed.

During system state saving, each process saves the state of its region in the common memory. The saved state of the common memory is loaded back into its region if rollback recovery is necessitated by the detection of an error. This guarantees that each process is consistent with the communications sent by it during recovery.

The overhead involved due to the above-described communication model is quite moderate. The size of the tables in the regions of the common memory is expected to be small; hence, the overall size of the common memory is also expected to be small. In terms of time overhead, the major detractor will be the time needed to search down the tables for the indexes of communication. If the size of the table is small, a sequential search can be adopted. The actual cost of the proposed common-memory system will depend on other factors, such as the communication intensity and the consumption rate of the communications.

Rollback recovery mechanism

A program model

The rollback point insertion strategy presented in this paper is an extension of Chandy and Ramamoorthy's basic model [4] used for checkpointing uniprocess systems. We consider a *system-oriented view*, where a program is carefully partitioned into a number of concurrent processes. These processes, which communicate with each other for maximal cooperation, may run on the same processor or may be assigned to distinct processors in a distributed multiprocessor environment. A process, which is a collection of tasks, is represented by a directed graph, as shown in Figure 3, where node i represents task i and a directed edge (i, j) exists if task i is followed by task j with nonzero probability. In deriving a process graph of a program, special care should be taken to represent repeated tasks. If a task is iterated, then either (1) each iteration of the task is treated as a distinct task, or (2) if the number of iterations is not known in advance, the iterations are coalesced into a single task. Thus, an arbitrary process is transformed into a graph with no cycles, leading to an acyclic graph.

Only temporary faults are considered in our model. On the other hand, software faults such as design bugs will cause a permanent error, unless an alternate module is used during the recovery. Special techniques exist to handle software errors; however, these techniques are not discussed here. We assume that if an error occurs within a task, it is detected before the completion of the task. In practice, errors can be detected by using a low-cost watchdog processor [19]. We also assume that a watchdog processor is responsible for the detection of errors that are local to a process. We now define the notations used in Figure 3; however, these notations are used explicitly only in the next section, "A rollback point insertion strategy."

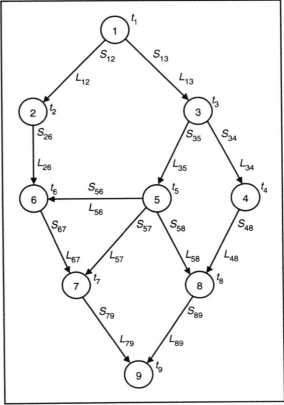

Figure 3. Directed acyclic graph for process execution.

(1)   Definition 1 [4]: For each node i of the process graph, a real number t_i is specified; t_i is the *anticipated time of completion* of task i. Within a task, there may be several execution paths; therefore, in the estimation of the value of t_i, the longest execution path should be taken into account.

(2)   Definition 2 [4]: The *savetime* S_{ij} associated with edge (i, j) of the process graph is the time taken to save the state of the system after task i has been completed and when it is known that task j follows task i. It may be noted that while S_{ij}'s are being estimated, the path within the nodes along which the maximum number of variables change must be considered.

(3)   Definition 3 [4]: The *loadtime* L_{ij} is the time taken to load the state of the system at edge (i, j) to the main memory.

(4)   Definition 4: The *recovery time* r at node i is the time required to load the saved state at the most recent rollback point and to rerun the program from this point to node i. Suppose that a rollback point is inserted in edge $(1, 2)$ and that tasks are denoted by consecutive numbers; then,

$$r = L(1,2) + \sum_{s=2}^{i} r_s$$

where r_s is the actual execution time of task s. We assume that during the recovery process, the time taken to execute task i is the same as the time taken during normal execution and that $r_s \le t_s$.

We now explain how the common memory can be used to establish the consistency of communications if erroneous communications are exchanged among various processes. Initially, all the communications received from another process are placed in an invalidated state. A process can validate the communications sent if no errors are detected locally at the completion of the current task. The validation of the communications sent is done as follows:

(1)   At the completion of a task, the communications are checked in chronological order for their validation. If no communications are received before a communication is sent, then all the communications sent prior to the next communication being received are validated.

(2)   If the communication received has the validation entry "true," then a validation is sent to all the processes that have been sent a communication prior to the next communication being received.

(3)   If the communication received is not validated, then the validity of the communication sent after that is postponed until the end of the next task, when the validity of the communication received is tested again.

The communications exchanged by a given process in the common memory are monitored, and a set of tuples is formed; each tuple contains the name of the process with which the given process communicated and the associated task number. The set of tuples and the table in the common memory corresponding to the given process are saved in a backup storage or a recovery cache [10] when a rollback point is inserted. When an error is flagged, the process detecting it looks into the set of tuples saved in the backup to determine the distance for rollback. During the recovery from an error, the table for the common memory is loaded back from the backup, along with the system variables, and the process starts reexecuting the program as determined by a recovery algorithm. Since the table is reloaded into the common memory, the entries for the communications sent after that point can be removed. Hence, a process looking for a communication during that time period will have to wait; during recovery, the processes can follow any task-execution sequence as determined by the real-time conditions at that instant.

Figure 4 illustrates the scenario of interprocess communication described above, which we refer to as *Scenario 1*. Using this illustration, we now explain the above-discussed formation of the set of tuples. Let the processes be named as $P_1, P_2, P_3, \ldots, P_n$ and let each task in a process be assigned a number. Thus, the tuple (P_j, l) in the set of process P_i corresponds to the lth task of process P_j. The order in which the tuples are written into this set is chronological. An entry that appears before another in the set implies that the corresponding communication was performed before the other. A single bit can be associated with each entry to indicate whether the data item was sent or received. The figure shows the set associated with each rollback point; the arrow indicates the direction of the communication. When a process starts executing, the set will be empty; as the communication takes place, the set will start building up. Assume that in a given snapshot, tasks x_1, y_1, and z_1 are being executed in processes P_1, P_2, and P_3, respectively. During the execution of task x_1 of process P_1, this process sends a communication to task y_1 of process P_2. At the end of the execution of task x_1, if no error is detected, process P_1 will validate the communication sent. But, during the execution of task x_2, process P_1 receives a communication from task y_2 of process P_2 and sends a communication to task z_2 of process P_3. At the end of task x_2, P_1 cannot validate the communication sent to P_3, since P_2 has not validated its communication yet. Hence, P_1 has to postpone the validation on the communication sent until the end of task x_3. When a new rollback point is inserted, its corresponding set will contain some or no entries generated at the previous rollback point.

The rules for adding and deleting entries to and from the set are as follows:

(1) When a task writes a data item into its region in the common memory, it appends the process and the task number of the process (a tuple) for which this data item is meant. If an identical tuple already exists, no new tuple is formed. In other words, all the communications between a pair of processes are indicated by a single tuple.

(2) When a task reads data from the common memory, it checks the validity of the data. If the data item is validated, then no entry is added to the set; if the data item is not validated, then the tuple that contains the process and the task number of the process that has written the data is appended to its set.

(3) When a task is completed, it checks for the validity of the communication received and then checks for the validity of the communication sent. All the communications that are validated are removed from the current set.

(4) When a fresh rollback point is inserted, a new set will be formed by retaining and transferring the tuples that were not validated from the previous set.

When a process detects an error, it has to roll back to the previous rollback point and also has to inform all other processes that have received a communication from it to roll back so as to obtain the correct data. For example, in Figure 4, if process P_1 detects an error during the execution of task x_1, then it forces a rollback on process P_2. A process that had received a communication from the erroneous process has to inform the processes that have received a communication from it after the erroneous communication has been received. For example, in Figure 4, if process P_2 detected an error during the execution of task y_2, it forces a rollback on process P_1 to reexecute task x_2. The process P_1 sent a communication to process P_3 after it had received the erroneous communication. Hence, it forces a rollback on process P_3 to reexecute task z_2. If process P_1 detected an error during the execution of task x_2, then it forces a rollback on process P_3. However, process P_2 need not roll back to reexecute task y_2, since it did not receive any communication from the erroneous process; hence, reaccessing the same data is not prevented in this model. During recovery, process P_1 will read again the same data from process P_2.

Figure 5 gives another scenario of interprocess communication, which we refer to as *Scenario 2*. Processes P_1 and P_2 establish rollback points at RP_1 and RP_2, respectively, and then a communication

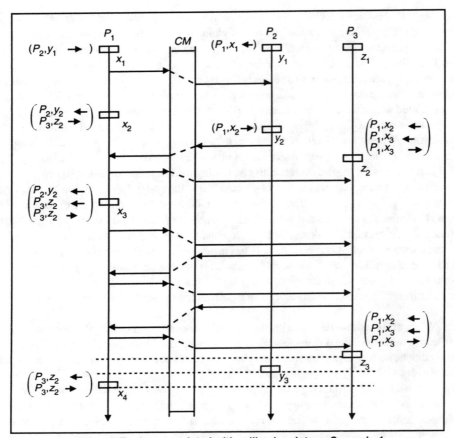

Figure 4. Tuples associated with rollback points — Scenario 1.

is sent by process P_1 to process P_2. Process P_2 then inserts a rollback point at RP_3 and then sends a communication to process P_1. Then, process P_2 detects an error and rolls back to RP_3, and this forces process P_1 to roll back to RP_1. Since process P_1 rolls back to RP_1, it will retransmit the communication it had sent to P_2 earlier. But, P_2 need not roll back to RP_2 so as to receive the communication. This can be explained as follows: Process P_1 sent the communication before receiving the erroneous communication; hence, there is no possibility for the communication to be erroneous. However, when the data item is written by process P_1 for the second time, process P_1 will write the same data as before in its common memory.

Theorem 1: Assume that all computations are deterministic. Under this assumption, whenever an error is detected, the processes roll back only a finite distance and no restart of the processes from their respective origins is necessary.

Proof: Let processes $P_1, P_2, P_3, \ldots, P_n$ communicate in a cooperative manner. Let τ_i be the time at which a process P_i inserts a rollback point and let τ $(\tau > \tau_i)$ be the time at which the process detects a local error. Since errors are detected before the completion of a task by the watchdog processor, process P_i must have been error-free prior to τ_i. Therefore, an error must have occurred during the interval between τ_i and τ; hence, the computation done during that period in process P_i must be

---

undone. The communications sent during that period may be erroneous also; hence, the processes (let's say $P_j, j \neq i$) that received communication during that time period must roll back. Process P_j must have to roll back to a point beyond τ_i, let's say τ_j ($\tau_j \leq \tau_i$), so as to obtain the correct data (see Figure 6). In doing so, process P_j need not undo the communications sent during the interval between τ_j and τ_i, since they were erroneous only after τ_i. If process P_j had received a communication during the interval between τ_j and τ_i, the process that

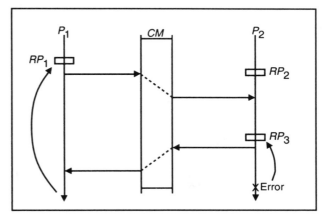

Figure 5. Communication Scenario 1.

sent the communication need not roll back to retransmit the communication, since it is taken care of by the communication model. Hence, all the processing done until the time τ_i is kept intact, and so the rollback is limited to the time τ_j and no further.

From the above theorem, we can conclude that the process that detects an error rolls back only to the most recent rollback point. The rollback of individual processes of a program in a global scenario depends on the communications as well as on the rollback point insertion strategy, a fact that we discuss next.

Meeting the deadline

Consider a process control system where rollback points are inserted in the individual processes such that, at any point in the program, recovery is possible within a specified time, let's say M, where M is the maximum specified recovery time. Such a local recovery time constraint is typical of process control systems where a certain task should be completed within a specified time, irrespective of errors [4]. Parameter M plays an important role in the recovery of process control systems. In a process control system, outputs generally have to be committed to the environment. Therefore, it is essential to keep M small in critical jobs and to delay the commitments accordingly. Thus, the time constraints can be met in real time and consistency on the commitments can be retained. The selection of a value for M depends on the application. (Some guidelines on this selection were given by Upadhyaya and Saluja [19].)

Let i and j be two consecutive tasks of a process. A decision is to be made about inserting a rollback in an edge (i, j). In uniprocess systems, rollback points are inserted in edge (i, j) if $r + t_j > M$ at the end of the execution of task i. Although rollback points can be inserted if $r + t_j \leq M$ at the end of task i, there is no gain in doing so; thus, no rollback point will be inserted. Since a rollback point has to be inserted within M units of time anywhere in the program, it is only reasonable to have the maximum task-execution time less than or equal to M. This condition for rollback point insertion can be applied to concurrent systems only if the processes do not communicate. When a process receives or transmits a data item, it may be forced to roll back because of an error in another process; therefore, the above-mentioned condition cannot be used to insert rollback points. Consequently, the maximum task-execution time can no longer be limited to M.

Theorem 2: If a process either receives or transmits data or both receives and transmits data, then the rollback points have to be inserted at least every $M/2$ units of time.

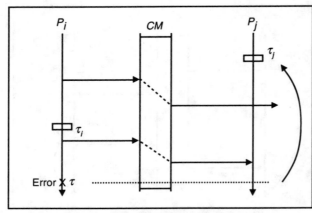

Figure 6. Error detection and recovery.

Proof: Let processes P_j and P_i, $i, j = 1, 2, \ldots, n, i \neq j$, respectively, transmit and receive data as shown in Figure 7. In this scenario, which we refer to as *Scenario 3*, if an error occurs in P_j, then it takes e_2 units of time for process P_j to recover and e units of time for process P_i to recover. Because we are interested in the recovery of all the processes within M units of time, we have to consider the worst case. The worst case of recovery corresponds to $e = e_1 + e_2$; that is, a process sends a communication just after inserting a rollback point and the process that receives the communication does so just before inserting a rollback point.

Figure 8 shows *Scenario 4*, where process P_i both receives and transmits data and process P_j both receives and transmits data. As explained earlier, it takes $e_1 + e_2$ units of time for both processes to recover from an error. Note that if more than two processes are involved in the communication, e_2 will be the maximum of the recovery times of all the processes involved. We require that $e_1 + e_2 \leq M$. Considering the worst case, let us assume that both of the processes execute for a time interval equal to the maximum allowable time. This means that $e_1 = e_2$. Thus, in order to recover within M units of time, rollback points have to be inserted in intervals of $M/2$ units of time.

Corollary 1: In situations where a process both receives and transmits data, the maximum execution time of each task should be less than or equal to $M/2$.

The rules for rollback point insertion so that recovery is possible within a specified deadline are summarized below.

- If there is no communication, rollback points are inserted in an interval of M units of time.
- If a process sends or receives data, rollback points have to be inserted in an interval of $M/2$ units of time.

In summary, the process that detects the error initiates the recovery by a self-rollback and also by invoking the rollback of all the processes that received a communication from the task that detects an error.

Deletion of rollback points

Although rollback points, in the worst case, are inserted within M units of time in a process, the actual rollback point insertion takes place following an optimization strategy. One such strategy is to minimize the total time spent in saving the system states, as discussed in the next section, "A rollback point insertion strategy." If a particular strategy is used for rollback point insertion, several rollback points may be inserted in an interval of M units of time. Thus, it is possible that at a given time, a number of rollback points may be present in the backup. If special hardware such as a recovery cache is used for backup, it is essential to minimize the number of rollback points that need to be

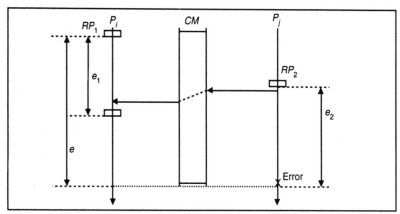

Figure 7. Communication Scenario 3.

retained at a given instant. A rollback point should be deleted as soon as its function is served. The following rules are used for deleting rollback points:

(1)   A rollback point is discarded if the set of tuples (see the earlier subsection entitled "A program model") becomes null and if another rollback point has been inserted most recently.

(2)   Let there be three consecutive rollback points in a process within a distance of M units of time, as denoted in Figure 9 by RB_1, RB_2, and RB_3. Assume that their associated sets are not null. If a fourth rollback point RB_4 is to be inserted in the current edge, the set of tuples at RB_3 is transferred into the set at RB_2, and the rollback point RB_3 is discarded. This means that if the process has to roll back because of a communication it received from another process after the instant RB_3, it would then roll back to RB_2 instead of RB_3.

Since the recovery time anywhere in the program should not exceed M units of time, having a rollback point beyond M units of time will be worthless. We now show that the set of tuples associated with each rollback point will become null before M units of time of its creation. When the program begins execution, the initial communications will be validated in the worst case within $M/2$ units of time — that is, as soon as a task has been completed. The next set of communications will be validated once the received communications have been validated and the current task has been completed. Given that a received communication is validated within $M/2$ units of time, if a task has been completed before the validation has been received, then the communication sent will be validated within $M/2$ units of time. If validations are received before the task has been completed, then the validation for the communications sent will be done at the end of the task. Since the task size is no greater than $M/2$ units of time, communications sent will be validated within $M/2$ units of time. Given that the communications are validated within $M/2$ units of time and because insertion and deletion of a rollback point are done at the end of execution of the tasks, it will take in the worst case M units of time to delete a rollback point ($M/2$ units of time for the communications received to be validated plus $M/2$ units of time for the current task to be completed and to decide on deleting a rollback point).

It is important to retain two least recently inserted rollback points, such as RB_1 and RB_2 in Figure 9. If we have instead only RB_1, for example, and transfer the tuples into the set at RB_1 as execution progresses, the set at RB_1 may never become empty and recovery within the specified time may not be possible.

In summary, no more than three rollback points per process are needed to recover from an error

---

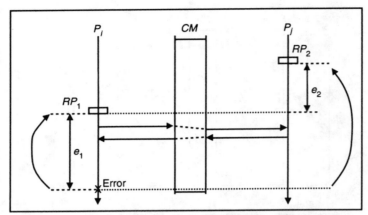

Figure 8. Process transmit and receive data — Scenario 4.

anywhere in the program. These three rollback points are the most recently inserted one and the two least recently inserted ones with nonempty sets of tuples.

A rollback point insertion strategy

Having derived the constraints for rollback point insertion, we now obtain a strategy for inserting rollback points. The objective is to minimize the maximum time that may be spent in saving the states of the system.

During the execution of a task, a process is said to be in one of the following two modes:

- Mode 1: In Mode 1, there is no communication in the interval between the most recent rollback point and the currently executing task.
- Mode 2: In Mode 2, data communication between the most recent rollback point and the currently executing task is sent and/or received. (There is no constraint on the type of communication.)

Let us consider a specific process. Assume that the following parameters are known by a preanalysis of the program: t_i, the maximum execution time of the task i; S_{ij}, the savetime at edge (i, j); L_{ij}, the loadtime at edge (i, j); and m_{ij}, the mode of the process before the execution of task i. Since the worst case situation is considered in the preanalysis stage, the assumptions made on the various parameters are justifiable.

The longest time interval between two rollback points depends on the current mode of the process. For Mode 1, the longest time interval is M; for Mode 2, the longest time interval is $M/2$. Therefore, during the execution of a process, the rollback points have to be inserted according to the current mode of the process. When a process starts, it will be in the mode of the first task; similarly, after a rollback point has been inserted, the mode of the process will be the mode of the next task. In case a rollback point is not inserted, the mode of the process will be a combination of the current mode and the mode of the task to be executed next. It is assumed that the mode of each of the various tasks, which can be obtained during the preanalysis of the program, is known a priori. For example, if a process is in Mode 2 and the task to be executed next is in Mode 1, the resultant mode of the process will be Mode 2 if a rollback point is not inserted.

For the sake of uniformity, we use the notation of Chandy and Ramamoorthy [4] in presenting our rollback strategy. For each vertex i of the process graph, we determine a function $f_i(r, m)$, for all possible values of recovery time r and mode m, where $f_i(r, m)$ is the minimum time spent in saving the states of the system after task i has been completed and before the completion of the process, in the worst case. For each edge (i, j) in the graph, we determine functions $g_{ij}(r, m)$ and $x_{ij}(r, m)$ (functions of recovery time and mode of the process). The function $g_{ij}(r, m)$ is the minimum time spent in saving the states of the system after task i has been completed and before the completion of the process, in the worst case, and if task i is followed by task j. The function $x_{ij}(r, m)$ is an optimal-decision variable defined as either 0 or 1, depending on the value of r and m such that when $x_{ij}(r,m) = 1$, a rollback point is inserted in edge (i, j), and

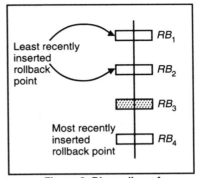

Figure 9. Discarding of rollback points.

when $x_{ij}(r, m) = 0$, a rollback point is not inserted. For each edge (i, j) in the graph, we determine a constant $B_{ij}(m)$ such that $B_{ij}(m)$ is the value of r below which $x_{ij}(r, m) = 0$.

Initially, we assume that $f_i(r, m) = \infty$ for $r > M$. For the exit vertex of a process graph, let $f_i(r, m)$ be defined as follows:

$$f_i(r, 1) = 0 \text{ for } r < M$$

$$f_i(r, 2) = 0 \text{ for } r < M/2$$

For all other tasks, $g_{ij}(r, m)$ is calculated from

$$g_{ij}(r, \ 1) = \begin{cases} S_{ij} + f_j(L_{ij} + t_j, 1) & \text{if } r + t_j \geq M \\ \min\{S_{ij} + f_j(L_{ij} + t_j, 1), \ f_j(r + t_j, 1)\} & \text{if } r + t_j < M \end{cases}$$

$$g_{ij}(r, 2) = \begin{cases} S_{ij} + f_j(L_{ij} + t_j, 2) & \text{if } r + t_j \geq M/2 \\ \min\{S_{ij} + f_j(L_{ij} + t_j, 2), \ f_j(r + t_j, 2)\} & \text{if } r + t_j < M/2 \end{cases}$$

For all values of m and r, $x_{ij}(r, m)$ is calculated from

$$x_{ij}(r,m) = \begin{cases} 0 & \text{if } g_{ij}(r,m) = f_j(r + t_j, m) \\ 1 & \text{otherwise} \end{cases}$$

$B_{ij}(m)$ is the maximum value of r below which $x_{ij}(r, m) = 0$; that is, $x_{ij}(r, m) = 0$ for $r \leq B_{ij}(m)$ and $x_{ij}(r,m) = 1$ for $r > B_{ij}(m)$.

The function $f_i(r, m)$ is then computed as follows:

$$f_i(r, m) = \text{maximum over all edges } (i, j) \text{ of } \{g_{ij}(r, m)\} \text{ for } 0 \leq r \leq M \text{ and for all values of } m.$$

At each edge of the program graph of a process, the following operations are done: The present mode of the program is combined with the mode of the task to be executed next in order to obtain the resultant mode, let's say w. The recovery time r is compared with $B_{ij}(w)$. If $r > B_{ij}(w)$, then a rollback point is inserted in edge (i, j); otherwise, no rollback point is inserted. If a rollback point is inserted,

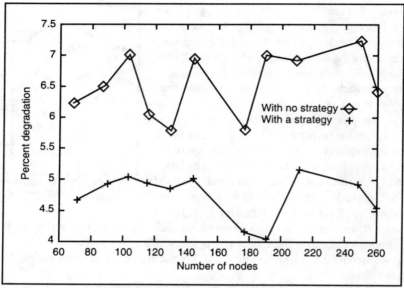

Figure 10. Percentage runtime degradation due to rollback point insertion.

then the mode of the program is set to the mode of the next task. If a rollback point is not inserted, then the mode of the program is a combination of the current mode and the mode of the next task.

Experimental study

We did a computer simulation to determine the performance of the checkpointing strategy for concurrent systems presented in the previous section. Since the size of tasks can be arbitrary in a given program, parameters such as t_i and S_{ij} were treated as random variables. For our analysis, we generated a number of process graphs using random numbers on a VAX-8600 system using Pascal. The number of nodes in the process graphs was varied between 72 and 260. Acyclic process graphs were generated using the following approach: First, a linear graph of p (random) nodes was generated; the entry and exit nodes were named as 1 and p, respectively. A small number (p_1, generated randomly) of extra nodes was added to the original graph. For these additional nodes, the edges were chosen randomly such that the new appended graph was also an acyclic graph. After the construction of the acyclic graph of $p + p_1$ nodes, the nodes were renumbered from 1 to $p + p_1$ such that $i < j$ for each edge (i, j).

Two different systems were developed, one using the extension of Chandy and Ramamoorthy's strategy [4] described in the previous section and the other with no specific strategy for rollback point insertion. In the latter, rollback points were inserted following the recovery time constraints only. The simulated systems had four processes running concurrently in a cooperative manner. The task-execution times and the savetimes were randomly generated. The common memory was simulated by building an array to store the communications and to retransmit whenever required. Also, the interprocess communication, which was in two modes, was initiated using random numbers. That is, the type of communication and the instants of communication between the processes were random.

The randomly generated program graph was executed on the simulation platform. Rollback points were inserted using only (1) the strategy presented in the previous section, and (2) the recovery time constraints. The communications and their validations using the common memory, the number of rollback points at a given time instant, and the deletion of rollback points were monitored. Important parameters, such as the program-execution time and the time spent on saving the system states, were determined. Figure 10 shows the percentage degradation due to system state saving, with no strategy and with a strategy, with respect to the number of tasks in a process. As can be seen from the figure, using a strategy such as the one presented in the previous section gives a reduced degradation in the program execution.

However, the strategy used to insert rollback points requires a considerable amount of precomputation to compute $B_{ij}(m)$'s; hence, time-varying constraints, if any, in a real-time system cannot be handled. The precomputation time increases exponentially with the number of edges of the program graph [17]. We developed a simplified strategy for rollback point insertion that relies on minimum precomputation, so that any time-varying constraints can be handled. We showed that a tradeoff between the amount of precomputation and the optimality of rollback point insertion can be worked out by means of a local minimization strategy [17].

Discussion

We present in this paper a method for error recovery within a deadline in cooperating concurrent processes. The avalanche of rollback, called the domino effect, is limited to only three steps using a new communication model based on a common memory. In our model, when an asynchronous communication takes place between the sender and the receiver process, the sender is not concerned with whether or not the receiver has accepted the data. But, if there is an error in the data sent, then the receiver is promptly notified. A watchdog processor is employed for the detection of local errors with low latency. Thus, the error propagation is well bounded. On the other hand, if the receiver process detects an error in the data received and the sender has completed its task, then there is no way the error can be corrected by the rollback procedure. It can be corrected either by a forward recovery or by invoking a special service routine to correct the data.

We performed a computer simulation on random graphs to check the performance of the rollback point insertion strategy. The results obtained show that the runtime performance degradation of programs employing rollback recovery is rather small. It is not known if the extension of Chandy and Ramamoorthy's technique [4] to concurrent systems will result in optimizing the time spent in saving the states of the system. The evaluation of the time complexity of the rollback point insertion algorithm and the investigation of optimality of the technique are problems for future study.

The main feature of our technique is that while the domino effect is being avoided, no process autonomy is sacrificed and no restrictions are placed on the interprocess communication. Further, no additional rollback points or pseudorecovery points are added during the normal execution of a program.

Distributed real-time systems are very common in process control applications. Such systems are generally subject to stringent deadlines, and rollback recovery is a viable approach to meet the reliability requirement in such applications. Since our approach is based on a system-oriented view, the techniques presented can be applied to distributed computing systems where the interprocess communications take place by sending messages. However, this extension would require the consideration of the message delays in the underlying model, a problem that is currently being investigated.

Acknowledgments

We would like to thank all the anonymous referees whose criticism helped improve substantially the quality of the paper. Research was supported in part by National Science Foundation Grant CCR-89-09243.

References

[1] M. Ahamad and L. Lin, "Using Checkpoints to Localize the Effects of Faults in Distributed Systems," *Proc. Eighth Symp. Reliable Distributed Systems*, IEEE Computer Soc. Press, Los Alamitos, Calif., 1989, pp. 2-11.

[2] T. Anderson and P.A. Lee, *Fault Tolerance: Principles and Practice*, Prentice-Hall, Inc., Englewood Cliffs, N.J., 1981.

[3] K.M. Chandy, "A Survey of Analytic Models of Rollback and Recovery Strategies," *Computer*, Vol. 8, No. 5, May 1975, pp. 40-47.

[4] K.M. Chandy and C.V. Ramamoorthy, "Rollback and Recovery Strategies for Computer Programs," *IEEE Trans. Computers*, Vol. C-21, No. 6, June 1972, pp. 546-556.

[5] K.M Chandy et al., "Analytic Models for Rollback and Recovery Strategies in Data Base Systems," *IEEE Trans. Software Eng.*, Vol. SE-1, No. 1, Mar. 1975, pp. 100-110.

[6] J. Gray, "Why Do Computers Stop and What Can Be Done about It?" *Proc. Fifth Symp. Reliability Distributed Software and Database Systems*, IEEE Computer Soc. Press, Los Alamitos, Calif., 1986, pp. 3-12.

[7] K. Kant, "A Model for Error Recovery with Global Checkpointing," *Information Sciences*, Vol. 30, No. 3, July 1983, pp. 225-237.

[8] K. Kant and A. Silberschatz, "Error Propagation and Recovery in Concurrent Environments," *Computer J.*, Vol. 28, No. 5, May 1985, pp. 466-473.

[9] K.H. Kim, "Programmer-Transparent Coordination of Recovering Concurrent Processes: Philosophy and Rules for Efficient Implementation," *IEEE Trans. Software Eng.*, Vol. 14, No. 6, June 1988, pp. 810-821.

[10] P.A. Lee, N. Ghani, and K. Heron, "A Recovery Cache for the PDP-11," *IEEE Trans. Computers*, Vol. C-29, No. 6, June 1980, pp. 546-549.

[11] Y.-H. Lee and K.G. Shin, "Design and Evaluation of a Fault-Tolerant Multiprocessor Using Hardware Recovery Blocks," *IEEE Trans. Computers*, Vol. C-33, No. 2, Feb. 1984, pp. 113-124.

[12] B. Randell, "System Structure for Software Fault Tolerance," *IEEE Trans. Software Eng.*, Vol. SE-1, No. 2, June 1975, pp. 220-232.

[13] K.G. Shin and Y.-H. Lee, "Evaluation of Error Recovery Blocks Used for Cooperating Processes," *IEEE Trans. Software Eng.*, Vol. SE-10, No. 6, Nov. 1984, pp. 692-700.

[14] K.G. Shin, T.-H. Lin, and Y.-H. Lee, "Optimal Checkpointing of Real-Time Tasks," *IEEE Trans. Computers*, Vol. C-36, No. 11, Nov. 1987, pp. 1328-1341.

[15] Z. Tong, R.Y. Kain, and W.T. Tsai, "A Low Overhead Checkpointing and Rollback Recovery Scheme for Distributed Systems," *Proc. Eighth Symp. Reliable Distributed Systems*, IEEE Computer Soc. Press, Los Alamitos, Calif., 1989, pp. 12-20.

[16] S.J. Upadhyaya, "A Study of Rollback Recovery Techniques: Hardware, Models, Algorithms, and Evaluation," doctoral thesis, Dept. of Electrical and Computer Eng., Univ. of New Castle, New South Wales, Australia, 1986.

[17] S.J. Upadhyaya, "Rollback Recovery in Real-Time Systems with Dynamic Constraints," *Proc. 14th Ann. Int'l Computer Software and Applications Conf. (COMPSAC90)*, IEEE Computer Soc. Press, Los Alamitos, Calif., 1990, pp. 524-529.

[18] S.J. Upadhyaya and K.K. Saluja, "A Hardware Supported General Rollback Technique," *Proc. 14th Int'l Conf. Fault-Tolerant Computing*, IEEE Computer Soc. Press, Los Alamitos, Calif., 1984, pp. 409-414.

[19] J.S. Upadhyaya and K.K. Saluja, "A Watchdog Processor Based General Rollback Technique with Multiple Retries," *IEEE Trans. Software Eng.*, Vol. SE-12, No. 1, Jan. 1986, pp. 87-95.

[20] S.J. Upadhyaya and K.K. Saluja, "An Experimental Study to Determine Task Size for Rollback Recovery Systems," *IEEE Trans. Computers*, Vol. 37, No. 7, July 1988, pp. 872-877.

[21] J.W. Young, "A First Order Approximation to the Optimum Checkpoint Interval," *Comm. ACM*, Vol. 17, No. 9, Sept. 1974, pp. 530-531.

Problem Solving with Distributed Knowledge

At the current level of communication and hardware technology, it has become possible to connect together large numbers of powerful, inexpensive processing units that execute asynchronously to provide cost-effective computational capacity to support artificial intelligence applications. The range of connection structures varies from tightly coupled processors communicating via shared/distributed memory to loosely coupled structures spanning over local/wide area networks. In this context, distributed problem solving has become an asset in handling AI applications that are inherently distributed. Typical applications may be

(1) Spatially distributed applications, such as
- Interpreting and integrating data from spatially distributed sensors or
- Controlling a set of robots that work together on a factory floor, and
(2) Functionally distributed applications, such as
- Bringing together a number of specialized medical-diagnosis systems on a particularly difficult case or
- Developing a sophisticated architectural expert system composed of individual experts in specialties such as structural engineering, electrical wiring, and room layout.

Manoj K. Saxena,

K.K. Biswas, and

P.C.P. Bhatt

A distributed problem solver has several advantages over a single monolithic, centralized problem solver. These advantages include faster problem solving by exploiting parallelism; decreased communication by transmitting only high-level partial solutions to nearby nodes, rather than raw data to a central site; greater flexibility by having problem solvers with different capabilities dynamically teaming up to solve current problems; and increased reliability by allowing problem solvers to take on the responsibilities of problem solvers that fail.

A critical consideration in distributed problem solvers is a good knowledge representation paradigm that facilitates identification of the states of reasoning. A good representation scheme induces modular growth, makes the system robust, and offers a higher level of maintainability. Traditional issues of knowledge representation in large distributed problem-solving systems include expressive adequacy, notational efficacy, incompleteness, defaults, primitives, and metarepresentation. In addition, issues like resource limitations, concurrency, consistency, uncertainty about future events, reasoning about time, global-control focus, timeliness, modularity, flexibility, distributability, fault tolerance, and knowledge acquisition and assimilation need to be considered in detail for distributed knowledge management and problem solving. Representative of recent approaches that address the above-mentioned issues are DVMT (distributed vehicle-monitoring testbed), MACE (multiagent computing environment), and AF (activation framework). Our approach is DISPROS (distributed problem solver).

Issues in knowledge management

In the absence of a good knowledge representation (KR) scheme, systems become progressively more difficult to construct, extend, and maintain. The two major aspects of any knowledge representation scheme that need careful consideration are the *expressive adequacy* and the *notational efficacy* [18], which are important in providing correct, rational inferences in a timely fashion in any knowledge-based-system design. Expressive adequacy has to do with the ability of a KR scheme to represent knowledge needed in the problem domain and to precisely capture states that focus on specific and meaningful knowledge. Notational efficacy is concerned with the actual shape and structure of the representation, as well as with the impact this structure has on system operations. Notational efficacy, in turn, breaks down into such components as *computational efficiency* for various kinds of inference, *conciseness of representation*, and *ease of modification*.

In reality, it is virtually impossible for anyone to provide exactly the right amount of knowledge and information to achieve the goals of problem solving. One must be able to reason with incomplete and inconsistent knowledge and handle modifications of the knowledge base. Exactly what a knowledge representation language allows one to leave unsaid about a domain determines how incomplete the system's knowledge can be. This, in turn, determines the extent of sophistication of the reasoning agent. For instance, the most commonly employed representation technique is a generalization/specialization relation, giving rise to the so-called IS-A hierarchy, which gives one mechanism of handling defaults [4], [11]. Another issue revolves around the structure, granularity, and level of abstraction of primitive knowledge structures [3]. A related issue is metarepresentation [6], which is the use of structures that represent knowledge about other structures in the system.

In addition to the above issues, distributed knowledge management requires consideration of limitations and optimal utilization of physical resources. The system should allow experts to exchange tasks across the network so that load is equally distributed and the experts are able to support each other in problem solving. A related issue for concurrent and consistent operation is coherent cooperation. There is a need to develop cooperative interaction mechanisms that allow multiple expert systems to work together to solve a problem with not necessarily consistent views and control information and still produce results within a specified time limit. This requires experts to exchange partial solutions, so that one or more of them has enough information to resolve the inconsistency. Thus, error resolution becomes an integral part of distributed problem solving as experts try to combine and assess the implications of partial and tentative results received from other experts. Another issue to be considered is the load on the communication network. Maximizing the speed of solution and reducing inconsistency may require frequent exchange of information, thereby increasing the communication load. There is a need to strike a balance between these two factors so as to optimize the communication resource usage.

The control structure becomes significantly more complex in a distributed environment because a problem solver must then consider how its local searching actions complement those of others. The global-control strategy should be such that it increases global coherence; that is, the activities of experts should be directed toward a given goal, avoiding both unnecessary duplications of work and experts being idle. This raises the issue of how global control can be implemented. A centralized control is easier to implement, but it has the disadvantages of limited computation, communication, and reliability. In decentralized control, the amount of global coherence in the network depends on the degree to which each node makes coherent local decisions based on its local view of problem solving. The control is generally implemented by message passing. The three major characteristics of the information communicated among nodes that affects global coherence are *relevance* (which is the amount of information that is consistent with the global solution), *timeliness* (which depends on how much the information will influence the current activity of the receiving expert), and *completeness* (which is that fraction of a complete solution that the message represents) [7].

The other issues that are relevant are uncertainty about future events, the sequence of events, and their relative timing. The system should be able to detect faults (hardware, software, and communication) and recover from them with minimum loss in performance and availability. Last, but not least, the system should be able to accept the data or knowledge without putting any restriction on the order in which it appears and to assimilate it into the system with minimum overheads. This is a complex issue in a loosely coupled system, because knowledge is distributed over a network and the new information can appear anywhere on the network.

Two issues that are relevant from the point of view of software engineering are modularity and distributability. It should be possible for separate teams—each knowledgeable in a particular domain — to develop modules that correspond to distinct expertise. The modules should be separately testable and should obey good software engineering practices in terms of data hiding and transparent man-machine interfaces; also, when they are written, it should not be necessary to know on which processors in the distributed system they will be run.

Recent approaches

Representative of recent approaches that address the issues of distributed problem solving are the work of

- Lesser and Corkill [13] at the University of Massachusetts on DVMT, a distributed vehicle-monitoring testbed;
- Gasser, Braganza, and Herman [9] at the University of Southern California on MACE, a flexible testbed for distributed artificial intelligence research; and
- Green [10] at Worcester Polytechnic Institute on AF, a framework for real-time distributed cooperative problem solving.

DVMT: Distributed vehicle-monitoring testbed

The distributed vehicle-monitoring testbed (DVMT) is a flexible and fully instrumented research environment constructed for the empirical evaluation of alternative designs [13] for functionally accurate, cooperative distributed problem-solving networks. The DVMT basically operates by simulating a network of HEARSAY-II nodes working on the vehicle-monitoring task. Each simulated node applies simplified signal-processing knowledge to acoustically sensed data in an attempt to identify, locate, and track patterns of a vehicle moving through a two-dimensional space. Each node has a HEARSAY-II, blackboard-based architecture [8], with knowledge sources and levels of abstraction appropriate for vehicle monitoring. The basic HEARSAY-II architecture has been extended in each node to include the capability of communicating hypotheses and goals among nodes, more sophisticated local control, and an interface to metalevel network coordination components [5], [13]. In particular, a planning module, a goal blackboard, a metalevel control

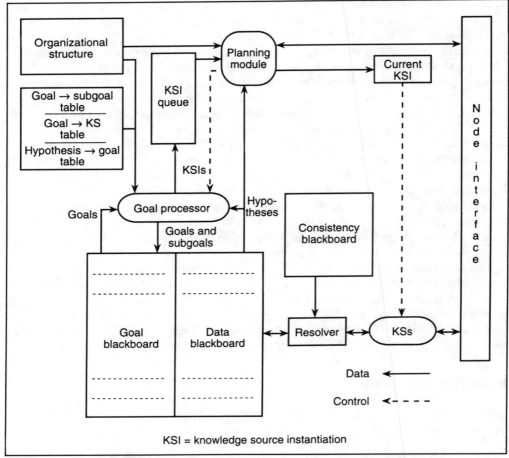

Figure 1. Distributed vehicle-monitoring testbed (DVMT) node architecture.

blackboard, and communication knowledge sources have been added (see Figure 1) to the HEARSAY-II structure.

Hypothesized vehicle movements are represented on the data blackboard, and knowledge sources (KSs) perform the basic problem-solving tasks of extending and refining hypotheses (partial solutions). The hypotheses are organized on a data blackboard with the following four levels of abstraction:

- *Signal*, for low-level analyses of the sensory data;
- *Group*, for collections of harmonically related signals;
- *Vehicles*, for collections of groups that correspond to given vehicle types; and
- *Pattern*, for collections of spatially related vehicle types, such as vehicles moving in a formation.

Each of these levels is in turn split into a level for *location hypotheses* (which have one time-location) and a level for *track hypotheses* (which have a sequence of time-locations).

Each node maintains a queue of pending KSIs (knowledge source instantiations) and ranks the KSIs to decide which one to invoke next. To improve upon these decisions, the HEARSAY-II architecture has been extended so that nodes can reason more fully about the intentions or goals of the KSIs [5]. Internode communication is added to the node architecture by the inclusion of communication knowledge sources. These knowledge sources allow the exchange of hypotheses and goals among nodes.

Given a particular problem-solving environment, each node begins by transforming its sensed data into a set of signal location hypotheses. The node will drive up its most promising signal data to form tracks and then will extend these tracks. It exchanges partial results to resolve any inconsistency and to converge on problem solutions. To minimize traffic, it uses organizational structuring of nodes. As soon as a node has found the solution, it broadcasts its success to the other nodes, and then it ceases its activity. In turn, the other nodes cease their activity either when they receive this message (which is subject to communication delays) or when they generate the solution themselves (if that should occur earlier).

MACE: Multiagent computing environment

MACE is an instrumented testbed for building a wide range of experimental distributed artificial intelligence systems at various levels of granularity. MACE computational units (called *agents*) run in parallel and communicate via messages. MACE's environment maps agents onto processors; handles interagent communication; and provides a language to describe agents, a facility for remote demons, and a collection of system-agents. These system-agents construct user-agents from descriptions, monitor execution, handle errors, and interface to a user [9]. MACE has been designed for experimenting with a variety of architectures and problem-solving paradigms at varying levels of granularity.

The emphasis of implementation is on flexibility for experimentation with distributed AI techniques. MACE is an attempt to provide the tools for prototyping experimental systems that run in a real parallel environment, but not for production-quality delivery systems.

The dominant metaphor of MACE is a collection of intelligent, semiautonomous agents interacting in organized ways. These agents know about some other agents in their environment and expect to draw upon and coordinate with the expertise of these other agents. This expertise is stored in each agent's world model, which is stored in an attribute called *acquaintances*. In addition, agents may be organized into subunits or coalitions that act in response to particular problems. There are predefined system-agents that provide MACE with several system-building tools. MACE incorporates extensive pattern-matching facilities for interpreting messages, for pattern-directed invocation of asynchronous events (for example, demons and other event-monitors), and for associative database access within agents. MACE kernels collectively handle communication and message routing; perform I/O to terminals, files, or other devices; map agents onto processors; and schedule agents for execution.

Agents take actions when the kernel evaluates a function called the *engine* of the agent. An agent's engine is the only executable part of the agent, apart from its initialization code and the action parts. The engine and its associated attributes provide the procedural knowledge incorporated in an agent. The engine deactivates the agent when it has completed its current activities. It is also responsible for communication, error handling, and the acquisition and dissemination of knowledge about its environment. Unless it deactivates itself, an agent's engine is evaluated on every scheduling cycle. The engine shell that is a part of the MACE kernel performs all the necessary initialization for the agent, getting the address of its initial acquaintances and executing its initialization code. It uses sophisticated local scheduling with multiagent planning to converge to a solution.

Agents communicate by sending messages. Messages can be addressed to individual agents, to a group of agents, or to all agents of a particular class. Messages can also be addressed to agents in MACE systems on other machines. MACE has been used to model both lower level parallelism (a distributed system of production rules without a global database or inference engine) and higher level distributed problem-solving architectures (domain-independent distributed blackboard and contract-net schemes).

AF: Activation framework

AF is a software framework that supports the implementation of real-time artificial intelligence programs on multiple interconnected computers that may be geographically distributed. It is based on the paradigm of expert objects communicating by messages in the manner of a community of experts. It uses message priority levels as the basis for distributed scheduling and focus-of-attention mechanisms. The major issues addressed by AF are distributed problem solving with timeliness response, keeping in view the uncertainty about future events with resource limitations.

In AF organization, hypotheses and procedural code for a local knowledge domain are integrated into an *activation framework object* (AFO). These AFOs form a community of experts that communicate by means of message exchange. Each AFO

- Can be thought of as being similar to a miniature HEARSAY-II system with its local blackboard and a limited set of KS procedures (see Figure 2),
- Has a name that is global and known to all other AFOs that need to communicate with it, and
- Is self-contained and has an external interface that is defined by the formats of the messages it sends and receives.

The incoming messages trigger the procedures contained in the AFO to act on local hypotheses and/or to send out other messages. The AFO can be written and tested independently by a team that is expert in the AFO's local knowledge domain. A system consisting of many AFOs can be distributed over a number of processors, with the scheduling of the AFOs being a function of message traffic. AFOs are attached to frameworks that are responsible for scheduling and delivery of messages to attached AFOs (see Figure 3). The framework is also responsible for delivering messages to other frameworks where appropriate. This message delivery is accomplished by using the host's operating-system message-passing mechanism. Each framework has a routing procedure that translates the symbolic name to a system-level identity for message delivery. The framework and attached AFOs form a process that is scheduled by the host's operating-system scheduler.

Multiple hypotheses are contained within an AFO. Each hypothesis has a name, a data structure, and an activation level that specifies the belief in its truth (*positive activation level*) or falseness (*negative activation level*). The AFO is itself given an activation level corresponding to the notion of this being evidence for the hypothesis that this AFO should be processed. In AF, message traffic has been used to control the scheduling of the

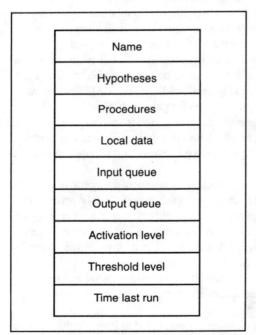

Figure 2. Activation framework object (AFO).

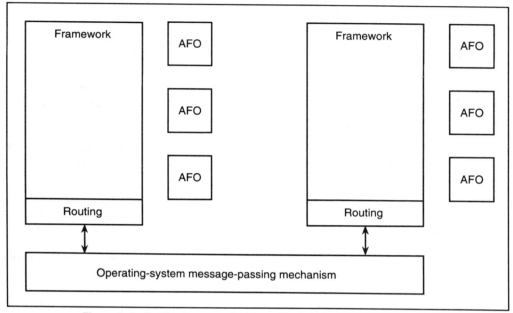

Figure 3. Activation framework objects (AFOs) attached to framework.

AFOs. If an AFO has no input message traffic, then it need not be executed. Where there is a choice, those AFOs with many messages should be run first.

The priority of an AFO is decided by the priority of messages on its input queue. AF also gives priority to those AFOs that have accumulated a large number of low-priority messages on their queues. There is no global scheduling, because a sending AFO places an activation level on messages that drive the scheduling of the system. The framework scheduler will continue to schedule and execute AFOs until there are no more AFOs with activation levels above their threshold. At this point, the framework process will sleep until another message arrives for one of the AFOs to process. AF has been applied to the problem of the navigator for an autonomous vehicle and to the smart conveyer belt robot.

DISPROS: Distributed blackboard problem-solving framework

DISPROS is a framework based on a blackboard (BB) architecture [12] that supports the implementation of concurrent fault-tolerant problem-solving systems on multiple interconnected computers that may be geographically distributed. It is based on the paradigm of level managers communicating by messages in the manner of a community of experts.

The development of DISPROS was motivated by the following two facts:

- In real-world scenarios for any reasonably complex problem, the knowledge is distributed, there is uncertainty about the facts, and communication is susceptible to faults.
- By partitioning a problem into loosely coupled subproblems and keeping multiple status (for different subproblems), substantial speedup can be achieved.

Also, we wanted to study the effect of incomplete and inconsistent knowledge on problem solving.

Other issues that were of concern to us were handling defaults in the knowledge representation, modularity, flexibility, and distributability.

DISPROS architecture

DISPROS retains the concepts of knowledge sources and blackboard levels of a conventional blackboard architecture. It does not strictly adhere to the structuring technique followed by most of the BB systems. It allows the BB to be partitioned into subboards, which are further partitioned into level managers, thereby imposing an organizational structure on the problem-solving network. This removes constraints imposed by the linear hierarchy requirements of a monolithic blackboard and gives modularity and flexibility to the architecture. Level managers (LMs) are active structures and are implemented as independent processes [17].

Level manager structure. Each LM consists of the following components (see Figure 4):

(1) *Local database.* The local database is a working memory purely local to the LM. All blackboard objects are stored in it. The objects are represented as frames [14] with a slot-and-filler representation structure. Links, which are special-purpose slots, are used to store relationships. The local database defines the relationship between objects (and also between instances). There are a number of system-defined relationships, such as

- Is an instance of
- Is a
- Is a neighbor of
- Is a part of
- Is a predecessor of

Also, the user can define arbitrary relationships between objects on a blackboard. An access function is automatically defined for each link in the same way that access functions are defined for the slots.

(2) *Local scheduler.* Each LM is considered to be an autonomous module with local control. Local control is effected by the local scheduler, which operates on instances of the KSs belonging to the LM in which it resides.

(3) *Scheduler database.* The scheduler database contains information useful to the local scheduler in making control decisions. The database is private to the LM in which it resides, but may contain information with a more global extent.

(4) Collection of *knowledge sources.* Knowledge sources are organized according to the tripartite structure *trigger-condition-action* and are rule based. Only the condition part is allowed to access data from other LMs. The action part can send data to other LMs to manipulate their database. The trigger is a symbolic token representing an event that has occurred on the blackboard and is restricted to the entries of the local database. If a trigger that has been posted matches with the one listed for a KS, it indicates that the KS is a potential contributor to problem solving provided that the condition part is met. The KSs held within an LM belong to that LM and may engage in indirect communication with other LMs via the communication control system (CCS). The KS stores the values of efficiency and confidence the system has in the rules contained within the KS in obtaining the solution. These values are used by the scheduler in deciding which KS to schedule next for execution.

(5) *Knowledge source matcher* and *knowledge source action interpreter.* The knowledge source matcher and the knowledge source action interpreter are responsible for matching preconditions of KSs and for executing actions. The presence of separate matchers and action interpreters allows different LMs to use different knowledge representations (like frames and semantic nets) if the problem domain so requires.

(6) *Communication control system.* The communication control system (CCS) has

its own database to handle the communication for each LM. This database, called the *communication control system (CCS) database*, stores information about the messages sent and received by the LM. All actions on the blackboard are atomic and the interaction with other LMs is done by the communication control system. The requests for an LM are serialized by the communication control system. This results in only one reader and writer in each LM; therefore, there is no need to lock an object or region within an LM. Each site has a *communication level manager* (CLM), responsible for message transfer between two sites, that controls the physical ports of the computer and uses heuristics to take care of communication link failures and congestion control.

Control model. The most important aspect of the architecture is its control model. The control is divided into *local control* and *global control*. Each LM has a representation of its local state and can make control decisions

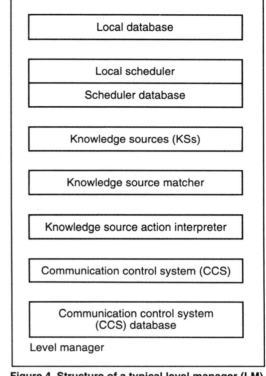

```
┌─────────────────────────────────────┐
│  ┌───────────────────────────────┐  │
│  │      Local database           │  │
│  └───────────────────────────────┘  │
│  ┌───────────────────────────────┐  │
│  │      Local scheduler          │  │
│  │      Scheduler database       │  │
│  └───────────────────────────────┘  │
│  ┌───────────────────────────────┐  │
│  │   Knowledge sources (KSs)     │  │
│  └───────────────────────────────┘  │
│  ┌───────────────────────────────┐  │
│  │   Knowledge source matcher    │  │
│  └───────────────────────────────┘  │
│  ┌───────────────────────────────┐  │
│  │ Knowledge source action interpreter │ │
│  └───────────────────────────────┘  │
│  ┌───────────────────────────────┐  │
│  │ Communication control system (CCS) │ │
│  └───────────────────────────────┘  │
│  ┌───────────────────────────────┐  │
│  │ Communication control system  │  │
│  │      (CCS) database           │  │
│  └───────────────────────────────┘  │
│  Level manager                       │
└─────────────────────────────────────┘
```

Figure 4. Structure of a typical level manager (LM).

based on it. These decisions are concerned with the scheduling of the most appropriate KS belonging to the LM for the next execution. Each LM has its own scheduling mechanism, which may be based on sequence, LIFO, or agenda. The scheduler can also base its decision on user-determined criteria such as characteristics of the events that trigger KSs, global or local problem-solving strategies, the current set of entries in the database, and knowledge of its own past behavior. The criteria for scheduling decisions within an LM may vary from one LM to another; this maximizes strategic flexibility and potential for opportunism.

In order for a collection of LMs to contribute effectively to the solution of a problem, it is necessary to provide a global control that can make the problem-solving process converge. The global control is implemented by message passing, which is used to communicate problem- and control-related information and is highly domain specific. Global coherence is achieved in DISPROS by using organizational structuring with partial global planning. The organizational structure is used to limit the range of the control decisions made by the level manager and to ensure that information necessary for making informed decisions is routed to the appropriate LMs.

Computational model. In DISPROS, the computation is done by a *process group*. A process group may consist of one or more processes (level managers) and is referred to as one *unit*. The processes in a group may reside on machines anywhere in the system; this results in replicating processes performing the same computation on different machines in the system. DISPROS uses a coordinator-cohort scheme to implement redundant processing within a group. In this scheme, the action associated with a request is performed by one group member (*coordinator*), while the others (*cohorts*) monitor the progress of this action and take over one by one as failures occur. The coordinator is chosen by ranking the members of a process group according to a simple rule: The lowest ranking member is labeled as coordinator and the other members then become cohorts. The coordinator executes requests; in case of a failure, cohorts take over one by one, in rank order. When the coordinator terminates, a copy of its reply message is sent to the cohorts using the atomic multicast protocol. This protocol ensures that a reply is received by the caller if it is received by the cohort. In case it is not received by the caller because of failure of the coordinator, then one of the cohorts is selected to take over the computation. There is no need to have intragroup synchronization because of the virtual synchronous environment.

DISPROS provides fault tolerance by running the same process on many processors. It provides error detection by having a site-monitoring facility that can trigger actions when a site or process fails or a site recovers. Once a failure is signaled, all interested processes will observe it, and all see the same sequence of failures and recoveries. When a process is restarted and joins a group, the current state of the operational processes of the group is transferred to it. A detailed discussion about fault-tolerance aspects of DISPROS is given in by Saxena, Biswas, and Bhatt [15].

Communication system. The communication system in DISPROS is based on atomic multicast protocols similar to those proposed by Birman and Joseph [2] to provide a virtual synchronous environment An atomic multicast protocol provides for general message-passing capabilities and ensures that all of its operational destinations receive the message unless the sender fails, in which case either all destinations receive the message or none do. Moreover, all recipients see the same message delivery ordering. This is very important in the case of blackboard implementation, as a process will often issue messages/broadcasts asynchronously. Birman et al. [1] show that atomicity of broadcast primitives holds in an asynchronous environment also and that delivery order is maintained. Maintaining delivery order is achieved by issuing the broadcast, waiting until a response is received from a single destination (usually self), and then continuing the main thread of computation while the broadcast completes asynchronously. The primitives ensure that there are no gaps in a sequence of causally related broadcasts.

There are two distinct types of messages provided for by the architecture: *problem-solving messages* and *control messages*. Problem-solving messages contain information relevant to the solution of the problem currently being solved. Control messages contain information relevant to the control of the problem-solving process. Messages of either type may be sent to inquire, to provide information, or to give an instruction. There are functions provided for establishing and maintaining communication among LMs. To request or inquire, DISPROS provides

REQUEST(LM, <function>)

which sends the request for the execution of the function to the specified LM. The specified LM executes the request and sends the reply using

SEND(LM, <data>)

to the requesting/client LM. Similarly, the ASCII representation of the object can be communicated using the call

SEND-OBJECT(LM, Level.Object)

which immediately transmits the object to the specified LM, where it is buffered until requested.

There is a primary communication level manager (PCLM) in every problem-solving computer.

It is responsible for dynamic reconfiguration of the network in case of failure or recovery, in addition to normal functions of a CLM. A recovery manager restarts processes after they have failed or if a site recovers. Both processes (CLM and recovery manager) should preferably reside on the same site to minimize message transfer during the recovery process.

Knowledge representation in DISPROS

DKRL, a distributed knowledge representation language [16] developed for DISPROS, supports a representation like that of some frame systems [14], with slots and fillers, providing a class mechanism with user-defined classes and compile-time and run-time inheritance, within an LM. A slot may be initialized at the definition time or it may be filled with a value as a result of events that are recorded on the BB.

In order to create a description of a situation that is more specific than a given one, it is necessary in DKRL to mention only those attributes being modified or added; one does not have to copy all of the attributes of the general situation. Besides conserving memory storage, this feature also helps to maintain consistency.

The link mechanism in DKRL is quite powerful, because it can explicitly associate user-defined property inheritance. Additionally, the procedures can be attached to particular operations that need to be performed. They are attached to the classes of objects, and it is possible for subclasses to inherit procedures, as well as data, from their associated superclass.

By default, properties/procedures are inherited from an included object. However, event inheritance keywords in DKRL allow the user to have some control. All event inheritance keywords have the form

{ :NO-DEFAULT-INHERITANCE |
(event-name :NEVER-INHERIT) |
(event-name :ALWAYS-INHERIT) } *

Specifying :NO-DEFAULT-INHERITANCE disables the normal inheritance from the included object. Specifying (event-name :NEVER-INHERIT) indicates that the specified event should never be inherited by this object from its included object. Specifying (event-name :ALWAYS-INHERIT) indicates that the specified event should always be inherited by any object that includes this object, even if those objects specify :NO-DEFAULT-INHERITANCE.

With the structured inheritance network provided by DKRL, it is possible to express necessary distinctions. For example, it is possible to maintain such subtle distinctions as those among "walk," "run," "amble," "drive," and "fly" and at the same time not to overlook the commonality between these specific concepts and the general concept "move." As the new distinctions become important, they can be introduced by refining or modifying existing concepts, and it is always possible to introduce more general concepts that abstract details from more specific concepts.

DKRL allows the assimilation of arbitrary new information in a very natural way. The new object can be added at any point of time during the problem-solving process by issuing

(ADD-OBJECT object-definition)

or a new instance of an already-existing object can be created by

(CREATE-OBJECT object-specification)

Consistency and concurrency in DISPROS

The object/slots have user-defined access functions that can make sure that operations performed on the data leave the data consistent. This helps in maintaining data consistency. Global-solution coherence is enhanced by periodically exchanging status information that enables LMs to determine if a modification will lead to a more precise solution. This causes a sort of distributed hill climbing that helps the system evolve toward a coherent solution.

In DISPROS, systems are generally organized into subproblems, with each level representing a class of intermediate solutions and the knowledge sources having their span of knowledge limited to only a few levels. This type of problem decomposition creates subproblem nodes (with relevant knowledge sources) that can have local objectives and a capability for self-evaluation. This helps in the absence of a global controller to evaluate the overall solution state as each asynchronous problem-solving node evaluates its own local state. Of course, there is no guarantee that the sum total of local correctness will yield global correctness.

As described earlier, each KS in an LM contains a number of rules, with each rule being a condition-action pair. KSs are triggered/selected based on the events, which are symbolic tokens defined by the user and posted by DISPROS, after a KS makes a modification to the blackboard that is relevant to the progress of the problem-solving process. The KSs are also labeled with the event tokens, using the :TRIGGER keyword of DKRL. The association between KSs and the events that trigger their invocation is done at compile-time, allowing efficient, concurrent invocation of all eligible KSs after a blackboard event. The events are recorded by the LM on a global-event queue, along with information about the posting agent (KS) and the cause of the event. This allows the LM to focus its attention on the parts of the blackboard that are active and provides the appropriate context in which to invoke any appropriate knowledge source.

The major source of concurrency in this scheme lies in the simultaneity of the activity of each LM. Simultaneity results in exploiting inherent data parallelism in the problem and leads to many KSs being executed concurrently, thereby providing the knowledge parallelism.

There are two potential ways for knowledge sources to run in parallel in DISPROS, as follows:

- Knowledge sources working on different regions of the blackboard asynchronously (working on subproblems in parallel) and
- Knowledge sources working in a pipelined fashion, exploiting the flow of information up or down the data hierarchy.

To exploit both sources of parallelism, the problem can be modeled in DISPROS in any of the following ways (or a combination thereof):

(1)   If the problem space is very large and requires a lot of computation to be done, the total space can be divided into smaller regions, and each region can be assigned to a processor or a group of processors.

(2)   If the problem is very complex, it can be partitioned into independent subproblems, where each subproblem is solved on a separate processor.

(3)   If the problem (for example, speech recognition) has a solution that is built up in a pipeline-like manner up the blackboard hierarchy, the knowledge source dependencies can form a chain from the knowledge sources working on the most detailed level of the blackboard to those working on the most abstract level. The implication is that knowledge sources can run in parallel along pipes formed by the blackboard data.

The user of DISPROS is then able to exploit the inherent concurrency in the problem optimally.

An application in DISPROS

The field engineering planner (FEP) plans the inventory, training, and manpower requirements of an organization, dealing with the maintenance of a large number of computers of different makes that are supplied to its clients all over the country. The FEP was developed using DISPROS.

The task. The scope of the FEP is restricted to supporting the planning of resources (both human and material) and training for a computer maintenance company. The planning of human resources involves

- Projecting the need for recruitment of maintenance engineers based on the "installed base" of computers under maintenance;
- Deploying the engineer in the field — that is, assigning a computer engineer (CE) to a customer location for maintenance of computers; and
- Training engineers to keep them abreast of the latest technology and the design and architecture of computers that have been taken in for maintenance.

The planning is done for both in-house training and training at the manufacturer's location.

The planning for material resources involves

- Management of inventory of parts and
- Procurement of spares for new machines taken for maintenance.

The FEP gets its input from the user, whenever

- A computer is taken for maintenance;
- A computer under maintenance is discontinued;
- The existing configuration of the computer changes;
- There is a change in the manpower deployed — that is, whenever a person joins or leaves the company; and
- A training course is completed for CEs.

The FEP then generates a plan for

- Additions to existing inventory, after checking the inventory status all over the country;
- Training requirements to maintain the new machine; and
- Additional manpower and expertise requirements.

The blackboard structure. The maintenance organization for which the FEP was designed has four regional offices and one corporate office. The four regions are northern region (NR), southern region (SR), eastern region (ER), and western region (WR). Field engineering is only one of the activities of the company. The company is also involved in software development, consultancy, and training.

The chairman cum managing director (CMD), based in the corporate office, is the highest authority. All directors report to him. The other functions/departments within the corporate structure of field engineering include material management center (MMC), technical support group (TSG), and vice president (VP). They all report to the director in the organizational hierarchy.

Each regional office has a divisional manager (DM). The DM is in charge of the field-engineering activities in the region. Each DM has a number of area managers (AMs) reporting to him. An AM is responsible for the maintenance of all computers in a specific geographical territory/area. A specialist is attached to each AM to help him solve the problems/faults within his territory; also, he may be asked by the TSG to help solve problems elsewhere in the country. A group of CEs is assigned to each AM to carry out the maintenance activities; the number of CEs assigned to each AM depends on the size of the territory.

Figure 5 shows the organizational hierarchy of the maintenance company. In this figure, the dotted line indicates that there is only functional interaction between the entities connected by it. This problem has been implemented in DISPROS as described below.

Each regional and corporate office is implemented as a level manager, whereas each manager/ corporate manager is represented as a set of knowledge sources. Thus, there are 12 different sets of knowledge sources in the system personifying each function in the hierarchy.

To understand how the knowledge is captured in each knowledge source, let us consider the role that an area manager plays. The area manager is responsible for the maintenance of computers in a specific territory/area and has many computer engineers reporting to him. Whenever a new machine is installed in this territory, he has to assign a computer engineer for its maintenance. He arrives at a decision based on various factors, such as the expertise available with his CEs for maintenance and the number of machines already assigned to a specific CE for maintenance. A typical rule of the KS that is used to represent the AM can be written as

If an engineer exists such that
the engineer is maintaining a lesser number of machines than that which he is capable of maintaining
and the engineer has expertise of the newly procured machine
Then assign the engineer for the new machine;
update the machines maintained by the engineer;
inform the user about the new assignment.

The blackboard within a level manager is partitioned into the following levels: *global, resource, system, subsystem, assembly,* and *component.* The global level contains information regarding the name and number of each type of computer and of such items as peripherals, along with the expertise available within the company on these systems. The resource level contains experts — for example, specialists and area managers — as the objects with information about their expertise. The other levels represent the hierarchy in the computer. The system level consists of objects like computers. The subsystem level has peripherals as the objects. The assembly level contains the assemblies of computer/peripherals represented as the objects. The component level contains the printed circuit boards (PCBs) and other components of the machine.

The objects at the higher levels have links connecting to objects at lower levels in the system hierarchy. For example, an IBM personal computer is an object at the system level with slots: type (micro), make (IBM), asset number (21203). It has links to the CE (an engineer who is responsible for its maintenance), an object at the resource level; the printer, an object at the subsystem level; and so on. Thus, all components of an IBM PC will be defined as objects at the four levels that represent the hierarchy within the computer.

Problem solving. The problem-solving process starts with the user specifying any change in the current status of computers under maintenance or in the manpower. The user-interface module captures the information from the user and posts it on the blackboard. This starts the execution cycle in DISPROS, which invokes the necessary knowledge sources in the system until the new requirements/constraints are satisfied. The system, depending on the input given by the user, informs him of the name of the CE assigned for maintenance, the new components to be ordered, or any change in the manpower/training requirement. In the FEP, each level manager is implemented as a process

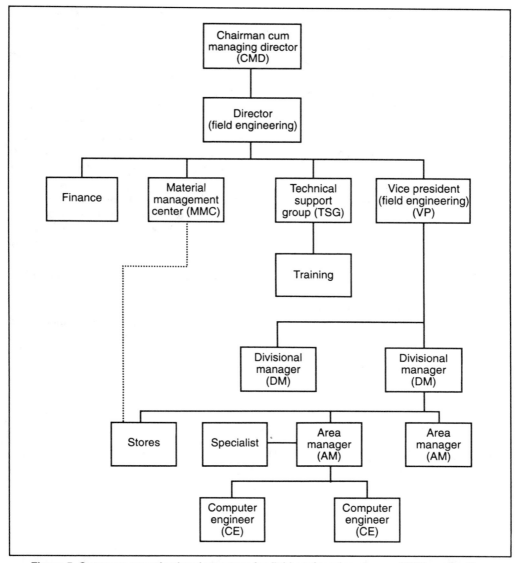

Figure 5. Company organizational structure for field engineering planner (FEP) application.

group, with members being replicated on more than one computer. DISPROS facilities provide fault tolerance.

Conclusions

The architecture of DISPROS draws its strength from the ease with which different sources of knowledge can be integrated. It permits different knowledge sources to embody qualitatively different sorts of expertise, to operate independently, and to contribute whenever they can. This enables knowledge about various aspects of the problem domain to be captured in different LMs, each using the representation technique best suited for that activity. Furthermore, in DISPROS, LMs are autonomous, encapsulated objects that are combined to make a system. The interactions between LMs are limited by the message-passing mechanism, resulting in the introduction of new level managers into the system far more easily and in a far more disciplined manner than in monolithic blackboard systems. This results in a modular structure, where the system is gradually built by adding new level managers and dealing with some other aspects of the problem over a period of time.

The presence of separate matchers and action interpreters allows different LMs to use different knowledge representation schemes if the problem domain so requires. This increases the flexibility and knowledge representation capability of the system. Also, DKRL generalizes the notion of abstract data types to the levels of abstraction and inheritance. It has the enormous advantages of flexibility and extensibility. It allows one to combine independently developed systems to produce integrated systems that are more powerful than the mere union of their parts.

We found that global control contributes to the network traffic significantly, because global control is implemented by message passing and is, for the same reason, difficult to implement. We have tried to minimize the network traffic and increase the global coherence by using organizational-structuring techniques. These techniques enable the user to specify the distribution of problem-solving capabilities among the LMs and to specify the pattern of information and control relationships that exists between them. The result is that each LM gets a high-level view of how the network solves the problem and of the role that the LM plays within the network's structure, thus allowing the LMs to decide to send — and to actually send — messages only to relevant LMs.

The system has been coded in C and runs on the Unix operating system, keeping portability and distributability in view. It is currently running on a local area network in the department that consists of heterogeneous systems — namely, micro-VAXs, HP9000, and Sun workstations.

Table 1 gives a comparison of our approach with DVMT, MACE, and AF. This comparison is based on the issues raised earlier.

Acknowledgments

The evolution of this paper was influenced by many of our colleagues, to whom we are deeply grateful. Special thanks go to Dr. P.P. Gupta, who was a constant source of inspiration and encouragement throughout the period of this work.

References

[1]   K. Birman et al., "Programming with Shared Bulletin Boards in Asynchronous Distributed Systems," Tech. Report TR 86-172, Dept. of Computer Science, Cornell Univ., Ithaca, N.Y., 1986.

[2]   K. Birman and T. Joseph, "Reliable Communication in the Presence of Failures," *ACM Trans. Computer Systems*, Vol. 5, No. 1, Feb. 1987, pp. 47-76.

[3]   D.G. Bobrow and T. Winograd, "An Overview of KRL, a Knowledge Representation Language," *Cognitive Science*, Vol. 1, No. 1, 1977, pp. 3-46.

[4]   R.J. Brachman, "What IS-A Is and Isn't: An Analysis of Taxonomic Links in Semantic Networks," *Computer,* Vol. 16, No. 10, Oct. 1983, pp. 30-36.

[5]   D.D. Corkill and V.R. Lesser, "A Goal Directed HEARSAY-II Architecture: Unifying Data and Goal-Directed Control," Tech. Report 81-15, Dept. of Computer and Information Science, Univ. of Massachusetts, Amherst, Mass., 1981.

[6]   R. Davis and B.G. Buchanan, "Meta-Level Knowledge: Overview and Applications," *Proc. Fifth Int'l Joint Conf. Artificial Intelligence (IJCAI-77)*, Vol. Two, Dept. of Computer Science, Carnegie Mellon Univ., Pittsburgh, Pa., 1977, pp. 920-927.

Table 1. Comparison of different approaches.

	DVMT	MACE	AF	DISPROS
Objective	Empirical evaluation of alternative designs for functionally accurate, cooperative (FA/C) distributed problem solving	Testbed for building a wide range of experimental distributed artificial intelligence (DAI) systems at different levels of granularity	Software framework for real-time distributed cooperative problem solving	Software framework for distributed cooperative problem solving
Knowledge representation scheme				
• Scheme	Rule based	Set of attributes	Rule based	Frames with production rules
• Inheritance	Multiple inheritance	Multiple inheritance with user control		Multiple inheritance with user control
• Multiple hypotheses	Yes	Yes	Yes	Yes
• Belief revision	No	No	No	Yes
• What determines an event	Monitor	Event monitors	Framework	Monitor
• Knowledge source (KS) condition (form)	Procedure	Procedure	Procedure	Condition part of rule
• Knowledge source (KS) body (form)	Procedure	Procedure	Procedure	Action part of rule
Distribution of knowledge				
• Geographically	Yes	Yes	Yes	Yes
• Multicomputer	Yes	Yes	Yes	Yes
Problem-solving strategy				
• Focus of attention	Goal	Agents	Activation framework object (AFO)	Level manager (LM)
• Partial solution evaluation	Yes	No	No	Yes
• Local scheduling	Local planner working with interest area	Sophisticated local scheduling	Activation level of an activation framework object (AFO)	Sophisticated local scheduling
• Global scheduling	Partial global planning	Multiagent planning	Not done	Partial global planning
• Flexibility	High	High	Moderate	High
Concurrency				
• Granularity	Knowledge source (KS)	Agent	Activation framework object (AFO)	Knowledge source (KS)
• Cooperation	Functionally accurate cooperation	Organizational structuring with message passing	Organizational structuring with message passing	Organizational structuring with message passing
Real-time aspects				
• Uncertainty about events	Working with alternative plans	Left to the user	Working with alternative plans	Working with alternative plans
• Reasoning about time	Not supported directly	Not supported directly	Not supported directly	Not supported directly
• Timeliness	Not supported directly	Not supported directly	Using suggestion mode	Not supported directly
Resource constraints	Focuses on minimizing message traffic and CPU utilization	Focuses on minimizing message traffic and CPU utilization	Focuses on minimizing message traffic and CPU utilization	Focuses on minimizing message traffic and CPU utilization
Communication protocols	Host operating system message-passing mechanism	MACE kernel communication handler	Host operating system message-passing mechanism	Based on virtual synchrony model; uses Isis for communication
Fault tolerance	Not provided	Not provided	Not provided	Yes, except for network partitioning
Distributability	Written in Common Lisp	Written in Common Lisp	Written in C and Common Lisp	Written in C
Modularity	Modules are independently developable and separately testable	Plans are to make agents independently developable and testable	Plans are to make activation framework objects (AFOs) independently developable and separately testable; highly modular	Level managers (LMs) are independently developable and separately testable; highly modular
Development tools	Good	Good	Moderate	Moderate
	Editor, debugger, simulator, performance-measurement tools	Editor, debugger, simulator, directory, performance-measurement tools	Editor, debugger, library	Editor, debugger, library

[7] E.H. Durfee, V.R. Lesser, and D.D. Corkill, "Trends in Cooperative Distributed Problem Solving," *IEEE Trans. Knowledge and Data Eng.*, Vol. 1, No. 1, Mar. 1989, pp. 63-83.

[8] L.D. Erman et al., "The HEARSAY-II Speech Understanding System: Integrating Knowledge to Resolve Uncertainty," *ACM Computing Surveys*, Vol. 12, No. 2, June 1980, pp. 213-253.

[9] L. Gasser, C. Braganza, and N. Herman, "MACE: A Flexible Testbed for Distributed AI Research," in *Distributed Artificial Intelligence*, M.N. Huhns, ed., Morgan Kaufmann, San Mateo, Calif., 1987, pp. 119-152.

[10] P.E. Green, "AF: A Framework for Real-Time Distributed Cooperative Problem Solving," *Distributed Artificial Intelligence*, M.N. Huhns, ed., Morgan Kaufmann, San Mateo, Calif., 1987, pp. 153-176.

[11] P.J. Hayes, "The Logic of Frames," in *Frame Conceptions & Text Understanding (Research in Text Theory: No. 5)*, D. Metzing, ed., Walter De Gruyter, Inc., Hawthorne, N.Y., 1980.

[12] B. Hayes-Roth, "A Blackboard Architecture for Control," *Artificial Intelligence*, Vol. 26, No. 2, Mar. 1985, pp. 251-321.

[13] V.R. Lesser and D.D. Corkill, "The Distributed Vehicle Monitoring Testbed: A Tool for Investigating Distributed Problem Solving Networks," *AI Magazine*, Vol. 4, No. 3, 1983, pp. 15-33.

[14] M. Minsky, "A Framework for Representing Knowledge," in *Psychology of Computer Vision*, P. Winston, ed., McGraw-Hill, New York, N.Y., 1975, pp. 211-277.

[15] M.K. Saxena, K.K. Biswas, and P.C.P. Bhatt, "DISPROS — A Fault Tolerant Blackboard Architecture," Tech. Report CSE/89/501, Dept. of Computer Science and Eng., Indian Inst. of Technology, Hauz Khas, New Delhi, India, 1989.

[16] M.K. Saxena, K.K. Biswas, and P.C.P. Bhatt, "Knowledge Representation in Distributed Blackboard Architecture — Some Issues," *Proc. Knowledge Based Computer Systems (KBCS '89)*, Lecture Notes Series 444, Springer Verlag, New York, N.Y., 1989, pp. 230-239.

[17] M.K. Saxena, K.K Biswas, and P.C.P. Bhatt, "DISPROS — A Distributed Blackboard Architecture," *Proc. Third Int'l Conf. Industrial and Eng. Applications Artificial Intelligence and Expert Systems (IEA/ AIE '90)*, ACM Press, New York, N.Y., 1990.

[18] W.A. Woods, "What's Important about Knowledge Representation?," *Computer*, Vol. 16, No. 10, Oct. 1983, pp. 22-27.

CHAPTER 6

Performance Measurements and Modeling

ZM4/Simple: A General Approach to Performance Measurement and Evaluation of Distributed Systems

P arallel and distributed data processing is intended to increase performance by distributing a workload onto many computers. This way of getting high performance from multicomputer architectures is a big leap forward; however, it produces new problems, such as races between concurrent programs, mutual waiting of processes, or access conflicts on interconnection networks. Obviously, it is highly desirable to understand why and where such problems exist. Event-driven measurements with appropriate monitors can provide insight and knowledge about the dynamic behavior of parallel activities and the communication between them.

One basic idea of our performance evaluation methodology is to do more than just monitoring, but also to integrate performance modeling and monitoring. Both rely on the same abstraction of dynamic program behavior: Strategic points are represented as *events of interest* and the overall dynamic behavior as an *event trace*. (In our project, event traces are analyzed in terms of performance. However, there is an interesting bridge to debugging of concurrent programs. Event-based debuggers examine recorded event histories — that is, traces — for finding errors [MH89]. Performance evaluation tools do almost the same. They examine event histories for getting insight into how and where to improve performance.) Thus, the dynamic behavior of the program(s) is abstracted to an event trace. In this paper, we show how models support a systematic event specification for monitoring and how monitoring validates the models. Monitoring helps to identify current performance problems and to find hints for tuning (for example, improved scheduling and mapping). The integration of modeling and monitoring is the basis for extending the (measured) knowledge about implemented programs in existing computer systems via models onto performance prediction of future programs and of programs in future systems. Using measured parameters makes the performance prediction more relevant.

Peter Dauphin,

Richard Hofmann,

Rainer Klar,

Bernd Mohr,

Andreas Quick,

Markus Siegle, and

Franz Sötz

Another basic idea of our performance evaluation concept is to bring performance evaluation "out of the ghetto of splendid isolation" [Fer86]. A systematic methodology is indispensable; however, it does not automatically solve real-world problems. It is the desire of our research to extend the theoretical relevance of the methodology to practical use. We agree with Ferrari [Fer86], who argued that in the past, "the study of performance evaluation as an independent subject has sometimes caused researchers in the area to lose contact with reality." Practical relevance means tools that help to make performance evaluation a natural part of system design and software engineering. Therefore, a set of tools puts our methodology into effect: We built a distributed hardware monitor (ZM4) and implemented a software tool environment for performance evaluation (SIMPLE).

Two architectural features were used in the design of the ZM4 monitor; they enable ZM4 to measure multiprocessor systems as well as computer networks. The first feature is a distributed and open-ended monitor architecture that matches the usually distributed architecture of the observed system. The observed computer system is called the *object system*. The second feature is a high-precision global monitor clock mechanism that provides globally valid time stamps. This feature allows for simultaneous observation of many computers over a common time scale. Our decision to use a hardware monitor does not mean that we are interested primarily in measuring hardware events. On the contrary, we are interested in the dynamic behavior and the performance of concurrent software in multicomputers. Therefore, hybrid monitoring is our favored method: The object software initiates source-referenced event tokens and the hardware monitor ZM4 collects them.

The tool environment SIMPLE is a modular, comprehensive set of tools for performance evaluation and visualization based on event traces, be they monitored or generated by simulators. These event traces of arbitrary structure, format, and representation are described by the versatile event trace description language (TDL). All tools of SIMPLE use the problem-oriented event trace (POET) access interface, a library of procedures for accessing and decoding information in event traces. This paper emphasizes the importance of this access interface TDL/POET as a means for evaluating event traces of arbitrary origin, for making trace format standardization superfluous, and for enabling the evaluation environment SIMPLE to cope with the flexibility of the distributed monitor ZM4.

The paper is divided into five sections. The first section describes fundamentals of event-driven monitoring. The second section deals with the integration of modeling and monitoring. The third section describes the hardware monitor system ZM4 and the fourth section describes the tools of the evaluation environment SIMPLE. The fifth section briefly presents three typical applications and the conclusions. It is shown that SIMPLE may be operationally independent of ZM4 and that using ZM4/SIMPLE in combination provides successful evaluation of high-speed communication software as well as of parallel programs.

Fundamentals of event-driven monitoring

Monitoring is either *time-driven* or *event-driven*. Time-driven monitoring (sampling) allows only statistical statements about the program behavior [Svo76], [FSZ83]. However, event-driven monitoring reveals the dynamic flow of program activities represented by sequences of events. An *event* is an atomic instantaneous action. It can be represented as a particular value on a processor bus or in a register or as a certain point in a program. With event-driven monitoring, the dynamic behavior of the program is abstracted to a sequence of events.

There are three monitoring techniques: *hardware*, *software*, and *hybrid*. With the use of hardware monitoring, the event definition and recognition can be difficult and complex. An event is defined as a bit pattern and is detected by the hardware monitor's probes, and it is difficult to find a problem-oriented reference to the monitored programs. (In many cases, identifiers in the source code of the object-program — like procedure names — are already-intelligible problem-oriented references. Then, "problem-oriented" and "source-referenced" are synonymous. Sometimes, an interesting event has no problem-oriented identifier as a counterpart. Then, it is necessary to give the respective event a problem-oriented name that is not yet defined in the source code of the object.) With the use of software or hybrid monitoring, the events are defined by instructions being inserted into the program to be measured. This is called *program instrumentation*. These measurement instructions write event tokens into a reserved memory area (in software monitoring) or to a hardware interface that is available for a hardware monitor (in hybrid monitoring). Program instrumentation is not needed in sampling; it always implies the use of event-driven monitoring. If events are defined by instrumenting a program, each measured event token can be clearly assigned to a point in a program; it provides a problem-oriented reference. Thus, the evaluation can be done on a level familiar to the program designer.

The following are the essential questions that occur in event-driven monitoring, regardless of the monitoring technique:

- What is the aim of measurement?
- Which events are necessary for modeling the functional behavior?
- Where should the program be instrumented so that the modeled behavior can be monitored?

Because the CPU time overhead increases with the number of events detected, the instrumentation of events must be limited to those events whose tracing is considered essential for an understanding of the problems to be solved. Therefore, to define events systematically, one needs knowledge about the aim of measurement; this was pointed out by Nutt [Nut75], who stated, "The most important questions to be answered before attempting to monitor a machine are *what* to measure and *why* the measurement should be taken." Also, knowledge about the functional behavior of the program is necessary, as noted by Ferrari, Serazzi, and Zeigner [FSZ83], who stated, "The workload and its evolution in time must be at least roughly known."

With the use of event-driven monitoring, the dynamic behavior is represented by events that are stored as an event trace. Whenever the monitor device recognizes an event, it stores a data record. We call such a data record an *event record*, or an *E-record* for short. It contains the information concerning what happened, when, and where, and it consists of at least an *event identification* (*token*) and a *time stamp*. This time stamp is generated by the monitor and does not reflect a duration, but rather reflects the acquisition time of the event record. Beside these fields, an E-record contains optional fields describing additional aspects of the occurred event — for example, a field describing the processor from which the event token came. An important performance measure is the runtime of a program. A program or a program part delimited by two events is called an *activity*. The duration of an activity is defined as the difference between the time stamps of its end-event and its start-event.

Integrating modeling and monitoring

Being interested in the functional and dynamic behavior of parallel and distributed systems, we decided to use function-oriented models that explicitly model the functional interdependence of activities in order for us to gain insight into this behavior. Figure 1 shows the use of models in monitoring: Specification of the problem and selection of an algorithm are prerequisites for building a *functional model* that disregards all implementation aspects. In this model, properties of an algorithm that determine the functional behavior of a program are described. Mapping the functional model onto a given computer configuration leads to one or several implementation strategies that are modeled in the *functional implementation model*. The functional implementation model forms the

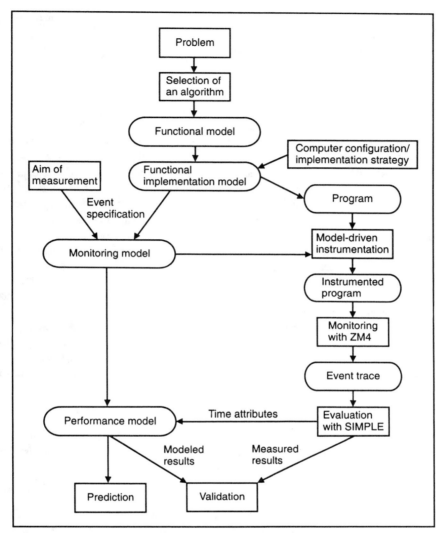

Figure 1. Model-driven monitoring.

basis for the implementation of the program and for the *monitoring model*. The monitoring model is a subset of the functional implementation model; that is, it covers some but not all of the details of the implementation model. It describes the functional dependencies of the implemented program on that level of abstraction on which the program should be monitored. The chosen level of abstraction is determined by the aim of measurement. The instrumented program results from an already-implemented program and the respective monitoring model. Running the instrumented program — that is, execution and measurement — produces an event trace as a result. The subsequent evaluation of the event traces provides overall results for validation and detailed performance parameters for assigning realistic time attributes to the program's activities. The monitoring model and time attributes build a *performance model* [Lut89]. The performance model is a prerequisite for tuning and predicting the performance of not-yet-implemented systems. Besides systematic event specification and performance prediction, the monitoring model can be used for automatic trace validation and as a graphical template for dynamic trace visualization (animation).

Systematic event specification

Instrumenting a program for event-driven monitoring means not only defining events, but also defining the respective level of abstraction. (The idea of analyzing parallel programs in different levels of abstraction is also called *analysis using multiple views* [LMF90].) Here, the relationship between *modeling* and *monitoring* is obvious: Both techniques are based on the same definition of events. In the same way that modeling describes the flow by transitions between model states, monitoring describes transitions between program activities by events. Because of the very close connection between the flow descriptions in modeling and in monitoring, it is desirable to use the same set of events for modeling and for monitoring. The monitoring model describes the flow of the program on a level of abstraction desired for measurement and performance evaluation. The level of abstraction described in the monitoring model depends on the intention of the analysis. Thereby, it is useful to first model and observe the flow on a coarse-level such as the process level. This model reveals process concurrency, process interdependence, and process interactions, but dispenses with instrumenting all procedures at the same time. Coarse-level monitoring avoids an intractable flood of events. Therefore, stepwise refinement, usually used in software engineering, should also be applied for monitoring.

With modeling and monitoring integrated, the instrumentation will be simplified, since the important phases of the program are regarded as black boxes and represented by states in the model. In this case, the difficult question of how to instrument a program is already answered implicitly by the monitoring model, and it is tempting to derive the instrumentation automatically from the model. Thus, the instrumentation need no longer be an intuitive action; it may be done systematically. A systematic procedure offers two great advantages, as follows:

- Program instrumentation can be carried out automatically with the support of tools.
- The necessary input parameters for a performance model — for example, runtime distributions of program phases or transition probabilities between them — can be derived from a measured event trace.

The systematic model-driven instrumentation guarantees by construction the same set of events in the monitored event trace as in the model. There is a one-to-one mapping between the model events and the measurement events. Therefore, no distinction is made between them.

The automatic instrumentation of a multigrid algorithm implemented on a multiprocessor system in the programming language C is described in reference [KQS91]. The modeling is done with stochastic graph models that can be generated and evaluated by the tool PEPP (performance evaluation of parallel programs). Beside modeling, PEPP provides a command file for the model-driven automatic instrumentation with the tool AICOS (automatic instrumentation of C object software). AICOS can be used for automatic instrumentation of programs written in C as a preprocessor. Both PEPP and AICOS have been developed at the University of Erlangen, Germany.

Another advantage of this method is the direct feedback between the monitoring results and the model. Building a model always includes intuitive deliberations. However, intuition can fail. Therefore, it is absolutely necessary to validate the model with the help of the monitoring results. Because of the same set of events being in monitoring and modeling, validation is possible; that is, whether or not the model matches with the monitored behavior of the program can be checked. If the model does not match the monitored behavior, there are two kinds of feedback between monitoring and modeling; that is, there are two kinds of feedback for bringing monitoring into line with modeling and vice versa, as follows:

- If it may be assumed that there is a correct implementation that is to be described by a model, the original model must be adapted to the implementation.
- If a specification given in a model is correct and should be implemented, then the implementation must be changed according to the model.

Such a correction demands a change of the program instrumentation before the next measurement. The advantages of using systematic and tool-supported automatic event specification and instrumentation are obvious: Instead of a demanding and fault-prone manual reinstrumentation of the object program, a modification of the monitoring model can be done. Then, a systematic, automatic instrumentation of all states described in the model is carried out. This tool support is especially helpful for the instrumentation of all ending points of a C-function, which is too tedious and error-prone a task using a text editor.

The model-driven approach enables us to instrument arbitrary statements in the program under investigation on the desired level of abstraction. So, the overhead caused by instrumenting all procedures, as in reference [AL89], can be significantly reduced. Also, monitoring is not restricted to interprocess communication as it is done in references [HC89] and [Joy+87]. In reference [Mil+90], an automatic approach to program instrumentation is presented that causes an overhead of up to 45 percent. We use the same multiple-view concept as LeBlanc, Mellor-Crummey, and Fowler [LMF90], but we support it by model-driven instrumentation, which allows very easy reinstrumentation of a program. In addition to finding suspicious behavior — as in debugging [MH89] and finding performance bottlenecks [BM89] — the integration of modeling and monitoring enables us to predict the performance of not-yet-available systems and implementations.

Performance prediction

Adding runtime distributions to the activities of a functional model, we get a performance model. Modeling enables us to compare the performance of various implementations and mappings. The use of measured distribution functions means model evaluation with realistic data and more relevant results. One application of integrating monitoring and modeling is shown in the following example:

We used stochastic graph models as performance models to predict the speedup of a parallel multigrid implementation on a 16-processor system. Each node of the model represented an activity such as relaxation and interpolation. The analysis was started by implementing and measuring a parallel algorithm A_1. The achieved speedup was disappointing. Analyzing the measured data, we detected that a poor parallelization strategy was responsible for the bad speedup. When the same level of abstraction was used in the monitoring model as in the graph model, the measured distribution functions of algorithm A_1 were valuable parameters for modeling different implementation alternatives. We were able to predict the speedup of an improved implementation. The predicted speedup could be confirmed by further measurements. In addition, the runtime of the algorithm on not-yet-available configurations with more than 16 processors was predicted based on the measured runtimes. According to this prediction, the speedup for this algorithm cannot be further improved by using more than 20 processors.

In this way, performance prediction is integrated with monitoring. Depending upon on the modeled problem, we use various modeling techniques, such as queueing models, timed petri nets, or stochastic graph models. Here, we describe the tools we currently use for modeling parallel programs.

For modeling parallel programs, we prefer *stochastic graphs*. A stochastic graph consists of nodes and arcs. The nodes represent the activities of the parallel program. An arc from activity *A* to *B* means that activity *A* must be finished before activity *B* can be started. The runtime behavior of each activity is modeled by a *distribution function*.

By analyzing a graph, we compute the runtime distribution function or the mean runtime of the modeled program. Let us consider problems that can be modeled with seriesparallel graphs. (For analyzing nonseriesparallel graphs, we use the state space analysis.) If we have a seriesparallel graph, the overall runtime distribution function can be obtained by reducing the graph to one single node. The operators convolution (*series reduction*) and product (*parallel reduction*) are applied to the activities' runtime distributions. The operator convolution can be applied to the nodes *A* and *B* if the only successor of *A* is *B* and *A* is the only predecessor of *B*. The operator product can be applied to the nodes *A* and *B* if the predecessor and the successor nodes are the same.

There are two methods of using the measured data for performance prediction, as follows:

- The empirical distribution functions are approximated with appropriate parametric distribution functions.
- The operators are directly applied to the empirical distribution functions.

Good approximations can be obtained by using exponential polynomials [Sah86]; branching Erlang distributions, as in MEDA (mixed erlang distribution approximation) [Sch87], [Sch89]; or distributions consisting of one deterministically and one exponentially distributed phase, as in PEPP [Söt90]. The problem is that in many cases of practical relevance, the analysis must be done by simulation, because of the high computational costs of the known mathematical methods.

The advantage of the second method is that the activities' runtime distributions may be arbitrarily distributed. In spite of this advantage, the graph can be evaluated very efficiently [Kle82]. In order to compare the execution time of different implementation schemes, we developed the tool SPASS (series parallel structures solver) [Pin88]. Using the empirical method, we can evaluate graphs consisting of 1000 and more nodes [SW90] in some minutes, independent of the runtime distribution shape.

ZM4 — A universal distributed monitor system

A monitor system, universally adaptable to computer systems with more than one processor, must fulfill several architectural demands. It must be able to

- Deal with a large number of processors (nodes in the object system),
- Cope with spatial distribution of the object nodes,
- Supply a global view of the object system, and
- Adapt to different node architectures.

In order to deal with a large number of processors, the monitor should be decentralized into a network of an arbitrary number of nodes, instead of being one huge monitor for the whole object system. Extending the concept of decentralization to spatial distribution of the monitor nodes allows the monitor system to cope with spatial distribution of the object system also.

Supplying a global view needs methods for showing causal relationships between activities in different processors. The following considerations show that a global clock with an accuracy better than 500 nanoseconds (ns) provides a means to do this in any of today's parallel and distributed systems.

In distributed systems as well as in multiprocessors, there is an event stream associated with each processor. As the processors are coworkers on a common task, they have to exchange information about each other, resulting in an interdependence of their event streams. In order to globally reveal all causal relationships, it suffices to order the events internal to each processor locally and to order events concerning interprocessor communication globally. Local ordering is automatically achieved if the events are recorded in the order of their occurrence.

A global ordering of the communication events can be achieved by the inherent causality of Send and Receive operations in systems communicating via message passing [Lam78]: A message can be received only after it was previously sent. But monitoring also has to show performance indices, introducing the necessity of physical time. Duda et al. [Dud+87] described a mechanism to estimate a global time from local observations in systems communicating via message passing. Systems communicating via shared variables lack this easy mechanism to globally order events and to derive a global time. Here, one processor's change of a shared variable alters the state of all processors using this variable, too. As the sequence of such accesses is arbitrary, it cannot be foreseen, and there is no means to globally order such events without a global time scale.

The change of a shared variable actually affects another processor's state when it reads this variable. As the read access to this variable can immediately follow the (state-changing) write access, two consecutive accesses to a shared variable must be ordered correctly. Because of the asynchronous nature of multiprocessor and multicomputer systems, access conflicts can occur. They are solved with an arbitration logic, which serializes conflicting access requests, but needs time to reach a stable state. So, a monitor clock with a global accuracy of better than about half a microsecond (μs) allows communication events to be globally ordered in systems with shared variables. As these demands on time resolution exceed by orders of magnitude those from ordering Send/Receive events, a monitor using a clock with this accuracy can be used universally.

A powerful monitor system should not be dedicated to just one object computer architecture. In order to enable an easy adaptation to arbitrary object systems and to fulfill the already-mentioned demands, one prerequisite is a distributed architecture with a global clock. Other capabilities must be provided by the monitor nodes. These can be functionally separated into the following tasks:

(1)   Interfacing to the object system: The monitor system must be adapted to the object system; that is, appropriate signals in the object system must be transformed to be compatible with the monitor kernel.

(2)   Event detection: There must be a unit in the monitor system that is responsible for recognizing the predefined events. This unit has to prepare the event-defining signals in such a manner that the later steps of the monitoring process are supplied with compact and useful information about the events occurring in the object system.

(3)   Time stamping and event recording: Each event must instantaneously be assigned a globally valid time stamp allowing the ordering of all events with global interdependence. Recording of the events is necessary for postprocessing, and multistage buffering is necessary to uncouple the event rate of the object system from the speed for writing high-volume trace files.

A pragmatic aspect is the handling of the monitor system. It must be applicable to large (that is, having many processors and/or spatial distribution) object systems, as well as to small object systems. Therefore, it must be flexible enough to support upgrading from small and rudimentary monitor configurations to very large ones.

These demands can nearly be fulfilled by the features of typical monitor systems being combined. Plattner [Pla84] developed a hardware monitor for monitoring software in real time. His monitor is dedicated to a single processor, which is fully adequate for his investigation: He showed that noninvasive monitoring of systems with dynamic resources — that is, with procedures with local variables, recursive calls, and dynamic memory allocation, for example — is very complicated.

Tsai, Fang, and Chen [TFC90] described a monitor system that is also called a noninvasive monitor. It is aimed at monitoring of multimicroprocessors with the Motorola 68000, which uses neither virtual addressing with memory protection nor caching mechanisms. This monitor works with a shadow processor for each processor in the object system. Once armed, it is loaded with the internal status of the object processor and then runs in parallel with it. After the specified trigger condition has been met, the status of the shadow processor, which is identical to that of the object processor, can be investigated without disturbing the object system. The arming for the next investigation is done by issuing an interrupt to the object processor, which transfers its internal status to the shadow processor. Tsai, Fang, and Chen [TFC90] restricted the range of possible investigations to software without dynamic resources, and there is no discussion concerning how to establish a global view of the object system.

The advantages and drawbacks of hardware, software, and hybrid monitoring were analyzed by Mink et al. [Min+90], who stated that hybrid monitoring allows investigations that are not possible with pure hardware monitoring — for example, when caches are involved. They preferred hybrid monitoring, because it causes little interference on the object system. Their monitor system was built of measurement nodes that carry out the data collection. Together with a central analysis computer, they are interconnected with a VMEbus. A measurement node consists of a set of very large scale integration (VLSI) chips, responsible for gathering the event-defining information from the object system, time stamping the generated event records, and data buffering. As a special feature, event counters are implemented in one of the VLSI chips in order to reduce the amount of data to be transferred and evaluated. With a time resolution of 100 ns, this monitor system allows all communication events in locally concentrated multiprocessor systems to be correctly ordered.

Netmon-II (networking monitor II) [ESZ90] is a hybrid monitoring tool for distributed and multiprocessor systems. It is a distributed master/slave system with a central control station (master) and monitor stations (slaves). Each monitor station contains a monitoring unit, a load generation unit, and a network interface for the communication with the central station, responsible for controlling the measurement and for data evaluation. The monitoring unit is implemented as an add-on card for PCs that is dedicated to hybrid monitoring and has an eight-bit-wide Centronics printer port as the interface to the object system. Thus, interfacing, event detection, and event recording — that is, all tasks of a monitor node — are combined on one board.

An autonomous clock with a resolution of eight μs is part of each monitoring unit, making the monitor suitable for object systems that communicate via Send/Receive mechanisms. In order for a global timebase to be established, these clocks are corrected every 15 milliseconds (ms) via the time channel that connects all monitoring units. As this correction is carried out by directly accessing registers from a signal that is distributed over distances in the local area network (LAN) area, erroneous corrections due to spikes on the time channel can occur. This results in incorrect time stamps that cannot be detected, because the clock circuitry does not distinguish between correct and incorrect pulses on the time channel.

In our opinion, universal monitor systems need two more features, as follows:

- Modular design of interfacing, detection, and time stamping in order to provide easy adaptability to arbitrary object systems and
- A global clock mechanism that combines high resolution, precise synchronization over large distances, and detection of synchronization errors.

Architecture of the ZM4

We have designed and implemented a universal distributed monitor system, called ZM4 (see Figure 2), that fulfills all the previously mentioned demands. It is structured as a master/slave system, with the central *control and evaluation computer* (CEC) as the master and an arbitrary number of

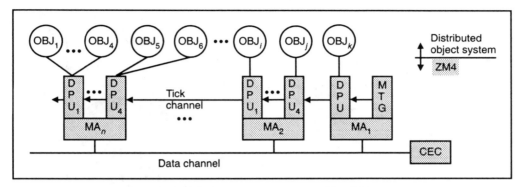

Figure 2. Distributed architecture of the ZM4.

monitor agents (MAs) as slaves. The distance between these MAs can be up to 1000 meters. Conceptually, the CEC has the task of building the user interface of the whole monitor system — that is, of controlling the measurement activity of the MAs, storing the measured data, and supporting the user with a powerful and universal toolset for evaluation of the measured data (see the section entitled "SIMPLE — A performance evaluation environment").

The MAs are the nodes of the distributed monitor system. They are equipped with up to four *dedicated probe units* (DPUs). The MAs control the DPUs and buffer the measured event traces on their local disks. The DPUs interface the nodes of the object system and are responsible for event recognition, time stamping, and event recording with the first, high-speed stage of buffering. As can be seen in the next subsection, the DPUs are separated into specialized and general parts.

In order to establish a global time scale with the necessary resolution, a time-stamping mechanism is integrated into the DPU by combining a globally synchronized clock with the event-recording mechanism. The clock of each DPU gets all information necessary for preparing precise time stamps via the tick channel from the *measure tick generator* (MTG) that forms the master part of the clock synchronization.

While the tick channel together with the synchronization mechanism is our own development, we used commercially available parts for the data channel; that is, we used Ethernet with TCP/IP. The data channel forms the communication subsystem of the ZM4 and it is used to distribute control information between the MAs and the CEC, as well as measured data. Together with the MAs, the MTG, and the CEC, the general part of the DPU forms the universal kernel of the ZM4.

The ZM4's architectural flexibility has been achieved by two properties: easy interfacing and a scalable architecture. The DPU can easily be adapted to different object systems (see the next subsection). ZM4 is fully scalable in terms of MAs and DPUs. The smallest configuration consists of one MA and one DPU and can monitor up to four object nodes. Larger object systems are matched by more DPUs and MAs, respectively.

Dedicated probe units in the monitor agent

The monitor agents are standard PC/AT-compatible machines. We use their expandability for adapting the kernel of the ZM4 to the various object systems. Each PC/AT provides processing power, memory resources, and a hard disk, in addition to a network interface for access to the data channel.

In order to achieve the goal of a universal monitor system, the DPUs physically implement the demanded functional separation (see "General DPU" in Figure 3). According to the three tasks of event processing, there are also three levels of achievable generality.

The *interface* depends to a high degree on the object system, so a universal implementation is

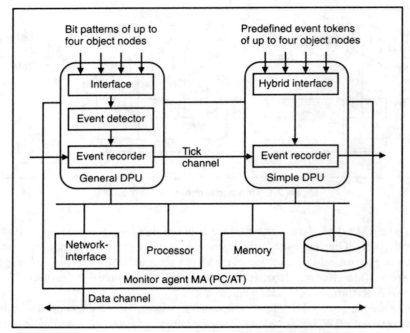

Figure 3. Monitor agent equipped with DPUs.

impractical (other than by using clumsy probes similar to those of logic analyzers). Interfacing the object system is usually a small fraction of the whole monitoring effort and it can be done without interaction of the MA's processor. As building a simple interface is the only effort for adapting a new object system, the functional separation makes the ZM4 a truly universal monitor system.

The *event detector* investigates the rapidly changing information supplied by the interface, in order to recognize the events of interest and to supply the event recorder with appropriate information about each event. This information must reveal two things: the event itself — that is, one element out of the set of possible and predefined events — and the point of time at which the event occurred. The complexity of the event detector depends largely on the type of measurement: For recognizing predefined statements in the program running on a processor without instruction cache and memory management unit, a set of comparators or a memory-mapped comparison scheme suffices. If the object system uses a processor with a hardware cache, or if predefined sequences of statements are intended to trigger an event, much more complex recognition circuits will be necessary [KL86].

At the output of the event detector, a stream of events — consisting of a bit pattern and a signal for their occurrence — is available for the *event recorder*. This part is needed in general, and — if implemented carefully — it can be used for any type of event and object (see the next subsection).

Using hybrid monitoring, the object system itself carries out the event recognition and sends suitable event tokens to the monitor. In this case, the interface and event detector can be combined to a *hybrid interface* that captures the information from the object system and transforms it to the protocol used by the *event recorder* (see "Simple DPU" in Figure 3).

In a simple version, which we successfully use, a hybrid interface is a board containing four input connectors for a printer port on one side and the connectors for interfacing the event recorder on the other side. Between these connectors, the signal lines for the data are directly routed, while the strobe

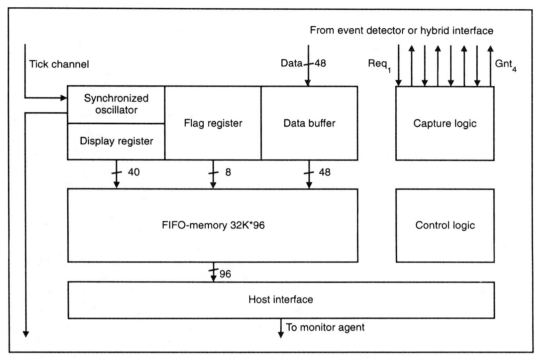

Figure 4. Architecture of the event recorder.

lines, signaling the occurrence of the events, are filtered and buffered before being routed to the event recorder. An example of a more complex interface is our socket adapter for hybrid monitoring of Transputers. Here, the signal pins of the Transputer are monitored in order to capture memory write cycles of the processor, triggered by the software instrumentation of the program.

Universal event recorder with a global clock

The event recorder has to fulfill tasks common to every kind of event-driven monitoring: assigning globally valid time stamps to the incoming events, thereby building event records, and supplying a first level of high-speed buffering. We designed and implemented the event recorder for arbitrary monitoring applications, made possible by the architecture shown in Figure 4 and the decisions for dimensioning this component.

We start our description with one of the key features of this event recorder: the interface to the event detector. This interface is built by two functionally disjoint bundles of signals: the *data path*, responsible for the event description itself, and the *control path*, signaling the occurrence of events. The signaling path is connected to the capture logic and consists mainly of four request lines (Req_i), each of them servicing an asynchronous and independent event stream. This means that up to four object nodes can be monitored with only one DPU. Additionally, each request line is paired with a grant line (Gnt_i). The grant line signals the capture of an event record. While ignoring the grant line does not cause a problem, Gnt_i can be used to facilitate the design of the event detector or the hybrid interface. We used this feature to ease the task of writing out event tokens via parallel ports that autonomously handle a request/grant protocol. This helped cut down an instrumentation statement to a single output statement.

Each of the four event streams can be furnished with an arbitrary fraction of the data field, which in total supplies 48 bits. The decision of how to split up this data field and do the assignment to the event streams is postponed to the definition of the event detector's architecture. For example, the event recorder can be used for one event stream with an event-coding scheme using the whole width of the data path, or four event streams with eight or 16 bits, or any combination thereof.

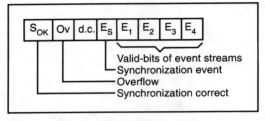

Figure 5. The flag register.

If at least one of the request lines signals an event, the capture logic latches the data field into the data buffer in order to establish a stable signal condition for further processing of the event record. The event record is composed of the output of the data buffer, the flag register, and the clock's display register. It is written into the FIFO-memory within one cycle of the globally synchronized clock of 100 ns.

Each event stream is associated with a bit in the flag register (see Figure 5) whose active condition in the event record signals that its event stream contributed to the recording of this event (E_1 to E_4). This mechanism allows for recognizing the relevant part of an event record and ignoring the rest of the data field. A fifth event stream – internal to the monitor system – is established for the information transmitted via the tick channel (E_S). The concept of these synchronization events is described later. Coincidence of events simply causes more than one bit in the flag register to be set, meaning that their corresponding parts in the data field are valid event descriptions. (The meaning of the E_S bit is defined by itself and has no corresponding part in the data field.) The overflow bit (Ov) means that at least one event has been lost because of to buffer overflow. S_{OK} signals the correct operation of the event recorder clock (see later).

The synchronized oscillator and the display register together form the slave part of a master/slave clocking scheme that is responsible for preparing globally valid time stamps with a resolution of 100 ns. This clocking scheme works on two levels: the PLL level and the token level. The PLL level is implemented as a distributed frequency synthesizer [Gar79], allowing the clock frequency of the master (one megahertz [MHz]) and the slave (10 MHz) to be chosen according to their individual needs. Especially the data transfer rate on the tick channel (100 kilohertz [kHz]) can be chosen to meet specifications for low-cost cabling and interfacing (RS 485) without significantly affecting the clock's precision. We have analyzed this scheme, and the measurements taken confirm a clock skew of less than five ns in the worst case. On the PLL level, the availability of the signal on the tick channel and the lock condition of the PLL circuitry are supervised and combined into the S_{OK} bit in the flag register. The token level of the synchronization uses the PLL level for the decoding of tokens, which are Manchester coded and distributed by the MTG via the tick channel. We use two different tokens: the **start_token** for starting the measurement and the **stop_token** for terminating it. While the PLL level of the clocking scheme ensures that all clocks run at the same rate, the token level is responsible for globally starting all clocks at the same 100-ns interval, thus creating a unique time scale over all event recorders.

In order to ensure the correctness of the generated time stamps, the clocking scheme was extended by the concept of *synchronization events*, which use the previously mentioned internal event stream in the following fault-tolerant protocol:

(1)   On a command from the CEC, transmitted via the data channel, all monitor agents reset their event recorders. This resets all clocks to zero and arms the event recorders waiting for the **start_token**.

(2)   After all event recorders have been armed, the MTG sends the start_token to all event recorders via the tick channel.

(3)   On the receipt of the start_token, all event recorders start their clocks and start recording events.

(4)   The receipt of a start_token creates an event on the internal event stream that is recorded as an event record with the E_s bit in the flag register set. If this sync_event coincides with events from other streams, the corresponding bits E_i of the active channels are also set.

(5)   After fixed time intervals (selectable from two ms to 65,536 ms, in millisecond steps), the MTG repeats broadcasting the start_token, which results in the corresponding sync_events at the event recorders.

(6)   A measurement is globally terminated by the MTG, which broadcasts the stop_token to all event recorders.

In this fault-tolerant protocol, the concept of sync_events allows the correctness of all time stamps at sync_events to be proved, because the correct time stamp assigned to a sync_event is known a priori as a result of the fixed intervals for generating them. Supervising the state of the synchronization and recording this in the flag field for each event allow the extension of the proof for sync_events to any event between them.

If a sync_event is lost, the interval for proving the correctness of time stamps is prolonged until the next sync_event. Unless there is a synchronization error in the prolonged interval, losing a sync_event is irrelevant. Additionally, error recovery for corrupted time stamps is possible by this means.

Providing a bandwidth of 120 megabytes per second at the input to the FIFO-memory, the event recorder has a peak performance of 10 million events per second. The high-speed buffering, having a depth of 32 K event records not only allows hybrid monitoring, but also works for all kinds of event-driven monitoring, which always deals with deliberately selected events and the resulting comparatively low event rates. The event rate exceeding this bare minimum necessary for event-driven monitoring can be used to record additional information. For example, if the program is instrumented in order to get a global overview and additionally a detailed view on a certain procedure, then a burst of events will be generated each time the procedure is executed. Within these bursts, the mean event rate will be exceeded by orders of magnitude.

Going down one step in Figure 4 leads us to the *host interface*, which is used for configuring the event recorder and for reading out the collected event records. This readout can be done only at the maximal rate of the host-PC/AT, resulting in a mean event rate of about 10,000 events per second for one monitor agent. The buffering mechanism of the FIFO-memory allows high peak event rates; the ability to read out the FIFO-buffer while monitoring removes the restriction on the maximal length of a trace. So, a high input event rate on the one side and on-line buffering on the other side add to the universality of this event recorder.

The control logic is responsible for the correct operation of the event recorder. It handles the configuration information transferred over the host interface and supplies the monitor agent with status information. The configuration information defines the actually used width of the data field (16, 32, 48 bits) and other parameters for setting up a measurement or correctly terminating it. As status information, the clock is monitored, as well as the amount of accumulated data in the FIFO-memory.

SIMPLE — A performance evaluation environment

SIMPLE is a tool environment designed and implemented for performance evaluation of arbitrary event traces. We use it on our central evaluation computer of the ZM4. The name "SIMPLE" —

derived from "source-related and integrated multiprocessor and computer performance evaluation, modeling, and visualization environment" — indicates that it is easy to use. SIMPLE has a modular structure and standardized interfaces, so that tools, which were developed and implemented by others, can be integrated into SIMPLE very easily.

The concept for a general logical structure of measured data — The basis for independence of measurement and evaluation

The task of designing and implementing an evaluation system for measured data is too complex and expensive to be done for only one special object system or monitor system. But if the evaluation system is able to handle data produced by monitoring arbitrary parallel and distributed computer systems, the following three requirements are essential:

(1)　*Monitor independence*: As there is a great variety of parallel and distributed computer systems and applications, it is necessary to use different monitoring techniques and methods. But the measured data, recorded by different monitor devices — and, therefore, usually differently structured, formatted, and represented — should be accessible in a uniform way.

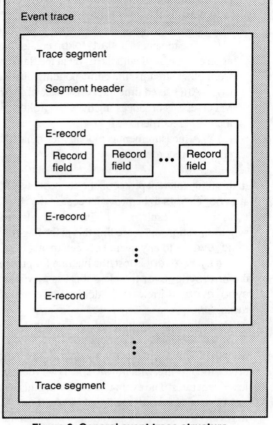

Figure 6. General event trace structure.

(2)　*Source reference*: Data recorded by monitor systems are usually encoded and in a compressed form. But in the analysis and presentation of the data, the user wants to work with the problem-oriented identifiers of hardware and software objects of the monitored system.

(3)　*Object system independence*: There are many differences in structure and function of the single nodes and in the configuration of the interconnection system. There is a variety of operating systems and applications. But an evaluation system should be applicable to differently configured computer systems with a wide variety of functions.

To handle these requirements, we have to look at the measured data, because this is what the evaluation system sees of the monitored system. All requirements mentioned have an effect on the structure, format, representation, and meaning of the measured data. In order to abstract from these properties, we have to find a general logical structure for all the different types of measured data. This general event trace structure is shown in Figure 6. It can then be used to define a *standardized access method* to the measured data.

With the use of event-driven monitoring, the data resulting from the monitor are a sequence of E-records, each describing one event. An E-record consists of an arbitrary number of components, called *record fields*, each containing a single value describing one aspect of the event that occurred.

In most cases, an E-record has record fields containing the event identification and the time the event was recognized. It is also possible that a record field or a group of record fields is not always present in the current E-record or that a record field is interpreted differently, depending on the actual value of another record field. Therefore, it is possible that E-records have different lengths, even in one event trace.

E-record fields can be classified into four basic *field types*, as follows:

(1)   *Token*: Record fields of the token type contain only one value out of a fixed and well-defined set of constant values. A token record field is a construction similar to the enumeration types in the usual programming languages. They can be used to describe encoded information, such as event or processor identifications. Each value has a special, fixed meaning called *interpretation*.

(2)   *Flags*: Record fields of the flags type are like token record fields, but they can contain more than one value out of a fixed, well-defined set. This is done by encoding the individual values as bits that are set or not set. Similar to token values, each bit — set or not set — can have a special meaning, also called *interpretation*.

(3)   *Time*: Record fields of the time type are used to describe timing information contained in an E-record. This timing information can be of arbitrary resolution and mode (for example, point in time or distance from previous time value).

(4)   *Data*: Record fields of the data type contain, in most cases, the value of a variable of the monitored software or the contents of a register of the object system. They can be compared with variables in programming languages. It is specified only how to interpret their value. This format specification is a simple data type, such as integer, unsigned, or string.

Additionally, there are other types of E-record fields that are relevant only to the decoding system. First, there are record length fields, which contain the length of the current or previous E-record, and checksums. Second, fields containing irrelevant or uninteresting data, such as blank fields, are called *filler*.

If during the measurement, one stores the event records sequentially in a file (*event trace file*), one gets a sequence of E-records sorted according to increasing time. A section in the event trace that has been continuously recorded is called a *trace segment*. A trace segment describes the dynamic behavior of the monitored system during a completely observed time interval. The knowledge of segment borders is important, especially for validation tools based on event traces. It is possible that each trace segment begins with a special data record, the so-called *segment header*, which contains some useful information about the following segment or is simply used to mark the beginning of a new trace segment.

With the hierarchy *event trace/trace segment/E-record/record field*, we have a general logical structure that enables us to abstract from the physical structure and representation of the measured data. An E-record with its fields represents an event with its assigned attributes, and the event trace file represents the dynamic behavior expressed in streams of events.

TDL/POET — A basic tool for accessing measured data

Based on the logical structure introduced in the preceding subsection, we designed and implemented the TDL/POET tool in order to meet the requirements listed there. The basic idea is to consider the measured data a generic abstract data structure or an object as in object-oriented programming languages. The evaluation system can access the measured data only via a uniform and standardized set of generic procedures. With the use of these procedures, an evaluation system is able to abstract from different data formats and representations and thus becomes independent of the monitor

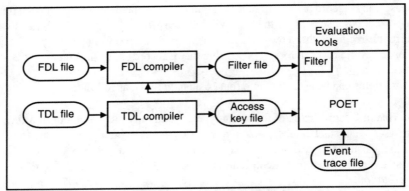

Figure 7. Event trace access with TDL/POET/FILTER.

device(s) and of the object systems monitored. The tool consists of three components, as shown in Figure 7, as follows:

(1)   POET (problem-oriented event trace interface): The POET library is a simple and monitor-independent function interface that enables the user to access measured data, stored in event trace files, in a problem-oriented manner. In order to be able to access and decode the different measured data, the POET functions use the *access key file*, which contains a complete description of formats and properties of the measured data. For efficiency, the key file is in a binary and compact format. In addition to describing data formats and representation of the single values, the access key file includes the user-defined (problem-oriented) identifiers for the recorded values. These identifiers can now be used by the evaluation tools, thus enabling the required source reference. There is a great variety of POET functions: For example, there are functions to process the E-records in an event trace in any desired order. It is possible to process the E-records in an event trace in the order in which they have been recorded (get_next) or to move the current decoding position in the event trace relative (forward, backward) or absolute (goto) to a desired E-record. For each type of E-record field, POET provides an efficient and representation-independent way of getting the decoded values of a certain E-record field (get_token, get_time,...). POET also provides a user-friendly way of handling time values (set_resolution, print_time, . . .).

(2)   TDL (event trace description language): In order to make the construction of the access key file more user-friendly, we developed the language TDL, which is designed for a problem-oriented description of event traces. The TDL compiler checks the TDL description for syntactic and semantic correctness and transforms it into the corresponding binary access key file. The development of TDL had two principal aims. The first was to make a language available that clearly and naturally reflects the fundamental structure of an event trace. The second was to make a language for which even a user not familiar with all details of the language should be able to read and understand a given TDL description. Therefore, TDL is largely adapted to the English language. The notation of syntactic elements of the language and the general structure of a TDL description are closely related to similar constructs in the programming languages PASCAL and C. By writing an event trace description in TDL, one provides at the same time a documentation of the performed measurement.

(3)   FDL (filter description language): Beyond the above, we use a similar approach for filtering

event records, depending on the values of their record fields. There is an additional function to the POET library (get_next_filtered) that can be used to move the current decoding position within the event trace to an E-record that matches the user-specified restrictions given in a so-called *filter file*. These filter rules can be specified in FDL. Since the FDL compiler does not read the filter description (FDL file) only, but also the event description (key file), the problem-oriented identifiers of the TDL file are also used for filtering.

The monitor independence enables us to analyze measured data with SIMPLE that were recorded by other monitor systems, such as network and logic analyzers, software monitors, or even traces generated by simulation tools. We are independent of all properties of an object system, especially of its operating system and the programming languages used. In order to adapt our environment to another kind of measurement, one has only to write a TDL description of the event trace to be analyzed. Being independent of the object system and the monitor device(s), the TDL/POET interface inherently has another advantage: Because it provides a uniform interface, the evaluation of measured data is independent of their recording. This enabled us to design and implement the tool environment SIMPLE in parallel to the design of our distributed monitor system ZM4. Additionally, POET is an open interface. This means that the user can build his own customized evaluation tools using the POET function library.

The tools TDL/POET/FILTER are implemented under the operating system Unix in the programming language C. A prototype was designed and implemented in 1987. The growing interest and two years of experience in the use of the tool led to a complete redesign and reimplementation of the language and the related tools in 1989. The now-available version 5.2 is much faster and provides more functions than the prototype [Moh90] (for details, see reference [Moh89]).

Rating of the TDL/POET approach

The idea of using configuration files or some sort of data description language in order to make a system independent of the format of its input data is used very often. Our work on TDL was inspired by the ISO (International Standards Organization) standard ASN.1 (Abstract Syntax Notation One), which is used in some protocol analyzers to describe the format of the data packets. To the best of our knowledge, the first to use a description language for describing and filtering monitoring data was Miller [MMS86] in the Distributed Program Monitor (DPM) project. His language allows the description of name, number, and size of the components in an E-record. The description of trace structures, such as segments, and of the physical representation of data values is not supported. Its main targets are distributed systems with send/receive communication. Unfortunately, regarding today's great number of evaluation tools, each depending on its own trace format, his approach seems not to be noticed.

In our opinion, the most important work on describing events was the definition of the event trace description language EDL by Bates and Wileden [BW82]. They also introduced the term *behavioral abstraction*. Their work inspired many others, among them our group. The main purpose of EDL is the definition of complex events out of primitive events. In EDL, attributes of the primitive events can be defined, but not their format or representation [Bat89].

Finally, a word on standardization. At the moment, efforts are being taken to standardize the format of event traces for debugging and evaluation systems. We feel that standardization of the event trace format is not the right approach. No standard format can be flexible enough to represent all possible event trace formats, unless format information is included in the trace, which is somewhat unhandy. Also, there is a great variety of existing (hardware) monitors that cannot produce a standardized format. Therefore, many conversion programs would have to be implemented. The TDL/POET interface shows that a generalized access method for arbitrary event traces works well.

The only assumption about the trace is that it is a sequence of records, each of which is a sequence of a variable number of fields. No further assumptions are made. This is flexible enough to handle all existing and future event trace formats. So, instead of the trace format being standardized, we plead for the event trace access interface being standardized.

The performance evaluation tools of SIMPLE

Performance evaluation of measured data, especially in large projects, can be done only if a powerful set of tools is provided. In this subsection, we give a short overview of the main components of, and the flow of data within, the SIMPLE environment (see Figure 8). For a more complete overview and an example of how to use these tools, see [Moh91].

Sometimes, the measured data are recorded with only one monitor, but using a distributed monitor system returns a set of more than one independently recorded event trace. The first step is to generate a global event trace in order to have a global view of the whole object system (*merging*). It is necessary to have such a global view in order to detect and evaluate the interactions between the interdependent activities of the local object nodes. This task can be done by the tool MERGE. It takes the local event trace files and the corresponding access key files as input and generates the global event trace and the corresponding access key. The E-records of the local event traces are sorted according to increasing time.

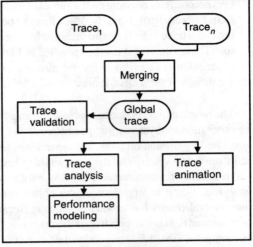

Figure 8. SIMPLE: An overview.

The next step is often forgotten, but nevertheless necessary. Before any analysis is done, it should be tested whether or not the measurement was performed without errors and the monitor devices worked correctly (*trace validation*). There is a tool CHECKTRACE, which performs some simple standard tests that can be applied to all event traces, and a tool VARUS (validating rules checking system), in which the user can specify some rules in a formal language (*assertions*) to validate the event trace. If the validation tests are successful, we can start to analyze the data. There are three basic uses for event traces, as follows:

(1) *Trace analysis*: The main use for event traces is what we call trace analysis. This can be a *standard trace analysis* for the generation of readable trace protocols (tool LIST) and computation of frequencies, durations, and other performance indices (tool TRCSTAT). The standard tools work well, if overall questions are to be answered. If more complex investigations have to be done, it is better to analyze the measured data interactively and with graphics support. We call this approach *interactive trace analysis*: The event trace is stored in a relational database (we use the commercial data analysis package S from AT&T [BCW88]) and can be used to analyze the dynamic behavior, as well as to compute performance indices. We extended the S package with additional functions to access the event traces and their description via the TDL/POET interface. The user can analyze the data interactively with a high-level programming language and has powerful graphical methods to visualize the data, such as histograms or time-state diagrams. (An example taken from the Berliner Kommunikationssystem [BERKOM] study, referred to in the

next section, can be seen in the figure presented there, entitled "Example of time-state diagram.") Here, the transfer of one data block from the sender (host attachment) to the receiver (workstation) is depicted in time-state diagrams with a common time scale.

(2)   *Performance modeling and prediction*: The trace analysis gives performance measures such as frequencies of events and runtime distributions. These results can then be used for performance modeling and prediction, as described in the section entitled "Integrating modeling and monitoring."

(3)   *Trace animation*: The event traces can also be used for trace animation. The dynamic visualization of an event trace presents the monitored dynamic behavior in a speed that can be followed by the user, exposing properties of the program or system that might otherwise be difficult to understand or might even remain unnoticed. By displaying only a single instant of time, more state information can be displayed simultaneously than in a time-state diagram. We developed the tools SMART (slow motion animated review of traces), which can be used on any character-oriented terminal, and VISIMON, which offers enhanced graphic capabilities and is based on X-Windows. Here, the user can specify the course and the layout of the animation in an animation description language.

For each measurement, one gets a lot of related files, such as event trace, key, filter description, and VARUS assertion files. For the *administration* of all these files, SIMPLE provides an additional tool (ADMIN). It is based on the Unix file system and has a menu-driven interface. It classifies all files in the hierarchy *project/experiment/measurement* and stores additional information, such as date, reason, and experimenter, for a measurement.

Experiences and conclusions

In this paper, we present the monitor system ZM4 and the performance evaluation environment SIMPLE. The design of these tools was guided by the idea of integrating modeling and monitoring. ZM4 is a universal hardware monitor that we have used for measurements on several parallel and distributed computer systems. Because of the modular structure of the DPUs, we could easily adapt it to different object systems. SIMPLE, a set of tools, proved to be capable of evaluating event traces either recorded by the ZM4 or originating from other hardware and software monitors. Three applications are briefly presented below.

(1)   Synchronous software monitoring of a parallel operating system [Qui89]: Accompanying the implementation of a parallel version of the Unix operating system for a concurrent 3280 MPS (multiprocessor system), the behavior of that system was analyzed. The 3280 MPS is a three-processor asymmetric architecture in which only one processor can do I/O. For our analysis, we used a software monitor that was implemented as an operating system function executable on all three processors independently. From each processor, an event trace was written into a reserved memory area. Since the 3280 MPS has a common clock with a resolution of 1 μs that is available on all three processors, there exists a common time scale for all three event traces. In the 3280 MPS system, a process can be scheduled to run on all three processors alternately. One aim of the measurement was to verify and improve the operating system's scheduling strategy. This goal was achieved by detecting portions of inefficient code in a mutual-exclusion mechanism of the operating system. Furthermore, an implementation bug that caused unfairness was detected by trace evaluation and could be removed.

(2)   Monitoring a high-speed communication system [Hof+90]: As a second example, we present a study of the BERKOM network, which was carried out together with the European

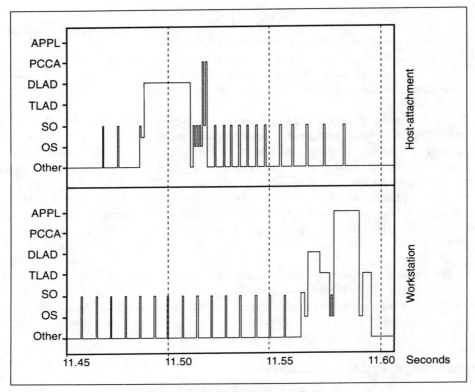

Figure 9. Example of time-state diagram.

Networking Center of IBM. BERKOM is a government-funded project for the development of fiber-based broadband ISDN. For this study, event traces were recorded using the ZM4 hardware monitor. The workload considered for our measurements was the transmission of rasterized images from one network node (host attachment) to another (workstation). Figure 9 shows a typical result of this analysis.

Luttenberger and Stieglitz [LS90] reported that monitoring helped to eliminate two major bottlenecks in the communication system: The amount of memory-to-memory copy operations in the receive path of the transport system could be reduced. Also, the message-oriented buffer management scheme, which caused interrupts on every "buffer-return" message, could be replaced by a procedure-oriented buffer management scheme. Thus, monitoring gave valuable hints for improving the throughput.

(3)   Monitoring a communication system for a Transputer network [OQM91]: In another recent project, the behavior of a packet-oriented communication system, TRACOS, developed at the University of Erlangen, Germany, was observed. On Transputers, without a communication system being used, process communication is implemented following the rendezvous concept, and communication between neighboring Transputers only is supported. With TRACOS, packets are buffered so that the sender does not have to wait for a packet to be received by the receiver. The other major task of TRACOS is the routing of packets between any pair of Transputers in the network. For our measurements, we used a basic testbed consisting of three Transputers (T1, T2,

and T3). All properties of interest could be monitored in this configuration. The hardware monitor ZM4 was adapted to each Transputer via a link and the Inmos link adapter. The application running on the Transputer network was a data transfer between Transputers T1 and T3 via T2 and an application process on Transputer T2. The effect of the communication on the application process was to be studied. For a given packet size, the CPU availability for the workload process decreased linearly with increasing packet rate. This behavior can be explained by the fact that the time for packet management and memory allocation is constant for each packet. It was found that only 65 percent of the theoretically possible transfer rate on a Transputer link was achieved for one-kilobyte (Kbyte) packets. A reimplementation was suggested by the results of the measurements, which improved the performance of TRACOS by about 30 percent, so that the overall performance was close to optimal (about 85 percent of the link bandwidth).

Experiences gained during these and other projects showed that the design principles of ZM4 and SIMPLE are sound. Practical use of ZM4/SIMPLE confirmed that the hardware monitor ZM4 can be easily adapted to arbitrary object systems and that SIMPLE is a highly flexible and comfortable tool with which all kinds of event traces can be evaluated. Using the TDL/POET interface makes it possible to access event traces of any format and origin by simply giving a TDL description of the trace. The concept of object system independence and of integrating monitoring and evaluation tools proved to be a big step forward. Methods like ZM4/SIMPLE provide a valuable aid to designers and users of parallel and distributed systems.

References

[AL89]   T.E. Anderson and E.D. Lazowska, "Quartz: A Tool for Tuning Parallel Program Performance," Tech. Report TR 89-10-05, Dept. of Computer Science, Univ. of Washington, Seattle, Wash., Sept. 1989.

[Bat89]   P. Bates, "Debugging Heterogeneous Distributed Systems Using Event-Based Models of Behavior," *ACM Sigplan Notices, Workshop Parallel and Distributed Debugging*, Vol. 24, No. 1, Jan. 1989, pp. 11-22.

[BW82]   P. Bates and J.C. Wileden, eds., "A Basis for Distributed System Debugging Tools," *Proc. 15th Hawaii Int'l Conf. System Sciences*, 1982, pp. 86-93.

[BCW88] R.A. Becker, J.M. Chambers, and A.R. Wilks, *The New S Language, a Programming Environment for Data Analysis and Graphics*, Wadsworth & Brooks/Cole Advanced Books & Software, Pacific Grove, Calif., 1988.

[BM89]   H. Burkhart and R. Millen, "Performance Measurement Tools in a Multiprocessor Environment," *IEEE Trans. Computers*, Vol. 38, No. 5, May 1989, pp. 725-737.

[Dud+87] A. Duda et al., "Estimating Global Time in Distributed Systems," *Proc. Seventh Int'l Conf. Distributed Computing Systems*, IEEE Computer Soc. Press, Los Alamitos, Calif., 1987, pp. 299-306.

[ESZ90] O. Endriss, M. Steinbrunn, and M. Zitterbart, "NETMON-II — A Monitoring Tool for Distributed and Multiprocessor Systems," *Performance Evaluation,*Vol. 12, No. 3, June 1991, pp. 191-202.

[Fer86] D. Ferrari, "Considerations on the Insularity of Performance Evaluation," *IEEE Trans. Software Eng.*, Vol. SE-12, No. 6, June 1986, pp. 678-683.

[FSZ83] D. Ferrari, G. Serazzi, and A. Zeigner, *Measurement and Tuning of Computer Systems*, Prentice-Hall, Inc., Englewood Cliffs, N.J., 1983.

[Gar79] F.M. Gardner, *Phaselock Techniques*, second ed., John Wiley & Sons, Inc., New York, N.Y., 1979.

[Hof+90] R. Hofmann et al., "Integrating Monitoring and Modeling to a Performance Evaluation Methodology," in *Entwurf und Betrieb Verteilter Systeme*, T. Härder, H. Wedekind, and G. Zimmermann, eds., Informatik-Fachbericht IFB 264 Springer-Verlag, Berlin, Germany, 1990, pp. 122-149.

[HC89]   A.A. Hough and J.E. Cuny, "Initial Experiences with a Pattern-Oriented Parallel Debugger," *ACM*

Sigplan Notices, Workshop Parallel and Distributed Debugging, Vol. 24, No. 1, Jan. 1989, pp. 195-205.

[Joy+87] J. Joyce et al., "Monitoring Distributed Systems," *ACM Trans. Computer Systems*, Vol. 5, No. 2, May 1987, pp. 121-150.

[KL86] R. Klar and N. Luttenberger, "VLSI-Based Monitoring of the Inter-Process-Communication of Multi-Microcomputer Systems with Shared Memory," *Proc. EUROMICRO '86, Microprocessing and Microprogramming*, Vol. 18, No. 1-5, 1986, pp. 195-204.

[KQS91] R. Klar, A. Quick, and F. Sötz, "Tools for a Model-Driven Instrumentation for Monitoring," *Proc. Fifth Int'l Conf. Modelling Tools and Performance Evaluation Computer Systems*, Elsevier Science Pub. B.V., Amsterdam, The Netherlands, 1991, pp. 165-180.

[Kle82] W. Kleinöder, *Stochastic Analysis of Parallel Programs for Hierarchical Multiprocessor Systems*, dissertation (in German), Universität Erlangen-Nürnberg, Erlangen, Germany, 1982.

[Lam78] L. Lamport, "Time, Clocks, and the Ordering of Events in a Distributed System," *Comm. ACM*, Vol. 21, No. 7, July 1978, pp. 558-565.

[LMF90] T.J. LeBlanc, J.M. Mellor-Crummey, and R.J. Fowler, "Analyzing Parallel Program Executions Using Multiple Views," *J. Parallel and Distributed Computing*, Vol. 9, No. 2, June 1990, pp. 203-217.

[Lut89] N. Luttenberger, *Monitoring Multiprocessor and Multicomputer Systems*, dissertation (in German), Universität Erlangen-Nürnberg, Erlangen, Germany, 1989.

[LS90] N. Luttenberger and R.V. Stieglitz, "Performance Evaluation of a Communication Subsystem Prototype for Broadband-ISDN," *Proc. Second IEEE Workshop Future Trends Distributed Computing Systems (Future Trends '90)*, IEEE Computer Soc. Press, Los Alamitos, Calif., 1990, pp. 440-449.

[MH89] C.E. McDowell and D.P. Helmbold, "Debugging Concurrent Programs," *ACM Computing Surveys*, Vol. 21, No. 4, Dec. 1989, pp. 593-622.

[MMS86] B.P. Miller, C. Macrander, and S. Sechrest, "A Distributed Programs Monitor for Berkeley Unix," *Software — Practice and Experience*, Vol. 16, No. 2, Feb. 1986, pp. 183-200.

[Mil+90] B.P. Miller et al., "IPS-2: The Second Generation of a Parallel Program Measurement System," *IEEE Trans. Parallel and Distributed Systems*, Vol. 1, No. 2, Apr. 1990, pp. 206-217.

[Min+90] A. Mink et al., "Multiprocessor Performance-Measurement Instrumentation," *Computer*, Vol. 23, No. 9 Sept. 1990, pp. 63-75.

[Moh89] B. Mohr, "TDL/POET — Version 5.1," Tech. Report 7/89, Universität Erlangen-Nürnberg, IMMD VII, Erlangen, Germany, July 1989.

[Moh90] B. Mohr, "Performance Evaluation of Parallel Programs in Parallel and Distributed Systems," *Proc. CONPAR 90-VAPP IV, Joint Int'l Conf. Vector and Parallel Processing*, LNCS 457, Springer-Verlag, Berlin, Germany, 1990, pp. 176-187.

[Moh91] B. Mohr, "SIMPLE: A Performance Evaluation Tool Environment for Parallel and Distributed Systems," *Proc. Second European Distributed Memory Computer Conf.*, LNCS 487, Springer-Verlag, Berlin, Germany, 1991, pp. 80-89.

[Nut75] G.J. Nutt, "Tutorial: Computer System Monitors," *Computer*, Vol. 8, No.11, Nov. 1975, pp. 51-61.

[OQM91] C.-W. Oehlrich, A. Quick, and P. Metzger, "Monitor-Supported Analysis of a Communication System for Transputer-Networks," *Proc. Second European Distributed Memory Computer Conf.*, LNCS 487, Springer-Verlag, Berlin, Germany, 1991, pp. 120-129.

[Pin88] H. Pingel, *Stochastic Analysis of Seriesparallel Programs*, internal study (in German), Universität Erlangen-Nürnberg, Erlangen, Germany, 1988.

[Pla84] B. Plattner, "Real-Time Execution Monitoring," *IEEE Trans. Software Eng.*, Vol. SE-10, No. 6, Nov. 1984, pp. 756-764.

[Qui89] A. Quick, "Synchronized Software Measurements for Performance Evaluation of a Parallel Unix Operating System" (in German), *Proc. 5. GI/ITG-Fachtagung Messung, Modellierung und Bewertung von Rechensystemen und Netzen*, G. Stiege and J.S. Lie, eds., Informatik-Fachbericht IFB 218 Springer-Verlag, Berlin, Germany, 1989, pp. 142-159.

[Sah86]   R.A. Sahner, *A Hybrid, Combinatorial Method of Solving Performance and Reliability Models*, doctoral thesis, Dept. Computer Science, Duke Univ., Durham, N.C., 1986.

[Sch87]   L. Schmickler, "Approximation of Empirical Distribution Functions with Branching Erlang and Cox Distributions" (in German), *Proc. GI/ITG-Fachtagung Messung, Modellierung und Bewertung von Rechensystemen*, U. Herzog and M. Paterok, eds., Informatik-Fachbericht IFB 154 Springer-Verlag, Berlin, Germany, 1987, pp. 265-278.

[Sch89]   L. Schmickler, "Extension of MEDA for Describing Empirical Distribution Functions with Analytical Distribution Functions" (in German), *Proc. 5. GI/ITG-Fachtagung Messung, Modellierung und Bewertung von Rechensystemen und Netzen*, G. Stiege and J.S. Lie, eds., Informatik Fachbericht IFB 218 Springer-Verlag, Berlin, Germany, 1989, pp. 175-189.

[Söt90]   F. Sötz, "A Method for Performance Prediction of Parallel Programs," *Proc. CONPAR 90-VAPP IV, Joint Int'l Conf. Vector and Parallel Processing*, LNCS 457, Springer-Verlag, Berlin, Germany, 1990, pp. 98-107.

[SW90]   F. Sötz and G. Werner, "Load Modeling with Stochastic Graphs for Improving Parallel Programs on Multiprocessors" (in German), *Proc. 11. ITG/GI-Fachtagung Architektur von Rechensystemen*, 1990.

[Svo76]   L. Svobodova, *Computer Performance Measurement and Evaluation Methods: Analysis and Applications*, Elsevier North-Holland, New York, N.Y., 1976.

[TFC90]   J.J.P. Tsai, K. Fang, and H. Chen, "A Noninvasive Architecture to Monitor Real-Time Distributed Systems," *Computer*, Vol. 23, No. 3, Mar. 1990, pp. 11-23.

Experimental Systems and Case Studies

Tools for Distributed Application Management

A program that performs *correctly* differs greatly from one that performs *well*. The former simply operates without failure and produces correct results, while the latter also uses resources efficiently and behaves predictably over a range of environmental and operating parameters. Writing distributed programs that perform well is especially difficult. These programs may run in widely varying configurations — from a single machine to tens or hundreds — and on machines with different performance levels or vendors. Often the programs must continue to operate when some machines have failed.

We call the activity of producing a distributed program that performs well in a given environment *distributed application management*. It involves

- Configuring the system components for a given hardware and software environment,
- Initializing the application in an orderly way,
- Monitoring the application's behavior and performance, and
- Scheduling work efficiently among the components.

Keith Marzullo,

Robert Cooper,

Mark D. Wood, and

Kenneth P. Birman

An application must be managed throughout its execution because the system must continually react to varying work loads, environment changes, and failures.

Traditionally, application management is performed manually or hardwired into the application code. A person thoroughly familiar with the application must continually monitor and control it; some adaptations can be made only by reprogramming. In practice, many aspects of application management are ignored, which results in poorly engineered systems that usually work but often exhibit unpredictable performance, become inconsistent, expose partial failures, and prove fragile when small changes are made to the hardware or software base. We seek to avoid the deficiencies of this *ad hoc* approach by creating a framework favoring the construction of robust distributed management software and applications. We have also developed a set of tools — the Meta system — that directly supports our approach.

A distributed computing environment causes more problems for application management than a nondistributed environment.

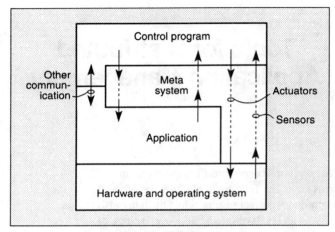

Figure 1. Meta application architecture.

The performance data required for system monitoring is distributed throughout the system, making it hard to access. Variable communication delays produce less-than-accurate data that is difficult to collate. The potential for improved performance through concurrency is attractive, but this concurrency significantly complicates all aspects of the application. For instance, components must be initialized in a well-defined order that observes the dependencies between them.

Failures are a fact of life in distributed systems and greatly complicate management. Most applications do not have strong reliability requirements, but unless special efforts are taken, the

Description of sensors and actuators

Sensors

The CPU utilization on a machine is a built-in Meta sensor.

The load on an application component would equal the size of the component's input job queue. This user-defined sensor can be implemented by supplying a component procedure to calculate the value when needed, or by directly monitoring a variable in the process's address space.

The total throughput of the application would be computed by combining the data from a number of more primitive sensors located in each component. Meta provides ways to specify such derived sensors.

The liveness of a component is determined by built-in sensors that test for the existence of a process or a user-defined sensor that implements an application-specific liveness criterion.

Acuators

Changing a process's priority would occur through a built-in actuator that controls fine-grained scheduling.

A lightweight thread's priority would be changed by modifying a variable within a designated process's address space or by invoking a user-specified procedure in a process.

Migrating a process to another machine requires an operating system that implements process migration.

Restarting a failed process involves selecting a machine on which to restart a failed process, initializing the process, and integrating the new process into existing components.

overall reliability of a distributed program will be much lower than that of some equivalent nondistributed program. Failure frequency directly relates to the number of hardware components.

Additional problems arise when existing nondistributed programs are reused in a distributed program. Although this is an important way of reducing costs, the application often does not perform well and may be difficult to manage. For example, the dependencies among reused components may be poorly defined, making program start-up and recovery difficult. In addition, the kinds of internal state information necessary for performance monitoring and resource scheduling may not be made available by programs that were originally designed for nondistributed applications. The Meta approach is well suited to applications that reuse software in this way.

We use the term *application program* to mean a distributed application composed of one or more processes. A *process* is a single nondistributed address space (as occurs in Unix) with one or more control threads. A *component* is a subsystem of the overall application that comprises one or more processes. We occasionally use the last term to refer to an environmental component such as a file server or a workstation.

Application architecture

Figure 1 depicts the Meta model of a distributed application. The application-management aspects are separated from its major functional parts, and the interface between these two layers is well defined. Separating policy from mechanism in this way makes modifying the management of an application easier and is less likely to impair the correctness of the rest of the program.

We call the management layer the control program. While the underlying application is built with conventional programming tools, the control program is best written in a reactive rule-based style. The Meta system is interposed between the control program and the application, and presents the control program with an abstract view of the application and the environment in which it runs. (As Figure 1 shows, not all communication between the control program and the application need go through Meta.) The structure of the application program — its constituent components and their interconnections — is declared to Meta in the form of an object-oriented data model.

The control program observes the application's behavior through interrogating sensors, which are functions that return values of the application's state and its environment (see descriptions on preceding page). Similarly, the behavior of the underlying application and its environment can be altered by using procedures called actuators. Meta provides a uniform, location-independent interface to both built-in and user-defined sensors and actuators. This interface also provides ways to combine multiple sensor values to compute more complicated sensors or provide fault tolerance. The particular sensors and actuators that are used depend on the application being controlled.

Meta offers several interfaces by which programs can query sensors and invoke actuators. The basic interface is from the application's programming language. Other interfaces include our low-level postfix language NPL, which is executed by a fault-tolerant distributed interpreter, and our high-level control language Lomita, which is compiled into NPL expressions. Lomita combines real-time interval logic with a rule-based syntax for querying sensors. The semantics of Lomita cleanly captures the temporal nature of significant complex events in the distributed application. Although the Lomita implementation is not yet complete, we use it rather than NPL in the examples because it is easier to read.

Meta uses the Isis distributed programming tool kit.[1] Isis provides primitives for reliable programming including process groups and ordered atomic multicast (sending a message to multiple destinations). On top of these primitives, Isis provides solutions to common subproblems in distributed computing such as distributed synchronization, resilient computation, and logging and recovery. Meta and Isis execute on the Unix operating system.

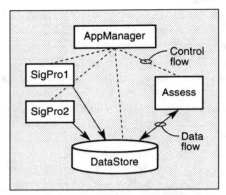

Figure 2. Simplified seismological monitoring operation.

Seismological analysis

To make our discussion of sensors and actuators more concrete, we present a hypothetical application and show how it is managed within the Meta framework. NuMon is a seismological analysis system for monitoring compliance with nuclear test-ban treaties. Science Applications International Corp.[2] developed a real nuclear monitoring system, on which this simplified example is based, by using Isis and an earlier version of Meta that lacked NPL and Lomita languages. It was our experience with this project that motivated us to work on higher levels of Meta.

NuMon consists of four component process types (see Figure 2). The SigPro processes (such as SigPro1 and SigPro2) collect seismological data and perform signal processing on it. The much smaller resulting processed data is stored in the DataStore. The Assess process is an interactive expert system that interprets the data produced by multiple SigPro processes and forms hypotheses about various events. To confirm these hypotheses, further tasks are assigned to SigPro processes. Assess stores its event classifications in the DataStore. The structure of the real application is more complex, with several more kinds of SigPro processes that fit into the same framework.

The AppManager contains the control program for NuMon. During normal operation the control program schedules work efficiently among the machines. When individual machines crash, it reapportions work automatically. When total failure occurs, it restarts the application.

AppManager. This program embodies the control policy for configuration, scheduling, and response to failures. This policy is expressed in the form of a rule base. Its second function is to support a graphical user interface that displays the current system state and lets users alter policy rules or issue commands to tune performance. Thus AppManager is semiautomatic. Common activities such as system startup and shutdown, and individual machine failures can be handled without human intervention. The user can handle other — perhaps unforeseen — circumstances. Typical examples include a persistent software error that causes some component to crash no matter how many times it is restarted.

SigPro. These computation engines service requests from Assess and interactive users, and process the input data. They derive from large sequential Fortran programs developed by seismologists with little experience in distributed programming. A crucial requirement, therefore, is that application-management functions can be easily added to these large programs without requiring substantial modification of Fortran code.

To schedule work among these tasks and start auxiliary SigPro processes when needed to improve throughput, each SigPro exports two performance sensors: backlog and load. The backlog sensor measures the backlog of input data to be processed. It corresponds to a program variable in SigPro. The load sensor procedure returns a measure of SigPro load by combining load factors such as the current size of the input task queue and the recent activity within the process.

The AppManager typically examines sets of sensor values, such as the average of all SigPro load sensors or the maximum of a load sensor over the last 2 minutes. These operations are directly supported by Meta through the notion of *derived sensors*, which are computed from primitive sensor values using a number of built-in functions.

Assess. This expert system executes at length and builds up considerable internal state, making fault tolerance important. If the Assess process fails (for example, the machine crashes), a new copy of Assess is started elsewhere. In order for this to occur, the AppManager must monitor the Assess process, choose a new location to restart Assess after a crash, and reconnect this new process to the SigPro and DataStore subsystems. Then the work that was in progress must be assigned to the newly created Assess.

AppManager uses Meta and Isis to accomplish these actions in a fault-tolerant manner. Assess uses the Isis message spooler to log its actions and to periodically "checkpoint" its state. In this way, AppManager leaves a stable record of the tasks it was engaged in should it fail. Some built-in Meta sensors detect failure and identify suitable alternative machines on which Assess can be run. Meta actuators are invoked to restart Assess with the correct spool file and reestablish connections to the rest of the application.

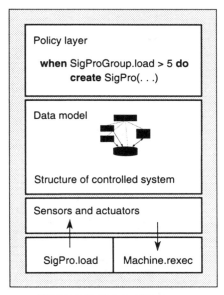

Figure 3. Meta function layers.

AppManager fault tolerance and atomicity. AppManager itself must tolerate failures. The easiest way to handle this is to replicate AppManager using the primary backup scheme supported by Meta. If all copies of AppManager crash, they can regain much of their state by interrogating the application and environment through sensors. The Isis spooler can checkpoint other important state. Thus the programmer can concentrate on writing a consistent set of policy rules for AppManager, leaving most of the fault-tolerance issues to Meta.

Instrumenting a distributed application

Using Meta to manage an application like NuMon takes three steps. The programmer instruments the application and its environment with sensors and actuators. These functions, along with a set of built-in sensors and actuators, provide the interface between the control program and the application program.

The programmer then describes the application structure using Lomita's object-oriented data modeling facilities. (Meta can be viewed as providing an object-oriented temporal database in which the application and environment provide the data values.)

Finally, the programmer writes a control program referencing the data model. The control program may be written as a Lomita script or in a conventional language embedded with calls to the Lomita language translator. The control program can make direct calls on sensors, actuators, and other functions in the data model. It can also use higher level policy rules that specify a set of conditions over sensors and the action to take when a given condition is true. Figure 3 shows the functional layering in the Meta system.

Figure 4 shows this functional architecture of the NuMon application. Most Meta functions are

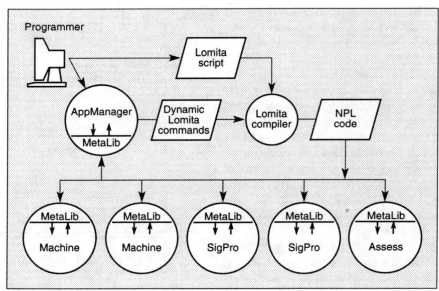

Figure 4. Meta process architecture.

provided by the Meta library (a copy of the library is linked to every application process). The library contains routines with which an application component declares its primitive sensors and actuators. Besides application processes such as SigPro and Assess, the Meta-supplied Machine processes provide built-in sensors and actuators.

The other major part of Meta concerns the translation and execution of Lomita. The Lomita compiler takes source language statements that are read from a file or dynamically generated by a program such as AppManager and translates them into the NPL language. Each copy of the Meta library contains an NPL interpreter. The object program is downloaded to the application processes and executed in a distributed fashion by these interpreters.

Sensors. A Meta sensor represents part of the state of the monitored application. Each sensor is identified by the kind of application component it monitors (such as SigPro), the kind of value it monitors (say, backlog), and the instance of the component it is monitoring (such as SigPro1).

Built-in sensors. Meta provides a set of built-in sensors that correspond to information obtained directly from the environment. Examples are sensors that return statistics such as the memory and processor usage of a Unix process. Furthermore, Meta provides the read_var sensor for reading the values of certain kinds of global variables in an active process. This is implemented with the Unix system call that permits access to another process's address space for debugging purposes. The built-in alive sensor returns the true value as long as it monitors an unfailed component.

User-defined sensors. Meta allows the programmer to define and implement primitive sensors. Such sensors correspond to dynamic properties of the application whose values cannot be supplied by simply polling the state of the underlying operating system. Sensors in this class are registered with Meta at runtime. Each application process that contains a user-defined sensor must connect itself to Meta when it is started up by calling the meta_stub_init routine in the Meta runtime library:

    meta_stub_init (name, instance);

The name argument is the component type name (say, SigPro) and instance is an instance identifier (say, SigPro1). The application writer must ensure that instance identifiers are unique for a given component type.

Having issued this call, the process can explicitly export sensors. For example, the following C programming language procedure implements a simple SigPro load sensor:

```
int work_load (int *value)
{
      *value = work_queue_size + 2*mbytes_in_use;
      return (0);
}
```

In this example, work_queue_size and mbytes_in_use are global variables maintained elsewhere in the process. This sensor procedure is made available to Meta by calling:

    sensor_id = meta_new_sensor   (work_load, "load",   TYPE_INTEGER, 10000);

The meta_new_sensor procedure returns an internal identifier by which the process can refer to the sensor instance in later communication with Meta. The first two arguments establish the binding between the sensor name and the procedure that returns the sensor value. The third argument specifies the type of sensor value, and the fourth argument defines the maximum polling interval in milliseconds. The sensor should be polled at this (or a shorter) period to avoid missing significant events.

If the polling interval is specified as the constant NEVER_POLL, Meta does not periodically poll this sensor. Instead the application must call the meta_notify routine when the value being sensed changes in a significant way. This routine takes a list of sensor identifiers. For example:

    sensor_ids[0] = memory_in_use;
    sensor_ids[1] = load_factor;
    meta_notify (2 /* Size of array */ ,   sensor_ids);

If the value of a sensor is simply the contents of a single global variable in a process, which is the case with the SigPro backlog sensor, Meta's built-in read_var sensor can be used. This avoids the need to link the Meta library with this process, which simplifies adding application management to existing programs.

Actuators. Meta supplies a number of built-in actuators that are named and referenced in the same fashion as sensors. These include an actuator to start up a process with a given argument list and a write_var actuator that allows global variable modification.

Users can instrument a process by defining actuator procedures in a similar way to sensor procedures. For example, we could have a SigPro checkpoint actuator that checkpoints the process state to disk for fault tolerance. The SigPro program declares this actuator by calling:

```
Machine: external entityset
   attributes
      key name: string
      sensor load: real
      sensor users: {string}
      sensor n_users: integer := size(users)
      sensor jobs: {string}
      actuator exec(string, string)
   end
end

FreeMachines : Machine aggregate
   attributes
      key unique
   end
   select m suchthat size(Machine[m].jobs) < = 1 & Machine[m].load < = 0.5
end

Process: dependent Task entityset
   attributes
      key instance: UID := new_uid()
      property params: string
      property executable_file_name: string
      sensor alive: integer
      sensor read_var(string): any
      actuator write_var(string, any)
      actuator exit
   end
end

SigPro: Process entityset
   attributes
      sensor load: integer
      sensor high_load: integer := max(history(load, 600))
      property executable_file_name: string := "/usr/numon/bin/sigpro"
      actuator reset_file (string)
   end
end

SigProTask: Task relation SigPro - > Machine
   attributes
      sensor load_ratio: real := SigPro.load / Machine.load
   end
end

SigProGroup: SigPro aggregate
   attributes
      key program_name: string
      sensor median_load: integer := median(Process.load)
   end
   select all
end
```

Figure 5. Data model for seismological application.

actuator_id = meta_new_ actuator (checkpoint, "checkpoint")

An actuator can take a variable number of arguments and return a Boolean indicating the action's success or failure.

Concurrency issues. To avoid inconsistent values or actions, user-defined sensors and actuators should be invoked only at well-defined points in the execution of a process. To prevent inconsistencies, Meta and the underlying process execute strictly as coroutines. The application process must call meta_notify (possibly with an empty sensor list) at least as often as the smallest sensor polling interval. With read_var and write_var, however, the only synchronization provided is the atomicity (if any) of reads and writes to a word of memory. Thus the global variable's value should be represented in one word or less.

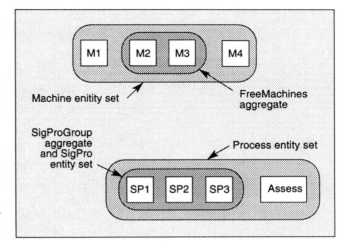

Figure 6. Lomita process group structure.

Describing the application

The next step is declaring the application's structure to Meta.

Lomita data model. The programmer develops a schema using the Lomita data modeling language to describe an application. Components in the application and the environment are modeled by entities, following entity-relationship database terminology.[3] Lomita provides ways to specify a rich set of connections and groupings between components, expressing the structure of the application. Figure 5 shows how part of the seismological monitoring application would be described in Lomita. The accompanying glossary describes some details of the Lomita data modeling facilities.

Mapping application components to process groups. Meta includes the notion of an aggregate: a collection of same-type components. In Figure 5 the FreeMachines aggregate collects a subset of the Machine components that are lightly loaded. Meta arranges for all processes in an aggregate to join a corresponding Isis process group. A process group also exists for each component type.

An Isis group provides an easy way to organize components and to communicate with them. Isis multicast simultaneously accesses all instances of a sensor or actuator in components of a given type. The multicast is atomic: An actuator invocation is received by all group members or by none. In addition, concurrent multicasts are ordered consistently at all group members, and Isis group semantics ensure that Meta has accurate knowledge of the current membership of an aggregate or type. Changes to the membership of a group, either planned (such as when a new component joins a group) or unplanned (such as a process failure), are serialized with group communication. Figure 6 shows the group structure.

Derived sensors. Primitive sensor values obtained from the application program can combine in the form of derived sensors, which provide a higher level view of program behavior. A derived sensor can combine values from a number of different primitive sensors, or from a single sensor over time. Derived sensors are defined by simple arithmetic expressions augmented with more powerful combining operations.

The following example (taken from the definition of SigProTask in Figure 5) defines a sensor load_ratio computed from the ratio of SigPro load to the Machine load:

sensor load_ratio: **real** := SigPro.load / Machine.load

Lomita data model glossary

Actuator — A Meta actuator.

Aggregate — Groups related entities into a single new entity, which can define attributes of its own. For example, the FreeMachines aggregate collects a subset of lightly loaded Machine entities. The members of an aggregate can be specified by a select operation and must be drawn from the same entity set. An aggregate inherits all attributes of its base entity. Thus the FreeMachines aggregate includes an exec actuator derived from the Machine.exec actuator. An attribute such as FreeMachines.exec behaves like a set-valued attribute, with one element for each member of the aggregate.

Attribute — A field or instance variable in an entity. Lomita supports three kinds of attributes: properties, sensors, and actuators.

Dependent entity set — Specifies that members of one entity set cannot exist without a corresponding member in some other entity set. For instance, the definition for Process specifies that a Process entity is dependent upon the existence of some Machine entity through the relationship set Task.

Entity — Similar to a record or an object in a programming language and represents a component in the application or environment. The example includes a Machine entity that models a computer and a Process entity that is a process running on a computer.

Entity set — Contains like entities. This is similar to a data type or class in a programming language.

Primary key — One or more properties belonging to an entity set that uniquely identify an entity. For instance, the primary key of the machine entity might be its name.

Property — An attribute whose value is stored in an internal database rather than being sensed directly from the application or its environment.

Relationship set — Specifies a one-to-one (< - >), many-to-one (- >), or many-to-many (—) relationship between components. For instance, there is a many-to-one relationship between processes and the machine on which they run.

Sensor — A Meta sensor.

Subtype — Declares one entity set to be an extension of another. The subtype inherits all the original entity's attributes and optionally adds new ones. An inherited attribute that had type "any" in the parent can be refined to a specific type in the new entity set. An example is the SigPro entity set based on the Process entity.

```
when size(SigProGroup[program_name]) < 2 or
(during SigProGroup[program_name].load > 5 for 60
        always SigProGroup[program_name].load > 5)
do
P: Process := create SigPro(params := "/usr/numon/data" )
M: Machine := FreeMachines.exec(P.executable_file_name, P.params)
                on 1 orderedby FreeMachines.load
create Task(Machine := M, Process := P)
end
```

Figure 7. Rule for creating new SigPros.

In addition to simple arithmetic operations, Lomita and NPL provide functions that operate over sets of values, including max, min, size, and median. There are several sources of set-valued data in Lomita to which these functions can be applied. First, there are set-valued sensors such as Machine.users. The following sensor definition (taken from the Machine component in Figure 5) computes the current number of users on a machine:

sensor n_users: **integer** := size(users)

Second, the function history (s, t) computes a set containing the values that sensor s has taken over the previous t seconds. The following example (from SigPro in Figure 5) defines a derived sensor high_load that is the maximum load over the last 10 minutes:

sensor high_load: **integer** := max(history(load, 600))

Finally, the individual sensors of the components constituting an aggregate can be treated as a set. Thus median(s) is the median value of the sensors s of each component of the containing aggregate. The following sensor definition (from SigProGroup in Figure 5) computes the median load of all SigPros in the group:

sensor median_load: **integer** := median(Process.load)

Expressing policy rules

We now describe the highest level of Meta: the rule-based control language. The programmer writes a description of the intended behavior of the system consisting of a set of Lomita policy rules of the form:

when condition **do** action

This statement declares that when the specified condition is observed, the stated action should be taken. The condition part of each rule is a predicate expressed on the underlying data model. The action component is simply a sequence of expressions involving actuators and sensors.

Figure 7 shows how part of the control program for the NuMon application would look. The **when** rule states that when the number of SigPros becomes too low or their collective load becomes too high and remains continuously high for at least 60 seconds, a new SigPro is to be started.

Table 1. Temporal operators in Lomita.

Expression	Meaning
During I always P	True if and only if predicate P is true throughout time interval I
During I occurs P	True if and only if predicate P is true at some point within time interval I
P until Q	Expresses the time interval beginning when predicate P next becomes true, until predicate Q subsequently becomes true
P for T	Expresses the time interval beginning when predicate P next becomes true, until T seconds have passed

Conditions. The form of conditions is limited to simple predicates, optionally appearing in a temporal logic expression (the temporal operators are explained in the Table 1).

Derived sensors can present their values as ranges or intervals. This can be useful to express known tolerances of the underlying primitive sensors or the value range obtained from an aggregate sensor. Marzullo[4] fully discusses this approach to tolerating inaccurate sensors.

Actions. The body of the **when** statement specifies a linear sequence of actions. A chain of rules in which each action triggers the condition of the next rule achieves a more complex control flow.

In Figure 7, the action part starts up a new SigPro process on a lightly loaded machine. The first action creates a SigPro object in the Lomita data model, initializing the params field. Note that at this point there is no associated Unix process. The second action selects a suitable machine from the FreeMachines aggregate and starts up a process on that machine using the appropriate executable file and initial job parameters. The FreeMachines.exec actuator is really a collection of Machine.exec actuators, one for each machine in the aggregate. Here we wish to select one machine and invoke the actuator. The **on** ... **orderedby** syntax achieves this. The clause specifies how many actuators are to be invoked (one in this case) and a sensor expression to prioritize ordering for the selection. In this example, the machine with the lightest load is chosen. The final step is to create a Task object that relates the newly created SigPro with the Machine on which it is running.

This rule is too simplistic for a real application. For instance, if a SigPro process continually fails upon startup because of a software bug, this rule continually attempts to restart it. In reality, such a rule would need a more complex condition that could check for repeated restarts within a short period, such as 5 minutes, and other rules would watch for repeated failures and notify an operator.

Lomita rule interpreter. A Lomita control program is compiled into NPL. Interpreters residing in the Meta library execute the compiled program in a distributed fashion. NPL's basic program object, like Lomita's, is a set of condition-action rules. However, where Lomita supports a rich syntax of expressions over the objects in the data model, NPL provides simple postfix expressions over primitive sensors and actuators. Furthermore, a given NPL expression is tied to a specific process, and it must reference nonlocal sensors explicitly. The Lomita compiler distributes pieces of the compiled control program among the interpreters in the application components. In so doing, it endeavors to minimize references to nonlocal sensors and actuators to improve response time. In particular, a rule that references sensors and actuators belonging to a single component will be executed entirely locally by the interpreter at that component.

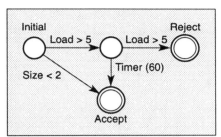

Figure 8. Finite-state automaton.

Rule interpretation. The execution of a Lomita **when-do** rule can be viewed as the execution of a finite-state automaton. Simple conditions that do not deal with time map into a single transition arc in the automaton. An interval temporal logic expression translates into multiple transitions in the automaton.

We explain the details of Lomita interpretation by describing the execution of the rule shown in Figure 7. The **when** condition has two parts. The first detects when the number of SigPros drops below two:

when size(SigProGroup [program_name]) < 2

To detect when this term is satisfied, a list is formed of the tasks belonging to the SigProGroup aggregate, and the size function is applied to that aggregate. The Meta interpreter handling the SigProGroup aggregate reevaluates the size function whenever a process joins or leaves the aggregate process group.

The second part of the **when** condition detects when the composite load on the SigPros exceeds five for 1 minute or more:

during SigProGroup [program_name].load > 5 **for** 60
    always SigProGroup   [program_name].load > 5

The whole **when** expression is converted to the finite-state automaton shown in Figure 8. In this case, the interpreter that handles the SigProGroup aggregate executes the entire rule.

Fault tolerance of the NPL implementation. Multiple interpreters are assigned the task of handling the sensors and actuators associated with each component type or aggregate. One of the interpreters is chosen to have primary responsibility, while the extra processes are backups.

Despite this redundancy, all NPL interpreters can fail at once. To cope with this, each application process can monitor for the total failure of the interpreter group. If this happens, the application normally terminates itself. Simply restarting Lomita from its initialization files starts up the application in an orderly way. Because the application terminates itself, no "orphan" application processes can survive the failure of the control program. Such processes would generate much confusion when the application was restarted.

A second option is to leave surviving application processes running and have the control program search on startup for existing processes. In our example, it would look for any members in the SigPro process group. Once the orphans were identified, they could be terminated or reinitialized and integrated into the new version. We have not provided support for orphan detection in the Lomita language; however, an Isis program could perform this function at application startup. A third option we have not explored is having the interpreters checkpoint their state to disk.

Atomicity of actions. For simple actions consisting of one actuator call (to one process or to the set of processes in an aggregate), Isis atomic broadcast provides necessary concurrency control.

However, when Meta operations trigger multiple actuators, concurrency and failure atomicity are more difficult. For example, suppose a Meta rule reacts to a failure by selecting a lightly loaded machine, reserving it, and instantiating a program on it. If several such rules are triggered simultaneously, a machine must not be reserved more than once. A similar case can arise when one member of an aggregate takes over after another member has failed. We are currently implementing a form of atomic transactions to permit atomic invocation of multiple actuators.

Performance and real-time behavior

With Meta, a distributed application-management control program is a soft, real-time reactive system. Producing a robust control program mandates handling such issues as the accuracy intervals for sensors and the latency before actuators take effect.

Performance. Meta must provide a predictable, short delay between the occurrence of a condition and its notification to the control program. We measured the cost of executing the rule:

when S **do** A,

where S is a trivial sensor and A is a trivial actuator. The times were measured on two Sun Microsystems 4/60s with a 10-megabit-per-second Ethernet, and Isis Version 3.0. Variance was less than 2 percent. The local cost of executing a rule was 84 microseconds. To this must be added the cost of checking for external events (involving the Unix select call), which can be substantial. When S and A actually resided on a machine that did not execute the rule, the cost was 17.1 milliseconds. It is clear that performance of the control program depends strongly on the locality of NPL expressions. References to local sensors and actuators, that is, ones that exist in the current process, are very fast. Accessing sensors and actuators on processes on other machines is relatively more expensive but quite adequate for the applications we have seen so far.

Real-time behavior on Unix and Isis. The predictability of Meta performance is at least as important as its absolute speed. These performance figures exhibited little variance because they were executed under controlled conditions. The current Isis implementation and the Unix operating system on which Meta executes do not provide predictable performance. One can conservatively assume that the end-to-end sensor latency can be as long as several seconds. It remains for the application programmer to specify the accuracy intervals for sensors and the maximum meaningful polling period. For managing most kinds of applications, polling intervals of several seconds or minutes are reasonable.

Other technologies

Although distributed application management is relatively new, Meta employs techniques drawn from existing work in distributed computing including performance monitoring, debugging, and operating systems.

The idea of viewing the data gathered from monitoring as a temporal database is due principally to Snodgrass.[5] A related project, the Issos system,[6] is similar to Meta in that it combines monitoring with control. Meta's use of rule-based techniques resembles expert systems used in soft real-time control applications.[7] Rule-based techniques are also used in debuggers for concurrent programs, such as Bruegge's Pathrules language,[8] that provide a kind of production rule breakpoint. This consists of a condition over variables and program counters of several processes. This condition triggers an action such as suspending the program.

Many functions of what we call the control program are more usually associated with an operating system: in particular, scheduling and resource management. In a general-purpose distributed operating system such as Locus,[9] the set of resources and control parameters is fixed by the operating system and is usually limited to the lowest common denominator of the applications envisaged. A common facility is remote execution, in which unrelated nondistributed programs are allocated to or migrated between machines to share the available load more evenly.[10] Load sharing is easily implemented using Meta, but the system provides much richer facilities for describing the interrelationships and dependencies between the processes that make up a true distributed application.

A few systems for controlling or configuring distributed applications take a more structured view of the application, permitting a finer degree of control. The RM2 distributed resource manager[11] permits the construction of compound software resources, which are similar to our notion of a distributed application. In the Conic language and system,[12] an application is structured as a set of modules and communication ports. Conic supports dynamic reconfiguration by allowing new modules to be created and existing ports to be reconnected at runtime through a graphical user interface. RM2 and Conic lack a general notion corresponding to either sensors or actuators. This makes it difficult for configuration scripts to react to changes in the application or its environment, and reconfiguration is restricted to modifying module connections and creating new modules.

Other Meta project work

The real-time requirements of distributed application management are minimal, certainly for the applications we have considered to date. However, the Meta model can be extended to handle real-time environments and continuously valued sensors.[4] The main obstacle is real-time multicast and a real-time operating system platform. Robbert van Renesse of the Free University, Amsterdam, has developed a graphical user interface for distributed control called Magic Lantern that works with Meta. A graphical editor complements a textual control language by letting users experiment with control strategies before writing a control program.

Distributed computing holds the promise of improved flexibility, reliability, and performance. But many system developers find that promise unfulfilled because the necessary tools are lacking. We believe that distributed application management is one of the more important — but neglected — areas in the field. The Meta system fills this gap by making it easier to build robust distributed applications using components that cannot individually tolerate faults. Designers can more easily plan and establish the correctness of the resulting control structures. These are important steps towards the open, heterogeneous distributed operating systems that will characterize the next generation of distributed environments.

Version 2.0 of Meta using the Isis system is being distributed in source code from within the Isis user com-munity of several hundred sites. This version contains a complete implementation of the Meta sensor and actuator subroutine interface we described, the built-in Machine and Process sensors, and the NPL interpreter. The Lomita language is still being implemented.

Acknowledgments

This work is supported by the US Defense Department's Advanced Research Projects Agency under DARPA/US National Aeronautics and Space Administration subcontract NAG2-593. (Our views should not be construed as official DoD policy.) The work has profited from the comments and suggestions of many colleagues and users of the first system releases. We particularly thank Cris Kobryn, Jerry Jackson, and Jim Wang of Science Applications International Corp. (architects of the nuclear seismological application). We also thank Miriam Leeser, Fred Schneider, Robbert van Renesse, and the *Computer* editors and referees who read and commented on earlier drafts of this paper.

References

1. K.P. Birman et al., *Isis — A Distributed Programming Environment: User's Guide and Reference Manual, Version 2.1*, Dept. of Computer Science, Cornell Univ., Ithaca, N.Y., Sept. 1990.

2. T.C. Bache et al., "The Intelligent Monitoring System," *Bull. Seismological Soc. America*, Vol. 80, No. 6, Dec. 1990, pp. 59-77.

3. P.P.-S. Chen, "The Entity-Relationship Model—Toward a Unified View of Data," *ACM Trans. Database Systems*, Vol. 1, No. 1, Mar. 1976, pp. 9-36.

4. K. Marzullo, "Tolerating Failures of Continuous-Valued Sensors," *ACM Trans. Computer Systems*, Vol. 8, No. 4, Nov. 1990, pp. 284-304.

5. R. Snodgrass, "A Relational Approach to Monitoring Complex Systems," *ACM Trans. Computer Systems*, Vol. 6, No. 2, May 1988, pp. 157-196.

6. K. Schwan et al., "A Language and System for the Construction and Tuning of Parallel Programs," *IEEE Trans. Software Eng.*, Vol. SE-14, No. 4, Apr. 1988, pp. 455-471.

7. A. Cruise et al., "YES/L1: Integrating Rule-Based, Procedural, and Real-Time Programming for Industrial Applications," *Proc. Third Conf. Artificial Intelligence Applications*, IEEE Computer Soc. Press, Los Alamitos, Calif., 1987, pp. 134-139.

8. B. Bruegge and P. Hibbard, "Generalized Path Expressions: A High-Level Debugging Mechanism," *Proc. ACM/SIGPlan Software Eng. Symp. High-Level Debugging*, ACM Press, New York, N.Y., 1983, pp. 34-44.

9. B. Walker et al., "The Locus Distributed Operating System," *Proc. Ninth ACM Symp. Operating System Principles*, ACM Press, New York, N.Y., 1983, pp. 49-70.

10. F. Douglis and J. Ousterhout, "Process Migration in the Sprite Operating System," *Proc. Seventh Int'l Conf. Distributed Computing Systems*, IEEE Computer Soc. Press, Los Alamitos, Calif., 1987, pp. 18-25.

11. D.H. Craft, "Resource Management in a Decentralized System," *Proc. Ninth ACM Symp. Operating System Principles*, ACM Press, New York, N.Y., 1983, pp. 11-19.

12. J. Kramer, J. Magee, and K. Ng, "Graphical Configuration Programming, *Computer*, Vol. 22, No. 10, Oct. 1989, pp. 53-65.

The Architectural Overview of the Galaxy Distributed Operating System

T he development and use of distributed systems has been motivated by

- The demand of today's applications for very high performance, fault tolerance, and a good price-to-performance ratio;
- The growing availability and functionality of relatively low cost, high-performance computer workstations; and
- The rapidly increasing speed and capacity of communication lines.

Judging from the enormous amount of distributed-system research carried out over the past decade, information-processing experts have come to recognize the advantages these systems possess. These research activities have led to the availability of more than 50 network and distributed systems. However, most of these systems can only partially succeed in attaining the major goals of a distributed system, which include higher performance, transparency, higher reliability and availability, and higher scalability. Of course, attaining all these features in the first attempt is impossible. Nonetheless, gradual improvements are possible if one learns from the existing systems and tries to overcome their limitations. The University of Tokyo's Galaxy project is a research effort to design, implement, and use a distributed computing environment based on this idea.

Pradeep K. Sinha,

Mamoru Maekawa,

Kentaro Shimizu,

Xiaohua Jia,

Hyo Ashihara,

Naoki Utsunomiya,

Kyu Sung Park, and

Hirohiko Nakano

Design goals and novel aspects

In designing Galaxy, we had several major and minor goals, all of which influenced our design. Our first major goal was to design a distributed operating system suitable for use in both local-area and wide-area networks of workstations. Our observation of the poor scalability of the existing distributed operating systems, which limits their use to local-area networks, motivated us to set this design goal. To achieve this goal, we

- Eliminated the use of broadcast protocols from all our mechanisms;
- Avoided the use of global-locking or time-stamp-ordering mechanisms, while maintaining the consistency of replicated information; and
- Decentralized the management of all globally useful information.

Our second major goal was to ensure high performance. We list below design decisions and novel system features that helped us achieve this goal.

(1)   Developing the Galaxy kernel from scratch, rather than modifying an existing Unix kernel, because we had observed that those distributed systems that had been built on an existing operating system normally suffer from poor performance and other design problems at various stages of system design;

(2)   Using multiple-level interprocess-communication (IPC) mechanisms to meet the various communication needs of different applications;

(3)   Supporting an efficient process-migration facility that helps in load sharing among the nodes of the system;

(4)   Employing the concept of variable-weight processes to allow flexibility and efficiency in data sharing and process scheduling;

(5)   Inventing an ID-table-based direct-object-locating mechanism that is based on the idea of replication of the locating information of an object only on those nodes from which there is some possibility of accessing the concerned object; and

(6)   Using a dynamic-replica mechanism to allow on-demand partial replication of file data on a page-by-page basis.

Our third major goal was to support network transparency — a common goal in the design of many existing distributed operating systems. This goal had a major influence on the design of our object-naming mechanism. Like several other distributed operating systems, such as Locus [8], V [3], and Sprite [15], our system uses a single, global, hierarchical name space for user-defined object names. However, the name-resolution mechanisms of the existing distributed systems that use a single, global name space for object naming normally suffer from poor reliability, poor scalability, and poor efficiency. Learning from these systems' drawbacks and from the limitations of their name-resolution mechanisms, we invented a highly reliable, highly scalable, and highly efficient name-resolution mechanism for Galaxy. This mechanism provides complete flexibility to users to choose and specify their own reliability requirements for the resolution of the various object names used by them.

Our fourth major goal was for Galaxy to have higher reliability and higher availability, a goal that influenced the design of several of our mechanisms. For example, our direct-object-locating mechanism is highly reliable, because the object-locating operation can be performed by searching only local information, without needing to consult any other node. Similarly, our user-definable reliability parameters allow users to have their own choice of the reliability of the name-resolution mechanism for the various object names. Also, our consistency-control mechanisms were designed to make them fault-tolerant. The use of data caches, name caches, a uniform address space, and dynamic- and static-replica mechanisms further help in improving our system's overall reliability and availability.

As a result of observing the existing systems, we adopted two minor goals. Our first minor goal was to make the application interface of Galaxy compatible with that of Unix. Because of the popularity of Unix and the availability of the vast amount of Unix-oriented software, for a new operating system to be acceptable by the present user community would be extremely difficult if its interface to application programs were different from that of Unix. To accomplish this first minor goal, we therefore designed the best interface from the viewpoint of distributed operating systems and then properly modified it to make it a superset of the present Unix interface. In addition, to accomplish this goal — and as long as our other goals did not suggest the use of any special techniques — we modeled our system as closely as possible after Unix.

Our second minor goal was for Galaxy to provide the mechanism of object grouping with group-communication protocols to facilitate group access control, group resource management, and generic group operations. We had recognized that several existing applications deal with groups of entities in the same manner as that in which other applications deal with individual entities. Moreover, group-oriented dealing is a common and natural feature in a distributed system in which the sets of object servers, network nodes, printers, and other resources constitute additional groups, replacing the single instances of these resources in conventional systems.

Galaxy system architecture

The Galaxy design belongs to the server-pool class of systems, with an underlying computational model based on *objects*. We had two main reasons for adopting the server-pool approach. First, Galaxy's design allows for the existence of diskless workstations in the network. This design issue precludes the use of an integrated-system approach in which each node of the network is an autonomous, stand-alone system. Second, our design policy was to place a particular module of the system only on those nodes of the network at which there is some possibility of using that module. Blindly maintaining all system utilities at every node appears to waste various system resources.

Galaxy objects

In Galaxy, the entities that need to be identified at the operating-system level — such as processes, files, devices, and nodes — are viewed as objects. Every object in Galaxy belongs to a particular type. The term *type* describes a set of objects with the same characteristics. It also describes the structure of data carried by objects, as well as the operations (or *methods*, in object-oriented terminology) applied to these objects. Users of a type see only the interface of the type — that is, they see a list of methods together with their signatures (in other words, they see the types of input parameters and the type of the result).

In Galaxy, each type of object is managed by a special module dedicated to the type. We call such modules by the general term *object managers*. There are several types of object managers, each corresponding to a particular object type. For example, disk managers implement physical disk transfers, file managers handle file objects, and process managers manage process objects. A particular type of object manager resides on all the nodes at which the objects of that type exist. A particular node may have more than one object manager for the same type of objects, depending on the average load for handling the objects of that type on that node. In case of two or more object managers on the same node for the same object type, each one cooperatively manages a subset of the objects of that particular type on the node. When an operation-invocation message is issued to an object, the corresponding object manager is invoked.

Our object-management policy has several attractive features, as follows:

- It ensures that access to managed resources (that is, to objects) is efficient, because the manager and the managed object reside on the same node;

- It ensures that the presence of an object manager at a particular node is not wasteful;
- It eases the problem of coping with hardware failures, because — for example — if a node crashes, then the managers for all the objects of that node will also be unavailable; and
- It is easily adaptable to different hardware configurations.

System structure

One of the most important issues in designing the structure of a distributed operating system is the size of the kernel that is replicated at each node of the network. In a large-kernel approach, taken by such systems as Locus [8] and Sprite [7], services are provided more efficiently than in cases in which they are offered outside the kernel. However, use of this approach reduces the overall flexibility and configurability of the resulting operating system. In a small-kernel approach, taken by V [2], most of the services are executed by separate servers. The servers usually are implemented as processes and can be programmed separately. A small kernel provides process scheduling, IPC, and some other basic, primitive operations. Use of this approach accomplishes the maximum flexibility but degrades efficiency.

In Galaxy, we use the small-kernel approach. For the sake of efficiency, we structured our system into multiple levels, with various communication facilities between the processes of these levels. As Figure 1 shows, Galaxy features the following five levels:

(1)   *User level.* The user level provides services such as object naming, user management, and implementation of the object-based environment. The modules at this level are implemented as distributed servers; they can be located at any node, and their programs are location-independent. Other modules at this level are implemented as local servers, but a user can invoke both categories of modules by using the same IPC facility.

(2)   *Network manager level.* The routines at the network manager level perform network-wide object management. Network-wide virtual memory, object migration, object replication, and the like are realized at this level.

(3)   *Local servers/managers level.* The routines at the local servers/managers level perform local object management. For example, the file manager routine is responsible for handling the local files and the process manager routine is responsible for handling the local processes. The ID manager routine at this level provides the location of a remote object for the realization of location-independent object accessing in our system. Most modules at the network manager level and at the local servers/managers level are implemented as processes that have separate address spaces.

(4)   *Device drivers level.* The device drivers level consists of the device driver routines, including the clock driver, disk driver, terminal driver, and network driver routines. The availability of a particular routine at this level at a particular node depends on the availability of the corresponding device on that node. The device drivers communicate with the kernel frequently by sending kernel I/O commands and responding to the kernel's interrupts. Thus, they share the address space with the kernel, so that they can access kernel data structures and respond to the kernel faster.

(5)   *Kernel level.* The kernel level, which is replicated on all the nodes, contains the most primitive functions of the system. These functions are implemented as procedures in the kernel and can be classified into the following types:

- Interrupt-handling routines, which set commands to hardware and catch interrupt signals from hardware;
- Routines for handling the most primitive IPCs;
- Process-handling routines, which manage system structure for processes, save and restore process context, and perform process scheduling; and

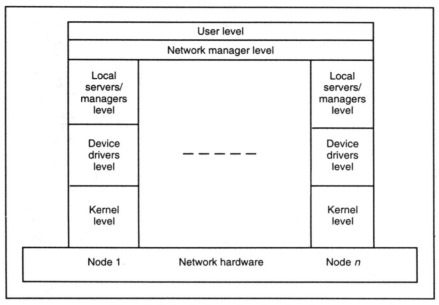

Figure 1. Galaxy's layered system structure.

- Memory-management routines, which manage physical memory and perform read/write operations on the physical memory.

The routines at the device drivers level and at the kernel level run in privileged mode.

Object naming and locating

In designing Galaxy's object-naming and object-locating mechanisms, we were particularly concerned about transparency, reliability, scalability, and efficiency. To satisfy our requirement for transparency, we used the single, global name space model used by such recent distributed systems as Locus [8], V [3], and Sprite [15], because it supports location transparency of both request-receiving objects and request-issuing objects. In this type of name space, the hierarchically structured global name space appears to the users and to the applications software as a single, tree-structured name space with one root across all the nodes of the distributed system.

Direct mapping of a user-defined object name to the object's location every time the object is accessed requires the name-resolution operation to be carried out for every access to the object, which degrades efficiency. Moreover, user-defined names are not unique for a particular object and are variable in length, not only for different objects but even for different names of the same object. Hence, they cannot be easily manipulated, stored, and used by the machines for identification. Therefore, to take care of the needs of both the users and the system, Galaxy uses system-defined flat names in addition to user-defined hierarchical names.

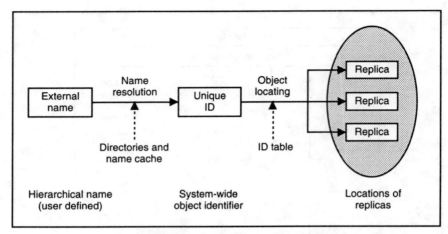

Figure 2. Galaxy's three-level naming scheme.

With these design policies, the naming scheme of Galaxy turns out to be a three-level one, as Figure 2 shows. User-defined names in Galaxy are called *external names* and system-defined names are called *unique identifiers* (or simply *IDs*). An external name is first mapped to its corresponding ID, which in turn is mapped to the physical locations (called *node numbers*) of the replicas of the concerned object. Galaxy's process of mapping an external name to its corresponding ID is called *name resolution* and the process of mapping an ID to the physical locations of the replicas of the concerned object is known as *object locating*.

The object-locating mechanism

The general requirement for object locating is a mapping table (called an *ID table* in Galaxy), each entry of which consists of the locating information of an object. In particular, a Galaxy ID table entry (IDTE) contains information about the type of the object, an access control list for the object, locations of the object's replicas (called a *replica list*), and locations where the copies of this IDTE exist (called a *copy list*). The replica list helps in returning all the locations of the desired object as a result of the object-locating operation. Galaxy uses the copy list to link together all IDTEs of the same object so that any modification can be made consistently to all copies. Thus, given an object's ID, Galaxy can know that object's physical locations by simply searching the given ID in the ID table and extracting the physical locations of its replicas from the ID table. The most difficult facet of this locating mechanism is choosing the method for maintaining this mapping table.

Examples of other object-locating mechanisms that have been proposed for and used in existing distributed systems are

- Broadcasting;
- Hint cache and broadcasting;
- Chaining;
- Centralized server, in which the entire ID table is kept on a single node; and
- Full replication, in which the entire ID table is replicated on all the nodes.

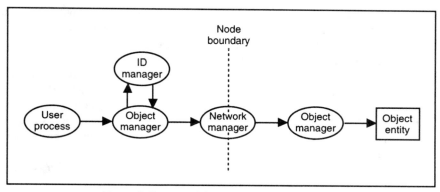

Figure 3. Remote-object-accessing mechanism.

However, these mechanisms all suffer from one or more of the common limitations of poor reliability, poor scalability, and poor efficiency. To overcome the limitations of these existing mechanisms, Galaxy uses a mechanism unlike any of those mentioned above: Galaxy keeps on a particular node only the locating information for those objects that have some possibility of being accessed from the concerned node. We determined that, in Galaxy, only the following two categories of IDs are necessary in the ID table of a particular node:

(1)   IDs contained in a directory or in a name cache of that node. The presence of these IDTEs in the local ID table of a node is necessary for the direct locating of the directory file objects during the name-resolution process.

(2)   IDs being used by the processes running on the node. These IDTEs are necessary in a node's ID table for the direct locating of the objects being used by that node's processes.

Based on this idea of direct-object locating and our object-management policy (discussed in the subsection entitled "Galaxy objects"), a process accesses a remote object as illustrated in Figure 3. This direct-object-locating mechanism enjoys the advantages of very high reliability, very high scalability, and very high efficiency, because the locating information stored in the local node can be used to directly locate any object, without the entire ID table needing to be replicated on all the nodes.

We observed that each IDTE is a collection of fields and that an update of each field can be done incrementally as well as independently. To maintain IDTE consistency, Galaxy uses a problem-oriented approach that is based on this observation. This approach takes advantage of Galaxy's special structure and the use of IDTEs.

We determined the following primitives to be sufficient for IDTE management: ReadIDTE(*ID, field*), InsertItem(*ID, field, item*), and DeleteItem(*ID, field, item*). We found that the two update operations *InsertItem* and *DeleteItem* are commutative operations; that is, the final result produced by a sequence of these update operations does not depend on the order in which the operations are executed. The execution order of two update operations should be serialized only when the two update operations are performed on the same item in the same field of the same IDTE. This property makes it possible to design an update mechanism on replicated IDTEs with high concurrency and efficiency. In this mechanism, read and update operations are done directly to the local replica of the ID table. The system executes an update operation issued by a local user on the local replica and immediately returns the control to the user. The update operation is propagated later to other nodes holding a replica, with no need of synchronization. To allow updates to an IDTE even during an insertion of a new replica of the IDTE, we defined the node that makes a new replica of an IDTE at another node as the *parent* of the newly created replica. The node in which the parent resides must keep informing the other replicas of the IDTE until they all come to "know about" the newly created replica. The access consistency is checked when the location information in an IDTE is used to locate the corresponding object.

Compared with other concurrency- and consistency-control mechanisms that guarantee strict consistency among replicas of data, Galaxy's mechanism has the following characteristics that these other mechanisms do not have:

- Neither global locking nor time-stamp ordering is required;
- Updating operations can be issued and executed without being synchronized; and
- Accesses to directories are allowed, even during the insertion of a new object replica or an IDTE replica as well as during the deletion of an object replica or an IDTE replica.

Jia et al. [5] discuss the correctness and applicability of Galaxy's object-locating algorithm.

The name-resolution mechanism

In conventional operating systems, directories are used to map an object's name to its physical location. In these systems, a directory entry consists of a component name and the corresponding object descriptor pointer, such as *i*-nodes in Unix [10] and *v*-nodes in the Sun Network File System (NFS) [11]. Galaxy differs from these systems in that a Galaxy directory entry is a (*component name, ID*) pair that maps a component name of an object to its system-wide unique ID. These directory objects are regular Galaxy objects that are distributed among the various nodes of the system and can be replicated and migrated just like any other object. In addition, in Galaxy, *name caches* are used at each node for caching recently used directory entries. Like the directories, Galaxy's name caches are hierarchical in structure.

Galaxy uses *remote pathname expansion* [12] as the basic name-resolution mechanism. The use of name cache at each node helps to improve the efficiency of this mechanism. Given an object's pathname, the pathname components are searched one by one in the local name cache, just as they are searched using regular directories. If the pathname of the desired object consists of n component names — out of which n_1 components are found in the local name cache — then the searching must be continued for the remaining $(n - n_1)$ components somewhere outside the local name cache. The ID corresponding to the last component name found in the local name cache is extracted from the name cache, and the local ID table is searched for this ID to get the locations of the corresponding object. Because of our replication policy of IDTEs at various nodes, this ID will definitely be available in the local ID table. Next, a message is sent to one of the locations (nodes) of the object whose ID was extracted from the name cache. This message contains the remaining $(n - n_1)$ pathname components to continue the expansion of the pathname at the new node. The remaining pathname components are searched in the concerned directories at the new node. This object-locating operation continues until all the pathname components have been resolved and the desired object's ID has been extracted. Note that a complete miss (that is, not even one component of the pathname being found in the local name cache) will never occur, because the root directory's unique ID is cached in the name cache of all the nodes.

Name-resolution reliability

In the remote-pathname-expansion mechanism, the locations of the directories — or of their replicas — that correspond to the given pathname components greatly influence the reliability of resolving the pathname from a particular node. On the basis of the various possible locations of the replicas of the concerned directories, we defined the following reliability factors of the name-resolution operation:

(1)   *Subpath reliability*: A name-resolution operation is said to be *subpath-reliable* when — for a *(node, pathname)* pair — the directories that are necessary for tracing the components of the pathname up to the subpath right at the specified node — without communicating with any other node — are present on the specified node.

(2)   *m-stage reliability*: A name-resolution operation is said to be *m-stage-unreliable* when m hops are required during pathname expansion for resolving the given pathname. In our method of remote pathname expansion, a *hop* is defined as the passing of the remaining pathname components from one node to another node having the next component's directory when the remaining components of the pathname cannot be further resolved on the present node.

(3)   *k-path reliability*: A name-resolution operation is said to be *k-path-reliable* when there are at least k possible paths between any two contiguous directories corresponding to the components of the given pathname starting from its root directory to the last directory of the given pathname. Note that the term *path* here means the logical name-resolution path (that is, the path of the pathname from one directory to another) and not the physical path of the network.

Figure 4 shows some typical examples of these three name-resolution reliability factors. In this figure, each circle represents a node of the system. A directed line from one node to another represents a hop, with the solid lines representing hops needed during the name-resolution process and the broken lines representing hops for object accessing and not for name resolution. Therefore, the hops corresponding to the broken lines are not taken into account for the name-resolution reliability factors.

Using the reliability factors listed above, a Galaxy user can specify reliability requirements for the various *(node, external name)* pairs of interest to the user. Depending on the user's specifications, the system automatically replicates the necessary directories at the proper nodes. This approach seems logical, because all the objects in a system are not of equal importance to all users and because a particular user normally works at only a few nodes of a large distributed system. Use of this approach makes it possible to give users the degree of reliability they want for resolving various names without the overall system efficiency being greatly affected.

Interprocess communication (IPC)

The IPC facility has several uses in a system, including informing processes of asynchronous-event occurrences, requesting processes to perform operations, and transferring data from one process to another. Because the amount of data to be transferred and the timing constraints are usually different for all these cases, using a single IPC mechanism for handling all types of uses and for communicating among the processes at all different levels of the system structure would be very inefficient. Based on this observation, Galaxy provides different types of IPC mechanisms, giving

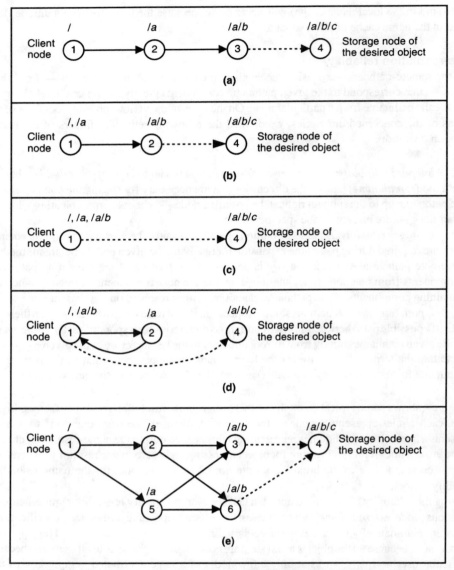

Figure 4. Typical examples of name-resolution reliability factors while an object with pathname /a/b/c is being located. (a) Values of reliability factors are subpath = /, m-stage = 2, k-path = 1; (b) Values of reliability factors are subpath = /a, m-stage = 1, k-path = 1; (c) Values of reliability factors are subpath = /a/b, m-stage = 0, k-path = ∞; (d) Values of reliability factors are subpath = /, m-stage = 2, k-path = 1; (e) Values of reliability factors are subpath = /, m-stage = 2, k-path = 2.

users the flexibility to choose and use the most suitable mechanism for their specific application needs. Below, we discuss the following types of IPC mechanisms provided in Galaxy: interrupt message passing, fixed-size message passing, message passing by memory sharing, group communication, and network-wide IPCs.

Interrupt message passing

In this type of IPC mechanism, a process explicitly "wanting" to avoid waiting for messages can set a *software interrupt* that will be triggered upon message reception. The interrupt-service routine, executing in the context of that process, then can either receive the incoming message and process it or notify the main program of the event in a user-defined manner. A mechanism like this can allow processes that are inherently bound to computation to react quickly to incoming messages without using some form of message polling. It can also be used to trigger language-defined exceptions across process boundaries.

Fixed-size message passing

Using this type of IPC mechanism, processes may send, receive, reply to, and forward fixed-length messages. For flexibility and efficiency, Galaxy supports the following three types of communication mechanisms for fixed-size message passing:

(1)   *Blocking.* In this type of communication mechanism, the sender and the receiver processes must be synchronized for a message transfer to take place. The blocking type of message-passing mechanism can be used to implement IPC that — to the sender — looks like procedure calls. Just as a procedure caller passes on control to the procedure, so our sender yields to the receiver. The *send* request message passes the equivalent of procedure arguments, and the *reply* message returns the results.

(2)   *Asynchronous.* In the case of asynchronous send, if the receiver process is waiting for the message, the message is sent out; otherwise, control is immediately returned to the sender, and the request is recorded as an *event*. After the receiver process has received the message, an interrupt to the sending process is executed. A similar scheme is used for an asynchronous receive.

(3)   *Polling.* In this case, if the receiver process is not ready to receive the message, control is immediately returned to the sender. In contrast to what happens in the asynchronous type, the request is not recorded; hence, there is no trace of the message. If the process "wants" to send the message later, it has to repeat the poll to ascertain if the receiver is now ready to receive the message. A similar scheme is used for a polling receive.

Message passing by memory sharing

This type of IPC mechanism is very useful for passing large amounts of data among processes. Galaxy uses the following two approaches for message passing by memory sharing:

(1)   *Virtual page transfer.* In this approach, when a page of data is sent from a sender process to a receiver process, the system modifies the page table of the sender process to detach the page from the sender process, and the page table of the receiver process consequently points to that page. The page data are neither copied nor moved to another place. The sender and the receiver should be synchronized for the page transfer. Virtual page transfer is especially useful for transferring I/O buffers among the file servers, the device drivers, and the users.

(2)   *Segment sharing.* In this approach, data sharing is implemented by changing the mapping of the virtual memory. After a sender process has sent a segment of data to a receiver process, both the sender process and the receiver process can access the data. Two processes that "want" to share a memory segment must synchronize with each other.

Group communication

In this type of IPC mechanism, Galaxy assembles objects into *object groups* [13], thus integrating object processing and management in a distributed environment. For the purpose of group

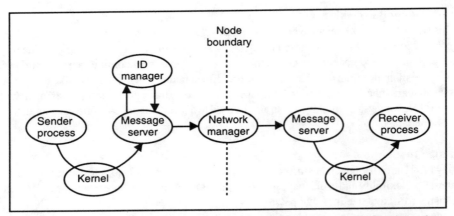

Figure 5. Galaxy's network-transparent interprocess communication (IPC) mechanism.

communication, which is one of the most important functions of object groups, process objects are grouped together and identified by a *GroupID*. Processes can freely join groups or leave groups and are free to join multiple groups. A sender can multicast a message to the processes of a group by specifying the group's *GroupID* in a special *send* primitive meant for this purpose. When a process sends a request message to a group, that process may "choose" to receive zero, one, more than one, or all reply messages by specifying a value of 0, 1, more than 1, or all, respectively, for the variable k. (For example, if the process chooses to receive one reply message, it would specify the value of k as 1.) We define a group operation to be k-*reliable* if at least k members of the group are guaranteed to have an operation performed on them. (In our example, the group operation would be 1-reliable, because one member of the group would be guaranteed to have an operation performed on it.) All-reliable, synchronous communication is useful for controlling a group of objects. One can suspend, resume, or terminate all the active objects that run in parallel. 1-reliable or k-reliable operations are especially useful for implementing servers. 0-reliable, asynchronous operations are used to broadcast a message that is not very important to member objects; the message broadcast by this operation is lost if it is not immediately received by a receiving object. Similarly, a process may choose to receive messages from one or more members of a group using the group communication *receive* primitive.

Network-wide IPC

An IPC command causes a trap to enter kernel processing. The kernel searches the local process table for the receiver process of a communication. If the receiver is at the local node, it handles the communication locally; otherwise, the IPC request is forwarded to a special user-level module called the *message server*. The message server locates the receiver by interacting with the ID manager and then forwards the request message to the message server of the node on which the receiver resides. The request is serviced at the receiver's node, and the result is returned to the sender via the message servers of the two nodes. Thus, when a sender transmits a message to a receiver, the sender has no direct means of determining whether the receiver is local to its node or is actually on a remote node. Hence, Galaxy's IPC mechanism is network-transparent, and the primitives for both local and remote message passing are the same. Figure 5 illustrates Galaxy's network-transparent IPC mechanism.

Computation model

Concurrent processing is one of the key concepts for achieving greater efficiency in the present computing era. The desirable properties of the process-management mechanism of a system with concurrent-processing facilities include low overhead in process-creation, process-deletion, and context-switching operations; flexible and efficient information sharing among the processes; and flexibility for users to define their own process-scheduling policies. In conventional operating systems, implementation of the concepts of lightweight processes and coroutines in process management currently provides these properties [1].

However, because of the limitations of these two concepts, neither is suitable for the needs of current and future parallel computing. For example, the concept of lightweight processes has limited applicability. Reasons for this limited applicability include the inability to support a large number of processes; the fairly large overhead involved in process-creation, process-deletion, and context-switching operations; the lack of flexibility for users to control scheduling and other aspects of processes; and the difficulty of distributing lightweight processes on the various nodes of a distributed system with no shared-memory facility. Similarly, coroutines suffer from several deficiencies, including lack of true parallelism; poor intercoroutine-communication facilities; lack of a mechanism to protect coroutines from each other, if required; and the inability to distribute coroutines over different nodes of a distributed system. Furthermore, at present, concurrent-processing capabilities provided by operating systems, distributed systems, and language systems are isolated and are not under a uniform interface, thus making it difficult to write programs that contain various types of processes and interactions among them.

Based on these observations, we realized that to fulfill the various application needs, the ideal process-management mechanism would provide a variety of processes whose properties vary. Thus, we proposed the notion of *variable-weight processes* in Galaxy. (*Weight* is defined as the amount of resources owned and accessed by a process; the amount of the resources is measured in two dimensions: space and time.) Variable-weight processes allow a program to use a suitable set of processes with different weights. Furthermore, a generic interface can be provided for a suitable weight of processes to be chosen at loading time or even at runtime.

Executor/domain model

To meet the flexibility, efficiency, and parallelism requirements of current computing and to support variable-weight processes, we proposed a new computation model in Galaxy called *executor/domain*. An *executor* is an active entity that either owns or has access rights to domains. A *domain* is a unit of information that is identifiable by its name; for example, one or more pages of a file may form a domain. The set of domains either owned or accessed by an executor is called the *executing domain* of the executor. The set of domains common to two executors is said to be *shared* by the two executors. Since the executing domain is arbitrarily defined for each executor, the shared domains can be very flexibly defined for a group of executors.

An executor itself is described by a data structure called an *executor descriptor*, which is maintained in some domains. The executor descriptor specifies the detailed information, such as registers and stack area, for its execution. If desired, a user may select as the executor either a bare CPU or a fully equipped process (that is, a process with its address space and all other necessary resources). Being very flexible, this structure enables a user to choose variously weighted processes for job execution.

Executor scheduling is primarily a function of the operating system's kernel; however, enabling a user to write his own scheduler is desirable in some cases. Galaxy allows user scheduling at the lightweight-process level. User-defined schedulers control most scheduling of lightweight processes.

Because the kernel supports only the operations of trapping interrupt signals, access control, switching execution mode, and so on, the kernel is very light.

Hybrid approach for lightweight activities

Conventional operating systems take the following two approaches to implementing lightweight processes or threads:

(1)   *In-kernel implementation.* In in-kernel implementation, the kernel performs scheduling; therefore, parallelism and preemption are given by the kernel scheduler. Potential added cost is a serious concern with this approach, because a trap or system call is necessary to cross the user process/kernel-protection boundary when scheduling operations are performed by the kernel and because the kernel must maintain the management data in its virtual address space.

(2)   *Out-of-kernel implementation.* On the other hand, coroutine packages are widely used in out-of-kernel implementation of lightweight processes. There are disadvantages in using coroutine packages (see the section entitled "Computation model"). Moreover, making a coroutine preemptive requires added cost. For example, SunOS 4.0 and some other extensions of Unix use coroutines as lightweight processes and implement their preemptive capability by using the set-timer mechanism of the Unix operating system. This approach degrades efficiency, because it requires system calls to generate the timer interrupts for switching coroutines. Also, completely implementing truly asynchronous event handling at the library level is very difficult. By using the *SIGIO* signal, SunOS 4.0 provides the asynchronous-read facility; however, because signals cannot be delivered to individual lightweight processes, only one lightweight process can actually use a nonblocking-read facility at a time.

To overcome the limitations of in-kernel and out-of-kernel implementations, Galaxy uses a hybrid approach for implementing lightweight activities. Galaxy features the following two classes of lightweight executors:

(1)   Kernel-supported user-mode executors. A kernel-supported user-mode executor, known as a *microprocess*, is an executor whose runtime context is maintained in the user address space; scheduling is performed in the user mode. However, in this class of executors, the kernel provides a clock-handling facility for creating preemptive executors. When a user address space is shared with the kernel, a system call for clock handling is executed with a small overhead.

(2)   User-mode executors in a single kernel-supported base executor. One or more user-mode executors can be defined within each kernel executor. These user-mode executors share the whole address space of the kernel-supported base executor, which is defined by the domain to which the kernel executor is attached.

In addition, the above two classes of user-mode executors have the following special features:

- Even if a user-mode executor takes a page fault or another kind of trap, other user-mode executors within the same kernel executor can continue their execution.
- User-mode executors can issue distinct system calls and I/O requests.
- User-mode executors can be defined hierarchically and scheduling is performed at each level of the user-mode-executor hierarchy.

The latter feature is especially useful for implementing hierarchical objects in an object-oriented environment.

Process migration

Process migration involves the following three major steps:

- Selection of a process that should be migrated,
- Selection of a receiver node to which the selected process should be migrated, and
- Actual transfer of the selected process to the receiver node.

The first two steps are taken care of by the *process-migration policy*. The third step is taken care of by the *process-migration mechanism*. The policy and the mechanism of Galaxy's process-migration facility are discussed below.

Process-migration policy

Selection of a proper migration policy is very important in reducing average response time and in increasing total throughput. To achieve these objectives, several existing systems normally use a load-balancing policy in which information about the job-arrival and service rates of each node is used to balance the load of each node. However, because the number of jobs in a node always fluctuates, a temporal unbalance among the nodes exists at every moment, even if a load-balancing policy has been adopted. Moreover, load-balancing policies are costly in the sense that global information exchange is to be carried out among the various nodes of the system.

For process migration in Galaxy, we use an adaptive load-sharing policy instead of a load-balancing policy. We chose this approach because we had observed that balancing the load among the nodes of the system is not required. Rather, preventing nodes from being empty (that is, idle) while other nodes have more than two jobs is necessary and sufficient. In existing systems, the two commonly used policies for load sharing are

(1) *Sender initiative policy.* In the sender initiative policy, when a new job arrives at a node that currently is neither empty nor sending any job to any other node, the node probes other, randomly selected nodes at least N_p times, where N_p is a constant whose value is normally determined by the size of the network. If any of the probed nodes is empty, one job is transferred to that node from the probing node.

(2) *Receiver initiative policy.* In the receiver initiative policy, when the last job of a node has been completed, that node probes other, randomly selected nodes at least N_p times. If any of the probed nodes has more than two jobs and is not already in the process of sending one of them to another node, then one job is transferred from that node to the probing node.

In Galaxy, we use a dual load-sharing policy that performs both sender- and receiver-initiated load sharing. We chose this policy after comparing it with the above two policies. We found that our policy, which performs both sender- and receiver-initiated probing and job transferring, works efficiently in both lightly and heavily loaded systems and is favorable even in the presence of static unbalance. Although the dual load-sharing policy adopted by us is not the optimal policy, it is simple — because it does not need global system information — and it is intrinsically stable.

Process-migration mechanism

Process migration involves the transfer of the process's state and address space. The time taken to transfer a process's address space is greater than that taken to transfer its state; thus, the overhead of transferring a process's address space dominates process-migration costs. In existing distributed operating systems that support process migration, one of the following three methods is used for the transfer of address space during process migration:

(1)   *Freezing.* In this method, used by DEMOS/MP [9] and Locus [8], the execution of a process is stopped while its address space is being migrated. The problem with use of this method is that a process may be stopped for a long time to transfer its whole address space.

(2)   *Pretransfer.* In this method, used by V [14], the address space is copied from the sender node to the receiver node while the process is still running on the sender node. Although use of this method reduces the time during which a process is stopped, the total time for migration may be increased because pages that repeatedly become "dirty" during pretransfer may have to be transferred several times.

(3)   *Transfer-on-reference.* In this method, used by Accent [16], the address space is copied after the process has begun execution on the receiver node. When a page is referenced by the process, the page is copied from the sender node. Although use of this method — like use of pretransfer — reduces the time during which a process is stopped, large communication overhead may result if most of the pages need to be transferred one by one on an on-demand basis.

Galaxy takes an intermediate approach to process migration in that the switching of execution is done in the middle of the address space transmission. Galaxy's approach is based on the following principles:

(1)   Those pages (determined by the *working-set* principle) that have a very high probability of being referenced in the near future are not pretransferred, because they may be immediately accessed and modified. These pages are transferred with the process's state. During the transfer time, the process is frozen.

(2)   Those pages that have a reasonably high probability of being referenced in the future are pretransferred. The pretransfer operation is done for only one round for memory-resident pages. Some pages that become "dirty" during the pretransfer operation are transferred with the process's state.

(3)   The remaining pages are *posttransferred.* That is, these pages are transferred after the process has started its execution on the receiver node.

Note that posttransfer is different from transfer-on-reference. Basically, the use of posttransfer avoids the problem of residual dependencies on the sender node. Posttransfer of pages with a low probability of access is better than pretransfer of all pages in that the execution of the migrated process can be started immediately. In addition, posttransfer decreases the possibility of redundant page transfers.

Management of replicated file data

File data are often replicated at the various nodes of a distributed system for efficient access to shared data as well as to enhance system reliability and availability. For the management of replicated file data, most existing distributed systems use a single mechanism in which the number and locations of replicas normally are determined statically. However, to improve system performance, we intuitively felt

• That data replication at the various nodes must be done dynamically and automatically by the system and

- That always replicating the whole file may be needless or even harmful in many cases, because of the locality of data access.

Based on our intuitions, we designed Galaxy to take a totally different approach from that of most existing distributed systems for the management of replicated file data. Galaxy manages replicated file data using a combination of the two types of mechanisms that are described below.

(1) *Dynamic-replica mechanism.* Use of the dynamic-replica mechanism allows for the dynamic, automatic creation by the system of a partial replica of a file. A dynamic replica initially contains no data and is created page by page on an on-demand basis. Thus, the contents of partial replicas and the locations of these replicas are dynamically determined by the system, according to the changing needs of the system, to achieve optimum efficiency. The replication of a page at a remote node is determined by consideration of the rates of read and write accesses to the page, the distance of the storage node of the concerned file object from the client node at the time of access, and the rough estimate of the cost of consistency control if the page is replicated. A dynamic-replica object differs from a cached object in that a dynamic replica is a global object in the system, exists beyond the lifetime of a process, and can be shared among processes and nodes. Because decisions are made locally, without regard for other replicas of the same object and without the use of any global data structure, our dynamic-replica algorithm is simple and efficient; however, it does not guarantee a global optimum.

(2) *Static-replica mechanism.* The static-replica mechanism of Galaxy is basically a user-definable file-replication mechanism. That is, unlike in the dynamic-replica mechanism, the creation of static replicas of a file object on the various nodes of the system is determined by the users of that file, who specify — through a special primitive meant for this purpose — the nodes on which a replica of the concerned file should be created. Moreover, unlike in the dynamic-replica mechanism, a file is always replicated in its entirety.

For the consistency control of replicas, Galaxy uses an invalidation mechanism. In this mechanism, each page of a static replica "remembers" the locations of all the dynamic replicas that have this page, and each dynamic replica "remembers" the location of the static replica from which it was created. When a page of a static replica is updated, the corresponding page is invalidated in all the dynamic replicas that have this page. On the other hand, when a page of a dynamic replica is updated, it sends a message to its corresponding static replica. This message is used to update the static replicas, and that page in other dynamic replicas of the same file is invalidated through the static replicas. Hence, in Galaxy, a dynamic replica is not "aware" of the existence of other dynamic replicas of the same file.

Present status and future plans

Our goal in designing the Galaxy distributed operating system was to achieve network transparency and higher reliability, higher scalability, higher efficiency, and higher availability. Although Galaxy is still under development, prototypes of its major system components have been implemented. In these prototypes, Galaxy runs on IBM RT PC workstations and all but a few hundred lines of code are in C, with the remaining lines written in assembly language. With a view toward testing our design ideas, we have been using these prototype implementations to conduct experiments that measure the performance of each system component. As of this writing, these implementations have demonstrated the viability and attractiveness of individual components. Extensive performance comparisons with other systems have not yet been undertaken; however, our experience to date indicates that Galaxy's design is fundamentally sound, although some refinement and further efforts are necessary in a number of areas. The full system is currently being implemented.

Our future research with Galaxy will be in several major areas. These areas, which are listed below, are basically those that we had given low priority while setting the design goals for Galaxy. Once the full system has been implemented, we will begin research in these areas.

(1)   Supporting a network of heterogeneous nodes. Galaxy currently supports only one basic node type; that is, it supports a network of homogeneous nodes.

(2)   Supporting resistance to maliciousness. Being a research project, Galaxy is intended to be used by a community of computer scientists. Hence, we did not pay much attention in the initial design to the various security features to be supported by the system. This does not mean that we totally ignored the protection issue. On the contrary, the presence of the access control list in an IDTE allows the checking of the accessibility of remote objects right at the client's node.

(3)   Supporting real-time applications. We did not attempt in the initial design to make Galaxy suitable for use for real-time applications. However, the increasing use of such applications has forced us to rethink and to modify our design to make our system suitable for such applications.

References

[1] D.L. Black, "Scheduling Support for Concurrency and Parallelism in the Mach Operating System," *Computer*, Vol. 23, No. 5, May 1990, pp. 35-43.

[2] D.R. Cheriton, "The V Distributed System," *Comm. ACM*, Vol. 31, No. 3, Mar. 1988, pp. 314-333.

[3] D.R. Cheriton and T.P. Mann, "Decentralizing a Global Naming Service for Improved Performance and Fault Tolerance," *ACM Trans. Computer Systems*, Vol. 7, No. 2, May 1989, pp. 147-183.

[4] P. Dasgupta, R.J. LeBlanc, Jr., and W.F. Applebe, "The Clouds Distributed Operating System: Functional Description, Implementation Details and Related Work," *Proc. Eighth Int'l Conf. Distributed Computing Systems*, IEEE Computer Soc. Press, Los Alamitos, Calif., 1988, pp. 2-9.

[5] X. Jia et al., "Highly Concurrent Directory Management in the GALAXY Distributed System," *Proc. 10th Int'l Conf. Distributed Computing Systems*, IEEE Computer Soc. Press, Los Alamitos, Calif., 1990, pp. 416-423.

[6] S.J. Mullender et al., "Amoeba: A Distributed Operating System for the 1990s," *Computer*, Vol. 23, No. 5, May 1990, pp. 44-53.

[7] J.K. Ousterhout et al., "The Sprite Network Operating System," *Computer*, Vol. 21, No. 2, Feb. 1988, pp. 23-36.

[8] G.J. Popek and B.J. Walker, *The Locus Distributed System Architecture*, MIT Press, Cambridge, Mass., 1985.

[9] M.L. Powell and B.P. Miller, "Process Migration in DEMOS/MP," *Proc. Ninth Symp. Operating Systems Principles*, ACM Press, New York, N.Y., 1983, pp. 110-119.

[10] D. Ritchie and K. Thompson, "The Unix Time-Sharing System," *Comm. ACM*, Vol. 17, No. 7, July 1974, pp. 365-375.

[11] R. Sandberg et al., "Design and Implementation of the Sun Network File System," *Proc. Usenix Conf.*, Usenix, Berkeley, Calif., 1985, pp. 119-130.

[12] A.B. Sheltzer, R. Lindell, and G.J. Popek, "Name Service Locality and Cache Design in a Distributed Operating System," *Proc. Sixth Int'l Conf. Distributed Computing Systems*, IEEE Computer Soc. Press, Los Alamitos, Calif., 1986, pp. 515-522.

[13] K. Shimizu, M. Maekawa, and J. Hamano, "Hierarchical Object Groups in Distributed Operating Systems," *Proc. Eighth Int'l Conf. Distributed Computing Systems*, IEEE Computer Soc. Press, Los Alamitos, Calif., 1988, pp. 18-24.

[14] M.M. Theimer, K.A. Lantz, and D.R. Cheriton, "Preemptable Remote Execution Facilities for the V-System," *Proc. 10th Symp. Operating Systems Principles*, ACM Press, New York, N.Y., 1985, pp. 2-12.

[15] B. Welch and J. Ousterhout, "Prefix Tables: A Simple Mechanism for Locating Files in a Distributed System," *Proc. Sixth Int'l Conf. Distributed Computing Systems*, IEEE Computer Soc. Press, Los Alamitos, Calif., 1986, pp. 184-189.

[16] E.R. Zayas, "Attacking the Process Migration Bottleneck," *Proc. 11th Symp. Operating Systems Principles*, ACM Press, New York, N.Y., 1987, pp. 13-22.

Communication Facilities for Distributed Transaction-Processing Systems

Distributed transaction-processing systems must manage such functions as concurrency, recovery, and replication. One way to improve the efficiency and reliability of such systems is to increase software modularity, which means the separate components should execute in separate address spaces to permit hardware-enforced separation. This structure offers advantages but demands efficient interprocess communication (IPC) services.

In our research at Purdue University, we are investigating mechanisms and paradigms for efficient communication support in conventional architectures, such as virtual-memory, single-processor machines with no special IPC hardware support. (Some mainframes have hardware assistance where more than one address space can be accessed at the same time.)

We are studying communication designs in the context of the Raid system, a robust and adaptable distributed database system for transaction processing.[1] Raid has been developed at Purdue on Sun workstations under the Unix operating system in a local area network.

In Raid, each major logical component is implemented as a server, which is a process in a separate address space. Servers interact with other processes through a high-level communication subsystem. Currently, Raid has six servers for transaction management: the user interface (UI), the action driver (AD), the access manager (AM), the atomicity controller (AC), the concurrency controller (CC), and the replication controller (RC). High-level name service is provided by a separate server, the oracle.

Enrique Mafla and

Bharat Bhargava

Raid's communication software, called *Raidcomm*, has evolved as a result of the knowledge we gained from other systems and from our own experiments, which are summarized in the sections that follow. The first version, Raidcomm V.1, was developed in 1986. Implemented on top of the SunOS socket-based IPC mechanism using UDP/IP (user datagram protocol/Internet protocol), it provides a clean, location-independent interface between the servers.[2] To permit defining server interfaces in terms of arbitrary data structures, we used Sun's external data representation standard, XDR. We developed Raidcomm V.2 in 1990 to provide multicasting support for the AC and RC servers. We designed Raidcomm V.3 to support transmission of complex database objects. It is based on the explicit control-passing mechanism and shared memory.

Related research work

Research in operating systems, multiprocessor systems, and computer networks has made useful contributions to the field of communication facilities:

- Carnegie Mellon's Camelot project[3,4] identified communication subsystem requirements.
- Remote-procedure-call- (RPC)-based session services support the interaction among data servers and applications.
- Highly specialized datagram-based communication facilities increase the performance demanded by data servers and applications.
- Efficient local and remote IPC have been investigated in many distributed computing systems — for example, the V system,[5] Mach,[6] Amoeba,[7] Sprite,[8] and x-kernel.[9]

We classify the existing communication paradigms into three groups: local interprocess communication, remote interprocess communication, and communication protocols for both local area and wide area networks.

Local interprocess communication

To improve local machine performance, Bershad[10] introduced two new mechanisms: lightweight remote procedure call (LRPC) and user-level remote procedure call (URPC). LRPC takes advantage of the control transfer and communication model of capability-based systems and the address-space-based protection model of traditional IPC facilities. URPC, another cross-address-space communication facility, eliminates the role of the kernel as an IPC intermediary by including communication and thread management code in each user address space.

Both LRPC and URPC were implemented on a Digital Equipment Corporation (DEC) SRC Firefly multiprocessor workstation running the Tao operating system.[10] A simple cross-address-space call using SRC RPC takes 464 microseconds on a single C-VAX processor. LRPC takes 157 microseconds for the same call and using URPC reduces the call's latency to 93 microseconds.

We've found the ideas used in LRPC and URPC applicable in systems such as Raid.

Remote interprocess communication

Several message-based operating systems can reliably send messages to processes executing on any host in the network. The V system[5] implements address spaces, processes, and the interprocess communication protocol in the kernel to provide a high-performance message-passing facility. All high-level system services are implemented outside the kernel in separate processes. Mach[6] uses virtual-memory techniques to optimize local IPC. Remote communication goes through a user-level server process, which adds extra overhead. Amoeba[7] uses capabilities for access control and message addresses. It has a small kernel, and most features are in user processes.

However, not all the systems use the microkernel approach with remote IPC outside the kernel. In Sprite,[8] the IPC is through a pseudodevice mechanism. Sprite kernel communication is through Sprite kernel-to-kernel RPC. RPC in x-kernel[9] is also implemented at the kernel level. Table 1 shows the performance of various RPCs over Ethernet.

Communication protocols

Communication protocols provide a standard way to communicate between hosts connected by a network. Datagram protocols such as IP are inexpensive but unreliable. However, more reliable protocols, such as virtual-circuit and request-response protocols, can be built on top of datagram protocols.

Table 1. Performance data for remote procedure calls. (The Sun 3/75 is a 2-million-instructions-per-second [MIPS] machine and the Sun 3/60 is a 3-MIPS machine.)

System	RPC type	Architecture	Latency (milliseconds)	Latency by MIPS (milliseconds)
V	User-level	Sun 3/75	2.50	5.0
Mach	User-level	Sun 3/60	11.00	33.0
Amoeba	User-level	Sun 3/60	1.10	3.3
Sprite	Kernel-level	Sun 3/75	2.45	4.9
x-kernel	Kernel-level	Sun 3/75	1.70	3.4

The versatile message transaction protocol (VMTP) is a transport-level protocol that supports the intrasystem model of distributed processing.[5] Page-level file access, remote procedure calls, real-time datagrams, and multicasting dominate the communication activities. VMTP provides two facilities — stable addressing and message transactions — useful for implementing conversations at higher levels. A stable address can be used in multiple message transactions, as long as it remains valid. A message transaction is a reliable request-response interaction between addressable network entities (for example, ports, processes, and procedure invocations). Multicasting, datagrams, and forwarding services are provided as variants of the message-transaction mechanism.

Using virtual protocols and layered protocols, the x-kernel implements general-purpose, yet efficient, RPCs.[9] Virtual protocols are demultiplexers that route the messages to appropriate lower level protocols. For example, in an Internet environment, a virtual protocol will bypass the IP for messages originating and ending in the same network. The support of atomic broadcasting and failure detection within the communication subsystem simplifies transaction-processing software and optimizes network broadcasting capabilities.[11] For example, a two-phase commit protocol can be implemented by atomic broadcasting.

Studies and enhancements

We have conducted a series of experiments on the performance of the facilities available for building the Raid communication software.[2,12]

Experimental measurements and observations

The measurements were done on Sun 3/50s (1-million-instructions-per-second [MIPS] machines) that use the SunOS 4.0 operating system. We configured one workstation with a special microsecond-resolution clock to measure elapsed times. (This timer board, developed by Peter Danzig and Steve Melvin, uses Advanced Micro Devices' AM9513A timer chip. The timer has a resolution of up to four ticks per microsecond, and the overhead to read a time stamp is approximately 20 microseconds.)

Our experimental work focused on general-purpose interprocess-communication facilities, multicasting, and the impact of interprocess communication on distributed transaction-processing performance.

Communication. We measured the overhead introduced by the layers of the socket-based interprocess-communication model for datagram communication (UDP). These layers include the

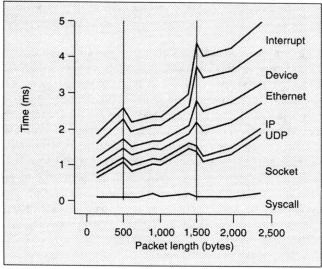

**Figure 1. Timing for a user datagram protocol (UDP) send.
(IP = Internet protocol and ms = milliseconds.)**

system call mechanism, the socket abstraction, communication protocols (UDP, IP, and Ethernet), and interrupt processing.

Figure 1 shows each layer's contribution to the total time of the send operation of user-level messages. We found that the socket abstraction, which included copying the message between user and kernel spaces, was expensive. Starting the physical device required approximately 20 percent of the total send time. The peaks are due to the SunOS's special memory-allocation policy.[12]

The mechanisms we investigated included message queues, named pipes, shared memory synchronized by two semaphores, and UDP sockets in both the Internet and Unix domains. We measured the round-trip time for a null message for each of these methods. We measured message queues at 1.7 milliseconds, named pipes at 1.8 milliseconds, shared memory with semaphores at 2.5 milliseconds, the Internet domain UDP socket at 4.4 milliseconds, and the Unix domain UDP socket at 3.6 milliseconds.

Multicasting. We studied several approaches to multicasting. The first two alternatives are based on the simple Ethernet (SE), a suite of protocols that provide low-level access to the Ethernet.[12] The user-level SE multicast utility is implemented on top of the SE device driver, which provides point-to-point Ethernet communication. The kernel-level SE multicast utility uses the multi-SE device driver. Finally, we experimented with physical multicasting. Although physical multicasting minimizes bandwidth, it demands a priori knowledge of the multicast address by all group members. This requirement may incur extra messages to set up the address.

Impact. To observe the impact of Raidcomm V.1 IPC on Raid's transaction-processing performance, we ran the DebitCredit benchmark.[12] (Known as *TP1* or *ET1*, DebitCredit is a simple yet realistic transaction-processing benchmark that uses a small banking database of three relations and 100-byte tuples.) The ratio of user times to system times for different servers is 2:1. Most of the system times are incurred by the communication activities.

Results. Details on the setup, procedures, and analysis of our experiments can be found elsewhere.[2,12] Below, we summarize only the major lessons and observations.

(1)   *Expensive.* General-purpose communication facilities are too expensive,[10,12] even though many abstractions and mechanisms are useful to support a variety of applications and users. Messages have to go through several unnecessary layers of the communication subsystem. To overcome these problems, we recommend using a simple IPC memory-management mechanism. Virtual and/or layered protocols in x-kernel and VMTP provide support to avoid such overhead.

(2)   *Communication intensive.* Transaction-processing systems are communication intensive,[4] and most of the communication is local rather than remote.[10] If the local communication is handled as a particular instance of the remote case, the operating system kernel becomes the system bottleneck, because of the high message traffic and the high cost to process messages. Communication facilities specialized for the local case can be simpler and more efficient.

(3)   *Communication support.* Some operating systems do not provide enough communication support for distributed transaction processing. The transaction-processing system implementer has to supply these services. It is desirable to define high-level interfaces between the modules. For communication, the modules use typed messages rather than simple buffers of bytes supported by the operating system. To be sent, a message has to be marshaled into kernel buffers. The receiving side must perform the inverse operation.

(4)   *Multicasting.* General-purpose multicasting mechanisms require group initialization and maintenance. In distributed transaction processing, multicasting groups are typically dynamic and short lived. In this case, the overhead of group initialization can obliterate the performance advantages of multicasting. Our experiment showed that simulating multicasting inside the kernel reduces CPU overhead.[12] Cheriton[5] proposed multicasting for many applications. We suggest that the group (multicasting) addresses used during commitment time be established as a function of the unique transaction ID. This eliminates the need for extra messages to set up group addresses.

(5)   *Name resolution.* Name resolution can become an expensive and complicated process. In general, we can have three different name spaces: the application name space, the interprocess-communication name space, and the network name space. The Raid system uses a special protocol to map Raid names into interprocess communication addresses (UDP/IP addresses). These addresses have to be mapped into network addresses (for example, Ethernet addresses) via a second address-resolution protocol. For a local area network, a straightforward correspondence between logical and physical communication addresses can be established.

Enhancements

The Raidcomm V.2 implementation for local area networks employs low overhead, simple naming, and transaction-oriented multicast support. Some of these ideas are based on LRPC and URPC.[10] Below, we briefly discuss ports, naming, multicasting schemes, and communication primitives. (Details can be found elsewhere.[12])

Ports. Processes communicate through ports, which are the basic communication abstraction. These ports reside in a memory segment shared by the process and kernel address spaces. Thus, data can be exchanged without copying. This method reduces copying by 50 percent compared with other kernel-based IPC methods. The mapped-memory segment contains a transmission buffer and a set of receiving buffers. The number and length of these buffers are specified by a process at the time it opens a port. The receiving buffers form a circular queue, which is coherently managed by the kernel and the process according to the conventional producer/consumer paradigm. Associated with the transmission buffer and each of the receiving buffers is an integer, which specifies the actual length of the message. In addition, there is a counter for the number of active messages (messages that have arrived, but which the server has not yet processed).

Naming. Within a given node, ports are uniquely identified by the triplet *<Raid instance number, server type, server instance>*. The other component of a Raid address, the site number or the transaction ID, determines the address of the physical node for monocast or the addresses of the group of nodes for multicast. In the case of Ethernet, we use only multicasting addresses for link-level communication. Site numbers or transaction IDs are used to build multicasting addresses by copying them into the four more-significant bytes of the Ethernet address.

Multicasting. In physical multicasting for processing a given transaction's data requests, each participant site sets a multicasting address using the transaction ID as its four more-significant bytes. At commitment time, the coordinator uses this address to multicast messages to all participant sites. This avoids the overhead of other multicasting methods. Currently, multicast addresses are added or deleted by Raid servers. The RC adds a new multicasting address for a transaction when it receives the first operation request for that transaction. Under normal conditions, the AC deletes the multicasting address once the transaction is committed or aborted. In the presence of failures, the CC does this job as part of its cleanup procedure. In the future, we plan to manage the multicasting addresses in the communication subsystem.

Communication primitives. System calls are provided to open and close a port, to send a message, and to add or delete a multicasting address. There is no need for an explicit receive system call. If idle, a receiving process must wait for a signal (and the corresponding message) to arrive. To send a message, a process writes it into the transmission buffer and passes control to the kernel. If the message is local, it is copied into a receiving buffer of the target port, and the port's owner is signaled (the owning process' ID is stored in the port's data structure). We use the Unix Sigio signal for this purpose. Otherwise, one of the existing network device drivers sends the message to its destination. The send operation will be aborted if there are not enough receiving buffers. The destination address is constructed as described above, and the message is enqueued into the device's output queue. When a message arrives over the network, it is demultiplexed to its corresponding port. Again, a signal alerts the receiving process about the incoming message. All this is done at interrupt time, so there is no need to schedule further software interrupts.

Performance of the communication primitives

We measured the latency of a user-to-user round-trip of local interprocess communication in Raidcomm V.1 and V.2. In version 2 it was 1.4 milliseconds, compared with the 4.4 milliseconds of the UDP socket used in version 1. In version 1, the round-trip time increased by a 1-millisecond average for each kilobyte of data; in version 2, the round-trip time increased by 0.34 millisecond for each additional kilobyte. The latency of a user-to-user round-trip remote communication reduced from 5.1 milliseconds in version 1 to 2.7 milliseconds in version 2. The round-trip-time increase for each kilobyte of data also reduced from about 3.0 milliseconds to 2.5 milliseconds. (See Figure 2.)

The socket-based IPC in version 1 and the new communication facility in version 2 provide the same functionality in a local area network environment, and both are equally affected by significant network-device-driver overhead. Despite this fact, the new communication facility achieved improvements of up to 50 percent. For multicasting, the performance advantages of the new communication facility become even more significant. The sending time does not depend on the number of destinations. On the other hand, the multicasting time for the socket IPC method grows linearly with the number of destinations.

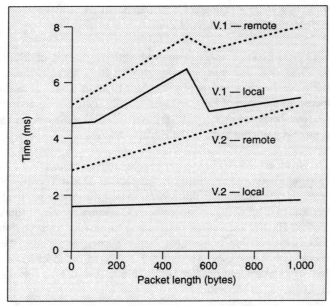

Figure 2. Round-trip times. (ms = milliseconds.)

Socket-based IPC does not optimize for the local case. Local round-trip costs were 68 to 88 percent of those for remote round-trips. In the new communication subsystem, local round-trip times were only 35 to 50 percent of the corresponding remote round-trip times.

Impact on transaction processing

We ran the DebitCredit benchmark on a single-site system and a five-site system. For the five-site system, we used the ROWA (read-once, write-all) replication method. This limited remote communication to the AC server. The benchmark contained 115 transactions that had write operations and required access to remote sites in the two-phase commit protocol. Using Raidcomm V.2 reduced the system time for transaction processing by an average of 62 percent, bringing the user-time-to-system-time ratio to 3:1.[12]

Other issues

In Raidcomm V.3, we are addressing some problems with XDR, scheduling, and context switching.

XDR. New applications require the underlying communication subsystem to provide cheap transportation for complex data objects. The transmitted data structures are usually bounded linear buffers. We can build our local communication channel in shared memory to avoid multiple encoding/decoding. Unlike lower level buffer-based communication resources, which are one-dimensional and usually accessible only as a whole, the shared-memory segments are multidimensional, randomly addressed storage resources just like the main memory. These schemes can eliminate the overhead of XDR in local communication.

Scheduling. Scheduling policies should consider high-level relationships that may exist among a group of processes. Conflicts may exist between the optimization criteria at the operating system and application levels. The application should have some way to partially control CPU allocation. The

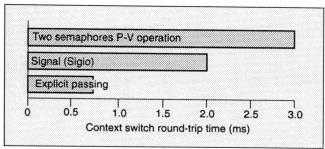

Figure 3. Performance of a context switch on the Sun 3/50 running SunOS 4.0. (ms = milliseconds.)

sender and the receiver process can collaborate under some high-level mechanism provided by the operating system to transfer the thread of control. In Unix, for example, the receiver process often goes to sleep to lower its priority. It is then put in a list and waits for the event (I/O, signals) that will grant it CPU time.

Context switching. We also conducted a series of experiments on context switching, based on the idea of explicit thread control passing. This is similar to the hand-off scheduling in Mach, but we extended it to schedule ordinary processes in Unix. Figure 3 shows round-trip times for a context switch between two processes. Raidcomm V.3 uses an explicit control-passing mechanism and shared memory. This reduced the latency of sending a high-level monocast Raid message to 0.68 millisecond. It was 2.4 milliseconds in Raidcomm V.1 and 1.1 milliseconds in Raidcomm V.2.

Conclusions

Overall, we have identified several communication services and mechanisms that can make Raid efficient. Separate address spaces can be used to structure a DTP system. High interaction among servers also triggers costly context-switching activity in the system. Increasing availability through distribution and replication of data demands special-purpose multicasting mechanisms. The idea of shared memory between the kernel and user processes is appealing, since it reduces context-switching activity. The identification of sites involved in transaction processing for accessing replicated data can be used in physical multicasting.

Our work has studied Unix-like operating systems. Obviously, Unix is not the only system on which commercial systems might be built, but it does provide a good benchmark for experimental study of new ideas in an academic setting. Our work has been conducted in a local area network environment. Similar studies must be undertaken to identify and reduce the overhead in wide area networks.

We believe technology in communications hardware and media is advancing at a rapid pace. Our research, along with related work in industry and academia, is intended to promote software advances.

Acknowledgments

Many students working on the Raid project have contributed to the system's communications facilities. Tom Muller, John Riedl, and Brad Sauder contributed to the earlier versions, and

Yongguang Zhang is helping us with the design of Raidcomm V.3. Zhang has also helped in collecting data from the designers of the various systems discussed in the section on related work and in revising the paper.

We thank each referee for giving us detailed guidelines that helped improve the paper.

This research is supported by NASA and AIRMICS under grant NAG-1-676, National Science Foundation Grant IRI-8821398, and AT&T.

References

1. B. Bhargava and J. Riedl, "The Raid Distributed Database System," *IEEE Trans. Software Eng.*, Vol. SE-15, No. 6, June 1989, pp. 726-736.

2. B. Bhargava, E. Mafla, and J. Riedl, "Communication in the Raid Distributed Database System," *Computer Networks and ISDN Systems, J. ICCC*, Vol. 21, 1991, pp. 81-92.

3. A.Z. Spector, "Communication Support in Operating Systems for Distributed Transactions," in *Networking in Open Systems*, G. Müller and R.P. Blanc, eds., Springer-Verlag, New York, N.Y., 1986, pp. 313-324.

4. D. Duchamp, "Analysis of Transaction Management Performance," *Proc. 12th ACM Symp. Operating Systems Principles*, ACM Press, New York, N.Y., 1989, pp. 177-190.

5. D.R. Cheriton, "The V Distributed System," *Comm. ACM*, Vol. 31, No. 3, Mar. 1988, pp. 314-333.

6. R.F. Rashid, "Threads of a New System," *Unix Review*, Vol. 4, No. 8, Aug. 1986, pp. 37-49.

7. A.S. Tanenbaum et al., "Experiences with the Amoeba Distributed Operating System," *Comm. ACM*, Vol. 33, No. 12, Dec. 1990, pp. 46-63.

8. J.K. Ousterhout et al., "The Sprite Network Operating System," *Computer*, Vol. 21, No. 2, Feb. 1988, pp. 23-36.

9. L. Peterson et al., "The x-kernel: A Platform for Accessing Internet Resources," *Computer*, Vol. 23, No. 5, May 1990, pp. 23-33.

10. B.N. Bershad, "High-Performance Cross-Address Space Communication," doctoral thesis, Tech. Report 90-06-02, University of Washington, Seattle, Wash., 1990.

11. K.P. Birman and T.A. Joseph, "Reliable Communication in the Presence of Failures," *ACM Trans. Computer Systems*, Vol. 5, No. 1, Feb. 1987, pp. 47-76.

12. E. Mafla and B. Bhargava, "Implementation and Performance of a Communication Facility for Distributed Transaction Processing," *Proc. Usenix Symp. Experiences with Distributed and Multiprocessor Systems*, Usenix Assoc., Berkeley, Calif., 1991, pp. 69-85.

Supporting Utility Services in a Distributed Environment

Cui-Qing Yang,

Debra Hensgen,

Thomas S. Thomas, and

Raphael Finkel

T his paper surveys approaches to designing and implementing utility servers for large-scale distributed operating systems under the *open-system* model. Large-scale computing resources with hundreds or thousands of processing units are becoming more common. Processor-coupling techniques range from a central bus to local area networks linking workstations. Efforts in software development have been directed at taking advantage of the vast computing power and resources in large-scale distributed environments. In particular, well-designed system services in a distributed environment allow user programs to access the resources effectively.

The software organization that has become traditional for centralized environments is often inappropriate in a distributed environment. In uniprocessors, the operating system typically controls all the resources, such as the CPU, memory, peripherals, and files, and it may support higher level abstractions, such as locks, transactions, and time-outs. The operating system is usually organized as a collection of subroutines that run in privileged mode, often with internal layers of hierarchical structure. This approach to organization forces the uniprocessor system to be *closed*; that is, it disallows user-provided replacements to the operating system, and user-provided enhancements must be built as a virtual layer above the existing operating system. Such enhancements often suffer a performance penalty.

In contrast, distributing resources across machine boundaries in a distributed environment often follows the open-system model, in which many traditional operating-system functions are moved into ordinary (unprotected) processes, which can be replaced or enhanced by users. The processes that control the resources (*servers*) need not be on the same machine as the processes that make use of them (*clients*). Hydra [31] originated the open-system model. Medusa [14] generalized individual servers into *task forces*, which are separate processes sharing common data structures to provide higher throughput service for a large client community. The open-system model gives rise to the philosophy that the kernel itself should provide mechanisms only for interprocess communication (IPC), memory management, and process control. This minimal kernel is often referred to as a *communication kernel*. The minimal-kernel philosophy is shared by many distributed operating systems, including V [4], Charlotte [6], [33], Accent [17], Mach [10], Amoeba [29], and Plan 9 [16].

Some servers are intended for specific applications. Others, which we call *utility servers*, control essential services such as remote kernel calls, creation of new processes, name searching, file access, and connection establishment among groups of processes. Some of these services have their counterparts in uniprocessor operating systems, whereas others are unique to a distributed environment. In a large multicomputer or multiprocessor, a single server cannot efficiently serve all clients. *Server squads*, which we describe in detail later, are groups of processes that cooperate to provide a single service by partitioning their efforts.

Although server processes have been designed and implemented for many environments, challenges remain. Unresolved problems include how to partition function between utility services and the operating-system kernel; how to construct a server process or squad automatically, given functional and system attributes; what support from both kernel and programming languages is appropriate for programming servers; and how to balance load among server processes.

This paper highlights the issues involved in designing and constructing utility services in a distributed operating system that is based on a communication kernel and contrasts various approaches to the resolution of these issues. The topics we cover include

- The relation between the open-system model and the distributed environment,
- The functional division of labor between utility services and the kernel,
- The internal structure of a utility server, and
- The construction of dynamic server squads.

We discuss various approaches taken by utility servers in Medusa, Charlotte, Mach, Amoeba, Yackos [9], and other related projects. To elucidate the main design considerations and implementation choices, we concentrate on basic services, such as extended kernel calls, invocation of new processes, name services, and connection establishment. Our observations are generalized to discuss functionality, reliability, and scalability of current server design. Finally, research trends for utility servers in future large distributed systems are explored.

Distributed environments and the open-system model

The traditional closed-system approach is convenient and efficient in a uniprocessor environment where all physical resources are confined under the centralized control of the CPU. (Figure 1 shows the system structure under the closed-system approach.) However, in a distributed environment, no memory is physically shared across machine boundaries, and processes communicate by passing messages. Many distributed systems are built based on the client-server paradigm. System services are provided by unprivileged server processes. Ordinary processes become clients to these server processes by sending them request messages. Often, remote procedure call (RPC) semantics are provided, either by the kernel or by programming-language support routines. RPC associates request messages with their replies, marshals and unmarshals parameters, ensures that the messages are well formed and appropriate to the service requested, deals with exceptions raised in the server, and blocks the client until the reply arrives [1], [12].

The client-server model is especially suitable for computations in a distributed environment, because no shared memory between client and server processes is required, and the only communication between processes is via message passing. It is also useful in parallel environments, particularly those

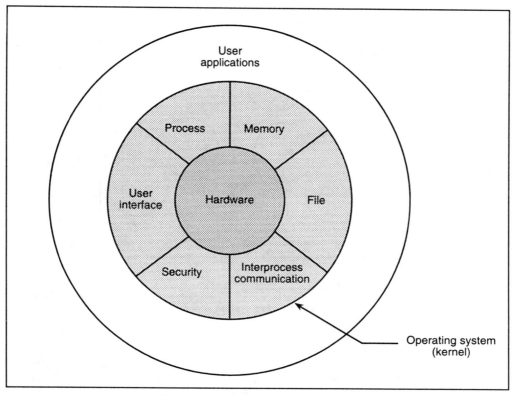

Figure 1. The closed-system approach.

with nonuniform memory access characteristics [25]. With the software structured in client and server processes, only the most basic system services, such as process management, memory management, and IPC, must be provided by the kernel. Other utility services can be provided by server processes or dedicated server machines. (Figure 2 shows the system structure under the open-system approach.)

The following are several attractive features that result from separating utility servers from the kernel:

(1) Memory is not wasted. Because the kernel is replicated on each machine, a small and efficient kernel can save substantial amounts of memory. Utility code need not be replicated on each machine in the system.

(2) Policies and mechanisms are clearly separated. Policies are naturally placed under the jurisdiction of utility servers, and the kernel provides only mechanisms. For example, a memory-management server can determine which page to replace, and the kernel can then accomplish the actual replacement. Policies and mechanisms need not reside on the same machine, although the data needed to inform a policy decision might need to be moved to the machine on which the server resides.

(3) Services can be customized. Users can modify and enhance services by providing their own servers without extra penalty. Of course, insofar as a service requires some privilege (for example, a file server needs the privilege of writing to the disk, and a memory-management server must be trusted by the kernel), the user-provided server may need to direct requests to privileged servers.

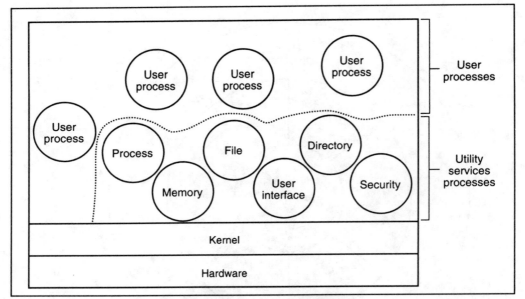

Figure 2. The open-system approach.

Services can be easily added, with no changes to the kernel. Multiple servers for the same service, but with distinct policies, can coexist.

(4) Services can be dynamically added. The configuration of resources and services need not be determined at the time the operating system is configured or booted. New servers or services can be dynamically added to handle changing client needs.

The developers of the Hydra operating system for the C.mmp multiprocessor first experimented with the open-system concept [31]. The basic goal of the Hydra design was to permit nearly all the facilities that one normally associates with an operating-system kernel to exist as normal user-level processes and, in addition, to allow an arbitrary number of user-level definitions of a single facility to simultaneously coexist. Today, this open-system approach is widely recognized as the basic model for the design and development of operating systems in distributed computing systems. Many contemporary distributed systems, such as V, Charlotte, Mach, and Amoeba, are built based on this model. In addition, distributed object-oriented approaches have a similar organization. In Clouds [5], Eden [1], and Chorus [19], for example, threads of computation accomplish work by invoking procedures in objects; objects can be designed that function as utility servers. (The object-oriented approach to supporting system services is discussed in the subsection entitled "The kernel-server relationship.")

The immense popularity of workstation-based distributed computing has been attributed to decreasing hardware costs, the rapid development of network technology, and the ease of cross-vendor standardization with the open-system model. The Open Software Foundation (OSF) is currently promoting the open-system approach of the Mach microkernel, with its multiserver interface, for the workstation-based environment.

Nonetheless, the developers of many distributed operating systems have not pursued using the strategy of the open-system-model. Locus [30] and Sprite [15], for example, are descendants of the Unix philosophy. Other projects, such as Argus [11] and Isis [2], are not full operating systems but rather packages providing functionality for distributed applications. (The approaches of projects such as Locus, Sprite, Argus, and Isis are beyond the scope of this paper.)

Major issues in the design of utility servers

Providing system services in an open environment differs from that in closed systems. Because the open-system approach places system services in ordinary user processes, many new questions are raised. For example,

- What support should the operating-system kernel provide?
- How should servers be built?
- How should clients access the services?

Answering these questions involves three important issues for the design of utility servers: the kernel-server relationship, server structure, and server configuration. We address these issues in this section.

The kernel-server relationship

In addressing the issue of the kernel-server relationship, the following two questions are raised:

(1) How should function be partitioned between the kernel and the server processes? One extreme abolishes the operating-system kernel completely and places all system services in server processes. This proposal ignores the fact that in a multiprogramming environment, some services must be retained in the operating system to ensure that resources are fairly shared and adequately utilized. Under the *minimal-kernel* philosophy, only the most basic system services are in the operating-system kernel so that it is as small as possible. There are many different views on what belongs in the minimal set of services. Designers who consider performance to be the top priority put more resource control directly in the kernel, whereas others who aim for maximum flexibility prefer a smaller kernel. For example, V provides process, memory, and device servers in the kernel [4]; in Mach, most of these functions are supported by servers outside the kernel [10]. Nevertheless, it is widely agreed that a concise communication kernel is appropriate for open distributed operating systems. The communication kernel provides mechanisms for process control, memory management, and interprocess communication.

(2) How much support should the kernel provide to the utility servers? The design of utility servers is greatly influenced by the system services in the kernel. On one hand, servers can be made more efficient by powerful primitives being placed in the kernel. On the other hand, kernel primitives should not cater to server needs if these primitives cause other processes to be complex and inefficient. Certain kinds of kernel support facilitate implementing server processes. Five examples of kernel support — threads of control, process groups and broadcast messages, communication primitives, object orientation, and device control — are discussed below.

Threads of control. Threads of control, also called *lightweight processes*, provide concurrent execution of multiple tasks within a single address space. Many designs — such as Mach, Amoeba, and Isis — have supported the use of threads in operating systems. Threads allow a server to maintain a separate context for each client and to isolate problems caused by misbehavior of a client from the service provided to others. To allow better global scheduling, threads are usually implemented in the kernel rather than by language runtime support.

Process groups and broadcast messages. A process group is a set of processes acting as a unit with a single identifier or a name. Various primitives are provided for operations on process groups, including multicasts of various strengths. A *multicast* is a broadcast message sent to an entire group. Different-strength multicasts guarantee either reception by some proportion of the group or similar ordering of messages in all members of a group. Process groups are implemented in several projects, including V and Isis. Isis even guarantees that all members of a dynamically changing group in an asynchronous environment will have a consistent view of membership. Kernel primitives for group membership and multicast can ease the implementation of server squads (see the section entitled "Dynamic server squads").

Communication primitives. Although every communication kernel supports basic message communication among processes, the communication primitives in a distributed environment vary significantly from system to system. Some systems offer primitives for synchronous (blocking) send and receive only; others provide asynchronous- (nonblocking-) communication facilities also. RPC is a higher level communication paradigm supported by the kernel or by programming languages. RPC relieves the programmer of a significant amount of effort, both for marshaling and unmarshaling data and for checking type consistency between client (*caller*) and server (*callee*). Other communication primitives that affect the implementation of server processes include expedited messages and a facility for screening the contents of a message. In the absence of threads, asynchronous communication can be used to allow the server to treat each client independently.

Object orientation. The object-oriented paradigm provides objects, which are at a higher level of abstraction than processes. An object encapsulates the data and operations (called *methods*) of an abstract data type. Types may be hierarchically structured. Object-oriented distributed operating systems often follow the open-system approach; that is, the kernel supports only basic functions such as object creation and method invocation. All other services are provided by objects themselves. Servers are implemented as objects belonging to certain server classes, and services are provided through the invocation of methods in server objects. Distributed implementations of object-oriented designs tend to address exactly the same questions as do traditional client-server designs [1], [5].

Device control. Servers that provide access to physical peripheral devices need to be able to effect I/O. One option is for the kernel to provide a basic I/O service. If the kernel does not provide lightweight processes, asynchronous (nonblocking) I/O is necessary to allow the server to multiplex client requests; in this case, completion interrupts need to be reflected to the servers. This option violates the principle of minimal kernels, since device code tends to be bulky. It also suffers from extra context switches on device interrupts. A second option is to allow the server to undertake raw I/O. The server must run in privileged mode and be able to handle interrupts directly. Such a design, although efficient, is fairly risky. Under either of these two options, the kernel must be able to deny I/O rights to other processes, so servers must have special privileges. Servers must either reside on the machine that has the peripheral device or have a proxy process on that machine. A third option is to dedicate server machines for device control. The software running on such machines need not be the same as the communication kernel in other machines, except that it must support the same message-based communication interface as does the communication kernel. The Charlotte primitive link, for example, supports communication between Charlotte and non-Charlotte processes; the latter are on separate machines devoted to device control [6]. None of the three options are both efficient and elegant.

Server structure

A message-passing facility provides a uniform interface for server construction, hiding the low-level details of the environment. However, the structure of utility servers relies heavily on the underlying hardware architecture, the interprocess-communication semantics, and the basic kernel functions. For example, the hierarchical cost of accessing memory in the clustered configuration of the Cm* machine influenced the design of Medusa's utility servers [14]. A Medusa server is designed

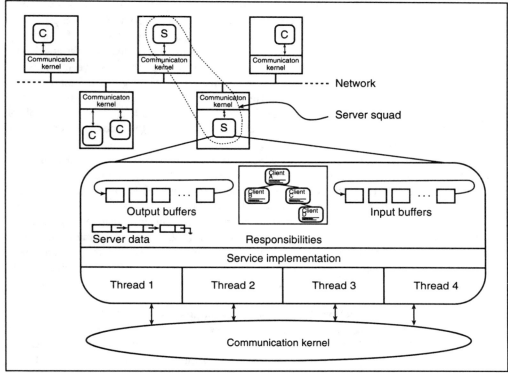

Figure 3. A typical structure of a multithreaded server.

as a task force of processes sharing global data but with separate copies of instructions. For efficiency reasons, task forces do not cross cluster boundaries [14]. Service can be provided concurrently by the processes of a task force with only a moderate cost of sharing information. On the other hand, most of the servers in Charlotte are structured with a single process per server to avoid the higher communication cost in its loosely coupled distributed environment [6]. In order to cope with contention for popular services, Charlotte also uses server squads, in which each member is a heavyweight process [6].

As mentioned above, many distributed operating systems support multiple threads within a single address space [4], [10], [29]. Such threads can share resources by accessing their shared memory. Implementation of a server process with a multithreaded structure increases concurrency of service and helps to configure the server program in a more structured manner. By its nature, a server process should be able to simultaneously handle many concurrent events (for instance, many requests from different clients, as well as communications with other servers). A multithreaded server elegantly accommodates a large number of concurrent events. Typically, each client is served by a single thread that retains client-specific information and that remains inactive between requests from that client. Alternatively, each request can create a thread that serves just that request. For the sake of efficiency, threads that are finished with their work can be saved and reused. Figure 3 depicts the typical structure of a multithreaded server. The server is configured as a hierarchy, with multiple server processes in a squad; each of these server processes consists of multiple threads.

The same elegant organization can be achieved by a programming language with its own thread scheduler in a monolithic process, if the kernel provides asynchronous-communication primitives [23]. In contrast, if a server program is written as a single sequential process, code for handling different events becomes entangled. Such server programs are extremely difficult to write and debug.

Deadlock and robustness are critical concerns in managing communication between clients and servers and among servers themselves. In particular, buffer-management strategies and communication protocols must be chosen. Synchronous send and receive are easy to use. However, there is a danger of deadlock when a process is blocked waiting for these requests to complete. A simple example of a deadlock is the situation that occurs when a server is blocked waiting for a message from a client and the client is also blocked waiting for a message from the server. Although there is no simple way to guarantee a deadlock-free program in general, script-based methods can be used to coordinate the protocol followed by client and server to properly sequence their actions and provide for efficient underlying message transfer [18]. In addition, synchronous communication puts servers at the mercy of malfunctioning clients. For example, a client that sends a request but never tries to receive the response could block the server. The solution is either to use threads (only the thread serving that client becomes blocked), to use a nonblocking method such as Reply in V, or to employ time-outs. Further protection from faulty clients requires preventive programming in a server. Servers need to check each request for sanity; inexpensive runtime methods for type checking, for example, are available [24]. The server can reject requests or even close the communication link with the client if abnormal messages arrive.

Asynchronous communication has its own problems. Each process (server or client) must manage message buffers in its own address space. Care must be taken to avoid ordering errors, such as those arising from reuse of a send buffer before its contents have been safely transmitted [8]. Communication activities of various threads can be orchestrated through synchronized message queues built with semaphores.

At some level of the software, messages are typeless byte strings. Servers and clients need to agree on message types and protocols. The designs of message formats are application-specific and typically depend on reliable message delivery. As mentioned above, an RPC interface can help define and enforce these designs.

A server process often must maintain state information for each resource it manages and for each client. In a distributed environment, it is difficult and expensive to have a server keep all state information in a consistent condition in the presence of possible message loss, network partitioning, and client failure. An alternative is the *stateless* approach, in which the server maintains no client-specific state information. Instead, state information is retained by the clients and is included in requests as appropriate. For example, Medusa servers read state information from client-specific memory regions. In the Network File System (NFS) [13], file servers keep no detailed information for open files; the clients (in this case, Unix kernels) store such information and provide it when needed during requests. It is hard to abolish all the information associated with a resource in a server process. Clients of stateless servers often can survive temporary server failure, but it is awkward for clients to gain exclusive control over resources (such a lock constitutes a client-specific state). Research is needed to determine how to make completely stateless servers both efficient and reliable.

Server configuration

Issues concerning server configuration include: where a particular server should execute, the granularity of service that should be provided by an individual server, and the number of servers that is necessary to provide one service: a single server or a server squad. These issues are discussed below.

(1)   Where should a particular server execute? For efficiency, servers that provide the lowest levels of device service should reside on the machines connected to the devices. Servers that

provide virtual services — such as lock, multicast, or time-out services — and servers that determine policy but do not implement mechanisms — such as memory-management and load-balancing (migration) servers — may execute on any machine. (Load-balancing and migration methods and policies are beyond the scope of this paper.)

(2)   What granularity of service should be provided by an individual server? It is often elegant to structure a service into a hierarchy of cooperating restricted-function servers. We call such a structure *fine grained*. For instance, the file service may be divided into separate servers that provide transactions, directories, files, bytes, stable storage, blocks, and locks. If lock service is separated from the rest of the file service, it becomes possible to create a variant lock service without modifying the file server, and it is also possible to reuse the lock service for other purposes. Such reuse of software is a primary motivation for object-oriented programming. In addition, finer granularity allows different components to be placed on different machines to balance load. Furthermore, finer granularity avoids penalizing clients that want only low-level services such as services of nontransaction files. The bullet file service in Amoeba is an example of a fine-grained structure [29]. The increased cost of interprocess communication must be balanced against the advantages of fine granularity.

(3)   What number of servers is necessary to provide one service: a single server or a server squad? When installations grow to hundreds or thousands of machines, one server probably will not always efficiently serve all requests. Servers become the bottlenecks for all applications, much the same way that a single bus cannot handle all requests for shared memory in a huge multiprocessor. Popular servers (file servers in particular) need to be enhanced into squads [32]. In the case of files, the bottleneck is ultimately the number of physical devices, so manual intervention (that is, attaching more disks and moving data to them) is necessary. For servers controlling virtual resources — such as locks, time-outs, policies, and names — the squad size often can be enlarged or reduced automatically in response to changing load, as we describe later. Two systems that pioneered the manual squad techniques are Eden and Medusa. In Eden, servers take the form of multiple-thread objects called *Ejects* (Eden objects) [1]. The Eject programmer determines the number of threads and how they partition the work. Eden does not provide a unifying theory for determining how and when new threads should be created in an Eject, whether they should ever terminate, and — if so — how they are to redistribute their work among remaining active threads. Medusa servers, including the memory manager, the file system, the debugger, and the exception reporter, are designed as task forces [14]. The task force manager (itself a task force), together with the kernel, can dynamically adjust the number of processes of each task force. Task forces grow and shrink in response to changes in their load and processor availability. Unfortunately, task forces were never completely implemented.

Utility services in contemporary distributed designs

In order to show how utility services can be implemented in a distributed environment, we now discuss the following services provided in several contemporary distributed designs: processor, memory, file, user-interface, name, security, connection, time-out, and lock. Some of these services (for example, processor, file, and user-interface services) have counterparts in centralized designs. Others (for example, name, security, and connection services) are unique to the distributed environment in the sense that either they are not applicable to a centralized design or their implementation in a centralized design is quite different from that in a distributed environment.

Processor service

Perhaps the most fundamental facility that an operating system provides is creating processes and controlling their execution. Creation includes loading an executable image of a process; allocating its memory; initializing its data, code segments, and registers; and scheduling its execution. In a centralized design, all these tasks are performed by a single kernel. The state of all processes (running, suspended, and so forth), is both known and controlled by the kernel. In a distributed design, multiple kernels are involved, cooperating processes execute on different machines, and the global state of all processes is difficult or impossible to determine. Not surprisingly, the ways in which processes are created and managed under a distributed operating system vary significantly from those under a centralized approach.

Amoeba [29] illustrates various features of distributed process control. Here, the kernel provides basic mechanisms for creating and scheduling processes. All process-management policies are implemented in servers. These servers can ask the kernel to allocate segments of memory of given sizes; initialize this memory with instructions, data, and stack; and then request that a new process be built out of the initialized segments. Each processor server controls a pool of processors and maintains information about all processes running on machines in that pool. Process-specific information is encapsulated in a process descriptor, which contains memory segment descriptors, thread descriptors (Amoeba supports multithreaded address spaces), and other state information. Amoeba runs on heterogeneous hardware platforms, so executable images cannot be run on all nodes. Therefore, the process descriptor also contains indicators for the class of machines that the process can run on, the instruction set used, memory requirements, and other prerequisites for the execution environment. When clients make appropriate requests, the process server can create, suspend, and migrate processes. All policies that control the processor services are fully implemented in the server processes [29].

Similarly, Charlotte includes a starter service that creates processes on behalf of clients, maintains process state information, supports process migration, and implements load-balancing policies [33]. Plan 9 dedicates some processors to run CPU server processes, which are connected by IPC to remote terminals [16]. The CPU servers provide a conventional command interpreter environment to the user and interact with other servers to access resources.

Memory service

Memory is another key hardware resource. Low-level operations such as establishing page tables require privileged instructions and are best left to the kernel. However, allocating physical memory and managing memory objects are often left to utility servers outside the kernel. These processes can pursue more global policies for memory allocation and memory sharing among processes.

The distributed shared-memory server in Mach [7] is a good example of memory service. The Mach kernel provides a virtual-memory manager that allows processes to create virtual-memory segments that can reside within the same machine or on other machines in the network. Mach maintains transparency across networks of machines with different memory architectures.

The memory manager is implemented in an external pager process that provides the means of storing and retrieving memory pages on backing storage in response to processor paging requests (such as Pageout and Pagein). The external pager process obeys a well-defined kernel-pager interface that delegates the kernel's paging duties to the pager. It provides primitives to other processes for memory object allocation and deallocation, replication, mapping, and type casting. Memory objects are uniquely identified by ports. Processes can share ports by passing their identifiers to other processes via IPC. A process can map the contents of memory object into its local virtual address space via the external pager, and the pager will migrate objects, making any translations necessary to accommodate differing memory architectures such as page sizes and data type representations.

The external pager maintains coherency of memory objects when virtual spaces are shared or replicated. The current owner of the object is given write access, and as other processes make write requests, they obtain ownership. Thus, the external pager is able to provide a complex and fundamental service without residing inside the kernel [7].

File service

Files are an indispensable resource defined by all operating systems. In a traditional centralized design, processes access files through a service-call interface to the kernel, which manages the single, central copy of a file and provides integrity, locking, and sharing. *Centralization* implies that all processes see a single, consistent view of the files. Distributed environments do not centralize the file system to a single site. Since distributed designs are larger and aim to support many more users (and resources) than centralized designs, files are often replicated across multiple sites to reduce bottlenecks and to increase availability and reliability. Maintaining integrity and presenting a single, consistent file system image are difficult in the face of replicated files. Designers and implementers of distributed file systems face unique challenges. A thorough discussion of distributed file systems can be found in the literature [28]. Here, we describe examples of distributed file systems taken from Andrew and other designs.

The Andrew project at Carnegie Mellon University, Pittsburgh, Pennsylvania, includes a distributed Unix-like file system [20]. Its architecture is based on an underlying network (called *Vice*) of trusted, dedicated servers and a collection of fully autonomous Unix-based workstations. Each workstation runs a process (called *Venus*) that extends the workstation's local file name space by adding a subtree with the global file name space. Venus provides ordinary Unix file semantics to processes and communicates with the Vice servers to locate files, cache them locally, and provide I/O. The global name space provides location transparency by presenting a single file system image.

Caching is key in providing adequate performance and in supporting concurrent file access. During the evolution of Andrew, various approaches were taken in maintaining consistency among multiple caches of a file [20]. Originally, Andrew used a pessimistic approach, in which — at every use of a cached file — Venus would verify with Vice that the cache value was current. Frequent Venus-Vice communication degraded network and client performance. Later, Andrew adopted an optimistic policy, in which Vice servers would notify Venus when cached data changed. Cache values were written back to Vice only when the local client closed the file. Originally, Andrew cached entire files, but now it can cache portions of files. Each version of Andrew has increased scalability by reducing message traffic for cache coherency policies and mechanisms, exploiting caching and replication, and decentralizing administration. The fact that Venus is outside the kernel has made such development relatively easy. More recently, Andrew's file system has grown into Coda, which additionally provides fault-tolerance mechanisms with goals of constant availability [21].

In Amoeba, various file systems have been implemented, including a high-performance file server (called *Bullet*) that stores immutable files contiguously on disk and caches them in server memory when needed, providing very fast accesses [29].

User-interface service

In a distributed environment, an application can be executed across multiple machines in the network, with the user interface, the application logic, and files and other resources all being disjoint. The provision of user-interface services in such an environment is an interesting issue in software design.

The X Window package is a sophisticated, widely used, distributed user-interface service [22]. It uses the client-server model in a network-transparent fashion to provide bitmapped windows containing text and graphics. X was developed at Massachusetts Institute of Technology (MIT), Cambridge, Massachusetts, starting in 1984 and has evolved into a de facto industry standard for distributed windowing packages. X specifies a protocol that defines the communications between clients and servers in which clients send requests to the servers to create and manipulate a hierarchy of rectangular windows. A server is typically in charge of one display. Windows serve as input and output interfaces between application programs (clients) and users. The server manages the physical devices of keyboard, screen, and pointing device. Asynchronous messages are exchanged between servers and clients. In general, the client and server processes may reside on different processors and communicate via messages over a reliable transport mechanism. Language support for X is provided by a library of procedures, shielding the programmer from the details of protocol-specific formats and interprocess communication with the X server. A client may communicate with multiple X servers.

Name service

In both centralized and distributed designs, processes needing services must communicate their requests to the appropriate servers. In centralized designs, all services generally are provided by protected code running in the kernel, and a single entry point to all services is available via a call interface. In distributed designs, services are not only outside the client's address space but also outside the client's physical node. Access cannot be resolved to an internal address in memory; instead, messages communicate requests, parameters, and results. The process of binding a client to a server process is more complex than that in centralized designs. Services are generally identified with some name (either textual or some other encoding meaningful to the client community); communication takes place via a logical *communication port*. *Binding* means establishing this connection between clients and servers. *Name servers* (also called *directory servers*) are utility processes that manage the resources of names and communication ports and help clients bind to servers.

We present here the Charlotte name server (called the *switchboard*) [33] as an example. Charlotte processes require a full-duplex logical communication channel (called a *link*) before they can exchange messages. Clients need to acquire such a link to servers. Links have two ends, either of which may be packaged into messages. All Charlotte servers are expected to register themselves with the switchboard, leaving one end of a link by which they can be reached and a textual name that describes their service. Clients contact the switchboard to acquire a link end associated with a given name. Thus, the switchboard allows processes to exchange links to provide full-duplex logical communications, much like a telephone switchboard.

The switchboard is implemented as a squad of processes across several machines. Each switchboard process maintains a database of registered services. Information is not replicated across switchboards. When a client queries a service-name, the switchboard returns the link end associated with the first match it encounters in a depth-first search of its own and its peers' databases. This implementation addresses issues of scalability in that squad growth policies can be defined that will adjust the number of name servers as a function of client demand.

Other name servers have been implemented as well. Athena's name server (called *Hesiod*) maintains user configuration files and location data for services in a central database [3]. Amoeba's directory service maps names to capabilities. It supports the creation of hierarchical directories, in which a directory can be a collection of capabilities for other directory servers [29]. Grapevine coordinates name and mail service by two interacting squads of servers [26].

Security service

Centralized and distributed designs differ fundamentally in how they protect data and resources from unauthorized or malicious access. In a uniprocessor, the trusted operating-system kernel can provide security by capitalizing on the centralized and self-contained nature of the resources. In a distributed environment, servers must be able to discover if their clients are authorized for the operations requested. The problem becomes more severe when a request must travel through a chain of servers; the last one must still act on behalf of the original client but only for the duration of that client's request.

There are several dangerous aspects of the distributed world. First, it is hard to prevent users from rebooting their machines with modified (and no longer trustworthy) kernels. Second, users can provide their own servers, as dictated by the open-system model; in such cases, security and access control information might no longer be housed in a protected domain. Third, transmission of such information across communication links is itself not necessarily secure.

The big challenge facing the design of a security service is how to meet the security requirements, given a configuration of nontrusted components in a distributed environment. The Kerberos authentication service and the security measure in Amoeba are two approaches used in many contemporary distributed environments.

The Kerberos authentication service confronts the issues of security in open distributed designs by assuming that clients and servers are not trusted, so their identity must be authenticated whenever service is requested [27]. The design of Kerberos is based on trusted third-party authentication. That is, the authentication server is the only trusted component, and clients and servers are expected to use it to authenticate each other. Authentication is achieved among Kerberos (the authentication server), clients, and ordinary servers through a set of protocols. An encryption scheme generates private keys when server or client processes first register with Kerberos. Protocols involving encryption prevent tampering with keys and exposing information resulting from eavesdropping on network communication. These private keys allow Kerberos to create messages that convince the server and its clients that the other party is really who it claims to be. Kerberos provides three distinct levels of protection: authentication only for the initial connection; authentication of each message; and private messages, where each message is not only authenticated but also encrypted. The Kerberos service has been used in Athena, Sun NFS, and other distributed environments.

The protection mechanism in Amoeba is based on cryptographically protected capabilities [29]. Accesses to any resource require a capability to that resource. Capabilities are generated through one-way encryption into a large space, making it infeasible to forge a capability. Therefore, capabilities themselves need not be protected and may be handled by untrusted processes. Amoeba has not been implemented on a huge scale, so there may be limitations on protection of capabilities. However, since a capability exposes only a single object, the effects of compromise will be limited.

Other services

Connection service, time-out service, and lock service are among other services provided by servers. These three services are discussed below. (Many other services in a distributed environment can be supported by various servers, such as printing and information-retrieval services. Because of the space limitations of this paper, our discussion focuses on system-related utility services.)

In many distributed designs, communication between processes requires that a logical connection be established between them before messages can be exchanged. Charlotte's link-based IPC and Unix's stream sockets are two examples of approaches in which such a logical connection is established. Initializing the connections within a complex group of cooperating processes can be supported by an appropriate server. Charlotte provides a connection service to establish initial links between processes [33]. The communications configuration is represented by a connection-description file, which specifies the identity of processes to be started and the communication relationships among them. The connector uses the starter server to create new processes and distributes communication links among them according to the configuration specified in the file.

A service that is well suited for implementation by servers is the time-out service in Yackos [9]. The time-out server squad allows client processes to set or cancel timers. Clients are notified of the expiration of timers; thus, clients are allowed to detect, for example, transmission failure or user

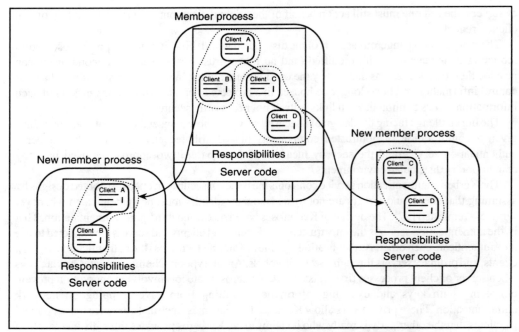

Figure 4. Creation of new members in a dynamic server squad.

inactivity. The timer squad uses a common hardware clock to ensure synchronization of the squad members; thus, a source of time and time-lapse measurements is provided to all components of a cooperating process group. Such common clocks are particularly important in heterogeneous environments in which the hardware timers in the various machines do not agree precisely.

Another service that is well suited for implementation by servers is the lock service in Yackos [9]. The lock service is typically needed by distributed applications that share resources among many processes. For example, locks are used in transactions to provide synchronization atomicity. The Yackos lock server generates locks at the request of a client process. Locks are associated with resources not by the server but rather by the clients. It is the clients' responsibility to generate unique lock names for the resources they wish to lock. Locks have various dimensions, such as whether they are read or write locks, whether they are protected from unauthorized access by a key, how long the requester is willing to wait for them, and how long a successful requester wishes to hold them before possible preemption. Preemption generates an unsolicited message from the server back to the client.

Dynamic server squads

A server squad is a group of heavyweight processes that together implement a service. In a *static squad*, the number of servers and the way they partition their work are fixed. In a *dynamic squad*, the number of servers and how they partition work vary according to demand for service and availability of underloaded CPUs. Figure 4 illustrates the operation of creating new members in a dynamic server squad. Although static squads are often easier to implement, dynamic squads can adapt to a changing environment. Adaptability is particularly important in a large-scale distributed system, where there are likely to be large fluctuations in sharing of resources and in cooperation among processes. Squads can be constructed either so that clients can send to any member (as in Yackos [9]) or so that clients are assigned to a particular member (as in Medusa [14]).

Several server squads, including those for time-outs and locks, have been implemented in Yackos. In addition, the Yackos software library includes enhancement tools to aid in the construction of future squads. (To *enhance* a server is to convert it to a squad.) The tools were used to build a multicast squad. The lessons learned building Yackos squads are broadly applicable to dynamic squads for any communication-kernel operating system.

A designer must resolve the following four issues when converting an ordinary server to a dynamic squad:

- *Adapting*: The issue of adapting determines how and when to grow and shrink the squad.
- *Coverage*: The issue of coverage refers to deciding which member of the squad will respond to any particular request and how the request will reach the responding member.
- *Adaptation communication*: The issue of adaptation communication addresses the communication that must surround the growth and shrinkage of a squad.
- *Nonadaptation communication*: The issue of nonadaptation communication considers all other communication, such as forwarding requests to appropriate members and reapportioning work among squad members.

The first three of these issues are peculiar to dynamically growing squads, while the fourth one applies to both dynamically growing and static squads. Each issue has *control*, *mechanism*, and *policy* aspects [32]; these are discussed below.

Server squad control

Squad control determines who has responsibility for actions that modify the squad. The choice is always between letting the squad members control the group themselves and applying external control from either the kernel or some other (squad-controller) server.

One responsibility is deciding when to grow and shrink a squad. The squad members collectively will know the demand that clients are placing on them. The kernels collectively will know how busy the processors are. Another responsibility is to decide which member covers which client request. The kernel can help by inspecting and properly delivering requests or even by randomizing the destinations, the members can keep track of coverage and forward requests, and a name server can randomly distribute the allocation of new clients to existing squad members. A third responsibility is deciding where each member should run. A load-balancing server can treat the squad members as it would any other processes to solve this problem. So the candidates for responsibility include the kernel, the members of the squad itself, and another server (which could also be implemented as a squad).

The open-system model and the minimal-kernel philosophy agree that the kernel should not be involved in squad control. If squads control themselves, they can elect controlling members or make decisions in a distributed way. External control is most appropriate when a control problem is generic to many squads and can be profitably implemented once in a specialized server. Three such control problems are

- Load balancing, which can be addressed by a *load-balancing service*;
- Nonadaptive communication, which can be addressed by a *multicast service*; and
- Coverage, which can be addressed by a *name service* that keeps track of squad-member coverage.

In the squads built so far in Yackos, the squad itself is responsible for deciding when to grow or shrink (the method is described below) and for deciding which member covers each request (typically by partitioning the workspace and forwarding requests between members). The problem of load balancing has not been addressed.

Server squad mechanism

The squad mechanism determines how a squad grows, shrinks, and serves its clients. The squad designer must decide

- How an individual squad member should gather information about the load on both squad members and individual CPUs;
- How an existing member should start a new member;
- How a member contemplating deleting itself should finally decide to do so and how it should transfer coverage to members that remain; and
- If a member receives a client request that is covered by another member, whether the member should respond to the client or quietly pass the request to the covering member.

All the mechanisms involved in the above decisions can be embedded in the code of an individual server squad when it is being written. A more attractive approach is to generate various mechanisms automatically by a squad generator, much as a stub generator automatically generates stubs for RPCs.

The Yackos squads vary in the mechanism of squad adaptation. Those that were built manually have fairly *ad hoc* methods for packaging coverage for dissemination among the members when a change takes place. The enhancement tools provide a general framework for partitioning work and handling dissemination invisibly.

Server squad policy

Squad policy determines when a squad should change size and which member of the squad covers which requests. Growth is appropriate for a squad in high demand only when there are underutilized nodes. Directing requests to the covering members can often be orchestrated by automatically generated code. Members of stateless server squads can generally handle any request that they get. They can notify the name service of their current load so that it can reapportion new clients accordingly. Servers with state must partition coverage among themselves. Some services have easily partitioned data structures. If so, the squad can furnish the name service with a mapping that permits the latter to determine which squad member is likely to cover any given request.

The Yackos enhancement tools provide a set of mechanism routines for adding a new member and deleting an existing member. Generic routines call server-implemented functions to determine which member covers each client request. A generic function aids in deciding when to grow or shrink.

Example: Multicast squad

To concretely demonstrate the problems involved in implementing dynamic server squads, we describe here in some detail the Yackos multicast squad, which was built with the assistance of the enhancement tools. A multicast service is responsible for delivering messages addressed to process groups. The Yackos multicast squad provides operations on groups (joining and departing) and various flavors of message reliability (guaranteed and best effort), ordering (unordered, atomic, and causal), and destination (any member, a majority, and the entire group). Atomic and causal ordering are functionally equivalent to Isis' Abcast and Cbcast [2], respectively. The Yackos multicast squad is characterized as being

- *Updating*: Information should be passed between members in order to serve clients,

- *Skilled*: A new member needs to be informed of some of the state of the existing members before it can serve any clients,
- *Exclusive*: Some requests can be answered only by particular members of the squad, and
- *With state*: The membership of multicast groups constitutes state retained by the service.

Specifying these characteristics and providing routines that decide, for example, which squad member covers a request are the bulk of the work needed to convert a server to a squad.

The multicast squad routes multicast requests to the right member of the squad based on the destination group specified by the request. When the squad grows, new members are assigned coverage over a set of existing multicast groups. Terminating members disseminate their coverage among the remaining members.

The decision to grow is based on information provided by clients. Each request includes a count of busy signals — that is, the number of times the client has attempted to send the request but failed because of a backlog of messages at the server. Many consecutive, large busy-signal counts indicate that the squad member is very busy. They can also indicate that the entire squad is busy, because messages are forwarded from other members of the squad. Serendipitously, they also indicate that there are underutilized nodes, or else the kernel (which in multiprocessor Yackos occupies a node) would not be able to deliver so many untreated messages. The enhancement tools automatically insert code to collect busy-signal statistics, and growth decisions are based on these statistics.

Conclusions and future trends

This paper summarizes the evolution of servers in distributed environments, giving many examples of contemporary open systems and contrasting them with their closed counterparts. Servers are motivated by the open-system model and by the minimal-kernel philosophy, both of which appear especially appropriate in a large distributed environment. The research questions that lie ahead are how well server squads scale, what other services should be embedded in servers, and how to provide extensive help for designers and implementers of those servers.

Improvements in the area of server program development will continue to be made. Already, languages for server implementation and tools to support building squads are available. Tools similar to Lex and YACC (Yet Another Compiler Compiler) for creating distributed object-oriented compilers executing as squads are being developed. New forms will include dynamic server squads that can share load with clients and allow migration of code into and out of the kernel. Different versions of servers will be appropriate for different environments, and these environments can change dynamically. Hence, some dynamic facility, either in the kernel or a server, will need to be responsible for choosing and executing different versions of the servers.

References

[1] G.T. Almes et al., "The Eden System: A Technical Review," *IEEE Trans. Software Eng.*, Vol. SE-11, No. 1, Jan. 1985, pp. 43-59.

[2] K.P. Birman, "Replication and Fault-Tolerance in the ISIS System," *Proc. 10th ACM Symp. Operating Systems Principles*, ACM Press, New York, N.Y., 1985, pp. 79-86.

[3] G.A. Champine, D.E. Geer, Jr., and W.N. Ruh, "Project Athena as a Distributed Computer System," *Computer*, Vol. 23, No. 9, Sept. 1990, pp. 40-51.

[4] D.R. Cheriton, "The V Distributed System," *Comm. ACM*, Vol. 31, No. 3, Mar. 1988, pp. 314-333.

[5] P. Dasgupta, R.J. LeBlanc, Jr., and W.F. Appelbe, "The Clouds Distributed Operating System: Functional

Description, Implementation Details and Related Work," *Proc. Eighth Int'l Conf. Distributed Computing Systems*, IEEE Computer Soc. Press, Los Alamitos, Calif., 1988, pp. 2-9.

[6] R. Finkel et al., "Experience with Charlotte: Simplicity and Function in a Distributed Operating System," *IEEE Trans. Software Eng.*, Vol. 15, No. 6, June 1989, pp. 676-685.

[7] A. Forin et al., "Design, Implementation, and Performance Evaluation of a Distributed Shared Memory Server for Mach," Tech. Report CMU-CS-88-165, School of Computer Science, Carnegie Mellon University, Pittsburgh, Pa., 1988.

[8] A. Gordon, *Ordering Errors in Distributed Program*, doctoral thesis, Computer Sciences Dept., Univ. of Wisconsin-Madison, Madison, Wisc., 1985.

[9] D. Hensgen and R. Finkel, "Dynamic Server Squads in Yackos," *Proc. Workshop Experiences Distributed and Multiprocessor Systems*, Usenix, Berkeley, Calif., 1989, pp. 73-90.

[10] M.B. Jones and R.F. Rashid, "Mach and Matchmaker: Kernel and Language Support for Object-Oriented Distributed Systems," *Proc. Object-Oriented Programming Systems, Languages and Applications (OOPSLA '86)*, ACM Press, New York, N.Y., 1986, pp. 67-77.

[11] B. Liskov et al., "Implementation of Argus," *Proc. 11th ACM Symp. Operating Systems Principles*, ACM Press, New York, N.Y., 1987, pp. 111-122.

[12] P.R. McJones and G.F. Swart, "Evolving the UNIX System Interface to Support Multithreaded Programs," Tech. Report 21, Digital Equipment Corp. (DEC) Systems Research Center, Palo Alto, Calif., 1987.

[13] *Networking on the SUN Workstation*, Sun Microsystems, Inc., Mountain View, Calif., 1986.

[14] J.K. Ousterhout, D.A. Scelza, and P.S. Sindhu, "Medusa: An Experiment in Distributed Operating System Structure," *Comm. ACM*, Vol. 23, No. 2, Feb. 1980, pp. 92-105.

[15] J. K. Ousterhout et al., "The Sprite Network Operating System," *Computer*, Vol. 21, No. 2, Feb. 1988, pp. 23-36.

[16] D. Presotto, "Plan 9, a Distributed System," *Proc. Usenix Workshop Micro-Kernels and Other Kernel Alternatives*, Usenix, Berkeley, Calif., 1992, pp. 31-38.

[17] R.F. Rashid and G.G. Robertson, "Accent: A Communication Oriented Network Operating System Kernel," *Proc. Eighth ACM Symp. Operating Systems Principles*, ACM Press, New York, N.Y., 1981, pp. 64-75.

[18] B. Rosenburg, *Automatic Generation of Communication Protocols*, doctoral thesis, Computer Sciences Dept., Univ. of Wisconsin-Madison, Madison, Wisc., 1986.

[19] M. Rozier et al., "The Chorus Distributed Operating System," *Computing Systems*, Vol. 1, No. 4, Dec. 1988, pp. 305-370.

[20] M. Satyanarayanan, "Scalable, Secure, and Highly Available Distributed File Access," *Computer*, Vol. 23, No. 5, May 1990, pp. 9-20.

[21] M. Satyanarayanan et al., "Coda: A Highly Available File System for a Distributed Workstation Environment," *IEEE Trans. Computers*, Vol. 39, No. 4, Apr. 1990, pp. 447-459.

[22] R.W. Scheifler, J. Gettys, and R. Newman, *X Window System — C Library and Protocol Reference*, Digital Press, Bedford, Mass., 1988.

[23] M.L. Scott and R.A. Finkel, "LYNX: A Dynamic Distributed Programming Language," *Proc. 1984 Int'l Conf. Parallel Processing*, IEEE Computer Soc. Press, Los Alamitos, Calif., 1984, pp. 395-401.

[24] M.L. Scott and R.A. Finkel, "A Simple Mechanism for Type Security across Compilation Units," *IEEE Trans. Software Eng.*, Vol. 14, No. 8, Aug. 1988, pp. 1238-1239.

[25] M.L. Scott, T.J. LeBlanc, and B.D. Marsh, "Psyche Multiprocessor Operating System," *Proc. Workshop Experiences Distributed and Multiprocessor Systems*, Usenix, Berkeley, Calif., 1989, pp. 227-236.

[26] M.D. Shroeder, A.D. Birrell, and R.M. Needham, "Experience with the Grapevine: The Growth of a Distributed System," *ACM Trans. Computer Systems*, Vol. 2, No. 1, Feb. 1984, pp. 3-23.

[27] J.G. Steiner, C. Neuman, and J.I. Schiller, "Kerberos: An Authentication Service for Open Network Systems," *Proc. Winter 1988 Usenix Conf.*, Usenix, Berkeley, Calif., 1988, pp. 191-202.

[28] A.S. Tanenbaum and R. Van Renesse, "Distributed Operating Systems," *Computing Surveys*, Vol. 17, No. 4, Dec. 1985, pp. 419-470.

[29] A.S. Tanenbaum et al., "Experiences with the Amoeba Distributed Operating System," *Comm. ACM*, Vol. 33, No. 12, Dec. 1990, pp. 46-63.

[30] B. Walker et al., "The LOCUS Distributed Operating System," *Proc. 10th ACM Symp. Operating Systems Principles*, ACM Press, New York, N.Y., 1983, pp. 49-70.

[31] W.A. Wulf, R. Levin, and S.P. Harbison, *HYDRA/C.mmp: An Experimental Computer System*, McGraw-Hill Book Co., New York, N.Y., 1981.

[32] C.-Q. Yang and M.S. Ali, "Issues on Designing Server Squads for Future Large-Scale Distributed and Parallel Computing Systems," *Proc. Second IEEE Workshop Future Trends Distributed Computing Systems (Future Trends '90)*, IEEE Computer Soc. Press, Los Alamitos, Calif., 1990, pp. 284-289.

[33] C.-Q. Yang and R. Finkel, "Utility Servers in Charlotte," *Software Practice & Experience*, Vol. 21, No. 5, May 1991, pp. 429-441.

CHAPTER 8

Distributed Shared Memory

Distributed Shared Memory: A Survey of Issues and Algorithms

As we slowly approach the physical limits of processor and memory speed, it is becoming more attractive to use multiprocessors to increase computing power. Two kinds of parallel processors have become popular: tightly coupled shared-memory multiprocessors and distributed-memory multiprocessors. A tightly coupled multiprocessor system — consisting of multiple CPUs and a single global physical memory — is more straightforward to program because it is a natural extension of a single-CPU system. However, this type of multiprocessor has a serious bottleneck: Main memory is accessed via a common bus — a serialization point — that limits system size to tens of processors.

Distributed-memory multiprocessors, however, do not suffer from this drawback. These systems consist of a collection of independent computers connected by a high-speed interconnection network. If designers choose the network topology carefully, the system can contain many orders of magnitude more processors than a tightly coupled system. Because all communication between concurrently executing processes must be performed over the network in such a system, until recently the programming model was limited to a message-passing paradigm. However, recent systems have implemented a shared-memory abstraction on top of message-passing distributed-memory systems. The shared-memory abstraction gives these systems the illusion of physically shared memory and allows programmers to use the shared-memory paradigm.

As Figure 1 shows, distributed shared memory (DSM) provides a virtual address space shared among processes on loosely coupled processors. The advantages offered by DSM include ease of programming and portability achieved through the shared-memory programming paradigm, the low cost of distributed-memory machines, and scalability resulting from the absence of hardware bottlenecks.

DSM has been an active area of research since the early 1980s, although its foundations in cache coherence and memory management have been extensively studied for many years. DSM research goals and issues are similar to those of research in

Bill Nitzberg and

Virginia Lo

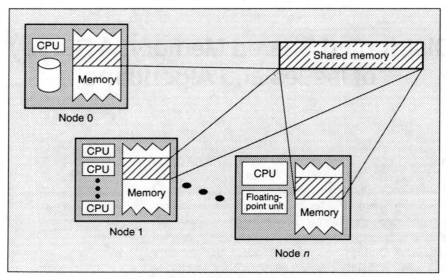

Figure 1. Distributed shared memory.

multiprocessor caches or networked file systems, memories for nonuniform memory access multiprocessors, and management systems for distributed or replicated databases.[1] Because of this similarity, many algorithms and lessons learned in these domains can be transferred to DSM systems and vice versa. However, each of the above systems has unique features (such as communication latency), so each must be considered separately.

The advantages of DSM can be realized with reasonably low runtime overhead. DSM systems have been implemented using three approaches (some systems use more than one approach):

- Hardware implementations that extend traditional caching techniques to scalable architectures,
- Operating system and library implementations that achieve sharing and coherence through virtual-memory-management mechanisms, and
- Compiler implementations where shared accesses are automatically converted into synchronization and coherence primitives.

These systems have been designed on common networks of workstations or minicomputers, special-purpose message-passing machines (such as the Intel iPSC/2), custom hardware, and even heterogeneous systems.

This paper gives an integrated overview of important DSM issues: memory coherence, design choices, and implementation methods. In our presentation, we use examples from the DSM systems listed and briefly described in the box on the next page. Table 1 compares how design issues are handled in a selected subset of the systems.

Design choices

A DSM system designer must make choices regarding structure, granularity, access, coherence semantics, scalability, and heterogeneity. Examination of how designers handled these issues in several real implementations of DSM shows the intricacies of such a system.

DSM systems

This partial listing gives the name of the DSM system, the principal developers of the system, the site and duration of their research, and a brief description of the system. Table 1 gives more information about the systems followed with an asterisk.

Agora (Bisiani and Forin, Carnegie Mellon University, 1987-): A heterogeneous DSM system that allows data structures to be shared across machines. Agora was the first system to support weak consistency.

Amber (Chase, Feeley, and Levy, University of Washington, 1988-): An object-based DSM system in which sharing is performed by migrating processes to data as well as data to processes.

Capnet (Tam and Farber, University of Delaware, 1990-): An extension of DSM to a wide area network.

Choices (Johnston and Campbell, University of Illinois, 1988-): DSM incorporated into a hierarchical object-oriented distributed operating system.

Clouds (Ramachandran and Khalidi, Georgia Institute of Technology, 1987-): An object-oriented distributed operating system where objects can migrate.

Dash* (Lenoski, Laudon, Gharachorloo, Gupta, and Hennessy, Stanford University, 1988-): A hardware implementation of DSM with a directory-based coherence protocol. Dash provides release consistency.

Emerald (Jul, Levy, Hutchinson, and Black, University of Washington, 1986-1988): An object-oriented language and system that indirectly support DSM through object mobility.

Ivy* (Li, Yale University, 1984-1986): An early page-oriented DSM on a network of Apollo workstations.

Linda* (Carriero and Gelernter, Yale University, 1982-): A shared associative object memory with access functions. Linda can be implemented for many languages and machines.

MemNet* (Delp and Farber, University of Delaware, 1986-1988): A hardware implementation of DSM implemented on a 200-megabit-per-second token ring used to broadcast invalidates and read requests.

Mermaid* (Stumm, Zhou, Li, and Wortman, University of Toronto and Princeton University, 1988-1991): A heterogeneous DSM system where the compiler forces shared pages to contain a single data type; type conversion is performed on reference.

Mether (Minnich and Farber, Supercomputing Research Center, Bowie, Maryland, 1990-): A transparent DSM built on SunOS 4.0. Mether allows applications to access an inconsistent state for efficiency.

Mirage* (Fleisch and Popek, University of California, Los Angeles, 1987-1989): A kernel-level implementation of DSM. Mirage reduces thrashing by prohibiting a page from being stolen before a minimum amount of time (Δ) has elapsed.

Munin* (Bennett, Carter, and Zwaenepoel, Rice University, 1989-): An object-based DSM system that investigates type-specific coherence protocols.

Plus* (Bisiani and Ravishankar, Carnegie Mellon University, 1988-): A hardware implementation of DSM. Plus uses a write-update coherence protocol and performs replication only by program request.

Shared Data-Object Model (Bal, Kaashoek, and Tanenbaum, Vrije University, Amsterdam, The Netherlands, 1988-): A DSM implementation on top of the Amoeba distributed operating system.

Shiva* (Li and Schaefer, Princeton University, 1988-): An Ivy-like DSM system for the Intel iPSC/2 hypercube.

Structure and granularity

The structure and granularity of a DSM system are closely related. *Structure* refers to the layout of the shared data in memory. Most DSM systems do not structure memory (it is a linear array of words), but some structure the data as objects, language types, or even an associative memory. *Granularity* refers to the size of the unit of sharing: byte, word, page, or complex data structure.

Ivy,[2] one of the first transparent DSM systems, implemented shared memory as virtual memory. This memory was unstructured and was shared in one-kilobyte pages. In systems implemented using

Table 1. DSM design issues.

System name	Current implementation	Structure and granularity	Coherence semantics	Coherence protocol	Sources of improved performance	Support for synchronization	Heterogeneous support
Dash	Hardware, modified Silicon Graphics Iris 4D/340 workstations, mesh	16 bytes	Release	Write-invalidate	Relaxed coherence, prefetching	Queued locks, atomic incrementation and decrementation	No
Ivy	Software, Apollo workstations, Apollo ring, modified Aegis	1-kilobyte pages	Strict	Write-invalidate	Pointer chain collapse, selective broadcast	Synchronized pages, semaphores, event counts	No
Linda	Software, variety of environments	Tuples	No mutable data	Varied	Hashing		?
MemNet	Hardware, token ring	32 bytes	Strict	Write-invalidate	Vectored interrupt support of control flow		No
Mermaid	Software, Sun workstations DEC Firefly multiprocessors, Mermaid/native operating system	8 kilobytes (Sun), 1 kilobyte (Firefly)	Strict	Write-invalidate		Messages for semaphores and signal/wait	Yes
Mirage	Software, VAX 11/750, Ethernet, Locus distributed operating system, Unix System V interface	512-byte pages	Strict	Write-invalidate	Kernel-level implementation, time window coherence protocol	Unix System V semaphores	No
Munin	Software, Sun workstations, Ethernet, Unix System V kernel and Presto parallel programming environment	Objects	Weak	Type-specific (delayed write update for read-mostly protocol)	Delayed update queue	Synchronized objects	No
Plus	Hardware and software, Motorola 88000, Caltech mesh, Plus kernel	Page for sharing, word for coherence	Processor	Nondemand write-update	Delayed operations	Complex synchronization instructions	No
Shiva	Software, Intel iPSC/2, hypercube, Shiva/native operating system	4-kilobyte pages	Strict	Write-invalidate	Data structure compaction, memory as backing store	Messages for semaphores and signal/wait	No

the virtual-memory hardware of the underlying architecture, it is convenient to choose a multiple of the hardware page size as the unit of sharing. Mirage[3] extended Ivy's single shared-memory space to support a paged segmentation scheme. Users share arbitrary-size regions of memory (segments) while the system maintains the shared space in pages.

Hardware implementations of DSM typically support smaller grain sizes. For example, Dash[4] and MemNet[5] also support unstructured sharing, but the unit of sharing is 16 and 32 bytes, respectively — typical cache line sizes. Plus[6] is somewhat of a hybrid: The unit of replication is a page, while the unit of coherence is a 32-bit word.

Because shared-memory programs provide locality of reference, a process is likely to access a large region of its shared address space in a small amount of time. Therefore, larger "page" sizes reduce paging overhead. However, sharing may also cause contention, and the larger the page size, the greater the likelihood is that more than one process will require access to a page. A smaller page reduces the possibility of *false sharing*, which occurs when two unrelated variables (each used by different processes) are placed in the same page. The page appears shared, even though the original variables were not. Another factor affecting the choice of page size is the need to keep directory information about the pages in the system: The smaller the page size, the larger the directory size must be.

A method of structuring the shared memory is by data type. With this method, shared memory is structured as objects in distributed object-oriented systems, as in the Emerald, Choices, and Clouds[7] systems, or it is structured as variables in the source language, as in the Shared Data-Object Model and Munin systems. Because with these systems the sizes of objects and data types vary greatly, the grain size varies to match the application. However, these systems can still suffer from false sharing when different parts of an object (for example, the top and bottom halves of an array) are accessed by distinct processes.

Another method is to structure the shared memory like a database. Linda,[8] a system that has such a model, orders its shared memory as an associative memory called a *tuple space*. This structure allows the location of data to be separated from its value, but it also requires programmers to use special access functions to interact with the shared-memory space. In most other systems, access to shared data is transparent.

Coherence semantics

For programmers to write correct programs on a shared-memory machine, they must understand how parallel memory updates are propagated throughout the system. The most intuitive semantics for memory coherence is *strict consistency*. (Although *coherence* and *consistency* are used somewhat interchangeably in the literature, we use *coherence* as the general term for the semantics of memory operations and *consistency* to refer to a specific kind of memory coherence.) In a system with strict consistency, a read operation returns the most recently written value. However, "most recently" is an ambiguous concept in a distributed system. For this reason, and to improve performance, some DSM systems provide only a reduced form of memory coherence. For example, Plus provides processor consistency and Dash provides only release consistency. In accordance with the reduced instruction-set computing (RISC) philosophy, both of these systems have mechanisms for forcing coherence, but their use must be explicitly specified by higher level software (a compiler) or perhaps even the programmer.

Relaxed coherence semantics allows more efficient shared access, because it requires less synchronization and less data movement. However, programs that depend on a stronger form of coherence may not perform correctly if executed in a system that supports only a weaker form. Figure 2 gives brief definitions of strict, sequential, processor, weak, and release consistency and illustrates the hierarchical relationship among these types of coherence. Table 1 indicates the coherence semantics supported by some current DSM systems.

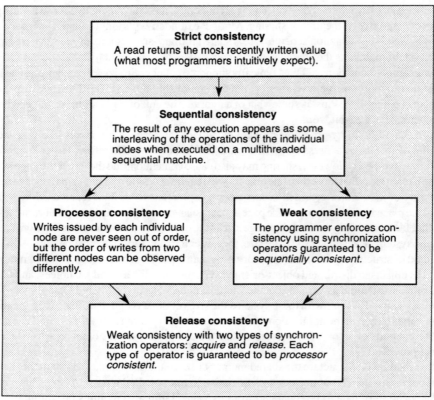

**Figure 2. Intuitive definitions of memory coherence.
(The arrows point from stricter to weaker consistencies.)**

Scalability

A theoretical benefit of DSM systems is that they scale better than tightly coupled shared-memory multiprocessors. The limits of scalability are greatly reduced by two factors: central bottlenecks (such as the bus of a tightly coupled shared-memory multiprocessor) and global common knowledge operations and storage (such as broadcast messages or full directories, whose sizes are proportional to the number of nodes).

Li and Hudak[2] went through several iterations to refine a coherence protocol for Ivy before arriving at their dynamic distributed-manager algorithm, which avoids centralized bottlenecks. However, Ivy and most other DSM systems are currently implemented on top of Ethernet (itself a centralized bottleneck), which can support only about 100 nodes at a time. This limitation is most likely a result of these systems being research tools rather than an indication of any real design flaw. Shiva[9] is an implementation of DSM on an Intel iPSC/2 hypercube, and it should scale nicely. Nodes in the Dash system are connected on two meshes. This implies that the machine should be expandable, but the Dash prototype is currently limited by its use of a full bit vector (one bit per node) to keep track of page replication.

Heterogeneity

At first glance, sharing memory between two machines with different architectures seems almost impossible. The machines may not even use the same representation for basic data types (integers, floating-point numbers, and so on). It is a bit easier if the DSM system is structured as variables or objects in the source language. Then, a DSM compiler can add conversion routines to all accesses to shared memory. In Agora, memory is structured as objects shared among heterogeneous machines.

Mermaid[10] explores another novel approach: Memory is shared in pages, and a page can contain only one type of data. Whenever a page is moved between two architecturally different systems, a conversion routine converts the data in the page to the appropriate format.

Although heterogeneous DSM might allow more machines to participate in a computation, the overhead of conversion seems to outweigh the benefits.

Implementation

A DSM system must automatically transform shared-memory access into interprocess communication. This requires algorithms to locate and access shared data, maintain coherence, and replace data. A DSM system may also have additional schemes to improve performance. Such algorithms directly support DSM. In addition, DSM implementers must tailor operating system algorithms to support process synchronization and memory management. We focus on the algorithms used in Ivy, Dash, Munin, Plus, Mirage, and MemNet, because these systems illustrate most of the important implementation issues. Stumm and Zhou[1] gave a good evolutionary overview of algorithms that support static, migratory, and replicated data.

Data location and access

To share data in a DSM system, a program must be able to find and retrieve the data it needs. If a piece of data does not move around in the system — it resides only in a single static location — then locating it is easy. All processes simply "know" where to obtain any piece of data. Some Linda implementations use hashing on the tuples to distribute data statically. This has the advantages of being simple and fast, but may cause a bottleneck if data are not distributed properly (for example, all shared data end up on a single node).

An alternative is to allow data to migrate freely throughout the system. This allows data to be redistributed dynamically to where it is being used. However, locating data then becomes more difficult. In this case, the simplest way to locate data is to have a centralized server that keeps track of all shared data. The centralized method suffers from two drawbacks: The server serializes location queries, reducing parallelism, and the server may become heavily loaded and slow the entire system.

Instead of using a centralized server, a system can broadcast requests for data. Unfortunately, broadcasting does not scale well. All nodes — not just the nodes containing the data — must process a broadcast request. The network latency of a broadcast may also require accesses to take a long time to complete.

To avoid broadcasts and distribute the load more evenly, several systems use an owner-based distributed scheme. This scheme is independent of data replication but is seen mostly in systems that support both data migration and replication. Each piece of data has an associated owner — a node with the primary copy of the data. The owners change as the data migrate through the system. When another node needs a copy of the data, it sends a request to the owner. If the owner still has the data, it returns the data. If the owner has given the data to some other node, it forwards the request to the new owner.

The drawback with this scheme is that a request may be forwarded many times before reaching the current owner. In some cases, this is more wasteful than broadcasting. In Ivy, all nodes involved in forwarding a request (including the requester) are given the identity of the current owner. This collapsing of pointer chains helps reduce the forwarding overhead and delay.

When it replicates data, a DSM system must keep track of the replicated copies. Dash uses a distributed directory-based scheme, implemented in hardware. The Dash directory for a given cluster (node) keeps track of the physical blocks in that cluster. Each block is represented by a directory entry that specifies whether the block is *unshared-remote* (local copy only), *shared-remote*, or *shared-dirty*. If the block is shared-remote, the directory entry also indicates the location of replicated copies of the block. If the block is shared dirty, the directory entry indicates the location of the single dirty copy. Only the special node known as the *home cluster* possesses the directory block entry. A node accesses nonlocal data for reading by sending a message to the home cluster.

Ivy's dynamic distributed scheme also supports replicated data. A *ptable* on each node contains for each page an entry that indicates the probable location for the referenced page. As described above, a node locates data by following the chain of probable owners. The copy-list scheme implemented by Plus uses a distributed linked list to keep track of replicated data. Memory references are mapped to the physically closest copy by the page map table.

Coherence protocol

All DSM systems provide some form of memory coherence. If the shared data are not replicated, then enforcing memory coherence is trivial. The underlying network automatically serializes requests in the order in which they occur. A node handling shared data can merely perform each request as it is received. This method will ensure strict memory consistency — the strongest form of coherence. Unfortunately, serializing data access creates a bottleneck and makes impossible a major advantage of DSM: parallelism.

To increase parallelism, virtually all DSM systems replicate data. Thus, for example, multiple reads can be performed in parallel. However, replication complicates the coherence protocol. Two types of protocols — write-invalidate and write-update protocols — handle replication. In a write-invalidate protocol, there can be many copies of a read-only piece of data but only one copy of a writable piece of data. The protocol is called *write-invalidate* because it *invalidates* all copies of a piece of data except one before a write can proceed. In a write-update scheme, however, a write updates all copies of a piece of data.

Most DSM systems have write-invalidate coherence protocols. All the protocols for these systems are similar. Each piece of data has a status tag that indicates whether it is valid, whether it is shared, and whether it is read-only or writable. For a read, if the piece of data is valid, it is returned immediately. If it is not valid, a read request is sent to the location of a valid copy, and a copy of the piece of data is returned. If it was writable on another node, this read request will cause it to become read-only. The copy remains valid until an invalidate request is received.

For a write, if the piece of data is valid and writable, the request is satisfied immediately. If the piece of data is not writable, the directory controller sends out an invalidate request, along with a request for a copy of the piece of data if the local copy is not valid. When the invalidate completes, the piece of data is valid locally and writable, and the original write request may complete.

Figure 3 illustrates the Dash directory-based coherence protocol. The sequence of events and messages shown in Figure 3(a) occurs when the block to be written is in the shared-remote state (multiple read-only copies on nodes A and B) just before the write. Figure 3(b) shows the events and messages that occur when the block to be written is in shared-dirty state (single dirty copy on node C) just before the write. In both cases, the initiator of the write sends a request to the home cluster, which uses the information in the directory to locate and transfer the data and to invalidate copies. Lenoski et al.[4] gave further details about the Dash coherence protocol and the methods they used to fine-tune the protocol for high performance.

Li and Hudak[2] showed that the write-invalidate protocol performs well for a variety of applications. In fact, they showed superlinear speedups for a linear-equation solver and a three-dimensional partial-differential-equation solver, resulting from the increased overall physical

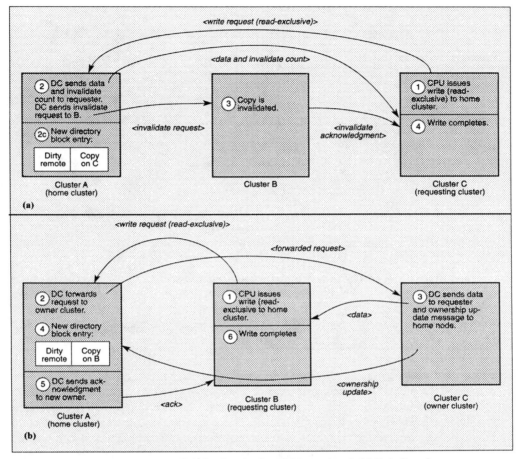

Figure 3. The simplified Dash write-invalidate protocol. (a) Data item is shared-remote. (b) Data item is dirty-remote (after events depicted in [a]). (DC = directory controller.)

memory and cache sizes. Li and Hudak rejected use of a write-update protocol at the onset with the reasoning that network latency would make it inefficient.

Subsequent research indicated that in the appropriate hardware environment, write-update protocols can be implemented efficiently. For example, Plus is a hardware implementation of DSM that uses a write-update protocol. Figure 4 traces the Plus write-update protocol, which begins all updates with the block's master node and then proceeds down the copy-list chain. The write operation is completed when the last node in the chain sends an acknowledgment message to the originator of the write request.

Munin[11] uses *type-specific memory coherence*, coherence protocols tailored for different types of data. For example, Munin uses a write-update protocol to keep coherent a piece of data that is read much more frequently than it is written (read-mostly data). Because an invalidation message is about the same size as an update message, an update costs no more than an invalidate. However, the overhead of making multiple read-only copies of the data item after each invalidate is avoided. An eager paging strategy supports the Munin producer-consumer memory type. A piece of data, once written by the producer process, is transferred to the consumer process, where it remains available

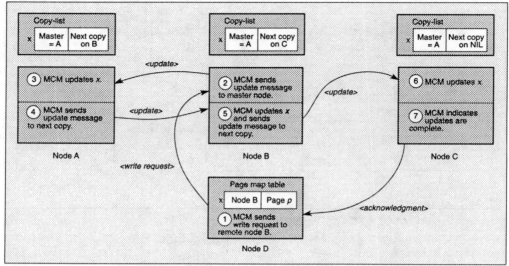

Figure 4. The Plus write-update protocol.
(MCM = memory coherence manager.)

until the consumer process is ready to use it. This reduces overhead, since the consumer does not request data already available in the *buffer*.

Replacement strategy

In systems that allow data to migrate around the system, two problems arise when the available space for "caching" shared data fills up: Which piece of data should be replaced to free space and where should it go? In choosing the data item to be replaced, a DSM system works almost like the caching system of a shared-memory multiprocessor. However, unlike most caching systems, which use a simple least recently used or random-replacement strategy, most DSM systems differentiate the status of data items and prioritize them. For example, priority is given to shared items over exclusively owned items, because the latter have to be transferred over the network. Simply deleting a read-only shared copy of a data item is possible because no data item is lost. Shiva prioritizes pages on the basis of a linear combination of type (read-only, owned read-only, and writable) and least recently used statistics.

Once a piece of data is to be replaced, the system must make sure it is not lost. In the caching system of a multiprocessor, the item would simply be placed in main memory. Some DSM systems, such as MemNet, use an equivalent scheme. The system transfers the data item to a "home node" that has a statically allocated space (perhaps on disk) to store a copy of an item when it is not needed elsewhere in the system. This method is simple to implement, but it wastes a lot of memory. An improvement is to have the node that wants to delete the item simply page it out onto disk. Although this does not waste any memory space, it is time-consuming. Because it may be faster to transfer something over the network than to transfer it to disk, a better solution (used in Shiva) is to keep track of free memory in the system and to simply page the item out to a node with space available to it.

Thrashing

DSM systems are particularly prone to thrashing. For example, if two nodes compete for write access to a single data item, it may be transferred back and forth at such a high rate that no real work can get done (a Ping-Pong effect). Two systems, Munin and Mirage, attack this problem directly.

Munin allows programmers to associate types with shared data: write-once, write-many, producer-consumer, private, migratory, result, read-mostly, synchronization, and general read/write. Shared data of different types get different coherence protocols. To avoid thrashing with two competing writers, a programmer could specify the type as write-many and the system would use a delayed-write policy. (Munin does not guarantee strict consistency of memory in this case.)

Tailoring the coherence algorithm to the shared-data usage patterns can greatly reduce thrashing. However, Munin requires programmers to specify the type of shared data. Programmers are notoriously bad at predicting the behavior of their programs, so this method may not be any better than choosing a particular protocol. In addition, because the type remains static once specified, Munin cannot dynamically adjust to an application's changing behavior.

Mirage[3] uses another method to reduce thrashing. It specifically examines the case when many nodes compete for access to the same page. To stop the Ping-Pong effect, Mirage adds a dynamically tunable parameter to the coherence protocol. This parameter determines the minimum amount of time (Δ) a page will be available at a node. For example, if a node performed a write to a shared page, the page would be writable on that node for Δ time. This solves the problem of having a page stolen away after only a single request on a node can be satisfied. Because Δ is tuned dynamically on the basis of access patterns, a process can complete a write run (or read run) before losing access to the page. Thus, Δ is akin to a time slice in a multitasking operating system, except that in Mirage, it is dynamically adjusted to meet an application's specific needs.

Related algorithms

To support a DSM system, synchronization operations and memory management must be specially tuned. Semaphores, for example, are typically implemented on shared-memory systems by using spin locks. In a DSM system, a spin lock can easily cause thrashing, because multiple nodes may heavily access shared data. For better performance, some systems provide specialized synchronization primitives along with DSM. Clouds provides semaphore operations by grouping semaphores into centrally managed segments. Munin supports the synchronization memory type with distributed locks. Plus supplies a variety of synchronization instructions and supports delayed execution, in which the synchronization can be initiated and later tested for successful completion. Dubois, Scheurich, and Briggs[12] discussed the relationship between coherence and synchronization.

Memory management can be restructured for DSM. A typical memory-allocation scheme (as in the C library *malloc()*) allocates memory out of a common pool, which is searched each time a request is made. A linear search of all shared memory can be expensive. A better approach is to partition available memory into private buffers on each node and allocate memory from the global buffer space only when the private buffer is empty.

Conclusions

Research has shown distributed shared-memory systems to be viable. The systems described in this paper demonstrate that DSM can be implemented in a variety of hardware and software environments: commercial workstations with native operating systems software, innovative customized hardware, and even heterogeneous systems. Many of the design choices and algorithms needed to implement DSM are well understood and integrated with related areas of computer science.

The performance of DSM is greatly affected by memory-access patterns and replication of shared data. Hardware implementations have yielded enormous reductions in communication latency and the advantages of a smaller unit of sharing. However, the performance results to date are preliminary. Most systems are experimental or are prototypes consisting of only a few nodes. In addition, because of the dearth of test programs, most studies are based on a small group of applications or on a synthetic work load. Nevertheless, research has proved that DSM effectively supports parallel processing, and it promises to be a fruitful and exciting area of research for the coming decade.

Acknowledgments

This work was supported in part by National Science Foundation (NSF) grant CCR-8808532, a Tektronix research fellowship, and the NSF Research Experiences for Undergraduates program.

We appreciate the comments from the anonymous referees and thank the authors who verified information about their systems. Thanks also to Kurt Windisch for helping prepare this manuscript.

References

1. M. Stumm and S. Zhou, "Algorithms Implementing Distributed Shared Memory," *Computer*, Vol. 23, No. 5, May 1990, pp. 54-64.

2. K. Li and P. Hudak, "Memory Coherence in Shared Virtual Memory Systems," *ACM Trans. Computer Systems*, Vol. 7, No. 4, Nov. 1989, pp. 321-359.

3. B. Fleisch and G. Popek, "Mirage: A Coherent Distributed Shared Memory Design," *Proc. 14th ACM Symp. Operating System Principles*, ACM Press, New York, N.Y., 1989, pp. 211-223.

4. D. Lenoski et al., "The Directory-Based Cache Coherence Protocol for the Dash Multiprocessor," *Proc. 17th Int'l Symp. Computer Architecture*, IEEE Computer Soc. Press, Los Alamitos, Calif., 1990, pp. 148-159.

5. G. Delp, *The Architecture and Implementation of MemNet: A High-Speed Shared Memory Computer Communication Network*, doctoral dissertation, Univ. of Delaware, Newark, Del., 1988.

6. R. Bisiani and M. Ravishankar, "Plus: A Distributed Shared-Memory System," *Proc. 17th Int'l Symp. Computer Architecture*, IEEE Computer Soc. Press, Los Alamitos, Calif., 1990, pp. 115-124.

7. U. Ramachandran and M.Y.A. Khalidi, "An Implementation of Distributed Shared Memory," *Proc. First Workshop Experiences with Building Distributed and Multiprocessor Systems*, Usenix Assoc., Berkeley, Calif., 1989, pp. 21-38.

8. N. Carriero and D. Gelernter, *How to Write Parallel Programs: A First Course*, MIT Press, Cambridge, Mass., 1990.

9. K. Li and R. Schaefer, "A Hypercube Shared Virtual Memory System," *Proc. Int'l Conf. Parallel Processing*, Pennsylvania State Univ. Press, University Park, Pa., 1989, pp. 125-132.

10. S. Zhou et al., "Heterogeneous Distributed Shared Memory," *IEEE Trans. Parallel and Distributed Systems*, Vol. 3, No. 5, Sept. 1992, pp. 540-554.

11. J. Bennett, J. Carter, and W. Zwaenepoel, "Munin: Distributed Shared Memory Based on Type-Specific Memory Coherence," *Proc. 1990 Conf. Principles and Practice Parallel Programming*, ACM Press, New York, N.Y., 1990, pp. 168-176.

12. M. Dubois, C. Scheurich, and F.A. Briggs, "Synchronization, Coherence, and Event Ordering in Multiprocessors," *Computer*, Vol. 21, No. 2, Feb. 1988, pp. 9-21.

Using Broadcasting to Implement Distributed Shared Memory Efficiently

As computers have continued to get cheaper, interest has increased in harnessing together multiple CPUs to build large, powerful parallel systems that are high in performance and low in cost. The two major design approaches taken so far are multiprocessors and multicomputers. NUMA (nonuniform memory access) architectures are an attempt at combining the two types of parallel machines, each of which has its strengths and weaknesses. This hybrid form uses an unusual software organization on conventional hardware to achieve a system that is easy to build and easy to program. We have built a prototype system that is similar to NUMA in some important respects. The central concept in our method is to efficiently do reliable broadcasting on unreliable hardware. Here, we describe some applications we have written for our system, give measurements of its performance, look at a paradigm for programming using this method, and discuss a parallel programming language that we have designed and implemented to allow programmers to use our system conveniently.

Much confusion exists in the literature about the terms *distributed system* and *parallel system*. For our purposes, a distributed system is one in which independent jobs execute on independent CPUs — on behalf of independent users — but share some resources, such as a common file server. A typical example of a distributed system is a collection of (possibly heterogeneous) engineering workstations connected by a fast local area network (LAN) and sharing a file server. In contrast, a parallel system is one in which a user attempts to utilize multiple (usually identical) CPUs in order to speed up the execution of a single program. The CPUs may be in a single rack and connected by a high-speed backplane bus, they may be distributed around a building and connected by a fast LAN, or they may be used in some other topology. What is important is that a large number of CPUs cooperate to solve a single problem. Thus, the difference between the two types of systems is really a question of how the software — not the hardware — is organized. Here, we concentrate on parallel systems, using as a metric how much speedup can be achieved on a single problem by using *n* identical processors rather than only one processor.

Andrew S. Tanenbaum,

M. Frans Kaashoek, and

Henri E. Bal

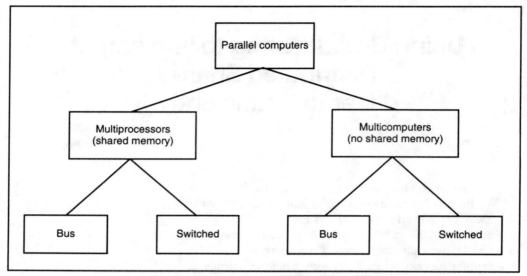

Figure 1. A taxonomy of parallel computers.

Multiprocessors versus multicomputers

Parallel computers can be divided into two categories: *multiprocessors*, which contain physical shared memory, and *multicomputers,* which do not. A simple taxonomy is given in Figure 1. In multiprocessors, there is a single, global, shared address space visible to all processors. Any processor can read or write any word in the address space by simply moving data from or to a memory address. In multicomputers, the processors need some other way to communicate—for example, by message passing.

Multiprocessors

The key property required of any multiprocessor is *memory coherence*. When any processor writes a value *v* to memory address *m*, any other processor that subsequently reads the word at memory address *m*, no matter how quickly after the write, will get the value *v* just written.

Multiprocessor hardware. There are two basic methods of building a multiprocessor, both of them expensive. In the first method, all the processors are put on a single bus, along with a memory module. To read or write a word of data, a processor makes a normal memory request over the bus. Because there is only one memory module and there are no copies of memory words anywhere else, the memory is always *coherent*. The problem with this method is that the bus will be completely saturated with as few as four to eight processors. To get around this problem, each processor is normally given a cache memory, as shown in Figure 2. However, the caches introduce a new problem: If Processors 1 and 2 both read the contents of memory address *m* into their caches, and one of them modifies *m*, then when the other processor next reads that address, it will get a *stale* value. Memory is then not coherent. Because *incoherent* memory is hard for programmers to deal with, it is unacceptable.

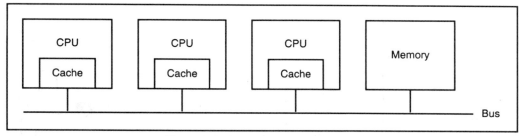

Figure 2. A single-bus multiprocessor.

The stale-data problem can be solved in many ways. One way is to have all writes go through the cache to update the external memory. Another is to have each cache constantly *snoop* on the bus (that is, monitor it) and take some appropriate action — such as invalidating or updating its cache entry — whenever another processor tries to write a word for which it has a local copy. Nevertheless, caching only delays the problem of bus saturation. Instead of saturating at four to eight processors, a well-designed single-bus system might saturate at 32 to 64 processors. Building a single-bus system with appreciably more than 64 processors is not feasible with current bus technology.

In the second method, a multiprocessor is built using some kind of switching network, such as the *crossbar switch*, which is shown in Figure 3(a). Each of the n processors can potentially be connected to any one of the n memory banks via a matrix of little electronic switches. When switch ij is closed (by hardware), processor i is connected to memory bank j and can read or write data there. Since several switches may be closed simultaneously, multiple reads and writes can occur at the same time between disjoint processor-memory combinations. The problem with the crossbar switch is that connecting n processors to n memory banks requires n^2 switches. As n becomes large — say 1024 processors and 1024 memories — the switch becomes prohibitively expensive and unmanageable.

An alternative switching scheme for multiprocessors is the omega network shown in Figure 3(b). In this figure, the CPUs (on the left) and the memories (on the right) are connected by the omega network, a sophisticated packet-switching network. To read a word of memory, a CPU sends a request packet to the appropriate memory via the switching network, which sends the reply back the other way. Many variations of this basic design have been proposed, but they all have the problem that for a system with n processors and n memories, the number of switching stages needed is on the order of $\log_2 n$ and the number of switching elements is $n \log_2 n$. For example, consider a system of 1024 reduced instruction-set computer (RISC) processors running at 50 megahertz (MHz). With $n = 1024$, 10 switches must be traversed from the CPU to the memory and 10 more on the way back. If this is to occur in one cycle (20 nanoseconds [ns]), each switching step must take no longer than one ns, and 10,240 such switches are required. A machine with such a large number of very high speed packet switches is clearly going to be expensive and difficult to build and maintain, even if the designers are able to make many optimizations.

Multiprocessor software. In contrast to building multiprocessor hardware — which, for large systems, is complicated, difficult, and expensive—building multiprocessor software is straightforward. Since all processes run within a single, shared address space, they can easily share data structures and variables. When one process updates a variable and another one reads it immediately afterward, the reader always gets the value just stored; that is, memory is coherent.

To avoid chaos, cooperating processes must synchronize their activities. For example, while one process is updating a linked list, it is essential that no other process even attempt to read the list, let alone modify it. Many well-known techniques — including spin locks, semaphores, and monitors —

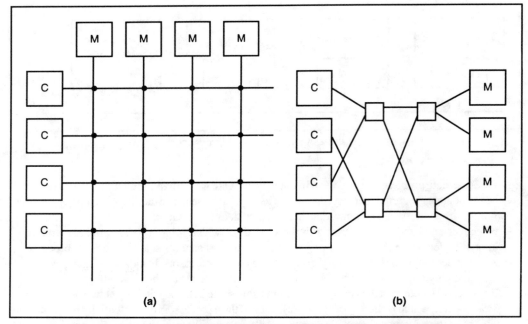

Figure 3. (a) Crossbar switch. (b) Omega network. (C = CPU and M = memory.)

can provide the necessary synchronization. (These techniques are discussed in any standard textbook on operating systems.) The advantages of multiprocessor software are that sharing is easy and cheap and uses a well-understood methodology that has been around for years.

Multicomputers

In contrast to multiprocessors, which — by definition — share primary memory, *multicomputers* do not. Each CPU in a multicomputer has its own, private memory, which it alone can read and write. This difference leads to a significantly different architecture, both in hardware and in software.

Multicomputer hardware. Just as there are bus and switched multiprocessors, there are bus and switched multicomputers. Figure 4 shows a simple bus-based multicomputer. Note that each CPU has its own local memory, which is not accessible by remote CPUs. Since there is no shared memory in this system, communication occurs via message passing between CPUs. The "bus" in this example can either be a LAN or a high-speed backplane; conceptually, these two are the same, differing only in their performance. Since each CPU-memory pair is essentially independent of all the others, building very large multicomputer systems — certainly much larger than multiprocessor systems — is straightforward.

Switched multicomputers do not have a single bus over which all traffic goes. Instead, they have a collection of point-to-point connections. Figure 5 shows a grid and a hypercube, two examples of the many designs that have been proposed and built. A grid is easy to understand and easy to lay out on a printed circuit board or chip. This architecture is best suited to problems that are two-dimensional in nature, such as graph theory and vision. A hypercube is an *n*-dimensional cube. One can imagine a four-dimensional hypercube as a pair of ordinary cubes with the corresponding vertices connected, as shown in Figure 5(b). (In the figure, the lower left nodes at the rear have been omitted for clarity.) Similarly, a five-dimensional hypercube can be represented as two copies of Figure 5(b) with the

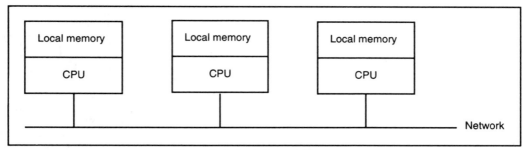

Figure 4. A single-bus multicomputer.

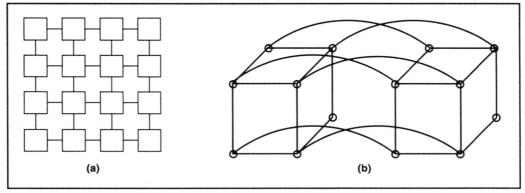

Figure 5. Multicomputers. (a) Grid. (b) Hypercube.

corresponding vertices connected, and so on. In general, an n-dimensional hypercube has 2^n vertices, each holding one CPU. Each CPU has a fan-out of n, so the interconnection complexity grows logarithmically with the number of CPUs.

Multicomputer software. Since by definition multicomputers do not contain shared memory, they must communicate by message passing. Various software paradigms have been devised to express message passing. The simplest one is to have two operating system primitives: *Send* and *Receive*. The *Send* primitive typically has three parameters: the destination address, a pointer to the data buffer, and the number of bytes to be sent. In its simplest form, the *Receive* primitive might just provide a buffer, accepting messages from any sender.

Many variations on this theme exist. For one, the primitives can be *blocking* (synchronous) or *nonblocking* (asynchronous). With a blocking *Send*, the sending process is suspended after the *Send* until the message has been actually accepted and acknowledged. With a nonblocking *Send*, the sender may continue immediately. The problem with allowing the sender to continue is that the sender may be in a loop, with messages being sent much faster than the underlying communication hardware can deliver them. The result may be lost messages. This problem may be alleviated somewhat by senders addressing messages not to processes but to *mailboxes*. A mailbox is a special kind of buffer that can hold multiple messages. However, overflow is still a possibility.

A fundamental problem with message passing is that conceptually it is really input/output. Many people believe that input/output should not be the central abstraction of a modern programming language. Birrell and Nelson [6] proposed a scheme called *remote procedure call (RPC)*, shown in Figure 6, to hide the bare input/output. The idea is to hide the message passing and make the

---

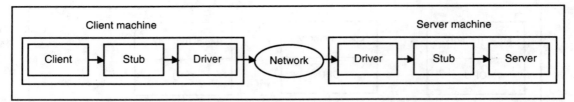

Figure 6. Remote procedure call (RPC) from a client to a server. The reply follows the same path in the reverse direction.

communication look like an ordinary procedure call. The sender, called the *client*, calls a *stub routine* on its own machine that builds a message containing the name of the procedure to be called and all the parameters. The stub then passes this message to the driver for transmission over the network. When the message arrives, the remote driver gives it to a stub, which unpacks the message and makes an ordinary procedure call to the *server*. The reply from server to client follows the reverse path. Because the client and server each think of the other as an ordinary local procedure, this scheme hides the message passing to some extent; however, making this scheme entirely transparent would be difficult. For example, passing pointers as parameters is difficult and passing arrays is costly. Thus, the programmer usually must be aware that the semantics of local and remote procedure calls are different.

In conclusion, the characteristics of multiprocessors and multicomputers differ significantly. Multiprocessors are hard to build but easy to program. In contrast, multicomputers are easy to build but hard to program. People want a system that is easy to build (that is, with no shared memory) and easy to program (that is, with shared memory). Reconciling these two contradictory demands is the subject of the rest of this paper.

NUMA machines

In developing intermediate designs, various researchers have tried to capture the desirable properties of both multiprocessor and multicomputer architectures. In most of these designs, an attempt was made to simulate shared memory on multicomputers. In all of the designs, a process executing on any machine can access data from its own memory without any delay. However, access to data located on another machine entails considerable delay and overhead, because a request message must be sent there and a reply must be received. In a system with *distributed shared memory*, a single address space is shared among otherwise disjoint machines.

Computers in which references to some memory addresses are cheap (that is, local) and others are expensive (that is, remote) have become known as *NUMA machines*. Three of the more interesting types of NUMA machines—*word-oriented*, *page-oriented*, and *object-oriented* machines —differ primarily in the granularity of access and the mechanism by which remote references are handled.

(1)   Word-oriented NUMA machines. One of the earliest word-oriented NUMA machines was Cm*, built at Carnegie Mellon University, Pittsburgh, Pennsylvania. Cm* consisted of a collection of LSI-11 minicomputers [16]. Each LSI-11 had a microprogrammed memory management unit (MMU) and a local memory. The MMU microcode could be downloaded when execution began, allowing part of the operating system to be run there. The LSI-11s were grouped together into clusters, the machines in each cluster were connected by an intracluster bus, and the clusters were connected by intercluster buses.

When an LSI-11 referenced its own local memory, the MMU simply read or wrote the required word directly. However, when an LSI-11 referenced a word in a remote memory, the microcode in the MMU built a request packet specifying which memory was being addressed, which word was needed, the opcode (*Read* or *Write*), and the value to be written for *Writes*. The packet was then sent out over the buses to the destination MMU via a store-and-forward network. At the destination, it was accepted and processed, and a reply containing the requested word (for *Read*) or an acknowledgment (for *Write*) was generated. The more remote the memory, the longer the operation was, with the worst case taking about 10 times as long as the best case. It was possible for a program to run out of remote memory entirely, with a performance penalty of a factor of about 10. There was no caching and no automatic data movement. It was up to the programmer to place code and data appropriately for optimal performance. Nevertheless, this system appeared — to the programmer — to have a single, shared address space accessible to all processors, even though — in actuality — it was implemented by an underlying packet-switching network.

(2)   Page-oriented NUMA machines. Cm* represents one extreme — sending requests for individual words from MMU to MMU in "hardware" (actually MMU microcode) over a set of tightly coupled backplane buses. At the other extreme are systems that implement virtual shared memory on a collection of workstations on a LAN. As in Cm*, users are presented with a single, shared virtual address space, but the implementation is quite different.

In its simplest form, the virtual memory in page-oriented NUMA machines is divided up into fixed-size pages, with each page residing on exactly one processor. When a processor references a local page, the reference is done by the hardware in the usual way. However, when a remote page is referenced, a page fault occurs, and a trap to the operating system occurs. The operating system fetches the page, just as in a traditional virtual-memory system, only now the page is fetched from another processor (which loses the page) instead of from the disk.

As in Cm*, pages are fetched by request and reply messages, only here these messages are generated and processed by the operating system instead of by the MMU microcode. Since the overhead is so much higher, an entire page is transferred each time, in the hope that subsequent references will be to the same page. If two processors are actively using the same page at the same time, the page will thrash back and forth wildly, degrading performance.

Li and Hudak [14] proposed, implemented, and analyzed a significant improvement to the basic algorithm. In their design, thrashing is reduced by permitting read-only pages to be replicated on all the machines that need them. When a read-only page is referenced, a copy is made instead of the page being sent, so the original owner may continue using it. Other pages may also be shared, but when a page is written, other copies of it are invalidated.

Li and Hudak [14] presented several algorithms for locating pages. In the simplest, a centralized manager keeps track of the location of all pages. All page requests are sent to the manager, which then forwards them to the processor holding the page. A variation of this scheme is to have multiple managers, with the leftmost n bits of the page number telling which manager is responsible for the page. This approach spreads the load over multiple managers. Even more decentralized page-location schemes are possible, including the use of hashing or broadcasting.

It is worth pointing out that the basic page-oriented strategy could (almost) have been used with Cm*. For example, if the MMUs noticed that a particular page were being heavily referenced by a single remote processor and not at all referenced by its own processor, the MMUs could have decided to ship the whole page to the place it was being used instead of constantly making expensive remote references. This approach was not taken because the message-routing algorithm used the page number to locate the page.

To reduce thrashing, NUMA machines have been designed so that a page may be transported a maximum of only k times. After that, the page is wired down, and all remote references to it are done as in Cm*. Alternatively, one can have a rule saying that once moved, a page may not be moved again for a certain time interval.

(3)   Object-oriented NUMA machines. An inherent problem with page-oriented NUMA

systems is that the amount of data transferred on each fault is fixed at exactly one page. Usually this is too much, sometimes it is too little, but hardly ever is it exactly right. The next step in the evolution of NUMA machines was an object-based system, in which the shared memory contains well-defined objects, each one with certain operations defined on it. When a process invokes an operation on a local object, it is executed directly, but when it invokes an operation on a remote object, the object is shipped to the invoker. Alternatively, the operation name and parameters can be sent to the object, with the operation being carried out on the remote processor and the result being sent back. In both of these schemes, no unnecessary data are moved (unlike in the page-oriented NUMA machines, which move one K or four K or eight K to fetch even a single byte).

It should be noted that our definition of a NUMA machine is somewhat broader than that some other writers have used. We regard as a NUMA machine any machine that presents the programmer with the illusion of shared memory but implements it by sending messages across a network to fetch chunks of data. Whether the code that implements this is in the MMU — as in Cm* — or in the operating system — as in the work of Li and Hudak — is simply an implementation decision. Similarly, whether the unit fetched is a word, a page, or an object is also an implementation decision. The essential commonality of NUMA machines is that when a remote read is made, the system sees an exception, sends a message to the remote memory, gets back a reply containing the data needed, and restarts the instruction. In this view, Cm* and the model of Li and Hudak simply differ in where the exception handler runs and the block size returned on a fault.

Weakened semantics

A completely different approach to implementing distributed shared memory is to weaken the semantics, giving up the demand for absolute coherence. For example, suppose three processes — Processes A, B, and C—all simultaneously update a word, followed by Process D reading it. If total coherence is required, the word will probably have to be sent first to A, then to B, then to C, and finally to D to carry out the three writes and the read. However, from D's point of view, it has no way of knowing which of the three writers went last (and thus whose value did not get overwritten). In the Munin system, Bennett, Carter, and Zwaenepoel [4] proposed that returning any one of the values written should be legal. The next step is to delay remote writes until a read is done that might observe the values written. It may even be possible to perform an optimization and avoid some of the writes altogether. This strategy was implemented in the Munin system, which uses a form of strong typing on shared objects to make it easier to perform these and other optimizations.

Other systems go even farther in this direction. For example, Mether [15] maintains a primary copy of each page and possibly one or more secondary copies. The primary copy is writable; the secondary copies are read-only. If a write is done to the primary copy, the secondary copies become obsolete and stale data are returned by reads to them. Applications simply have to accept this. In Mether, three ways are provided for getting resynchronized: The owner of a secondary copy can ask for an up-to-date copy; the owner of the primary copy can issue an up-to-date copy to the readers; or the owner of a secondary copy can just discard it, getting a fresh copy on the next read.

A new model

Although weakening the semantics of the shared memory may improve the performance, it has the disadvantage of ruining the ease of programming that the shared-memory model was designed to provide. In effect, it offers only the syntax of shared variables, while forcing the programmer to deal with semantics even less convenient than message passing.

We have devised an alternative model that preserves the coherency of (object-based) shared

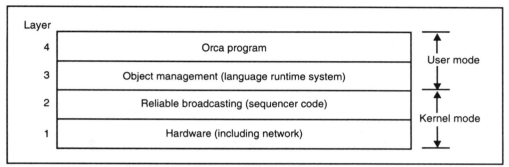

Figure 7. The layer structure of reliable broadcasting.

memory yet has been implemented efficiently. Our model, which we call *reliable broadcasting*, consists of four layers, as shown in Figure 7.

Layer 1 is the bare CPU and networking hardware. Our scheme is most efficient on networks that support *broadcasting* (sending a message to all machines) or *multicasting* (sending a message to a selected group of machines) in hardware, but supporting broadcasting or multicasting is not required. Ethernet, earth satellites, and cellular radio are examples of networks having broadcasting or multicasting. (For simplicity, we henceforth use the term *broadcasting* to mean either one.) Broadcasting is assumed to be *unreliable*; that is, it is possible for messages to be lost.

Layer 2 is the software necessary to turn the unreliable broadcasting offered by Layer 1 into reliable broadcasting. It is normally part of the operating system kernel. As a simple example of a possible (but highly inefficient) protocol, reliably broadcasting a message to n machines can be done by having the kernel send each machine, in turn, a point-to-point message and then wait for an acknowledgment. This protocol takes $2n$ messages per reliable broadcast. Below, we describe a different protocol that takes (on the average) a fraction more than two messages per reliable broadcast, instead of $2n$. The main issue to understand is that when Layer 3 hands a message to Layer 2 and asks for it to be reliably broadcast, Layer 3 does not have to worry about how this is implemented or what happens if the hardware loses a message. All of this is taken care of by Layer 2.

In addition to its inefficiency, the protocol that sends a point-to-point message to every machine has a more serious problem. When two machines — Machines A and B — simultaneously do a broadcast, the results can be interleaved. That is, depending on network topology, lost messages, and so on, some machines may get the broadcast from Machine A before that from Machine B and other machines may receive the broadcasts in the reverse order. This property makes programming difficult. In the protocol that we describe below, this cannot happen. Either all the machines get Machine A's broadcast and then B's broadcast or all the machines get B's broadcast and then A's broadcast. Broadcasts are globally ordered, and it is guaranteed that all user processes get them in the same order.

Layer 3 is the language runtime system, which is usually a set of library procedures compiled into the application program. Conceptually, programmers can have variables and objects can be *Private* or *Shared*. *Private* objects are not visible on other machines, so they can be accessed by direct memory reads and writes. *Shared* objects are replicated on all machines. Reads to them are local, the same as reads to *Private* objects. Writes are done by reliable broadcasting. Objects are entirely passive; they contain only data, not processes.

Layer 4 provides language support. Although it is possible for programmers to use the distributed shared memory by making calls directly on Layer 3, having language support is much more convenient. We designed a language, called *Orca* [1], for parallel programming using distributed shared objects and implemented a compiler for it. In Orca, programmers can declare shared objects,

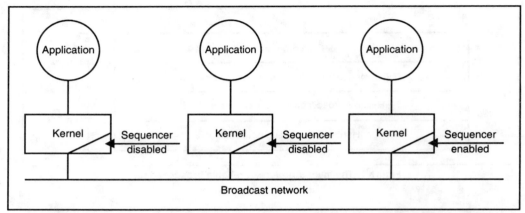

Figure 8. System structure. Each kernel is capable of becoming the sequencer; however, at any instant, only one of them functions as sequencer.

with each shared object containing a data structure for the object and a set of procedures that operate on it. Operations on shared objects are indivisible and serializable. In other words, when multiple processes update the same object simultaneously, the final result is as if the updates had been performed sequentially, in some unspecified order, with each update having been completed before the next one began.

Reliable broadcasting

The heart of our proposal is the efficient implementation of indivisible, reliable broadcasting (Layer 2). Once that has been achieved, the rest is relatively straightforward. In this section, we describe the mechanism used to achieve reliable broadcasting (in software) over an unreliable network. (Kaashoek et al. [12] described this mechanism more comprehensively.)

The hardware/software configuration required for reliable broadcasting is shown in Figure 8. The circles represent the application programs and their runtime systems (Layers 3 and 4). The kernel represents Layer 2. The network is Layer 1. The hardware of all the machines is identical, and they all run exactly the same kernel and application software. However, when the application starts up, one of the machines is elected as sequencer, like a committee electing a chairman [13]. If the sequencer machine subsequently crashes, the remaining members elect a new one. (Many election algorithms are known. For example, the one used in the IEEE 802.4 Token Bus standard is to pick the machine with the highest network address. We do not discuss this point further here.)

The actual sequence of events involved in achieving reliable broadcasting can be summarized as follows:

- The user traps to the kernel, passing it the message.
- The kernel accepts the message and blocks the user.
- The kernel sends the message to the sequencer using an ordinary point-to-point message.
- When the sequencer gets the message, it allocates the next available sequence number, puts the sequencer number in a header field reserved for it, and broadcasts the message (and sequence number).
- When the sending kernel sees the broadcast message, it unblocks the calling process to let it continue execution.

Let us now consider these events in more detail. When an application process executes a *Broadcast* primitive, a trap to its kernel occurs. The kernel then blocks the caller and builds a message containing a kernel-supplied header and the application-supplied data. The header contains the message type (*Request for Broadcast*, in this case), a unique message identifier (used to detect duplicates), the number of the last broadcast received by the kernel (a kind of piggybacked acknowledgment), and some other information. The kernel sends the message to the sequencer using a normal point-to-point message and simultaneously starts a timer. If the broadcast comes back before the timer runs out (as happens in practice well over 99 percent of the time, because LANs are highly reliable), the sending kernel stops the timer and returns control to the caller.

On the other hand, if the broadcast has not come back before the timer expires, the kernel assumes that either the message or the broadcast has been lost. Either way, it retransmits the message. If the original message was lost, no harm has been done, and the second (or subsequent) attempt will trigger the broadcast in the usual way. If the message got to the sequencer and was broadcast, but the sender missed the broadcast, the sequencer will detect the retransmission as a duplicate (from the message identifier) and simply tell the sender that everything is all right. The message is not broadcast a second time.

A third possibility is that a broadcast comes back before the timer expires, but it is the wrong broadcast. This situation arises when two processes attempt to broadcast simultaneously. One of them, Process A, gets to the sequencer first, and its message is broadcast. Process A sees the broadcast and unblocks its application program. However, its competitor, Process B, sees Process A's broadcast and realizes that it has failed. Nevertheless, Process B knows that its message probably got to the sequencer (since lost messages are rare), where it will be queued and broadcast next. Thus, Process B accepts Process A's broadcast and continues to wait for its own broadcast to come back or its timer to expire.

Let us consider what happens at the sequencer when a *Request for Broadcast* arrives there. First, a check is made to see if the message is a retransmission; if so, the sender is informed that the broadcast has already been done, as mentioned above. If the message is new (as is the normal case), the next sequence number is assigned to it, and the sequencer counter is incremented by one for next time. The message and its identifier are then stored in a *history buffer*, and the message is then broadcast. (The management of the history buffer is described shortly.) The message is also passed up to the application running on the sequencer's machine (because the broadcast does not cause an interrupt on the machine that issued the broadcast).

Now, let us consider what happens when a kernel receives a broadcast. First, the sequence number is compared to the sequence number of the most recently received broadcast. If the new one is one higher (as is the normal case), no broadcasts have been missed, so the message is passed up to the application program. If the application program is multithreaded, usually one thread will be waiting for the message; if it is single threaded, the kernel waits for the program to try to receive a message.

Suppose that the newly received broadcast has sequence number 25, while the previous one had number 23. The kernel is immediately alerted to the fact that it has missed number 24, so it sends a point-to-point message to the sequencer asking for a private retransmission of the missing message. The sequencer fetches the missing message from its history buffer and sends it. When it arrives, the receiving kernel processes 24 and 25, passing them up to the application program in numerical order. Thus, the only effect of a lost message is a minor time delay. All application programs see all broadcasts in the same order, even if some messages are lost.

The reliable-broadcast protocol is illustrated in Figure 9. Here, the application program running on Machine A passes a message M to its kernel for broadcasting. The kernel sends the message to the sequencer, where it is assigned sequence number 25. The message (containing the sequence number 25) is now broadcast to all machines and also passed up to the application program running on the sequencer itself. This broadcast message is denoted by M25 in the figure.

Message M25 arrives at Machines B and C. At Machine B, the kernel sees that it has already

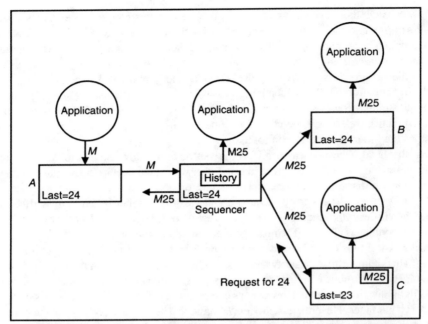

Figure 9. The application of Machine *A* sends a message *M* to the sequencer, which then adds a sequence number (25) and broadcasts it. At *B* it is accepted, but at *C* it is buffered until 24, which was missed, can be retrieved from the sequencer.

processed all broadcasts up to and including 24, so it immediately passes *M*25 up to the application program. However, at *C*, the last message to arrive was 23 (24 must have been lost), so *M*25 is buffered in the kernel, and a point-to-point message requesting 24 is sent to the sequencer. Only after the reply has come back and been given to the application program will *M*25 be passed upward as well.

Now, let us look at the management of the history buffer. Unless something is done to prevent it, the history buffer will quickly fill up. However, if the sequencer knows that all machines have correctly received broadcasts — say zero through 23 — it can delete these from its history buffer. Several mechanisms are provided to allow the sequencer to discover this information. The basic one is that each *Request for Broadcast* message sent to the sequencer carries a piggybacked acknowledgment k, meaning that all broadcasts up to and including k have been correctly received. This way, the sequencer can maintain a piggyback table, indexed by machine number, telling for each machine which broadcast is the last one received. Whenever the history buffer begins to fill up, the sequencer can make a pass through this table to find the smallest value. It can then safely discard all messages up to and including this value.

To inform the sequencer, a machine is required to send a short acknowledgment message when it has sent no broadcast messages for a certain period of time. Otherwise, if one machine happens to be silent for an unusually long period of time, the sequencer will not know what its status is. Furthermore, the sequencer can broadcast a *Request for Status* message, which directs all other machines to send it a message giving the number of the highest broadcast received in sequence. In this way, the sequencer can update its piggyback table and then truncate its history buffer. In practice, *Request for Status* messages are rare; however, when they do occur, the mean number of messages required for a reliable broadcast is raised to slightly above two, even when there are no lost messages. This effect increases slightly as the number of machines grows.

We would like to clarify a subtle design point concerning the reliable-broadcast protocol. There are two methods for doing the broadcast. In Method 1 (described above), the user sends a point-to-point message to the sequencer, which then broadcasts it. In Method 2, the user broadcasts the message, including a unique identifier. When the sequencer sees this, it broadcasts a special *Accept* message containing the unique identifier and its newly assigned sequence number. A broadcast is only "official" when the *Accept* message has been sent. Although these protocols are logically equivalent, they have different performance characteristics. In Method 1, each message appears in full on the network twice: once to the sequencer and once from the sequencer. Thus, a message of length m bytes consumes $2m$ bytes worth of network bandwidth. However, only the second of these is broadcast, so each user machine is interrupted only once (for the second message). In Method 2, the full message appears only once on the network, in addition to a very short *Accept* message from the sequencer; therefore, only half the bandwidth is consumed. On the other hand, every machine is interrupted twice: once for the message and once for the *Accept*. Thus, Method 1 wastes bandwidth to reduce interrupts compared to Method 2. We have implemented both methods and are now running experiments comparing them. Depending on the results of these experiments, we may go to a hybrid scheme that uses Method 1 for short messages and Method 2 for long ones.

In summary, our reliable-broadcast protocol allows reliable broadcasting to be done on an unreliable network in just over two messages per reliable broadcast. Each broadcast is indivisible, and all applications receive all messages in the same order, no matter how many are lost. The worst that can happen is that a short delay is introduced when a message is lost, which rarely occurs. If two processes attempt to broadcast at the same time, one of them will get to the sequencer first and win. The other will see a broadcast from its competitor coming back from the sequencer and will realize that its request has been queued and will appear shortly, so it simply waits.

Comparison

Kaashoek et al. [12] gave a detailed comparison of our scheme with other published protocols for doing reliable broadcasting. Here, we compare our scheme with some of the major other ones. Three other kinds of work to which we can compare ours are

- Distributed shared memory,
- Broadcasting to achieve fault tolerance, and
- Broadcasting as an operating system service.

Most research on distributed shared memory is based on the work of Li and Hudak [14]. In their method, fixed-size pages are moved around the network in point-to-point messages. If broadcasting is used at all, it is only for invalidating pages. In contrast, broadcasting is the basis of the entire system in our method. Furthermore, messages are variable sized, containing only the data that are needed. Most of the time, the amount of data needed is much less than a page; therefore, being able to send short messages is a significant performance improvement.

Some recent work in distributed shared memories emphasized weakening the semantics of what shared memory means [15]. We consider this unacceptable, since the goal is to give the programmer an easy-to-understand model to work with, and weak-semantics systems put all the burden of coherency back on the programmer. Other work concentrated on using broadcasting to achieve fault tolerance. Chang and Maxemchuk [8] described a family of protocols for reliable broadcasting, of which nonfault tolerance is a special case. Like our protocol, their protocol for the nonfault-tolerant case uses a sequencer, but they have the nodes ordered in a logical ring, with the sequencer advancing along the ring with every message sent. This motion of the sequencer is almost free when the traffic is heavy, but costs an extra message per broadcast when it is not. On the average, their protocol requires two to three messages per reliable broadcast, whereas ours requires just a fraction over two. In addition, their protocol uses more storage: They have to store the history buffer on all machines, because of the moving sequencer. With a one-megabyte (Mbyte) history buffer and 100 machines, we need one Mbyte of memory for the history buffer and they need 100 Mbytes.

Finally, in our Method 1, each reliable broadcast uses one point-to-point message and one broadcast message. With $n \gg 1$ machine, we generate about n interrupts per reliable broadcast. In their protocol (similar to what we have called Method 2), all messages are broadcast, so they need between $2n$ and $3n$ interrupts per reliable broadcast. When there are hundreds of broadcasts per second, their scheme uses much more CPU time than ours.

Another family of fault-tolerant protocols is the Isis system of Birman and Joseph [5]. They used a distributed two-phase commit protocol to achieve global ordering, something we achieve in two messages per broadcast. Since they realized that their protocol is inefficient, they proposed alternative protocols with weaker semantics. Our method shows that it is not necessary to weaken and complicate the semantics to achieve efficiency. However, in Isis's favor, it does provide a high degree of fault tolerance, which our basic protocol does not. Our method can also provide fault tolerance, if desired [11]. Furthermore, Isis supports simultaneous use of overlapping process groups, whereas — in our scheme — groups are disjoint. Each application forms its own group, and no attempt is made to provide global ordering between different applications.

A few researchers proposed providing broadcasting as an operating system service. For example, the system of Cheriton and Zwaenepoel [9] supports broadcasting, but it does not guarantee reliability. A problem with their system is that the programmer's job is made more difficult than that in a system in which broadcasts are guaranteed to be reliable.

Performance of reliable broadcasting

We modified the Amoeba kernel to support our reliable-broadcast protocol. Amoeba runs on a collection of 16-MHz Motorola 68030 processors connected by a 10-megabit- (Mbit)-per-second Ethernet. We measured the performance of this system by running various experiments on it. First, to measure the maximum broadcast rate by a single process, we had one process continuously broadcast null messages as fast as it could. In this experiment, we achieved 370 reliable broadcasts per second with up to 16 processors. Note that this experiment tested the worst possible case. Since all machines but one were silent, they were not sending back piggybacked acknowledgments to the sequencer. Without these acknowledgments, the sequencer had to send out a *Request for Status* every 64 messages. It is instructive to point out that even though we were measuring broadcasting, the performance was better than that for most (point-to-point) RPC systems, partly because our protocol requires only two messages per broadcast, whereas RPCs often require three, with the last being an acknowledgment. (As an aside, these results differed from our earlier results, because we had designed and implemented a new kernel that can handle broadcasting over an arbitrary internetwork consisting of LANs and buses. Also, this scheme supports transparent process migration and automatic network reconfiguration and management. The differences between the results here and the previously published ones are entirely accounted for by these changes.)

Second, to see the effect of contention, we had not one but multiple processes broadcasting at the same time. In this experiment, we varied the number of senders from two to 14, with the number in the receiving group equal to the number of senders. Table 1 gives the results of our second experiment. Multiple senders get a higher throughput than just one, because if two machines send messages to the sequencer almost simultaneously, the first one to arrive will be broadcast first, but the second one will be buffered and broadcast immediately afterward. This simple form of pipelining increases the parallelism of the system and thus increases the broadcast rate. As the number of senders increases, performance drops slightly because of contention for the Ethernet. (We were unable to make consistent measurements for 15 and 16 processors because of technical limitations of our equipment.)

A word about scaling is appropriate here. It has been pointed out to us that the sequencer will become a bottleneck in very large systems. While this is true, few current systems or applications suffer from this limit. With current technology (two-million-instructions-per-second [MIPS] CPUs and 10-Mbit-per-second Ethernet), we can support on the order of 800 reliable broadcasts per second, as shown above. Because broadcast messages are usually short, there is bandwidth to spare. For many problems, the read-to-write ratio is quite high. Suppose (conservatively) that 90 percent of the operations are reads and 10 percent are writes. Then, we can support 8000 operations per second on shared objects (7200 reads, done locally, and 800 writes, done by broadcasting). We know of very few applications that would be hindered by being able to perform only 8000 operations per second on shared objects. Furthermore, with 20-MIPS RISC processors and 100-Mbit-per-second fiber-optic networks, this limit will be closer to 80,000 operations per second on shared objects within a few years.

Table 1. Performance with multiple processes broadcasting at the same time.

Number of senders	Broadcasts per second
2	714
3	769
4	769
5	793
6	789
7	795
8	800
9	782
10	781
11	780
12	780
13	718
14	710

Object management

On top of the broadcast layer is the object-management layer, implemented by a package of library procedures (in user space). This layer manages shared objects. Our design is based on the explicit assumption that shared objects are read much more often than they are written. Ratios of 10 to one or even 100 to one are not at all unusual. Therefore, we have chosen to replicate each object on all machines that use the object. (Note that multiple, independent applications may be running at the same time, so not every machine needs every object.) All replicas have equal status: There is no concept of a primary object and secondary copies of it.

Two operations are defined on objects: *Read* and *Write*. *Reads* are done on the local copy, without any network traffic. A *Read* on a shared object is only slightly more expensive than a *Read* on a *Private* object (because of some locking). A *Write* to a shared object can be done by sending a reliable broadcast with the new value of the object, in whole or in part, or it can be done by sending an operation code and some parameters, letting each machine recompute the new value. The former strategy is attractive for small objects and the latter is attractive for large objects; it is up to the runtime system to pick one. Since all machines process all broadcasts in the same order, all objects will settle down to the same value when equilibrium is reached.

This scheme does not provide complete memory coherence, because if Machine *A* initiates a reliable broadcast to update a shared object and Machine *B* reads the (local copy of the) object one ns later, *B* will get the old value. On the other hand, it does provide for indivisible update and serializability, which is almost as good, as can easily be seen in the example that follows. Consider a multiprocessor with a true shared memory. At a certain moment, Process *A* wants to write a word and Process *B* wants to read it. Since the two operations may take place a microsecond apart, the value read by *B* depends on who went first. Despite the memory being coherent, the value read by *B* is determined by the detailed timing. Our shared-object model has a similar property. In both cases, programs whose correct functioning depends on who wins the race to memory are living dangerously, at best. Thus, although our memory model does not exhibit true coherence, serializability plus global message ordering are in reality sufficient properties, and our model does have these properties.

Orca

While it is possible to program directly with shared objects, it is much more convenient to have language support for them. For this reason, we have designed the Orca parallel programming language and written a compiler for it. The following are the four guiding principles behind the Orca design:

(1) *Transparency.* With transparency, programs (and programmers) should not be aware of where objects reside. Location management should be fully automatic. Furthermore, the programmer should not be aware of whether the program is running on a machine with physical shared memory or one with disjoint memories. The same program should run on both, unlike nearly all other languages for parallel programming, which are aimed at either one or the other, but not both. (Of course, one can always simulate message passing on a multiprocessor, but this is far from optimal.)

(2) *Semantic simplicity.* With semantic simplicity, programmers should be able to form a simple mental model of how the shared memory works. This principle rules out incoherent memory, in which reads to shared data sometimes return good values and sometimes return stale (incorrect) ones.

(3) *Serializability.* In a parallel system, many events happen simultaneously. By making operations serializable, we guarantee that operations on objects are indivisible and that the observed behavior is the same as some sequential execution would have been. Operations on objects are guaranteed not to be interleaved, which contributes to semantic simplicity, as does the fact that all machines see the same sequence of serial events. Of course, the compiler and runtime system do not actually serialize events any more than they have to guarantee the semantics.

(4) *Efficiency.* Efficiency is also important, since we are proposing a system that can actually be used for solving real problems.

Now let us look at the principal aspects of Orca that relate to parallelism and shared objects. Orca is a procedural language whose sequential constructs are roughly similar to those of languages like C or Modula 2. Parallelism is based on two orthogonal concepts: *processes* and *objects*. Processes are active entities that execute programs. They can be created and destroyed dynamically. It is possible to read in an integer n and then execute a loop n times, creating a new process on each iteration. Thus, the number of processes is not fixed at compile time, but is determined during execution.

The Orca construct for creating a new process is the

     fork func(param, ...)

statement, which creates a new process running the procedure *func* with the specified parameters. The user may specify which processor to use or let the runtime system use its own load-balancing heuristics. Objects may be passed as parameters (call by reference). A process may fork many times, passing the same objects to each of the children. This is how objects come to be shared among a collection of processes. There are no global objects in Orca.

Objects are passive; they do not contain processes or other active elements. Each object contains some data structures, along with definitions of one or more operations that use the data structures. The operations are defined by Orca procedures written by the programmer. An object has a specification part and an implementation part; in this respect, Orca is similar to Ada packages or Modula 2 modules.

A common way of programming in Orca is the *replicated worker paradigm* [7]. In this model, the main program starts out by creating a large number of identical worker processes, each getting the same objects as parameters, so they are shared among all the workers. Once the initialization phase has been completed, the system consists of the main process, along with some number of identical worker processes, all of which share some objects. Processes can perform operations on any of their objects whenever they want to, without having to worry about all the mechanics of how many copies are stored and where, how updates take place, which synchronization technique is used, and so on. As far as the programmer is concerned, all the objects are effectively located in one big shared memory somewhere, but they are protected by a kind of monitor that prevents multiple updates to an object at the same time.

As a minimal example of an object specification, consider a simple object consisting of an integer variable with two operations on it: *read* and *write*. If this object is subsequently shared among multiple processes, any of them can read or write the value of the integer. The Orca specification part looks like the following:

```
object specification SharedInt;
        operation read(): integer;
        operation write(val: integer): integer;
end;
```

The implementation part looks like the following:

```
object implementation SharedInt;
        n: integer; # the value

        operation read(): integer;
        begin
                return n;
        end;

        operation write(val: integer);
        begin
                n := val;
        end;
end;
```

To declare and use an object of type *SharedInt*, the programmer might write the following:

```
s: SharedInt;
i: integer; # ordinary integer

s$write(100); # set object to 100
i := s$read(); # set i to 100
```

Although the programming style suggested by this trivial example is sufficient for some programs, for many others some kind of synchronization method is required. A common example is *barrier*

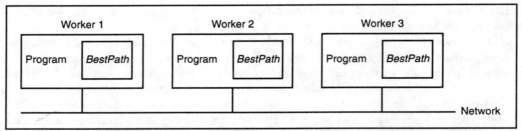

Figure 10. Model of the traveling salesman problem (TSP) program using the replicated worker paradigm.

synchronization, in which *n* workers are busy computing something, and only when all of them have finished may the next step begin. Synchronization in Orca is handled by *guarded commands*, in which an operation consists of a number of (guard, statement) pairs. Each guard is a side-effect-free Boolean expression and each statement is an arbitrary piece of sequential Orca code. When the operation is invoked, the language runtime system evaluates the guards one at a time (in an unspecified order); as soon as it finds one that is true, the corresponding statement is executed. For example, to implement barrier synchronization, the main process could create a shared object with operations to initialize it, increment it, and synchronize on it (that is, wait until it reached *n*). The main process would *initialize* it to zero and then fork off all the workers. When each worker had finished its work, it would invoke the *increment* operation and then the *synchronize* operation. The latter would block the calling process until the value reached *n*, at which point all the processes would be released to start the next phase.

As a slightly more elaborate example, consider an implementation of the *traveling salesman problem (TSP)* in Orca. In this problem, the computer is a given a starting city and a list of cities to visit; it has to find the shortest path that visits each city exactly once and returns to the starting city. Usually, the TSP is solved using the branch-and-bound algorithm. Suppose the starting city is New York and the cities to be visited are London, Sydney, Tokyo, Nairobi, and Rio de Janeiro. The main program begins by computing some possible path (for example, using the closest-city-next algorithm) and determining its length. Then, it initializes a soon-to-be-shared object, *BestPath*, containing this path and its length. As the program executes, this object will always contain the best path found so far and its length. Next, it forks off some number of workers, each getting the shared object as parameter, as shown in Figure 10.

Each worker is given a different partial path to investigate. The first worker tries paths beginning New York-London, the second one tries paths beginning New York-Sydney, the third one tries paths beginning New York-Tokyo, and so on. Very roughly, the algorithm used by a worker that is given a partial path plus *k* cities to visit is to first check if the length of the partial path is longer than the best complete path found so far. If so, the process terminates itself. If the partial path is still a potential candidate, the process generates *k* new partial paths to be investigated — one per city in the list — and forks off these to *k* new workers. To avoid forking off too many processes, when the list of remaining cities to be visited is less than *n*, the process tries all the possible combinations itself. Other optimizations are also used. Whenever a new best path is found, an update operation on the shared object *BestPath* is executed to replace the previous best path by the new one. When the Orca compiler detects an assignment to a variable in a shared object, it generates code to cause the runtime system to issue a reliable broadcast of the new value. In this manner, all the details of managing shared objects are hidden from the programmer.

A moment's thought reveals that reads of *BestPath* will occur very often, while writes will hardly occur at all, certainly not after the program has been running for a while and has found a path close to the optimal one. Remember that reads are done entirely locally on each machine, whereas writes require a reliable broadcast. The net result is that the vast majority of operations on the shared object do not require network traffic, and the few that do take only two messages. Consequently, the solution is highly efficient. We have achieved almost linear speedup with 10 processes. In fact, actual measurements showed the distributed version to outperform one run on a shared-memory machine (without caching), because the latter suffers from serious memory contention as large numbers of processors constantly try to read the memory word containing the length of the best path so far.

Comparison

It is instructive to briefly compare Orca with some alternative approaches to parallel programming. A large number of languages are based on message passing, which is of a conceptually lower level than shared objects. The approach usually used in languages that support shared memory is the use of semaphores or monitors to protect critical regions. Both work adequately on shared-memory machines with a small number of processors but poorly on large distributed systems, because they use a locking scheme that is inherently centralized.

A system that is somewhat similar to Orca is Emerald [10]. Like Orca, Emerald supports shared objects. However, unlike Orca, it does not replicate objects. This means that when a caller on Machine 1 invokes an operation on an object located on Machine 2 using a parameter on Machine 3, messages must be sent to collect all the necessary information in the same place. There is no automatic migration, so if the programmer does not arrange for things that go together to be colocated, execution will be inefficient. Alternatively, for efficiency, the programmer can specify on each call that the parameter objects are to be sent to the machine where the object resides and to remain there after the invocation. The programmer can also specify whether or not the result is to remain there. In a truly transparent system, these issues would not arise.

In Orca, in contrast, the runtime system decides whether or not it wants to replicate objects and, if so, where. When the broadcast system described above is used, all objects are replicated on machines that need them (but other Orca implementations do it differently). In any event, object management is not the programmer's responsibility; it is handled automatically, and the decision on whether to perform operations locally or remotely is made by the system. The Orca approach comes much closer than does Emerald to providing the semantics of a shared-memory multiprocessor.

Yet another shared-object scheme is Linda [7]. Linda supports the concept of a shared tuple space that is equally accessible to processes on all machines. Linda is fully location-transparent, but the primitives are low-level: inserting and deleting tuples. In Orca, in contrast, the operations on shared objects can be simple or arbitrarily complex, as the programmer wishes.

In summary, Orca supports the model of having dynamically created parallel processes perform user-defined operations on shared objects. These objects are implemented by maintaining identical copies on all machines. An operation that reads an object — but does not change it — is done entirely locally, with no network traffic. The efficiency of this operation is only slightly worse than that of an operation on an unshared object.

An operation that modifies an object is handled differently. The operation name and parameters are put in a message that is passed to the runtime system (object-management layer) for transmission to all other machines in one indivisible reliable broadcast. The method by which the kernel provides this abstraction is discussed in detail above. When the message arrives, the operation is carried out locally. This method is preferable to carrying out the operation on the sending machine and broadcasting the new object to reduce the size of the message. This division of labor between the layers yields a great conceptual simplicity: The programmer defines and invokes operations on shared objects, the runtime system handles reads and writes on these objects, and the reliable-broadcast layer implements indivisible updates to objects using the sequencer protocol.

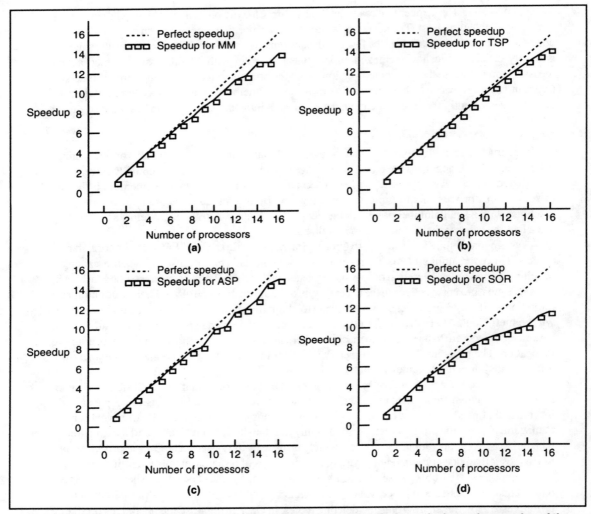

Figure 11. Performance (measured speedup) for four Orca programs. Each graph shows the speedup of the parallel Orca program on *N* CPUs over the same program running on one CPU. (a) Matrix multiplication (MM), using input matrices of size 250 × 250. (b) The traveling salesman problem (TSP), averaged over three randomly generated graphs with 12 cities each. (c) The all-pairs shortest paths (ASP) problem, using an input graph with 300 nodes. (d) Successive overrelaxation (SOR), using a grid with 80 columns and 242 rows.

Parallel applications in Orca

Orca is a procedural, type-secure language intended for implementing parallel applications on distributed systems [1], [2], [3]. Below, we briefly discuss four examples of problems for which Orca has been used. Figure 11 presents the measured speedup of the Orca program for these four problems.

(1) *Matrix multiplication (MM).* MM is an example employing "trivial parallelism." Each processor is assigned a fixed portion of the result matrix. Once the work-to-do has been

distributed, all processors can proceed independently from each other. The speedup is not perfect, because it takes some time to initialize the source matrices (of size 250×250) and the portions are fixed but not necessarily equal if the matrix size is not divisible by the number of processors.

(2)   *The traveling salesman problem (TSP).* The main characteristic of the TSP is the shared variable containing the current best solution. This variable is stored in a shared object that is read very frequently. If a new better route is found, all copies of the object are updated immediately, using the efficient broadcast protocol. It is important that the updating take place immediately, lest some processors continue to use an inferior bound, reducing the effectiveness of the pruning. The TSP achieves a speedup close to linear. (The TSP is discussed in detail in this paper.)

(3)   *The all-pairs shortest paths (ASP) problem.* In the ASP problem, communication overhead is much higher than in the TSP. The ASP problem uses an iterative algorithm. Before each iteration, some process selects one row of the distances matrix as pivot row and sends it to all other processes. If implemented with point-to-point messages, the communication overhead would be linear with the number of processors. However, with our multicast protocol, the overhead is reduced to a few messages, resulting in high speedups.

(4)   *Successive overrelaxation (SOR).* Of course, not all parallel applications benefit from broadcasting. In SOR, each processor communicates mainly with its neighbors. SOR is a worst-case example for our system, because point-to-point messages between neighboring nodes are implemented as broadcast messages received by all nodes. Still, the program achieves a reasonable speedup.

Summary and conclusions

Multiprocessors (with shared memory) are easy to program but hard to build, while multicomputers (no shared memory) are easy to build but hard to program. Here, we introduce a new model that is easy to program, easy to build, and has an acceptable performance on problems with a moderate grain size in which reads are much more common than writes. The essence of our approach is to implement reliable broadcasting as a distinct semantic layer and then use this layer to implement shared objects. Reliable broadcasting is achieved by having users send their messages to a sequencer, which then numbers them sequentially and broadcasts them. Machines that miss a message can get it by asking the sequencer, which maintains a history buffer. This scheme requires slightly over two messages per reliable broadcast. We built a kernel based on these principles and measured its performance at up to 1500 reliable broadcasts per second.

Also, we designed and implemented a shared-object layer and a language, Orca, that allows programmers to declare objects shared by multiple processes. Objects are replicated on all the machines that need to access them. When the language runtime system needs to read a shared object, it simply uses the local copy. When it needs to update a shared object, it reliably broadcasts the new object (or operation code and parameters). This scheme is simple and has a semantic model that is easy for programmers to understand. It is also efficient, because the amount of data broadcast is exactly what is needed. It is not constrained — as in the work of Li and Hudak [14] — to be one K or eight K because the page size happens to be that. Most of our broadcasts are much smaller (typically a few hundred bytes, at most).

In conclusion, the use of reliable broadcasting to support replicated, shared objects is a good way to approach parallel programming. Reliable broadcasting is simple to understand and efficient to implement. The use of a language like Orca makes it easier to use shared objects; however, even without Orca, this paradigm offers a new and effective way to exploit parallelism in future computing systems.

Acknowledgments

We would like to thank Erik Baalbergen, Dick Grune, and Wiebren de Jonge for carefully reading the paper and making many helpful suggestions.

References

[1] H.E. Bal, *Programming Distributed Systems*, Silicon Press, Summit, N.J., 1990.

[2] H.E. Bal, M.F. Kaashoek, and A.S. Tanenbaum, "A Distributed Implementation of the Shared Data-Object Model," *Proc. USENIX/SERC Workshop Experiences with Building Distributed and Multiprocessor Systems*, Usenix, Berkeley, Calif., 1989, pp. 1-9.

[3] H.E. Bal, M.F. Kaashoek, and A.S. Tanenbaum, "Experience with Distributed Programming in Orca," *Proc. 1990 Int'l Conf. Computer Languages*, IEEE Computer Soc. Press, Los Alamitos, Calif., 1990, pp. 79-89.

[4] J.K. Bennett, J.B. Carter, and W. Zwaenepoel, "Munin: Distributed Shared Memory Based on Type-Specific Memory Coherence," *Proc. Second ACM Symp. Principles and Practice Parallel Programming*, ACM Press, New York, N.Y., 1990, pp. 168-177.

[5] K.P. Birman, and T.A. Joseph, "Reliable Communication in the Presence of Failures," *ACM Trans. Computer Systems*, Vol. 5, No. 1, Feb. 1987, pp. 47-76.

[6] A.D. Birrell and B.J. Nelson, "Implementing Remote Procedure Calls," *ACM Trans. Computer Systems*, Vol. 2, No. 1., Feb. 1984, pp. 39-59.

[7] N. Carriero and D. Gelernter, "Linda in Context," *Comm. ACM*, Vol. 32, No. 4, Apr. 1989, pp. 444-458.

[8] J. Chang and N.F. Maxemchuk, "Reliable Broadcast Protocols," *ACM Trans. Computer Systems*, Vol. 2, No. 3, Aug. 1984, pp. 251-273.

[9] D.R. Cheriton and W. Zwaenepoel, "Distributed Process Groups in the V Kernel," *ACM Trans. Computer Systems*, Vol. 3, No. 2, May 1985, pp. 77-107.

[10] E. Jul, H. Hutchinson, and A. Black, "Fine-Grained Mobility in the Emerald System," *ACM Trans. Computer Systems*, Vol. 6, No. 1, Feb. 1988, pp. 109-133.

[11] M.F. Kaashoek, *Group Communication in Distributed Computer Systems*, doctoral thesis, Vrije Universiteit, Amsterdam, The Netherlands, 1992.

[12] M.F. Kaashoek et al., "An Efficient Reliable Broadcast Protocol," *Operating Systems Rev.*, Vol. 23, No. 4, Oct. 1989, pp. 5-19.

[13] M.F. Kaashoek and A.S. Tanenbaum, "Group Communication in the Amoeba Distributed Operating System," *Proc. 11th Int'l Conf. Distributed Computing Systems*, IEEE Computer Soc. Press, Los Alamitos, Calif., 1991, pp. 222-230.

[14] K. Li and P. Hudak, "Memory Coherence in Shared Virtual Memory Systems," *ACM Trans. Computer Systems*, Vol. 7, No. 4, Nov. 1989, pp. 321-359.

[15] R.G. Minnich and D.J. Farber, "Reducing Host Load, Network Load, and Latency in a Distributed Shared Memory," *Proc. 10th Int'l Conf. Distributed Computing Systems*, IEEE Computer Soc. Press, Los Alamitos, Calif., 1990, pp. 468-475.

[16] R.J. Swan, S.H. Fuller, and D.P. Siewiorek, "Cm* — A Modular, MultiMicroprocessor System," *Proc. Nat'l Computer Conf.*, AFIPS, Reston, Va., 1977, pp. 645-655.

Memory as a Network Abstraction

C omputer systems are extremely complex. One technique that has proven effective at managing this complexity is based on the idea of *modularity*. Activities are decomposed into a collection of cooperating *modules*, each of which provides an abstraction to the other modules through some interface. In the area of networking, the modularization — called *layering* — is refined along functional lines. Layering is an intellectual technique that allows the various behaviors and complexities of different protocols to be decomposed into pieces, called *layers*, each of which takes a step toward the translation of application data into "bits on a wire" or reverses this translation. Layering can be a useful technique for matching one type of abstraction to another. For example, in systems using distributed file systems, a file system abstraction is mapped to the low-level message-based Ethernet abstraction via a series of layers. The layers, in turn, map the following:

- A file system operation to a remote procedure call (RPC) request;
- An RPC request to a host-independent packet (essentially converting it to a string of characters);
- A packet to one or more messages; and
- A message to one or more network packets, via a multiplexed I/O interface (for example, an Ethernet card).

At each layer, the abstraction changes, with some attendant processing of the data in the packet (in current protocol implementations, this overhead is a large percentage of the total overhead), copying or fragmentation of that data to smaller units, and encapsulation of that data in a larger packet.

Some idea of the amount of copying overhead can be obtained from the fact that current protocol stacks are more memory-bandwidth constrained than processor constrained, because of the number of copies that must be performed. Even with fast processors, interprocess communication (IPC) over fast communications networks has often achieved only a fraction of the peak network bandwidth.

A problem with layering is that it can conceal some set of initial assumptions that may no longer be valid. For example, in the case

Gary Delp,

David Farber,

Ronald Minnich,

Jonathan Smith, and

Ivan Ming-Chit Tam

of distributed file systems, much effort has been expended on avoiding network overhead. The effort has been put into (1) caching local copies of a file, (2) making the RPC more efficient, or (3) minimizing the path length from the RPC code to the Ethernet interface. The basic assumption — that of a message-based hardware interface that is multiplexed and accessed only by the operating system — has not changed.

Farber [11] suggested a fundamentally different approach to the problem of IPC over fast networks. He argued that the essence of the problem was the network abstraction — that is, what model the hardware network interface provided to the computer. Current network interfaces are based on the I/O abstraction, which requires the host processor to direct the input and output of each message on the network. No data may flow through the interface directly to an application; rather, the operating system must become involved in every step of the process. The nature of this interface forces the computer to perform expensive processing to transform the data into a form acceptable to computations. Farber argued that the network should provide the abstraction of computer memory directly to the application, with no explicit operating system intervention required to effect the movement of data. This abstraction had been successfully applied to secondary storage such as drums and disks with the idea of "virtual memory." This idea seemed ripe for exploration with the advent of high-speed local networks and high-speed switches that enable fast packet-switched wide area networks (WANs).

Delp [11] performed the explorations, starting in 1985, that resulted in MemNet (discussed in a later section) in 1988. MemNet demonstrated that the memory abstraction was effective when implemented entirely in hardware and that it would provide good performance. MemNet connected a number of computers using a parallel, 200-megabit-per-second, insertion-modification token ring. The success of MemNet led to a number of further efforts, which we now discuss. Minnich had worked with the MemNet system and wanted to preserve its applications interface while exploring a variety of optimizations. His Mether system [16] was originally intended to be a software MemNet that used broadcast Ethernet. The system has evolved from a software MemNet to a unique distributed shared memory (DSM) in its own right, with new mechanisms for allowing applications to specify the type of service they require from the DSM on a memory-fetch basis, as well as mechanisms for supporting synchronization based on the memory operation. The result is minimized messages and easier synchronization, which imply better performance in high-latency settings. The changes from the original version of Mether to the current Mether 3.0, described in a later section, are the result of extensive applications experience. Tam [21] investigated the extension of DSM to high-speed, packet-switched WANs with his CapNet system, which augments the switching fabric with support for memory operations. The CapNet research has implications for the design of future high-speed interconnection networks. The CapNet design is discussed in a later section. Smith's UPWARDS operating system [9], also discussed in a later section, attempts to extend optimizations used elsewhere in the memory hierarchy into the network.

There has been a spate of DSM studies and implementations recently; many of these are discussed in a survey by Tam, Smith, and Farber [22], to which the reader is referred. For the most part, these studies have focused on extending shared-memory properties to distributed systems and, other than MemNet, all of these implementations have been as software systems. There are essentially two varieties of these software systems: page oriented and object oriented. Page-oriented systems have used the assistance provided by existing memory-management hardware to shuttle requests for fixed-size chunks of data (*pages*) to be shuttled around a local area network (LAN). Object-oriented systems have attempted to minimize the unnecessary transfer of data (due to mismatch between the units of shared data and page sizes) by defining objects that encapsulate the shared state and manage its consistency. The difficulty with the object-oriented approach is the inability of applications (for example, existing binaries) to use it transparently. In addition, such approaches often require rewriting in a specialized language, such as Bal, Kaashoek, and Tanenbaum's Orca [1]. Another problem with the object-oriented approach is that it must still, at some point, have access to a network system; if the system is software based, it will not be able to make effective use of the network. The use of a system such as Orca does not have any implications, pro or con, about the use of a MemNet-like network to effect communications.

While the MemNet consistency control mechanism is similar to the cache management used by several other systems, such as Li's Ivy, it is important to remember that MemNet represents a network abstraction, not an operating system extension.

This paper is organized into five sections. The first section discusses MemNet. The section begins by presenting shared memory as a networking abstraction. It then turns its attention to the MemNet system, focusing

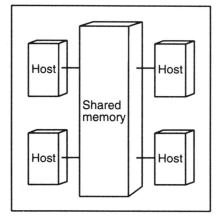

Figure 1. Programmer's view of MemNet.

first on the performance of the system and second on lessons learned from its implementation. The second section discusses Mether 3.0. The third section, which discusses CapNet, argues that message count is the crucial performance measure in a high-speed WAN setting. CapNet demonstrates a scheme that minimizes the number of messages necessary to maintain consistent shared memory. The fourth section focuses on UPWARDS, a system that provides extremely high performance IPC based on DSM and attempts to include multimedia in the abstraction. The fifth section concludes the paper, pointing out a number of difficulties with DSM and providing our expectations for future developments.

MemNet

In the programming model of the MemNet system, all of the processors have equal and fast access to a large amount of memory (see Figure 1). While this abstraction is convenient for the programmer, if the system were implemented in this simple manner, the system response time would suffer from memory contention and transmission latency. As additional hosts are added to the network, the potential required memory bandwidth will increase linearly in the number of hosts.

A solution for the memory contention that works in the large majority of cases is for each host to cache the memory that it is currently using. With a cache of the appropriate size, the number of references that must be satisfied by the central resource can be reduced dramatically. Caching memory is a relatively simple task. Keeping multiple cached copies of the same memory location consistent with each other is a more difficult matter. Consistency protocols used for tightly coupled multiprocessors do not scale well [3].

Bus-based systems suffer from decreased transmission bandwidth as the length of the bus is increased. The MemNet system uses a token ring interconnect system to avoid the bandwidth decrease coincident with bus extension. Memory access latency may increase as the physical distribution of hosts increases, but the bandwidth of the access media does not decrease, as is the case with a bus-based system that needs to allow access control signals to propagate to the ends of the bus and echo back for each bit. Figure 2 gives a macro view of a MemNet system.

In the system, each computing node has a MemNet device as a memory controller on its local bus. These devices are interconnected with a dedicated, parallel, high-speed token ring. The interface from the node to the ring is through dual-ported memory. Each computing node references this memory as real memory on its local bus, with the MemNet interface hardware managing a local cache

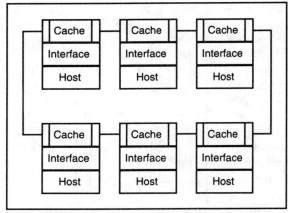

Figure 2. Macro view of a MemNet system.

of recently used data. The interfaces communicate among themselves using the token ring. To keep ring contention from limiting the average access speed to memory, network use is reduced by the caching of data at each node. A multiplexed, distributed interrupt channel is provided to distribute control information.

The MemNet token ring interface uses hardware state machines to manage the ring traffic. The data consistency information on each interface can be affected only by ring traffic. The host cannot access the ring directly. All ring traffic is generated by the interface, not the local host, and all ring traffic is interpreted by the interface with minimal impact on the local bus. The only impact that the ring traffic does have is the possibility of some MemNet memory references being delayed because of concurrent network and local node accesses to the MemNet device.

A ring is used for two reasons. First, the token ring provides an absolute upper bound on the time of network access. Second, because the packets that traverse the ring arrive at each interface in the same order, the tags used to manage the consistency protocol are themselves kept consistent.

The ring is a token insertion-modification ring. The default action of the interface is to echo what is received on its input port onto its output port. The latency at each interface is long enough to modify the output as appropriate. When an interface wishes to use the ring, it waits for a token, assembles and transmits a ring packet, and then releases the token. Each interface has a hardware state machine watching the input port. As packets arrive on the input, they are examined for effects on local memory and requests that this interface can satisfy. If the incoming packet is a packet that this interface generated, then this interface does not echo this packet to the output, thereby removing the packet from the ring. If the incoming packet is a request that this interface can satisfy, then the filler in the incoming packet is replaced with data supplied by this interface. All of this communication with the ring takes place without any intervention from the local host.

The address space of the MemNet environment is divided into 32-byte "chunks." The word "chunk" is used to describe this division to avoid some of the connotations of the terms "page" or "cache frame." A discussion of the choice of chunk size is part of the analysis by Delp [10].

The entire address space of the MemNet environment is mapped onto the local address space of each node. Each MemNet interface has two tag tables that are used to maintain consistency information for each chunk in the entire MemNet space and to manage the resources of the local interface. The tags used in the first of the two tables include Valid, Exclusive, Reserved, Clean, Interrupt, and Cached Location. These tags are maintained on each interface for all of the chunks in the entire MemNet address space. The second tag table is associated with the local chunk cache and contains an entry for each location in the cache. These tags include Clean, Inuse, and Chunk Contained (a backward pointer).

The consistency protocol run by the interfaces is a single-writer, multiple-readers protocol. The operation is similar to "snooping caches"; however, there are two major differences. First, while the multicomputers that use snooping cache techniques have all of the processors on a single (short) bus, the MemNet scheme allows systems with the physical range of a LAN. Second, the snooping systems rely on some separate main memory to which all of the caches have access. In the MemNet environment, the "main memory" is distributed among the interfaces.

Traffic is kept to a minimum on the ring through the use of large chunk caches on each interface. With effective caching, most of the node accesses to the MemNet address space will be satisfied by the data cached at the local interface and will not generate any ring traffic. If the ring traffic is minimized, then the average time that an interface must wait for a token to satisfy a cache miss is also minimized. Behavior of the MemNet environment under varying hit/miss ratios, varying chunk sizes, and varying numbers of nodes is projected by Delp [10].

Overall performance

The MemNet system provides a very fast channel into and out of the domain of the processor. The processor $\leftrightarrow$ memory interconnect is one that has been greatly optimized; it is no surprise that communications that use the characteristics and processor interface of memory are fast. In a 10-node system such as the one described by Delp [10], a one-way communication action has the time domain overhead of less than 20 bus memory accesses. The projected communications overhead for a 100-node system, assuming availability of the network, is in the neighborhood of 125 memory access times. If memory is being used in the ratio of one MemNet access for every 99 local memory accesses, the access times degrade to only 20 and 150 local memory access times (for 10- and 100-node systems, respectively).

The average memory access times for the 99:1 and 999:1 cases are affected only slightly by an increase in the number of nodes in the system. In both of these cases, the *network* (in the case of a cache miss) accesses are resolved in less time than 200 local bus cycles would take, even for a network of 100 nodes. To put this figure in perspective, the network transaction, including transit latency, is approximately equivalent to executing less than 40 lines of "C" code. By comparison, typical context switch code in an operating system is at minimum over 100 lines. Thus, it is usually cheaper to wait for the chunk to return than to switch to another process while waiting for the returned chunk.

It has been argued that using nodes that have very little or no local memory, the entire system memories of which are made up of MemNet memory, will offer the most seamless interface between local processes and the distributed system within which they operate. It is clear that some local storage will be required on each node, but nodes with mostly MemNet memory do not need to distinguish between memory that is shared and memory that must be copied to be shared. This means that many management and communication tasks can be performed more simply and efficiently. The potential of lightweight-task migration and distributed shared memory, as well as the simplicity issues, all argue toward systems with mostly active, global memory.

System considerations and error recovery

Many of the systems aspects of the use of the MemNet scheme have yet to be fully explored. Many of the problems and opportunities of the MemNet scheme are the same as those for a shared-memory multicomputer such as the Sequent [2], the Alliant [19], or the BBN TC2000 [24]. The requirements of the shared-memory schemes of System 5 and 4.3 BSD and the Linda system [7] of content-addressable shared data spaces are directly supported by the MemNet system. The multiprocessor process fork and join primitives for manipulating control flow find support in the atomic-memory operations and multiplexed signaling portions of MemNet. However, the physical extent of the MemNet system adds a degree of bus bandwidth and physical distribution not found in single-bus, single-location systems.

The degree of risk sharing among nodes is more evident with a physically distributed system than with a single system, but the system size considerations are similar. The MemNet interfaces are interconnected with a token ring. Errors on the ring can, for the most part, be detected by the transmitting interface. The consistency protocol is not idempotent, so if packets are corrupted, the data in the corresponding chunk are probably not recoverable. The reliability of the memory system is arguably at the same level as the reliability of a disk subsystem. Schemes for handling disk block errors exist; schemes for handling network memory errors will be developed. For applications requiring the degree of reliability that justifies the expense, checkpointed systems such as the one described by Bernstein [5] can easily be implemented in a MemNet-compatible system.

The conclusions that one reaches related to system reliability are not absolute; however, it is important to remember that ring reliability is well understood. These interfaces rarely miss packets. Of the packets missed, even rarer are those missed without notification. A two- or three-pass ring protocol that was closer to being idempotent could be devised, but performance in the general case would suffer greatly. Realistic reliability calculations need to be performed on the basis of experience, but it seems that this reliability factor, rather than the raw performance factor, will be the factor that limits the practical size of single memory-sharing rings. This is not to say that the potential size of virtual systems implemented in the MemNet manner is limited, just that the degree of risk shared on a distributed system must be contained.

There is a myriad of possible modifications that can be made to the basic MemNet architecture in the interests of error prevention, error detection, and error recovery. The work that has been done in ring robustness and fault-tolerant computing applies equally to the MemNet architecture. The design choices made from the host of possibilities will, to a large extent, be economic and engineering choices.

MemNet summary

The goals of the initial MemNet work were to explore the viability of using shared memory in support of distributed systems and to demonstrate that a fundamental change in the network abstraction (from I/O to memory) would result in an improved interface, both in performance and usability. The work demonstrated that the memory abstraction, when implemented in hardware, can provide access to the full network bandwidth for the application, completely bypassing the operating system and providing a speedup of distributed system interaction by up to a factor of 1000.

Therefore, we can conclude that for local area distributed systems, shared-memory support of communications makes sense immediately. Moving to other environments requires that we consider changes needed in order to support growth in network size, speed of nodes, and complexity of interconnection. For example, we need to consider how to extend the memory model to a wide area, with unreliable connections and no true broadcast. MemNet depends on the broadcast properties of token rings for its consistency protocol. It assumes a very high degree of reliability in message transmission (that is, no drops). In a wide area system, reliable broadcast will not be available, but unreliable multicast may be. Point-to-point messages will be much less reliable. We have concluded from these facts, among other things, that in a wide area environment, we should explore a relaxation of the consistency properties that a MemNet-like system provides. The range of network primitive operations (which on MemNet consists of physical read, physical write, read-modify-write, and signal) should be extended to allow distributed management of the network resources. The way in which consistency ought to be relaxed and the nature of the extended network primitive operations form the focus of the work embodied by Mether, described in the following section.

It is not practical to model the nation's network as a large, flat address space, as we have already learned in the transition from the flat host-name address space to the domain name system in Internet [18], which is hierarchical. In MemNet follow-on systems, flat address spaces should give way to more sophisticated addressing schemes. A candidate scheme is described later, in the section on CapNet.

There are many other research areas. Graceful degradation under network and node failure will need to be incorporated into the designs. In addition, new expressive tools (languages) will need to be developed so that the users of these distributed resources can describe interesting problems and their solutions.

Mether

Mether is a DSM implemented on Sun workstations under the SunOS 4.0 operating system. (Sun and SunOS are trademarks of Sun Microsystems, Inc.) It is distributed, since pages of memory are not all at one workstation, but rather move around the network in a demand-paged fashion. Processes through the network share read, write, and execute access. User programs access the data in a way indistinguishable from that used for other memory.

Mether design began in March 1988. Experience with MemNet pointed toward experiments with a DSM in a wholly different network environment: one with a higher latency, lower bandwidth, and software-based page fault managers. Work on Mether had several goals, as follows:

(1)   To develop a system to function as a "reality check" on the idea of DSM. MemNet had fulfilled its function in demonstrating that a DSM was practical. The next question was: Was MemNet a one-of-a-kind system or a specific instance of a general case? We felt that if Mether were a success, then the latter was true.

(2)   To better determine what the applications interface to a DSM should be. MemNet had certain properties, such as memory interrupts and strong consistency, that might have been either necessities or implementation decisions for one particular DSM.

(3)   To build a system that was useful in and of itself. We believed that a DSM running on conventional workstations (for example, Suns) using conventional networking protocols (for example, transmission-control protocol/internet protocol [TCP/IP] [8]) would be useful.

The first implementation of Mether, V0, was operational in November 1988 and is described by Minnich and Farber [16]. This version was essentially a software MemNet, supporting strong consistency and replicated read-only pages, and was thus similar to systems such as Li and Hudak's Ivy [14] and Bisiani and Forin's Mach-based DSM [6]. Processes mapped in a set of pages that were distinguished by being shareable over a network. A page could be moved from one processor to another at any time. If a process accessed a page and it was not present on the processor, it was fetched over the network.

The use of Mether V0 made a number of problems clear once a measurement study had been done. These problems are listed below.

(1)   Many shared-memory programs attempted to synchronize using memory variables as locks or semaphores and, in doing so, saturated the network with packets. Since they were synchronizing using the *value* of the memory variable, we sought to use this fact to our advantage.

(2)   Synchronization traffic also affected the Mether communications servers, resulting in queued packets.

(3)   Long queues of packets and blocked communications servers increased the latency of the shared memory.

(4)   Programs trying to synchronize spent most of their execution time in loops examining unchanged variables. This increased host load.

(5)   On workstations, packet delivery was unreliable. Even point-to-point messages could be easily dropped or misordered. Protocols had to be designed to tolerate such unreliability.

Several resolutions for these problems are possible. Synchronization mechanisms can be added as an out-of-band subsystem, as in Ivy's use of RPC. However, for aesthetic reasons, we wanted synchronization to be supported as an integral part of the DSM. The shared-memory model used by our DSMs needed to be extended and changed.

It might be seen as contradictory to advocate "dilution" of the shared-memory model as a network interface. But this is not so; the abstraction has not changed, but rather the implementation for a specific setting has changed. Also, as we are finding, many applications do not require the high degree of consistency provided by MemNet; they can make effective use of a more relaxed consistency model. For this reason, we were willing to have Mether depart from an emulation of the shared-memory model where differences can provide a performance improvement in the face of high latency and poor operating system performance. As testing of applications (ported from machines such as the Cray-2) progressed, the shared-memory model was adapted accordingly. In many cases, processes need only examine a few variables in a page. Consistent memory is not always needed. Even the demand-driven nature so basic to the DSM model is not always desirable. We describe these changes — inconsistent memory, short pages, user-driven page propagation, latency-insensitive address space, and data-driven page faults — in further detail below. None of the changes detract from the utility of memory as a network abstraction.

Inconsistent memory

Mether V3 allows a process to access memory as consistent or inconsistent. A process indicates its desired access by mapping the memory as read-only or writable. There is one consistent copy of a page; for reasons described by Minnich and Farber [17], we move the consistent copy of a page around, rather than the write capabilities for a page.

When a process gets an inconsistent copy of a page, the process holding a consistent copy may continue to write to it. Over time, a read-only copy will become out-of-date, or inconsistent. There are four ways that an update can occur, as follows:

(1)   A process may request the consistent copy, causing an up-to-date copy of the page to be transmitted over the network, at which time all the Mether servers having a copy of the page will refresh their copy.

(2)   The process holding the consistent copy can cause a new version of the copy to be sent out over the network via a system call, using network refresh (see the subsection entitled "User-driven page propagation").

(3)   As part of the page-management policy, the local inconsistent copy will be discarded when it has been present for more than (currently) five seconds. Thus, there is an absolute bound on how out-of-date a copy may be.

(4)   The process holding the inconsistent copy can purge its copy; the next time it accesses the page, a new copy will be fetched over the network.

The first three mechanisms constitute a passive update. The last mechanism is an active update.

Short pages

Another capability added to Mether was support for *short pages*. Short pages are only 32 bytes long. They are actually the first 32 bytes of a full-sized page. A typical use is to store important state variables in the first 32 bytes of the page. The process can access these variables with extremely low overhead, because few packets must be transmitted upon a fault, and determine whether to access the full (8192-byte) page. The low overhead comes from the fact that page faults cause only 32 bytes, as opposed to 8192 bytes, to transit the network. The address space for short pages is a complete overlay of the address space for full pages, which is how the short pages can share variables with full

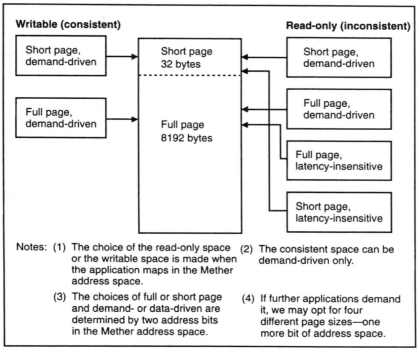

Notes: (1) The choice of the read-only space or the writable space is made when the application maps in the Mether address space. (2) The consistent space can be demand-driven only.

(3) The choices of full or short page and demand- or data-driven are determined by two address bits in the Mether address space. (4) If further applications demand it, we may opt for four different page sizes—one more bit of address space.

Figure 3. The Mether address space.

pages. Figure 3 shows the relationship of short pages to full pages in the address space, and it shows how different virtual addresses in the Mether address space reference a single page.

User-driven page propagation

Because pages can become out-of-date in the Mether model, there must be a way to propagate new copies of a page. Since the servers do not always know when propagation should occur, Mether supports user-driven propagation. First, processes can cause local, read-only copies of a page to be discarded, so that the next reference causes a new copy of the page to be fetched over the network. Second, on those systems that support some form of broadcast or multicast, a writer can cause its copy to be broadcast to all holders of the inconsistent copy; this is called *network refresh*.

Latency-insensitive address space

Mether 3.0 provides an address space that is *latency insensitive*. When a reference in this space results in a page fault, Mether will use a high-latency communications channel to send out the request for the page. Pending references in the latency-insensitive address space may be resolved by a network refresh. The latency-insensitive address space is used to support *data-driven page faults*, described next. This new address space type provides a base for experimentation assuming high-latency environments.

Data-driven page faults

An even greater departure from the standard DSM is the support Mether provides for data-driven page faults. In the shared-memory systems described above, a page fault always results in a request

---

Operation	Rule for subsets	Rule for supersets
Mapping a page in	All subsets must be present	Supersets need not be present
Pagein from the network	All subsets paged in	No supersets paged in
Pageout	All subsets paged out	All supersets left paged in but unmapped
Lock	All subsets must be present; if all are present, all are locked; otherwise, the lock fails and any nonpresent subsets are marked wanted	No supersets locked but must be present; all are unmapped; nonpresent supersets are marked wanted
Page fault	All subsets must be present	Supersets need not be present
Purge	All consistent subsets are purged	Supersets are not affected

Figure 4. The rules for subspace operations.

over the network for a page. In a data-driven page fault, one process takes an action that causes another process's page fault to be satisfied. Thus, one process takes an action that causes another process's memory cycle to complete.

Data-driven page faults are accomplished when a process blocks on a memory read request to the latency-insensitive address space. The request may be satisfied by some other process performing a network refresh of the page. Thus, one process's memory read request has been directly satisfied by an action taken by some other process. A synchronization has been performed at the memory request level, using behavior of processes at the operating system level.

The rules for paging pages in and out, mapping them into a process's address space, and locking them into one process's address space are more complex for Mether than for simple DSMs. These rules are shown in Figure 4. In the table presented in this figure, *subset* refers to the contained page (that is, the short page) and *superset* refers to the containing page (that is, the 8192-byte page in the current implementation). Note that we may later have more than two page lengths.

Mether summary

Mether V3 implements a DSM with extended semantics for memory operations, specifically: short pages, a latency-insensitive address space, network refresh, and data-driven page requests [15]. Mether has supported a variety of applications for over three years. Mether has demonstrated that

- MemNet was not a one-of-a-kind system, but rather was a specific instance of a general case;
- The MemNet model of strongly consistent memory had to be extended and changed for a high-latency environment;
- A DSM running on conventional workstations under a standard Unix operating system is useful; and
- Applications can make effective use of an inconsistent address space with the other Mether properties.

CapNet — A distributed shared memory for wide area networks

One of the key questions that arose in the MemNet research was the applicability of the shared-memory abstraction to the WAN environment. There are number of crucial differences between WANs and LANs that might frustrate the abstraction, as follows:

- WANs have much larger latency (the round-trip time required to send data and receive a response),
- WANs cannot effectively support broadcast, and
- WANs have traditionally been bandwidth constrained.

DSM remains useful as a system abstraction for writing distributed applications involving information sharing. One example of such an application is support of distributed databases, as proposed by Tam [23] and Hsu at Harvard University, Cambridge, Massachusetts. Coupled with the evidence from Mether that applications could operate with relaxed consistency, extending DSM to the wide area environment is both technically interesting and desirable.

CapNet issues

Issues addressed by CapNet include those that are issues in any DSM, such as memory coherency, and some that are specific to the WAN environment. Most DSMs, as pointed to in the survey by Tam, Smith, and Farber [22], mentioned earlier, use a single-writer/multiple-readers serialization protocol. Our research has suggested new notions of memory coherency that would allow users to improve concurrency by exploiting characteristics of applications; Bennett, Carter, and Zwaenepoel [4] of Rice University, Houston, Texas, and Hutto and Ahamad [13] of Georgia Institute of Technology, Atlanta, Georgia, as well have addressed reexamination of memory coherence policies. We will concentrate on issues specific to a WAN-based DSM and assume a single-writer/multiple-readers protocol. However, the schemes are independent of the coherency protocols used.

Wide area DSMs are built on a point-to-point switching network where broadcasting is inherently expensive. Hence, a directory of page locations must be maintained by some *page manager*. Requests for a page go to the page manager, which forwards the requests to the *owner*. An owner is the host that made the last modification to the page and, therefore, has the most current version. The page manager designates the requesting host as the new owner before it forwards a write request to the current owner. The current owner is the host whose write request has just been forwarded. An owner honors a read request by sending the page and updating its *copyset*, the set of hosts with read copies. Set membership is used to multicast invalidation information (and avoid broadcast) when a write request is honored by the page manager. This scheme (in terms of delay) requires a round-trip to the page manager and a round-trip to the owner before a request can be honored. In a WAN, where latency is high, the number of request/response round-trips detailed above may imply a very long response time. Higher performance could be achieved if we could optimize the protocol or architecture to remove these delays. We set ourselves the goal of the requests reaching the owner directly, without reference to an intermediary directory service. Our scheme is described next.

Page-location scheme of CapNet

The scheme proposed in CapNet [21] is to integrate the network and the operating system software. We do this by augmenting the packet switches with information necessary for locating pages. By distributing the page table into the network switches, the network can route a page request to the owner directly. Under our scheme, a memory request is routed according to its virtual address, which is shared by the participants in an area of DSM. Each switch has its own version of the page table and each page table entry contains an identifier for an outgoing hop leading to the owner of the page. (This table resembles a routing table.) Entries in the page table are updated as pages are transferred to satisfy write requests. Therefore, the current location of a page is always accurate, and it is maintained by the network fabric. A host requesting a shared page may generate a page request. The request is sent to the network; the network locates the page and transfers it to the requester. The whole process takes only two messages, and no broadcasting is required. Address information in the network is self-maintaining. It is possible that there are more than one outstanding request for a page. These requests can be held in a FIFO queue appended to the page. When the page is transferred, the queue of requests is transferred with it.

If a page request is issued when the requested page is in transit, the request may either "chase" the page to its new owner or it may be directed to the switch closest to the previous owner and then redirected to the new owner. This will depend on whether the path of the second request intersects with that of the first request and, if so, whether the page table of the switch at the intersection has already been altered.

Putting the entire page table in the switches may pose some problems, because of the extent of the address spaces that might be envisioned, as well as because of the number of participants. Fast memory, especially fast content-addressable memories (CAMs), is quite expensive. We have devised a hybrid approach that preserves much of the latency reduction of the original scheme and does so with reduced memory requirements. The basic "hybridization" comes from distributing lookup entries across the switching nodes. To the degree that we can map entries to switches near their points of frequent use, we will succeed. Locations for pages that are infrequently referenced can be kept in a page manager. It is possible to partition the virtual address space by some scheme and to designate a host as the manager for the pages in each of these partitions. The scheme we suggest is to use the page manager's identifier as part of the virtual address. The page manager of a group of pages that exhibit geographic locality can be migrated as the referencing (and hence the locality) changes, reducing the average propagation delay in comparison to that using a page manager that has a fixed location.

UPWARDS

UPWARDS (for University of Pennsylvania wide area distributed system) is an attempt to develop software that can provide access to the bandwidth available in future high-speed WANs. The target environment for UPWARDS is the AURORA testbed [9], which is described in a summary published by the Corporation for National Research Initiatives [12]. Briefly, four sites (University of Pennsylvania, Philadelphia, Pennsylvania; IBM Research, Hawthorne, New York; Bell Communications Research [Bellcore], Morristown, New Jersey; and the Massachusetts Institute of Technology [MIT], Cambridge, Massachusetts) will be connected by a number of OC12 links. These links operate at 622 megabits per second, which is about 80 megabytes per second. Such speeds will place a considerable burden on the operating system software of connected computers, as they represent very large fractions of the bus bandwidths of even the fastest workstations.

UPWARDS is exploring a number of technologies in an attempt to offer a significant fraction of the available bandwidth to computations. First, UPWARDS uses DSM, because — with DSM — the number of instructions necessary for passing state between processes is minimized. This is because — independent of any communications scheme used — shared memory communicates using machine instructions. Traditional approaches to IPC build abstract instructions such as Read and Write out of many simple machine instructions. Thus, shared-memory communication should place a smaller burden on the machines that employ it. Evidence from MemNet argues for the feasibility, and many DSMs have been built in the LAN environment [22].

Second, UPWARDS uses lightweight processes, because high-context switch overheads are intolerable at gigabit/second speeds. For example, an operating system that requires five milliseconds per context switch and has two processes, A and B, can easily accumulate 1.25 megabytes of information. To see this, assume A is receiving data and is context switched out and B is context switched in. This takes five milliseconds; assuming no work is accomplished, B is then switched out and A is context switched in, for another five milliseconds. In this 10 milliseconds, $10^{**}7$ bits, or 1.25 megabytes, of data have arrived.

Third, UPWARDS makes heavy use of caches and cache preloading in an attempt to address the issue of latency. Caches are portions of fast local memory containing data that have been obtained from slower memory areas. If the correct data are in the cache (that is, if the cache has a high "hit rate"), the illusion of a single memory of low cost, large size, and fast access can be achieved. In the case of memory implemented using a network, a cache must be employed to defeat the latency imposed by propagation delays. We believe that caches must also be preloaded, anticipating future memory requests, in an attempt to reduce observed latency using available bandwidth.

We are developing special hardware assists [25] in order to support the memory-oriented abstraction for networks. These assists are in the form of host interfaces, which connect the network fabric into the computer's bus.

We see the high throughput, cache management, and lightweight processes of UPWARDS as ideal for a number of applications of our network. One of particular interest is that of multiparty multimedia interaction. Each of the four research sites in the AURORA network has an experimental teleconferencing facility provided by Bellcore called a *VideoWindow*. The VideoWindow consists of a pair of wide-screen television displays, a pair of television cameras, and high-quality audio equipment. The displays and cameras operate using National Television System Committee (NTSC) video, which requires about 150 megabits per second uncompressed. In order to bring the full capabilities of the computer to bear in teleconferencing, we are developing video interfaces to the RS/6000 Microchannel Architecture so that the images on the screen can be processed, controlled, and augmented by computer. Ideally, one should be able to comprise a presentation using voice, images, data displays, and full-motion video in order to share a multimedia environment with other participants in the teleconference. Processing the large amounts of shared state inherent in such a system should provide a challenging driving application for UPWARDS.

Conclusions and open questions

From the initial idea of memory as a network abstraction came the MemNet DSM, which treated the network as an extended processor bus and, because of the nature of its components, was able to exhibit very good performance in an LAN environment. Minnich originally constructed the Mether software as an attempt to preserve the MemNet interface, and much of the early design effort was spent on building software that could be implemented easily in silicon. However, experience with a number of applications led to the conclusion that DSMs that supported strongly consistent memory can exhibit poor performance, for reasons that are implementation-independent. Thus, there are common issues that can be addressed between MemNet and Mether.

The current version of Mether, Mether 3.0, addresses these common issues by using short pages of 32 bytes (as opposed to the 8192-byte pages of the host operating system) for synchronization data and by relaxing consistency constraints where possible. Thus, by moving the MemNet design from a specialized LAN fabric and custom operating system, the Mether system is able to attack variable latency, host load, and program performance. Lessons learned from Mether can guide the design of future hardware DSMs.

The CapNet design extends the MemNet scheme in another direction — that of WANs. As

---

previously discussed, the most difficult issue is the latency, or delay in message propagation, between nodes. Latency wreaks havoc on the performance of page-management schemes designed for broadcast LANs. CapNet addresses the latency by augmenting packet switches in the network with a directory system used for page location. The effect is a significant reduction in the number of messages required for page table management and, thus, a significant improvement in response time. A hybrid scheme can be used to reduce the memory requirements of each switch node. Thus, CapNet suggests an extremely attractive hardware architecture for a high-performance WAN DSM.

The UPWARDS system is, in a sense, the software complement to the CapNet research. It focuses on software resource-management schemes and service primitives with which processes can communicate efficiently. It is specifically targeted at high-speed — for example, gigabit-rate — WANs.

The growth of these systems from the original MemNet design and implementation suggests that this approach has merit that transcends any particular instantiation. What was originally a hardware DSM on a specialized LAN has been extended to constructions using WANs and implementing DSM with software. Other research [20] has shown that memory techniques such as caching and prefetching can be used to control the traffic generated by a computer. After 25 years of research, memory management is one of the best understood areas of computer science. We are trying to bring this understanding, and the power that it implies, to bear on the problems of computer networking.

Some of the open questions that remain are listed below.

(1)   How large does it make sense to let these nets grow? MemNet gave indications that, depending on the style of usage of a DSM, a network of either 30 or 300 computers is the reasonable upper bound. Additional characterization will need to be done before this question can be answered, but one possibility was suggested by Mether's relaxed consistency scheme.

(2)   What lessons from virtual memory can be directly transferred to DSM systems? What new schemes will be necessary to support the virtual memory model of data access?

(3)   What form should schemes for error prevention, error detection, and error recovery take? How can these forms be generalized so that the solution is a general solution, rather than an individual solution for each instance of a DSM application?

(4)   How can networks of heterogeneous machines be interconnected? Issues of data alignment can affect even homogeneous processor complexes. Can this be done without huge performance penalties?

(5)   Can models of security be preserved?

(6)   What new problems will this system solve? The introduction of a new resource with new capabilities generally enables new classes of solutions. What form will these solutions take?

References

[1] H.E. Bal, M.F. Kaashoek, and A.S. Tanenbaum, "Experience with Distributed Programming in Orca," *Proc. 1990 Int'l Conf. Computer Languages*, IEEE Computer Soc. Press, Los Alamitos, Calif., 1990, pp. 79-89.

[2] R. Beck and R. Kasten, "VLSI Assist in Building a Multiprocessor UNIX System," *Proc. Summer Usenix Conf.*, Usenix, Berkeley, Calif., 1985, pp. 255-275.

[3] G. Bell, "ULTRACOMPUTERS: A Teraflop before Its Time," *Comm. ACM*, Vol. 35, No. 8, Aug. 1992, pp. 27-47.

[4] J. Bennett, J. Carter, and W. Zwaenepoel, "Munin: Distributed Shared Memory Based on Type-Specific Memory Coherence," *Proc. 1990 Conf. Principles and Practice of Parallel Programming*, ACM Press, New York, N.Y., 1990, pp. 168-176.

[5] P.A. Bernstein, "Sequoia: A Fault-Tolerant Tightly Coupled Multiprocessor for Transaction Processing," *Computer*, Vol. 21, No. 2, Feb. 1988, pp. 37-45.

[6] R. Bisiani and A. Forin, "Multilanguage Parallel Programming of Heterogeneous Machines," *IEEE Trans. Computers*, Vol. 37, No. 8, Aug. 1988, pp. 930-945.

[7] L. Borrmann and M. Herdieckerhoff, "Parallel Processing Performance in a Linda System," *Proc. 1989 Int'l Conf. Parallel Processing, Vol. I: Architecture*, The Pennsylvania State Univ. Press, University Park, Pa., 1989, pp. 151-158.

[8] V.G. Cerf and R.E. Kahn, "A Protocol for Packet Network Intercommunication, " *IEEE Trans. Comm.*, Vol. COM-22, May 1974, pp. 637-648.

[9] D.D. Clark et al., "The AURORA Gigabit Testbed," *Computer Networks and ISDN Systems*, Vol. 25, No. 6, Jan. 1993, pp. 599-621.

[10] G.S. Delp, *The Architecture and Implementation of MemNet: A High-Speed Shared Memory Computer Communication Network*, doctoral thesis, Dept. of Electrical Eng., Univ. of Delaware, Newark, Del., 1988.

[11] G.S. Delp and D.J. Farber, "MemNet: An Experiment in High-Speed, Memory-Mapped Local Network Interfaces," Tech. Report 85-11-1, Dept. of Electrical Eng., Univ. of Delaware, Newark, Del., 1985.

[12] "Gigabit Testbed Initiative Summary," Corp. for Nat'l Research Initiatives, Reston, Va., Jan. 1992.

[13] P.W. Hutto and M. Ahamad, "Slow Memory: Weakening Consistency to Enhance Concurrency in Distributed Shared Memories," *Proc. 10th Int'l Conf. Distributed Computing Systems*, IEEE Computer Soc. Press, Los Alamitos, Calif., 1990, pp. 302-309.

[14] K. Li and P. Hudak, "Memory Coherence in Shared Virtual Memory Systems," *ACM Trans. Computer Systems,* Vol. 7, No. 4, Nov. 1989, pp. 321-359.

[15] R.G. Minnich, *Mether: A Memory System for Network Multiprocessors*, doctoral thesis, Univ. of Pennsylvania, Philadelphia, Pa., 1990.

[16] R.G. Minnich and D.J. Farber, "The Mether System: A Distributed Shared Memory for SunOS 4.0," *Proc. Usenix Conf.,* Usenix, Berkeley, Calif., 1989.

[17] R.G. Minnich and D.J. Farber, "Reducing Host Load, Network Load, and Latency in a Distributed Shared Memory," *Proc. 10th Int'l Conf. Distributed Computing Systems*, IEEE Computer Soc. Press, Los Alamitos, Calif., 1990, pp. 468-475.

[18] P.V. Mockapetris, "DNS Encoding of Network Names and Other Types," Internet Request for Comments (RFC)1101, Network Information Center, SRI Int'l, Menlo Park, Calif., Apr. 1989.

[19] O. Serlin, "Alliant Unveils Parallel Multiprocessor," *Unixworld*, Dec. 1985, pp. 17-27.

[20] J.M. Smith and D.J. Farber, "Traffic Characteristics of a Distributed Memory System," *Computer Networks and ISDN Systems*, Vol. 22, No.2, Sept. 1991, pp. 143-154.

[21] I.M.-C. Tam and D.J. Farber, "CapNet — An Alternative Approach to Ultra High Speed Networks," *Proc. Int'l Comm. Conf. '90*, IEEE Service Center, Piscataway, N.J., 1990, pp. 955-961.

[22] I.M.-C. Tam, J.M. Smith, and D.J. Farber, "A Taxonomy-Based Comparison of Several Distributed Shared Memory Systems," *ACM Operating Systems Rev.*, Vol. 24, No. 3, July 1990, pp. 40-67.

[23] V.-O. Tam, *Transaction Management in Data Migration Systems,* doctoral thesis, Computer Science, Harvard Univ., Cambridge, Mass., 1991.

[24] "TC2000 Technical Product Summary," BBN Advanced Computers, Inc., Cambridge, Mass., Nov. 1989.

[25] C.B.S. Traw and J.M. Smith, "A High-Performance Host Interface for ATM Networks," *Proc. ACM SIGCOMM Conf.*, ACM Press, New York, N.Y., 1991, pp. 317-325.

Distributed File Systems

Managing Highly Available Personal Files

T he proliferation of computer networks enables users
who are geographically located across wide areas to
share resources. Users routinely access machines within
their local area networks and — by means of internetworks —
access machines distributed across wide regions. For example, a
user at our university (Michigan State University, East Lansing,
Michigan) typically has accounts on machines managed by the
Computer Science Department, the Computing Center, and the
College of Engineering. In addition, the internet allows a user to
easily access accounts on machines located throughout the country
and even the world.

The opportunity for increased sharing of resources is an obvious
benefit that results from growth in the number of computer
networks. Users are likely to have accounts that are provided by
separate administrative units. For security and management reasons,
each administrative unit typically does not allow its file systems to
be mounted by systems managed by other administrative units.
Therefore, users have computer accounts that are likely to be
served by independent file systems. Many difficulties occur for
users who must manage their personal files that are distributed
among independent file systems. Users' views of a file system
often depend on the machine that they are currently accessing.
Figure 1 illustrates an environment in which a user has home
directories at three separate administrative units (called *management
units*). The user is logged into Machine C-1, where a local disk
holds a personal directory for the user. The user's home directory
within Management Unit C is at a remote file server, such as
Machine C-2. The home directory is accessed transparently by a
network file system (NFS) [18]. In addition, the user has a personal
directory located at Machine C-3. Within Management Unit C, the
user sees three separate file systems at Machines C-1, C-2, and
C-3. A user in this environment often does not effectively manage
local disk capacity, but places most personal files under the home
directory without using the additional available personal directories.
The user in the example illustrated in Figure 1 has access to other,
independent file systems located within Management Units A

Matt W. Mutka and

Lionel M. Ni

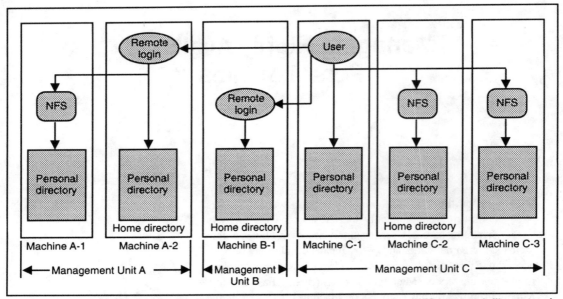

Figure 1. Personal files dispersed across several separate management units. (NFS = network file system.)

and B. Management Unit A contains two machines and two file systems and Management Unit B contains one machine and one file system. In the example shown, the user accesses Machines A-2 and B-1 by remote login. Files stored within Management Units A and B are not directly accessible but can be accessed through remote login services.

Users need services to help them manage their files that are placed among several separate file systems. Typically, users replicate their personal files at different machines. Users must remember which machine has the most recent version of a file as well as the location of a file within the file system on that machine. Support is needed to provide transparent access to all files, no matter which machine a user is logged into. In addition, files should remain accessible, despite a failure at a file server. To provide such a service, one approach is to modify the existing operating system on all machines. However, managers usually are reluctant to modify the operating system. It is almost impossible to have managers for all different administrative units modify their operating systems. Therefore, we propose a method that neither involves help from the managers nor the modification of the operating system and file structures.

We built PFS (for "personal file system") to provide transparent and highly available access to files that are dispersed across multiple file servers. By means of PFS, users create a global file structure of their personal files that looks the same, no matter which machine a user accesses. Figure 2 illustrates the role of PFS. Components of PFS are placed at each independent administrative unit for which a user has access, so that the user receives a unified and highly available file system for personal files. PFS manages a user's disk capacity, whether it is the capacity at several remote file servers or the capacity at the local workstation. Each file in a user's PFS is duplicated, so that a single failure at any file server does not restrict access to files. A more reliable system can be obtained by replicating files more than once, but there is a trade-off between the cost of duplication and the degree of reliability desired. We support single replication in our prototype system.

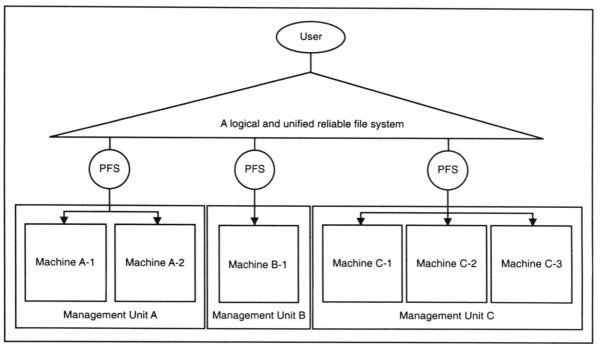

Figure 2. PFS provides a unified and reliable view of the personal files.

PFS: Objectives and related work

To understand the goals of PFS and the services it provides, one must realize that the Unix file system has a "relaxed" view of file integrity. Unix is more concerned with measurements of performance and the price-to-performance ratio than with maintaining consistency of files in the presence of system failures. When closing a modified Unix file, the modifications are likely to be permanent if the system does not fail for a few minutes. If the system fails, then all, some, or perhaps none of the file modifications will be present [4]. PFS operates within the service constraints provided by the Unix file system to enable users to access files as servers disappear from the network. Because the services that PFS provides are for a single user's personal files, problems with consistency and synchronization are at the personal level—a level at which each user can be called upon for aid when needed. Users know from which machines they access their personal files, and they are probably aware of their atypical file access behavior. Scaling is not a problem in PFS. Each PFS environment is customized for each user. A user would likely have fewer than five independent file systems in which personal files are stored, and rarely would there be more than 10 independent file systems that hold a user's files. PFS's achievement is to significantly enhance the personal file-management facilities available to a user, without the underlying operating system being modified.

Objectives for the PFS environment

The objectives that are desired for the PFS environment concern the operating environment, file availability, performance, the disk-management facility, and the user interface. These objectives are discussed below.

Operating environment. PFS should provide its global interface to personal files by operating in Unix environments, a de facto standard, in which the user lacks administrative control. It requires the underlying file systems that support its service to be conventional Unix file systems. Services in PFS can be built on top of systems such as AT&T System V Unix, Unix Berkeley Software Distribution (BSD) 4.3, SunOS 4.1, and the NeXT Mach operating system.

File availability. PFS should provide access to highly available files. Replicas are maintained to enable users to access the files in the presence of failures at a file server. Since PFS does not implement a new underlying file system, several problems arise when PFS tries to support some of the Unix system calls in a global file system. This paper addresses these problems and discusses solutions that can be applied for a personal file system.

Performance. PFS should provide service that is perceived by a user to differ little in performance from the expected service from a Unix file system without PFS. To improve performance, PFS takes advantage of behavior characteristics that have been observed in users of personal files. The following are examples of these behavior characteristics:

- Users tend to use the same files repeatedly at the same location and
- User generally do not create or change a specific file at different machines simultaneously.

Disk-management facility. The disk-management facility of PFS makes decisions for placing files at file server locations according to the amount of disk space available at these locations, the observed access patterns to files, and the access rates for files at the file servers. These file-placement decisions are part of the *file-assignment problem* for workstation and file servers in networked environments. Studies of this problem were conducted by Pattipati and Wolf [12], [22]. Surveys of the file-assignment problem were described by Dowdy and Foster [6] and Wah [20].

User interface. PFS should be integrated into user environments with little "learning overhead" required by a user. To achieve this objective, PFS presents the user with the traditional Unix interface, so there is no need to learn special commands. A few new commands support management operations.

Other notable systems

Coda [15], [16] is a system whose services resemble those that PFS provides, but whose objectives are different. Coda is a highly available distributed file system that emulates Unix file semantics and evolved from the Andrew file system [11]. Unlike PFS, Coda provides its services by building a new underlying file system. Coda must be supported by all the machines in its environment. PFS provides a new personal-file-management facility, but does not implement a new distributed file system.

Other notable examples of systems that replicate files for reliability and performance are Pulse [19], Locus [13], Echo [8], IBM Aix-DS [17], replicated network file system (RNFS) [10], a file-replication facility built for Unix BSD 4.3 [14], and Dragon Slayer [21]. Pulse is an operating system built for sharing of file systems among personal computers. Files can be duplicated in Pulse, but duplicates are only kept consistent when they are referenced. Inconsistent copies of the same file are denoted by different version numbers. Locus provides a distributed file system with elaborate mechanisms for keeping duplicates of files transparently consistent. Echo is a distributed file system being implemented by Digital Equipment Corporation (DEC). It uses a replication scheme to maintain availability of files in case of failure at the primary site. IBM Aix-DS provides a distributed file system that is based on System V Unix. Replication of files provides fault tolerance, but users have

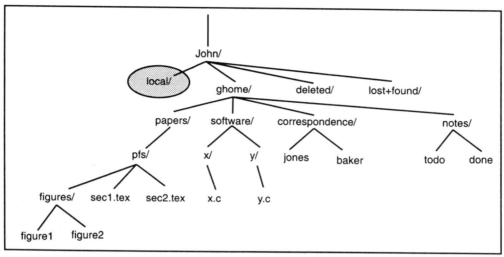

Figure 3. View of a user's home directory.

no control over access to replicas. RNFS adds replication of files to Sun NFS to enhance the availability of files in a standard NFS. The file-replication facility built for Unix BSD 4.3, described by Purdin, Schlichting, and Andrews [14], provides a set of commands for users so that they can specify which files should be duplicated and at which machines to place the duplicates. Dragon Slayer [21] provides a network layer on the underlying operating system. Files may be fragmented and stored at different servers. The user has to explicitly specify the number of replications needed. Dragon Slayer requires all systems in its environment to use its newly created commands to manage the environment.

Abdullah and Juang [1] discuss an NFS with a file access mechanism built into the command interpreter. Although they do not study a highly available personal-file-management system, their approach has similarities to our approach. The command interpreter resolves the location of files in a networked environment and requests copies of files from the daemons at the sites at which the files are located.

The user's view of the personal file system

PFS maintains high availability to a global file system of a user's personal files. Figure 3 illustrates how a user named *John* views files in his home directory within PFS. No matter which file server John accesses, he sees the home directory partitioned into the following four parts: *local, ghome, deleted,* and *lost+found* files.

The local file directory is illustrated in Figure 3 as the shaded ellipse that branches from the home directory. Local files are not part of the global file system and are accessible only from the local file server being accessed. These files are likely to be machine-specific files that will not be accessed at other locations and files that the user wants to share with others at only the specific local site.

Globally accessible files are located under the ghome directory. The files in the global file system can be accessed from any location at which the user has installed PFS. The global file system can be installed at several independent file systems and at the local disk of the user's workstation. No matter

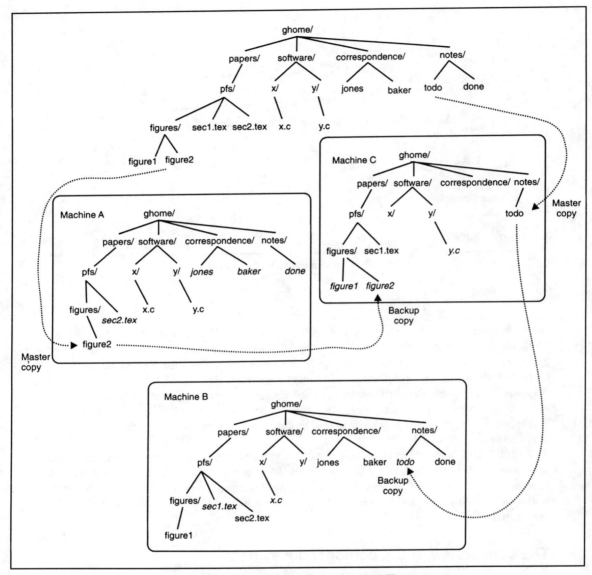

Figure 4. Placement of global files at physical file servers.

which machine the user is accessing within the global file system, a user has the same view of the file system structure. For example, suppose *John* has installed PFS at three different machines: Machines A, B, and C. Each machine is served by an independent file system. Consider the file ghome/notes/todo, which is under the ghome directory. PFS makes the file todo accessible at each of the Machines A, B, and C. Figure 4 shows an instance of the placement of files that are located under the ghome directory at the three machines. Notice that each file system has the same directory tree, which means directories are replicated at each site. Each file listed within the ghome directory in Figure 3 has two copies shown in Figure 4. One copy is designated as a *master copy* and the other is the *backup copy*. Use of PFS requires that a site obtain the master copy of a file in order to modify it. The backup copy enables a user to access to a file if a master copy becomes inaccessible. Notice that the file ghome/notes/todo has a copy at both Machine B and Machine C. On Figure 4, the copy listed at Machine C is in normal type (that is, nonitalics), which indicates it is a master copy, and the copy listed at Machine B is in italics, indicating it is the backup copy. Similarly, notice the placement of other files in the system.

Table 1. .gmap entries.

File name
File size
Location of master copy
Location of backup copy
Current state (master, backup, temporary, neutral, ...)
Delete flag
In-use flag
Last accessed
Length of forward chain

Within the directory ghome/papers/pfs/figures, Machine A has the master copy of figure2 and the backup copy is placed at Machine C.

Files in the deleted and lost+found directories are managed by PFS. (See the sections entitled "Operations on files" and "Maintaining availability.")

The PFS server processes

Typically, a user interacts with a Unix system by means of the *sh* (for "Unix shell") or the *csh* (for "Unix C-shell"), which are user processes created when a user logs into a system. A *gsh* (for "global shell") is created when a user logs into an account at a machine running PFS and the current directory is set to the ghome directory. After the user has entered a command, the gsh locates the relevant files, brings the master copies to the local file system if they are not already local, and then passes the command to the sh or the csh.

The global view of a user's personal file system is enabled by the creation of system files, called *.gmap files*. A .gmap file is located in each directory in the global file system and is normally hidden from the user. The .gmap file is created and modified by a PFS server, called the *file server daemon* (FSD), which is located at each file server in the system. Table 1 lists information that the FSD manages in each .gmap file in order to maintain global transparency. The information in the file includes the names of the files in the directory, their sizes, the locations of their master and backup copies, and the states of the files from the FSD's perspective. If there is a local copy of the file, the state can be a master, backup, or a temporary copy of the file; if the file is not present, the local state is neutral. If the file has been deleted recently, the PFS server marks the entry by the *deleted flag*. While a file is in the deleted state, it is possible to reverse the deletion and recover the file. A file that the FSD detects as being actively used is marked by the *in-use flag*. One entry records the time the file was last detected to be accessed, which is used for disk-management strategies that are described in the section entitled "Disk management." (Additional information regarding the actions that occur when files are accessed is presented in the section entitled "Operations on files.") One entry is labeled *length of forward chain*, which is modified when the master copy of the file is moved. (The use of this entry is described in the "Operations on files" section.)

Figure 5 illustrates the PFS processes that are active at an example installation. In the illustrated example, a PFS system is formed from three machines. Each machine has an independent file system. The PFS processes are the gsh, the FSD, the recovery daemon (RD), and the disk daemon (DD). A gsh is the user interface to the Unix operating system. One gsh exists for every login process on a

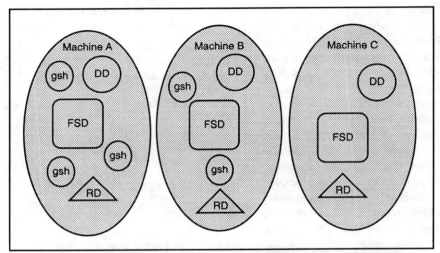

Figure 5. Processes in PFS at an example installation. (gsh = global shell, DD = disk daemon, FSD = file server daemon, and RD = recovery daemon.)

machine. Machine A has three gsh processes executing, because the user has opened three windows on Machine A. Likewise, two gsh processes are executing on Machine B. Since the user has not logged into Machine C, no gsh processes are executing there. An FSD process manages the .gmap files located in each directory at a file server. The RD has the responsibility of helping users maintain access to their files in spite of failure of servers. (We discuss the responsibilities of the RD in the sections entitled "Operations on files" and "Maintaining availability.") The DD manages disk space. It determines where to place backup copies of files and where to move files when disk space becomes scarce. In addition, the DD clears the disks of temporary files created by users. (We describe the DD in the section entitled "Disk management.") Each machine has one FSD, one RD, and one DD process executing.

Operations on files

In operations on files in a global file system, files should appear to the user as if they were located in a local file system. A user does not need specific commands to create, examine, or delete files within the global file system, but uses the commands normally provided by the Unix operating system. The gsh emulates the user interface to the global file system as if it were the sh or csh Unix interface. Nevertheless, problems and limitations arise, specifically because PFS supports a global file system without modifying the kernel of the machines in the system. This section describes some problems, solutions, and limitations encountered when implementing the commonly used operations of file creation, access, and deletion. Apacible et al. [3] provided a detailed description of the states, transitions, and actions for the operations implemented in the system.

File creation

PFS must be able to detect the creation of a file in order to update the .gmap files on the file server in the system. This usually is done by the gsh as command lines are interpreted. When a new file is created by an editor, or by redirection of output, the gsh makes a new entry in its .gmap file and broadcasts this information to the other file servers. A user does not wait unnecessarily as the information is updated to the other file servers. The only noticeable effect is a small delay before the user can list the newly created file from a different file server. (These small delays are described in greater detail in the section entitled "Performance profile.") Since users tend to first access newly created files from the machine in which they were created, the user could immediately list the files in the local machine and detect no significant delay due to updating the .gmap entries.

The main problem encountered by PFS occurs when file creation cannot be detected at the user interface. PFS has not implemented a new kernel or modified an existing kernel, as is done in many systems [5], [8], [13], [15], [19], and PFS does not require a user to relink a program to new system library routines, as is done in the Condor system [9] and the replication facility for Unix BSD 4.3 [14]. Unix system calls that create files, such as Creat and Open, are neither intercepted nor detected by PFS. We must have another means of detecting the presence of newly created files. Two schemes have worked well in our current experience. The first scheme is to detect newly created files and then update the .gmap entries at the time the user lists the files. Often, a user executes a program that creates a file and then executes a file-listing command, such as the Unix ls command. We have modified the ls command so that it detects the existence of files not included in a .gmap file. If the ls command detects a new file, a new entry will be added to the .gmap file, and the information is disseminated to the other file servers. The user receives the listing of all the files in the directory, including the newly created files. The user does not perceive any delay for the files to appear in the global file system. The second scheme is to detect newly created files, establish a backup of the files, and then update .gmap entries. This scheme is used if a user does not list the files in a directory in which new files have been created. It is the responsibility of the RD to periodically examine the existence of files in each directory and to compare them with the .gmap entries in each directory. When new files are detected, the new entries are updated to all file servers. The interval between examinations of the file system for newly detected files is a parameter set during the initialization of PFS. This interval is usually set to be several minutes. (The RD has several other responsibilities, which are described in the section entitled "Maintaining availability.")

File access

For every file access, a copy is brought to the server that provides the minimum access time. (The placement of the file at the server is described in the subsection entitled "A model for disk management and file placement.") Initially, PFS attempts to obtain a master copy of the file at the server with the minimum access time; we call this server the *local server*. If the file server has a local copy of a file, and if it is the master copy, the user can proceed with access to the file by either reading from it or writing to it. If the local copy is a backup, then the local FSD negotiates with the FSD at the site holding the master copy. If negotiations are successful, the backup copy becomes the new master copy and the previous master copy becomes the backup. If negotiations fail because the master copy is currently active by another requester, then only the backup copy is readable, because a site must be the master to modify a file. (Note that only one master copy can be active for modifications at any time.) If a local file server does not have a copy of the file that is to be accessed, the local FSD negotiates with the FSD at the site with the master copy. The local FSD attempts to obtain the master copy. If negotiations fail, then the site receives a temporary copy of the file that will not have any modifications reflected in the master copy. Temporary files are deleted daily by the DD. If negotiations with the FSD at the master copy's site are successful, the backup is notified of the new location of the master, and then the file can be accessed.

To reduce the overhead of broadcasting the change of the master's location each time a master is moved, we inform only the backup and the old master of the new master's location. If the master location changes several times, some sites might need to traverse a chain of previous master locations when they search for the current master. Nevertheless, it is unlikely that there will be a long chain in a typical system. If the chain becomes longer than a specified length of forward chain (which is an entry in the .gmap table), then the master site broadcasts the master's location to all the sites (note that the chain length specification in our prototype system is ForwardChain = 2) and the length-of-forward-chain entry is reset to zero. We do not expect the chain length to grow in a personal file system in which accesses to particular files typically are made from the same location. Therefore, it is beneficial for performance to update the .gmap entries of only the master and backup copies. Nevertheless, during periods of late-night inactivity, the RDs at all the sites in the system make the entries of all the .gmap tables consistent. Therefore, early in a workday's morning, all the .gmap entries should reflect identical entries of the placement of master and backup copies of files, until accesses to files change the locations of master and backup copies.

A problem is encountered when programs access files by means of the Open system call. For this situation, access to files in the global directory is not transparent to a user. Since the Open call is not detected by PFS, a file must be local before a program can open the file. A user has the option of executing the PFS bringlocal file -mode command to bring a copy of the file to the local server, with the permissions mode read/write or read-only. If a read/write copy is requested, then the local FSD attempts to obtain a master copy of the file. If a master copy cannot be obtained, then a temporary version is obtained locally. Our initial experience indicated that the bringlocal command is adequate for a personal file system in which a user is aware that files are dispersed among servers. Because we are restricted from modifying the operating system and therefore do not have completely transparent access to the global file system, we believe that the PFS service is beneficial and acceptable for access to personal files.

Another approach to providing global access to personal files is to implement a personal library that contains the Open call and to link the library to personal programs. The personal version of the Open call will detect the opening of files and inform the FSD. (We will consider implementing the personal library in future versions of PFS.) In addition, some machines in a user's personal file system are under the control of the user. In these cases, the user could extend the operating system to enable the FSD to detect file operations. We can implement a new *device driver* for an FSD device. Users on the machine who use PFS can have their home directories linked from the new "device." Access to files by means of the new device driver will cause the FSD to be notified. This scheme only works for those machines that a user has permission to modify; therefore, it will not be the only scheme implemented. Nevertheless, it will be useful for a subset of the machines in a PFS environment.

File deletion

File deletion in PFS has the following two stages:

- Logical deletion of a file by marking the delete-flag entry in the .gmap as "deleted" and
- Physical deletion of the file from disk.

Files are logically deleted by using the rm command. This causes the entry for a file to be put in the "deleted" state on each file server. The backup copy is removed and the master copy is transferred to a special deleted directory under the user's home directory. Subsequent access to the file will fail, as if the file had been physically deleted. A "deleted" file can be returned to the global file system by the recover command. Therefore, our implementation provides another level of recovery capability, which is not provided in — for example — Unix BSD 4.3, SunOS 4.1, and System V Unix. When a logically deleted file is recovered, a master copy is returned from the deleted directory at the master's site. In addition, a new backup copy of the file is created.

A logically deleted file can be physically deleted in three different ways. First, the file can be removed when the DD does its daily "cleanup" work. Logically deleted files will exist at most for only one day, until the DD automatically removes them. Second, the file can be physically removed when a user creates a new file with the same name as a "deleted" file. The older version of the named file becomes obsolete. Third, the file can be explicitly removed by the user by means of the purge command. The purge command forces the DD to remove the "deleted" files to create free disk space. Once a file has been purged, it cannot be recovered.

Disk management

Disk space can become completely exhausted on a machine that holds the master or backup copies for most files in the file system. Some users might have a quota on the amount of disk space they can consume. File-migration operations [7] must be implemented to create, transfer, and delete copies in the system in order to manage the amount of disk spaced consumed. PFS has implemented a disk-management daemon (that is, the DD) for managing disk space.

The DD normally operates during periods of user inactivity, such as in the late evenings, to clean up temporary copies of files and remove files in the deleted directory. During periods of user inactivity, the RD—acting in conjunction with the DD—removes forward chains by broadcasting locations of master copies and checking for inconsistencies among user files and .gmap entries. The DD can be triggered to operate under either of two conditions: the user's quota of space is nearly depleted or a file server has little available disk space. Limitations recorded in a configuration file .gshrc indicate the existence of either of these two conditions; when one does exist, the DD follows the prioritized list of steps given below to free disk space on the server.

- Remove local copies of "temporary" and "deleted" files.
- Move backup copies of files to other server locations. The priority of moving backups is to move the least recently accessed backups to remote sites before moving those most recently accessed.
- Move least recently accessed master copies of files.
- Compress files and request user intervention.

This strategy takes advantage of the observation that users most likely access files in the future that have been recently accessed in the past, on the same machine as in the past. When disk space is being freed, it is better to keep recently accessed master copies of a file at a site than files that have not been used recently.

Normally, during the DD's periodic execution, it frees space on a server by executing only the first step of the above itemized list. It will execute the second and third steps if a site's quota or the amount of available disk space is within a range that is specified in the local file server configuration file. The last step will be executed only if the previous steps do not free enough disk space.

Disk-management tools

Users are very likely to have personal directories at several sites. File servers provide personal directories to an individual from disk space shared among many users. Some directory space is designated as users' home directories, which are the working directories for users when they log into a server or when they log into a domain served by the file server. Other personal-directory space provided by file servers might not be specified as the location of a user's home directory. Users often need to be aware of the details of the disk resources available at each personal-directory location. In addition, local disks are provided at a user's personal workstation. The local disks are either embedded within the workstation or attached as auxiliary devices. Typically, this disk space is controlled exclusively by the workstation owner.

Table 2. List of parameters.

Notation	Meaning
M_i	Maximum capacity of the ith personal directory
G_i	Capacity occupied by global files/directories
L_i	Capacity occupied by local files/directories
$A_i = M_i - G_i - L_i$	Available capacity of ith personal directory
t_{ki}	Average file access time from Machine k to ith personal directory
w_{ki}	Average network latency from Machine k to ith personal directory
v_i	Average disk access time of disk system holding ith personal directory
f_j	Size of file j
D	Size of directories of global file system
$\alpha_k(f)$	Placement policy of master file f evaluated at Machine k
$\beta_k(f)$	Placement policy of backup file f evaluated at Machine k

With an increasing number of personal directories becoming accessible to individuals, users need management tools to more effectively utilize their personal directories. Tools that provide automatic file placement for sharing and balancing of disk capacity can ease many cumbersome details. PFS implements facilities for disk capacity sharing and balancing, which can be described more formally by the following model.

A model for disk management and file placement

Consider a general case for a user with n personal directories. Table 2 lists the set of parameters that can be used to characterize a personal file system. These parameters, which can be easily measured or estimated, are recorded in the configuration file .gshrc. Note that the number of machines may be different from the number of personal directories. For simplicity of notation, we assume that the personal directory j is physically located at Machine j. The maximum capacity $M_i (1 \leq i \leq n)$ can be estimated by the allocated disk quota (if enforced) and the available capacity of the disk system. The average file access time t_{ki} is approximately equal to $w_{ki} + v_i$. If Machine k has a slow disk (for example, a slow Small Computer Systems Interface [SCSI] disk with a 25-millisecond disk access time), it may be beneficial to access a high-speed remote disk through the network (that is, $v_k > w_{ki} + v_i$ for some i).

For a highly available PFS in which each file is duplicated, the following global constraint must be satisfied:

$$\sum_{i=1}^{n} M_i \geq 2\sum_{\forall j} f_j + nD + \sum_{i=1}^{n} L_i \tag{1}$$

This constraint states that the sum of the maximum capacities of each personal directory available to a user must be greater than or equal to twice the size of the user's personal files, plus the size of the global directories that are replicated at all n personal directories and the sum of the capacities of each local directory. If the above constraint cannot be satisfied, either some files should be compressed or some files should be removed from the disk. In the latter case, the user will receive a warning message and should take appropriate actions.

Threshold capacity of personal directories. Each personal directory should keep a certain amount of available capacity to hold some master files without file migration. One approach is based on the relative occupancy of files based on the following equation, where T_1 is the threshold for the utilization of a personal directory:

$$\frac{L_i + G_i}{M_i} \leq T_1 \text{ for } 1 \leq i \leq n \tag{2}$$

This approach works well if the whole file system is allocated to this particular personal directory or if M_i is large. A better approach is to use an absolute measurement based on the following equation, where T_2 is the threshold for the amount of disk capacity that should remain available:

$$M_i - L_i - G_i \geq T_2 \tag{3}$$

Placement of master files. The *master-file-placement policy* decides at which personal directory to locate a master file. This policy should provide a good response time for the user. Because a file may be opened by the user from any machine, the master-file-placement policy is invoked when a file is activated. Let $\alpha_k(f)$ define the location of the master-file f when accessed from Machine k. Our current prototype implementation adopts $\alpha_k(f) = k$. However, a better master-file-placement policy is

$$\alpha_k(f) = j, \text{ where } j = \min_{\forall i} t_{ki} \text{ and } f + G_j + L_j \leq M_j \tag{4}$$

The second condition can be easily satisfied if the constraint in Equation (3) is satisfied. Otherwise, some files have to be migrated. (See the subsubsection entitled "File migration.")

Placement of backup files. The *backup-file-placement policy* decides the location of a backup file. Let $\beta_k(f)$ define the location of the backup file f when accessed from Machine k. The following policy may be used:

$$\beta_k(f) = j, \text{ where } j = \max_{\forall i} v_i \text{ and } f + G_j + L_j \leq M_j \text{ and } j \neq \alpha_k(f) \tag{5}$$

The basic idea is to place the backup files on the slowest disk in order to provide more available disk space at the sites holding the master copies. Nevertheless, in our prototype implementation, we define

$$\beta_k(f) = j, \text{ where } j = \max_{\forall i} A_i \tag{6}$$

as the initial location of the backup file f. The backup is placed at the site with the largest amount of unused disk capacity.

File migration. In PFS, file migration is automatically invoked if a file is opened and $\alpha_k(f)$ is different from the original location of the master file f. File migration also may be invoked during the daily cleanup process in order to satisfy Equation (3) for all i. The following are two issues to consider when file migration is being performed:

(1)   Which file should be migrated? Intuitively, all backup files are candidates. We must

consider the file size and the age of the file. If all files are master files (which is very likely if one's workstation has a small local disk), the factors to be considered include the file size and the last time the file was referenced.

(2)   Where can the migrated file be placed? Equation (3) then may be used. However, to avoid unnecessary movement of files, two thresholds (one high-water mark and one low-water mark) may be used instead of the single T_2 used in Equation (3). (Heuristics for file migration will be studied further in this project in the future.)

Cost of file storage. In this model, we do not consider the cost of file storage. In most Unix systems, file storage is free. However, some file systems may have to charge for storage. Therefore, the above model has to be modified. If some file systems are free and some are charged, one approach is to store files in the free file systems. The charged file systems store only active master files; when these files are closed, they are migrated to free file systems. If the total capacity of the free file systems is exceeded, the issue then becomes whether the user should place files at the charged file system or remove extra files. (Issues such as this will be considered in more detail in this project in the future.)

Maintaining availability

To provide a reliable file system, files must be replicated. In our prototype implementation, each file is duplicated, so that there are one master and one backup. Hence, our system is called a *2-reliable file system*. Furthermore, both copies must be placed on different personal directories (or different file systems). Let $A_i = S_i - P_i$ be the capacity allocated to global files. To provide a 2-reliable system, the following condition must be satisfied:

$$\frac{A_i}{\sum_{i=1}^{n} A_i} < 50 \text{ percent} \tag{7}$$

In some environments, a user may have only two personal directories. If a machine were to fail in such an environment, the condition expressed in Equation (7) would not be satisfied and, therefore, a 2-reliable system could not be provided. A possible solution is to provide a *deficient 2-reliable system* in which only selected files are duplicated. The issue then becomes which files should be duplicated. (This is an issue that we will study further in this project in the future.)

Periods of inaccessibility might occur as daemons or machines quit operating or as servers become disconnected from a network. Although time intervals of inaccessibility in local networks are often short (specifically, lasting for several minutes)—as, for example, when systems reboot—they can continue for extended periods.

Disconnecting and reconnecting servers

Our current design of PFS makes personal files in the global file system available in the event of disconnection of a single server from the system. Our approach is to place a file server site logically within a loop with the other servers in the system. The configuration file .gshrc defines the logical loop, in addition to the parameters described in Table 2. The loop described in .gshrc defines a predecessor and a successor relationship among the servers in the system. Figure 6 illustrates the predecessor and successor relationships among the file server machines in an example installation of five independent file servers. The logical link order is *Machine A* → *Machine B* → ... → *Machine E* → *Machine A*. Machine B is shown to be a predecessor to Machine C and a successor to

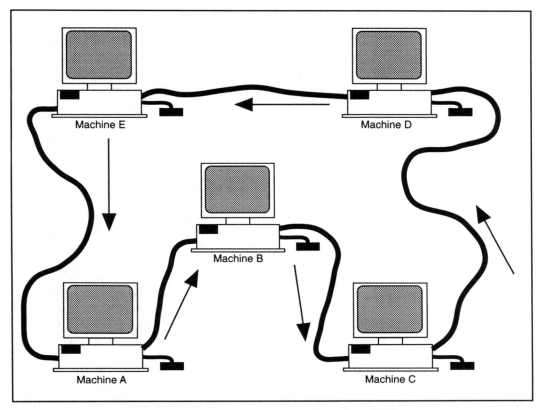

Figure 6. Example of a logical configuration of PFS.

Machine A. Consider the situation in which Machine B fails and Machine E attempts to access the master copy of a file held at Machine B. Suppose the backup copy is held at Machine D. Since the master copy is not available, the FSD of Machine E contacts the FSD at the site holding the backup copy of the file (which is Machine D). The FSD at Machine D returns a master copy of the file to the requester. Machine D contacts an RD at the successor to the failed site, which is Machine C. Machine C sends messages to each FSD to cause their configuration files to be modified to delete Machine B from the logical link. This means that the successor to Machine A is modified to be Machine C and the predecessor to Machine C is modified to be Machine A. In addition, future attempts to contact Machine B are directed to the RD at Machine C. The RD at Machine C records attempts to access files at Machine B and records creation and deletions of files that will affect the .gmap files at Machine B when it eventually recovers. Files that have had their master and backup copies moved from Machine B are recorded by the RD at Machine C.

The RD of Machine C periodically tries to contact Machine B to determine when it resumes operating so that it can recover the site. Future contact to the disconnected site is restricted until it is brought back into the system. If Machine B is operating, but the PFS daemons are inactive, the RD of Machine C remotely restarts the daemons on Machine B. When Machine B resumes operations and the PFS daemons are active, the RD of Machine C updates Machine B with the changes in its files and the modifications to .gmap entries. The RD causes changes to the configuration files located at each server to insert Machine B into the logical loop of the system.

Our system considers a machine to be disconnected for an extended period if the interval exceeds 15 minutes. Further investigation of the characteristics of disconnections is needed to determine an appropriate interval. For periods of extended disconnection from the network, the RD of the successor of a failed site traverses the global directory and examines the .gmap files to determine the files for which the failed site holds a master copy and a backup copy. For these files, the RD contacts the RDs at the sites with the corresponding backup copy or master copy, respectively, and has new copies made. Changes are recorded in the .gmap files at all servers. For failures of extended periods, the failed site has all its master and backup copies placed elsewhere, and it will no longer have global files for which it will be responsible when it recovers.

Inconsistencies

During normal operations, inconsistencies can develop between copies of files and between entries in the .gmap on different machines for a specific file. When the DD manages disk capacity during "nonworking hours," it checks the state of files recorded in the .gmap files and instructs the RD to make the entries consistent across all the .gmap files. Other inconsistencies can develop when a user submits commands to PFS. For example, an inconsistency can occur when two different files at different servers are located in the same global directory under the same name. A program might create a file with a name that is not present at the local server but is present at another server. Since the program does not use the .gmap to create or access the file, an inconsistency can occur when the new file is discovered. Likewise, programs running simultaneously at different machines can create files in the same logical directory with the same name. Although this situation is unlikely in a personal file system, the files are inconsistent when they have their entries added to .gmap files. PFS has no means of knowing how to resolve the inconsistencies without user intervention. Therefore, we follow a strategy that is similar to one employed in the Coda [16] file system. In our strategy, the file that is most recently created is kept as the current version of the file. The other file is put in a lost+found directory under the user's home directory. The user has an option to execute a recovery program, which is a tool to resolve inconsistencies. This tool enables files placed in the lost+found directory to be brought back to the global file system and enables files of the same name to be moved to other directories or to be given other names.

Performance profile

We made preliminary observations of PFS on a cluster of 10 Sun SparcStations and a Sun 4/390 file server in a local area network. (Note that Sun SparcStation and Sun 4/390 are trademarks of Sun Microsystems.) Each SparcStation has its own local SCSI disk. Performance results vary as changes occur in the load of the machines and the network. Differences in performance emerge because the access rates of the disk vary between an SCSI disk and a disk server on the Sun 4/390 file server. The physical connections in a system, such as a terminal to a machine through a terminal server or a workstation to a file server, can influence the performance observed by a user. In addition, logically local files might be mounted into a local directory from a remote machine by means of the Sun NFS. Therefore, logically local files can require network access and service from a remote machine; performance in such a case differs from that when access is to a physically local file system. A performance profile comparing the execution of Unix commands in PFS with that in a Sun NFS installation did not indicate specific performance values over a wide range of conditions; however, it did provide relative performance differences between environments with and without PFS. By means of these relative performance differences, we justify that the performance of PFS is acceptable for a user.

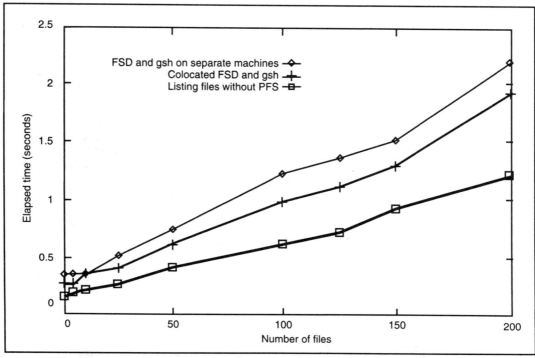

Figure 7. Elapsed time to list files. (FSD = file server daemon and gsh = global shell.)

File-listing command

Our performance profile was obtained by executing common Unix commands and measuring the time required for the PFS operations to implement the commands. For example, the file-listing command, ls, is a commonly used Unix command that required special consideration in PFS. Figure 7 shows the observed elapsed time for the ls -la command to be executed as we varied the number of files to list in a directory in our experiments. (la is an option for the ls command.) The file-listing command causes files to be listed with information about the files' owners and access permissions. The implementation of PFS is flexible, such that the FSD and gsh server processes can be configured on different machines. In some environments, such as those using the Sun NFS, a user's home directory might be located at a machine that is different from the machine on which the user executes the gsh. Although not a typical situation, the user might wish to place the FSD at the site holding the home directory, which is a different machine from the site executing the gsh. Shown in Figure 7 are three plots, indicated by thick, medium, and thin lines. The thick plot shows the elapsed time to list files without PFS, the medium plot shows the elapsed time to list files when the FSD and the gsh are colocated, and the thin plot shows the elapsed time when they are at separate machines. In both of the latter two cases, the directory listed was located at the Sun 4/390 file server and the ls command was submitted from a SparcStation. If a gsh is colocated with the FSD process on the SparcStation, our implementation uses a shared-memory facility provided by SunOS 4.1 to hold recently used .gmap files. When a user types the ls command, the gsh indicates to the FSD that this command has been requested by the user. If the .gmap is already loaded in the shared memory, the

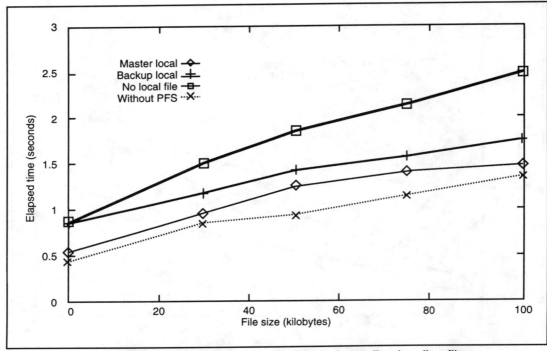

Figure 8. Elapsed time to access a file for editing for small and medium files (file size ≤ 100 kilobytes).

FSD returns to the gsh an index to the location of the .gmap file in the shared memory. The elapsed time to list the files increases as the number of files in the directory increases. When the FSD and the gsh are located at separate machines, an increase in the elapsed time to execute the ls command is correlated to the size of the .gmap file, which is a function of the number of files in the directory. The difference between the elapsed time to list files when the FSD and gsh processes are colocated and that when they are at separate machines is determined by the performance of the Sun remote procedure call (RPC) for transferring files. When as many as 200 files were located in the directory, the elapsed time to list the files was nearly two seconds. This value is comparable to, although a little larger than, the elapsed time to list files in a Sun NFS environment without PFS (shown by the thick plot), which is the average elapsed time of repeated ls -la commands on a SparcStation of a directory located at the Sun 4/390 file server.

File editing

Another important characteristic of PFS that we measured in our performance profile was the time required to access a file for editing. This time depends on whether or not a copy of the file is local and, if it is local, whether the copy is a master copy or a backup copy. We conducted experiments using SparcStations with local SCSI disks, with colocated FSD and gsh. We measured the elapsed time for an editor to open a file and then immediately close the file for the following four cases:

- PFS with a master copy at the local server,
- PFS with a backup copy at the local server,

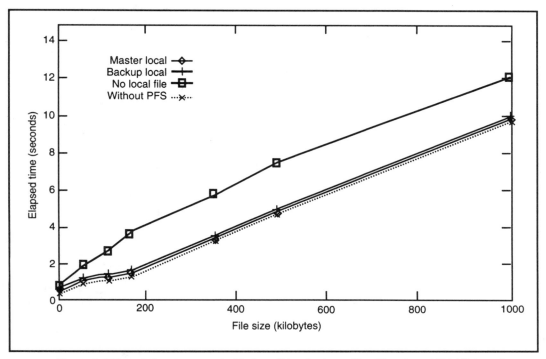

Figure 9. Elapsed time to access a file for editing for large files (file size ≤ 1000 kilobytes).

- PFS with neither a master copy nor a backup copy at the local server, and
- A local server without PFS.

We found that the measured elapsed time depended on the location of the file and the size of the file that was being loaded into memory for editing. If the local file was the master copy or the backup copy, then the observed elapsed time to access the file for editing differed little from that observed in an environment without PFS. Figure 8 shows the file access times for small and medium files for the four cases and Figure 9 shows the file access times for large files for the four cases. Observe in Figure 9 that for large files, there is little difference among the four cases when the editor accesses a file when the master copy is local, the backup copy is local, and the file is accessed without PFS. The time cost for a PFS system with a master copy of the file at the local server is approximately 0.2 to 0.3 seconds greater than that for a system without PFS, and the time cost for a PFS system with a local backup copy is 0.4 to 0.5 seconds greater than that for a system without PFS. The differences in time cost between when the local file was a backup copy and when it was a master copy are mostly determined by the RPC, which changes ownership of the file with the existing master, so that the existing master becomes the backup and the local copy becomes the master. The additional time needed to access a file that had neither a local master nor a backup copy depended on the size of the file (because the file must be copied from the site of the master) and the time required to change ownership of the file. Despite the location and status of a file, the elapsed time to access a small file (that is, less than or equal to about 15 kilobytes) was less than one second and that to access a file as large as 100 kilobytes was less than two seconds. The time cost difference between systems with and without PFS is insignificant

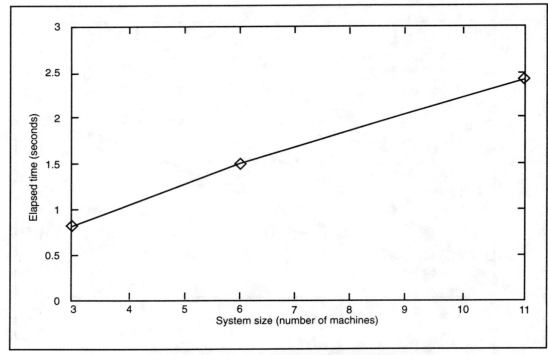

Figure 10. Elapsed time to update .gmap entries.

if the local file is a master, and this difference is small if the local file is a backup. If the local file is neither a master nor a backup, the time cost difference is small for small and medium files and acceptable for large files.

File creation

When a new file is created, an entry must be added to .gmap files for all file servers in order that the new file can be accessed from any file server in the system. The time required to add a new entry to all .gmap files depends on the number of file servers in the system and on the time required to create a backup copy of the file. We measured the time required to update all file servers when a new file (30 kilobytes) was detected by the ls command. Our prototype PFS implements a ring structure for updating the .gmap files. Typically, a user's personal file system contains less than 10 file servers. Our experiments measured a system containing up to 11 machines, with each machine using its local disk as an independent file server. Figure 10 shows the elapsed time before all servers are updated when one new file has been detected. Within 2.5 seconds, we could execute an ls command at any file server in the system of 11 machines and detect the existence of the new file. For a personal file system, these delays are acceptable. With PFS, the user obtains a highly available system for personal files without enduring significant performance delay. Although the ring structure is adequate for a personal file system in which there are only a few independent file servers that a user accesses, we plan to implement a more efficient strategy for updating N independent file servers (if N grows large), such as a $O(\log N)$ treelike broadcasting strategy [2] rather than the $O(N)$ ring structure.

Conclusions

Our objective in developing PFS was to develop a personal file system that fulfilled the following criteria:

- Users should have a global view of their personal files, no matter which file server a particular user accesses.
- Users should not need to learn a new set of commands to operate in a PFS environment.
- So that PFS would be acceptable, the performance of the PFS commands should not differ significantly from that in an environment without PFS.
- By supporting placement and access control for a copy of a file at more than one location, PFS should enhance the availability of the global file system, in spite of failures at a single site.

We have met this objective in our development of the PFS prototype. We paid special attention to performance in our implementation so that responses to Unix commands in the global PFS environment would perform comparably with those in environments without PFS. Users do not need to learn a new set of file operations, although a few new commands are provided to support management operations such as initializing, forcing a file to be a master copy at a site, and immediately removing stale files that eventually would be deleted. We are continuing to enhance our development of PFS. We will expand our disk-management facilities and will build tools for administration of the consumption and sharing of disk space among file servers. We will enhance our RD to handle cases of failures of file servers beyond a single site. Choice of the locations at which master and backup copies of files are placed will consider disk access times and network communication latency. Additional work will be directed toward tailoring PFS for a wide area network (the characteristics of which differ from those of local area networks), so that file servers can be dispersed across the country and can be disconnected from the network. We will explore the implementation of PFS service for installations in which portable computers are detached from a network and reconnected as they are moved among different locations.

Acknowledgments

This research was supported in part by National Science Foundation grants CCR-9010906 and MIP-8811815.

References

[1] N. Abdullah and J.-Y. Juang, "A User-Level Network File System in Command Interpreter," *Proc. IEEE Computer Soc. Office Automation Symp.*, IEEE Computer Soc. Press, Los Alamitos, Calif., 1987, pp. 68-75.

[2] N. Alon, A. Barak, and U. Manber, "On Disseminating Information Reliably without Broadcasting," *Proc. Seventh Int'l Conf. Distributed Computing Systems*, IEEE Computer Soc. Press, Los Alamitos, Calif., 1987, pp. 74-81.

[3] J. Apacible et al., "The Personal File System (PFS) State Transition Tables," tech. report, Dept. of Computer Science, Michigan State Univ., East Lansing, Mich., 1990.

[4] M. Baker, "Comment at the 4th ACM SIGOPS European Workshop on Fault Tolerance Support in Distributed Systems," *ACM Operating Systems Rev.*, Vol. 25, No. 1, 1991, pp. 31-33.

[5] D.R. Brownbridge, L.F. Marshall, and B. Randell, "The Newcastle Connection or UNIXES of the World Unite!," *Software Practice and Experience*, Vol. 12, No. 12, Dec. 1982, pp. 1147-1162.

[6] L.W. Dowdy and D.V. Foster, "Comparative Models of the File Assignment Problem," *ACM Computing Surveys*, Vol. 14, No. 2, June 1982, pp. 287-313.

[7] B. Gavish and O.R.L. Sheng, "Dynamic File Migration in Distributed Computer Systems," *Comm. ACM*, Vol. 33, No. 2, Feb. 1990, pp. 177-189.

[8] A. Hisgen et al., "Availability and Consistency Tradeoffs in the Echo Distributed File System," *Proc. Second Workshop Workstation Operating Systems (WWOS-II)*, IEEE Computer Soc. Press, Los Alamitos, Calif., 1989, pp. 49-54.

[9] M.J. Litzkow, M. Livny, and M.W. Mutka, "Condor— A Hunter of Idle Workstations," *Proc. Eighth Int'l Conf. Distributed Computing Systems*, IEEE Computer Soc. Press, Los Alamitos, Calif., 1988, pp. 104-111.

[10] K. Marzullo and F. Schmuck, "Supplying High Availability with a Standard Network File System," *Proc. Eighth Int'l Conf. Distributed Computing Systems*, IEEE Computer Soc. Press, Los Alamitos, Calif., 1988, pp. 447-453.

[11] J.H. Morris et al., "Andrew: A Distributed Personal Computing Environment," *Comm. ACM*, Vol. 29, No. 3, Mar. 1986, pp. 184-201.

[12] K.R. Pattipati and J.L. Wolf, "A File Assignment Problem Model for Extended Local Area Network Environments," *Proc. 10th Int'l Conf. Distributed Computing Systems*, IEEE Computer Soc. Press, Los Alamitos, Calif., 1990, pp. 554-560.

[13] G.J. Popek and B.J. Walker, *The LOCUS Distributed System Architecture*, MIT Press, Cambridge, Mass., 1985.

[14] T.D. Purdin, R.D. Schlichting, and G.R. Andrews, "A File Replication Facility for Berkeley Unix," *Software Practice and Experience*, Vol. 17, No. 12, Dec. 1987, pp. 923-940.

[15] M. Satyanarayanan, "Scalable, Secure, and Highly Available Distributed File Access," *Computer*, Vol. 23, No. 5, May 1990, pp. 9-21.

[16] M. Satyanarayanan et al., "Coda: A Highly Available File System for a Distributed Workstation Environment," *IEEE Trans. Computers*, Vol. 39, No. 4, Apr. 1990, pp. 447-459.

[17] C.H. Sauer et al., "RT PC Distributed Services Overview," *ACM Operating Systems Rev.*, Vol. 21, No. 3, July 1987, pp. 18-29.

[18] *Sun Microsystems Network Programming Guide*, Sun Microsystems, Inc., Mountain View, Calif., 1988.

[19] G.M. Tomlinson et al., "The PULSE Distributed File System," *Software Practice and Experience*, Vol. 15, No. 12, Dec. 1985, pp. 1087-1101.

[20] B.W. Wah, "File Placement on Distributed Computer Systems," *Computer*, Vol. 17, No. 1, Jan. 1984, pp. 23-32.

[21] H.F. Wedde et al., "Transparent Distributed Object Management under Completely Decentralized Control," *Proc. Ninth Int'l Conf. Distributed Computing Systems*, IEEE Computer Soc. Press, Los Alamitos, Calif., 1989, pp. 335-342.

[22] J.L. Wolf, "The Placement Optimization Program: A Practical Solution to the Disk File Assignment Problem," *Proc. 1989 ACM SIGMETRICS Conf. Measurement and Modeling Computer Systems*, ACM Press, New York, N.Y., 1989, pp. 1-10.

Pushing the Limits of Transparency in Distributed File Systems

R ecent years have seen a growth in the scale and importance of distributed computer systems. Users have become increasingly dependent on these systems to meet their information storage and sharing needs. Current research and development focus on distributed file systems as a solution to these needs.

Existing distributed file systems provide, at a minimum, transparent access to files on a network. By *transparent access* to files, we mean that files on remote machines can be accessed using the same techniques as those used for accessing local files. Sun Microsystems' Network File System (NFS) [9], for example, provides a way to mount remote file systems in the naming tree of a user's machine. This technique is commonly used in Unix-based distributed file systems. (The section entitled "Related work" describes some other examples.)

The major advantage of this approach to providing transparent access is that it can, with a careful choice of naming conventions, allow a user to share files and execute applications independent of relative user and file locations. However, there are a number of serious drawbacks to this style of transparent access. Binding sections of the naming tree to a host means that the resources available to users of that tree are limited to those on that machine. Limitations in storage space and processor capacity crop up in unexpected places, and reconfiguration to correct problems is difficult. A more serious drawback is decreased availability due to machine crashes and other faults. Users generally require access to multiple machines to perform their work. The *effective availability* is the probability that all required machines are accessible. An analysis [4] of the effective availabilities of a variety of file distribution schemes showed that an unreplicated, but distributed, file system has significantly poorer availability than does a central file server.

Users can, and frequently do, cope with these problems by moving and copying files. Unfortunately, this approach to load balancing and avoiding downtime requires current knowledge of the hosts and resources available on the network. In addition, the manual replication of files to ensure availability raises the difficult problem of keeping file copies consistent or, if they do become inconsistent, the problems of locating the most current one and reconciling conflicting changes.

Rick Floyd and

Carla Schlatter Ellis

Clearly, it is not enough to simply provide users with the means to specify and access files on remote machines. The complexity introduced by the distribution of computing resources and files can quickly overwhelm users, unless we provide a mechanism that allows simple abstractions of the environment to be constructed. Moreover, this mechanism must allow users to make effective use of the resources available and to take advantage of the distributed nature of the environment.

The focus of the work described in this paper was to test the premise that a *fully network transparent distributed file system* is a viable solution for providing these simple, familiar abstractions. By *fully network transparent*, we mean that the distributed file system allows users to create and access files with no constraints due to the name or the location of the user or file and with no knowledge of the underlying systems. Our basic goal was to preserve the abstraction of a single, shared file system across the network. A major benefit of full network transparency is that it frees users from the need to understand the details of the underlying network, thus allowing them to develop a simpler model of their environment. To accomplish our goal, we identified subgoals that serve to further define full network transparency: *name and location transparency* (which is uncoupling name from location), adequate availability (which implies replication for both files and file name lookup), consistency, balanced performance, and masking heterogeneity in the environment.

Existing distributed file systems that we examined provide only limited degrees of network transparency. The question, often debated, is how far one can go toward providing full transparency without compromising other desirable goals. In order to gain more experience with the concept of full network transparency, and to explore its costs and benefits, we designed and implemented as close to a fully network transparent distributed file system as we felt possible. Our distributed file system, Casper (called *Roe* in an earlier life), appears to users as a single, globally accessible file system providing highly available, consistent files. Casper provides a coherent framework for uniting techniques in the areas of naming, replication, consistency control, file placement, and migration. It maintains the information necessary to allow these techniques to work effectively.

The architecture of Casper

Since the driving force for this project was to understand the design implications of transparency, the most important goal for Casper is *full* network transparency. The intent is that the user need not be aware of any network-related characteristics of accessed files. The other goals of the system can be viewed as benefits derived from transparency (for example, a simple user model), prerequisites for achieving transparency (for example, consistency and support for heterogeneity), or both (for example, reconfigurability, which exploits *location transparency* while further contributing to transparency by providing a mechanism that can enhance availability and balance performance). The emphasis in this section is on the general techniques used to meet these goals and on how these techniques interact.

The target environment determines the flavor and scope of the potential solution space. We assume a heterogeneous collection of workstations (the most important ones for our purposes have disks, possibly removable, that can participate in file storage), general time-sharing machines, and servers on a medium-scale local area network (LAN). These hosts do not necessarily run a common operating system. Thus, heterogeneity, at both the hardware and software level, is an unavoidable characteristic of our environment. We assume that these hosts are connected by a high-bandwidth, low-delay network (for example, several Ethernets connected by high-speed gateways). While individual hosts or gateways may fail, we assume that the network itself will generally be available. We allow for the possibility of a network partition. The file access and file-naming patterns are assumed to be typical of an academic or research laboratory environment [3], [5]. This implies that there is low write contention for any given file and that files normally either belong to a single user or are read-only. Files typically are small, with several components in the pathname used to locate them. Thus, the file-open operation can be more important to overall performance than the read and write operations of its data. Finally, we assume that all hosts are under a single administrative control and that *autonomy* (control over local resources) is not an issue.

Single-site file systems that attempt to present an abstraction of consistent, shared files make it possible for information to be easily shared among users and their applications. Casper preserves this model across the network. It supports a single, globally accessible file system that provides highly available, consistent, distributed, sharable files in a heterogeneous environment. The use of this model allows users to ignore the presence of the network that supports Casper, with network details being handled by Casper. This greatly simplifies the use of a network.

Casper uses file replication, atomic transactions, a replicated global directory, a detailed model of the current status of the network, automatic initial placement of newly created files, and migration in approaching our goal of full network transparency. It runs on top of existing operating systems and uses the resources of the existing heterogeneous hosts for storage.

File replication and consistency

Individual file replication is used to enhance the availability of Casper files and directories. Flexibility to tune the availability and performance characteristics on a file-by-file basis is the motivation for choosing the file as the unit of replication instead of other alternatives (such as choosing volume as the unit of replication [12], [14]). It is not clear if applying uniform replication to the data falling into any of the obvious coarser granularity units can be justified by real reference patterns.

Casper guarantees a consistent view of these replicated files. Enforcing consistency ensures that each user will see the same results, irrespective of location, and that earlier results will not reappear because of host or network failures. Consistency in this context has two aspects: keeping a copy internally consistent and maintaining mutual consistency between replicated copies.

We can ensure that users see a consistent view of a file copy at any given time by serializing access to the copy. It is also necessary to ensure that any changes made are applied atomically and to coordinate these changes with the changes made to other copies. Locking each copy of the file, as a whole, is the serialization method used. Data on file reference patterns [4], [11] showing a high percentage of files being completely read or written, small file sizes, and a lack of demand for fine-grained sharing in an academic Unix environment, such as ours, justify the choice of whole-file locking. Locking requests are rejected if they cannot be immediately satisfied. A two-phase commit protocol [8] is used to ensure that writes are applied atomically and that updates are coordinated among the copies designated to be written. Details of the actual locking scheme and the recovery mechanism used at a site are determined by the operating system support available at the particular host and have to satisfy only the basic functionality required by Casper.

We desire a mutual-consistency algorithm that improves availability, has good performance in terms of the delay perceived by users, imposes minimal restrictions on the range of other algorithms and techniques that can be used by Casper, and behaves correctly under network partitioning and other failures. There are three general classes of methods for ensuring mutual consistency between copies: *unanimous update*, *voting*, and *primary copy*. Unanimous-update algorithms are not serious candidates, since they actually decrease the availability of a file in our environment. Both voting and primary-copy algorithms can provide the strong consistency desired for Casper, even in the presence of network partitions. In addition to these three classes, there are algorithms that provide consistency under certain circumstances (for example, in the absence of partitions) or that relax the consistency requirement (for example, attempting to detect and compensate for inconsistencies at a later time). Optimistic replication, in which updates eventually propagate to copies, is attractive and becoming popular for the high availability it offers, even in disconnected situations [15], [18]. However, the price paid for this higher availability is the loss of consistency guarantees and network transparency, issues that are of primary interest in Casper.

Weighted voting [6] is a generalized form of voting that allows tuning of parameters. It operates by associating a version counter and some number of votes with each copy of a file. A read quorum r and a write quorum w are defined for the overall replicated file. When a file is opened, the version numbers and votes are collected from the copies. At least r votes must be collected to read a file and at least $MAX[r, w]$ votes must be collected to write it. Reads can be from any current copy and writes go to current copies that hold a total of at least w votes. Making $r + w$ greater than the total number of votes in all copies of the file ensures that at least one current copy will be in any quorum. The version counter of each participating copy is incremented when the copy is updated. Voting solutions do not require that a copy be brought up to date when a failed or disconnected site recovers. The existence of obsolete copies is acceptable as long as at least a write quorum of current copies can be found. As long as a quorum of copies is reachable, operations can proceed normally, even without accurate information about the current location of all the copies.

In contrast, solutions that can be classified as primary copy share two important characteristics: the need for agreement on a single authority governing the object (for example, the identity of the primary copy) and a method for ensuring the currency of copies that may have to take over the primary role in the event of failure. In our environment, this reduces to the requirements that each copy of an object reliably know the locations of all other copies, making migration difficult, and that all accessible copies be kept up to date. An attractive feature of primary copy lies in the small, constant number of messages required to open a file in the normal case. In weighted voting, in contrast, an open request is sent out to each of the n participating copies, resulting in $2n$ messages (although n will usually be quite a small number). However, if these messages are sent in parallel, the delay perceived by the user is approximately the same in the primary-copy and weighted-voting algorithms.

Our desire for decentralized control, operation in the presence of partial knowledge, and our use of migration for reconfiguration led us to select weighted voting as the basis for mutual-consistency control in Casper. Weighted voting provides the desired consistency and availability properties. Our analysis [4] showed that, for typical host availabilities over 0.9 and observed file-naming characteristics, a weighted-voting scheme based on three copies provides file availability substantially exceeding that of a central-server system. It does this without requiring expensive state maintenance in the presence of caching, migration, network partitions, and host crashes. It is able to tolerate out-of-date copies and can operate with partial or out-of-date knowledge of copy locations.

The global directory

Casper maintains a replicated network-wide directory that is used to name Casper files and directories. This name space is separate from the name spaces of the hosts that support Casper. Retaining control over the directory allows Casper to transparently place, migrate, and replicate both files and the directory itself. This is in contrast to the approach, used in some other distributed file systems, of patching together existing naming subtrees, making it more difficult to reconfigure resources or to replicate for availability. The Casper global directory supports a Unix-like hierarchical directory tree with user-chosen names and organization. There is no encoding of location or host information in names visible to the user.

The distribution of files and directory components raises issues that do not occur in centralized directories, such as what strategies to use for partitioning the directory and for locating resources referenced through the directory. Casper addresses the partitioning issue by breaking directory information logically along boundaries that reflect the way the information is used and that do not unduly restrict the location of this information. The common use of an operation to enumerate entries contained in a node of the directory tree (for example, Unix ls command) and the practice of grouping related files in a subdirectory led us to make the unit of partitioning be the set of entries in a directory node. Each directory node is independently replicated and its copies placed. The directory tree is not fully replicated at all sites or even at all servers of directory components. Casper addresses the issue of locating named resources by the use of hints and caching in pathname resolution. Resolving an absolute pathname involves starting at the root and looking up each directory node, in turn, to reach the one containing the needed entry. Casper caches information on frequently used directories, forming a tree of directory information that may be used to avoid repeated lookups and minimize the overhead of name resolution. There are two types of information in a Casper directory: information about the directory node itself and information for each entry in the directory.

Figure 1 shows an example of a Casper directory describing a replicated file. Note that the voting information in a directory entry is just a hint. Voting hints aid in optimizing opens. The actual voting information, including the version, is stored with the copies of the file. This allows a file to be referenced from multiple positions in the directory tree. The location information in a directory entry is also a hint. When a file is migrated, updating each affected directory entry at the time of migration may not be possible.

The global directory is replicated using a modified weighted-voting algorithm. Consistency in this case includes seeing the effects of adding, deleting, or modifying an entry when we subsequently do a lookup on the entry or enumerate a directory.

Weighted voting, as described by Gifford [6], locks the entire object being accessed. While this is appropriate for files in our environment, it is not appropriate for directories. The specialized entry-oriented nature of operations on a directory, combined with the need for shared access, concurrency (especially at higher levels in the directory tree), and long-term connections, makes whole-node locking both unnecessary and inadequate.

Our variation of weighted voting provides the concurrency control we need, with support for caching and long-term connections that do not lock out other users. When an instantiation of Casper connects to a directory, at least a read quorum of votes is collected from the node copies. At this time, the user of the directory is *registered* with these copies. Registration differs from holding a lock in that the registration may be "broken," with notification. From the read quorum, a current copy is selected and read requests are directed to it.

Writing requires that updates be made atomically to current copies containing at least a write quorum of votes (currency is verified during read quorum collection). We send update requests (to add, delete, or modify an entry) to all current copies. If they are willing to make the change, they respond with an acknowledgment. If a write quorum is collected, then the user can instruct the servers to commit. At this point, the changes are actually made (that is, become permanent and visible to readers), and the versions of the participating copies are incremented. If a write quorum cannot be collected, the request is aborted and, depending on the error, may be retried. To preserve the meaning of the version number, only one write may be active (that is, in the process of collecting votes or committing) for a directory node at a time.

An operation, such as modifying an entry, that depends on previous information needs a bit of special handling to guard against making changes based on invalid data. We send, in the request to modify an entry, both the new information and the data in the entry upon which the changes are based. If these data do not agree with the information currently in the directory, the request is rejected. Since an individual directory entry is small, little extra overhead is involved in doing this.

The registration information is used when a writer finds that he cannot update all current copies of a node, even though he is able to collect a write quorum. In this case, the writer, in the commit message, tells the participating directory copies to notify registered readers that they may no longer be reading a current copy. Since the sum of read and write quorums is greater than the total number

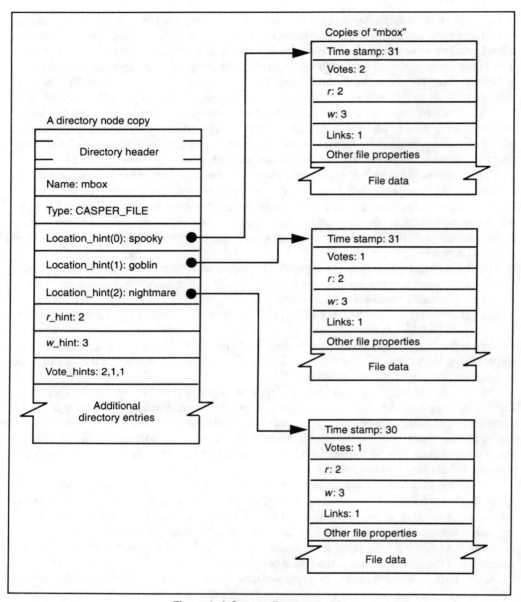

Figure 1. A Casper directory entry.

of available votes, there is always some overlap between the quorums, and so all readers will be notified. Readers also receive notification when copies they have registered with become inaccessible because of partitioning or node crashes. This notification is handled by using the automatic failure-detection facilities of the underlying interprocess communication (IPC) mechanism. The combination of these two notifications ensures that readers will be reliably informed of problems.

The registration mechanism can also be used to handle directory cache invalidation due to renames or other updates resulting in structural changes. In this case, users register interest in directory node modifications and are notified when significant changes are made.

Support for heterogeneity

Casper is intended for use in a heterogeneous environment. This makes it impractical to undertake a significant implementation for each new operating system and hardware base encountered. Our approach is based on providing local servers with a uniform interface, allowing us to make use of the existing file systems of each host. The host dependencies are isolated in these local servers and the full complement of Casper services need not be provided by every type of host.

The Casper design provides for the automatic conversion of basic data types between hosts. Not all files can or should be converted when moving between hosts. Executable files containing machine code, for example, are useful only on machines of certain types running a particular operating system. To retain transparency and allow the Casper naming tree to be shared between hosts of dissimilar types, we introduce a new file type: the *machine-dependent file*. A machine-dependent file appears to the casual user to be a single Casper file, but it contains separate file suites for each distinct machine/operating system combination on which it may run.

Casper associates a *property list* (which is a list of name/value pairs) with each file and directory. Voting and usage information for a file or directory copy is stored in properties of the copy. Data such as file size and last modification date are also represented as file properties, with Casper converting between property and actual system representation as necessary. In addition, information that is specific to particular host operating systems (for example, record structure) is stored in file properties, thereby providing an unobtrusive method for accommodating the needs of a wide range of heterogeneous systems.

Casper maintains a network model that contains both static and dynamic information on hosts and networks. Each Casper host maintains its own network model that describes only the components of the environment that it is actively using. This local view aids in decentralized decision making and the partial knowledge enhances scalability. The network model is important in making placement decisions (see the subsection entitled "Initial placement and migration") and for supporting heterogeneity. For dealing with heterogeneity, the network model includes information on the hardware and software base and on delay, availability, and free space for each participating host. The information on the hardware and software base is used in making decisions that depend on this base. The other information provides a representation of the relevant capabilities of each host, allowing hosts of dissimilar performance, capacity, and reliabilities to be integrated, while still making effective use of their strengths.

Initial placement and migration

When Casper creates a new file or directory, a decision must be made on how many copies to create and where they are to be placed. Users generally do not know — and do not wish to know — what resources are available for storing new information. Instead, the replication and placement of files and directories is managed by Casper to preserve network transparency. Varying the placement of files can have a dramatic effect on performance. Studies of some versions of the Andrew file system [7] showed as much as a five-to-one difference in utilization between file servers, which results in dramatic differences in response time under load. It is important that Casper take into account factors such as this when placing files.

Whereas most of the work on initial placement has been concerned with finding optimal solutions that minimize various cost functions, Casper is designed to make use of placement heuristics. In our case, optimal solutions are not appropriate for several reasons. Optimal file placement is NP-complete [2]. We expect that issues (for example, congestion) that depend on the interaction of accesses to many files will play an important part in determining expected delays and, hence, placements. In general, we also have only partial knowledge of the network on which Casper is running and limited or no knowledge of the activities of other users. These factors further complicate attempts to find optimal placements. However, an optimal solution is not always needed or desired when quick placement is required. Casper has the ability to migrate files based on usage information that is not available when the file is initially placed, so suboptimal placements need not have a permanent impact.

When a file is created, a replication factor is selected. This is, by default, based on the replication factor of the directory where the file is initially cataloged. The creator of the file may specify additional information on the type of the file (temporary or permanent) and on important characteristics of the file (high availability versus high performance, usually read versus usually written, and so on) as part of creation, without making replication factors explicit in the interface. This information can be used to modify the default replication factor and to assign tentative vote quorums. For example, files uhat are marked as being temporary are normally given only one copy. Files for which high availability is requested are given a higher replication factor.

Each copy of the potentially replicated file is then independently placed. This is done using state, free-space, delay, and availability information in the network model maintained locally by Casper. A variety of initial-placement policies are possible based on this information, and the Casper design allows alternatives to be investigated. Files would typically be placed to minimize access delay. If the creator of the file has asked that placement emphasize availability, this can be given primary consideration. Also, an attempt can be made to locate copies on hosts that currently support the parent directory, as this tends to decrease failure points and so increases availability.

The conditions that determine the initial placement of file and directory copies change over time. For example, congestion makes some servers less attractive than they originally were. Users change locations. Usage patterns of a file change, and a history of usage provides more accurate information than that used for initial placement. File creation and file deletion change the available space on a device. Faster or more reliable servers become available. If the changes are significant, it may be worthwhile to move, or *migrate*, copies to adjust to the changes.

The arguments for using heuristic algorithms able to operate in a decentralized fashion and with partial (possibly incorrect) knowledge that we used for replication and initial placement also apply to migration. Making intelligent migration decisions requires an estimate of future accesses that will be made to a file or directory. Previous work [16] suggested that future accesses may be estimated using past access history. Casper keeps with each file and directory, as a property, information on recent accesses.

Migration is done by first opening and locking the copy to be migrated. This ensures that the copy will not be able to vote multiple times while it is being moved. (Otherwise, it may be possible for the old copy to participate in one quorum and the new one in another, resulting in inconsistencies.) Also, the old copy is flagged for deletion at this time. A copy is tentatively made on the destination host, and the directory is updated to indicate the new location. These changes are then atomically committed.

If a file is referenced by more than one directory, then updating the directory through which the file is referenced is not enough. The other directories still contain obsolete information on the old location of the copy. In this case, a *forwarding address* is left behind on the old host. References to a file through this forwarding address cause the obsolete directory to be updated. Forwarding addresses in Casper are discarded after all directories containing obsolete information have been updated. Reference counts are used to detect no-longer-needed forwarding addresses.

Implementation experience

It is frequently argued in systems research circles that an implementation is the most effective way (and sometimes the *only* way) to validate a system design. An implementation often uncovers problems and complications that were not anticipated in the original design and points up areas where future work is badly needed. Our experiences gained in implementing Casper confirm this view.

An implementation of a Casper prototype was started at the University of Rochester, Rochester, New York, in late 1981 to experimentally evaluate the architectural design and its adequacy in providing network transparency. Thus, it was one of the first distributed file system projects employing replicated files and directories. The prototype was under development or serving as a basis for experiments until 1987; by then, the equipment in the laboratory had radically changed and the investigators had left Rochester. The recent renewed interest in replicated file systems makes reporting our early experiences relevant.

At the time the project began, the University of Rochester Computer Science Department's network consisted of several Data General Eclipses running RIG (Rochester's Intelligent Gateway), a locally developed message-passing system; VAXs running BSD (Berkeley Software Distribution) Unix; and a number of Xerox Alto workstations running Alto/Mesa. These hosts were connected together with a three-megabit Ethernet. The software base upon which Casper was built consisted of the file systems of the three different host operating systems and an IPC mechanism known as CMU-IPC that was extended across our network using user-level servers. CMU-IPC was developed by Rashid at CMU (Carnegie Mellon University, Pittsburgh, Pennsylvania) for 4.1 BSD Unix and was a precursor of Accent IPC [13]. We made minimal changes to the host environments. This was in keeping with our goal of gracefully accommodating heterogeneity with limited effort. The most striking example of this was our reliance on the file systems of the hosts. Casper files and directories were implemented as files residing on the regular file systems of the hosts. In a similar spirit (and because we were not the sole users), we used CMU-IPC without any modifications as a base for the implementation.

Our general approach was to implement enough of Casper to both validate the approach used and to make the system usable. In practice, this meant that a fairly complete implementation of the system was done in the Unix environment and a limited subset of the system was implemented in the RIG and Alto/Mesa environments. This allowed us to validate the overall design, investigate the heterogeneity aspects of Casper, and implement a working system in a reasonable amount of time.

Structure

The framework for the implementation consisted of five different types of components. Three of these components provided access to local information (files, directories, and host status), one managed transactions on replicated resources, and one performed the work necessary for name translation and opens. The three local components provided a uniform, host-independent interface to the two higher level components. The two higher level components pieced together the local resources to give users a transparent, globally consistent view. The five types of components and their purposes are listed below.

(1) *Local file servers*, which provided access to individual copies of files located on a host and managed the file space used by Casper on the host. For each host, there was one local file server that provided file storage. This was the component responsible for ensuring the internal consistency of file copies and responding to vote gathering and commit requests.

(2) *Local directory servers*, which provided access to individual copies of directory nodes on a host. On each machine, there was one local directory server that had directory information. This component was responsible for directory node caching, providing the registration and notification functions (not fully implemented), performing requested operations on directory entries, maintaining voting information for its copies of directory nodes, and ensuring consistency on directory updates. The implementation imposed a limit of one pending update per directory node, and crash recovery was not supported.

(3) *Local representatives*, which provided higher levels with information on the status of the host (hardware and software base, space available, and so on) and spawned new servers on request. There was one local representative per host supporting Casper.

(4) *Transaction coordinators*, which distributed user read and write requests to replicated copies of opened files, coordinated the commit protocol, and masked single-copy failures. There was one transaction coordinator per active user.

(5) *Global directory servers*, which accepted user requests to open files or access directories and mapped the requests into operations on a quorum of file or directory copies. Thus, the global directory server was responsible for coordinating the collection of votes. The global directory server was the glue holding Casper together. Global directory servers maintained the hierarchical name space and used it in name resolution. Each global directory server maintained a network model by polling the necessary local representatives. The global directory servers used their network models to replicate and to perform initial placement for files and directories and to migrate file copies. Initial placement was based on dynamic delay, availability, and free-space information collected from hosts. By default, hosts that currently had the lowest delay were chosen, but only if their availability exceeded a threshold and if sufficient space was available. If a machine-dependent file was being created, there was the further restriction that the new host be of the same type as the one creating the file. The only migration policy provided in the implementation was migration on reference, with a copy of a file being moved to the user's site when the file was opened. Directory migration was not implemented in the prototype.

Local file servers and local representatives were implemented for all three host environments. This allowed files to be stored on all hosts on the target network. The file data of a Casper file and the representation of the properties were mapped into the structure of the host's native files. Local directory servers, transaction coordinators, and global directory servers were implemented only in the Unix environment.

The support for heterogeneity in the Casper design was clearly demonstrated in the prototype implementation by our ability to successfully incorporate the three distinct host environments. Minimal host changes allowed new types of hosts to be easily added. The combination of local servers with a uniform interface, typed file data, and automatic type conversion at machine boundaries allowed heterogeneity to be ignored where it was not important. Machine-dependent files, property "escapes," and the network model maintained by Casper provided mechanisms for recognizing situations in which heterogeneity was important and for exploiting it when possible.

Functional evaluation

Our experience developing the prototype demonstrated how successfully the individual mechanisms and algorithms, chosen to satisfy particular subgoals, actually meshed into a system that could provide close-to-full network transparency. The user could, in fact, operate without needing to know any of the details of the underlying network or even whether there was one. This functionality was accomplished without encountering major surprises in the way various techniques interacted in practice.

Properties proved to be a remarkably powerful concept, contributing to a number of the subgoals. The property list contained the voting information for file and directory copies needed in the weighted-voting, mutual-consistency algorithm. It also held usage information that could be exploited in migration decisions (although policies using such information were left unexplored). Also, properties were used as a way to specify host-specific characteristics of a file, contributing to the ability to accommodate heterogeneity. They allowed both users and the system itself to associate information with files that aided in interpreting data. They provided a method for easily extending the Casper protocols.

The lack of need for global knowledge simplified the Casper implementation. In particular, we were able to avoid complicated and potentially expensive global consistency and snapshot algorithms. Casper maintained a partial view of the network, with status changes propagated only where they were likely to be needed. Information on objects managed by Casper was kept with the object and verified only when the object was used.

Most of the negative experiences could be attributed to attempting to build Casper on a relatively weak software base. In some cases, there was a lack of support for lightweight threads, leading to the development of complex multiplexed servers. The underlying host file system support expected by Casper was not always present. At a minimum, Casper requires a means of ensuring that information written to a file will survive a machine crash (usually, this means ensuring that it has reached the disk). This expectation did not seem unreasonable, but was not always met in the unmodified host file systems. Finally, although some aspects of CMU-IPC proved useful in implementing Casper (for example, failure notification and typed data), a number of shortcomings were identified as well [4]. Some of the problems were weaknesses of the particular implementation we used and others were basic design flaws. The weaknesses included race conditions created by an interaction of our use of dynamic port allocation/deallocation, a limited local port name space requiring reuse of local capabilities, and the inability of a process to determine outside interest in one of its ports. Other weaknesses involved difficulties interpreting emergency messages — particularly emergency messages that contain notification of failures — and difficulties locating services through the primitive name server for ports. The lesson to be learned was that there is a need for a more solid base of tools (including support for distributed debugging and transactions) that also do not restrict the ability to accommodate heterogeneity by establishing requirements that are too high to be generally met.

The Casper implementation was an accurate realization of the architecture described in the section entitled "The architecture of Casper," but it was by no means a complete production-quality file system (even by university standards). Compromises were made in the areas of crash recovery, autonomy, security, the number of migration policies supplied, and optimizations for performance. In some cases, such as support for autonomy, decisions were made to emphasize other issues that seem incompatible. This lack of autonomy was a consequence of three factors: the use of a separate global directory to ensure transparency, replication to increase overall availability, and our insistence on consistency for replicated files and directories. In other cases, omitted features were compatible with the Casper design, but suffered from our need to set priorities on the expenditure of resources and effort. For example, it would be straightforward to add access control mechanisms given a single administrative domain, but the prototype implementation did not address this particular aspect. In a different kind of environment (multiple administrative domains or a network that included untrusted hosts), security would be a more serious problem.

Performance issues

Performance was an issue that was never satisfactorily resolved in the implementation. The Casper implementation and the IPC it used were intended as prototypes to study the synthesis of functional distributed systems and were not optimized for performance. Measurements of the time delays incurred in opening a Casper file were indicative of some of the major causes of poor performance and pointed the way to possible improvements. Opening a file was one of the most complicated and frequently used operations in Casper; therefore, the time required to open a file determined, to a large extent, the overall performance of the system. When the elapsed time required to open a Casper file was broken down by phases, name resolution typically accounted for about one fourth of the time, with the rest being spent in communication and disk I/O to actually open a file copy. Opening and initiating reading on a Casper file residing locally on Unix was roughly three times slower than the equivalent Unix operations (286 milliseconds [ms] as compared to 96 ms on the VAX 11/750s used for the studies). The major culprit was IPC-related activity (message send/receive, message formatting, and port management), which accounted for half of the total cost of the open. Much of the rest of the overhead came from retrieving voting information and other properties associated with a file copy. IPC overhead became an increasingly serious problem for opens of remote and replicated files. Performance could be significantly improved by avoiding message passing (for example, among components on the same machine), avoiding the more expensive IPC functions (for example, port management), and tuning or reimplementing the IPC system itself. Retaining voting information on a file that Casper would expect to be reopened quickly and exploiting file and directory caching would address the remaining non-IPC sources of overhead. These enhancements were never incorporated into the prototype.

In summary, the Casper implementation met the transparency, availability, heterogeneity, and reconfigurability goals set out for the system. Performance studies identified that the primary bottlenecks were related to implementation, rather than to inherent design issues.

Related work

The area of distributed file systems has received a considerable amount of both commercial and research attention in recent years. In this section, we concentrate on the differences between Casper and a few existing systems. The systems presented here either are representative of approaches that have been, or are currently being, investigated or are significant in their own right.

Network File System

One approach to providing access to remote files, taken by Sun Microsystems' Network File System (NFS) [9], is to patch remote directory trees into the local name space. This approach allows the same access methods to be used, independent of where a file is located (*access transparency*). NFS allows file systems on remote machines to be *mounted* in a local directory, in the same way that local SunOS (a BSD Unix derivative) file systems may be mounted. Each kernel maintains a *mount table* that describes where in the naming tree file systems are mounted. File systems are generally mounted as part of the boot sequence.

NFS can, with a careful choice of naming and mounting conventions, provide the appearance of a common name space for most files (the root file system and some administrative file systems are always local to a host). Users can then take advantage of the file resources of other hosts, without needing to know the details of their location. However, location transparency is not a major emphasis of NFS. All files in a mounted subtree reside on a fixed physical file system and so are bound to the host and disk supporting the file system. Binding sections of the naming tree to a file system means that the resources available to users of that tree are limited to those on that file system and host. Reconfiguration to correct problems or improve performance is difficult, because of both the forced grouping of files and the relatively static nature of the mount table. Also, the mount table approach introduces scaling and administration problems as networks grow. These limitations are avoided by Casper's more dynamic global directory.

The availability of an NFS-style system is less than that of a host running alone. Recent versions of NFS partially address this problem by supporting replication using a technique called *automounter*. Automounter allows one of a set of servers to be mounted on first reference to a remote file system. It is intended for primarily read-only file systems. With automounter, any changes to a file system must be propagated manually. Casper, in contrast, supports consistent replication of any file in a manner that is transparent to the user. This feature can be used to provide availability that is much higher than that of any single server.

Another difference between NFS and Casper is the level of consistency and concurrency control supported. NFS delays writeback of updated file blocks to improve performance. This delay can allow transient inconsistencies to arise. Also, NFS uses stateless protocols to decrease complexity and to simplify crash recovery. No state (beyond caching to improve performance) is maintained on the remote host, and so concurrency control is not directly supported by NFS. Casper, in contrast, enforces consistency and serializes requests to maintain network transparency in the presence of replicated resources and network failures.

Locus

Locus [18] is also an extension of BSD Unix. Locus supports a Unix-like hierarchical file system organized around *logical filegroups*. Logical filegroups resemble Unix file systems in that each one implements a subtree of the global file space and is glued in place using the Unix mount mechanism. The resulting mount table is stored at all hosts in the network. The use of a global mount table limits the scalability of Locus. Casper, in contrast, has the ability to operate in the presence of partial knowledge.

Locus allows files to be replicated to increase availability. To support replication, Locus associates one or more physical containers (Unix file systems) with each logical filegroup. A file or directory in a logical filegroup may be present in any subset of the containers for its filegroup. Because of this, Locus provides a somewhat higher degree of location transparency than does NFS; in turn, this provides a greater degree of reconfigurability. However, Locus does not provide the degree of location transparency supported by Casper (that is, in Locus, files are bound to the logical filegroup where they are created), and so there are limits to the amount of reconfiguration allowed.

Locus guarantees consistency of replicated files and directories in the absence of partitions; in this case, its consistency behavior is identical to Casper's. If a partition occurs that splits the physical container for a filegroup, Locus allows operations to continue in both partitions [18]. This can allow Locus to potentially provide higher availability than Casper for a given configuration of files, but at the expense of a violation of network transparency if inconsistencies arise. A version vector scheme is used to detect inconsistencies, and certain cases allow automatic reconciliation; however, in the general case, the users must be involved in resolving the inconsistencies.

Apollo Domain

Apollo Domain [10] implements a flat space of distributed, typed objects, named by unique identifiers (UIDs). Objects may move and are located using hints from various sources. In addition, there is a name service that maps names in a Unix-like hierarchy into UIDs. Directories (except for a replicated root database) are themselves objects and so may migrate also. This design allows Domain to provide complete location transparency. Its primary difference from Casper in this respect is in the way objects are located. Domain relies on hints, which may cause problems in large networks or in pathological situations. Casper's directory allows objects to be located in a more direct fashion.

Domain objects are not replicated. This limits Domain's ability to mask network failures. Data may be cached at nodes that access an object, with consistency being enforced by a separate lock manager.

Andrew file system

The Andrew file system (AFS) [7] is intended for large-scale networks of personal computers. AFS is structured around a client-server model. Dedicated Andrew servers support a global file system. Clients use their disk resources primarily for whole-file caching of recently referenced files. Casper, on the other hand, is oriented toward cooperating peers, with caching being another instance of replication. This gives Casper more flexibility in managing resources. The AFS approach minimizes client load on servers and networks. In typical situations, Casper — with its use of active migration and replication—could be expected to place a greater load on the network than does AFS. However, the computational and I/O load imposed by Casper may be spread over a greater number of machines.

The structuring primitive in Andrew is the *volume*. Each volume supports a subtree of the overall global naming tree. All files in a volume reside on the same server. Volumes in Andrew are typically dedicated to one user and may grow and shrink in size, depending on the disk space available on a server and on the needs of the user. A *volume location database* dynamically maps volumes to servers. This allows volumes to be manually moved to balance server utilization and disk consumption. This movement, unlike migration in Casper, is a relatively "heavyweight" operation. The use of a volume structure simplifies name resolution, but precludes the short-term load balancing possible with Casper.

AFS supports the replication of read-only volumes. This is used to provide higher availability for volumes containing system executables and other slowly changing files. This can be contrasted with Casper's general replication support.

Coda

Coda [15] is a descendant of AFS. Coda retains the key features of AFS and provides additional support for replication and disconnected operation. Coda retains both the benefits and drawbacks of AFS that we describe above, but provides higher availability.

Replication in Coda is modeled after that in Locus, with a *volume* being the unit of replication. As with Locus, operation is allowed in the presence of partitions, with inconsistencies detected and resolved when the partition heals. This can provide increased availability over Casper's approach of enforcing consistency, but at the expense of exposing the replicated nature of resources to the user.

Disconnected operation allows a client with cached files to continue while disconnected from the network. There is no equivalent capability in Casper. It would be difficult to provide disconnected operation while attempting to retain consistency.

Deceit

Deceit [17] allows a collection of servers to work together to provide the illusion of a highly available NFS file system. Files are replicated and distributed among the participating servers. As with Casper, clients may contact any host supporting the service; the actual location of files is completely transparent to the client. The servers forward requests as necessary. Files may be migrated between servers on reference to minimize the cost of future accesses.

Perhaps the most significant difference between Deceit and Casper is Casper's ability to operate with partial knowledge. Deceit uses ISIS [1] process groups to manage files. Process groups require mutually consistent knowledge of the state of participants to operate correctly. This makes file creation and migration relatively expensive operations and limits the scalability of the system. The design of Deceit recognizes this by incorporating the notion of a *cell*, which is a small number of related machines. Replication is within cells only, which limits the reconfigurability and transparency of Deceit. Deceit also differs from Casper in Deceit's ability to support files with varying consistency properties.

Conclusions

The work we describe here was motivated by a belief in the potential benefits of full network transparency. Casper is a demonstration of a working system that delivers many of these benefits. Casper uses network transparency to provide a coherent framework for uniting techniques in the areas of naming, replication, consistency control, file and directory placement, and file and directory migration. Using these techniques, Casper can transparently integrate new resources, make effective use of existing ones, reconfigure to balance load and adapt to failures, and replicate resources to increase availability. Casper does these things while ensuring consistency, network-transparent naming, and transparent access, thus supporting a particularly simple user model.

Casper makes extensive use of algorithms, such as weighted voting, that are able to work in the presence of partial network knowledge. Control of data is placed with the data. The use of partial knowledge and distributed control eliminates state maintenance overhead and bottlenecks that can cripple a growing system and cause it to topple under its own weight. Thus, although the opportunity never arose to experimentally investigate scalability issues in the context of the Casper design, these features lend themselves to use within larger scale networks.

An aspect of large-scale systems that currently is not represented in the Casper design is the presence of multiple administrative domains. In an environment containing multiple domains, it generally will not be appropriate for Casper to place resources created in one domain in another domain or for operation in one domain to be dependent on operation in another. A more appropriate model in this environment may be that of mutually suspicious Casper systems interacting to provide a global service. Representing multiple administrative domains in Casper and understanding the effect that this would have on transparency require further work.

Adding support for hosts that may need to occasionally operate autonomously is another area that merits further investigation. One approach to take here is limiting the amount of control that a host is willing to give up to Casper.

In summary, the distributed-systems community as a whole has almost no experience with network transparency at the level we describe here. The Casper design and implementation is one step in this direction, providing some insights concerning the costs and benefits of full network transparency. Unfortunately, the Casper prototype never saw extensive use; however, the limited experience we had with Casper demonstrated to us its potential benefits. We used trace data to evaluate various aspects of Casper's design [4], but this cannot replace experiences gained in day-to-day use. Emerging trends toward larger scale LANs — combined with impressive advances in the capabilities of workstations (making the peer-oriented approach of Casper even more attractive) and growing user dissatisfaction with the de facto standard solutions — suggest that the time is right for further studies to realize the potential Casper has shown.

Acknowledgments

We would like to acknowledge the members of the implementation team and others who provided technical assistance in the development of the Casper prototype: Liud Bukys, Mike Dean, Doug Ierardi, and Josh Tenenberg.

This research was supported in part by the National Science Foundation under grant DCR-8320136 and in part by the Office of Naval Research under grant N00014-82-K-0193.

References

[1] K. Birman, "Replication and Fault-Tolerance in the ISIS System," *Proc. 10th ACM Symp. Operating Systems Principles*, ACM Press, New York, N.Y., 1985, pp. 79-86.

[2] W. Dowdy and D.V. Foster, "Comparative Models of the File Assignment Problem," *ACM Computing Surveys*, Vol. 14, No. 2, June 1982, pp. 287-313.

[3] R. Floyd, "Short-Term File Reference Patterns in a UNIX Environment," Tech. Report 177, Dept. of Computer Science, Univ. of Rochester, Rochester, N.Y., 1986.

[4] R. Floyd, *Transparency in Distributed File Systems*, doctoral thesis and Tech. Report 272, Univ. of Rochester, Rochester, N.Y., 1989.

[5] R.A. Floyd and C.S. Ellis, "Directory Reference Patterns in Hierarchical File Systems," *IEEE Trans. Knowledge and Data Eng.*, Vol. 1, No. 2, June 1989, pp. 238-247.

[6] D. Gifford, "Weighted Voting for Replicated Data," *Proc. Seventh ACM Symp. Operating Systems Principles*, ACM Press, New York, N.Y., 1979, pp. 150-162.

[7] J. Howard et al., "Scale and Performance in a Distributed File System," *ACM Trans. Computer Systems*, Vol. 6, No. 1, Feb. 1988, pp. 51-81.

[8] B. Lampson, "Atomic Transactions," in *Distributed Systems — Architecture and Implementation*, B. Lampson, M. Paul, and H. Siegert, eds., Springer-Verlag, New York, N.Y., 1981, pp. 246-264.

[9] B. Lyon et al., "Overview of the Sun Network File System," tech. report, Sun Microsystems, Inc., Mountain View, Calif., 1985.

[10] D.L. Nelson and P.J. Leach, "The Evolution of the Apollo DOMAIN," *Proc. 28th IEEE Computer Soc. Int'l Conf. (Spring Compcon84)*, IEEE Computer Soc. Press, Los Alamitos, Calif., 1984, pp. 132-141.

[11] J. Ousterhout et al., "A Trace Driven Analysis of the UNIX 4.2 BSD File System," *Proc. 10th ACM Symp. Operating Systems Principles*, ACM Press, New York, N.Y., 1985, pp. 15-24.

[12] G. Popek et al., "Locus: A Network Transparent, High Reliability Distributed System," *Proc. Eighth ACM Symp. Operating Systems Principles*, ACM Press, New York, N.Y., 1981, pp. 169-177.

[13] R. Rashid and G. Robertson, "Accent: A Communication-Oriented Network Operating System Kernel," *Proc. Eighth ACM Symp. Operating Systems Principles*, ACM Press, New York, N.Y., 1981, pp. 64-75.

[14] M. Satyanarayanan, "Coda: A Highly Available File System for a Distributed Workstation Environment," *Proc. Second Workshop Workstation Operating Systems (WWOS-II)*, IEEE Computer Soc. Press, Los Alamitos, Calif., 1989, pp. 114-117; also appeared as M. Satyanarayanan et al., "Coda: A Highly Available File System for a Distributed Workstation Environment," *IEEE Trans. Computers*, Vol. 39, No. 4, Apr. 1990, pp. 447-459.

[15] M. Satyanarayanan, "Scalable, Secure, and Highly Available Distributed File Access," *Computer*, Vol. 23, No. 5, May 1990, pp. 9-21.

[16] O. Sheng, *Models for Dynamic File Migration in Distributed Computer Systems*, doctoral thesis, Graduate School of Management, Univ. of Rochester, Rochester, N.Y., 1986.

[17] A. Siegel, K. Birman, and K. Marzullo, "Deceit: A Flexible Distributed File System," Tech. Report 89-1042, Dept. of Computer Science, Cornell Univ., Ithaca, N.Y., 1989.

[18] B. Walker et al., "The LOCUS Distributed Operating System," *Operating Systems Rev.*, Vol. 17, No. 5, Dec. 1983, pp. 49-70.

Scale in Distributed Systems

I n recent years, *scale* has become an increasingly important factor in the design of distributed systems. Large computer networks such as the Internet have broadened the pool of resources from which distributed systems can be constructed. Building a system to fully use such resources requires an understanding of the problems of scale. A system is said to be *scalable* if it can handle the addition of users and resources without suffering a noticeable loss of performance or increase in administrative complexity. Scale comprises the following three parameters:

- The number of users and objects that are part of the system,
- The distance between the farthest nodes in the system, and
- The number of organizations that exert administrative control over pieces of the system.

B. Clifford Neuman

If a system is expected to grow, its ability to scale must be considered when the system is designed. Scale affects all of the following: naming, authentication, authorization, accounting, communication, the use of remote resources, and the user's ability to easily interact with the system.

Grapevine was one of the earliest distributed computer systems consciously designed to scale. More recent projects — such as the Internet Domain Name System (DNS), Kerberos, Sprite, and Digital Equipment Corporation's (DEC's) global name service and global authentication service — concentrated on particular subsystems. Other projects attempted to provide complete scalable systems. Among these are Locus, Andrew, Project Athena, Dash, and Amoeba. Scale affects the way users perceive a system: As the number of objects that are accessible grows, locating the objects of interest becomes increasingly difficult. Plan 9, Profile, Prospero, QuickSilver, and Tilde are a few systems that address this aspect of scale.

This paper examines the methods used to handle scale in the systems mentioned above and in other systems. It begins by describing the effects of scale on the systems themselves and discussing the problems of scale and their general solutions. Then, it looks at the problems specific to individual subsystems and the particular solutions used by several systems; these solutions generally fall into three categories: replication, distribution, and caching. Next, it examines some of the problems that confront users of large systems. Lastly, it lists suggestions to be followed and questions to be asked when scalable systems are being built. The box at the end — entitled "Systems designed with scale in mind" — briefly describes the systems mentioned in this paper.

Definitions

In this paper, the term *system* refers to a distributed system. A *distributed system* is a collection of computers, connected by a computer network, working together to collectively implement some minimal set of services. A *node* is an individual computer within the system. A *site* is a collection of related nodes, a subset of the nodes in the system.

A service or resource is *replicated* when it has multiple logically identical instances appearing on different nodes in a system. A request for access to the resource can be directed to any of its instances.

A service is *distributed* when it is provided by multiple nodes, each of which is capable of handling a subset of the requests for service. Each request can be handled by one of the nodes implementing the service (or a subset of the nodes, if the service is also replicated). A *distribution function* maps requests to the subset of the nodes that can handle it.

The results of a query are *cached* by saving them at the requesting node so that they may be reused instead of the query being repeated. Caching improves the performance of a local node by reducing the time spent waiting for a response and improves scalability by reducing the number of repeated queries sent to a server. Caches employ *validation techniques* to make sure that data from the cache are not used if the results of the query might have changed. Caching is a temporary form of replication.

The effects of scale

Scale affects systems in many ways. This section examines the effects of scale on reliability, system load, administration, and heterogeneity. These effects are felt by all parts of the system.

Effects on reliability

As the number of components in a distributed system increases, the likelihood that all components will be working simultaneously decreases. As the system scales geographically, the likelihood that all components will be able to communicate decreases. A system should not cease to operate just because certain nodes are unavailable.

Increasing the autonomy of the nodes in a system can often improve reliability. A collection of nodes is *autonomous* if it can run independently from the other nodes in the system. A failure in an autonomous system affects access to resources only in the neighborhood of the failure. For example, failure of a name server in one part of a network would not prevent access to local resources in another.

Replication can improve the reliability of a system. Replication allows a resource to be used even if some of the instances are not running or are inaccessible. Replicas can be scattered across the network so that a network failure is less likely to isolate any part of the system from all of the replicas. Dynamically reconfiguring the set of servers used by a client might also be possible, so that if a server goes down, clients can continue with as little disruption as possible.

Effects on system load

Scale affects system load in several ways. As a system gets bigger, the amount of data managed by network services grows, as does the total number of requests for service. Replication, distribution, and caching are all used to reduce the number of requests that must be handled by each server. Replication and distribution allow requests to be spread across multiple servers, while caching reduces repeated requests. The existence of the same system binaries on more than one server is an example of replication. With replication, the choice of server can be based on factors such as load and proximity. The use of multiple file servers, each providing storage for different files, is an example of distribution.

Effects on administration

The administrative dimension of scale adds its own problems. As the number of nodes in a system grows, maintaining information about the system and its users on each node becomes impractical: There are too many copies to keep up-to-date. Administration of a collection of nodes is made easier when common information is centrally maintained — for example, through a name server, through an authentication server, or through a file server that provides a central repository for system binaries.

As a system continues to grow, information about the system changes more frequently, thus making it less practical for a single individual to keep it up-to-date. Additionally, as a system crosses administrative boundaries, organizations want control over their own part of the system. They are less willing to delegate that control to individuals outside their organization. These problems can be addressed by distribution: Responsibility for maintaining pieces of the database are assigned to each organization, and each organization maintains that part of the database that concerns its part of the system. (The section entitled "Distribution" describes the methods that can be used to distribute the database.)

Effects on heterogeneity

The administrative dimension of scale compounds the problem of heterogeneity. Not only will systems that cross administrative boundaries probably include hardware of different types, but they may also be running different operating systems or different versions of the same operating system. Guaranteeing that everyone runs exactly the same software is not practical.

Coherence is one approach to dealing with heterogeneity. In a coherent system, all computers that are part of the system are required to support a common interface. This requirement takes several forms:

(1)   All nodes might be required to support the same instruction set. This is not often practical.
(2)   A looser requirement is for all nodes to support a common execution abstraction. Two computers share the same execution abstraction if software that runs on one computer can be easily recompiled to run on the other. Massachusetts Institute of Technology's (MIT's) Project Athena [5] is an example of a system that uses coherence of the execution abstraction to deal with heterogeneity.
(3)   A still looser requirement is for coherence at the protocol level —that is, for all nodes to support a common set of protocols, and for these protocols to define the interfaces to the subsystems that are tied together in the system.

The Heterogeneous Computer Systems (HCS) Project [20] provides explicit support for heterogeneity. A mechanism is provided that allows the use of a single interface when communication is with nodes that use different underlying protocols. The HCS approach shows that multiple mechanisms can be supported in heterogeneous systems. This ability is important when different mechanisms have different strengths and weaknesses.

Above, we have looked at some of the issues that affect the scalability of a system as a whole. The next few sections examine the effects of scale on particular subsystems.

Naming and directory services

A *name* refers to an object. An *address* tells where that object can be found. The *binding* of a name is the *object* to which it refers. A *name server* (or *directory server*) maps a name to information about the name's binding. This information might be the address of an object or it might be more general — for example, personal information about a user. An attribute-based name service maps information about an object to the object(s) matching that information. (The section entitled "The user's view" discusses attribute-based naming.)

Granularity of naming

Name servers differ in the sizes of the objects they name. Some name servers name only hosts. The names of finer grained objects such as services and files must then include the name of the host so that the object can be found. A problem with this approach is that moving objects is difficult. Other name servers name individual users and services. The names of such entities do not change frequently, so the ratio of updates to references is usually fairly low. This simplifies considerably the job of a name server. A few name servers name individual files. There are a huge number of files, and the files are often transient in nature. Naming at this level requires support for frequent updates and a massive number of queries.

An intermediate approach is used by Sprite [21] and a number of other file systems. Groups of objects sharing a common prefix are assigned to servers. The name service maps the prefix to the server, and the remainder of the name is resolved locally by the server on which the object is stored. One advantage of this approach is that clients can easily cache the mappings they have learned; this is useful because the prefixes change less frequently than do the full names of the objects and because the name service handles fewer names than when this approach is not used. Another advantage is that names need not include the name of the server on which the object resides, thus allowing groups of objects (sharing a common prefix) to be moved. The main disadvantage is that objects sharing common prefixes must be stored together. (Actually, a prefix can be an entire file name; however, doing this is possible with a very limited number of objects and does not scale.)

The granularity of the objects named affects the size of the naming database, the frequency of queries, and the read-to-write ratio, which in turn affect the techniques that can be used to support naming in large systems.

Reducing load

The following three techniques are often used to reduce the number of requests that must be handled by a name server:

(1) Replication. Replication is the simplest of these three techniques. When multiple name servers handle the same queries, different clients are able to send their requests to different servers. The choice of server can be based on physical location or on the relative loads of the different servers or it can be made at random. The difficulty with replication lies in keeping the replicas consistent. (The section entitled "Replication" discusses consistency mechanisms.)

(2) Distribution. Distribution is a second technique for spreading the load across servers. In distribution, different parts of the name space are assigned to different servers. Advantages of distribution are that only part of the naming database is stored on each server, thus reducing the number of queries and updates to be processed. Further, because the size of each database is reduced, each request usually can be handled faster. With distribution, the client must be able to determine which server contains the requested information. (The section entitled "Distribution" describes techniques for making this determination.)

(3)   Caching. Caching is a third technique for reducing the load on name servers. If a name is resolved once, it will often need to be resolved again. If the results are remembered, additional requests for the same information can be avoided. As later pointed out, caching is of particular importance in domain-based distribution of names. Not only is the same name likely to be used again, but so are names with common prefixes. By caching the mapping from a prefix to the name server handling that prefix, future names sharing the same prefix can be resolved with fewer messages. This is extremely important, because — as prefixes become shorter — the number of names that share them grows. Without the caching of prefixes, high-level name servers would be overloaded and would become a bottleneck for name resolution. Caching is a form of replication; as with replication, the biggest difficulty is the need to for consistency. (The section entitled "Caching" describes caching in greater detail.)

Unique-identifier- (UID)-based naming

Not all distributed systems use a hierarchical name service like those that have been described. Some systems use unique identifiers (UIDs) to name objects. Capability-based systems such as Amoeba [30] fall into this category. A *capability* is a UID that both names and grants access rights for an object. UIDs may be thought of as addresses. They usually contain information identifying the server that maintains the object and an identifier to be interpreted by the server. The information identifying the server might be an address or it might be a UID to be included in requests broadcast by the client. A client needing to access an object or service is expected to already possess its UID.

A problem with UID-based naming is that objects move, but the UIDs often identify the server on which an object resides. Since the UIDs are scattered about without any way for them all to be found, they might continue to exist with incorrect addresses for the objects they reference. A technique often used to solve this problem is *forwarding pointers* [7]. With forwarding pointers, a user attempting to use an old address to access an object is given a new UID containing the new address. A problem with forwarding pointers is that the chain of links to be followed can become lengthy, thus reducing performance. Also, if one of the nodes in the chain is down, access to the object is prevented. This problem is solved in Emerald by requiring each object to have a home site, with the forwarding pointer at that site kept up-to-date. Another way to solve this problem is for the client to update the forwarding pointers traversed when subsequent forwarding pointers are encountered.

Prospero [19] supports UIDs with expiration dates. Its directory service guarantees that the UIDs it maintains are kept up-to-date. The use of expiration dates makes getting rid of forwarding pointers possible, once all possible UIDs with the old address have expired.

Directory services

Even in UID-based systems, translating from symbolic names that humans use into the UIDs for the named objects is often desirable. Directory servers do this. Given a UID for a directory, it is possible to read the contents of that directory, map from a symbolic name in the directory to another UID, and add a symbolic name-UID pair to the directory. A directory can contain UIDs for files, other directories, or — in fact — any object for which a UID exists.

The load on directory servers is easily distributed. There is no requirement that a subdirectory be on the same server as its parent. Different parts of a name space can reside on different machines. Replication can be supported by associating multiple UIDs with the same symbolic name or by using UIDs that identify multiple replicas of the same object or directory.

The primary difference between a name server and a directory server is that the directory server usually possesses little information about the full name of an object. A directory server can support pieces of independent name spaces, and those name spaces can overlap or even contain cycles. Both Prospero and Amoeba use directory servers to translate names to UIDs.

Growth and reorganization

For a system to be scalable, it must be able to grow gracefully. If two organizations with separate global name spaces merge, reorganize, or otherwise combine their name spaces, a problem arises if the name spaces are not disjoint. This problem arises because one or both name spaces suddenly change; the new names correspond to the old names, but with a new prefix corresponding to the point in the new name space at which the original name space was attached. This in turn causes problems for any names that were embedded in programs or otherwise specified before the change.

DEC's global name service [13] addresses the above problems by associating a unique number with the root of every independent name space. When a file name is stored, the number for the root of the name space can be stored along with the name. When name spaces are merged, an entry is made in the new root, pairing the UID of each previous root with the prefix required to find it. When a name with an associated root UID is resolved, the UID is checked; if it does not match that for the current root, the corresponding prefix is prepended, allowing the embedded name to work.

The security subsystem

As the size of a system grows, security becomes increasingly important and increasingly difficult to implement. The bigger the system, the more vulnerable it is to attack. This is because as system size grows, the number of points from which an intruder can enter the network increases, the number of legitimate users of the system increases, and the users are more likely to have conflicting goals. Increased vulnerability is particularly troublesome when a distributed system spans administrative boundaries, because the security mechanisms employed in different parts of a system will have different strengths. Containing the effects of a security breach to the part of the system that was broken is important.

Among the security-related functions of a distributed system are

- *Authentication*, which is how the system verifies a user's identity;
- *Authorization*, which is how the system decides whether or not a user is allowed to perform the requested operation; and
- *Accounting*, which is how the system records what the user has done and how it makes sure that a user does not use excessive resources. Accounting can include mechanisms to bill the user for the resources used.

Many systems implement distributed mechanisms for authentication, but leave authorization to the individual server. Few systems provide for accounting in a distributed manner. Authentication, authorization, and accounting are discussed below.

Authentication

Distributed systems use several techniques to authenticate users. Among these are

- *Password-based authentication*,
- *Host-based authentication*, and
- *Encryption-based authentication*.

Password-based authentication. This technique, which is the simplest, uses passwords on each host. It requires maintenance of a password database on multiple nodes. To make this technique easier to administer, Grapevine [2] supported a central service to verify passwords. Password-based authentication can be cumbersome if the user is required to present a password each time a new service

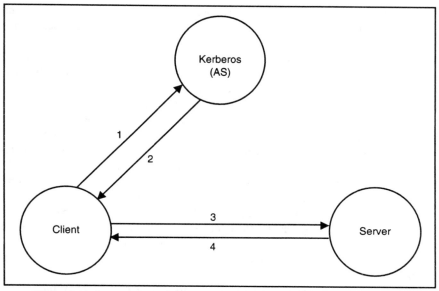

Figure 1. Kerberos authentication protocol. (AS = authentication server.)

is requested. Unfortunately, letting the workstation remember the user's password is risky. Also, password-based authentication is vulnerable to the theft of passwords by attackers that can eavesdrop on the network.

Host-based authentication. As used for *rlogin* and *rsh* commands in Berkeley Unix, this technique has problems too. In this technique, the client is authenticated by the local host. Remote servers trust the host to properly identify the client. As one loses control of the nodes in a system, one should be less willing to trust the claims made by other systems about the identity of its users.

Encryption-based authentication. This technique does not suffer from the same problems as the other two techniques. Passwords are never sent across the network; instead, each user is assigned an encryption key, and that key is used to prove the user's identity. However, encryption-based authentication is not without its own problems. Principals (that is, users and servers) must maintain a key for use with every other principal with which they might possibly communicate, which is impractical in large systems. Altogether, $(n \times m)$ keys are required, where n is the number of users and m is the number of servers.

Needham and Schroeder [16] showed how the number of keys to be maintained can be reduced through the use of an authentication server (AS), which securely generates keys as they are needed and distributes them to the parties wishing to communicate. Each party shares a key (or key pair) with the AS. Authentication in Kerberos [29] is based on a modified version of the Needham and Schroeder protocol. In the Kerberos authentication protocol (see Figure 1), a client wishing to communicate with a server contacts the AS, sending its own name and the name of the server to be contacted (Message 1 on the figure). The AS randomly generates a session key and returns it to the client encrypted in the key that the client registered with the AS (Message 2 on the figure). Accompanying the encrypted session key is a *ticket* that contains the name of the client and the session key, all encrypted in the key that the server registered with the AS.

In Kerberos, the session key and the ticket received from the AS are valid for a limited time and are cached by the client, reducing the number of requests to the AS. Additionally, the user's secret key is needed only when initially logging in. Subsequent requests during the same login session use a session key returned by the AS in response to the initial request.

To prove its identity to the server, the client forwards the ticket together with a time stamp encrypted in the session key from the ticket (Message 3 on the figure). The server decrypts the ticket and uses the session key contained therein to decrypt the time stamp. If the time stamp indicates that the message is recent, the server knows that the message was sent by a principal who knew the session key and that the session key was issued only to the principal named in the ticket. This authenticates the client. If the client requires authentication from the server, the server adds one to the time stamp, reencrypts it using the session key, and returns it to the client (Message 4 on the figure).

As a system scales, it becomes less practical for an AS to share keys with every client and server. Additionally, it becomes less likely that all users will trust a single AS. Kerberos allows the registration of principals to be distributed across multiple *realms*. (The section entitled "Distribution" describes the distribution mechanism.)

The Kerberos authentication protocol is based on conventional cryptography, but authentication can also be accomplished by the use of *public-key cryptography*. In public-key cryptography, separate keys are used for encryption and decryption, and the key distribution step of authentication can be accomplished by publishing each principal's public key. When issues such as revocation are considered, authentication protocols based on public-key cryptography make different trade-offs than protocols based on conventional cryptography but provide little reduction in complexity. However, authentication based on public-key cryptography is much better suited for authentication of a single message to multiple recipients.

Authorization

Distributed systems approach authorization in a number of ways. In one approach, a request is sent to an authorization service whenever a server needs to make an access control decision. The authorization service makes the decision and sends its answer back to the server. This approach allows the access control decision to take into account factors such as global quotas and recent use of other servers. The disadvantages of this approach are that it can be cumbersome and the access control service can become a bottleneck.

In a second approach, first the client is authenticated and then the server makes its own decision about whether or not the client is authorized to perform an operation. The server knows the most about the request and is in the best position to decide if access should be allowed. For example, in the Andrew File System [11], each directory has an associated list, known as an access control list (ACL) that identifies the users authorized to access the files within the directory. When access to a file is requested, the client's name is compared with those in the ACL.

ACL entries in Andrew can contain the names of groups. The use of groups allow rights to be granted to named collections of individuals without the need to update multiple ACLs each time membership in the group changes. Each Andrew file server maintains the list of the groups to which each user belongs, and that list is consulted before the ACL is checked.

The server making an authorization decision should be provided with as much information as possible. For example, if authentication required the participation of more than one AS, the names of the ASs that took part should be available. It should also be possible for the server to use external sources to obtain information — for example, group membership information as provided by

Grapevine. Its use is similar to that of an authorization service, but differs in that not all requests require information from the group server and the final decision is left to the end server.

In Grapevine — as in Andrew — authorization is based on membership in ACLs. ACLs identify authorized individuals or groups. Group membership is determined by sending to a name server a query that contains the name of the individual and the name of the group. The name server recursively checks the group for membership by the individual. If necessary, recursive queries can be sent to other name servers. One of the most noticeable bottlenecks in Grapevine was the time required to check membership in large groups, especially when other name servers were involved [27].

External authorization information can be made available to a server through credentials, without the server needing to contact other servers. The client can request cryptographically sealed credentials either authorizing its access to a particular object or verifying its membership in a particular group. These credentials can be passed to the server in a manner similar to that for the capability-based approach described next. The difference between the credentials-based approach and the capabilities-based approach is that these credentials might be usable only by a particular user or they might require further proof that they were really issued to the user presenting them. Version 5 of Kerberos supports such credentials. Their use is described separately by Neuman [18].

The authorization approaches discussed so far have been based on an ACL model. The advantages of this model are that it leaves the final decision with the server itself and that revoking access — should that be required — is straightforward. A disadvantage of this model is that the client must first be authenticated, then looked up in a potentially long list; the lookup may involve the recursive expansion of multiple groups and may require interaction with other servers.

Amoeba [30] uses the capability model for authorization. In this model, the user maintains the list of the objects for which access is authorized. Each object is represented by a capability that, when presented to a server, grants the bearer access to the object. To prevent users from forging capabilities, Amoeba includes a random bit pattern. By choosing the bit pattern from a sparse-enough address space, it is sufficiently difficult for a user to create its own capability. A client presents its capability when it wishes to access an object. The server then compares the bit pattern of the capability with that stored along with the object; if they match, the access is allowed.

The advantage of the capability model is that the server, once contacted by the client, can make its access control decision without contacting other servers. Yet, the server does not need to maintain a large authorization database that would be difficult to keep up-to-date in a large system. A disadvantage is that capabilities can only be revoked en masse. Capabilities are revoked by changing the bit pattern, but this causes *all* outstanding capabilities for that object to be immediately invalidated. The new capability must then be reissued to all legitimate users. In a large system, this might be a significant task.

Authorization in capability-based distributed systems is still dependent on authentication and related mechanisms. Authentication is required when a user logs into the system before the user is granted an initial capability that can be used to obtain other capabilities from a directory service. Additionally, as was the case with passwords, capabilities can be easily intercepted when they are presented to a server over the network. Thus, they cannot simply be sent in the clear. Instead, they must be sent encrypted, together with sufficient information to prevent replay. This mechanism is quite similar to that used for encryption-based authentication.

Accounting

Most distributed systems handle accounting on a host-by-host basis. A distributed, secure, and scalable accounting mechanism is needed, especially in large systems that cross administrative boundaries. To date, few systems have even considered this need. The difficulty lies in the inability to trust servers run by unknown individuals or organizations. Among the few approaches that have been described are the bank server approach [15] and accounting based on proxies [18]. Amoeba provides an example of the bank server approach: Bank servers handle accounting by maintaining accounts on behalf of users and servers; users transfer money to servers, which then draw upon the balance as resources are used. Compared to the bank server approach, proxy-based accounting is tied much closer to authentication and authorization. The client grants the server a proxy that allows the server to transfer funds from the client's account.

Both of these approaches require support for multiple *currencies*. This support is important as systems span international boundaries or as the accounting service is called on to maintain information about different types of resources. The currencies can represent the actual funds for which clients can be billed or they can represent limits on the use of resources such as printer pages or CPU cycles. Quotas for reusable resources (such as disk pages) can be represented as a deposit that is refunded when the resource is released.

Authorization and accounting depend on one another. In one direction, the transfer of funds requires the authorization of the owner of the account from which funds will be taken. In the other, a server might verify that the client has sufficient funds (or quota) to pay for an operation before it will be performed.

On replication, distribution, and caching

Above, the problems specific to scaling the security subsystems of large systems are described and the mechanisms used to solve them are discussed. Many problems with naming also arise with security. As with naming, replication, distribution, and caching are often used with security. When these techniques are applied in the area of security, the following considerations must be kept in mind:

- When a server that maintains secret keys is replicated, the compromise of any replica can result in the compromise of important keys.
- The security of the service is that of the weakest of all replicas.
- When distribution is used, multiple servers may be involved in a particular exchange.
- It is important that both principals know which servers were involved so that they can correctly decide how much trust to place in the results.
- The longer credentials are allowed to be cached, the longer it will take to recover when a key is compromised.

As a system grows, less trust can be placed in its component pieces. For this reason, encryption-based security mechanisms are the appropriate choice for large distributed systems. Even encryption-based mechanisms rely on trust of certain pieces of a system. The more clear it is which pieces need to be trusted, the better able end services are to decide when a request is authentic.

Remote resources

Naming and security are not the only parts of the system affected by scale. Scale also affects the sharing of many kinds of resources, including processors, memory, storage, programs, and physical devices. The services that provide access to these resources often inherit scalability problems from the naming and security mechanisms they use. For example, one cannot access a resource without first finding it. This involves both identifying the resource that is needed and determining its location, given its name. Once a resource has been found, authentication and authorization might be required for its use.

The services used to access resources sometimes have scalability problems of their own, and techniques similar to those mentioned above are employed to solve these problems. Problems of reliability and load are often addressed through replication, distribution, and caching. Some services further reduce load by shifting as much computation to the client as possible; however, this should be done only when all the information needed for the computation is readily accessible to the client.

The services used to access remote resources are very dependent on the underlying communications mechanisms they employ. This section looks at the scaling issues related to network communication in such services. Then, to provide an example of the problems that arise when access to remote resources is supported, it looks at the effect of scale on a heavily used resource: the network file system.

Communication

As a system grows geographically, the medium of communications places limits on the system's performance. These limits must be considered when a decision is made on how best to access a remote resource. Approaches that might seem reasonable given a low-latency connection might not be reasonable across a satellite link.

Because they can greatly affect the usability of a system, the underlying communications parameters must not be completely hidden from the application. The Dash system [1] does a good job of exposing the communication parameters in an appropriate manner. When a connection is established, the application can require that the connection meet certain requirements; if the requirements are not met, an error is returned. When one set of required communication parameters cannot be met, the application still might be able to access the resource via an alternate mechanism — for example, via whole-file caching instead of remote reads and writes.

Communication typically takes one of two forms: *point-to-point communication* or *broadcast communication*. In point-to-point communication, the client sends messages to the particular server that can satisfy the request. If the contacted server cannot satisfy the request, it might respond with the identity of a server that can. In broadcast communication, the client sends the message to everyone, and only those servers that can satisfy the request respond. The advantage of broadcast communication is that finding a server that can handle a request is easy: The request is sent and the correct server responds. Unfortunately, broadcast communication does not scale well. Preliminary processing is required by all servers, whether or not they can handle a request. As the total number of requests grows, the load due to preliminary processing on each server also grows.

The use of global broadcast communication also limits the scalability of computer networks. Computer networks improve their aggregate throughput by distributing network traffic across multiple subnets. Only those messages that need to pass through a subnet to reach their destination are transmitted on a particular subnet. Local communications in one part of a network are not seen by users in another. When messages are broadcast globally, they are transmitted on all subnets, consuming available bandwidth on each. Although global broadcast should be avoided in scalable systems, broadcast communication need not be ruled out entirely. Amoeba [30] uses broadcast on its subnets to improve the performance of local operations. Communications beyond the local subnet use point-to-point communication.

Multicast is a broadcastlike mechanism that can also be used. In multicast, a single message can be sent to a group of servers. This reduces the number of messages required to transmit the same message to multiple recipients. For multicast to scale, the groups to which messages are sent should be kept small (that is, limited to only those recipients that need to receive a message). Additionally, the network should transmit multicast message across only those subnets necessary to reach the intended recipients.

The file system

The file system provides an excellent example of a service affected by scale. It is heavily used and it requires the transfer of large amounts of data.

In a global file system, distribution is the first line of defense against overloading file servers. Files are spread across many servers, and each server processes requests only for the files that it stores. (The section entitled "Distribution" describes mechanisms used to find the server storing a file, given the file's name.) In most distributed systems, files are assigned to servers based on a prefix of the file name. For example, on a system where the names of binaries start with "bin," it is likely that such files will be assigned to a common server. Unfortunately, since binaries are more frequently referenced than files in other parts of the file system, such an assignment might not evenly distribute requests across file servers.

Requests can also be spread across file servers through the use of replication. Files are assigned to multiple servers, and clients contact a subset of the servers when making requests. The difficulty with replication lies in keeping the replicas consistent. (The section entitled "Replication" describes techniques for doing so.) Since binaries rarely change, manual techniques are often sufficient for keeping their replicas consistent.

Caching is extremely important in network file systems. A local cache of file blocks can be used to make network delays less noticeable. A file can be read over the network a block at a time, and access to data within that block can be made locally. Caching significantly reduces the number of requests sent to a file server, especially for applications that read a file several bytes at a time. The primary difficulty with caching lies in making sure the cached data are correct. In a file system, a problem arises if a file is modified while other systems have the file—or parts of the file—in their cache. (The section entitled "Caching" describes mechanisms for maintaining the consistency of caches.)

An issue of importance when files are cached is the size of the chunks to be cached. Most systems cache pieces of files. This is appropriate when only parts of a file are read. Coda [26] and early versions of the Andrew File System [11] support whole-file caching, in which the entire file—when opened—is transferred to the client's workstation. Files that are modified are copied back when closed. Files remain cached on the workstation between opens so that a subsequent open does not require the file to be fetched again. Approaches such as whole-file caching work well on networks with high latency; this is important in a geographically large system. But, whole-file caching can be expensive if an application wants to access only a small part of a large file. Also, it is difficult for diskless workstations to support whole-file caching for large files. Because of the range in capabilities of the computers and communication channels that make up a distributed system, multiple file access mechanisms should be supported.

Replication

Replication is an important tool for building scalable distributed systems. Its use in naming, authentication, and file services reduces the load on individual servers and improves the reliability and availability of the services as a whole. The issues of importance for replication are the placement of the replicas and the mechanisms by which the replicas are kept consistent.

Placement of replicas

The placement of replicas in a distributed system depends on the purpose of replicating the resource. If a service is being replicated to improve the availability of the service in the face of network partitions or to reduce the network delays when the service is accessed, then the replicas should be scattered across the system. Replicas should be located so that a network partition will not make the service unavailable to a significant number of users. If the majority of users are local and if the service is being replicated to improve the reliability of the service, to improve its availability in the face of server failure, or to spread the load across multiple servers, then replicas may be placed near one another. The placement of replicas affects the choice of the mechanism that maintains the consistency of replicas.

Mechanisms for maintaining replica consistency

A replicated object can be logically thought of as a single object. If a change is made to the object, the change should be visible to everyone. At a particular point in time, a set of replicas is said to be *consistent* if the value of the object is the same for all readers. The following are some of the approaches that have been used to maintain the consistency of replicas in distributed systems:

(1) Replication of read-only information. Some systems support this approach only. Andrew and Athena take this approach for replicating system binaries. Because such files change infrequently and because they cannot be changed by normal users, external mechanisms are used to keep the replicas consistent.

(2) Replication of immutable information. This approach, which is closely related to the read-only approach, is used by the Amoeba file server. Files in Amoeba are immutable; as a result, they can be replicated at will. Changes to files are made by creating new files and then changing the directory so that the new version of the file will be found.

(3) Allowing updates, but requiring updates to be sent to all replicas. This is a less restrictive approach than the above two. One of the limitations of this approach is that updates can take place only when all of the replicas are available, thus reducing the availability of the system for write operations. Another limitation is that an absolute ordering on updates is required, so that inconsistencies do not result if updates are received by replicas in different orders. A third limitation is that a client might fail during an update, resulting in the receipt of the update by only some of the replicas.

(4) Primary-site replication. In this approach, all updates are directed to a primary replica, which then forwards the updates to the other replicas. Updates may be forwarded individually, as in Echo [10], or the whole database may be periodically downloaded by the replicas, as in Kerberos [29] and the Berkeley Internet Name Domain (BIND) Server [31], an implementation of DNS [14]. The advantages of the primary-site approach are that the ordering of updates is determined by the order in which they are received at the primary site and that updates require only the availability of the primary site. One disadvantage of this approach is that the availability of updates still depends on a single server, although some systems select a new primary site if the existing primary goes down. Another disadvantage is that if changes are distributed periodically, the updates are delayed until the next update cycle.

(5) Loose consistency. For some applications, absolute consistency is often not an overriding concern. Some delay in propagating a change is often acceptable, especially if one can tell when a response is incorrect. This observation was exploited by Grapevine, allowing it to guarantee only loose consistency. With loose consistency, replicas are guaranteed to *eventually* contain identical data. Updates are allowed even when the network is partitioned or servers are down. Updates are sent to any replica, and that replica forwards the update to the other replicas as they become available. If conflicting updates are received by different replicas in different orders, time stamps indicate the order in which they are to be applied. The disadvantage of loose consistency is that there is no guarantee that a query will return the most recent data. However, it is often possible — with name servers — to check if the response is correct at the time it is used.

(6) Quorum consensus. Maintaining a consistent view of replicated data does not require that all replicas be up-to-date; it requires only that the up-to-date information always be visible to the users of the data. In the mechanisms described so far, updates eventually make it to every replica. In quorum consensus, or voting [8], updates may be sent to a subset of replicas. A consistent view is maintained by requiring that all reads be directed to at least one replica that is up-to-date. This is accomplished by
- Assigning votes to each replica,

- Selecting two numbers—a read-quorum and a write-quorum—such that the read-quorum plus the write-quorum exceeds the total number of votes, and
- Requiring that reads and writes be directed to a sufficient number of replicas to collect enough votes to satisfy the quorum.

Taking these steps guarantees that the set of replicas read will intersect with the set written during the most recent update. Time stamps or version numbers stored with each replica allow the client to determine which data are most recent.

Distribution

Distribution allows the information maintained by a distributed service to be spread across multiple servers, which is important for several reasons. For one, there may be too much information to fit on a single server. In addition, distribution reduces the number of requests to be handled by each server, allows administration of parts of a service to be assigned to different individuals, and allows information that is used more frequently in one part of a network than in others to be maintained near that part of the network. This section describes the use of distribution in naming, authentication, and file services. Some of the issues of importance in distribution are the placement of the servers and the mechanisms by which the client finds the server with the desired information.

Placement of servers

Distributed systems exhibit locality. Certain pieces of information are more likely to be accessed by users in one part of a network than by users in another. Information should be distributed to servers that are near the users that will most frequently access the information. For example, a user's files could be assigned to a file server on the same subnet as that of the workstation usually used by that user. Similarly, the names maintained by name servers can be assigned so that names for nearby objects can be obtained from local name servers. In addition to reducing network traffic, such assignments improve reliability, since they make it less likely that a network partition will make a local server inaccessible. In any case, it is desirable to avoid the need to contact a name server across the country in order to find a resource in the next room.

By assigning information to servers along administrative lines, an organization can avoid dependence on other organizations. When distributed along organizational lines, objects maintained by an organization are often said to be within a particular *domain* (in DNS) or *cell* (in Andrew). Kerberos uses the term *realm* to describe the unit of distribution when an explicit trust relationship exists between the server and the principals assigned to it.

Mechanisms for finding the right server

The difficulty with distribution lies in the distribution function: The client must determine which server contains the requested information. Hierarchical name spaces make the task easier, since names with common prefixes are often stored together, but identifying the server maintaining that part of the name space is still necessary. (In this discussion, *prefix* means the most significant part of the name. For file names or for names in DEC's global name service, the most significant part of the name is the prefix. For domain names, the most significant part of the name is really the suffix.) The methods most frequently used are *mounts*, *broadcast*, and *domain-based distribution*.

To identify the server on which a named object resides, Sun's Network File System (NFS) [25], Locus [32], and Plan 9 [23] use a mount table. The system maintains this table, which maps name prefixes to servers. When an object is referenced, the name is looked up in the mount table, and the request is forwarded to the appropriate server. In NFS, the table can be different on different systems, meaning that the same name might refer to different objects on different systems. Locus supports a uniform name space by keeping the mount table the same on all systems. In Plan 9, the table is maintained on a per-process basis.

Sprite [21] uses broadcast communication to identify the server on which a particular file can be found. The client broadcasts a request, and the server with the file replies. The reply includes the prefix for the files maintained by the server. This prefix is cached so that subsequent requests for files with the same prefix can be sent directly to that server. As discussed in the subsection entitled "Communication," this approach does not scale beyond a local network. In fact, most of the systems that use this approach provide a secondary name-resolution mechanism to be used when a broadcast goes unanswered.

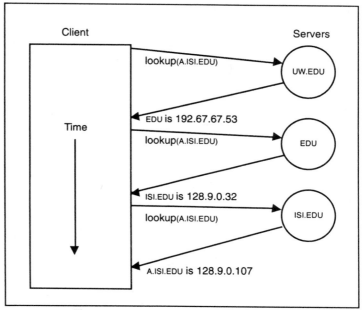

Figure 2. Resolving a domain-based name.

Distribution in Grapevine, DNS, DEC's global name service, and X.500 [24] is domain based. Like the other techniques described, the distribution function in domain-based naming is based on a prefix of the name to be resolved. Names are divided into multiple components. One component specifies the name to be resolved by a particular name server and the others specify the server that is to resolve the name. For example, names in Grapevine consist of a registry and a name within the registry. A name of the form NEUMAN.UW would be stored in the UW registry under the name NEUMAN. DNS and DEC's global name service both support variable-depth names. In these systems, the point at which the name and the domain are separated can vary. In DNS, the last components of the name specify the domain and the first components specify the name within that domain. For example, VENERA.ISI.EDU is registered in the name server for the ISI.EDU domain.

To find a name server containing information for a given domain or registry, a client sends a request to the local name server. The local name server sends back an answer or information redirecting the query to another name server. With the two-level name space supported by Grapevine, only two queries are required: one to find the server for a given registry and one to resolve the name. The server for a given registry is found by looking up the name in the GV registry that is replicated on every Grapevine server.

Figure 2 shows the resolution of a name with a variable number of components. The client sends to its local server a request for resolution of the host name A.ISI.EDU. That server returns the name and address of the EDU server. The client repeats its request to the EDU server, which responds with the name and address for the ISI.EDU server. The process repeats, with successively longer prefixes, until a server (in this case, ISI.EDU) returns the address for the requested host. The client caches intermediate responses that map prefixes to servers so that subsequent requests can be handled with fewer messages.

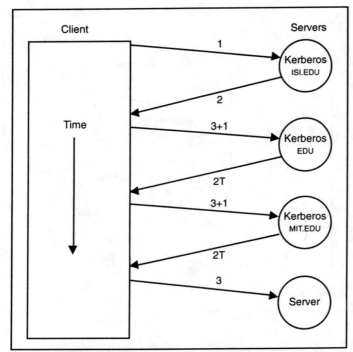

Figure 3. Multiple-hop cross-realm authentication in Kerberos.

Domain-based distribution of names scales well. As the system grows and queries become more frequent, additional replicas of frequently queried registries or domains can be added. However, Grapevine's two-level name space limits scalability. Because every name server must maintain the GV registry and because the size of this registry grows linearly with the total number of name servers, the total number of name servers that can be supported is limited. Clearinghouse, a production version of Grapevine, addressed this problem by supporting a three-level name space, which allows the name service to scale to a larger number of names. Nevertheless, a limit is still eventually reached because of the size of the root or second-level registries. The primary disadvantage of domain-based distribution of names with a greater number of levels is that resolving a single name can take many queries. Fortunately, many of these additional queries can be eliminated with the appropriate use of caching.

Domain-based distribution can also be used for authentication. In Kerberos, principals are registered in multiple *realms*, thus allowing an organization to set up its own Kerberos server and thereby eliminating the need for global trust. The server's realm is used to determine the sequence of ASs to be contacted. If a client in one Kerberos realm wishes to use a server in another, it must first authenticate itself to the AS in the server's realm using the AS in its own realm.

Figure 3 shows multiple-hop cross-realm authentication in Kerberos. In this figure, the message numbers loosely correspond to those in Figure 1. Message 3+1 is a message authenticating the client to the next Kerberos server, accompanied by a request for credentials. Message 2T is the same as Message 2 in Figure 1, except that instead of the response being encrypted in the client's key, it is encrypted in the session key from the ticket sent to the AS in the previous message.

The initial version of Kerberos supported only single-hop cross-realm authentication. This required each realm to know about every other realm with which it was to communicate. This requirement does not exist in Version 5 of Kerberos or in DEC's global authentication service [3]. With multiple-hop cross-realm authentication, what is known after a client has been authenticated may be as weak as the following statement: "The local AS claims that a remote AS claims that another AS has authenticated the client as A." To allow the end server to make an informed decision, it must know the complete list of realms that took part in authenticating the client. In global authentication, this information is part of the name of the authenticated principal. The principal's name is constructed by concatenating the names of the links that were traversed at each step in the authentication process. In Version 5 of Kerberos, the credentials include a list of the transited realms. Both Version 5 of Kerberos and DEC's global authentication service allow intermediaries to be skipped, thus not only speeding up the authentication process, but also making it more secure.

Caching

Caching — a form of replication — is another important tool for building scalable systems. As with replication, two issues of importance with caching are the placement of caches and the mechanisms by which the caches are kept consistent. The difference between caching and replication is that cached data are temporary replicas. Updates need not be propagated to caches. Instead, consistency is maintained by cached data being invalidated when consistency cannot be guaranteed.

Placement of caches

Caching can occur in multiple places. Caching is usually performed by the client, eliminating repeated requests to network services. Caching can also take place on the servers implementing these services. For example, in addition to caching on the workstation, Sprite [21] caches blocks in the memory of the file server. Reading a file from the memory-cached copy on the file server is often faster than reading it from the client's local disk. The additional caching on the file server can improve performance, because the file server might have more memory than does the client and because many of the blocks cached on the file server might be read by multiple clients.

Caching in multiple places is also useful for name servers. Most name servers unable to answer a query will return the address of the name server sharing the longest prefix in common with the name being resolved. In many cases, this name server might be the one for the root. BIND [31] may be configured so that a local name server makes queries on behalf of the client and caches the response (and any intermediate responses) for use by other local clients. This additional level of caching allows higher levels of the naming hierarchy to be bypassed, even if the client does not know the server for the desired prefix. For example, if a client in the CS.WASHINGTON.EDU domain wishes to resolve VENERA.ISI.EDU, the local name server could make the query to the root name server on behalf of the client, return the address for that name server, and cache it. If a second host in the CS.WASHINGTON.EDU domain wanted to resolve A.ISI.EDU, the local name server would then be able to return the address of the correct name server without an additional query to root. For this to work, clients must be willing to first look for information locally, instead of initially asking the root name server.

Mechanisms for maintaining cache consistency

As with replication, many techniques are used to maintain the consistency of caches. The four most common approaches used to keep caches consistent in distributed systems are *time-outs*, *check-on-use (hints)*, *callbacks*, and *leases*.

Time-outs are used to maintain cache consistency in DNS, DEC's global name service, Prospero, and a number of other systems. In these systems, responses from servers always include the time for which they may be considered valid, referred to as the *time-to-live (TTL)*. The TTL can vary from item to item. It will usually be longer for infrequently changing information and shorter for information expected to change. Clients can cache information until the TTL expires. When information changes, the TTL sets an upper bound on the time required before everyone will be using the new information. If a change is expected in advance, the TTL can be reduced so that the change will take effect quickly.

If it is possible to tell when incorrect information has been obtained, cached entries can be treated as hints. Hints do not have to be kept consistent; if data entries are out-of-date, that fact will be detected when the data are used, and the entry can be flushed. Both Grapevine and QuickSilver [4] use hints.

Hints are useful in naming systems if an object's identifier can be stored along with the object itself. The cached data tell where the object can be found; however, if the object has moved, that fact will be apparent when the client attempts to retrieve it. By the cached data being treated as hints, the cached data may be used until a change is detected, and the need for more complicated mechanisms to keep the cache consistent is thus avoided.

In some systems, the only way to check the validity of cached data is to go back to the server that originally provided the information. For small amounts of data, the cost of doing so is the same as if the information were not cached at all. For larger amounts of data, the check takes significantly less time than transferring the data themselves. The Andrew File System [11] originally used this form of check-on-use to decide if a locally cached copy of a file could be used. Experience showed that the checks were the primary bottleneck and that, in the common case, the files were unchanged. For this reason, the next implementation (and subsequently Coda) used callbacks. When a file is cached, the file server adds the caching site to a list stored along with the file. If the file changes, a message is sent to all sites with copies telling them that the cached copy is no longer valid. By requiring that clients check the validity of files when they reboot (or if contact with the file server has been lost), problems due to lost callbacks can be minimized.

Leases [9] are similar to callbacks, but there are several important differences. A lease eventually expires, and a server granting a lease guarantees that it will not make a change during the period the lease is valid—unless it first gets approval from the lease holder. A client holding a lease can cache the data to which the lease applies for the term of the lease or until the client authorizes the server to break the lease. Trade-offs similar to those for choosing a TTL apply to the selection of the term of a lease.

The user's view

Many mechanisms are used to help systems deal with scale. Unfortunately, the effect of scale on the user has received relatively little attention. The user has finite mental capacity. The potential exists for the size of the system to overwhelm the user as the number of computers in a system grows, the system expands geographically, and the system begins to cross administrative boundaries. Mechanisms are needed to allow objects and resources that are of interest to be organized in a manner that allows them to be easily found again. One does not want these objects and resources quickly lost in a sea of objects and resources in which there is little interest. It is also important that the user be able to identify additional objects and resources of potential interest.

Traditional systems such as Andrew, Locus, and Sprite support a uniform global name space that uniquely names all objects. This approach allows simple sharing of names and has the advantage that it is no harder for users to understand than the systems they previously used. Unfortunately, as systems cross administrative boundaries, obtaining agreement on what should appear where in the name space becomes difficult. The solution is for the names of sites to appear at the top level and for each site to name its own objects. Unfortunately, this results in related information being scattered across the global name space and users not knowing where to look for it.

Even with a familiar system model, the number of objects and the number of resources that are available can overwhelm the user. For this reason, mechanisms are needed to help the user organize information and to reduce the amount of information with which the user has to deal. The solution is to allow individual users to customize their name space so that they see only the objects that are of interest. This approach is taken in Plan 9 [23], Prospero [19], Tilde [6], and QuickSilver [4]. Naming in these systems is often described as user centered; however, with the exception of Prospero, it might better be described as user-exclusive, because an object must be added to the user's name space before it can be named. In Prospero, most objects are expected to start out in a user's name space, but with lengthy names. When a user expresses an interest in an object, a link is added to the name space, bringing the object closer to the center (root). An objection to user-centered naming is that the same name can refer to different objects when used by different users. To address this objection, Prospero supports *closure*: Every object in the system has an associated name space. Names are normally resolved within the name space associated with the object in which the name is found.

A few systems have looked at mechanisms for identifying objects that are needed when the object's full name is not known. Profile [22] supports attribute-based naming, in which the user specifies known attributes of an object instead of its name. For attributes to be used in place of a name, enough of them must be specified to uniquely identify the object. In order for the system to scale, information must be distributed across multiple name servers. In Profile, each user has a working set of name servers, and each is contacted. Responses from a name server may require further resolution (perhaps by a different server). This successive resolution of links is similar to the mechanism used to resolve names in traditional distributed systems. The key difference is that in attribute-based naming, the links do not necessarily form a hierarchy.

Alternative approaches are being examined by the Resource Discovery Project at the University of Colorado, Boulder. These approaches use information already available over the network. In one approach, resource discovery agents [28] collect and share information with other agents scattered across the system. A user wishing to find a resource asks one of these agents; the agents route queries among themselves, exploiting the semantics of the query to limit the activity that must take place. If the resource is found, a response is returned to the client.

Prospero takes a slightly different approach to identifying objects of interest. Tools are provided to allow users to customize and organize their views of the system. Prospero supports a user-centered name space and closure. Naming of all objects and resources is handled through a UID-based directory service. Name spaces may overlap and cycles are allowed. The Prospero directory service supports *filters* and *union links*. A filter is a program that can modify the results of a directory query when the path for the queried directory passes through the filtered link. A union link allows the results of a (possibly filtered) query to be merged with the contents of the directory containing the link. The nature of the directory service and its support for filters and union links allow users to organize their own objects and those of others in many ways. The ability for objects to have multiple names makes finding objects and resources much easier; one can look for an object using the organization that best fits the information that is known. Users and organizations set up directories within which they organize objects, and they make these directories available to others. It is through this sharing that users find new objects.

Conclusions

This paper examines the problems that arise as systems scale, using examples from many systems to demonstrate these problems and their solutions. The systems mentioned are not the only systems for which scale was a design factor; however, they are the most readily available examples for the mechanisms discussed. Out of necessity, this paper takes a narrow view of the systems, examining individual subsystems instead of the systems as a whole. Nevertheless, the effects of scale are felt throughout the system.

This paper shows how scale affects large systems. Each component of scale — numerical, geographical, and administrative—introduces its own problems, and this paper discusses the solutions employed by a number of systems. The three primary techniques used repeatedly to handle scale are replication, distribution, and caching. The box entitled "Building scalable systems" presents a collection of suggestions for designing scalable systems. These suggestions expand upon the three primary techniques and provide additional ways in which these techniques can be applied. The suggestions should help system designers address scale in the design of future distributed systems.

Building scalable systems

This box presents — in a form that can be used as a guide — suggestions for building scalable systems. (These suggestions are discussed in greater detail elsewhere in the paper.) Here, they are broken into groups corresponding to the primary techniques of replication, distribution, and caching, followed by a group of general suggestions.

When systems are being built, considering factors other than scalability is important. Lampson [12] presented an excellent collection of suggestions on the general design of computer systems.

Replication suggestions

Replicate important resources. Replication increases availability and allows requests to be spread across xmultiple servers, thus reducing the load on each.

Distribute the replicas. Placing replicas in different parts of the network improves availability during network partitions. By at least one replica being placed in any area with frequent requests, these requests can be directed to a local replica, thus reducing the load on the network and minimizing response time.

Use loose consistency. Absolute consistency does not scale well. Using loose consistency can reduce the cost of updates, while guaranteeing that changes will *eventually* make it to each replica. In systems that use loose consistency, being able to detect out-of-date information at the time it is used is desirable.

Distribution suggestions

Distribute across multiple servers. Distributing data across multiple servers decreases the size of the database that must be maintained by each server, reducing the time needed to search the database. Distribution also spreads the load across the servers, reducing the number of requests each handles.

Distribute evenly. The greatest impact on scalability will be felt if requests can be distributed to servers in proportion to their power. With an uneven distribution, one server may be idle while others are overloaded.

Exploit locality. Network traffic and latency can be reduced if data are assigned to servers close to the location from which they are most frequently used. DNS does this. Each site maintains the information for its own hosts in its own servers. Most queries to a name server are for local hosts. As a result, most queries never leave the local network.

Bypass upper levels of hierarchies. In hierarchically organized systems, information from the root is needed for many queries. If cached copies are available from subordinate servers, the upper levels can be bypassed. In some cases, it might be desirable for a server to answer queries only from its immediate subordinates and to let the subordinates make the responses available to their subordinates.

Caching suggestions

Cache frequently accessed data. Caching decreases the load on servers and the network. Cached information can be accessed more quickly than if a new request were made.

Consider access patterns when caching. The amount of data normally referenced together, the ratio of reads to writes, the likelihood of conflicts, the number of simultaneous users, and other factors affect the choice of caching mechanisms. For example, if files are normally read from start to finish, caching the entire file might be more efficient than caching blocks. If conflicts between readers and writers are rare, using callbacks to maintain consistency might reduce requests. The ability to detect invalid data on use allows cached data to be used until such a condition is detected.

Cache time-out. Associating a TTL with cached data allows an upper bound to be placed on the time required for changes to be observed. This is useful when only eventual consistency is required or as a backup to other cache consistency mechanisms. The TTL should be chosen by the server holding the authoritative copy. If a change is expected, the TTL can be decreased accordingly.

Cache at multiple levels. Additional levels of caching often reduce the number of requests to the next level. For example, if a name server handling requests for a local network caches information from the root name servers, it can request it once, then answer local requests for that information instead of requiring each client to request it separately. Similarly, caching on file servers allows a block to be read (and cached) by multiple clients, but requires only one disk access.

Look first locally. When nearby copies of data are looked for before central servers are contacted, the load on central servers can be reduced. For example, if a name is not available from a cache in the local system, a name server on the local network should be contacted before a distant name server. Even if it is not the authority for the name to be resolved, the local name server may possess information that allows the root name server to be bypassed.

Limit updates to extensively shared data. When an extensively shared object is changed, a large number of cached copies become invalid, and each must be refreshed. A system should be organized so that extensively shared data are relatively stable. A hierarchical name space exhibits this property. Most changes occur at the leaves of the hierarchy. Upper levels rarely change.

General suggestions

Shed load, but not too much. When computation can be done as easily by the client as by the server, leaving computation to the client is often best. However, if allowing the client to perform the computation requires the return of a significantly greater amount of information (as might be the case for a database query), having the server to do the computation is more appropriate. Additionally, if the result can be cached by the server and later provided to others, doing the computation on the server is appropriate, especially if the computation requires contacting additional servers.

Avoid global broadcast. Broadcast does not scale well. It requires all systems to process a message, whether or not they need to. Multicast is acceptable, but groups should include only those servers that need to receive the message.

Support multiple access mechanisms. Applications place varying requirements on access mechanisms. What is best for one application might not be best for another. Also, changing communication parameters can affect the choice of mechanism. Multiple mechanisms should be supported when objects and resources are being accessed. The client should choose the method based on the prevailing conditions.

Keep the user in mind. Many mechanisms are used to help the system deal with scale. The mechanisms that are used should not make the system more difficult to understand. Even with a familiar system model, the number of available objects and resources can overwhelm the user. Large systems require mechanisms that reduce the amount of information to be processed and remembered by the user. These mechanisms should not hide information that might be of interest.

Evaluating scalable systems

Rather than provide an equation that yields a number to use for evaluating the scalability of a distributed system, this box presents several important questions to ask in the evaluation of such systems. In fact, different systems scale in different ways: One system may scale better administratively, while another may scale better numerically. So many unknowns affect scaling that experience is often the only true test of a system's ability to scale.

The first set of questions concerns the use of the system.

- How will the frequency of queries grow as the system grows?
- What percentage of those queries must be handled by central servers?
- How many replicas of the central servers are there? Is this enough, can more be added, what problems are introduced by doing so, and are there any bottlenecks?

The next set of questions concerns the data that must be maintained.

- How do the sizes of the databases handled by the individual servers grow? How does this affect query time?
- How often will information change?
- What update mechanism is used? How does it scale?
- How will an update affect the frequency of queries?
- Will caches be invalidated? Will this result in a sudden increase in requests as caches are refreshed?

The final set of questions concerns the administrative component of scale.

- Is a single authority that makes final decisions concerning the system required? (Many systems require this.)
- Is this requirement practical in the environment for which the system will be used?

This is not a complete list of questions. However, addressing the questions listed here will point out some of the problem areas in a system. It is entirely possible that important factors not addressed here will cause a system to stop scaling even earlier.

Systems designed with scale in mind

Scalability is included among the design criteria for a number of recent systems. These systems range from a collection of computers on a local-area network to computers distributed across the entire Internet. This box describes some of these systems, states the degree to which each system is intended to scale, and lists some of the ways in which each system addresses the problems of scale. Table 1 summarizes this information.

Amoeba. Developed at Vrije Universiteit and CWI in Amsterdam, The Netherlands, Amoeba is a capability-based distributed operating system that has been used across long-haul networks spanning multiple organizations. Objects are referenced by capabilities that include identifiers for the server and object and access rights for the object. The capabilities provide both a distributed naming mechanism and an authorization mechanism. [15], [30]

Andrew. Developed at Carnegie Mellon University, Pittsburgh, Pennsylvania, the Andrew system runs on thousands of computers distributed across the campus. Its most notable component is the Andrew File System, which now ties together file systems at sites distributed across the United States. As a follow-on to the Andrew file system, **Coda** has improved availability, especially in the face of network partitions. [11], [26]

MIT's Project Athena. Project Athena, developed at MIT, is a system built from thousands of computers distributed across the campus. Distributed services provide authentication, naming, filing, printing, mailing, and administrative functions. **Kerberos** was developed as part of Project Athena. [5]

Coda. (See **Andrew system**.)

Dash. Under development at the University of California, Berkeley, Dash is a distributed operating system designed for use across large networks exhibiting a range of transmission characteristics. It is notable for exposing these characteristics by allowing the application to require that the connection meet certain requirements and by returning an error if those requirements cannot be met. [1]

DEC's global authentication service. (See **DEC's global name service**.)

DEC's global name service. Developed at DEC's Systems Research Center, DEC's global name service was designed to support naming in large networks spanning multiple organizations. It is notable for the attention paid to reorganization of the name space as independent name spaces are merged or as the external relationship between organizations changes (for example, through mergers or acquisitions). **Echo** is a distributed file system supporting consistent replication of local partitions, but with partitions tied together using the loosely consistent global name service. **DEC's global authentication service** is notable for a principal's name not being absolute, but instead being determined by the sequence of authentication servers (ASs) used to authenticate the principal. [3], [10], [13]

Echo. (See **DEC's global name service**.)

Grapevine. Grapevine was one of the earliest distributed systems designed to scale to a large network. It was developed at Xerox Corporation's Palo Alto Research Center (PARC) to support electronic mail, to provide a name service for the location of network services, and to support simple password-based authentication on a worldwide network connecting Xerox sites. [2], [27]

Heterogeneous Computer Systems (HCS) Project. The HCS Project at the University of Washington, Seattle, demonstrated that a single interface could be used to communicate among systems using different underlying protocols and data representations. This is important for large systems when dictating the choice of hardware and software across multiple sites is not practical or when the underlying mechanisms have different strengths and weaknesses. [20]

Internet Domain Name System (DNS). DNS is a distributed name service, running on the Internet, that supports the translation of host names to Internet addresses and mail forwarders. Each organization maintains replicated servers supporting the translation of names for its own part of the name space. [14], [31]

Kerberos. Developed by MIT's Project Athena, Kerberos is an encryption-based network-authentication system that supports authentication of users both locally and across organizational boundaries. [29]

Locus. Developed at the University of California, Los Angeles, Locus was designed to run on systems distributed across a local-area network. Locus is notable for being one of the earliest distributed systems to support a uniform view of the file system across all nodes in the system. [32]

Sun's Network File System (NFS). Developed by Sun Microsystems, Inc., Sun's NFS supports transparent access to files stored on remote hosts. Files are named independently on each host. Before a remote file can be accessed, the remote file system containing the file must be mounted on the local system, establishing a mapping of part of the local file name space to files on the remote system. The NFS server maintains very little information (state) about the clients that use it. [25]

Plan 9 from Bell Labs. Plan 9 was intended for use by a large corporation. It supports a process-centered name space (perhaps better described as a *process-exclusive* name space, since objects must first be added to the user's name space before they can be named), allowing users to incorporate into their name space those parts of the global system that are useful. [23]

Profile. Developed at the University of Arizona, Tucson, Profile is an attribute-based name service that maps possibly incomplete information about coarse-grained objects on a large network to the object(s) matching that information. [22]

Prospero. Developed at the University of Washington, Seattle, Prospero runs on systems distributed across the Internet. It supports an object-centered view of the entire system, allowing users to define their own virtual system by specifying the pieces of the global system that are of interest. Prospero's support for closure resolves the problems caused by the use of multiple name spaces. [19]

QuickSilver. Developed at IBM's Almaden Research Center, QuickSilver is notable for its proposed use of a user-centered name space (perhaps better described as a *user-exclusive* name space, since objects must first be added to the user's name space before they can be named). In a system spanning a large, multinational corporation, such a name space allows users to see only those parts of the system that concern them. [4]

Sprite. Developed at the University of California, Berkeley, Sprite is a network operating system that was designed for use across a local-area network. Its file system is notable for its use of caching on both the client and the server to improve performance and for its use of prefix tables to distribute requests to the correct file server. [21]

Tilde naming system. Developed at Purdue University, West Lafayette, Indiana, the Tilde naming system supports process-centered naming (perhaps better described as a *process-exclusive* naming, since objects must first be added to the user's name space before they can be named), allowing one to specify, on a per-process basis, how names will map to pieces of the global system. This ability provides applications with the advantages of a global name space for those file names that should be resolved globally, while allowing parts of the name space to be specified locally for file names that would be better resolved to local files. [6]

X.500. X.500 is an International Standards Organization (ISO) standard describing a distributed directory service that is designed to store information about users, organizations, resources, and similar entities worldwide. Scalability is addressed in largely the same manner as that in the **Internet Domain Name System (DNS)**. [24]

Table 1. Important distributed systems and the methods they use to handle scale.
(DEC = Digital Equipment Corporation, TTL = time-to-live, HCS = Heterogeneous Computer Systems, DNS = Domain Name System, NFS = Network File System, and UID = unique identifier.)

System	Service	Intended environment			Methods used		
		Number of nodes	Geographic	Administrative	Replication	Distribution	Caching
Amoeba	General	∞	Wide area	Multiple organizations	Immutable	Capabilities	Yes
Andrew	File system	10,000	Wide area	Multiple organizations	Read-only	Cell/volume	Blocks
Athena	General	10,000	Campus	University	Service	Clusters	Yes
Coda	File system	10,000	Global	Multiple organizations	Optimistic	Volume	Whole file
Dash	General	∞	Wide area	Multiple organizations	Yes	Yes	Yes
DEC's global authentication service		∞	Global	Multiple organizations	Loose	Directories	—
DEC's global name service		∞	Global	Multiple organizations	Loose	Directories	TTL
Echo	File system	∞	Wide area	Multiple organizations	Loose/ primary	Volume	Yes
Grape-vine	General	2000	Company	Multiple departments	Loose	Registry	Yes
HCS	General	—	Wide area	Multiple organizations	—	Yes	—
Internet DNS	Naming	∞	Global	Multiple organizations	Primary	Domain	Yes
Kerberos	Authen-tication	∞	Global	Multiple organizations	Primary	Realm	Tickets
Locus	General	100	Local	Department	Primary	Mount	Yes
NFS	File system	—	Local	Single organization	No	Mount	Blocks
Plan 9	General	10,000	Company	Multiple departments	No	Mount	No
Profile	Naming	∞	Wide area	Multiple organizations	Information	Principal	Client managed
Prospero	Naming	∞	Global	Multiple organizations	Yes	UID	Yes
Quick-Silver	File system	10,000	Company	Multiple departments	No	Prefix	Immutable
Sprite	File system	100	Local	Department	Read-only	Prefix	Client and server
Tilde	Naming	100	Local	Single organization	No	Trees	Yes
X.500	Naming	∞	Global	Multiple organizations	Yes	Yes	Yes

Acknowledgments

The author would like to thank Brian Bershad, Robert Cooper, Barbara Gordon, Bruce Gordon, Terry Gray, Andrew Herbert, Richard Ladner, Ed Lazowska, Hank Levy, Mary Ann G. Neuman, David Notkin, John Zahorjan, and the anonymous referees who commented on earlier drafts of this paper. The research was supported in part by National Science Foundation Grant Number CCR-8619663, the Washington Technology Centers, and Digital Equipment Corporation (DEC).

References

[1] D.P. Anderson and D. Ferrari, "The Dash Project: An Overview," Tech. Report 88/405, Computer Science Division, Dept. of Electrical Eng. and Computer Science, Univ. of California, Berkeley, Calif., 1988.

[2] A.D. Birrell et al., "Grapevine: An Exercise in Distributed Computing," *Comm. ACM*, Vol. 25, No. 4, Apr. 1982, pp. 260-274.

[3] A.D. Birrell et al., "A Global Authentication Service without Global Trust, *Proc. 1986 IEEE Symp. Security and Privacy*, published in *Security and Privacy, Vol. 2: Proc. Sixth, Seventh, and Eighth Symposia, 1985-1987*, IEEE Computer Soc. Press, Los Alamitos, Calif., 1990, pp. 223-230.

[4] L.-F. Cabrera and J. Wyllie, "QuickSilver Distributed File Services: An Architecture for Horizontal Growth," *Proc. Second IEEE Conf. Computer Workstations*, IEEE Computer Soc. Press, Los Alamitos, Calif., 1988, pp. 23-37.

[5] G.A. Champine, D.E. Geer, Jr., and W.N. Ruh, "Project Athena as a Distributed Computer System," *Computer*, Vol. 23, No. 9, Sept. 1990, pp. 40-51.

[6] D. Comer, R.E. Droms, and T.P. Murtagh, "An Experimental Implementation of the Tilde Naming System," *Computing Systems*, Vol. 4, No. 3, Fall 1990, pp. 487-515.

[7] R.J. Fowler, *Decentralized Object Finding Using Forwarding Addresses*, doctoral thesis and Tech. Report 85-12-1, Dept. of Computer Science, Univ. of Washington, Seattle, Wash., 1985.

[8] D.K. Gifford, "Weighted Voting for Replicated Data," *Proc. Seventh ACM Symp. Operating Systems Principles*, ACM Press, New York, N.Y., 1979, pp. 150-159.

[9] C.G. Gray and D.R. Cheriton, "Leases: An Efficient Fault-Tolerant Mechanism for Distributed File Cache Consistency," *Proc. 12th ACM Symp. Operating Systems Principles*, ACM Press, New York, N.Y., 1989, pp. 202-210.

[10] A. Hisgen et al., "Availability and Consistency Tradeoffs in the Echo Distributed File System," *Proc. Second Workshop Workstation Operating Systems*, IEEE Computer Soc. Press, Los Alamitos, Calif., 1989, pp. 49-54.

[11] J.H. Howard et al., "Scale and Performance in a Distributed File System," *ACM Trans. Computer Systems*, Vol. 6, No. 1, Feb. 1988, pp. 51-81.

[12] B.W. Lampson, "Hints for Computer System Design," *Proc. Ninth ACM Symp. Operating Systems Principles*, ACM Press, New York, N.Y., 1983, pp. 33-48.

[13] B.W. Lampson, "Designing a Global Name Service," *Proc. Fourth ACM Symp. Principles Distributed Computing*, ACM Press, New York, N.Y., 1985.

[14] P. Mockapetris, "Domain Names — Concepts and Facilities," Internet Request for Comments (RFC) 1034, Information Sciences Inst., Univ. of Southern California, Los Angeles, Calif., Nov. 1987.

[15] S.J. Mullender and A.S. Tanenbaum, "The Design of a Capability-Based Distributed Operating System," *The Computer J.*, Vol. 29, No. 4, 1986, pp. 289-299.

[16] R.M. Needham and M.D. Schroeder, "Using Encryption for Authentication in Large Networks of Computers," *Comm. ACM*, Vol. 21, No. 12, Dec. 1978, pp. 993-999.

[17] B.C. Neuman, "Issues of Scale in Large Distributed Operating Systems," General Examination Report, Dept. of Computer Science, Univ. of Washington, Seattle, Wash., May 1988.

[18] B.C. Neuman, "Proxy-Based Authorization and Accounting for Distributed Systems," *Proc. 13th Int'l Conf. Distributed Computing Systems*, IEEE Computer Soc. Press, Los Alamitos, Calif., 1993, pp. 283-291.

[19] B.C. Neuman, "The Prospero File System: A Global File System Based on the Virtual System," *Computing Systems*, Vol. 5, No. 4, Fall 1992, pp. 407-432.

[20] D. Notkin et al., "Interconnecting Heterogeneous Computer Systems," *Comm. ACM*, Vol. 31, No. 3, Mar. 1988, pp. 258-273.

[21] J.K. Ousterhout et al., "The Sprite Network Operating System," *Computer*, Vol. 21, No. 2, Feb. 1988, pp. 23-35.

[22] L.L. Peterson, "The Profile Naming Service," *ACM Trans. Computer Systems*, Vol. 6, No. 4, Nov. 1988, pp. 341-364.

[23] D. Presotto et al., "Plan 9: A Distributed System," *Proc. Spring 1991 EurOpen*, 1991.

[24] *Recommendation X.500: The Directory*, Comité Consultatif International de Téléphonique et Télégraphique (CCITT), Geneva, Switzerland, Dec. 1988.

[25] R. Sandberg et al., "Design and Implementation of the Sun Network File System," *Proc. Summer 1985 Usenix Conf.*, Usenix, Berkeley, Calif., 1985, pp. 119-130.

[26] M. Satyanarayanan, "Scalable, Secure, and Highly Available Distributed File Access," *Computer*, Vol. 23, No. 5, May 1990, pp. 9-21.

[27] M.D. Schroeder, A.D. Birrell, and R.M. Needham, "Experience with Grapevine: The Growth of a Distributed System," *ACM Trans. Computer Systems*, Vol. 2, No. 1, Feb. 1984, pp. 3-23.

[28] M.F. Schwartz, "The Networked Resource Discovery Project," *Proc. IFIP XI World Congress*, 1989, pp. 827-832.

[29] J.G. Steiner, B.C. Neuman, and J.I. Schiller, "Kerberos: An Authentication Service for Open Network Systems," *Proc. Winter 1988 Usenix Conf.*, Usenix, Berkeley, Calif., 1988, pp. 191-201.

[30] A.S. Tanenbaum et al. "Experience with the Amoeba Distributed Operating System," *Comm. ACM*, Vol. 33, No. 12, Dec. 1990, pp. 47-63.

[31] D.B. Terry et al., "The Berkeley Internet Domain Server," *Proc. Summer 1984 Usenix Conf.*, Usenix, Berkeley, Calif., 1984, pp. 23-31.

[32] B. Walker et al., "The Locus Distributed Operating System," *Proc. Ninth ACM Symp. Operating Systems Principles*, ACM Press, New York, N.Y., 1983, pp. 49-70.

Transparent Access to Large Files That Are Stored across Sites

T
he distributed nature of a variety of novel applications often necessitates some form of file fragmentation. In the Dragon Slayer distributed operating system, *fragments*, or their replicas, reside at different sites. The upcoming metropolitan area networks (MANs), systems-management applications, and even load-balancing considerations require that access to fragmented files be *transparent*. If the fragmentation is done like that in operating systems management to achieve — for example — better load balance or better disk space utilization, then the application designer need not be responsible for details regarding the fragment structure and the relocation of fragments and their replicas.

This paper begins by describing the fragmented-file-management techniques and facilities of Dragon Slayer. We explain Dragon Slayer's major kernel services, emphasizing the problem of supporting the transparent execution of the operations on fragmented files and describing in some detail the corresponding distributed-resource-scheduling algorithm. This algorithm is described in the format of a distributed game resulting in guaranteed access — for all players involved — to all resources (files or their fragments) requested. Next, we address the file-management strategies used in Dragon Slayer, demonstrating how Dragon Slayer maintains the consistency of replicated files and provides access to "whole" fragmented files. In the scenario of group editing of a book, we discuss recovery issues and describe novel forms and options for fragmented-file-access operations. Then, we describe some distributed simulation experiments that measured the effect of file fragmentation. Access reliability to a fragmented file clearly can be higher than in the nonfragmented case, and there are performance advantages that come with fragmentation. We present and discuss the simulation results, which clearly display these advantages, and then present conclusions. Finally, we compare our work with other research in distributed-file management.

Horst F. Wedde,

Bogdan Korel,

Shengdong Chen,

Douglas C. Daniels,

Srinivasan Nagaraj, and

Babu Santhanam

Fragmented files in heterogeneous environments

In this section, we begin by explaining the concept of transparent file operations. Next, we indicate major directions of the present

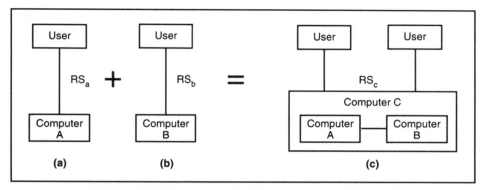

Figure 1. Distributed services. (RS = resources and services.)

and future use of this concept in various applications. Then, we explain how fragmentation of files can occur, whether for very large distributed files or for better support of local-operation structures on distributed files — in particular, for transparency support. We conclude this section by briefly mentioning previous and related work.

Transparent operations

In order to understand the concept of transparent operations, assume that a given computer, Computer A, provides a set of resources and services RS_a, as shown in part (a) of Figure 1. Now assume that another computer, Computer B, provides another set of resources and services RS_b, as depicted in part (b) of Figure 1. By connecting these two computers, each one can be made to provide a larger set RS_{ab}, consisting of the union of RS_a and RS_b. Furthermore, an extra set of resources and services RS_x, made possible only by the interconnection of the computers, can be constructed and provided. As illustrated in part (c) of Figure 1, the two computers form a distributed computer system (Computer C), with a set of resources and services RS_c that includes RS_{ab} and RS_x. The system can be expanded to any number of sites x, with the power and flexibility of the system increasing as the number and/or type of computers increase.

In the above example, all is dependent on user ability to manipulate the collective resources and services of the system as if they all belong to one computer. As an example, consider the operation of copying the data in one file to another file. If these files reside at the same computer, all that a user needs to know is the operating system command at that machine — for example,

Copy source file to target file

However, if the two files reside on different computers, the user must know the locations of the files and the communications commands for file transfer — for example,

Send source file from source machine to target machine

Furthermore, if the two computers are different (or run different operating systems), the user must also know the file format and naming conventions of each machine — for example,

Using source machine conventions, get data from source file and send it to target machine
Then, using target machine conventions, make target file with data from source file

If a distributed operating system would manage the resources of a system of computers as transparently as a traditional operating system manages the resources of one computer, it should be able to locate and transfer the files as well as recognize and convert the different machine conventions. Then, the command for the user would once again become, for example,

Copy source file to target file

Although the aspects of system heterogeneity are not central to these experiments, they are nonetheless important to them.

New dimensions in distributed-systems applications

Given the current progress toward high-speed and high-bandwidth interconnection technology, we can very soon expect commercial fiber-optics cables with a throughput of one gigabit (Gbit) per second or above. This will allow for a new dimension of networking well beyond the range of local area networks (LANs), widening LANs into MANs. Such networks typically would exhibit a much higher degree of hardware and operating software heterogeneity, because the systems in the larger range of a metropolitan area would need to be more heterogeneous than in a network of workstations. A good example is a bank organization that wants to connect all administrative systems of their branches in their main metropolitan area of business into one MAN. Their goals might include a considerable increase in cooperation of various loan departments among branches, while at the same time taking advantage of the decentralized branch structure that allows for higher service flexibility and reliability.

Fragmented files

Trends like those mentioned above have caused several specific changes to be incorporated into the way information and data are viewed, generated, managed, or maintained in distributed operating systems. As an extreme (and still utopian) example, consider the General Motors (GM) Company and its personnel administration. If the administrative systems of each GM plant in North America were connected into one distributed system, then *logically* combining all personnel information into one file would make sense. In order to understand this, consider GM having agreed, after nationwide negotiations with the United Auto Workers (UAW), to raise the salaries of all its UAW workers by 3.8 percent, effective immediately. Logically, the corresponding *update* operation could be conceived to be performed on the personnel file of the GM personnel employed in the range of the union contract. The operation could be issued at one site, while affecting all local personnel files in locations with UAW representation. However, the pure size of this logical unit precludes such a file being stored *physically* at any one of the sites. Given a user's interest in a GM personnel file, the aspects addressed suggest that this object (that is, this personnel file) would be defined and managed like a conventional file, except that it is physically spread across many sites. The local parts of the GM personnel file would be called its *fragments*.

Other than size, quite different reasons for file fragmentation may exist. As an example, consider student registration at a university. In this example, assume the following: Students will be registering during different days. For greater convenience and better accessibility for both students and administrative personnel, several different locations will be available for registration. Students will be allowed to register at locations depending on whether their last names start with a letter belonging to a certain section of the alphabet — for example, "A to H," "I to O," and "P to Z" — with all three groups at all three locations representing almost the same number of students. The registration office wants to make sure that one location will be open every day for every section and that every location

Table 1. Example registration schedule.

Day	Location 1	Location 2	Location 3
1	A - H	I - O	P - Z
2	I - O	P - Z	A - H
3	P - Z	A - H	I - O
4	A - Z		

eventually will cover the whole alphabet. In this way, students will be able to choose to register either at the location closest to their home or at their most convenient time slot according to their individual schedules. There will be four days and three locations for final registration. The registration office decides to use the schedule given in Table 1. (The office chose one central location for the fourth day, since experience has shown that few students are left for registration on the last day.)

The fragmentation in this example originates from functional reasons in the nature of the application. Also, one notes as a separate observation that for a file-level access mode, fragmentation is advantageous, since a high amount of the registration operations (typically more than 80 percent here) involve information contained in, or relating to, one fragment. Since the fragment size is a fraction of the size of the whole file, the access time for each such operation to a fragment may be considerably shorter than that to the whole file. Moreover, the access to a fragment is possible even if computers at other sites are down, resulting in a higher *reliability* or in a more *graceful degradation* of data accessibility as sites fail.

Also, through relocation and replication, both the accessibility and availability of fragments can be further enhanced. So, in total, fragmented files may be spread across various sites, permanently or temporarily, and fragments may be replicated.

Transparent operations on fragmented files

Relocation or replication of fragments may be of direct interest to a user or a user program. A particular fragmentation structure could be generated at file-creation time or the fragments could be recombined into one file to be stored at a later time at one site only. Other changes—say in the number or location of fragment replicas — could be the sole result of load-balancing considerations; these considerations are normally below the user/application level, but are instrumental within the management of distributed operating systems. Fragmentation and replication details, such as the number and location of fragments or replicas, should be hidden from the user in order not to be reflected in the application program structure. Therefore, transparency of file access as addressed in the subsection entitled "Transparent operations" becomes an issue of critical importance for fragmented files. In the format of the case study example of group editing of a book (see the section entitled "Issues in fragmented-file management"), we describe how conventional file operations are realized for the fragmented files in Dragon Slayer. We indicate in some detail how novel forms and options for several standard file operations come into the discussion under the extended paradigm of fragmented files. We also indicate how these novel forms and options are realized in Dragon Slayer.

Previous and related work

Van Renesse, Tanenbaum, and Wilschut [24], Satyanarayanan [18], and Theimer, Cabrera, and Wyllie [21] discussed file systems for distributed environments; Walsh et al. [25] provided a partial report on Sun's Network File System (NFS). However, these discussions were restricted to performance studies with nonreplicated, nonfragmented files. Scheurich and Dubois [20] considered file blocks distributed over more than one storage device. When file blocks are distributed in this way, tight coupling among processes and a shared-memory architecture are needed. The purpose of their work was a conceptual study rather than a distributed implementation project.

In this paper, we describe novel mechanisms for *creating*, *distributing*, and even *reconfiguring* fragmented files and for *transparently accessing* them. These mechanisms form a special case of the concept of *distributed objects*, which are named entities with a set of legal distributed operations. Wedde et al. [29] introduced and discussed the concept of distributed objects within Dragon Slayer. Similar fragmented objects with replicated parts were independently defined in Gothic [3], but without allowing for different versions of fragments. (This latter feature was instrumental in the novel adaptive real-time file system Melody [30] and in distributed version control [29].) Also, Gothic operations (multifunctions) always work on the *whole* file, not on fragments.

After the pioneering developments of the V system [6], several distributed operating systems, such as Clouds [8] and Mach [4], [17], were developed that use an *object/thread* model. Eden programs and data are encapsulated in *objects* [1], [16]. Argus [10] uses *guardians* as abstractions of resource handlers. In the V system, *UIO* objects correspond to open files. Dragon Slayer's file transfer philosophy is found also in Andrew [11] and Amoeba [12], [24]. While most of these systems are relying on a homogeneous hardware basis, Dragon Slayer was designed for operating in a heterogeneous environment, as was Mach. While Mach is currently implemented in Unix-like environments, Dragon Slayer is operational in a Token Ring network of IBM RT PCs and IBM 9370s.

Access transparency is also addressed in the Apollo Domain file system [15], Andrew [19], and Sprite [14]. In these systems, either objects or files are located at one site only.

The Dragon Slayer environment

All computer operating systems perform some subset of the same general set of functions. The operating system functions under discussion include

- Keeping track of the resources of the system,
- Deciding when and how resources are allocated to processes,
- Allocating resources to processes, and
- Reclaiming resources after processes have finished using them.

Dragon Slayer is a *virtual* operating system. It can use another traditional operating system as its "kernel," as depicted in Figure 2. It is *process-oriented* in that services normally performed by the kernel operating system are performed by Dragon Slayer processes, which make system calls to the kernel operating system.

Because each computer runs its own copy of the distributed operating system and system processes can communicate across computer boundaries, Dragon Slayer extends the kernel operating system to the distributed environment. It acts as an interface among the kernel operating systems at each computer. Since users at all computers must use the same set of Dragon Slayer commands, there appears to be only one operating system.

The issue of scheduling the allocation of resources to processes is much more complicated in the distributed environment than in centralized computing systems. The major problem is that processes may require mutually exclusive sets of resources that are spread over two or more computers. Dragon Slayer's approach to resource scheduling is based on decentralized control. Each computer is responsible for allocation of only those resources at that computer. The responsibilities for locating and procuring a set of resources are placed on the processes that need the resources. A user process makes a request for a set of needed resources. System processes then locate and acquire the resources

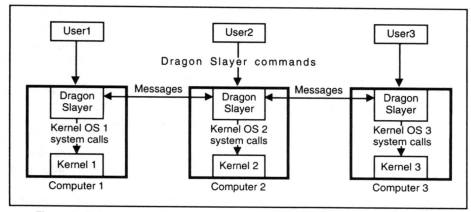

Figure 2. Only one operating system is visible to users. (OS = operating system.)

for the user process. These system processes send broadcast messages to all *resource managers* to locate resources. Then, the processes and all involved resource managers (those that respond in the affirmative to the location requests) adhere to a decentralized scheduling algorithm. This algorithm, which was explained and proven elsewhere to be deadlock- and starvation-free [26], [27], guarantees exclusive allocation of sets of resources to processes when and if necessary.

Processes that need to access an entire file without regard to either the fragments or the replicas — that is, applications that treat the fragmented or replicated file as a single object — may do so without regard to issues concerning fragmentation or replication. Just as normal operating systems provide their users with I/O transparency, so does Dragon Slayer. The application designer, or the interactive user editing a file, need know nothing of the internal mechanics of resource location, allocation, or scheduling. All resource scheduling takes place within a layer of Dragon Slayer that is completely transparent to the user. For instance, though the actual syntax varies among programming languages, the basic *file-write* operation generally involves an *open-for-write* operation — followed by a sequence of *write* operations — and a *file-close* operation. The Dragon Slayer system services for the distributed *open*, *write*, and *close* operations can be called, in the C language, from within the source code and handled directly by the C compiler. In this fashion, Dragon Slayer presents not only the interactive user, but also the application designer, with a high degree of transparency in which shared and distributed objects may be operated on as single and local entities.

The Dragon Slayer scheduling protocol

Resource scheduling in a fully distributed environment involves the resolution of conflicts among different processes over resources. As an example, assume that two processes P_1 and P_2 each require mutually exclusive access to a file F. Assume also that file F is partitioned into three file fragments. In order for a process to have complete exclusive access to the file, it must have exclusive access to all three fragments. In this sense, the file fragments become resources — that is, a set of resources $R_1, R_2,$ and R_3 — that both processes need for their *critical sections*. In this example, *mutual exclusion* implies that a process must be able to access all three resources in such a way that no other process is allowed access to any of the three resources at the same time.

In a completely distributed environment, the *serialization* of access, which guarantees the property of mutual exclusion, can be more difficult to achieve than it would appear. Though many mechanisms are known that guarantee the property of mutual exclusion, the situation is further complicated by other requirements. For instance, suppose that processes were allowed to *lock* a resource — that is, to reserve access to a resource for themselves, as a means of prohibiting other processes from accessing the resource. From the example above, process P_1 or P_2 might attempt to lock either R_1, R_2, or R_3 and, having succeeded in doing so, might then attempt to lock the other required resources. When it had locked all three resources, it could then enter its critical section. If both processes were to attempt to enter their critical sections at nearly the same time, then P_1 could first lock R_1 and P_2 could first lock R_2. Regardless of which process locked R_3, neither process could proceed until locking all three resources. As neither process could release any of the resources on which it had already obtained a lock, P_1 and P_2 would wait on each other forever; such a situation is known as a *deadlock*. A good distributed *resource scheduler* should be free of deadlock. In addition, there are still other desirable properties that a good distributed resource scheduler should have. Some of these properties are discussed below.

In Dragon Slayer, distributed resource scheduling is accomplished by forcing processes that are attempting to *lock* resources to do so according to the rules of a protocol that all processes will obey. Part of this protocol is that no application process will attempt to access a public (shared) resource until it has been granted the right to do so by a system process or server process that controls access to that resource. These server processes — the *resource managers* — control all access to all *shared resources* in Dragon Slayer. A shared resource may be a shared object or a subcomponent of a shared object — for example, a file replica or fragment.

It is perhaps most illustrative to describe the Dragon Slayer scheduling protocol as a game — more specifically as a card game — in which each process wishing to access shared resources must "win" before being allowed to access those resources. The core idea for this card game was borrowed from theoretical algorithms referred to by Winkowski [31]. In the game, each process has an infinite supply of calling cards whose face values are the process identification (*process id*) and the process's *priority*. In a given round of play, a process will give one of its cards to each of the involved resource managers — that is, to those resource managers that serve the resources required in the process's critical section. Each resource manager maintains a list of the cards that it accepts, ordered by priority. A resource manager will either accept or reject a process's card according to the following simple rule: If the card just received by a resource manager has a priority higher than that of any other card that is already in that resource manager's list of cards, then the resource managers will accept the card from the process and place it at the end of the aforementioned list. If there is already a card in a resource manager's list that has a greater priority, then the resource manager will reject the card. A process that has any one of its cards rejected by a resource manager is a "loser." Losers must inform all of the other resource managers that have accepted a card to remove that card from their lists. Thus, a loser is a loser everywhere and must inform all resource managers that have accepted its card that it has become a loser. The cards of losers are removed from all lists. A "winner" is a process whose card is accepted by all of the required resource managers and is at the front of the list of each required resource manager.

Processes execute the following procedure:

- Step 1. Distribute cards (send "take card" messages) to all required resources (resource managers).
- Step 2. Wait for each resource manager to respond with the status of the card.
    Step 2.1. If any card becomes a loser ("you lose" message is received), GOTO 3.
    Step 2.2. If all cards become winners ("you win" message is received), GOTO 5.
- Step 3. Send all other resources an "I lose" message. The loser's cards will be removed from all lists.
- Step 4. GOTO 1. (Try again.)

Figure 3. Distributed-resource-scheduling game. (P = processor and R = resource.)

- Step 5. Inform all resource managers that a final winner has been found (claim resource).
- Step 6. Enter critical section.
- Step 7. Release all resources (inform resource managers that the resource is free again).

Note: For Step 2, the scheduling algorithm guarantees that all cards distributed will become losers or winners in finite time.

Resource managers obey the following protocol rules:

- Rule 1. Reject all cards (send a "you lose" message) when there is a card of higher priority already enqueued in the list or when the requested resource is not free. Place accepted cards at the rear of the list.
- Rule 2. Upon receipt of an "I lose" message, remove the sender's card from the list.
- Rule 3. Send a "you win" message to the owner of the first card placed in the list or to the owner of any card that is promoted to the front of the list when the card in front of it is removed.
- Rule 4. Upon receipt of an "I win" message, send "you lose" messages to the owners of all other cards in the list, empty the list, and mark the resource as "not free."
- Rule 5. Upon receipt of a "release" message, mark the resource as "free."

Figure 3 illustrates an example in which four processes P_1, P_2, P_3, and P_4 will compete for three shared resources R_1, R_2 and R_3, which might represent three file fragments (as in the example at the beginning of this subsection). The four process priorities are such that $P_1 > P_2 > P_3 > P_4$. As in the earlier example, process P_1 will require all three resources for its critical section. P_2 will need resources R_1 and R_2. P_3 will need resources R_2 and R_3. P_4 will need resource R_3. Assume that all four processes attempt to access the shared resources and begin their first round of play at very nearly the same time. Assume further that at R_1, P_2's message has arrived first; at R_2, P_3's message has arrived first; and at R_3, P_1's message has arrived first. P_4's message arrives at R_3 after P_1's, but P_4's card is rejected by R_3 (that is, P_4 becomes a loser), because P_1's higher priority card is already in the list at R_3. Therefore, P_4 will cycle through the first four steps of the scheduling procedure while P_1's card is in the list at R_3. Next in this example round of play, R_2 accepts P_2's card and places it behind P_3's while R_1 accepts P_1's card and places it behind P_2's. However, P_3's card is rejected by R_3 (that is, P_3 — like P_4 — becomes a loser), because P_1's higher priority card is already in R_3's list. P_3 must inform R_2 that it has become a loser so that R_2 can remove P_3's card from its list (see Step 3). When R_2 receives P_3's "I lose" message, P_3's card will be removed from R_2's list, promoting P_2 to a local winner at R_2. Having already received a "you win" message from R_1, P_2 becomes a game winner when it receives a "you win" message from R_2. P_2 is now a winner everywhere and sends an "I win" message to all of the involved resource managers — that is, to R_1 and R_2. R_1 and R_2 must now send "you lose" messages to P_1 (see Rule 4). Though a winner at R_3, P_1 has become a loser somewhere and so has become a loser everywhere. P_1 must therefore send an "I lose" message to R_3 so that its card can be removed from the list at R_3. Processes P_1, P_3, and P_4 have all become losers somewhere and so may try again. However, as long as P_2 remains in its critical section, resources R_1 and R_2 will not be free; therefore, only P_4 can become a winner everywhere. Shortly after P_2 has entered its critical section, P4 *will* become a winner and will thus enter its critical section. The scheduling protocol attempts to keep every resource as busy as it can, thus maximizing concurrency and, in this example, allowing for concurrent update of the same file.

In a practical situation, when a resource R becomes busy, it informs its other current client processes (losing processes) that they should remove themselves from the scheduling game; that is, they should remove all cards placed at other resources and wait. Later, when R is freed, it will inform these waiting client processes that they have been enqueued at R and should begin playing the game for their remaining resources. This eliminates unnecessary messaging generated by processes that cannot win. Though the protocol's worst-case messaging can be somewhat large, it *is* bounded. Moreover, though the protocol may take a while to complete, a winner is generally found quickly, thus allowing for a high degree of resource utilization.

Since all of the communicating subprocedures are either active or in message-wait (message-driven procedures), a time-out mechanism can be used to detect all lost messages. The overhead of lost messages involves only the detection time and the retransmission time. The scheduling algorithm itself, though requiring that all messages eventually be received, would never proceed incorrectly as a result of a lost message.

The complete Dragon Slayer resource-scheduling protocol includes a mechanism that makes the resource scheduler starvation-free. As each process wins access to a resource, a record is generated for each losing process that associates that losing process with the winner. Also, each time a process wins, all *locking records* that indicate it as a loser are destroyed. Finally, there is a simple rule that a process that is indicated as a winner for a locking record at a given resource R is not allowed to enter the game again for R. In this way, after competitors of some process P have won the game, they are not allowed to return to the game until P has won the game. Locking records can be implemented easily by a pair of local time stamps indicating when a current client entered the game and when a now-departed client won. If any current client has entered the game before a given winner has won the game, then that winning process cannot play the scheduling game for that resource. Winner time stamps that are older than the oldest existing game entry time stamp may be discarded. Game entry time stamps are discarded as the process becomes a winner. (Wedde and Daniels [28] gave more information on distributed resource scheduling in Dragon Slayer.)

Issues in fragmented-file management

Files are conceived to be encapsulated in objects. Therefore, a file will be represented by a *name* and a set of *attributes*. The *abstract data type* for a file is defined as a set of related data records with the operations *read* and *write*. The *type=file* attribute specification indicates that the *file server* must be called upon to perform operations on this object. Each file server is capable of performing the *read* and *write* operations on real files located at its computer. To use a file, a user process makes a request for the name of the file and specifies whether it is needed for read or write access. A system process sends a broadcast message to all resource managers asking if a copy of the file resides at their computer. The resource managers check their lists of resident objects for the name. If a resource manager finds the object, it will check the attribute list of the object to see if the requesting process has authorization for the object in the manner requested. If so, the resource manager responds in the affirmative. The process cannot request allocation of the file until it has gained access to all other resources it needs during the same critical section. However, once the process can successfully request the file, it sends to the file server at the computer where the file resides a message to send a copy of the file to the requesting computer or to some other computer specified by the requesting computer. The local file server formats the file for transmission in a message and sends the message, along with the file's attribute list, to the specified computer's file server. This file server creates a temporary file with the attributes of the requested file and writes the data into it. The user process can access this temporary file in the local manner through its local file server. When the process releases the file, if it has been updated, the process's local file server transmits the temporary copy back to the original file server. The new version of the file is now available for other processes.

In Dragon Slayer, files may consist of more than one fragment. Fragmented (replicated and fragmented) files can be created and manipulated as one entity from any computer in the system. Figure 4 shows the representation of a replicated file with three copies. We can assume that the three computers (Computers A, B, and C) run different operating systems under Dragon Slayer. Suppose that these three computers have the following file-naming conventions: for Computer A, all file names must begin with a slash character "/"; for Computer B, all file names must consist of nine characters, with a "/" in the fifth position; and for Computer C, all file names must end with a "/." A request from some other computer, Computer D, to locate file "X" will be answered by all three resource managers RMA, RMB, and RMC. The abstract file "X" is mapped to three real files — /filename, file/name, and filename/—to create a replicated file, even though the three computers have incompatible file-naming conventions.

The benefits of replicated files, such as increased reliability and availability, and the various methods for accessing and maintaining consistency are well documented in the literature [2], [5], [16], [22]. Based on statistical comparisons [13], the available-copies method seems best suited for the Dragon Slayer environment. This method includes a technique for recovery when all replicas are lost due to computer crashes; this technique uses a read-any, write-all scheme for replicated files. As long as one copy remains, reads and writes are allowed. If a computer crashes, this technique is responsible for updating the computer's replicated files upon its return from the crash. This is accomplished by the use of a *version* attribute and a *current* attribute. The *version* attribute is a scalar value that indicates the chronology of updates to a file, while the *current* attribute indicates whether or not the object is known to be up-to-date. Whenever a copy is successfully updated, the *version* attribute is incremented. The *current* attribute is also checked upon a successful update. If it was marked "false," it is changed to "true." When the *current* attribute of a file is "false," the file's server will not respond to inquiries

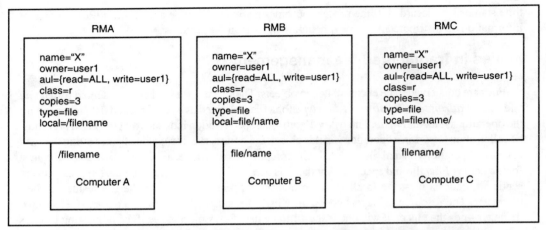

Figure 4. Replicated file "X" is contained in the resource list at each of three computers. (RM = resource manager.)

or requests for the file from any client process, except another of its replica servers. When a computer returns from a crash, the resource manager marks as "false" the *current* attributes of all of its replicas of files. It then tries to find a current copy of each replica to update, or validate, its copy of that file. If it finds a current copy, it compares the *version* attribute of its copy with the *version* attribute of the current copy. If the versions are equal, there is no need to update its copy. The *current* attribute is marked as "true." If the versions are not equal, the resource manager must replace its copy with the current copy, change the *version* attribute in its copy to that of the current copy, and then mark as "true" its copy's *current* attribute.

In the case in which all copies of a replicated file are unavailable during the same time interval because of computer crashes, the file cannot be accessed until all sites with resident copies have returned to the system. As a site returns, the resident resource manager checks to see if it can find all of the other replicas. If not, the resource manager is not on the last computer to recover, and the latest version of the file cannot be determined. If the resource manager can find all of the other copies, this means that all sites with resident replicas are active. With all versions known, the latest version of the file can be determined and distributed to each involved site. There is no race condition among returning sites, as only the count of returned sites is needed to determine when full recovery may take place.

Figure 5 shows the representation of a fragmented file with three parts. All three resource managers will respond to a request to locate file "X." However, this time the three real files have been mapped to the abstract file as three parts in a specified order. A process can determine from the attribute lists that three parts are needed to construct this file and which part is which. Note that with a fragmented file, the individual parts can be represented and accessed separately. They may even belong to many different files.

Since any named file must be accessed as a whole file, there is no problem of consistency, as such, with fragmented files. However, one or more parts of the fragmented file may be replicated, and replicated-file strategies are necessary for these parts. Information about file usage is easily collected by the resource managers and file servers at each computer in the system. The best locations and configurations for files can be determined easily from this information. The transparency of both the location and the implementation of the file abstraction makes it easy to move and reconfigure the abstractions and the real files for more efficient and reliable access.

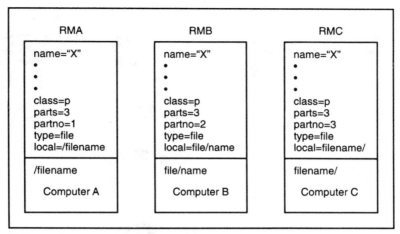

Figure 5. Parts of partitioned file "X" stored on three computers. (RM = resource manager.)

Distributed-file operations

The Dragon Slayer distributed-file system supports the following file operations:

(1) Basic operations. The basic file operations necessary to manipulate the file system are the *create*, *erase*, *open*, *close*, *read*, and *write* operations. The *create* operation creates a shared file. The *erase* operation erases a shared file or a private file. The *open* operation opens a file or a fragment of a file for the purpose of read or write. A list of files can be specified for the purpose of opening. The Dragon Slayer distributed-file system checks for the existence of all the files in the distributed network and opens all the files, avoiding any deadlock that may occur (the underlying kernel of the Dragon Slayer distributed-file system supports deadlock avoidance). If a file or a fragment is checked out for write, then it is locked, and other users cannot access the same file or its fragments for writing. Files accessed can be either private or shared. Shared files may be fragmented or nonfragmented. The *close* operation closes an already-open file(s). As mentioned earlier, both the *open* operation and the *close* operation can be used to operate on one or more files. The *read* and *write* operations provide features for manipulating the contents of a file. The *read* operation reads a character from a file, while the *write* operation writes a character to a file.

(2) Fragmentation operations. Files in the Dragon Slayer distributed-file system can be either maintained as a single physical unit or split into fragments. File fragments can be physically scattered throughout the computer network, but they are treated as one logical object by the users. Fragmentation operations are performed on shared files. The fundamental fragmentation operations are the *fragment* operation, which partitions a file into several fragments, and the *combine* operation, which combines a fragmented file into one physical file.

(3) Replication operations. Since the shared space is spread over more than one computer, being able to perform replication operations is essential. Replication operations can be achieved by the *replication*, *duplication*, and *copy* operations. The *replication* operation increases the number of copies of a shared file; this shared file may be fragmented or nonfragmented. The *duplication* operation makes a private copy of a shared file in the private workspace of the user. The *copy* operation makes a copy of a shared file or a private file in either the shared or private workspace.

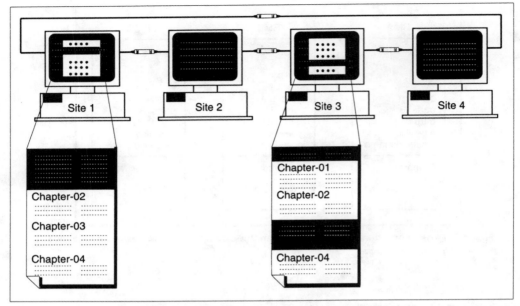

Figure 6: A distributed-group-editing environment.

The *replication*, *duplication*, and *copy* operations are used extensively in the Dragon Slayer distributed-file system. When a particular file or fragment is accessed by a user and is later committed to the shared file space, the file system takes care of automatically updating all the replicas of the file or fragments.

(4) Access rights operations. The *authorize* and *deauthorize* operations can provide the feature that different users have authorities on different shared files. These operations give access rights to users on shared files or fragments of a shared file. Users can have read or write access on a particular file or a fragment of a particular file.

Distributed group editing

In *group editing*, several users edit the same text — for example, a report or a joint article. A *distributed editor* is an editing environment that supports group editing in the distributed environment. A *distributed-editing environment* consists of a LAN of computers wherein editing is done on these interlinked computers — for example, a LAN of PCs. Distributed environments are changing the way in which text editing is done. Users can be working on one computer site, while the text files (or their fragments) can be on another site.

The distributed-editing environment that we have developed is designed to provide support for text editing in a distributed environment. Its major feature is that it allows for concurrent access to the same text file by several different users under the assumption that different users work on different parts of the text. Consider a group of authors who have set out to write a report. They first create an initial version of a text file (the report). After each author has been assigned a chapter, the file can be fragmented into chapters using the *fragment* command. Each author can work on his chapter (that is, the fragment) using the distributed editor. A lock is put on the edited file (or its fragment) so that no one else can access that file (or fragment) at the same time. This allows several authors to update different fragments of the same file, resulting in concurrent file access. The text file (or its fragment) can be accessed any time by any author for reading. As an example, Figure 6 shows a small network — with four workstations — where the author of chapter 01 is working on his fragment (that is, chapter 01) at site 1 and the author of chapter 03 is working on his fragment at site 3.

Managing text editing in a distributed environment creates several new problems that do not exist in *centralized* environments. For example, in the distributed environment, text files (or their fragments) are located on different computer sites; therefore, one of the main problems is the localization of these files in the network. This problem exists, for instance, when users request files that are not located on their computer sites. In this case, they must determine where those files are located (a time-consuming and tedious process), remotely log in to these computer sites, check out the fragments to be modified, and copy them to their computer sites in order to modify them. Similar sequences of operations are necessary to check in the updated fragments. A group of collaborating users can aggravate this problem even more.

The distributed-editing environment has been implemented on our Token Ring of IBM RT PCs and IBM 9370s. It has been developed on the top of the Dragon Slayer distributed-file system. Distributed editing supports editing of fragments in a location-transparent manner; that is, users may not know the physical location of fragments. By replicating fragments on different computer sites, it provides increased reliability and availability. Because the backup and the update of replicated files are automatic, the distributed-editing environment aides in maintaining consistency among the replicas, without users needing to worry about it.

Naming

The *naming* facility is the means by which files are bound by a high-level name and by which a particular file is located. This facility is the key component in any distributed-file system [7], [9], [23]. The file name space in the Dragon Slayer file system is partitioned into a local name space and a shared name space. The local name space is unique, being associated with each user, and is hierarchically structured. The shared name space is location-transparent and is distributed across the network. The shared name space is currently flat, but we have been extending the naming facility in order to support the hierarchical name structure in the shared name space.

Performance studies

In general, it is clear that fragmented files — through the distribution of both fragments and their replicas — can be more reliably accessed than nonfragmented and nonreplicated files. However, the overhead for maintaining fragmented files is in question. In the section entitled "Fragmented files in heterogeneous environments," we give an example of a student-registration system with a dynamically fragmented student file. Even without fragment replication, a simple query — say for the students who have signed up so far for the operating system class CSC 442 (relevant for classroom rescheduling on the fly) — would be executed as a distributed *read* operation on the operating system level. In the case of competing *write* commands, the Dragon Slayer distributed-resource-scheduling algorithm for guaranteeing mutually exclusive access to all fragments would be invoked. (See the section entitled "Issues in fragmented-file management.")

In a broad range of applications, one finds that operations at a specific site tend to operate on a specific subset of the data in a file. If this data subset can be determined and placed in a specific fragment, the file-fragmentation structure can be organized such that the data most frequently referenced at a specific site can be located at that site. Thus, references to this specific fragment could be localized, eliminating the overheads associated with *remote-data-access* operations. In our student-registration example, 80 percent of all operations comprised local operations (that is, file accesses). *Local dominance* is our term for the expected dominance of local operations. (Thus, local dominance was 80 percent in the student-registration example.) These local operations have the benefit of accessing only comparably small files, while not holding locks across the network. If the overheads associated with the management of fragmented files are more than offset by the overheads associated with remote-file access, then fragmented files clearly offer a promising performance advantage.

The above considerations set the stage for a series of simulation experiments in which we compared system performance under a given set of operations: namely, with and without fragmentation of files. We did not replicate files or fragments. (The benefit of replication alone has been studied separately [16].) Our simulation model had the following features and assumptions:

- There are no site failures.
- There is no block-level access. (Access is to the whole file.)
- The access time is proportional to the file length.
- There is no loss of messages. (For example, we have the uniform bound on communication delays among processes.)
- The system is controlled under completely decentralized service, authority, control, and facilities (that is, under no centralized service, authority, control, or facilities.)
- There is no assumption on the organization of local processes or process schedules.
- Scheduling times plus waiting times are added to process-execution times.

The primary purpose of our simulation experiments was the investigation of trade-offs in fragmented-file management. Basically, the principle overhead in fragmented-file management is associated with the more complex of the file-management operations. For example, the scheduling of mutually exclusive access to the file fragments involves greater communication between servers and clients. In the case of nonfragmented files, overheads derive mainly from the loss of concurrency among writers queuing for the single, nonfragmented copy (*blocking time*) and from the greater communication time required to transmit across the network entire files rather than individual fragments.

In terms of the scheduling overhead, two factors to be considered are the following:

(1)   Schedules are not static but are determined on the fly, as real, external events dictate; therefore, the *next* file access is scheduled after — not during — the execution of the previous file access (that is, there is no look-ahead). Thus, the amount of time required to schedule a file operation (by our model) must be added to the total access time of the file operation.

(2)   Though a winner of the scheduling game generally can be found early in a given round of scheduling play, considerable messaging can be generated by the losers even after the winner has been found. Because such messaging is generally after the fact of a start of a file operation, it does not contribute directly to the overhead of the operation scheduled; however, the available communication channel bandwidth is still reduced and all operations are proportionally slowed down.

For describing our simulation experiments, we use the following:

x = packet switch time
r = length of time interval (partition of simulation runtime)

q = total number of protocol messages per simulation time interval
t = best-case file-transmission time (computation time plus transmission time)
n = number of resources (fragments) per operation
f = file size (in kilobytes)
packet size = 512 bytes

The *competition time* (that is, the time required to find a new winner after a file or fragment has been released) was set at $3xn$ per file operation; this is a reasonable assumption of the time for the average case, based on experience with the resource scheduler discussed earlier (see the section entitled "The Dragon Slayer environment"). For all remote-file operations, a copy of the needed file or fragment was transmitted over the network, packet by packet, to the requesting site and, in the case of a *write* operation, was sent back to the originating site. Thus, the *file* (or *file fragment*) *transmission time* is given by $2fx$ and $4fx$ for *read* and *write* operations, respectively. Either a read lock or a write lock was maintained throughout the operation. The proportion of channel bandwidth dedicated to fragment management—that is, the ratio of scheduling protocol messaging to application messaging —is determined as follows: Because each protocol message is assumed to occupy a single packet, the percentage of available channel bandwidth dedicated to scheduling, in terms of the time division of the channel, is represented as qx/r. Thus, the *total scheduling overhead* is given as $3xn + (qx/r)$. The factor qx/r represents a degraded availability of the communication channel for application operations; therefore, it must be added to the ideal, best-case file-transmission time. The *adjusted file-transmission time* is represented by $t[1 + (qx/r)]$. Then, the *total file-operation time* is the competition time plus the computation time plus the adjusted file-transmission time for the operation in the fragmented case. (The *computation time* is the access time to the [locked] file fragment.)

We now give other assumptions and simulation parameters for our simulation model. We assumed that there were 10 nodes communicating with each other in the system, over a period of time that was subdivided into 10 periods. We further assumed that every node randomly generated files at the rate of between one and 20 per time period. The file length was randomly determined to be between 500 and 2000 records. Thus, each time period represents a changing system file set, and we simulated the effect of the *create* and *delete* operations on files in the course of each run by assuming that such operations executed "synchronously" every 20 seconds. At each site, any operation worked either on the whole file or on only one fragment. In order to compare the fragmented and nonfragmented cases, partitioning into two to four fragments was randomly chosen for each file such that the first fragment was located at the site where the file had been generated. Fragments were not relocated. We randomly generated a pattern of *read* and *write* operations for each site. The probability that an operation was a *read* was equal to the probability that it was a *write*. In the fragmented case, if the processes wanted to access the same fragments of a file, they would compete for these fragments according to the resource-scheduling algorithm outlined in the section entitled "The Dragon Slayer environment." This algorithm is based on message passing. If a reader won the competition, then all other readers were allowed to proceed concurrently. If a writer won, then all other operations were blocked until the writer released. The scheduling algorithm did not take into account any further difference between readers and writers.

In Figure 7, the upper curve represents the total blocking time as sampled across the different intervals of simulation time. The lower curve depicts the scheduling overhead as computed by $3xn + (qx/r)$. Taken together, the two curves indicate the relationship between blocking time and scheduling overhead, both of which are largely dependent on the level of competition among operations at any given time in the simulation.

Figure 8 depicts the effects of changing local dominance on the total operational access times. Each operation worked on one or all of a file's fragments. Only users at sites that were chosen to hold

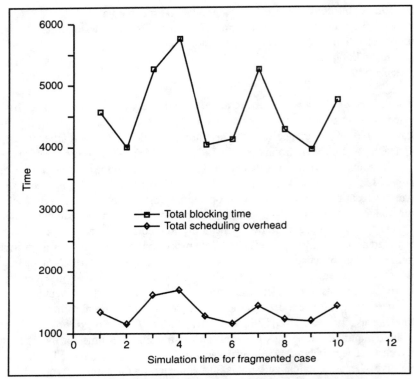

Figure 7: Blocking time and scheduling overhead.

a file fragment were assumed to access the corresponding file. Every point in the curve representing the fragmented case stands for the total access time during a complete simulation run, which was set up such that a prespecified local dominance of operations was observed. For each of the runs, the same set of user processes executed the same set of operations on the same files and fragment structures. For comparison purposes, runs using only the nonfragmented versions of the files were conducted correspondingly; however, a single copy of the file resided at a site that held a fragment of that file in other runs. Access times were constant in the nonfragmented case, because the percentage of local dominance of operations did not change between runs. That is, all that determines whether an access is local or remote is the site of origin of the operation. Since the nonfragmented file resided at one of the nodes that held a fragment of that file in the fragmented case and since the set of operations and files did not change between cases, the locality of operations could not change between runs. The nonfragmented approach outperformed the fragmented approach only when the percentage of local operations (that is, the local dominance) fell below 30 percent.

Figure 9 depicts the results of a second series of simulations, in which the number of fragments per file was varied between runs. The series comprised six sets of runs, with each set being characterized by a different local dominance. The file set was held constant along the runs on each curve. In the figure, the file access time is plotted against the number of fragments per file. Each point in each curve represents a simulation run. The different curves depict the performance of different transaction populations in which the local dominance varied between 50 and 85 percent. The results

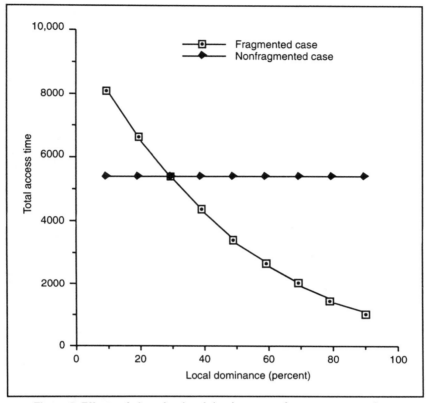

Figure 8. Effects of changing local dominance on fragment access times.

clearly indicate that the higher the degree of fragmentation and the higher the degree of local dominance, the better the performance. Only when the percentage of local accesses was low and the number of file fragments was small did the single-fragment case (that is, the nonfragmented case) perform better than the fragmented cases. This can be seen in the uppermost curve in the figure, where a maximum of only two fragments per file results in an even higher total access time than one fragment per file, because the overhead of managing operations on two fragments is not yet outweighed by the savings through local file access. In the case of 60-percent local dominance, the access times for one fragment per file and two fragments per file are approximately the same. Only when local dominance is at least 60 percent and there are at least three fragments per file as an upper bound is there a considerable advantage in fragmentation.

Discussion and future research

We designed and implemented a novel distributed-file system with fragmented files as part of our distributed operating system Dragon Slayer. Our system currently runs on a Token Ring of IBM RT PCs and IBM 9370s, a truly heterogeneous environment. Files are distributed objects, with replicated and dispersed fragments. Normally, operations work transparently on the files, but direct access to fragments is also provided. Fragmentation and replication structures can be arbitrarily reconfigured. While high reliability and high availability of information through distributed files are obvious

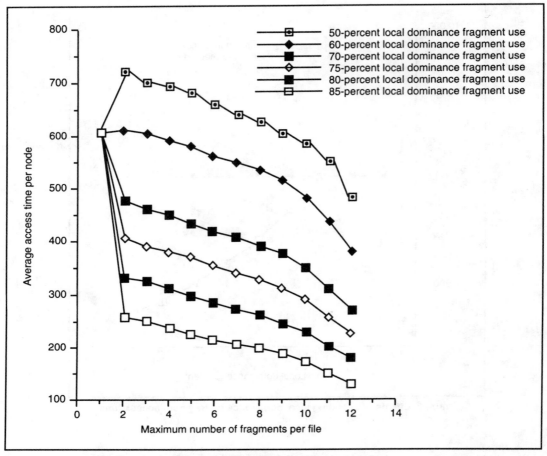

Figure 9. Different fragment structures.

features of our system, our simulation studies clearly showed that — even with a low dominance of local operations — a system incorporating the concept of distributed files exhibits a superior performance over that of nonfragmented-file systems. We are continuing our research with refined, more elaborate models of specific application areas of interest — for example, large administration systems, automatic transaction processing under completely decentralized control, and management of data structures in distributed banking systems.

In the scenario of a case study, we demonstrated how specific service needs for group cooperation could easily be met with the use of fragmented files and novel options for editing operations. We are currently exploring new options for several file operations that are to be used for fragmented files. As an example, for users in a MAN to be free to place copies of files or fragments wherever they like is very unlikely, because varying regulations of data security normally would be found in these upcoming widely heterogeneous networks. However, this means that — for example — a simple *copy* command will need to be given a large variety of different options that would correspond to the variety of authorization regulations for copying files or their fragments. In summary, the consideration of application scenarios like the ones mentioned in this paragraph will allow us to study further the novel application potential offered by fragmented files as used in the Dragon Slayer file system.

Acknowledgments

This work was partially supported by IBM Endicott under Research Agreement No. 9018-89 and by General Dynamics Land Systems under Grant No. DEY-605089.

References

[1] G.T. Almes et al., "The Eden System: A Technical Review," *IEEE Trans. Software Eng.*, Vol. SE-11, No. 1, Jan. 1985, pp. 43-58.

[2] P.A. Alsberg and J.D. Day, "A Principle for Resilient Sharing of Distributed Resources," *Proc. Second Int'l Conf. Software Eng.*, IEEE Computer Soc. Press, Los Alamitos, Calif., 1976, pp. 562-570.

[3] J.P. Banatre, M. Banatre, and G. Muller, "Main Aspects of the GOTHIC Distributed System," *Proc. EUTECO '88*, 1988.

[4] R.V. Baron et al., *MACH Kernel Interface Manual*, Carnegie Mellon Univ., Pittsburgh, Pa., Sept. 1988.

[5] P.A. Bernstein and N. Goodman, "An Algorithm for Concurrency Control and Recovery in Replicated Distributed Databases," *ACM Trans. Database Systems*, Vol. 9, No. 4, Dec. 1984, pp. 596-615.

[6] D.R. Cheriton, "The V Distributed System," *Comm. ACM*, Vol. 31, No. 3, Mar. 1988, pp. 314-333.

[7] D.R. Cheriton and T.P. Mann, "Decentralizing a Global Naming Service for Improved Performance and Fault Tolerance," *ACM Trans. Computer Systems*, Vol. 7, No. 2, May 1989, pp. 147-183.

[8] P. Dasgupta, R.J. LeBlanc, Jr., and W.F. Appelbe, "The Clouds Distributed Operating System: Functional Description, Implementation Details and Related Work," *Proc. Eighth Int'l Conf. Distributed Computing Systems*, IEEE Computer Soc. Press, Los Alamitos, Calif., 1988, pp. 2-9.

[9] X. Jia et al., "Highly Concurrent Directory Management in the GALAXY Distributed System," *Proc. 10th Int'l Conf. Distributed Computing Systems*, IEEE Computer Soc. Press, Los Alamitos, Calif., 1990, pp. 416-423.

[10] B. Liskov, "Distributed Programming in Argus," *Comm. ACM*, Vol. 31, No. 3, Mar. 1988, pp. 300-312.

[11] J.H. Morris et al., "Andrew: A Distributed Personal Computing Environment," *Comm. ACM*, Vol. 29, No. 3, Mar. 1986, pp. 184-201.

[12] S.J. Mullender et al., "Amoeba: A Distributed Operating System for the 1990s," *Computer*, Vol. 23, No. 5, May 1990, pp. 44-53.

[13] J.D. Noe and A. Andreassian, "Effectiveness of Replication in Distributed Computer Networks," *Proc. Seventh Int'l Conf. Distributed Computing Systems*, IEEE Computer Soc. Press, Los Alamitos, Calif., 1987, pp. 508-513.

[14] J.K. Ousterhout et al., "The Sprite Network Operating System," *Computer*, Vol. 21, No. 2, Feb., 1988, pp. 23-36.

[15] J.N. Pato, E. Martin, and B. Davis, "A User Account Registration System for a Large (Heterogeneous) UNIX Network," *Proc. Winter Usenix Conf.*, Usenix, Berkeley, Calif., 1988.

[16] C. Pu, J.D. Noe, and A. Proudfoot, "Regeneration of Replicated Objects: A Technique and Its Eden Implementation," *IEEE Trans. Software Eng.*, Vol. 14, No. 7, July 1988, pp. 936-945.

[17] R. Rashid et al., "Machine-Independent Virtual Memory Management for Paged Uniprocessor and Multiprocessor Architectures," *Proc. ACM Conf. Architectural Support Programming Languages and Operating Systems*, ACM Press, New York, N.Y., 1987.

[18] M. Satyanarayanan, "A Survey of Distributed File Systems," *Ann. Rev. Computer Science*, 1990, pp. 73-104.

[19] M. Satyanarayanan et al., "The ITC Distributed File System: Principles and Design," *Proc. 10th ACM Symp. Operating System Principles*, ACM Press, New York, N.Y., 1985.

[20] C. Scheurich and M. Dubois, "Dynamic Page Migration in Multiprocessors with Distributed Global

Memory," *Proc. Eighth Int'l Conf. Distributed Computing Systems*, IEEE Computer Soc. Press, Los Alamitos, Calif., 1988, pp. 162-169.

[21] M. Theimer, L.-F. Cabrera, and J. Wyllie, "QuickSilver Support for Access to Data in Large, Geographically Dispersed Systems," *Proc. Ninth Int'l Conf. Distributed Computing Systems*, IEEE Computer Soc. Press, Los Alamitos, Calif., 1989, pp. 28-35.

[22] R.H. Thomas, "A Majority Consensus Approach to Concurrency Control," *ACM Trans. Database Systems*, Vol. 4, No. 2, June 1979, pp. 180-209.

[23] P. Triantafillou and M. Bauer, *Distributed Name Management in Internet Systems: A Study of Design and Performance Issues*, Academic Press, Inc., New York, N.Y., 1990, pp. 357-368.

[24] R. van Renesse, A.S. Tanenbaum, and A. Wilschut, "The Design of a High Performance File Server," *Proc. Ninth Int'l Conf. Distributed Computing Systems*, IEEE Computer Soc. Press, Los Alamitos, Calif., 1989, pp. 22-27.

[25] D. Walsh et al., "Overview of the Sun Network File System," *Proc. Winter Usenix Conf.*, Usenix, Berkeley, Calif., 1985.

[26] H.F. Wedde, "An Iterative and Starvation-Free Solution for a General Class of Distributed Control Problems Based on Interaction Primitives," *Theoretical Computer Science*, Vol. 24, 1983, pp. 1-19.

[27] H.F. Wedde, "A Graph-Theoretic Model for Designing Fair Distributed Scheduling Algorithms," in *Springer Lecture Notes in Computer Science*, No. 314, G. Tinhofer and G. Schmidt, eds., Springer-Verlag, 1986, pp. 186-205.

[28] H.F. Wedde and D.C. Daniels, "Formal Specification and Analysis for Reliable and Transparent Resource Management," *Proc. Eighth Ann. Int'l Phoenix Conf. Computers and Comm.*, IEEE Computer Soc. Press, Los Alamitos, Calif., 1989, pp. 277-283.

[29] H.F. Wedde et al., "Transparent Distributed Object Management under Completely Decentralized Control," *Proc. Ninth Int'l Conf. Distributed Computing Systems*, IEEE Computer Soc. Press, Los Alamitos, Calif., 1989, pp. 335-342.

[30] H.F. Wedde et al., "MELODY: A Completely Decentralized Adaptive File System for Handling Real-Time Tasks in Unpredictable Environments," *Real-Time Systems*, Vol. 2, No. 4, Dec. 1990, pp. 347-364.

[31] J. Winkowski, "Protocols of Accessing Overlapping Sets of Resources," *Information Processing Letters*, Vol. 12, No. 55, 1981, pp. 239-243.

Distributed Databases

Distributed Data Management:
Unsolved Problems and
New Issues

M. Tamer Özsu and

Patrick Valduriez

Distributed database technology is one of the more important developments of the past decade. During this period, distributed database research issues have been topics of intense study, culminating in the release of a number of "first-generation" commercial products. Distributed database technology is expected to impact data processing the same way that centralized systems did a decade ago. It has been claimed that within the next 10 years, centralized database managers will be an "antique curiosity" and most organizations will move toward distributed database managers [STON88, page 189]. The technology is now at the critical stage of finding its way into commercial products. At this juncture, it is important to seek answers to the following questions:

(1)   What were the initial promises and goals of the distributed database technology? How do the current commercial products measure up to these promises? In retrospect, were these goals achievable?

(2)   Have the important technical problems already been solved?

(3)   What are the technological changes that underlie distributed data managers, and how will they impact next-generation systems?

The last two questions hold particular importance for researchers, since their answers lay down the road map for research in the upcoming years. Recent papers that addressed these questions emphasized scaling problems [STON89] and issues related to the introduction of heterogeneity and autonomy [GARC90a]. While these problems are important ones to address, there are many others that remain unsolved. Even much-studied topics like distributed query processing and transaction management have research problems that have yet to be addressed adequately. Furthermore, new issues arise with the changing technology, expanding application areas, and the experience that has been gained with the limited application of the distributed database technology. The most important new topics that can be identified for future research are distributed object-oriented database systems and distributed knowledge base systems. Additionally, database machines (which were hot research topics in the 1970s, but lost some of their lustre in the 1980s [BORA83]) are likely to reemerge as multiprocessor-based parallel data servers on distributed systems [DEWI90a]. Finally, distributed heterogeneous database systems are now being revisited as their autonomy considerations are being recognized as more important than their heterogeneity. This changing recognition has resulted in an emphasis on multidatabase systems as a platform for the development of interoperable information systems.

Our purposes here are to address the above questions and to provide answers rather than a tutorial introduction to distributed database technology or a survey of the capabilities of existing products. We introduce each topic very briefly to establish terminology and then proceed to discuss the issues raised in the above questions. For more detailed presentation of the technology, we direct the user to the various textbooks on the subject.

What is a distributed database system?

A *distributed database* (DDB) is a collection of multiple, logically interrelated databases distributed over a computer network [OZSU91]. A *distributed database management system* (distributed DBMS) is then defined as the software system that permits the management of the DDB and makes the distribution transparent to the users. We use the term *distributed database system* (DDBS) to refer to the combination of the DDB and the distributed DBMS. Assumptions regarding the system that underlie these definitions are given below.

(1)   Data are stored at a number of sites. Each site is assumed to *logically* consist of a single processor. Even if some sites are multiprocessor machines, the distributed DBMS is not concerned with the storage and management of data on this parallel machine.

(2)   The processors at these sites are interconnected by a computer network rather than a multiprocessor configuration. The important point here is the emphasis on loose-interconnection between processors that have their own operating systems and operate independently. Even though shared-nothing multiprocessor architectures are quite similar to the loosely interconnected distributed systems, they have different issues to deal with (for example, load balancing and task allocation and migration) that are not considered in this paper.

(3)   The DDB is a database, not some "collection" of files that can be individually stored at each node of a computer network. This is the distinction between a DDB and a collection of files managed by a distributed file system. To form a DDB, distributed data should be logically related (where the relationship is defined according to some structural formalism) and access to data should be at a high level (via a common interface). The typical formalism that is used for establishing the logical relationship is the relational model. In fact, most existing distributed database system research assumes a relational system.

(4)   The system has the full functionality of a DBMS. As indicated above, it is not a distributed file system, nor is it a transaction-processing system [BERN90]. Transaction processing is not only one type of distributed application, but it is also among the functions provided by a distributed DBMS. However, a distributed DBMS provides other functions (such as query processing and structured organization of data) with which transaction-processing systems do not necessarily deal.

These assumptions are valid in today's technology base. Most of the existing distributed systems are built on top of local area networks in which a site consists of a single computer. The database is distributed across these sites so that each site typically manages a single local database (Figure 1).

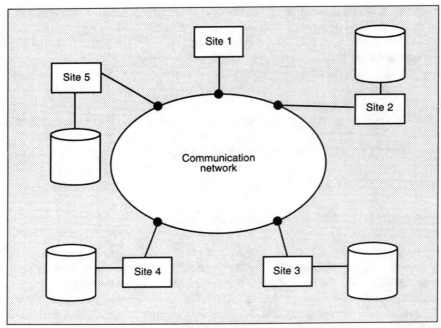

Figure 1. A distributed database environment.

This is the type of system that we concentrate on in this paper. However, next-generation distributed DBMSs will be designed differently as a result of technological developments (especially the emergence of affordable multiprocessors and high-speed networks), the increasing use of database technology in application domains (which are more complex than business data processing), and the wider adoption of the client-server mode of computing accompanied by standard interfaces between clients and servers. Thus, the next-generation distributed DBMS environment will include multiprocessor database servers connected to high-speed networks that link them and other data repositories to client machines that run application code and participate in the execution of database requests [TAYL87]. Distributed relational DBMSs of this type are already appearing and a number of the existing object-oriented systems [KIM89], [ZDON90] also fit this description.

A distributed DBMS as defined above is only one way of providing database management support for a distributed computing environment. In [OZSU91], we presented a working classification of possible design alternatives along three dimensions: autonomy, distribution, and heterogeneity.

(1) *Autonomy* refers to the distribution of control and indicates the degree to which individual DBMSs can operate independently. It involves a number of factors, such as if the component systems exchange information,[1] if they can independently execute transactions, and if one is allowed to modify them. Three types of autonomy are *tight integration*, *semiautonomy*, and *full autonomy* (or *total isolation*). In tightly integrated systems, a single image of the entire database is available to users who want to share the information that may reside in multiple databases.

---

[1]In this context, "exchanging information" does not refer to networking concerns but rather to if the DBMSs are designed to exchange information and coordinate their actions in executing user requests.

Semiautonomous systems consist of DBMSs that can (and usually do) operate independently but have decided to participate in a federation to make their local data shareable. In totally isolated systems, the individual components are stand-alone DBMSs that know neither of the existence of other DBMSs nor how to communicate with them.

(2)   The *distribution* dimension of the taxonomy deals with data. We consider two cases: Either data are physically distributed over multiple sites that communicate with each other over some form of communication medium or they are stored at only one site.

(3)   *Heterogeneity* can occur in various forms in distributed systems, ranging from hardware heterogeneity and differences in networking protocols to variations in data managers. The important ones from the perspective of database systems relate to data models, query languages, interfaces, and transaction management protocols. The taxonomy classifies DBMSs as *homogeneous* or *heterogeneous*.

The alternative system architectures based on this taxonomy are illustrated in Figure 2. The arrows along the axes do not indicate an infinite number of choices but rather simply the dimensions of the taxonomy that we discuss above.

The current state of distributed database technology

As with any emerging technology, DDBSs have their share of fulfilled and unfulfilled promises. In this section, we consider the commonly cited advantages of distributed DBMSs and discuss how well the existing commercial products provide these advantages.

Transparent management of distributed and replicated data

Centralized database systems have taken us from a paradigm of data processing in which data definition and maintenance were embedded in each application to one in which these functions are abstracted out of the applications and placed under the control of a server called the DBMS. This new orientation results in *data independence*, whereby the application programs are immune to changes in the logical or physical organization of the data and vice versa. The distributed database technology intends to extend the concept of data independence to environments where data are distributed and replicated over a number of machines connected by a network. This is provided by several forms of *transparency*: *network* (and, therefore, *distribution*) transparency, *replication* transparency, and *fragmentation* transparency. Transparent access to data separates the higher level semantics of a system from lower level implementation issues. Thus, the database users would see a logically integrated, single-image database (even though it may be physically distributed), enabling them to access the distributed database as if it were a centralized one. In its ideal form, full transparency would imply a query language interface to the distributed DBMS that is no different from that of a centralized DBMS.

Most commercial distributed DBMSs do not provide a sufficient level of transparency. Part of this is due to the lack of support for the management of replicated data. A number of systems do not permit replication of the data across multiple databases, while those that do require that the user be physically "logged on" to one database at a given time. Some distributed DBMSs attempt to establish their own transparent naming scheme, usually with unsatisfactory results, requiring the users either to specify the full path to data or to build aliases to avoid long pathnames. An important aspect of the problem is the lack of proper operating system support for transparency. Network transparency can easily be supported by means of a transparent naming mechanism that can be implemented by the operating system. The operating system can also assist with replication transparency, leaving the task of fragmentation transparency to the distributed DBMS.

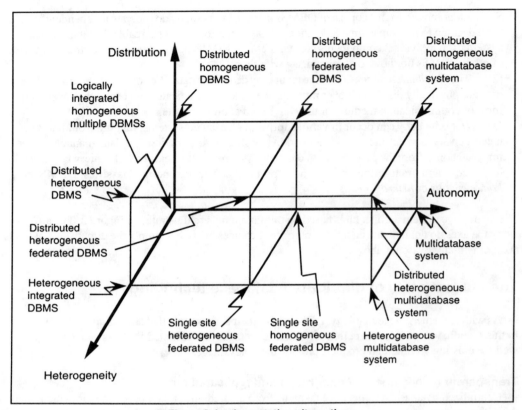

Figure 2. Implementation alternatives.

Full transparency is not a universally accepted objective, however. Gray [GRAY89] argues that full transparency makes the management of distributed data very difficult and claims that "applications coded with transparent access to geographically distributed databases have: poor manageability, poor modularity, and poor message performance." He proposes a remote procedure call mechanism between the requester users and the server DBMSs whereby the users would direct their queries to a specific DBMS. We agree that the management of distributed data is more difficult if transparent access is provided to users and that the client-server architecture with a remote-procedure-call-based communication between the clients and the servers is the right architectural approach. In fact, some commercial distributed DBMSs are organized in this fashion (for example, Sybase). However, the original goal of distributed DBMSs to provide transparent access to distributed and replicated data should not be given up because of these difficulties. The issue is who should be taking over the responsibility of managing distributed and replicated data: the distributed DBMS, or the user application? In our opinion, it should be the distributed DBMS whose components may be organized in a client-server fashion. The related technical issues are among the remaining research and development issues that need to be addressed.

Reliability through distributed transactions

Distributed DBMSs are intended to improve reliability, since they have replicated components and thereby eliminate single points of failure. The failure of a single site, or the failure of a communication link that makes one or more sites unreachable, is not sufficient to bring down the entire system.[2] In the case of a distributed database, this means that some of the data may be unreachable, but with proper care, users may be permitted to access other parts of the distributed database. The "proper care" comes in the form of support for *distributed transactions*.

A *transaction* is a basic unit of consistent and reliable computing, consisting of a sequence of database operations executed as an atomic action. It transforms a consistent database state, to another consistent database state, even when a number of such transactions are executed concurrently (sometimes called *concurrency transparency*) and even when failures occur (also called *failure atomicity*). Therefore, a DBMS that provides full transaction support guarantees that concurrent execution of user transactions will not violate database consistency in the face of system failures, as long as each transaction is correct and obeys the integrity rules specified on the database.

Distributed transactions execute at a number of sites at which they access the local database. With full support for distributed transactions, user applications can access a single logical image of the database and rely on the distributed DBMS to ensure that their requests will be executed correctly no matter what happens in the system. "Correctly" means that user applications do not need to be concerned with coordinating their accesses to individual local databases, nor do they need to worry about the possibility of site or communication link failures during the execution of their transactions. This illustrates the link between distributed transactions and transparency, since both involve issues related to distributed naming and directory management, among other things.

Providing transaction support requires the implementation of distributed concurrency control and distributed reliability protocols, which are significantly more complicated than their centralized counterparts. The typical distributed concurrency control algorithm is some variation of the well-known two-phase locking (2PL) algorithm, depending on the placement of the lock tables and the assignment of the lock management responsibilities. Distributed reliability protocols consist of distributed commit protocols and recovery procedures. Commit protocols enforce atomicity of distributed transactions by ensuring that a given transaction has the same effect (commit or abort) at each site where it exists, whereas the recovery protocols specify how the global database consistency is to be restored following failures. In the distributed environment, the commit protocols are two-phase (2PC protocols). In the first phase, an agreement is established among the various sites regarding the fate of a transaction. The agreed-upon action is taken in the second phase.

Data replication increases database availability, since copies of the data stored at a failed or unreachable site (due to link failure) exist at other operational sites. However, supporting replicas require the implementation of *replica control protocols* that enforce a specified semantics of accessing them. The most straightforward semantics is *one-copy equivalence,* which can be enforced by the ROWA protocol ("read-one write-all"). In ROWA, a logical read operation on a replicated data item is converted to one physical read operation on any one of its copies, but a logical write operation is translated to physical writes on all of the copies. More complicated replica control protocols that are less restrictive and that are based on deferring the writes on some copies have been studied but are not implemented in any of the systems that we know.

Concurrency control and commit protocols are among the two most researched topics in distributed databases. Yet, their implementation in existing commercial systems is not widespread. The performance implications of implementing distributed transactions (which are not fully understood) makes them unpopular among vendors. Commercial systems provide varying degrees of distributed transaction support. Some (for example, Oracle) require users to have one database open at a given time, thereby eliminating the need for distributed transactions while others (for example, Sybase) implement the basic primitives that are necessary for the 2PC protocol, but require

---

[2]We do not wish to discuss the differences between site failures and link failures at this point. It is well known that link failures may cause network partitioning and are, therefore, more difficult to deal with.

the user applications to handle the coordination of the commit actions. In other words, the distributed DBMS does not enforce atomicity of distributed transactions but rather provides the basic primitives by which user applications can enforce it. There are other systems, however, that implement the 2PC protocols fully (for example, Ingres and NonStop SQL).

Improved performance

The case for the improved performance of distributed DBMSs is typically made based on two points:

(1)   A distributed DBMS fragments the conceptual database, enabling data to be stored in close proximity to its points of use (also called *data localization*). This has two potential advantages:

- Since each site handles only a portion of the database, contention for CPU and I/O services is not as severe as for centralized databases, and
- Localization reduces remote access delays that are usually involved in wide area networks (for example, the minimum round-trip message propagation delay in satellite-based systems is about one second).

Most distributed DBMSs are structured to gain maximum benefit from data localization. Full benefits of reduced contention and reduced communication overhead can be obtained only by a proper fragmentation and distribution of the database.

(2)   The inherent parallelism of distributed systems may be exploited for *interquery* and *intraquery parallelism*. Interquery parallelism results from the ability to execute multiple queries at the same time, while intraquery parallelism is achieved by breaking up a single query into a number of subqueries, each of which is executed at a different site, accessing a different part of the distributed database.

If the user access to the distributed database consisted only of querying (read-only access), then provision of interquery and intraquery parallelism would imply that as much of the database as possible should be replicated. However, since most database accesses are not read-only, the mixing of read and update operations requires the implementation of elaborate concurrency control and commit protocols.

Existing commercial systems employ two alternative execution models (other than the implementation of full distributed transaction support) in realizing improved performance. The first alternative is to have the database open only for queries (read-only access) during the regular operating hours while the updates are batched. The database is then closed to query activity during off-hours when the batched updates are run sequentially. This is time multiplexing between read activity and update activity. A second alternative is based on multiplexing the database. Accordingly, two copies of the database are maintained, one for *ad hoc* querying (called the *query database*) and the other for updates by application programs (called the *production database*). At regular intervals, the production database is copied to the query database. The latter alternative does not eliminate the need to implement concurrency control and reliability protocols for the production database, since these are necessary to synchronize the write operations on the same data; however, it improves the performance of the queries, since they can be executed without the overhead of transaction manipulation.

The performance characteristics of distributed database systems are not very well understood. There is not a sufficient number of true distributed database applications to provide a sound base to make practical judgments. In addition, the performance models of distributed database systems are not sufficiently developed. The database community has developed a number of benchmarks to test the performance of transaction-processing applications, but it is not clear if they can be used to measure the performance of distributed transaction management. The performances of the commercial DBMS products, even with respect to these benchmarks, are generally not openly published. NonStop SQL is one product for which performance figures, as well as the experimental setup that is used in obtaining them, have been published [TAND88].

Easier and more economical system expansion

In a distributed environment, it should be easier to accommodate increasing database sizes. Major system overhauls are seldom necessary; expansion can usually be handled by adding processing and storage power to the system. We call this *database size scaling*, as opposed to *network scaling*. It may not be possible to obtain a linear increase in "power," since this also depends on the overhead of distribution. However, significant improvements are still possible.

Microprocessor and workstation technologies have played a role in improving economies. The price/performance characteristics of these systems make it more economical to put together a system of smaller computers with the equivalent power of a single big machine. Many commercial distributed DBMSs operate on minicomputers and workstations to take advantage of their favorable price/performance characteristics. The current reliance on workstation technology exists because most of the commercial distributed DBMSs operate within local area networks for which the workstation technology is most suitable. The emergence of distributed DBMSs that run on wide area networks may increase the importance of mainframes. On the other hand, future distributed DBMSs may support hierarchical organizations where sites consist of clusters of computers communicating over a local area network with a high-speed backbone wide area network connecting the clusters. Whatever the architectural model, distributed DBMSs, with proper support for transparent access to data, will assist the incremental growth of database sizes without major impact on application code.

Another economic factor is the trade-off between data communication and telecommunication costs. In the previous subsection, we argue that data localization improves performance by reducing delays. It also reduces costs. Consider an application (such as inventory control) that needs to run at a number of locations. If this application accesses the database frequently, it may be more economical to distribute the data and to process it locally. This is in contrast to the execution of the application at various sites and making remote accesses to a central database that is stored at another site. In other words, the cost of distributing data and shipping some of it from one site to the other from time to time to execute distributed queries may be lower than the telecommunication cost of frequently accessing a remote database. We should state that this part of the economics argument is still speculative. As we indicated above, most of the distributed DBMSs are local area network products, and how they can be extended to operate in wide area networks is a topic of discussion and controversy.

Unsolved problems

In the previous section, we discuss the current state of commercial distributed DBMSs and how well they meet the original objectives that were set for the technology. Obviously, there is still some way to go before the commercial state of the art fulfills the original goals of the technology. The issue is not only that the commercial systems have to catch up and implement the research results, but also that there are significant research problems that remain to be solved. This section discusses these issues in some detail.

Network scaling problems

As noted before, the database community does not have a full understanding of the performance implications of all the design alternatives that accompany the development of distributed DBMSs. Specifically, questions have been raised about the scalability of some protocols and algorithms as the systems become geographically distributed [STON89] or as the number of system components increases [GARC90a]. Of specific concern is the suitability of the distributed transaction-processing mechanisms (that is, two-phase locking algorithms and, particularly, two-phase commit protocols) in wide area network-based distributed database systems. There is a significant overhead associated with these protocols, and implementing them over a slow wide area network may be difficult [STON89].

Scaling issues are only one part of a more general problem — namely, that we do not have a good handle on the role of network architectures and protocols in the performance of distributed DBMSs. Almost all the performance studies that we know assume a very simple network cost model, sometimes as unrealistic as using a fixed communication delay that is independent of all network characteristics, such as the load, message size, and network size. The inappropriateness of these models can be demonstrated easily. Consider, for example, a distributed DBMS that runs on an Ethernet-type local area network. Message delays in Ethernet increase as the network load increases, and, in general, cannot be bounded. Therefore, realistic performance models of an Ethernet-based distributed DBMS cannot realistically use a constant network delay or even a delay function that does not consider network load. In general, the performance of the proposed algorithm and protocols in different local area network architectures is not well understood, let alone their comparative behavior in moving from local area networks to wide area networks.

The proper way to deal with scalability issues is to develop general and sufficiently powerful performance models, measurement tools, and methodologies. Such work for centralized DBMSs has been going on for some time but has not yet been sufficiently extended to distributed DBMSs. We already raised questions about the suitability of the existing benchmarks. Detailed and comprehensive simulation studies do not exist either. Even though there are plenty of performance studies of distributed DBMS, these usually employ simplistic models, artificial work loads, or conflicting assumptions, or they consider only a few special algorithms. It has been suggested that to make generalizations based on the existing performance studies requires a giant leap of faith. This does not mean that we do not have some understanding of the trade-offs. In fact, certain trade-offs have long been recognized and even the earlier systems have considered them in their design. For example, the query processor of the SDD-1 system [BERN81] was designed to execute distributed operations most efficiently on slow wide area networks. Later studies [WAH85], [OZSO87] considered the optimization of query processors in faster, broadcasting local area networks. However, these trade-offs can mostly be spelled out only in qualitative terms; their quantification requires more research on performance models.

Distribution design

The design methodology of distributed databases varies according to the system architecture. In the case of tightly integrated distributed databases, design proceeds top-down from requirements analysis and logical design of the *global database* to physical design of each *local database*. In the case of distributed multidatabase systems, the design process is bottom-up and involves the integration of existing databases. In this subsection, we concentrate on the top-down design process issues.

The step in the top-down process that is of interest to us is *distribution design*. This step deals with designing the *local conceptual schemas* by distributing the global entities over the sites of the distributed system. The global entities are specified within the *global conceptual schema*. In the case of the relational model, both the global and local entities are relations, and distribution design maps global relations to local ones. The most important research issue that requires attention is the development of a practical distribution design methodology and its integration into the general data modeling process.

There are two aspects of distribution design: *fragmentation* and *allocation*. Fragmentation deals with the partitioning of each global relation into a set of fragment relations, while allocation concentrates on the distribution (possibly replicated) of these local relations across the sites of the distributed system. Research on fragmentation has concentrated on horizontal (selecting) and vertical (projecting) fragmentation of global relations. Numerous allocation algorithms based on mathematical optimization formulations have also been proposed.

There is no underlying design methodology that combines the horizontal and vertical partitioning techniques; horizontal and vertical partitioning algorithms have been developed completely independently. If one starts with a global relation, there are algorithms to decompose it horizontally as well as algorithms to decompose it vertically into a set of fragment relations. However, there are no algorithms that fragment a global relation into a set of fragment relations (some of which are decomposed horizontally, while others are decomposed vertically). It is always pointed out that most real-life fragmentations would be mixed; that is, they would involve both horizontal and vertical partitioning of a relation. But the methodology research to accomplish this is lacking. What is needed is a distribution design methodology that encompasses the horizontal and vertical fragmentation algorithms and uses them as part of a more general strategy. Such a methodology should take a global relation together with a set of design criteria and come up with a set of fragments (some of which are obtained via horizontal fragmentation, while others are obtained via vertical fragmentation).

The second part of distribution design is allocation, which is typically treated independently of fragmentation. The process is linear when the output of fragmentation is input to allocation. At first sight, the isolation of the fragmentation and allocation steps appears to simplify the formulation of the problem by reducing the decision space. However, closer examination reveals that isolating the two steps actually contributes to the complexity of the allocation models. Both steps have similar inputs, differing only in that fragmentation works on global relations, whereas allocation considers fragment relations. They both require information about the user applications (such as how often they access data and what the relationship of individual data objects to one another is), but they both ignore how each makes use of these inputs. The end result is that the fragmentation algorithms decide how to partition a relation based partially on how applications access it, but the allocation models ignore the part that this input plays in fragmentation. Therefore, the allocation models have to include all over again detailed specification of the relationship among the fragment relations and how user applications access them. What would be more promising is to extend the methodology discussed above so that the interdependence of the fragmentation and allocation decisions is properly reflected. This requires extensions to existing distribution design strategies (for example, [CERI87]).

We recognize that integrated methodologies such as the one we propose here may be considerably complex. However, there may be synergistic effects of combining these two steps, enabling the development of quite acceptable heuristic solution methods. There are some studies that give us hope that such integrated methodologies and proper solution mechanisms can be developed [MURO85], [YOSH85]. These methodologies build a simulation model of the distributed DBMS, taking as input a specific database design, and measure its effectiveness. Development of tools based on such methodologies, which aid the human designer rather than attempt to replace him, is probably the more appropriate approach to the design problem.

Distributed query processing

Distributed query processors automatically translate a high-level query on a distributed database, which is seen as a single central database by the users, into an efficient low-level execution plan expressed on the local databases. Such translation has two important aspects. First, the translation must be a correct transformation of the input query, so that the execution plan actually produces the expected result. The formal bases for this task are the equivalence between relational calculus and relational algebra, and the transformation rules associated with relational algebra. Second, the execution plan must be "optimal"; that is, it must minimize a cost function that captures resource consumption. This requires investigating equivalent alternative plans in order to select the best one.

Because of the difficulty of addressing these two aspects together, they are typically isolated in two sequential steps, which we have called *data localization* and *global optimization* [OZSU91]. These steps are generally preceded by query decomposition, which simplifies the input query and rewrites it in relational algebra. Data localization transforms an input algebraic query expressed on the distributed database into an equivalent fragment query (a query expressed on database fragments stored at different sites), which can be further simplified by algebraic transformations. Global query optimization, generates an optimal execution plan for the input fragment query by making decisions regarding operation ordering, data movement between sites, and the choice of both distributed and local algorithms for database operations. There are a number of problems regarding this last step. They have to do with the restrictions imposed on the cost model, the focus on a subset of the query language, the trade-off between optimization cost and execution cost, and the optimization/ reoptimization interval.

The cost model is central to global query optimization, since it provides the necessary abstraction of the distributed DBMS execution system in terms of access methods and an abstraction of the database in terms of physical schema information and related statistics. The cost model is used to predict the execution cost of alternative execution plans for a query. A number of important restrictions are often associated with the cost model, limiting the effectiveness of optimization. It is a weighted combination of cost components such as I/O, CPU, and communication and can capture either response time (RT) or total time (TT). However, the performance objective of many distributed systems is to improve throughput. The open problem here is to factor out the knowledge of the work load of concurrent queries within the cost model. Although TT optimization may increase throughput by minimizing resource consumption, RT optimization may well hurt throughput because of the overhead of parallelism. A potentially beneficial direction of research is to apply multiple query optimization [SELL88] where a set of important queries from the same work load are optimized together. This would provide opportunities for load balancing and for exploiting common intermediate results. Other problems associated with the cost model are the accuracy of the cost functions for distributed algorithms and the impact of update queries on throughput, particularly in the case of replicated databases. Careful analysis of the cost functions should provide insights for determining useful heuristics to cut down the number of alternative execution plans (see, for example, [OZSU90a] and [OZSU90b]). Work in extensible query optimization [FREY87] can be useful in parameterizing the cost model, which can then be refined after much experimentation.

Even though query languages are becoming increasingly powerful (for example, new versions of SQL), global query optimization typically focuses on a subset of the query language — namely, select-project-join (SPJ) queries with conjunctive predicates. This is an important class of queries for which good optimization opportunities exist. As a result, a good deal of theory has been developed for join and semijoin ordering. However, there are other important queries that warrant optimization, such as queries with disjunctions, unions, aggregations, or sorting. Although these have been partially addressed in centralized query optimization, the solutions cannot always be extended to distributed execution. For example, transforming an average function over a relation into multiple average functions, each defined on a fragment of the original relation, simply does not produce the correct result. One way of dealing with these queries is to centralize the operands (that is, reconstruct the original relations) before processing the query, but this clearly is not desirable, since it eliminates intraquery parallelism. Methods have to be found for processing complex queries without giving up parallelism. One can then have multiple optimization "experts," each specialized in one class of queries (such as SPJ optimization and aggregate optimization). As query languages evolve toward more general purpose languages that permit multiple statements to be combined with control statements (such as Sybase's TRANSACT-SQL), the major problem becomes the recognition of optimizable constructs within the input query. A promising solution is to separate the language understanding from the optimization itself, which can be dedicated to several optimization experts [VALD89].

There is a necessary trade-off between *optimization cost* and *quality* of the generated execution plans. Higher optimization costs are probably acceptable to produce "better" plans for repetitive queries, since this would reduce query *execution cost* and amortize the optimization cost over many executions. However, it is unacceptable for *ad hoc* queries that are executed only once. The optimization cost is mainly incurred by searching the solution space for alternative execution plans. Thus, there are two important components that affect optimization cost: the size of the solution space and the efficiency of the search strategy. In a distributed system, the solution space can be quite large, because of the wide range of distributed execution strategies. Therefore, it is critical to study the application of efficient search strategies [IOAN90] that avoid the exhaustive search approach. More important, a different search strategy should be used depending on the kind of query (simple versus complex) and the application requirements (*ad hoc* versus repetitive). This requires support for controllable search strategies [LANZ90].

Global query optimization is typically performed prior to the execution of the query — hence called *static* — for two reasons. First, it can be done within a compiler, reducing optimization cost. Second, it can better exploit knowledge regarding physical schema and data placement. Earlier proposals have proposed dynamic techniques that mix optimization and execution. This can be achieved easily using the static approach by adding tests at compile time in order to make runtime decisions. A major problem with this approach is that the cost model used for optimization may become inaccurate, because of changes in the fragment sizes or database reorganization that is important for load balancing. The problem is to determine the optimal intervals of recompilation/reoptimization of the queries, taking into account the trade-off between optimization and execution cost.

Distributed transaction processing

It may be hard to believe that in an area as widely researched as distributed transaction processing there may still be important topics to investigate, but there are. We have already mentioned the scaling problems of transaction management algorithms. Additionally, replica control protocols, more sophisticated transaction models, and nonserializable correctness criteria require further attention.

In replicated distributed DBMSs, database operations are specified on logical data objects.[3] The replica control protocols are responsible for mapping an operation on a logical data object to an operation on multiple physical copies of this data object. In so doing, they ensure the *mutual consistency* of the replicated database. The ROWA rule that we discuss above is the most straightforward method of enforcing mutual consistency. Accordingly, a replicated database is in a mutually consistent state if all the copies of every data object have identical values.

The field of data replication needs further experimentation, research on replication methods for computation and communication, and more work to enable the systematic exploitation of application-specific properties. The field ripened for methodical experimental research only in the late 1980s; consequently, much still needs to be done. It remains difficult to evaluate the claims that are made by algorithm and system designers and we lack a consistent framework for comparing competing techniques. One of the difficulties in quantitatively evaluating replication techniques lies in the absence of commonly accepted *failure incidence models*. For example, Markov models that are

---

[3]We use the term *data object* here instead of the more common *data item* because we do not want to make a statement about the granularity of the logical data.

---

sometimes used to analyze the availability achieved by replication protocols assume the statistical independence of individual failure events and the rarity of network partitions relative to site failures. We do not currently know that either of these assumptions is tenable nor do we know how sensitive Markov models are to these assumptions. The validation of the Markov models by simulation cannot be trusted in the absence of empirical measurements, since simulations often embody the same assumptions that underlie the Markov analysis. Thus, there is a need for empirical studies to monitor failure patterns in real-life production systems, with the purpose of constructing a simple model of typical *failure loads*.

A failure load model should account for sequences of failures, which raises some interesting research questions. If failures are not statistically independent, must the models employ joint probability distributions, or do correlation coefficients suffice? How inaccurate are the models that make the independence assumption? A failure model should include a variety of what might be called *failure incidence benchmarks* and availability metrics that are readily measurable. The development of commonly accepted failure models will clarify how reconfiguration algorithms should exploit information about failures that have been detected and diagnosed. Some methods (for example, primary copy [ALSB76] and available copies [BERN84]) call for immediate reorganization after a failure before any further operations on the replicated data can be processed. On the other hand, voting methods [THOM79], [GIFF79], [HERL86] call for a reorganization only if the availability must (and can) be enhanced in the face of further failures that may occur before the first one is repaired.

Until failure loads are clarified and documented, validating the results obtained by analytical and simulation approaches, the most credible alternative is to construct testbed systems for the purpose of evaluating the relative availability and performance achieved by different replication techniques. These empirical studies must necessarily involve the tight integration of a number of different algorithms to maintain consistency while achieving replication, reconfiguration, caching, garbage collection, concurrent operation, replica failure recovery, and security. This high degree of integration is necessitated by the tight and often subtle interaction between many of the different algorithms that form the components of the replication suite of algorithms (for example, [WEIH89]).

The second area of research that needs work is replicating computation and communication (including input and output). To achieve the twin goals of data replication (namely *availability* and *performance*), we need to provide integrated systems in which the replication of data goes hand in hand with the replication of computation and communication (including I/O). Only data replication has been studied intensely; relatively little has been done in the replication of computation and communication. Replication of computation has been studied for a variety of purposes, including running synchronous duplicate processes as "hot standbys" [GRAY85], [COOP85] and processes implementing different versions of the same software to guard against human design errors [AVIZ85]. Replication of communication messages primarily by retry has been studied in the context of providing reliable message delivery [BIRM87], and a few papers report on the replication of input/output messages to enhance the availability of transactional systems [MINO82]. However, more work needs to be done to study how these tools may be integrated together with data replication to support applications such as real-time control systems that may benefit from all three kinds of replication. This work would be invaluable in guiding operating system and programming language designers toward the proper set of tools to offer in support of fault-tolerant systems.

In addition to work on replication, but related to it, work on more elaborate transaction models, especially those that exploit the semantics of the application, is required. Higher availability and performance, as well as concurrency, can be achieved this way. As database technology enters new application domains, such as engineering design, software development, and office information systems, the nature and requirements for transactions change. Thus, work is needed on more complicated transaction models and on correctness conditions different from serializability.

As a first approximation, the existing work on transaction models can be classified along two dimensions: the transaction model and the structure of objects on which they operate. Along the transaction-model dimension, we recognize flat transactions, closed nested transactions [MOSS85] and open transaction models such as sagas [GARC87], and models that include both open and closed nesting [BUCH91], [ELMA90a], in increasing order of complexity. Along the object-structure dimension, we identify simple objects (for example, pages), objects as instances of abstract data types (ADTs), and complex objects, again in increasing order of complexity. We make the distinction between the last two to indicate that objects as instances of abstract data types support encapsulation (and therefore are harder to run transactions on than simple objects) but do not have a complex structure (that is, do not contain other objects) and their types do not participate in an inheritance hierarchy. As stated above, this classification is not meant to be taken as a definitive statement but rather is only meant to highlight some of the transaction management issues. It is described in more detail in [BUCH91].

Within the above framework, most of the transaction model work in distributed systems has concentrated on the execution of flat transactions on simple objects. This point in the design space is quite well understood. While some work has been done in the application of nested transactions on simple objects, much remains to be done, especially in distributed databases. Specifically, the semantics of these transaction models are still being worked out [BEER87], [LYNC86]. Similarly, there has been work done on applying simple transactions to objects as instances of abstract data types [WEIH88] and to complex objects [BADR88]. Again, these are initial attempts that need to be followed up to specify their full semantics, their incorporation into a DBMS, their interaction with recovery managers, and, finally, their distribution properties.

Complex transaction models are important in distributed systems for a number of reasons. First, transaction processing in distributed multidatabase systems can benefit from the relaxed semantics of these models. Second, the new application domains that distributed DBMSs will support in the future (such as engineering design, office information systems, and cooperative work) require transaction models that incorporate more abstract operations that execute on complex data. Furthermore, these applications have a different sharing paradigm than the typical database access that we are accustomed to. For example, computer-assisted cooperative work environments [GRIE88] require participants to cooperate in accessing shared resources rather than competing for them, as is usual in typical database applications. These changing requirements necessitate the development of new transaction models and accompanying correctness criteria.

A related line of research concerns multilevel transactions [BEER88]. This research views a transaction as consisting of multiple levels of abstract operations rather than a flat sequence of atomic actions. In this model, an atomic abstract operation at one level of abstraction is executed as an atomic transaction at the next lower level of abstraction. This approach may be beneficial in implementing transactions as operating system primitives.

Integration with distributed operating systems

The undesirability of running a centralized or distributed DBMS as an ordinary user application on top of a host operating system (OS) has long been recognized [GRAY79], [STON81], [CHRI87]. There is a mismatch between the requirements of the DBMS and the functionality of the existing OSs. This is even more true in the case of distributed DBMSs that require functions (for example, distributed transaction support, including concurrency control and recovery; efficient management of distributed persistent data; and more complicated access methods) that existing distributed OSs do not provide. Furthermore, distributed DBMSs necessitate modifications in how the distributed OSs perform their traditional functions (for example, task scheduling, naming, and buffer management). The architectural paradigms that guide the development of many commercial OSs do not permit easy incorporation of these considerations in OS designs. The result is either the modification of the underlying OS services by DBMS vendors or the duplication of these services within a DBMS kernel that bypasses the OS. There is a need for a comprehensive treatment of these issues in the distributed setting.

A proper discussion of distributed DBMS/distributed OS integration issues can easily be the topic of a paper about the size of this one. We highlight only the fundamental issues in this subsection. They relate to the appropriate system architecture, transparent naming of resources, persistent data management, distributed scheduling, remote communication, and transaction support.

An important architectural consideration is that the coupling of distributed DBMSs and distributed OSs is not a binary integration issue. There are also communication network protocols that need to be considered, adding to the complexity of the problem. Typically, distributed OSs implement their own communication services, ignoring the standards developed for the services offered by the communication networks. However, if OSs diverge significantly from the standard network protocols, porting the operating system to different networks can require major rework to accommodate the idiosyncrasies of each individual network architecture. Interfacing the operating system with a network standard at a reasonable level is essential for portability and compatibility with the developments in networking standards. Thus, the architectural paradigm has to be flexible enough to accommodate distributed DBMS functions and distributed operating system services, as well as the communication protocol standards such as the International Standards Organization/Open Systems Interconnection (ISO/OSI) or IEEE 802. In this context, efforts that include too much of the database functionality inside the operating system kernel or those that modify tightly closed operating systems are likely to prove unsuccessful. In our view, the operating system should implement only the essential OS services and those DBMS functions that it can *efficiently* implement and then *should get out of the way*. The model that best fits this requirement seems to be the client-server architecture with a small kernel that provides the database functionality that can efficiently be provided and does not hinder the DBMS in efficiently implementing other services at the user level (for example, Mach [RASH89] and Amoeba [TANE90]). Object orientation may also have a lot to offer as a system structuring approach to facilitate this integration.

Naming is the fundamental mechanism that is available to the operating system for providing transparent access to system resources. Whether or not access to distributed objects should be transparent at the operating system level is a contentious issue. Proponents of transparency argue that it simplifies the user access to distributed objects, that it enables free movement of objects around the system, and that it facilitates load balancing. Opponents, on the other hand, point to the overhead of providing transparent access and claim that it is not reasonable to expect applications that do not require transparency to suffer the performance implications. They also indicate that it is not necessary to have transparency in order to have a coherent view of the system. This discussion is likely to continue for some time. From the perspective of a distributed DBMS, transparency is important. Many of the existing distributed DBMSs attempt to establish their own transparent naming schemes without significant success. More work is necessary in investigating the naming issue and the relationship between distributed directories and OS name servers. A worthwhile naming construct that deserves some attention in this context is the capability concept that was used in older systems such as Hydra [WULF81] and is being used in more modern OSs such as Amoeba [TANE90].

Storage and management of *persistent data* that survive past the execution of the program that manipulates them is the primary function of database management systems. Operating systems have traditionally dealt with persistent data by means of file systems. If a successful cooperation paradigm can be found, it may be possible to use the DBMS as the OS file system. At a more general level, the cooperation between DBMS and OS programming languages to manage persistent data requires further research. There are at least three dimensions in addressing the persistent data management issues:

- Problems that DBMSs have with traditional file systems,
- Issues in supporting persistence within the context of database programming languages and how such languages may impact operating system functionality, and
- Specific considerations of distributed file systems.

From the unique perspective of this paper, the third dimension is the most important one.
The distributed file systems operate in one of the following three modes [GIFF88]:

- *Remote-disk systems*, which enable sharing of unstructured remote disk blocks among a number of clients;
- *Block-level-access systems*, which enable accessing of portions of remote files (called *file blocks*); and
- *File-level-access systems*, which enable sharing of entire files among clients by transferring them from one machine to another.

These distributed file system organizations are not suitable for distributed DBMS implementation. Remote disk systems are not appropriate, because they do not permit any level of concurrency in updating data, which is a significant feature of any state-of-the-art distributed DBMS. Each remote disk block has to be marked as either read-only or mutable, and only the read-only blocks can be concurrently accessed. Similarly, file-level-access systems provide concurrent access at the file level only. In a relational distributed DBMS where each file stores a relation, this means locking out an entire relation, which would have significant performance penalties. Even though block-level-access systems permit concurrent access at the block level, this eliminates the possibility of implementing predicate locks that lock out only the accessed records in a block rather than the entire block. Commercial DBMSs do not implement predicate locking but provide page-level locking instead. This is due to the performance overhead of record-level locking in relational systems. However, the ability to lock at a level of granularity smaller than a page becomes important in object-oriented systems where each page stores multiple objects. Additionally, these remote file system implementations rely on transmitting either fixed-size blocks or entire files between machines. However, the results of distributed DBMS queries typically vary in size and the query processor attempts to minimize the amount of data transmission. It is clear that there is a need for some mode of communication between the query processor and the distributed file system, as well as new paradigms of implementing remote file access.

Two communication paradigms that have been widely studied in distributed operating systems are message passing[4] and remote procedure call (RPC). The relative merits of each approach have long been debated, but the simple semantics of RPC (blocking and one-time execution) have been appealing to distributed system designers. An RPC-based access to distributed data at the user level is sometimes proposed in place of providing fully transparent access [GRAY89]. However, implementation of an RPC mechanism for a heterogeneous computing environment is not an easy matter. The issue is that the RPC systems of different vendors do not interoperate. For example, even though both Sun and Apollo workstations are Unix based[5] and even though both implement RPC

---

[4]Note that we are referring to logical message passing, not to physical. Remote procedure calls have to be transmitted between sites as physical messages as well.
[5]Unix is a trademark of AT&T Bell Laboratories.

mechanisms based on Internet protocol- (IP)-class network protocols, they cannot interoperate. Among other reasons, one may cite their incompatible communication paradigms: One uses virtual circuits (supports session-based communication), while the other is datagram based. It can be argued that this type of interoperability is at the level of the distributed operating system and does not necessarily concern the distributed DBMS. This is true to a certain extent, and the issue has been studied at that level [STOY90], [RENE87]. On the other hand, the incompleteness of RPC, even with its simple and restricted communication semantics, needs to be emphasized. It may be necessary to look at communication at higher levels of abstraction in order to overcome heterogeneity or at lower levels of abstraction (message passing) to achieve more parallelism. This trade-off needs to be studied further.

In current DBMSs, the transaction manager is implemented as part of the DBMS. Whether transactions should and can be implemented as part of standard operating system services has long been discussed. It is fair to state that there are strong arguments on both sides, but a clear resolution of the issue requires more research as well as some more experience with the various general-purpose (non-DBMS) transaction management services. Some example systems include Camelot [EPPI91], which adds transaction management services to Mach [RASH89]; QuickSilver [HASK88], which includes transaction management as standard operating system service; and Argus [LISK88], where the transaction concept is supported as a language primitive.

A detailed discussion of the pros and cons of providing an operating system transaction management service is beyond the scope of this paper (see [WEIK86] for a discussion). However, any OS transaction mechanism needs to be sufficiently powerful to support abstract operations on abstract objects [WEIH88]. In this context, the multilevel transaction model discussed earlier may be appropriate. The operating system can efficiently implement the lowest level of abstraction and let the user-level applications extend this abstraction to a model that is suitable for their domain. For example, page-level locking can be one abstraction level, while predicate locking can be another level. The operating system then has to provide the mechanisms that enable the definition of successive levels of abstractions. An added advantage of such an approach may be that nested transactions, which are necessary for complex application domains, can be more easily reconciled with the multilevel transaction model.

Changing technology and new issues

Distribution is commonly identified as one of the major features of next-generation database systems that will be ushered in by the penetration of database technology into new application areas with different requirements than traditional business data processing and the technological developments in computer architecture and networking. The question, from the perspective of this paper, is what the nature of distribution in these systems will be. Answering this question requires the definition of the features of next-generation DBMSs, which is a controversial issue. A number of documents attempted to provide such definitions [SILB90], [ATKI89], [STON90a], [STON90b]; from these, it is possible to identify certain common features:

(1)   *Data model.* One of the common features is that the data model to be supported will need to be more powerful than the relational model, yet without compromising its advantages (data independence and high-level query languages). When applied to more complex application domains — such as CAD/CAM, software design, office information systems, and expert systems — the relational data model exhibits limitations in terms of complex object support, type system, and rule management. To address these issues, two important technologies — knowledge bases and object-oriented databases — are currently being investigated.

(2)   *Parallelism.* A major issue that faces designers of next-generation DBMS is going to be

system performance as more functionality is added. Exploiting the parallelism available in multiprocessor computers is one promising approach to providing high performance. Techniques designed for distributed databases can be useful but need to be significantly extended to implement parallel database systems.

(3) *Interoperability.* A consequence of applying database technology to various application domains may well be a proliferation of different, yet complementary, DBMSs and — more generally — information systems. Thus, an important direction of research is interoperability of such systems within a computer network. Multidatabase system technology requires significant extensions toward this goal.

In this section, we discuss each of these topics and highlight the research issues that have started receiving attention in the database community.

Distributed object-oriented database systems

Object-oriented databases (OODBs) [ATKI89], [KIM89], [ZDON90] combine object-oriented programming (OOP) and database technologies in order to provide higher modeling power and flexibility to data-intensive application programmers. There is controversy as to the nature of an object-oriented data model — that is, whether it should be an extension of the relational model with nested relations (for example, DASDBS [SCHE90]), abstract data types (for example, POSTGRES [STON90c]), or a new model borrowing from OOP concepts (for example, O$_2$ [LECL88], ORION [KIM90], and GEMSTONE [MAIE87]). In any case, in addition to traditional database functions, the primary functions to be supported are abstract data types, type inheritance, and complex objects.

Over the last five years, OODBs have been the subject of intensive research and experimentation that have led to an impressive number of prototypes and commercial products. However, the theory and practice of developing distributed object-oriented DBMSs (OODBMSs) have yet to be fully developed. This effort almost parallels that of relational systems. Even though some of the solutions developed for relational systems are applicable, the high degree of generality introduced by the object-oriented data models creates significant difficulties. In this subsection, we review the more important issues related to the system architecture, query models and management, transaction management, and distributed object management.

Distributed OODBMS architecture. Dealing with distributed environments will make the problems even more difficult. Additionally, the issues related to data dictionary management and distributed object management have to be dealt with. However, distribution is an essential requirement, since applications that require OODB technology typically arise in networked-workstation environments. The early commercial OODBMSs (for example, GEMSTONE) use a client/server architecture where multiple workstations can access the database centralized on a server. However, as a result of hardware advances in microprocessor technology, the processing power of such distributed systems gets concentrated in the client workstations rather than the server [DEWI90b]. A similar observation can be made for the capacity and speed of the local disks attached to workstations compared to the larger server's disks. Consequently, distributing an OODB within a network of workstations (and servers) becomes very attractive. In fact, some OODBMSs (for example, ONTOS and Distributed ORION) already support some form of data distribution transparency.

The design of distributed OODBMS should benefit from the experience gained from distributed databases. In particular, if the system is an extension of a relational DBMS, then most distributed database solutions can apply. However, in the case of a more general object-oriented data model, the management of distributed objects is complicated by the transparency and efficiency requirements.

Many distributed object-oriented systems simplify the problem by making the user aware of object location and performing remote accesses to nonlocal objects. This approach is not appropriate for distributed OODBMSs, because location transparency and distributed program execution — two essential functions for high performance and availability — would be precluded.

Queries and query processing. In order not to compromise the obvious advantages of relational systems, an OODBMS ought to provide a high-level query language for object manipulation. While there have been some proposals for calculus and algebras for OODBs, query optimization remains an open issue. OODB queries are more complicated and can include path traversals and ADT operations as part of their predicates. The initial work on query processing [OSBO88], [KORT88], [GRAE88], [SHAW89], [STRA90] does not consider object distribution. The efficient processing of distributed OODB queries can borrow from distributed relational query processing to exploit the fragmentation of collection objects. However, achieving correct program transformations is more involved due to the higher expressive power of object-oriented query languages, especially in the presence of objects that are referentially shared [KHOS87].

Transaction management. Difficulties are introduced in transaction management for the following three reasons:

- Objects can be complex, thereby making variable-granularity locking essential;
- Support for dynamic schema evolution requires efficient solutions for updating schema data; and
- To address the different requirements of the targeted application domains, several concurrency control algorithms need to be supported (for example, pessimistic and optimistic concurrency control as in GEMSTONE).

Furthermore, engineering applications typically require specific support for cooperative transactions or long-duration nested transactions. In the subsection entitled "Distributed transaction processing," we indicated the possible transaction models. In object-oriented systems, full generality is typically required such that complex transactions operate on complex object structures. Furthermore, the object model may treat transactions as first-class objects, adding both complexity and more opportunities to support multiple transaction types in one system. This area has started to attract some attention but is still in its infancy.

Replication of objects, replica control protocols, and their relationship to concurrency control algorithms in object-oriented systems open some interesting issues. The information hiding implicit in-typed data offers an opportunity for the storage system (including the replication algorithms) of the systematic exploitation of the type semantics. An example of a type-specific approach is that of *event-based data replication* [HERL86], [HEDD88], in which the unit of replication is a single-operation execution and not the entire value of the object. Thus, a replica contains a (possibly partial) history or log of operation execution and checkpoint events, rather than a value or a set of versions. By contrast, traditional (value-based) data replication methods maintain copies of object values, with an associated log that is used exclusively for local recovery from site failures. Event-based data replication promises more efficient utilization of disks (because log writes eliminate seek times), higher concurrency (achieved by permitting type-specific, concurrency control algorithms to operate directly on the log representation), and higher availability and faster response time for common update operations that are semantically blind-writes (log append). In addition, this approach forms a basis for the seamless integration of type-specific and type-independent algorithms for concurrency control, recovery, and replication in the same system. This is because the event log degenerates into a value if the checkpoints are constrained to be always current.

Distributed object management. Efficient management of objects with complex connections is difficult. When objects can be hierarchical and contain possibly shared subobjects, object clustering and indexing is a major issue [KEMP90]. With object sharing, garbage collection of objects that become orphans after updates is problematic. Furthermore, large-sized objects such as graphics and images need special attention, especially in distributed systems where objects are moved between the client and server machines. It is important to maintain physical contiguity of objects to reduce the data movement overhead.

Distributed object management should rely on a distributed storage model that can capture the clustering and fragmentation of complex objects [KHOS89], [GRUB91]. Solutions developed for relational systems can be applied to collections of objects. However, the main problems remain the support of global object identity and object sharing. Global object identity is expensive because of the current lack of global virtual address spaces. Therefore, the distinction between objects (with OIDs) and values is important since values can be manipulated as in relational systems. Managing distributed shared objects is difficult, since inconsistencies can occur when a shared object is moved and updated at another site. Possible solutions include the use of an indirection table or the avoidance of problems at compile time. With the first kind of solutions, distributed garbage collection is an open problem [LISK86], [SHAP90].

The development of distributed object-oriented DBMSs brings to the forefront the issues related to proper OS support. The issues are more interesting in this case, because the development of object-oriented distributed operating systems has also been studied independently. Object-oriented technology can serve as the common platform to eliminate the "impedance mismatch" between the programming languages, database management systems, and operating systems. The integration of the first two has been addressed by researchers; we indicate some of this work above. However, the integration of object-oriented DBMSs and object-oriented operating systems has not yet been studied and remains an interesting research issue. One problem in using object orientation to bring these systems together is their differing understandings of what an object is and their quite different type systems. Nevertheless, if the next-generation object-oriented DBMSs are to have an easier cooperation with the operating systems than today's relational DBMSs do, these issues need to be addressed.

Distributed knowledge base systems

An important feature that is likely to be present in next-generation DBMSs is some facility for reasoning. This is a feature that should enable us to move from data management to more general knowledge management by abstracting the reasoning mechanism from the application programs and encapsulating it within the DBMS. This does not mean that the reasoning capability needs to be centralized, but only that the responsibility for its application is taken out of the application program. The reasoning engine can be distributed, as well as the rules according to which it is applied. In object-oriented knowledge base implementations, for example, reasoning rules can be encapsulated in each object.

Capturing knowledge in the form of rules has been extensively studied in a particular form of knowledge base system called a *deductive database*. Deductive database systems [GALL84] manage and process rules against large amounts of data within the DBMS rather than with a separate subsystem. Rules can be declarative (*assertions*) or imperative (*triggers*). By isolating the application knowledge and behavior within rules, knowledge base management systems (KBMSs) provide control over knowledge that can be better shared among users. Furthermore, the high expressive power of rule programs aids application development. These advantages imply increased programmer productivity and application performance. Based on first-order logic, deductive database technology subsumes relational database technology. We can isolate two alternative approaches to KBMS design. The first one extends a relational DBMS with a more powerful rule language (for example,

RDL [KIER90] or ESQL [GARD90]), while the second approach extends first-order logic into a declarative programming language such as Datalog (for example, LDL [CHIM90]). The two approaches raise similar issues, some of which have been partially addressed by the artificial intelligence community, although with strong assumptions such as a small database and the absence of data sharing.

Rule management — as investigated in deductive databases — is essential, since it provides a uniform paradigm to deal with semantic integrity control, views, protection, deduction, and triggers. Much of the work in deductive databases has concentrated on the semantics of rule programs and on processing deductive queries — in particular, in the presence of recursive and negated predicates [BANC86]. However, there are a number of open issues related to the enforcement of the semantic consistency of the knowledge base, optimization of rule programs involving large amounts of data and rules, integration of rule-based languages with other tools (application generators), and providing appropriate debugging tools. Furthermore, much work is needed to combine rule support with object-oriented capabilities such as class mechanisms and complex objects.

For reasons similar to those for OODB applications, knowledge base applications are likely to arise in networked-workstation environments. These applications can also arise in parallel computing environments when the database is managed by a multiprocessor database server (see the next subsection). In any case, there are a number of similar issues that can get simplified by relying on distributed relational database technology. Unlike in most OODB approaches that try to extend an OOPL system, this is a strong advantage for implementing knowledge bases in distributed environments. Therefore, the new issues have more to do with distributed knowledge management and processing and debugging of distributed knowledge base queries than with distributed data management.

Distributed knowledge management includes the management of various kinds of rules such as assertions, deductive rules, and triggers. The question is how and where they should be stored in order to minimize a cost function. When one is dealing with fragmented relations, fragment definition and rule definition should be investigated jointly so that rules can efficiently apply to fragments. The preventive approach of compiling assertions — such as semantic integrity constraints — into efficient pretests [SIMO86] can possibly be extended to address more general rules. Another possibility is to implement rule firing based on updates (for example, triggers) as an extension of the transaction management mechanism [STON90c], [DAYA88], [MCCA89]. In any case, distributed database design must be revisited to take into account rules when defining fragmentation.

Distributed knowledge base query processing and debugging are made difficult by the presence of additional capabilities (such as recursive rules) and the larger range of distributed execution strategies for such capabilities. Most of the work in this area has focused on extending distributed query processing to support the transitive closure of fragmented relations in parallel [VALD88]. More general Datalog programs are considered for distributed execution [WOLF90]. However, much more work is needed to provide a general framework to process distributed knowledge base queries. As in the centralized case, debugging of distributed knowledge base queries is more difficult because of the complex transformations that can be applied to input queries.

Parallel database systems

Parallel database systems intend to exploit the recent multiprocessor computer architectures in order to build high-performance, fault-tolerant database servers [VALD91]. This can be achieved by extending distributed database technology — for example, by fragmenting the database across multiple nodes so that more inter- and intraquery parallelism can be obtained. For obvious reasons such as set-oriented processing and application portability, most of the work in this area has focused on supporting SQL. Bubba [BORA90] is a notable exception, because it supports a more powerful database language. There are already some relational database products that implement this approach (for example, Teradata's DBC [NECH85] and Tandem's NonStop SQL [TAND87]), and the number of such products will increase as the market for general-purpose parallel computers expands. We have started to see implementations of existing relational DBMSs on parallel computers (for example, Ingres on Encore and ORACLE on Sequent).

The design of parallel database systems faces a number of challenging issues with respect to operating system support, data placement, parallel algorithms, and parallelizing compilation. These issues are common to both kinds of multiprocessor architectures. Furthermore, if the supported language has object-oriented or deductive capabilities, we obviously have the issues previously discussed (such as placement of complex objects).

In the context of dedicated database servers, specific operating system support for parallel data management can be very cost-effective. Two approaches can be applied. The first one creates a brand new dedicated operating system almost from scratch (for example, the Bubba operating system), which implements a single-level store where all data are uniformly represented in a virtual address space [COPE90]. The second one tries to capitalize on modern, open distributed operating systems (for example, Mach) and extends it in a way that can provide single-level store efficiency with special attention to dataflow support.

Data placement in a parallel database server exhibits similarities with horizontal fragmentation. An obvious similarity is that parallelism can be dictated by fragmentation. It is much more involved in the case of a distributed-memory architecture, because load balancing is directly implied by the fragmentation. The solution proposed in [COPE88] insists that data placement (fragmentation and allocation of fragments) is initially based on the size and access frequency of the relations and can be revised by periodic reorganizations. The main issue here is to decide when and how to perform such reorganizations. Another issue is to avoid having to recompile all the queries because of reorganization.

Fragmented data placement is the basis for parallel data processing. Therefore, the first issue is to design parallel algorithms that can exploit such data placement. The problem is simple for select operations and more difficult for joins [BITT83], [VALD84]. More work is needed to study the effect of indexes or dynamic reorganization on parallel algorithms and their application to other expensive or complex operations such as transitive closure. Furthermore, some capabilities of the interconnect network (such as broadcasting) can be exploited here.

Parallelizing compilation transforms an input query into an efficient low-level equivalent program that can be directly executed by the parallel system. An open issue here is to define a good parallel language in which optimization decisions regarding the parallel algorithms and the dataflow control can be expressed. Parallel FAD [HART88] and Parallel LERA [CHAC91] are first attempts toward this goal. The main issue in language design is to provide a good trade-off between generality and abstraction. Generality is essential to be able to express all kinds of parallel execution strategies supported by the system; abstraction is important to avoid dealing with low-level details of optimization.

If parallel data servers become prevalent, it is not difficult to see an environment where multiples of them are placed on a backbone network. This gives rise to distributed systems consisting of clusters of processors [GRAY89]. An interesting concern in such an environment is internetworking. Specifically, the execution of database commands that span multiple, and possibly heterogeneous, clusters creates at least the problems that we discuss in the next subsection. However, an additional problem is that the queries have to be optimized not only for execution in parallel on a cluster of servers but also for execution across a network.

Distributed multidatabase systems

Multidatabase system organization is an alternative to logically integrated distributed databases. The fundamental difference between the two approaches is the level of autonomy afforded to the component data managers at each site. While integrated DBMSs have components that are designed to work together, multidatabase management systems (multi-DBMSs) consist of components that may not have any notion of cooperation. Specifically, the components are independent DBMSs. This means that while they may have facilities to execute transactions, they have no notion of executing distributed transactions that span multiple components (because they have neither global concurrency control mechanisms nor distributed commit protocol implementation).

As an alternative architectural model, distributed multidatabase systems share the problems of distributed DBMSs and introduce additional ones of their own. As such, they probably deserve more space and attention than we are able to devote in this paper. In this subsection, we briefly highlight the open problems that relate to global schema definition and management, query processing, and transaction processing.

Global schema definition and management issues. The arguments against full transparency gain much more credibility in multidatabase systems. The additional autonomy of individual components and their potential heterogeneity make it more difficult (some claim impossible) to support full transparency. A major difficulty relates to the definition of the global conceptual schema (GCS) as a specification of the content and structure of the global database. The definition and role of the GCS are well understood in the case of integrated distributed database systems: It defines a logical single image over physically distributed data. The same understanding does not exist in the case of multidatabase systems, however. First, the global conceptual schema may or may not define the entire database, since each system may autonomously decide which parts of its local database it wants to make globally accessible. Second, the definition of a global conceptual schema from a large number of frequently changing local schemas is considered to be very difficult [SCHE90b]. Third, the maintenance of consistency of the global conceptual schema is a significant problem in multidatabase systems. It is quite possible for local schemas to be modified independently so that the global schema definition is affected. In this case, the maintenance of the consistency of the GCS requires that it also be modified according to the changes to the local schema. Setting up the mechanisms for mapping these changes is not easy. One way the issue can be attacked is to treat the global conceptual schema not as a concrete definition but rather as a generalization view defined over local conceptual schemas. Studies along this line have been conducted before [MOTR81], [DAYA84], and their practical implications with respect to transparency need to be considered. Finally, the definition and enforcement of global integrity constraints need to be addressed. Most current research ignores data dependencies across autonomous databases.

If the global conceptual schema can be defined as a single view over the local database schemas, why cannot multiple views for different applications be defined over the same local schemas? This observation has led some researchers to suggest that a multi-DBMS be defined as a system that manages "several databases without a global schema" [LITW88]. It is argued that the absence of a GCS is a significant advantage of multidatabase systems over distributed database systems.

An example of integrating multiple databases without defining a global conceptual schema is MRDSM, which specifies a language (called *MDL* [LITW87]) with sufficiently powerful constructs to access multiple databases. A significant research problem is the nature of such a language. As indicated in [SCHE90b], the component DBMSs may implement special operators in their query languages, which makes it difficult to define a language that is as powerful as the union of the component ones. It is also possible that component DBMSs may provide different interfaces to general-purpose programming languages. The solution may be to implement languages that are extensible.

Query processing. The autonomy and potential heterogeneity of component systems create problems in query processing and especially in query optimization. The fundamental problem is the difficulty of global optimization when local cost functions are not known and local cost values cannot be communicated to the multi-DBMS. It has been suggested that semantic optimization based only on qualitative information may be the best that one can do [SCHE90b], but semantic query processing is not fully understood either. Potentially, it may be possible to develop hierarchical query optimizers that perform some amount of global query optimization and then to let each local system perform further optimization on the localized subquery. This may not provide an "optimal" solution but may still enable some amount of optimization. The emerging standards, which we discuss shortly, may also make it easier to share some cost information.

Transaction processing. Transaction processing in autonomous multidatabase systems is another important research area. The emerging consensus on the transaction execution model seems to be the following: Each component DBMS has its own transaction-processing services (that is, transaction manager, scheduler, and recovery manager) and is capable of accepting *local transactions* and running them to completion. In addition, the multi-DBMS layer has its own transaction-processing components (that is, global transaction manager and global scheduler) in charge of accepting *global transactions* accessing multiple databases and coordinating their execution.

Autonomy requires that the global transaction management functions be performed independently of the local transaction execution functions. In other words, the individual DBMSs (more specifically, the transaction-processing components) or their local applications are not modified to accommodate global transactions. Heterogeneity has the additional implication that the transaction-processing components may employ different concurrency control, commit, and recovery protocols.

In this model of execution, the global transactions are broken down into a set of *subtransactions*, each of which is submitted to a component DBMS for execution. Local DBMSs execute these subtransactions intermixed with the local transactions that they receive directly. The existence of local transactions that are unknown to the global scheduler complicates things and may create *indirect conflicts* among global transactions. Furthermore, the subtransactions that are submitted to a component DBMS on behalf of a global transaction are treated as local transactions by the component DBMSs. Therefore, there is the additional problem of ensuring that the ordering imposed upon the global transactions by the global scheduler be maintained for all of their subtransactions at each component DBMS by all the local schedulers [BREI88]. If serializability is used as the correctness criterion for concurrent execution of transactions, the problem is ensuring that the serialization order of global transactions at each site be the same.

A number of different solutions have been proposed to deal with concurrent multidatabase transaction processing. Some of these use global serializability of transactions as their correctness criterion [GEOR91], [BREI88], while others relax serializability [DU89], [BARK90]. Most of this work should be treated as preliminary initial attempts at understanding and formalizing the issues. There are many issues that remain to be investigated. One area of investigation has to deal with revisions in the transaction model and the correctness criteria. There are initial attempts to recast the transaction model assumptions [GARC90b], [ELMA90]; this work needs to continue. Nested transaction models look particularly promising for multidatabase systems, and their semantics based on knowledge about the transaction's behavior (similar to [FARR89]) needs to be formalized. In this context, it is necessary to go back and reconsider the meaning of *consistency* in multidatabase systems. A good starting point is the four degrees of consistency defined by Gray [GRAY79].

Another difficult issue that requires further investigation is the reliability and recovery aspects of multidatabase systems. The above-described transaction execution model is quite similar to the execution of distributed transactions. However, if the component DBMSs are fully autonomous, then they do not incorporate 2PC procedures, which makes it difficult to enforce distributed transaction atomicity. Even though the topic has been discussed in some recent works [BARK91], [GEOR90], [WOLS90], these approaches are initial engineering solutions. The development of reliability and recovery protocols for multidatabase systems and their integration with concurrency control mechanisms still need to be worked out.

Autonomy and standards. Probably one of the fundamental impediments to further development of multidatabase systems is the lack of understanding of the nature of autonomy, which plays a major role in making life miserable. It is probably because what we call "autonomy" is itself composed of a number of factors. An initial characterization identifies three different forms of autonomy: design autonomy, communication autonomy, and execution autonomy. Other characterizations have also been proposed [GARC88], [SHET90]. These characterizations need to be worked out more precisely and exhaustively. Furthermore, most researchers treat autonomy as if it were an "all-or-nothing" feature. Even the taxonomy that we considered in the "What is a distributed database?" section indicates only three points along this dimension. However, the spectrum between "no autonomy" and "full autonomy" probably contains many distinct points. It is essential, in our opinion, to

- Precisely define what is meant by "no autonomy" and "full autonomy";
- Precisely delineate and define the many different levels of autonomy; and
- Identify, as we indicated above, the appropriate degree of database consistency that is possible for each of these levels.

At that point, it would be more appropriate to discuss the different transaction models and execution semantics that are appropriate at each of these levels of autonomy. In addition, this process should enable the identification of a layered structure — similar to the ISO/OSI model — for the interoperability of autonomous and possibly heterogeneous database systems. Such a development would then make it possible to specify interfacing standards at different levels. Some standardization work is already under way within the context of the Remote Data Access (RDA) standard, and this line of work will make the development of practical solutions to the interoperability problem possible.

Object orientation and multidatabase systems. Another important ingredient is the development of the technology that can inherently deal with autonomous software components. A prime candidate technology is object orientation. We discuss its role in the development of database management systems at the beginning of the "Changing technology and new issues" section. Here, we comment only on its role in addressing the interoperability issues.

Object-oriented systems typically treat the entities in their domain as instances of some abstract type. In the case of database systems, these entities are usually data objects. However, it is quite common for object-oriented models to treat every entity uniformly as objects, so programs and user queries are considered to be objects in certain object models. The technology is concerned primarily with providing the necessary tools and methodology for the consistent management of these entities while there are user accesses (both to retrieve and to update) to them. This is to be done without allowing the user to "see" the physical structure of each object. In other words, user access to objects is only by means of well-defined interfaces that hide their internal structure. In the case of applying object orientation to the interoperability problem, one considers each autonomous DBMS to be an object. The relationship is then established between manipulating objects without "looking inside them" and being able to perform operations on autonomous DBMSs without "requiring changes in them." This is a very simple characterization of the problem. There has been some initial discussion of the potential benefits that may be gained from the application of the object-oriented technology to the interoperability problem [MAN90], [SCHE90b], [HEIL90], and this is a major direction that needs to be further investigated.

Conclusions

In this paper, we discuss the state of the art in distributed database research and products. Specifically, we address the following questions:

(1)   What were the initial promises and goals of the distributed database technology? How do the current commercial products measure up to these promises? In retrospect, were these goals achievable?

(2)   Have the important technical problems already been solved?

(3)   What are the technological changes that underlie distributed data managers, and how will they impact next-generation systems?

The initial promises of distributed database systems — namely, transparent management of distributed and replicated data, improved system reliability via distributed transactions, improved system performance by means of inter- and intraquery parallelism, and easier and more economical system expansion — are met to varying degrees by existing commercial products. Full realization of these promises is dependent not only on the commercial state of the art catching up with the research results but also on the solution of a number of problems. The issues that have been studied but still require more work are

(1)   Performance models, methodologies, and benchmarks to better understand the sensitivity of the proposed algorithms and mechanisms to the underlying technology;

(2)   Distributed query processing to handle queries that are more complex than select-project-join, the ability to process multiple queries at once to save on common work, and optimization cost models to be able to determine when such multiple query processing is beneficial;

(3)   Advanced transaction models that differ from those defined for business data processing and that better reflect the mode of processing common in most distributed applications (that is, cooperative sharing versus competition, interaction with the user, and long duration) for which the distributed database technology is going to provide support;

(4)   Analysis of replication and its impact on distributed database system architecture and algorithms and on the development of efficient replica control protocols that improve system availability;

(5)   Implementation strategies for distributed DBMSs that emphasize a better interface and cooperation with distributed operating systems; and

(6)   Theoretically complete and correct and practical design methodologies for distributed databases.

In addition to these existing issues, we identify the changing nature of the technology on which distributed DBMSs are implemented and discuss the issues that need to be investigated to facilitate the development of next-generation distributed DBMSs. Basically, we expect the following changes:

(1)   Advances in the development of cost-effective multiprocessors will make parallel database servers feasible. This will affect DDBSs in two ways. First, distributed DBMSs will be implemented on these parallel database servers, requiring the revision of most of the existing algorithms and protocols to operate on the parallel machines. Second, the parallel database servers

will be connected as servers to networks, requiring the development of distributed DBMSs that will have to deal with a hierarchy of data managers.

(2) As distributed database technology infiltrates nonbusiness data-processing-type application domains (such as engineering databases, office information systems, and software development environments), the capabilities required of these systems will change. This will necessitate a shift in emphasis from relational systems to data models that are more powerful. Current research along these lines concentrates on object orientation and knowledge base systems.

(3) The above-mentioned diversity of distributed database application domains is probably not possible through a tightly integrated system design. Consequently, distributed database technology will need to effectively deal with environments that consist of a federation of autonomous systems. The requirement for interoperability between autonomous and possibly heterogeneous systems has prompted research in multidatabase systems.

As this paper clearly demonstrates, there are many important technical problems that await solution as well as new ones that arise as a result of the technological changes that underlie distributed data managers. These problems should keep researchers as well as distributed DBMS implementers quite busy for some time to come.

Acknowledgments

We would like to extend our thanks to Abdelsalam Heddaya of Boston University who not only reviewed the entire paper and provided many comments but also helped us write the replication part of "Distributed query processing." Alex Biliris of Boston University, Michael Brodie, Alex Buchmann, Dimitrios Georgakopoulos, and Frank Manola of GTE Laboratories also read the entire manuscript and provided many suggestions regarding the content and the presentation that improved the paper significantly.

The research of the first author has been partially supported by the Natural Sciences and Engineering Research Council (NSERC) of Canada under operating grant OGP-0951.

References

[ALSB76] P. Alsberg et al., "Multi-Copy Resiliency Techniques," CAC Document 202, Center for Advanced Computation, Univ. of Illinois, Urbana, Ill., May 1976.

[APER81] P.M.G. Apers, "Redundant Allocation of Relations in a Communication Network," *Proc. Fifth Berkeley Workshop Distributed Data Management and Computer Networks,* 1981, pp. 245-258.

[ATKI89] M. Atkinson et al., "The Object-Oriented Database System Manifesto," *Proc. First Int'l Conf. Deductive and Object-Oriented Databases,* 1989, pp. 40-57.

[AVIZ85] A. Avizienis, "The N-Version Approach to Fault-Tolerant Software," *IEEE Trans. Software Eng.,* Vol. SE-11, No. 12, Dec. 1985, pp. 1491-1501.

[BADR88] B.R. Badrinath and K. Ramamritham, "Synchronizing Transactions on Objects," *IEEE Trans. Computers,* Vol. 37, No. 5, May 1988, pp. 541-547.

[BANC86] F. Bancilhon and R. Ramakrishnan, "An Amateur's Introduction to Recursive Query Processing," *Proc. ACM SIGMOD Int'l Conf. Management Data,* ACM Press, New York, N.Y., 1986, pp. 16-52.

[BARK90] K. Barker, "Transaction Management on Multidatabase Systems," doctoral thesis, Univ. of Alberta, Dept. of Computing Science, Edmonton, Alberta, Canada, 1990 (available as Technical Report TR90-23).

[BARK91]   K. Barker and M.T. Özsu, "Reliable Transaction Execution in Multidatabase Systems," *Proc. First Int'l Workshop Interoperability Multidatabase Systems,* IEEE Computer Soc. Press, Los Alamitos, Calif., 1991, pp. 344-347.

[BEER88]   C. Beeri, H.-J. Schek, and G. Weikum, "Multilevel Transaction Management, Theoretical Art or Practical Need?," in *Advances in Database Technology — EDBT '88,* J.W. Schmidt, S. Ceri, and M. Missikoff, eds., Springer-Verlag, New York, N.Y., 1988, pp. 134-154.

[BEER87]   C. Beerhi, P.A. Bernstein, and N. Goodman, "A Model for Concurrency in Nested Transaction Systems," *J. ACM,* Vol. 36, No. 2, Apr. 1989, pp. 230-269.

[BERN90]   P.A. Bernstein, "Transaction Processing Monitors," *Comm. ACM,* Vol. 3, No. 11, Nov. 1990, pp. 75-86.

[BERN81]   P.A. Bernstein et al., "Query Processing in a System for Distributed Databases (SDD-1)," *ACM Trans. Database Systems,* Vol. 6, No. 4, Dec. 1981, pp. 602-625.

[BERN84]   P.A. Bernstein and N. Goodman, "An Algorithm for Concurrency Control and Recovery in Replicated Distributed Databases," *ACM Trans. Database Systems,* Vol. 9, No. 4, Dec. 1984, pp. 596-615.

[BIRM87]   K. Birman and T.A. Joseph, "Exploiting Virtual Synchrony in Distributed Systems," *Proc. 11th ACM Symp. Operating System Principles,* ACM Press, New York, N.Y., 1987.

[BITT83]   D. Bitton et al., "Parallel Algorithms for the Execution of Relational Database Operations," *ACM Trans. Database Systems,* Vol. 8, No. 3, Sept. 1983, pp. 324-353.

[BORA83]   H. Boral and D.J. Dewitt, "Database Machines: An Idea Whose Time has Passed? A Critique of the Future of Database Machines," *Proc. Third Int'l Workshop Database Machines,* Springer-Verlag, Munich, Germany, 1983, pp. 166-187.

[BORA90]   H. Boral et al., "Prototyping Bubba, a Highly Parallel Database System," *IEEE Trans. Knowledge and Data Eng.,* Vol. 2, No. 1, Mar. 1990, pp. 4-24.

[BREI88]   Y. Breitbart and A. Silberschatz, "Multidatabase Update Issues," *Proc. ACM SIGMOD Int'l Conf. Management Data,* ACM Press, New York, N.Y., 1988, pp. 135-142.

[BUCH91]   A. Buchmann et al., "A Transaction Model for Active, Distributed Object Systems," in *Advanced Transaction Models for New Applications,* A. Elmagarmid, ed., Morgan Kaufmann, San Mateo, Calif., 1991.

[CERI87]   S. Ceri, B. Pernici, and G. Wiederhold, "Distributed Database Design Methodologies," *Proc. IEEE,* Vol. 75, No. 5, May 1987, pp. 533-546.

[CHAC91]   C. Chachaty, P. Borla-Salamet, and B. Bergsten, "Capturing Parallel Data Processing Strategies within a Compiled Language," in *Data Management and Parallel Processing,* P. Valduriez, ed., Chapman and Hall, London, UK, 1991.

[CHIM90]   D. Chimenti et al., "The LDL System Prototype," *IEEE Trans. Knowledge and Data Eng.,* Vol. 2, No. 1, Mar. 1990, pp. 76-90.

[CHRI87]   P. Christmann et al., "Which Kinds of OS Mechanisms Should Be Provided for Database Management," in *Experiences with Distributed Systems,* J. Nehmer, ed., Springer-Verlag, New York, N.Y., 1987, pp. 213-251.

[COOP85]   E. Cooper, "Replicated Distributed Programs," *Proc. 10th ACM Symp. Operating System Principles,* ACM Press, New York, N.Y., 1985, pp. 63-78.

[COPE88]   G. Copeland et al., "Data Placement in Bubba," *Proc. ACM SIGMOD Int'l Conf. Management Data,* ACM Press, New York, N.Y., 1988, pp. 99-108.

[COPE90]   G. Copeland, M. Franklin, and G. Weikum, "Uniform Object Management," in *Advances in Database Technology — EDBT '90,* 1990, pp. 253-268.

[DAYA84]   U. Dayal and H.Y. Hwang, "View Definition and Generalization for Database System Integration in a Multidatabase System," *IEEE Trans. Software Eng.,* Vol. SE-10, No. 6, Nov. 1984, pp. 628-645.

[DAYA88]   U. Dayal, A. Buchmann, and D. McCarthy, "Rules Are Objects Too: A Knowledge Model for an Active Object-Oriented Database System," *Proc. Second Int'l Workshop Object Oriented Database Systems,* 1988, pp. 129-143.

[DEWI90a] D.J. Dewitt and J. Gray, "Parallel Database Systems," *ACM SIGMOD Record,* Vol. 19, No. 4, Dec. 1990, pp. 104-112.

[DEWI90b] D.J. Dewitt et al., "A Study of Three Alternative Workstation Server Architectures for Object-Oriented Database Systems," *Proc. 16th Int'l Conf. Very Large Data Bases,* 1990, pp. 107-121.

[DU89] W. Du and A. Elmagarmid, "Quasi-Serializability: A Correctness Criterion for Global Concurrency Control in InterBase," *Proc. 15th Int'l Conf. Very Large Data Bases,* 1989, pp. 347-355.

[ELMA90] A.K. Elmagarmid et al., "A Multidatabase Transaction Model for InterBase," *Proc. 16th Int'l Conf. Very Large Data Bases,* 1990, pp. 507-518.

[EPPI91] J.L. Eppinger, L.B. Mummert, and A. Spector, eds., *Camelot and Avalon, A Distributed Transaction Facility,* Morgan Kaufmann, San Mateo, Calif., 1991.

[FARR89] A.A. Farrag and M.T. Özsu, "Using Semantic Knowledge of Transactions to Increase Concurrency," *ACM Trans. Database Systems,* Vol. 14, No. 4, Dec. 1989, pp. 503-525.

[FREY87] C. Freytag, "A Rule-Based View of Query Optimization," *Proc. ACM SIGMOD Int'l Conf. Management Data,* ACM Press, New York, N.Y., 1987, pp. 173-180.

[GALL84] H. Gallaire, J. Minker, and J.-M. Nicolas, "Logic and Databases: A Deductive Approach," *ACM Computing Surveys,* Vol. 16, No. 2, June 1984, pp. 153-186.

[GARC87] H. Garcia-Molina and K. Salem, "Sagas," *Proc. ACM SIGMOD Int'l Conf. Management Data,* ACM Press, New York, N.Y., 1987, pp. 249-259.

[GARC88] H. Garcia-Molina and B. Kogan, "Node Autonomy in Distributed Systems," *Proc. Int'l Symp. Databases Parallel and Distributed Systems,* IEEE Computer Soc. Press, Los Alamitos, Calif., 1988.

[GARC90a] H. Garcia-Molina and B. Lindsay, "Research Directions for Distributed Databases," *IEEE Q. Bull. Database Eng.,* Vol. 13, No. 4, Dec. 1990, pp. 12-17.

[GARC90b] H. Garcia-Molina et al., "Coordinating Multi-Transaction Activities," Tech. Report CS-TR-247-90, Princeton Univ., Princeton, N.J., Feb. 1990.

[GARD90] G. Gardarin and P. Valduriez, "ESQL: An Extended SQL with Object and Deductive Capabilities," *Proc. Int'l Conf. Database and Expert System Applications,* 1990.

[GEOR90] D. Georgakopoulos, *Transaction Management in Multidatabase Systems,* doctoral thesis, Univ. of Houston, Dept. of Computer Science, Houston, Texas, 1990.

[GEOR91] D. Georgakopoulos, "Multidatabase Recoverability and Recovery," *Proc. First Int'l Workshop Interoperability Multidatabase Systems,* IEEE Computer Soc. Press, Los Alamitos, Calif., 1991, pp. 348-355.

[GIFF79] D.K. Gifford, "Weighted Voting for Replicated Data." *Proc. Seventh ACM Symp. Operating System Principles,* ACM Press, New York, N.Y., 1979, pp. 150-159.

[GIFF88] D.K. Gifford, R.M. Needham, and M.D. Schroeder, "The Cedar File System," *Comm. ACM,* Vol. 31, No. 3, Mar. 1988, pp. 288-298.

[GRAE88] G. Graefe and D. Maier, "Query Optimization in Object-Oriented Database Systems: A Prospectus," in *Advances in Object Oriented Database Systems,* K.R. Dittrich, ed., Springer-Verlag, New York, N.Y., 1988, pp. 358-363.

[GRAY79] J. Gray, "Notes on Data Base Operating Systems," in *Operating Systems: An Advanced Course,* R. Bayer, R.M. Graham, and G. Seegmüller, eds., Springer-Verlag, New York, N.Y., 1979, pp. 393-481.

[GRAY85] J. Gray, "Why Do Computers Stop and What Can Be Done about It?," Tech. Report 85-7, Tandem Computers, Inc., Cupertino, Calif., 1985.

[GRAY89] J. Gray, "Transparency in Its Place — The Case against Transparent Access to Geographically Distributed Data," Tech. Report TR89.1, Tandem Computers, Inc., Cupertino, Calif., 1989.

[GRIE88] I. Grief, ed., *Computer-Supported Cooperative Work: A Book of Readings,* Morgan Kaufmann, San Mateo, Calif., 1988.

[GRUB91] O. Gruber and P. Valduriez, "Object Management in Parallel Database Servers," in *Data Management and Parallel Processing,* P. Valduriez, ed., Chapman and Hall, London, UK, 1991.

[HART88]   B. Hart, S. Danforth, and P. Valduriez, "Parallelizing FAD: A Database Programming Language," *Proc. Int'l Symp. Databases Parallel and Distributed Systems,* IEEE Computer Soc. Press, Los Alamitos, Calif., 1988, pp. 72-79.

[HASK88]   R. Haskin et al., "Recovery Management in QuickSilver," *ACM Trans. Computer Systems,* Vol. 6, No. 1, Feb. 1988, pp. 82-108.

[HEDD88]   A.A. Heddaya, "Managing Event-Based Replication for Abstract Data Types in Distributed Systems," doctoral thesis, Aiken Computation Lab., Harvard Univ., Cambridge, Mass., 1988 (available as Tech. Report TR-20-88).

[HEIL90]   S. Heiler and S. Zdonik, "Object Views: Extending the Vision," *Proc. Sixth Int'l Conf. Data Eng.,* IEEE Computer Soc. Press, Los Alamitos, Calif., 1990, pp. 86-93.

[HERL86]   M. Herlihy, "A Quorum-Consensus Replication Method," *ACM Trans. Computer Systems,* Vol. 4, No. 1, Feb. 1986, pp. 32-53.

[IOAN90]   Y.E. Ioannidis and Y.C. Kang, "Randomized Algorithms for Optimizing Large Join Queries," *Proc. ACM SIGMOD Int'l Conf. Management Data,* ACM Press, New York, N.Y., 1990, pp. 312-321.

[KEMP90]   A. Kemper and G. Moerkotte, "Access Support in Object Bases," *Proc. ACM SIGMOD Int'l Conf. Management Data,* ACM Press, New York, N.Y., 1990, pp. 364-386.

[KHOS87]   S. Khoshafian and P. Valduriez, "Sharing, Persistence and Object-Orientation, a Database Perspective," *Proc. Int'l Workshop Database Programming Languages,* 1987, pp. 181-205.

[KHOS89]   S. Khoshafian and P. Valduriez, "A Parallel Container Model for Data Intensive Applications," *Proc. Int'l Workshop Database Machines,* 1989, pp. 156-170.

[KIER90]   G. Kiernan, C. De Maindreville, and E. Simon, "Making Deductive Database a Practical Technology: A Step Forward," *Proc. ACM SIGMOD Int'l Conf. Management Data,* ACM Press, New York, N.Y., 1990, pp. 237-246.

[KIM89]   W. Kim and F.H. Lochovsky, eds., *Object-Oriented Concepts, Databases, and Applications,* ACM Press, New York, N.Y., 1989.

[KIM90]   W. Kim et al., "Architecture of the ORION Next-Generation Database System," *IEEE Trans. Knowledge and Data Eng.,* Vol. 2, No. 1, Mar. 1990, pp. 109-124.

[KORT88]   H.F. Korth, "Optimization of Object-Retrieval Queries," in *Advances in Object Oriented Database Systems,* K.R. Dittrich, ed., Springer-Verlag, New York, N.Y., 1988, pp. 352-357.

[KUIJ90]   H. Van Kuijk, F. Pijpers, and P. Apers, "Multilevel Query Optimization in Distributed Database Systems," *Proc. Int'l Conf. Computing and Information,* 1990, pp. 295-300.

[LANZ90]   R. Lanzelotte and P. Valduriez, "Extending the Search Strategy in a Query Optimizer," 1990.

[LECL88]   C.L. Cluse, P. Richard, and F. Velez, "O2: An Object-Oriented Data Model," *Proc. ACM SIGMOD Int'l Conf. Management Data,* ACM Press, New York, N.Y., 1988, pp. 424-433.

[LISK88]   B. Liskov, "Distributed Programming in Argus," *Comm. ACM,* Vol. 31, No. 3, Mar. 1988, pp. 300-312.

[LISK86]   B. Liskov and R. Ladin, "Highly Available Distributed Services and Fault-Tolerant Distributed Garbage Collection," *Proc. ACM Symp. Principles Distributed Computing,* ACM Press, New York, N.Y., 1986, pp. 29-39.

[LITW88]   W. Litwin, "From Database Systems to Multidatabase Systems: Why and How," *Proc. British Nat'l Conf. Databases (BNCOD 6),* Cambridge Univ. Press, Cambridge, UK, 1988, pp. 161-188.

[LITW87]   W. Litwin and A. Abdellatif, "An Overview of the Multidatabase Manipulation Language — MDL," *Proc. IEEE,* Vol. 75, No. 5, May 1987, pp. 621-631.

[LYNC86]   N. Lynch and M. Merritt, "Introduction to the Theory of Nested Transactions," Tech. Report MIT/LCS/TR-367, Laboratory for Computer Science, MIT, Cambridge, Mass., July 1986.

[MAIE87]   D. Maier and J. Stein, "Development and Implementation of an Object-Oriented DBMS," in *Research Directions in Object-Oriented Programming,* B. Shriver and P. Wegner, eds., MIT Press, Cambridge, Mass., 1987, pp. 355-392.

[MANO90] F. Manola, "Object-Oriented Knowledge Bases — Parts I and II," *AI Expert,* Vol. 5, No. 3, Mar. 1990, pp. 26-36, and Vol. 5, No. 4, Apr. 1990, pp. 46-57.

[MCCA89] D.R. Mccarthy and U. Dayal, "The Architecture of an Active Data Base Management System," *Proc. ACM SIGMOD Int'l Conf. Management Data,* ACM Press, New York, N.Y., 1989, pp. 215-224.

[MINO82] T. Minoura and G. Wiederhold, "Resilient Extended True-Copy Token Scheme for a Distributed Database System," *IEEE Trans. Software Eng.,* Vol. SE-8, No. 3, May 1982, pp. 173-189.

[MOSS85] E. Moss, *Nested Transactions,* MIT Press, Cambridge, Mass., 1985.

[MOTR81] A. Motro and P. Buneman, "Constructing Superviews," *Proc. ACM SIGMOD Int'l Conf. Management Data,* ACM Press, New York, N.Y., 1981, pp. 56-64.

[MURO85] S. Muro et al., "Evaluation of File Redundancy in Distributed Database Systems," *IEEE Trans. Software Eng.,* Vol. SE-11, No. 2, Feb. 1985, pp. 199-205.

[NECH85] P.M. Neches, "The Anatomy of a Data Base Computer System," *Digest of Papers, Spring COMPCON 85,* IEEE Computer Soc. Press, Los Alamitos, Calif., 1985, pp. 252-254.

[OSBO88] S.L. Osborn, "Identity, Equality and Query Optimization," in *Advances in Object Oriented Database Systems,* K.R. Dittrich, ed., Springer-Verlag, New York, N.Y., 1988, pp. 346-351.

[OZSO87] Z.M. Ozsoyoglu and N. Zhou, "Distributed Query Processing in Broadcasting Local Area Networks," *Proc. 20th Hawaii Int'l Conf. System Sciences,* IEEE Computer Soc. Press, Los Alamitos, Calif., 1987, pp. 419-429.

[OZSU90a] M.T. Özsu and D. Meechan, "Join Processing Heuristics in Relational Database Systems," *Information Systems,* Vol. 15, No. 4, 1990, pp. 429-444.

[OZSU90b] M.T. Özsu and D. Meechan, "Finding Heuristics for Processing Selection Queries in Relational Database Systems," *Information Systems,* Vol. 15, No. 3, 1990, pp. 359-373.

[OZSU91] M.T. Özsu and P. Valduriez, *Principles of Distributed Database Systems,* Prentice-Hall, Englewood Cliffs, N.J., 1991.

[RASH89] R. Rashid et al., "Mach: A Foundation for Open Systems — A Position Paper," *Proc. Second Workshop Workstation Operating Systems (WWOS-II),* IEEE Computer Soc. Press, Los Alamitos, Calif., 1989, pp. 109-113.

[RENE87] R. van Renesse et al., "Connecting RPC-Based Distributed Systems Using Wide-Area Networks," *Proc. Seventh Int'l Conf. Distributed Computing Systems,* IEEE Computer Soc. Press, Los Alamitos, Calif., 1987, pp. 28-34.

[SCHE90a] H.-J. Schek et al., "The DASDBS Project: Objectives, Experiences, and Future Prospects," *IEEE Trans. Knowledge and Data Eng.,* Vol. 2, No. 1, Mar. 1990, pp. 25-43.

[SCHE90b] P. Scheurmann and C. Yu, eds., "Report of the Workshop on Heterogeneous Database Systems," *IEEE Q. Bull. Database Eng.,* Vol. 13, No. 4, Dec. 1990, pp. 3-11.

[SELL88] T.K. Sellis, "Multiple Query Optimization," *ACM Trans. Database Systems,* Vol. 13, No. 1, Mar. 1988, pp. 23-52.

[SHAP90] M. Shapiro, O. Gruber, and D. Plainfosse, "A Garbage Detection Protocol for Realistic Distributed Object-Support Systems," Research Report No. 1320, INRIA, Rocquencourt, France, 1990.

[SHAW89] G. Shaw and S.B. Zdonik, "Object-Oriented Queries: Equivalence and Optimization," *Proc. First Int'l Conf. Deductive and Object-Oriented Databases,* 1989, pp. 264-278.

[SHET90] A. Sheth and J. Larson, "Federated Databases: Architectures and Integration," *Proc. 16th Int'l Conf. Very Large Data Bases,* 1990, pp. 183-236.

[SILB90] A. Silberschatz, M. Stonebraker, and J.D. Ullman, eds., "Database Systems: Achievements and Opportunities: Report of the NSF Invitational Workshop on the Future of Database Systems Research," Tech. Report TR-90-22, Dept. of Computer Sciences, Univ. of Texas at Austin, Austin, Tex., 1990.

[SIMO86] E. Simon and P. Valduriez, "Integrity Control Distributed Database Systems," *Proc. 19th Hawaii Int'l Conf. System Sciences,* IEEE Computer Soc. Press, Los Alamitos, Calif., 1986, pp. 622-632.

[STON81] M. Stonebraker, "Operating System Support for Database Management," *Comm. ACM,* Vol. 24, No. 7, July 1981, pp. 412-418.

[STON88] M. Stonebraker, *Readings in Database Systems,* Morgan Kaufmann, San Mateo, Calif., 1988.

[STON89] M. Stonebraker, "Future Trends in Database Systems," *IEEE Trans. Knowledge and Data Eng.,* Vol. 1, No. 1, Mar. 1989, pp. 33-44.

[STON90a] M. Stonebraker, "Architecture of Future Data Base Systems," *IEEE Q. Bull. Database Eng.,* Vol. 13, No. 4, Dec. 1990, pp. 18-23.

[STON90b] M. Stonebraker et al., "Third-Generation Data Base System Manifesto," *ACM SIGMOD Record,* Vol. 19, No. 3, Sept. 1990, pp. 31-44.

[STON90c] M. Stonebraker, L.A. Rowe, and M. Hiroshama, "The Implementation of POSTGRES," *IEEE Trans. Knowledge and Data Eng.,* Vol. 2, No. 1, Mar. 1990, pp. 125-142.

[STOY90] A. Stoyenko, "A General RPC for Model-Level Heterogeneous RPC Interoperability," *Proc. Second IEEE Symp. Parallel and Distributed Processing,* IEEE Computer Soc. Press, Los Alamitos, Calif., 1990, pp. 668-675.

[STRA90] D.D. Straube and M.T. Özsu, "Queries and Query Processing in Object-Oriented Database Systems," *ACM Trans. Information Systems,* Vol. 8, No. 4, Oct. 1990, pp. 387-430.

[TAND87] Tandem Performance Group, "NonStop SQL — A Distributed High-Performance, High-Availability Implementation of SQL," *Proc. Int'l Workshop High Performance Transaction Systems,* 1987.

[TAND88] Tandem Performance Group, "A Benchmark of Non-Stop SQL on the Debit Credit Transaction," *Proc. ACM SIGMOD Int'l Conf. Management Data,* ACM Press, New York, N.Y., 1988, pp. 337-341.

[TANE90] A.S. Tanenbaum, "Experiences with the Amoeba Distributed Operating System," *Comm. ACM,* Vol. 33, No. 12, Dec. 1990, pp. 46-63.

[TAYL87] R.W. Taylor, "Data Server Architectures: Experiences and Lessons," *Proc. CIPS (Canadian Information Processing Soc.), Edmonton '87 Conf.,* 1987, pp. 334-342.

[THOM79] R.H. Thomas, "A Majority Consensus Approach to Concurrency Control for Multiple Copy Databases," *ACM Trans. Database Systems,* Vol. 4, No. 2, June 1979, pp. 180-209.

[VALD91] P. Valduriez, ed., *Data Management and Parallel Processing,* Chapman and Hall, London, UK, 1991.

[VALD84] P. Valduriez and G. Gardarin, "Join and Semi-Join Algorithms for a Multi-Processor Database Machine," *ACM Trans. Database Systems,* Vol. 9, No. 1, Mar. 1984, pp. 133-161.

[VALD88] P. Valduriez and S. Khoshafian, "Parallel Evaluation of the Transitive Closure of a Database Relation," *Int'l J. Parallel Programming,* Vol. 12, No. 1, Feb. 1988, pp. 19-42.

[VALD89] P. Valduriez and S. Danforth, "Query Optimization in Database Programming Languages," *Proc. First Int'l Conf. Deductive and Object-Oriented Databases,* 1989, pp. 516-534.

[WAH85] B.W. Wah and Y.N. Lien, "Design of Distributed Databases on Local Computer Systems," *IEEE Trans. Software Eng.,* Vol. SE-11, No. 7, July 1985, pp. 609-619.

[WEIH88] W.E. Weihl, "Commutativity-Based Concurrency Control for Abstract Data Types," *IEEE Trans. Computers,* Vol. 37, No. 12, Dec. 1988, pp. 1488-1505.

[WEIH89] W.E. Weihl, "The Impact of Recovery on Concurrency Control," *Proc. Eighth ACM SIGACT-SIGMOD-SIGART Symp. Principles Database Systems,* ACM Press, New York, N.Y., 1989, pp. 259-269.

[WEIK86] G. Weikum, "Pros and Cons of Operating System Transactions for Data Base Systems," *Proc. Fall Joint Computer Conf.,* IEEE Computer Soc. Press, Los Alamitos, Calif., 1986, pp. 1219-1225.

[WOLF90] O. Wolfson and A. Ozeri, "A New Paradigm for Parallel and Distributed Rule-Processing," *Proc. ACM SIGMOD Int'l Conf. Management Data,* ACM Press, New York, N.Y., 1990, pp. 133-142.

[WOLS90]   A. Wolski and J. Veijalainen, "2PC Agent Method: Achieving Serializability in Presence of Failures in a Heterogeneous Multidatabase," *Proc. Int'l Conf. Databases, Parallel Architectures, and Their Applications,* 1990, pp. 321-330.

[WULF81]   W.A. Wulf, R. Levin, and S.P. Harbison, *HYDRA/C.mmp : An Experimental Computer System,* McGraw-Hill, New York, N.Y., 1981.

[YOSH85]   M. Yoshida et al., "Time and Cost Evaluation Schemes of Multiple Copies of Data in Distributed Database Systems," *IEEE Trans. Software Eng.,* Vol. SE-11, No. 9, Sept. 1985, pp. 954-958.

[ZDON90]   S. Zdonik and D. Maier, eds., *Readings in Object-Oriented Database Systems,* Morgan Kaufmann, San Mateo, Calif., 1990.

A Unified Approach to Distributed Concurrency Control

T he problem of distributed concurrency control has received much attention and many protocols have appeared in the literature [3], [6], [11]. Recently, research efforts have focused on ways to increase concurrency —beyond the level that the conventional protocols permit— by utilizing the semantics of applications [9], [10], [12], [13], [14], [16], [18], [19], [23], [25], [26], [27]. One approach in this direction suggests the use of "typed" data or *objects* [12], [13], [18], [23], [25], [26], [27], which are instances of abstract data types on which "high-level" operations — rich in semantic information — can be defined. Choosing the types that are most natural for an application makes it possible for greater concurrency to be obtained than that obtainable when applications are restricted to using only the types provided by the system (for example, database relations or files) with *read* and *write* operations only.

We have adopted the notion of using *transactions* as a means of controlling concurrency and failures. Transactions are widely accepted for structuring distributed computations in which the preservation of data consistency is essential. Computations in the form of transactions are guaranteed to execute completely or not at all — a property known as *failure atomicity*— and they appear to execute serially even if they are overlapped in actual execution — a property known as *serializability*. The purpose of *concurrency control* is to ensure serializability. In the literature, the properties of failure atomicity and serializability are often referred to by the term *atomicity*, and the data objects providing these properties are called *atomic objects* [11], [18], [25], [27].

The main concurrency control protocols for distributed environments fall into three classes [3]:

- *Two-phase locking protocols*,
- *Time-stamp-ordering protocols*, and
- *Optimistic protocols*.

Many variations of these protocols have been designed to suit particular applications. These protocols first appeared in the context of databases and are based on syntactic information only. They cannot be used in an object-based environment

P. Anastassopoulos and

Jean Dollimore

without modifications. A simple expansion to support high-level operations is not sufficient if operations are eventually classified into *readers* and *writers*. Further modifications are needed in order to provide the increased concurrency permitted by the semantics of objects; these modifications are summarized in the subsections entitled "The notion of *conflict*," "Eliminating the conflicts between operations," and "Execution, serialization, and commit orders need not be the same."

Which of the three main classes of protocols (or which variation thereof) is most suitable for the needs of a particular application? This important practical question has to be answered at design time. Once the protocol has been chosen, the objects are implemented to provide that concurrency control protocol. Unfortunately, no protocol is strictly better than the others; this is reflected in performance-evaluation work, which often yields contradictory results and conclusions [25]. If the chosen protocol gives unsatisfactory performance, the implementation has to be redesigned. Changes in the semantics of an application as the needs change may result in protocols being redesigned in order to achieve the level of concurrency required. This may in turn necessitate rewriting the application programs, if the details of a concurrency control protocol are not hidden from the application. Redesigning implementations from scratch is not desirable for the following reasons: It is an expensive task, it wastes all the previous effort, and every new implementation is prone to errors.

The model we propose for concurrency control can exploit the semantics of an application. Part of the semantic knowledge can be captured by the types of objects used and, in particular, their behavior in the presence of concurrency. We claim that our model can allow for the maximum concurrency conceived for an object of a certain type and can introduce a uniform pattern in implementing atomic objects that facilitates the task of writing implementations. But most importantly, the model is "flexible" enough to adapt to changes in the semantics of objects. It is not designed for any particular semantics, but instead it can understand and utilize semantic information given to it by the application programmer in a specification language. When new semantic knowledge needs to be provided to objects in order to increase concurrency, all that is necessary is to change the objects' specifications. No redesign of implementations is necessary; therefore, different levels of concurrency can be achieved with minimum effort of the application programmer.

The two main problems that we consider in this paper are

- Synchronizing operations invoked by transactions on objects and
- Synchronizing transactions.

The execution of transactions should satisfy the correctness criterion of serializability [20]. An important aspect of flexibility is the provision of more than one protocol. Our model can realize a wide range of protocols, including the three main classes of concurrency control protocols mentioned above as well as "hybrid" protocols that combine characteristics of the three main classes. The implementation of different protocols for transaction execution captures another part of the semantics of an application. Different protocols can be implemented when the right specifications for the synchronization of transactions are chosen. These specifications, which are provided by the application programmer, are referred to in this paper as *strategies* to distinguish them from specifications of objects.

Sometimes, more than one protocol must be employed within the same application at the same time in order for the semantics of that application to be best utilized [13], [14]. Different transactions may "wish" to run under different protocols. [21]. Objects may also "choose" different concurrency control protocols [3], [5]. At an even finer granularity, it may also be beneficial for different operations defined on objects of the same type to be executed using different concurrency control protocols [13]. Clearly, the requirement for more than one protocol to be employed within the same application at the same time cannot be met by an attempt to implement more than one protocol in a system in the usual way (that is, by associating locks and time stamps with each object for every operation defined on it), and a unified model is needed. In our model, different protocols can coexist within the same application; this is made possible by the selection of a mixture of specified strategies with the desired characteristics.

In addition to the problems of synchronizing operations invoked by transactions on objects and synchronizing transactions, we also consider the problem of the *incompatibility* of protocols. Of the problems we discuss, this is perhaps the most serious. Protocol incompatibility arises when several protocols are implemented at the same time: Different protocols may impose different relative orderings on transactions. This problem is overcome by the "scheduler" module being separated into two modules: one to perform the synchronization of operations invoked on each object and the other to perform the synchronization of transactions.

Below, we begin by describing our model. Then, we discuss how operations invoked on objects are synchronized according to the specifications given and we explain synchronization of transactions. Next, we demonstrate how to implement existing protocols or combinations thereof, and we show that — under our model — different protocols can coexist within the same application. We conclude by contrasting related work. The presentation here is rather informal; a formal presentation of this material was made by Anastassopoulos [2].

The system model

Our system consists of *objects* and *transactions*. Objects are dispersed over a number of sites interconnected through a communication network. Each object supports a set of operations, which are the only means of manipulating it. A transaction is a collection of operations invoked on one or more objects. Any operation invoked by a transaction on an object may initiate a new (sub)transaction in the general case. In turn, the operations of (sub)transactions may initiate new (sub)transactions, and so on. By allowing such arbitrary nesting, we may permit concurrency within a transaction. Our unified model can support nested transactions [17], [22]; however, for simplicity — and because our main points can be expressed using one-level transactions — we focus in this paper on transactions without structure. We view transactions as sequential processes and require that the execution of transactions be *serializable*; that is, transaction execution must be computationally equivalent to a serial execution. This means that transactions should *appear* to execute in a *global serialization order*, although they run concurrently.

Transaction managers

In our system model, transactions access objects through intermediate modules, called *transaction managers* (TMs), rather than accessing objects directly. TMs control the execution of transactions. They invoke operations on objects at various sites and, at the final stage of execution, perform a *commitment protocol* [11] to ensure that the effects of a transaction will be applied to every participating object, despite failures (see Figure 1). Also, TMs must determine the serialization order of transactions. We represent the serialization order by time stamps, which are unique identifiers similar in content to the time stamps discussed by Lamport [15]. Time stamps are assigned to transactions by their TMs, at the latest before the transactions commit. When two transactions T obtain time stamps ts, we can determine their relative ordering in the serialization order: We say that transaction T_i *precedes* T_j in the serialization order if the time stamp of T_i is smaller than the time stamp of T_j — that is, if $ts(T_i) < ts(T_j)$.

The objects are *atomic* and provide operations to manipulate their state. As each operation is invoked, it is placed in a queue of invocations, where it waits until is executed (see Figure 1). The *scheduler module* of an object synchronizes the operations invoked by transactions, according to the

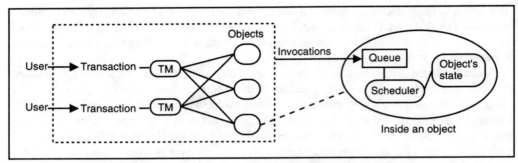

Figure 1. Transaction managers (TMs) and objects.

object's specification. Objects' specifications are provided by the application programmer. However, the serialization order of transactions is not determined by the *object schedulers*—as it is in previous models [18], [25], [27]—but rather is determined by the TMs. By suggesting, on request, acceptable relative orderings of transactions, object schedulers may assist TMs in selecting the appropriate time stamps.

With respect to the property of failure atomicity, the objects must guarantee that the partial effects of aborted transactions are *undone* and the effects of committed transactions can survive failures. For this purpose, the objects support the *precommit*, *commit*, and *abort* operations, which are invoked by the TMs at the final stage of the execution of transactions during the commitment protocol. To guarantee that the effects of committed transactions are not lost in the presence of failures, the system should use replication either at a lower level (by providing the abstraction of stable storage) or at a higher lever (by maintaining copies of the data at different sites). (Replication at a higher level, which is usually addressed by implementing *replica control algorithms* on top of the concurrency control protocols, is not considered in this paper.) We assume that the state of objects, which is a result of committed transactions, is recorded in stable storage.

Objects and their specifications

An object belongs to some *type* and consists of a set of possible *values* and a set of *operations*, some of which may be partial. An object is specified completely if we define

(1) The domain of possible states,
(2) The object's initial state, and
(3) The rules that determine for each operation
  • Whether the operation can be applied to the object and
  • The new state that is produced.

Every operation when executed produces a *response*. The response to an operation could be either the normal response of *ok* or an exception. If the operation-response pairs are applied to an object in some sequence that causes a state transition from the initial state to another state through other intermediate states, all of which belong to the domain of possible states, we say that the sequence in question is *valid* and the implementation of the object meets that object's *specification*.

When transactions run concurrently and failures may occur in the system, we do not consider the actual sequence of the operation-response pairs executed on an object, but rather we consider the sequence of the operation-response pairs of committed transactions executed in the global serialization

```
        deposit (amt: real)
                requires: -
                effect: acc_bal ← acc_bal + amt
                exceptions: -

        withdraw (amt: real); signals → "insufficient funds"
                requires: acc_bal ≥ amt
                effect: acc_bal ← acc_bal - amt
                exceptions: signals → "insufficient funds"

        get_balance (); returns: (acc_bal: real)
                requires: -
                effect: returns acc_bal
                exceptions: -
```

Figure 2. Specification of *bank_account* in a sequential environment.

order. (Recall that the serialization order of transactions is always determined prior to their commitment.) An implementation of an object meets its specification if this hypothetical sequence is valid. Therefore, transactions are allowed to commit only if their results, when added to the sequence of committed transactions in their serialization order, produce a valid sequence.

To illustrate the above with an example, we consider the specification of an object of type *bank_account* in a sequential environment (see Figure 2). The set of possible states of the account is any nonnegative real number. The current state of the account is given by its balance, denoted by *acc_bal*. The initial state of *acc_bal* is zero and the set of operations defined is *deposit(amt)*, *withdraw(amt)*, and *get_balance()*. For each of these operations, we describe the set of states on which they can be defined and the rules that determine the states they produce when applied to the object.

In our specifications, we describe procedures that raise exceptions by the *signals* clause, which can be omitted if there are no exceptions. The *requires* clause states the conditions under which the operation produces the normal effect, stated in the *effect* clause. If the constraints are not satisfied, the operation will not have any effect and will signal an exception. A sequence of operation-response pairs (on the initial state with zero balance) is valid if the responses returned to operations conform to the above specification. For example, the sequence *deposit(20)/ok, withdraw(30)/insuf, deposit(30)/ok, withdraw(40)/ok* is a valid sequence, but the sequence *deposit(40)/ok, withdraw(30)/ok, withdraw(20)/ok* is not.

In the presence of concurrency and failures, we want the sequence of operation-response pairs of committed transactions, when applied in the global serialization order, to be valid. Operations of aborted transactions are ignored. For example, if the serialization order for the above set of operations is *deposit(20)/ok, deposit(30)/ok, withdraw(30)/insuf, withdraw(40)/ok*, the responses returned to the operations do not meet the object's specification. To ensure that the responses to operations are such that only valid sequences are produced, we must also describe the kinds of concurrent executions permitted and the way the object will handle failures as part of the object's specification.

Synchronization of operations

The synchronization of operations of a particular object in our unified model is performed by the object scheduler. Its main task is to determine the "conflicts" between operations and suggest an ordering for the operations in which they could be accepted. The conflicts between operations are determined by the object's specification for a concurrent environment. Semantic knowledge about the operations may be exploited in order to reduce the number of conflicts. The actions taken to resolve conflicts are specified in the strategies used for the synchronization of transactions. The strategy can be *delay*, *accept*, or *abort* the operation, along with some preconditions that represent the conflict to be resolved. (Strategies are explained in more detail in the section entitled "Synchronization of transactions.")

The notion of *conflict*

Concurrency control protocols attain serializability by considering "conflicts" between pairs of operations [3], [7], [20]. Conflicts may arise between operations invoked on the same object only. When a conflict is found, actions are taken to resolve it. Informally, two operations conflict if the observations of the one are no longer valid because of the other or vice versa. In the conventional database protocols, two operations conflict if at least one of them is a *write*. An alternative definition of *conflict* that is used by most "pessimistic" concurrency control protocols (that is, locking and time-stamp-ordering protocols) is based on the notion of *commutativity* [6], [26]: Two operations *commute* if the result of their execution does not depend on the order in which they were processed. Such operations can proceed concurrently.

The above definition of *conflict* and the equivalent definition of *commutativity* are not suitable for our unified model, which intends to integrate pessimistic and optimistic protocols. We introduce a more primitive relationship for describing conflicts between operations: the *invalidate* relationship. An operation *p invalidates* another operation *q* if the sequences $s_1 p s_2 s_3$ and $s_1 s_2 q s_3$ are valid, but the sequence $s_1 p s_2 q s_3$ is not (where s_1, s_2, and s_3 are sequences of operation-response pairs invoked on the same object). In other words, operation *p* causes the observations of *q* to become incorrect, so that the response produced to *q* no longer meets the specification of the object. The definition applies even when some (or all) of the sequences s_1, s_2, and s_3 are empty. Based on the definition of the *invalidate* relationship, we can also define the complementary relationship *invalidated_by*: An operation *q* is *invalidated_by p* if *p* invalidates *q*. Informally, an operation *q* is *invalidated_by p* if its observation is not valid because of *p*, with the response produced by *q* therefore being no longer correct.

The *invalidate* (or *invalidated_by*) relationship can describe an asymmetry that is common between operations: namely, that one operation invalidates the other but not vice versa. For example, a *write* invalidates a *read*, but a *read* does not invalidate a *write*. This asymmetry between two operations suggests a *possible* way to run them concurrently (based on the same initial state). We can permit such operations to run concurrently if we know their serialization order or if the operations are executed under a relatively optimistic protocol. Other operations are related with a symmetric relationship (for example, a *dequeue* operation defined on a FIFO queue invalidates another *dequeue* operation). In the conventional notion of *conflict* (and in that of *commutativity*), the difference between asymmetric and symmetric relationships cannot be distinguished. In the discussion that follows, the word *conflict* is used to indicate that two operations are related by *invalidate*, *invalidated_by*, or both.

Eliminating the conflicts between operations

Concurrency control mechanisms impose restrictions on concurrency when conflicts between pairs of operations arise. When considering conflicts between operations, it is advantageous to use the semantic knowledge about a type in order to decide whether or not the conflicting operations can run concurrently. There are operations that under certain conditions conflict while under other conditions do not conflict. Distinguishing between such cases is important in order for operations to be permitted to run concurrently when possible. To eliminate conflicts, we may have to consider the arguments of the operations invoked, the responses returned, and/or the state (current or future) of objects.

Table 1. Conflicts between operations _m_ and _n_ defined on a _bank_account_ object.

n \ m	deposit	withdraw	get_balance
deposit		X	X
withdraw		X	X

The arguments of operations may be used to indicate which parts of the object are to be accessed. Operations that access different parts of the same object do not conflict. It is possible to allow such operations to run concurrently and, in this way, to implement finer granularity schemes. For example, in an object of type _directory_, two operations that modify two different entries can run concurrently. Multiple granularities can be implemented logically within an object in a similar way.

In Table 1, we consider the conflicts between operations _m_ and _n_ defined on a _bank_account_ object. We describe conflicts in terms of the _invalidate_ and _invalidated_by_ relationships in order to distinguish between operations related with an asymmetric relationship and those related with a symmetric one. In the table, the rows represent the relationship _n invalidates m_ and the columns represent the relationship _m is invalidated_by n_.

A _deposit_ operation and a _withdraw_ operation can invalidate another _withdraw_ operation or _get_balance_ operation. A _withdraw_ operation may be invalidated by either a _deposit_ operation or another _withdraw_ operation. We can reduce the number of conflicts if we consider operations with respect to operation-response pairs (of previously executed operations). Thus, a _deposit_ operation can invalidate a _withdraw/insuf_ pair and a _withdraw_ operation can invalidate a _withdraw/ok_ pair. But a _withdraw_ operation may be invalidated by any _deposit/ok_ or _withdraw/ok_ pair.

When we consider the response to an operation before the latter is synchronized, we can determine more precisely the operation-response pairs in conflict with it. This additional knowledge may result in a further increase in concurrency. For example, if the balance of an account cannot cover the amount to be withdrawn, the response to a _withdraw_ operation is _insuf_. The _withdraw/insuf_ pair may be invalidated by a _deposit/ok_ pair. If the response to a _withdraw_ operation is _ok_, the _withdraw/ok_ pair may be invalidated by another _withdraw/ok_ pair. This is shown in Table 2, in which we consider conflicts between operation-response pairs _m_ and _n_ defined on a _bank_account_ object. In the table, the rows represent the relationship _n invalidates m_ and the columns represent the relationship _m is invalidated_by n_.

More concurrency is possible if we consider future states of the object that may be produced when active operations commit. The conflicts marked with an asterisk in Table 2 may be eliminated in this way. For example, two _withdraw/ok_ operations do not conflict and may be allowed to run concurrently if the balance can cover both of them. To check if the balance can cover both withdrawals, we have to take into account other pending withdrawals. If all active withdrawals, when applied to the current balance, leave a sufficient amount of money for the withdrawal in question, the latter will neither be invalidated by nor invalidate another withdrawal. Similarly, a _deposit_ operation may invalidate a _withdraw(k)/insuf_, where _k_ is a real number that represents some amount of money, if the deposit credits the balance by an amount that could cover this withdrawal.

Execution, serialization, and commit orders need not be the same

In the standard concurrency control protocols [3], [14], _pairs_ of operations are synchronized and subsequently executed in the order in which they were invoked on objects. When operations are found to conflict, some actions must be taken to resolve the conflicts. The final state of the objects depends on the order in which operations were executed. However, the requirement that the execution order

Table 2. Conflicts between operation-response pairs _m_ and _n_ defined on a _bank_account_ object.

_n_ \ _m_	_deposit/ok_	_withdraw/ok_	_withdraw/insuf_	_get_balance_
deposit/ok			X*	X
withdraw/ok		X*		X

of operations correspond to their serialization order may be relaxed, and operations may be executed in an order that does not necessarily correspond to the serialization order of their transactions. That is, an operation executed after another one may precede it in the serialization order. The models used by Herlihy [12], [13] and Weihl [25], [27] make such a distinction between execution order and serialization order.

It is recognized that more operations will be able to run concurrently if we relax the requirement for the execution order of operations to correspond to their serialization order. To demonstrate this, we consider an empty FIFO queue and the sequence of operations _enqueue(a)_, _dequeue()_, and _enqueue(b)_ invoked by transactions T_1, T_2, and T_3, respectively, where _a_ and _b_ are items in the queue. Suppose that the first operation is executed. In the standard protocols, a _dequeue_ operation must wait for the _enqueue(a)_ operation to terminate since _enqueue_ and _dequeue_ operations conflict on an empty queue. The same applies to the _enqueue(b)_ operation, because _enqueue_ operations on a FIFO queue do not commute. Suppose now that the _enqueue(b)_ operation is permitted to execute concurrently with the _enqueue(a)_ operation and that transaction T_3 commits first. The _dequeue_ operation need not wait any longer but could proceed by removing item _b_ from the queue; in this case, transaction T_3 is assumed to precede transaction T_1 in the serialization order, although their operations on the FIFO queue object were executed in exactly the opposite order. Transaction T_2 must follow transaction T_3 in the serialization order. Notice that any assumption about the relative ordering of transactions T_1 and T_2 is acceptable.

As a second example, consider a _bank_account_ type where a _get_balance()_ operation is invoked after a _withdraw/ok_ has been executed earlier but has not committed yet. The _get_balance_ operation can run concurrently with the _withdraw/ok_ and return the current balance of the account, which does not reflect the changes underway by the withdrawal. That is, the _get_balance_ operation is assumed to precede _withdraw/ok_ in the serialization order, although the latter had been accepted earlier. Notice that — at the time an operation is executed — the serialization order may be known or it may not be known. In the latter case, the operation is accepted on the assumption that the serialization order, which is determined later, will be in agreement with the assumption made at the execution of the _get_balance_ operation: namely, that _get_balance()_ precedes _withdraw/ok_.

We can go one step further and distinguish the commit order of transactions from their serialization order. It is not necessary to prevent one transaction from committing its results because another transaction that precedes it in the serialization order is still active. All that is needed is to guarantee that a transaction will not observe results of other transactions that follow it in the serialization order. For instance, an _update_ transaction should not wait for a long _read-only_ transaction that precedes it in the serialization order to commit. On the other hand, a _read-only_ transaction should not access inconsistent data produced by transactions that both precede and follow it in the serialization order.

Several versions (states) of the objects must be retained in order to allow transactions to commit in an order other than their serialization order. The benefit of maintaining previous states is that the operations of different transactions can access different versions of an object. This increases concurrency. Multiversion protocols are based on this principle. Our unified model supports multiversion schemes. Furthermore, there are many applications (for example, engineering and office information) that require previous versions of objects to be available. Our unified model is able to support such applications, as well as the conventional business data-processing applications.

The history abstraction

In designing our unified model, we had several objectives. The unified model must be capable of exploiting the semantics of an application and allow for the maximum conceivable concurrency for a type. Any protocol implemented under the model should be able to recognize situations where no conflicts arise by considering the arguments of operations, the responses returned, and the state (current or future) of objects. For this purpose, the scheduler module must have, at any time, a complete view of the operations and responses of both committed and active transactions that have been executed. The operations of committed transactions, executed in the global serialization order, should produce a valid sequence, even if they were executed or committed in a different order from the serialization order. As long as only valid sequences are generated, the implementation of a type can concurrently execute as many operations as possible. The execution and commit order of transactions is immaterial.

To meet the above objectives, we use the *history abstraction* to capture the sequence of operations executed on an object, their serialization order, and their status (that is, *committed* or *active*). Every operation is represented by a separate entry in the history. The state of an object is represented by a sequence of operations of committed transactions applied to the initial state in their serialization order. This representation will result in a very long history for an object, unless the old entries in the history are removed and represented in a more compact way. We can substitute a sequence of old entries by a more "natural" representation of an object. For instance, the state of a *bank_account* object can be represented by a single value (the balance) or the state of an object of type *set* can be represented by an array of members. These representations may replace the old parts of the history only; the more recent states of the objects should be described by *history entries*. The history abstraction can be used by any instance of a type implementation, in parallel with its usual representation. For simplicity, we assume here that the whole sequence of the operations executed on an object is represented by a sequence of history entries.

Execution of operations and synchronization control. Operations invoked on an object may be executed either after they have been synchronized or without any synchronization control. In the latter case, operations have to be synchronized at a later time, but not after the corresponding transactions enter the commitment protocol. The synchronization control will locate the operations in the history that may be *invalidated_by* or may *invalidate* the one that is currently synchronized and will determine an order in which the operations are likely to be accepted at this object. We refer to this process as *scheduling*. The decision as to whether or not an operation can be accepted depends on both the conflicts encountered during scheduling and the strategy used. An operation that cannot be accepted must be either delayed and executed later or aborted. If an operation has already been executed before it is synchronized, then the operation can be either accepted or aborted.

Operations of transactions that have not been assigned time stamps (that is, their serialization order has not yet been determined) observe the most recently committed state of objects. This is the state produced by all committed transactions that have accessed an object that can be obtained by applying their operations in the serialization order. Operations with time stamps (that is, operations invoked by transactions with time stamps) are serialized according to their time stamp value and observe the state of an object produced by committed transactions with lower time stamps only. The state of objects observed in this case is not necessarily the most recently committed one. In fact, in our model, obtaining time stamps is the only way in which transactions can access previous states of objects. Also, obtaining time stamps ensures that transactions' operations access consistent states of objects (that is, that they access the state that an object had at a particular time).

The main task of the object scheduler is to determine the conflicts between operations. Submitted invocations to objects have the following structure:

op <args>	T-id/class	time stamp	strategy	schedule	return_ts

The *op <args>* field represents the operation to be invoked with possible arguments. *T-id/class* is the transaction-id of the invoking transaction and its protocol class (for example, locking and optimistic). The *time stamp* field may contain a single time stamp, if the serialization order of the transaction is known when the operation is executed. The *strategy* determines the actions that should be taken if the operation conflicts with another already in the history. (This is explained further in the section entitled "Synchronization of transactions.") *Schedule* is a Boolean variable. If its value is *true*, the operation *op* is synchronized (scheduled) first and then executed (if it can be accepted). If its value is *false*, the operation is executed without any control taking place; it will be synchronized later. The *return_ts* is also a Boolean variable. (The role of *return_ts* is explained in the subsection entitled "Detecting nonserializable executions.")

History entries. When an operation is executed, a new entry is created and inserted into the history. An entry has the following structure:

op <args>/res	T-id/class	status — execution/commit time	time stamp	strategy	before/after sets

The *op <args>/res* field contains the operation with the values of arguments (if any) and the response returned. *T-id* is the transaction identifier of the invoking transaction and its protocol class. The *status — execution/commit time* field indicates the status of the transaction and the time the operation in question was executed or committed, respectively. This is the time recorded from the local clock (it is not a "time stamp" that represents the serialization order). The status can be

- *Executed — not synchronized*, denoted by *EX*;
- *Active — serialized*, denoted by *AS*;
- *Active — not serialized*, denoted by *ANS*; or
- *Committed*, denoted by *COM*.

(The exact definitions of these terms are given in the next paragraph.) The *time stamp* field, which is discussed in more detail later, will eventually obtain a single value that represents the serialization order of the corresponding transaction. (In the section entitled "Synchronization of transactions," we explain how a single time stamp is derived.) The *before/after sets* for an operation are constructed according the concurrent specifications of that operation during the scheduling process. (See the subsubsection entitled "The *before/after sets* field of a history entry.")

When a transaction has entered the process of selecting a time stamp or has already obtained a single time stamp, we say that it has been *serialized*. Its operations have the *serialized* status. This happens by the time a transaction has entered the commitment protocol, but it could happen earlier. *Active* transactions are those that have been *executed* but not yet *committed*. Their operations are marked as *active*; that is, {active} = {EX} $\cup$ {AS} $\cup$ {ANS}. *Serialized* transactions may be *active*, but an *active* operation is not necessarily *serialized*. *Active* transactions that have been scheduled before execution may be *serialized* (that is, their status is *active—serialized* [AS]) or *not serialized* (that is, their status is *active—not serialized* [ANS]). The status of operations that have been *executed* without any synchronization control is *executed—not synchronized* (EX). The status of operations of *committed* transactions is *committed* (COM). Notice that *committed* transactions are also *serialized*, according to the definition for *serialized* given previously; that is, {serialized} = {COM} ∪ {AS}.

The entries in the history are updated when the status of transactions changes and when new operations that conflict with existing ones are synchronized. These updates are performed in an atomic way. Aborted transactions have no effect on objects, and their entries in the history are deleted when the outcome of the transaction is known. The removal of an entry from the history may have some effects on waiting or previously accepted operations. For example, waiting operations may be scheduled for execution and operations of active transactions may cease to be related to those of the aborted transactions. All these effects take place atomically when the entries of the aborted transaction are removed from the history.

This recovery scheme—namely, the removal of entries of aborted transactions—is very simple. When used in conjunction with a stable storage mechanism, it can guarantee the failure atomicity property of transactions and also that the effects of committed transactions always survive system crashes. For this, the contents of the history must be recorded to stable storage when transactions commit—in particular, just before the entries of a transaction are marked as *committed*. The copying to stable storage takes place in an atomic way and not at the same time as that at which updates to the history take place. When a system recovers from a failure, it retrieves a copy of the history from the stable storage, which should contain the effects of committed transactions and partial effects of transactions that were active at the time the failure occurred. As part of the recovery process, the entries of active transactions can be deleted before the object starts considering new operations for execution.

Operations provided by the history type. The type *history* provides a *create* operation, which creates a history without entries for an object and the set of operations listed below. The history must be enclosed in a monitor (or a similar mechanism) to guarantee that the operations are executed one at a time.

(1)   *Search (template).* This operation returns locations of entries that match with the given template. The template can be any possible value for any field or combinations thereof; for example, the template *withdraw/ok* matches all entries that correspond to successful withdrawals. The template *withdraw/ok.active* matches all entries for successful withdrawals of *active* transactions (that is, EX, AS, and ANS). The "." denotes concatenation of field values. The template can also be a set of templates (we explain later), in which case the search is repeatedly invoked with each one of the elements of the set.

(2)   *Modify (e:entry, <field=(±)value>).* This operation modifies a particular entry *e* of the history by

- Setting a specified field to a given value or
- Adding a given value to a specified field(s) or removing a given value from a specified field(s).

The "value" could take any value from the domain of possible values for a certain field (for example, the possible values for the status field are EX, AS, ANS, and COM).

(3)   *Insert (e:entry).* This operation inserts a given entry *e* into the history.

(4)   *Delete (e:entry).* This operation removes entry *e* from the history. It is invoked when a transaction aborts.

```
           deposit (amt: real)
                   requires: -
                   effect:
                                •invalidated_by: -
                                •invalidates: withdraw/insuf, get_balance
                                acc_bal ← acc_bal + amt
                   exceptions: -

           withdraw (amt: real); signals → "insufficient funds"
                   requires: acc_bal ≥ amt
                   effect:
                                •invalidated_by: withdraw/ok
                                •invalidates: withdraw/ok, get_balance
                                acc_bal ← acc_bal - amt
                   exceptions:
                                •invalidated_by: deposit/ok
                                •invalidates: -
                                signals → "insufficient funds"

       get_balance (); returns: (acc_bal: real)
                   requires: -
                   effect:
                                •invalidated_by: deposit/ok, withdraw/ok
                                •invalidates: -
                                returns acc_bal
                   exceptions: -
```

Figure 3. Concurrent specification of the conflicts defined on a *bank_account* object.

Concurrent specifications

In the subsection entitled "Objects and their specifications," we present a notation for the serial specifications of objects. In a concurrent environment, the serial specification for each operation has to be augmented with the sets *invalidated_by* and *invalidate* of the operations that respectively invalidate or are invalidated by the operation in question. These sets may contain operations (and possibly arguments) or operation-response pairs, if responses to operations are also taken into account when scheduling an operation. If the current state of an object is also considered, then the specification for an operation contains the sets *invalidated_by* and *invalidate* for every possible operation-response pair. We use the term *concurrent specifications* when we refer to specifications of objects in a concurrent environment in the discussion that follows. Figure 3 gives the concurrent specification that describes the conflicts shown in Table 2.

Future states of the object that may be produced later, when operations of currently active transactions commit, can also be taken into account to further eliminate the conflicts. Our notation can describe the concurrent executions permitted in this case, while compatibility tables cannot. The problem with compatibility tables is that they cannot describe conflicts that depend on the state of the objects. In our example, we can eliminate the conflicts between two *withdraw/ok* operations (when the balance can cover both) and the conflicts between a *deposit* operation and a *withdraw/insuf* operation (when the deposited amount cannot cover the withdrawal). For this purpose, we must enhance the specifications for the *deposit* and *withdraw* operations.

In the specification given in Figure 4, the *invalidate* and *invalidated_by* sets depend on some conditions. The object scheduler examines the history to find out which conditions hold in order to determine the right *invalidate* and *invalidated_by* for the operation that is currently being synchronized.

```
        deposit (amt: real)
                requires: -
                effect:
                            if acc_bal + changes (deposit/ok.(AS ∪ ANS)) + amt ≥ k
                                    •invalidated_by: -
                                    •invalidates: withdraw(k)/insuf, get_balance
                        else
                                    •invalidated_by: -
                                    •invalidates: get_balance
                            acc_bal ← acc_bal + amt
                exceptions: -

        withdraw (amt: real); signals → "insufficient funds"
                requires: acc_bal ≥ amt
                effect:
                            if acc_bal + changes (withdraw/ok.(AS ∪ ANS)) < amt
                                    •invalidated_by: withdraw/ok
                                    •invalidates: withdraw/ok, get_balance
                        else
                                    •invalidated_by: -
                                    •invalidates: get_balance
                            acc_bal ← acc_bal - amt
                exceptions:
                            if acc_bal + changes (deposit/ok.(AS ∪ ANS)) ≥ amt
                                    •invalidated_by: deposit/ok
                                    •invalidates: -
                        else
                                    •invalidated_by: -
                                    •invalidates: -
                            signals → "insufficient funds"
```

Figure 4. Specification of the conflicts defined on a *bank_account* object with enhanced concurrency. (k = a real number that represents some amount of money.)

The validity of a condition may depend on entries of other active or committed transactions. In our example, the scheduler has to take into account the *deposit* or *withdraw* operations of active transactions that have been scheduled previously on the same object. The entries of interest are denoted by *deposit/ok.(AS ∪ ANS)* or *withdraw/ok.(AS ∪ ANS)* and correspond to deposits or successful withdrawals of transactions in the AS status or ANS status, respectively. The scheduler must locate these entries and compute the "changes." By "changes," we mean the summation of the amounts that appear in the arguments of these operations. (In Figure 4, k is a real number that represents some amount of money; it is used to relate the result of "changes" of active deposits to the arguments of unsuccessful withdrawals.)

By using specifications and a uniform representation for all types (that is, the history abstraction), we can utilize semantic knowledge and achieve various degrees of concurrency without having to redesign the implementation of a type every time the semantics change. An implementation of a *bank_account* type by a conventional protocol that classifies operations into *readers* and *writers* is essentially the same as one that utilizes the operation-response pairs of "high-level" operations and allows for increased concurrency. The only difference is in the specifications — in particular, the *invalidate* and *invalidated_by* sets provided. No redesign of the type is necessary in order to increase concurrency.

The remarks in the previous paragraph also apply to the implementation of a *bank_account* type that meets the specification of Figure 4. An additional procedure is needed to compute the "changes." In order for the required entries to be located and read, this procedure makes use of the operations provided by the history. If the concurrency gains improve the overall performance of a system, this justifies the additional overhead incurred when the scheduler module has to examine the history. In general, semantic information can be utilized at an additional cost. The cost of searching for specific entries in the history can be reduced by making some optimizations in the actual implementation [2]. (Such implementation details are outside the scope of this paper.)

"Scheduling" operations

In this subsection, we describe how an operation is synchronized by the scheduler module. We use the term *scheduling* to describe this kind of synchronization control and to distinguish it from the *synchronization* of transactions, discussed in the next section. Operations are synchronized according to their conflicts and may be delayed, aborted, or accepted, depending on the strategy used for the synchronization of transactions. The task of the scheduler is to

- Determine for each operation *op* the operations op_1 in the history that conflict with *op* and
- Suggest a relative ordering for operations *op* and op_1 in which both of them could be accepted.

The operations in conflict with an operation *op* that is currently synchronized are determined by using the concurrent specifications: namely, the *invalidate* and *invalidated_by* sets provided by the application programmer. To determine the conflicts for an operation *op*, invoked by transaction *T*, the object scheduler must "search" the history and locate the entries whose first field is any of the elements of either the *invalidate* set or the *invalidated_by* set. (Recall that the template for a *search* operation can be a set for this purpose.) If the *invalidate* and *invalidated_by* sets depend on some conditions (for example, the specification for the *bank_account* object in Figure 4), the scheduler must first examine the history to find out which condition holds and then determine which are the valid *invalidate* and *invalidated_by* sets for the operation *op*.

The suggested ordering between operations is described by the relationships *scheduled before* and *scheduled after* in the discussion that follows. We can informally define these relationships by saying that operation op_1, which is invoked by transaction T_1, is *scheduled before* op_2, which is invoked by transaction T_2, if the only way in which they both can be accepted by the scheduler is if transaction T_1 precedes transaction T_2. Similarly, operation op_1, which is invoked by transaction T_1, is *scheduled after* op_2, which is invoked by transaction T_2, if the only way in which they both can be accepted by the scheduler is if transaction T_2 precedes transaction T_1. The rules for suggesting a suitable ordering are

- If operation *op* is *invalidated_by* another operation op_1 in the history, then *op* must be *scheduled before* op_1 and
- If *op* invalidates op_1, then *op* must be *scheduled after* op_1.

The rules for scheduling operations. An operation can be executed after it is synchronized or without any synchronization control. It may or may not contain a time stamp at the time it is executed. An operation *op* without a time stamp is scheduled after every committed operation that is invalidated by or invalidates *op* when it is executed. An operation *op* with a time stamp is scheduled after every committed operation with a lower time stamp that invalidates *op*. We assume that operations with time stamps are always scheduled before execution.

The entries in the history correspond to *committed* operations (COM) or *active* operations (AN, ANS, or EX). Table 3 describes the scheduling process for an operation *op* with respect to operations of the history for all four combinations of COM, AS, ANS, and EX.

The third column in Table 3 shows the templates for entries for which the scheduler is searching in order to determine the conflicts of operation *op*. The fourth column shows the action taken when

Table 3. The scheduling process for an operation *op*. (*ts(p)* = time stamp of operation *p*, *ct* = commit time, and *et* = execution time.)

Case	Status	Template	Action
A	Operation *op* is scheduled before execution and does not have a time stamp		
A1	*Committed* (COM)		
A2	*Active — serialized* (AS)	•if *op* is invalidated_by op_1.AS •if *op* invalidates op_1.AS	•delay *op* or *op* is scheduled before op_1 •delay *op* or *op* is scheduled after op_1
A3	*Active — not serialized* (ANS)	•if *op* is invalidated_by op_1.ANS •if *op* invalidates op_1.ANS	•delay *op* or *op* is scheduled before op_1 •delay *op* or *op* is scheduled after op_1
A4	*Executed — not synchronized* (EX)	•if *op* is invalidated_by op_1.EX •if *op* invalidates op_1.EX	•delay *op* or *op* is scheduled before op_1 •delay *op* or *op* is scheduled after op_1
B	Operation *op* is scheduled before execution and has a time stamp *t*		
B1	*Committed* (COM)	•if *op* invalidates op_1.COM.$ts(op_1) > t$	•abort *op*
B2	*Active — serialized* (AS)	•if *op* is invalidated_by op_1.AS.$ts(op_1) < t$ •if *op* invalidates op_1.AS.$ts(op_1) > t$	•delay *op* •abort *op*
B3	*Active — not serialized* (ANS)	•if *op* is invalidated_by op_1.ANS •if *op* invalidates op_1.ANS	•delay *op* or *op* is scheduled before op_1 •delay *op* or *op* is scheduled after op_1
B4	*Executed — not synchronized* (EX)	•if *op* is invalidated_by op_1.EX •if *op* invalidates op_1.EX	•delay *op* or *op* is scheduled before op_1 •delay *op* or *op* is scheduled after op_1
C	Operation *op* is scheduled after execution and does not have a time stamp		
C1	*Committed* (COM)	•if *op* is invalidated_by op_1.COM.$ct(op_1) > et(op)$ •if *op* invalidates op_1.COM.$ct(op_1) > et(op)$	•abort *op* or *op* is scheduled before op_1 •abort *op* or *op* is scheduled after op_1
C2	*Active — serialized* (AS)	•if *op* is invalidated_by op_1.AS •if *op* invalidates op_1.AS	•abort *op* or *op* is scheduled before op_1 •abort *op* or *op* is scheduled after op_1
C3	*Active — not serialized* (ANS)	•if *op* is invalidated_by op_1.ANS •if *op* invalidates op_1.ANS	•abort *op* or *op* is scheduled before op_1 •abort *op* or *op* is scheduled after op_1
C4	*Executed — not synchronized* (EX)	•if *op* is invalidated_by op_1.EX •if *op* invalidates op_1.EX	•abort *op* or *op* is scheduled before op_1 •abort *op* or *op* is scheduled after op_1
D	Operation *op* is scheduled after execution but has obtained a time stamp *t*		
D1	*Committed* (COM)	•if *op* is invalidated_by op_1.COM.$ct(op_1) > et(op).ts(op_1) < t$ •if *op* invalidates op_1.COM.$ct(op_1) > et(op).ts(op_1) > t$	•abort *op* •abort *op*
D2	*Active — serialized* (AS)	•if *op* is invalidated_by op_1.AS.$ts(op_1) < t$ •if *op* invalidates op_1.AS.$ts(op_1) > t$	•abort *op* •abort *op*
D3	*Active — not serialized* (ANS)	•if *op* is invalidated_by op_1.ANS •if *op* invalidates op_1.ANS	•abort *op* or *op* is scheduled before op_1 •abort *op* or *op* is scheduled after op_1
D4	*Executed — not synchronized* (EX)	•if *op* is invalidated_by op_1.EX •if *op* invalidates op_1.EX	•abort *op* or *op* is scheduled before op_1 •abort *op* or *op* is scheduled after op_1

the scheduler locates an entry. When there is a choice of action, the action taken by default is *schedule before/after*, unless a different action is specified in the strategy. (See the section entitled "Synchronization of transactions.")

The *before/after* sets. For each operation *op*, we can associate two sets of operations that must be scheduled before or after *op*; these sets are denoted by *op.before* and *op.after*. The domains of the *op.before* and *op.after* sets are the *invalidate* and *invalidated_by* sets, respectively, for operation *op*. (See Figure 5.)

Because the relationships *schedule before/after* between operations are defined in terms of their transactions, we can introduce a similar relationship for the corresponding transactions: Saying that op_1 is *scheduled before* op_2 implies that transaction T_1 is *scheduled before* transaction T_2, which is denoted by $T_1 \rightarrow T_2$. The suggested relative ordering between pairs of operations, which is induced by their conflicts, indicates an ordering between

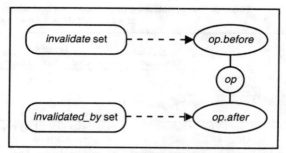

Figure 5. The *op.before* and *op.after* sets.

their transactions. For the transaction T that has invoked operation *op* on an object, we can associate two sets of transactions: the *T.before* set of transactions that should be scheduled before transaction T and the *T.after* set of transactions that should be scheduled after transaction T. These sets describe relative orderings of transactions at a particular object only.

To include the possibility that a transaction may invoke more than one operation on the same object, we can define $\smile T.before$ as the union of the *T.before* sets determined for each separate operation invoked by a transaction T on a particular object. Similarly, $\smile T.after$ is the union of the *T.after* sets determined for each operation invoked by a transaction T on the same object. In the discussion that follows, we assume for simplicity that transactions invoke one operation on an object, and we will be talking in terms of transactions and their *T.before/after* sets, instead of $\smile T.before/after$. The general case (that is, the case when transactions can invoke more than one operation) was considered by Anastassopoulos [2]. Because we assume that there is one operation per transaction, we can interchangeably refer to a particular entry in the history as the entry of either an operation or a transaction.

The *before/after sets* field of a history entry. The *T.before* and *T.after* sets are recorded in the *before/after sets* field of the entry for transaction T when the invoking operation is scheduled. (Recall that an entry for an operation *op* is created only when *op* is executed.) If a *delay* strategy has been specified for *op*, that operation is not executed and no entries are created. If *op* must be aborted, either no entry is created for *op* or, if *op* has been already executed, the corresponding entry is deleted.

The contents of the *before/after sets* field in an entry for transaction T refer to the entries of transactions that must be scheduled before or after transaction T. When the scheduler inserts a new entry for transaction T in the history, it has to incrementally update the contents of the *before/after sets* fields of entries that correspond to transactions in the *T.before/after* sets of transaction T. The *modify* operation is used for this purpose (see the subsection entitled "The history abstraction"). When an entry is removed from the history, all the references to this entry must be deleted.

Two entries that are related directly and that both have been scheduled should reference one another. We do not record transitive relationships between operations. If, for example, transaction T_1 is scheduled before transaction T_2 and transaction T_2 is scheduled before transaction T_3, then transaction T_1 has to be scheduled before transaction T_3. However, the corresponding operations op_1 and op_3 may not be in conflict, and the entries for transactions T_1 and T_3 in the history should not reference one another. In this way, transaction T_2 may be aborted at any time without these entries being left with wrong information: namely, that op_1 should be scheduled before op_3 because of some conflict encountered when the operations were scheduled.

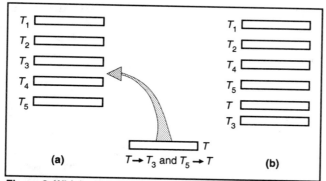

Figure 6. Which operations can be accepted by the scheduler.
(T = transaction.)

Determining a possible ordering between transactions. We explain above that the scheduler will attempt to schedule any two conflicting operations op and op_1 in an order in which they can be accepted (unless a strategy other than the default one has been specified or the only option for scheduling them is *delay/abort*). The suggested order for op and op_1 is determined by the kind of relationship (that is, *invalidated_by* or *invalidate*) by which they are related. However, there are operations that are related by a symmetric relationship, and these cannot be scheduled before/after one another. The example that follows shows that, in some cases, operations that could be scheduled in an acceptable way when considered in pairs cannot be accepted by the scheduler when we consider all the entries in the history. In our example, in which we talk again in terms of transactions (because we assume that there is one entry per transaction in the history), we examine the scheduling of transaction T. Figure 6 illustrates our example.

Suppose first that all the operations in the history have been scheduled (that is, the $T.before$ and $T.after$ sets have been constructed). Further suppose that their transactions are related as follows: $T_1 \rightarrow T_2, T_1 \rightarrow T_5$, and $T_4 \rightarrow T_5$ (see Figure 6). (Recall that the notation $T_1 \rightarrow T_2$ means that $T_2 \in T_1.after$ and $T_1 \in T_2.before$.) Suppose further that the new operation of transaction T is found to conflict with the operations of transactions T_3 and T_5 and that transaction T must be scheduled before transaction T_3 and after transaction T_5. To visualize the process of scheduling, we can assume that the entries in the history are reordered (Figure 6[b]) in order to accommodate transaction T in the history. Suppose now that there exists an additional relationship $T_3 \rightarrow T_4$. It is easy to see that in this case, there is no acceptable way in which we can schedule transaction T, because it must be scheduled before and after the same transaction.

To detect such cyclic situations between operations (and their corresponding transactions), the scheduler may call a special procedure *find_cycle* as part of the scheduling process. The procedure is invoked when the scheduler operates under the default strategy and repeatedly traverses entries in the history based on the information contained in their $T.before/T.after$ sets field. The procedure terminates when it has exhausted all existing paths between transactions or when it detects a cycle.

Transactions that have been assigned time stamps are related by the *precedes* relationship, even if they do not conflict. This relationship is not recorded in the history entries (the $T.before/after$ sets field); nevertheless, it has to be taken into account by the *find_cycle* procedure. In the example illustrated in Figure 6, transactions T_4 and T_5 may be related not because of a conflict but because of their time stamps — for example, $ts(T_4) < ts(T_5)$.

The following describes how a cyclic situation is detected in this case: When the *find_cycle* traverses entries based in the $T.after$ sets, it may visit transactions with time stamps. The transactions' time stamps are compared, and the minimum time stamp found — denoted by *min [ts(T.after)]* — is recorded. The same happens when the *find_cycle* traverses the entries in the opposite direction (that is, based in the $T.before$ sets), but this time the maximum time stamp found — denoted by *max [ts(T.before)]* — is recorded. When the procedure has exhausted all paths, the two recordings are compared. Transaction T can be accepted if

$$\max\ [ts(T.before)] < \min\ [ts(T.after)]$$

Details of the *find_cycle* procedure were provided by Anastassopoulos [2].

Synchronization of transactions

By locating the entries of operations that conflict with an operation *op* invoked by transaction T, the scheduler module constructs two sets for transaction T: the *T.before* and *T.after* sets. This happens when the scheduler can accept for execution operations that conflict (that is, it operates under the default strategy). However, the fact that an operation has been accepted for execution does not necessarily imply that the associated transaction will succeed. There is no guarantee that different object schedulers, accessed by transaction T, will decide to schedule operations in the same relative order. If, for example, an object suggests that the order for execution of transactions T_1 and T_2 should be T_1 is *scheduled before* T_2 and another object suggests that the order should be T_1 is *scheduled after* T_2, it is not possible to commit both transactions. Such situations should be avoided, prevented, or detected before both transactions make their results permanent. We address this problem in this section.

To avoid situations in which transactions are scheduled in opposite relative order at different objects, the TMs must predetermine their serialization order. Alternatively, the TMs could decide to run transactions without having made any assumption in advance about their serialization order; such a policy permits more flexibility in scheduling operations but may sometimes result in deadlock situations or nonserializable executions of transactions. In fact, deadlocks and nonserializable executions are two aspects of the same problem. Deadlocks, which may arise under a preventive policy, would lead to nonserializable executions if transactions have been allowed to freely execute to completion.

This observation implies that a similar mechanism (that is, a graph of transactions) can be used for the detection of both deadlocks and nonserializable executions. However, this approach is in general not very attractive because of the overhead associated with the maintenance and management of a graph that spreads over many sites. Furthermore, committed transactions cannot be removed from the graph when active transactions are scheduled before them. This means that in order to keep the graph small, we must prevent transactions from being serialized before committed ones. In our model, we adopt a different approach for the detection of nonserializable executions: Transactions are assigned intervals of time stamps.

Detecting nonserializable executions

At its birth, every transaction is assigned an interval $(0, \infty)$, which eventually will be reduced to a single time stamp. Until the final time stamp of a transaction has been determined, there is no certainty of the serialization order of that transaction in the history and there is no guarantee that the operations of that transaction will not be invalidated by either committed or active transactions. Once the serialization order of a transaction has been determined and *accepted* by an object, the transaction will not be invalidated by another transaction at this object.

An object scheduler can suggest some intervals for transactions that will allow them to commit locally later on. The suggested interval for a transaction T is determined according to the time stamps or intervals of serialized transactions. (Recall that {serialized} = {COM} $\cup$ {AS}.) When transaction T invokes an operation on an object, the interval is reduced to (T_c, ∞), where T_c is the maximum of the time stamps of committed transactions whose operations may be invalidated by or may invalidate the operations of transaction T. (Recall that transactions can access previous states of the object if they already have a time stamp.) Serialized transactions cause the interval of transaction T to be reduced further. In particular, the interval for transaction T must be {max [$ts(T.before.serialized)$], min [$ts(T.after.serialized)$]}. This interval will be computed and sent to the TM on request. This may occur in the following three cases:

- When an operation is executed (that is, the *return_ts* field of an invocation is set to *true*);
- During the execution of transaction T; or
- When transaction T enters the commitment protocol (in this case, the request is sent with the *precommit* messages).

In any case except the first, we say that transaction T enters the process of obtaining a time stamp and that its status becomes AS. The *time stamp* field of the entries for transaction T contains the results of such computations and eventually a single time stamp. The reader may have observed a race condition: Assume that a transaction T is *active — serialized* (AS) but has not yet obtained a single time stamp; further assume that the TM of another transaction T_1 has asked an object scheduler for a suitable interval. The strategy can be either *delay* or the default one. In the case of a default strategy, the suggested interval for transaction T_1 is based on the upper/lower bound of the interval suggested previously for transaction T. If the default strategy is used, intervals with no upper bound should be truncated to a finite value.

In order to determine the time stamp of a transaction, the TM may collect the suggested intervals from all the objects it has accessed and take their intersection. If the intersection is the empty set, the transaction cannot commit. On the other hand, a TM can unilaterally choose a time stamp for its transaction without consulting the objects at all (this may happen before the transaction is executed, during its execution, or when the execution completes). In such a case, the objects should decide if this time stamp is acceptable. Other variations, in which TMs consult only some objects, are also possible.

Resolving the conflicts

When an operation *op* is scheduled, the scheduler will create the *before* and *after* sets for the corresponding transaction T. These sets are empty if no conflicts are found. If any (or both) of the sets $T.before$ or $T.after$ are not empty, the conflicts must be resolved. The strategy for the execution of the operation *op* will then determine what kind of action (*accept*, *delay*, or *abort*) should be taken in order to resolve the conflict(s). When a strategy other than the default one is to be used, it must be given explicitly. It is relatively easy to specify the strategy in terms of its consequences to the interval for transaction T.

Transactions will obtain intervals of the form (T_c, ∞) when they first access objects. Thus, a transaction will always be able to find a suitable time stamp and to commit if none of the intervals suggested by the objects have an upper bound. When the interval for a transaction has been truncated from the right, then the probability that this transaction will be able to commit later becomes very small. It is possible to prevent this from happening: An operation *op* may or may not be accepted by the object scheduler, depending on whether or not the adjustments that should be performed to intervals of other transactions are "permitted." However, notice that the previous statement does not apply to single time stamps, because they cannot be adjusted any more. (We discuss this issue further in the subsection that follows.)

Scheduling transactions before others

We use an example to draw some conclusions regarding the scheduling of transactions *before* others. In Figure 7, we consider the histories of two objects — objects 1 and 2 — and suppose that transactions T_1 and T_2 are committed with time stamps $ts(T_1) = 10$ and $ts(T_2) = 15$. Transaction T_3 has executed operations on both objects. Their operations have been scheduled after transactions T_1 and T_2. Suppose now that transaction T_4 is executed and scheduled after transaction T_3 at object 1. Transaction T_4 is later assigned the time stamp value of 14 by its TM and commits with this time stamp. The suggested intervals for transaction T_3 by objects 1 and 2 would be (10, 14) and (15, ∞), respectively, which means that there is no suitable time stamp for transaction T_3 to commit. The reason for this is the scheduling (and subsequently

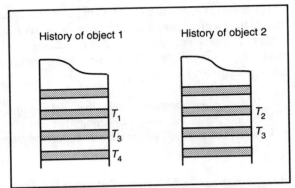

Figure 7. Scheduling transactions at objects 1 and 2 before other transactions. (T = transaction.)

the commitment) of transaction T_4 after transaction T_3 at object 1. Transaction T_4 caused the interval for transaction T_3 to be truncated from the right.

Situations like those presented in the preceding example occur when the following two problems arise:

- A transaction is scheduled before a committed one or
- A transaction is scheduled before another active transaction that has the right to restrict the time stamp interval of the former.

When either of these problems occurs, the interval of a transaction T has to be truncated from the right. Use of one of the following policies can completely or partially eliminate the above two problems:

(1)   Not allowing transactions to be scheduled before active transactions or before committed ones (we assume that, at some stage, both transactions were active). When no active transactions are ever scheduled before committed or active ones, then time stamp intervals are never truncated from the right. This is the case in most conventional protocols. If an active transaction is scheduled after another active one and wants to commit, its commitment must be deferred until the transaction that should precede it in the serialization order terminates. Some protocols use this policy. Its drawback is that a transaction that has completed execution is unable to commit and has to wait for another to terminate first (which may take too long).

(2)   Forcing transactions to obtain a time stamp when they are scheduled before others. A transaction T can be required to get a time stamp when it is scheduled before another transaction T_1. T may get its time stamp

- Immediately after transaction T has been scheduled before transaction T_1 (or immediately after transaction T_1 has been scheduled after transaction T, depending on their relative execution order) or
- When transaction T_1 is assigned a time stamp.

In the first case, the time stamp of transaction T_1 is determined based on the time stamp of transaction T (or based on the upper bound of the interval suggested for transaction T at that object). The time stamp of transaction T will cause the interval suggested for transaction T_1 to be adjusted accordingly. Details of such variations were discussed by Anastassopoulos [2].

(3)   Leaving some space for transactions that are scheduled before another, so that it is more

likely for them to find a nonempty interval. Some space can be left for transactions that are scheduled before a given transaction T_1 so that the probability of obtaining a nonempty interval for them increases. In this case, the suggested interval by an object scheduler for transaction T_1 is $(T_c + \Delta, \infty)$, where Δ may be a constant number or a function of the number of elements in the $T_1.before$ set.

Use of the three policies listed above produces a variety of hybrid protocols that favor — in a controlled manner — one transaction relative to another.

In our example (see Figure 7), notice that the *before/after* relationships between the transactions could be $T_1 \rightarrow T_3$, $T_2 \rightarrow T_3$, $T_1 \rightarrow T_4$, and $T_3 \rightarrow T_4$. We can see that there is no cycle in the graph of transactions; however, transaction T_3 is aborted. This happens because transaction T_1 precedes transaction T_2 in the serialization order, although transactions T_1 and T_2 may not be related by any conflict relationship. This is a limitation of the mechanisms that assign a global serialization order to transactions, as opposed to mechanisms that construct graphs: The time stamp values introduce more relationships between transactions, in addition to those determined by their conflicts, that are recorded in their *before/after* sets.

Some examples

In this section, we describe how existing protocols or combinations thereof can be obtained by our model.

Locking protocols

Locking protocols [7] use the *delay* strategy whenever conflicts arise. This strategy is not the default one and has to be specified. In locking protocols, the invoked operations do not have time stamps and they are scheduled before execution. The entries in the history are of status *committed* (COM), *active — serialized* (AS), or *active — not serialized* (ANS). Entries of status EX do not appear in pure locking protocols. We are concerned with Cases A1 through A3 in Table 3; in the case of conflict, the action to be taken is *delay*. To specify this, we explicitly give the scheduler the templates for entries for which it should be looking in the history and the action that should be taken if any such entry is located. To schedule transaction T under a locking protocol, we use Strategy 1:

Strategy 1: T: if $T.before.(ANS \cup AS) \neq \{\varnothing\}$
            effect: delay T
         if $T.after.(ANS \cup AS) \neq \{\varnothing\}$
            effect: delay T

To relate the above to the templates of Table 3 (third column), recall that the sets *invalidate* and *invalidated_by* are the respective domains of $T.before$ and $T.after$, as explained in the subsubsection entitled "The *before/after* sets" (see also Figure 5). The above strategy says that the scheduler must delay any operation that either is invalidated by or invalidates another active operation in the history.

For the standard locking protocols with *read/write* (R/W) operations, a *read* is invalidated by a *write* and a *write* is invalidated by another *write* (the second relationship may be omitted if we apply Thomas' Rule [3]). Every operation is scheduled after committed transactions; that is, the time stamp interval suggested by each object scheduler is (T_c, ∞), where T_c is the maximum of the time stamps of committed transactions that have performed *write* operations (for *read* operations) or *read* and *write* operations (for *write* operations) on the object.

In locking protocols, object schedulers return suggested intervals for transactions with the responses to invocations (that is, the *return_ts* field for each invocation is *true*). When all the operations of a transaction have been executed, the TM can determine the serialization order of that transaction. The time stamp is chosen according to some specific rule; for example, it could be the lower bound of the result of the intersection of the intervals collected from the participating objects. No transaction is scheduled before others in locking protocols, so that intervals of transactions are never truncated from the right. Consequently, the intersection of intervals is never empty. If transactions are to enter into incorrect executions, they get involved in deadlocks that can be resolved either by a time-out mechanism or by deadlock-detection and -resolution algorithms.

Time-stamp-ordering protocols

The implementation of time-stamp-ordering (TO) protocols is straightforward. The interval assigned to transactions at their birth is immediately reduced to a single time stamp before the transactions start executing. Operations are scheduled before execution according to their time stamp values, and it is possible for transactions to access older states of objects, as in multiversion schemes [22]. In the basic TO protocol [6], old versions are not available, and transactions cannot be scheduled before committed ones. The operations in the history may be *committed* (COM) or *active — serialized* (AS) (Cases B1 and B2, respectively, in Table 3). The strategy for scheduling operations under TO protocols is the specified one (there is no other option) and need not be explicitly given to the scheduler. The meaning of the templates in Cases B1 and B2 in Table 3 is that operations should be scheduled in increasing time stamp order. Thus, operations that are invalidated by others with smaller time stamps are delayed, while operations that invalidate others with bigger time stamps are not accepted by the object scheduler. Because the serialization order has been predetermined, there is no flexibility in scheduling, but no deadlocks arise.

Optimistic protocols

In optimistic protocols, no synchronization control is performed until transactions run to completion. Then, TMs may use either of two variations:

- Selecting a time stamp by first asking objects to "suggest" suitable intervals and then taking the intersection of these intervals [4] (see Case C in Table 3) or
- Choosing a time stamp and requiring objects to schedule their operations with that time stamp [1] (see Case D in Table 3).

In Case C, the object schedulers are requested to schedule the operations of transactions, but no time stamp is provided. More freedom in scheduling is possible in this case than in Case D, as the choice of actions in Table 3 indicates. The entries in the history are of status *committed* (COM), *active — serialized* (AS), and *executed — not synchronized* (EX) (Cases C1, C2, and C4, respectively, in Table 3). Depending on the strategy used, several variations arise. We may decide to do one of the following: abort COM, AS, or EX transactions; abort any two of them (usually COM and AS); or — when their intervals are to be truncated from the right — abort all three. When the default strategy is used in all three cases (that is, in Cases C1, C2, and C4 in Table 3) — meaning that no strategy has to be specified — transactions will be given every chance to find a suitable interval and commit. Of course, some may end up with empty intervals.

In Case D, the entries in the history may be *committed* (COM), *active — serialized* (AS), or *executed — not synchronized* (EX) (Cases D1, D2, and D4, respectively, in Table 3). The strategy used for Cases D1 and D2 is the specified one and need not be explicitly given to the scheduler. For Case D4, either we can use the default strategy, which corresponds to the standard optimistic schemes with *backward validation* control, or we can apply Strategy 2, which implements optimistic schemes with a kind of *forward validation* control:

Strategy 2: *T*: if *T.before.EX* ≠ {∅}
effect: abort *T*

Our model implements optimistic protocols that allow transactions to be validated concurrently. Other strategies (for example, a *delay* strategy for Case C2 in Table 3) could be specified, which would result in schemes that permit only one transaction at a time to be validated. However, in our opinion, such schemes do not fit very naturally to distributed environments; for this reason, no such strategies are included as possible options in Table 3.

At the end of scheduling, object schedulers determine an interval for a transaction *T* that is currently validated. The suggested interval for transaction *T* is selected according to the time stamps of other serialized transactions. If some of these transactions are still in the process of obtaining a time stamp, the interval for transaction *T* is selected according to the lower or upper bound of their intervals. For this purpose, intervals for optimistic transactions having an infinite upper bound are forced to obtain a finite value. As a result of this practice, more transactions may fail to obtain a nonempty interval. This is the cost we pay for allowing more transactions to be validated in parallel. Alternatively, we can wait until all these transactions have obtained single time stamps and then suggest an interval for transaction *T*.

Hybrid protocols

The three main classes of protocols — two-phase locking , time-stamp-ordering, and optimistic — usually correspond to three of the 16 cases presented in Table 3. Many other protocols can be implemented when a mixture of operations are executed either before or after scheduling and either with or without time stamps. The subsections entitled "Detecting nonserializable executions," "Resolving the conflicts," and "Scheduling transactions before others" outline a general hybrid protocol in which all of the above combinations are possible. Concurrency control protocols that fall into a subset of all combinations in Table 3 can also be implemented. It is difficult to assess how all these protocols would perform (some are expected to be of practical interest, while others may perform poorly), but it is easy to show that all of them will produce serializable executions. The proof is straightforward: Transactions eventually obtain unique time stamps that represent the global serialization order, and every object schedules conflicting operations in time stamp order.

Depending on the time at which we determine the serialization order of transactions and the strategy we specify, a variety of protocols can also be obtained. If the serialization order is determined early, a transaction does not have much flexibility in scheduling but has a priority over the transactions without time stamps. Once a transaction with a single time stamp has been accepted, it will not be aborted by any other transaction without a time stamp; the latter must be scheduled with respect to the former. In locking and optimistic protocols, the serialization order is determined before transactions commit (in locking protocols, when all the objects have been acquired). In TO protocols, the serialization order is determined before transactions start executing. However, it is possible to implement protocols in which the serialization order is determined during the execution of transactions. This strategy may be used when a TM observes many conflicts and would like to secure its transaction and prevent nonserializable executions.

The scheduling in optimistic schemes is performed when a transaction enters the *validation* phase. A different and relatively optimistic scheme could allow conflicting operations to proceed as long as the scheduler can find an acceptable ordering in which it can schedule them. Such a scheme is based on Cases A and B in Table 3 (that is, scheduling is performed before operations are executed) with the default strategy. In this way, operations that are related by a symmetric relationship are not accepted. This scheme is also beneficial for transactions that access one object only. These transactions may be delayed or aborted in standard protocols if they are in conflict with another active transaction. In our scheme, they can proceed immediately if the object scheduler can accommodate them in the history. More sophisticated strategies can be specified that may delay operations whose chance of success becomes too small (for example, when the number of conflicts for an operation exceeds a certain threshold). These strategies will enable a TM to switch to more pessimistic protocols, depending on the number of conflicts encountered on an object.

Mixing different protocols

In our model, the time stamps of transactions are determined by TMs; therefore, we can always obtain a unique serialization order for a set of transactions that might run under the same or different protocols. We can have different protocols in an application, because either objects are given the freedom to use different scheduling strategies (per object integration) or transactions are allowed to choose the strategies they prefer when they submit invocations to objects (we assume that objects have also been given the specification of the strategies requested). In the latter case, transactions may "decide" to run under different protocols (per transaction integration) and — like protocols — can be grouped into classes (for example, locking and optimistic). The scheduling strategies must determine how conflicts between transactions of the same or different classes should be resolved.

Integrated schemes for the three main classes of protocols can be implemented easily and without any additional overhead in terms of messages exchanged between sites, because their time stamps are determined either in advance or during the commitment protocol. We present below two examples of integrated schemes: one for locking and optimistic transactions and the other for locking and time-stamp-ordering transactions.

Integrated scheme for locking and optimistic transactions. In this scheme, we use a *delay* strategy for locking (LOC) transactions when there is a possibility that their intervals might be truncated from the right. This may happen when they conflict with other locking transactions. However, an exception can be made when locking transactions are scheduled after locking of AS status, because such transactions always have single time stamps. (This scheme is a variation of the pure locking scheme presented in the subsection entitled "Locking protocols.") With regard to optimistic transactions, a locking transaction is delayed if it is to be scheduled before an optimistic AS transaction (that is, a currently validated transaction). On the other hand, a locking transaction can be scheduled after an optimistic AS transaction; the strategy used in this case will be the default one. Finally, locking transactions never take any action when they conflict with optimistic EX transactions. The necessary actions will be taken by the optimistic transactions when they are scheduled. The strategy for locking transactions is Strategy 3:

> Strategy 3: $T(LOC)$: if $T.before.ANS \neq \{\varnothing\}$
> effect: delay T
> if $T.after.(ANS \cup AS) \neq \{\varnothing\}$
> effect: delay T

Notice that when Strategy 3 is used, the objects return suggested intervals for locking transactions with the responses to the invocations. When a locking transaction is scheduled after another locking AS transaction, the interval returned is bigger than the time stamp of the latter transaction. If a locking transaction is scheduled after an optimistic AS transaction, the interval for the locking transaction is based on the upper bound of the interval suggested for the optimistic transaction. For this purpose, the intervals of optimistic transactions that have no upper bound are truncated from the right.

In this scheme, we assume that optimistic (OPT) transactions are executed without time stamps under the default strategy with respect to other serialized transactions that are both locking and optimistic (see Case C in Table 3). It is reasonable to also assume that conflicts between optimistic and locking transactions are resolved by forcing the former to abort. That is, when an optimistic transaction invalidates a locking ANS transaction, the object scheduler must decide to abort it (see Case C3 in Table 3). The operation of the optimistic transaction cannot be accepted, because it causes an interval of the locking transaction to be truncated from the right. Similar action must be taken if the optimistic transaction is invalidated by a locking ANS transaction, because the time stamp that the former obtains may be bigger than the time stamp assigned to the latter. (Recall that intervals for locking transactions are collected with responses.) As a result, the locking transaction must abort after it has been executed. This scenario corresponds to a situation in which a locking transaction loses control over an object that has locked previously. The strategy for optimistic transactions is Strategy 4 (a similar scheme for R/W operations was suggested by Pons and Vilarem [21]):

Strategy 4: T(OPT): if $T.before.ANS \neq \{\varnothing\}$
  effect: abort T
  if $T.after.ANS \neq \{\varnothing\}$
  effect: abort T

Integrated scheme for locking and time-stamp-ordering transactions. A locking transaction is executed in the usual way (that is, under Strategy 1) with respect to other transactions. Notice that under Strategy 1, AS transactions may be locking or time-stamp-ordering (TO). When a TO transaction is scheduled, the object scheduler decides whether or not to accept its time stamp. In general, a TO transaction that is to be scheduled either before or after a locking transaction without a time stamp (that is, an ANS transaction) should be delayed (see Case B3 in Table 3). TO transactions are never delayed because of other TO transactions. The strategy for TO transactions is Strategy 5:

Strategy 5: T(TO): if $T.before.ANS \neq \{\varnothing\}$
  effect: delay T
  if $T.after.ANS \neq \{\varnothing\}$
  effect: delay T

When a locking transaction is serialized (and commits), the TO transaction can be considered for execution. Notice that a *delay* strategy that is in force while a locking transaction is in status ANS does not guarantee that the TO transaction will be able to commit later. It may eventually have to restart, depending on the time stamp assigned to the locking transaction. A similar protocol for R/W operations was suggested by Wang and Li [24]; it has been implemented with locks.

Related work and conclusions

The problem of synchronization of operations on objects was considered by Ng [18]; Weihl [25], [26], [27]; and Herlihy [12], [13]. Ng [18] used the history abstraction for concurrency control. Our work is different from that of Ng in many respects. For example,

(1)   Ng suggested a process for implementing atomic objects that is more stylized than the methods used by Weihl. We suggest an approach for implementing atomic objects in which the

synchronization requirements of operations are given by a specification language. In this way, changes in the semantics can be introduced and utilized with the minimum of effort made by the programmer. We believe that the approach of reimplementing the objects when the semantics change is expensive, wastes previous effort, and is prone to errors.

(2)   The assumption that all objects must perform the same concurrency control protocol was made by Ng [18]; Weihl [25], [26], [27]; and Herlihy [12], [13]. In Ng's approach, the same synchronization protocol was implemented by all objects below the history abstraction. In our approach, objects do not perform any particular protocol. A concurrency control protocol is implemented by selecting the appropriate specifications. The serialization order is not determined by the objects but instead by the TMs. In this way, we ensure that a unique time stamp is assigned to each transaction; thus, different protocols can coexist within the system.

Under our unified model, we can implement previous schemes as well as other combinations. Thus, our approach is more general than, for example, the integrated schemes suggested by Boral and Gold [5], Farrag and Ozsu [8], Herlihy [13], Pons and Vilarem [21], and Wang and Li [24]. These schemes were simple integrations of two different protocols that were implemented using the standard techniques (that is, locks or time stamps).

In conclusion, the work presented in this paper can be viewed as an approach to modeling concurrency control protocols and also as a unified protocol for concurrency control. Our model could facilitate a comparative study of existing concurrency control protocols. In addition, it provides a uniform framework for describing and implementing protocols able to utilize the semantics of an application in order to increase concurrency.

Acknowledgments

The authors wish to thank the referees for their helpful comments.

The material presented in this paper is based upon work supported by the State Scholarship Foundation of Greece under contract no. 2178-87.

References

[1] D. Agrawal et al., "Distributed Optimistic Concurrency Control with Reduced Rollback," *Distributed Computing*, Vol. 2, No. 1, 1987, pp. 45-59.

[2] P. Anastassopoulos, *Synchronisation of Operations on Objects*, doctoral thesis, Dept. of Computer Science, Queen Mary and Westfield College, Univ. of London, London, England, 1992.

[3] P.A. Bernstein and N. Goodman, "Concurrency Control in Distributed Database Systems," *ACM Computing Surveys*, Vol. 13, No. 2, June 1981, pp. 185-221.

[4] C. Boksenbaum et al., "Concurrent Certifications by Intervals of Timestamps in Distributed Database Systems," *IEEE Trans. Software Eng.*, Vol. SE-13, No. 4, Apr. 1987, pp. 409-419.

[5] H. Boral and I. Gold, "Towards a Self-Adapting Centralized Concurrency Control Algorithm," *ACM SIGMOD Record*, Vol. 14, No. 2, June 1984, pp. 18-32.

[6] S. Ceri and G. Pelagatti, *Distributed Databases—Principles and Systems*, McGraw-Hill, Inc., New York, N.Y., 1984.

[7] K.P. Eswaran et al., "The Notion of Consistency and Predicate Locks in a Database System," *Comm. ACM*, Vol. 19, No. 11, Nov. 1976, pp. 624-633.

[8] A.A. Farrag and M.T. Özsu, "Towards a General Concurrency Control Algorithm for Database Systems," *IEEE Trans. Software Eng.*, Vol. SE-13, No. 10, Oct. 1987, pp. 1073-1079.

[9] A.A. Farrag and M.T. Özsu, "Using Semantic Knowledge of Transactions to Increase Concurrency," *ACM Trans. Database Systems*, Vol. 14, No. 4, Dec. 1989, pp. 503-525.

[10] H. Garcia-Molina, "Using Semantic Knowledge for Transaction Processing in a Distributed Database," *ACM Trans. Database Systems*, Vol. 8, No. 2, June 1983, pp. 186-213.

[11] J.N. Gray, "Notes on Data Base Operating Systems," in *Lecture Notes in Computer Science, No. 60, Operating Systems — An Advanced Course*, R. Bayer, R.M. Graham, and G. Seegmuller, eds., Springer-Verlag, New York, N.Y., 1978, pp. 393-481.

[12] M. Herlihy, "Extending Multiversion Time-Stamping Protocols to Exploit Type Information," *IEEE Trans. Computers*, Vol. C-36, No. 4, Apr. 1987, pp. 443-448.

[13] M. Herlihy, "Apologizing versus Asking Permission: Optimistic Concurrency Control for Abstract Data Types," *ACM Trans. Database Systems*, Vol. 15, No. 1, Mar. 1990, pp. 96-124.

[14] H. Korth, "Locking Primitives in a Database System," *J. ACM*, Vol. 30, No. 1, Jan. 1983, pp. 55-79.

[15] L. Lamport, "Time, Clocks, and the Ordering Of Events in a Distributed System," *Comm. ACM*, Vol. 21, No. 7, July 1978, pp. 558-565.

[16] N.A. Lynch, "Multilevel Atomicity — A New Correctness Criterion for Database Concurrency Control," *ACM Trans. Database Systems*, Vol. 8, No. 4, Dec. 1983, pp. 484-502.

[17] J.E.B. Moss, "Nested Transactions: An Approach to Reliable Distributed Computing," Tech. Report TR-260, Laboratory of Computer Science, MIT, Cambridge, Mass., Apr. 1981.

[18] T.P. Ng, "Using Histories to Implement Atomic Objects," *ACM Trans. Computer Systems*, Vol. 7, No. 4, Nov. 1989, pp. 360-393.

[19] P.E. O'Neil, "The Escrow Transactional Method," *ACM Trans. Database Systems*, Vol. 11, No. 4, Dec. 1986, pp. 405-430.

[20] C. Papadimitriou, *The Theory of Database Concurrency Control*, Computer Science Press, New York, N.Y., 1986.

[21] J.-F. Pons and J.F. Vilarem, "A Dynamic and Integrated Concurrency Control for Distributed Databases," *IEEE J. Selected Areas Comm.*, Vol. 7, No. 3, Apr. 1989, pp. 364-374.

[22] D.P. Reed, "Naming and Synchronisation in a Decentralised Computer System," Tech. Report TR-205, Laboratory of Computer Science, MIT, Cambridge, Mass., Sept. 1978.

[23] P.M. Schwarz and A.Z. Spector, "Synchronizing Shared Abstract Types," *ACM Trans. Computer Systems*, Vol. 2, No. 3, Aug. 1984, pp. 223-250.

[24] C.P. Wang and V.O.K. Li, "A Unified Concurrency Control Algorithm for Distributed Database Systems," *Proc. Fourth Int'l Conf. Data Eng.*, IEEE Computer Soc. Press, Los Alamitos, Calif., 1988, pp. 410-417.

[25] W.E. Weihl, "Specification and Implementation of Atomic Data Types," Tech. Report TR-314, Laboratory of Computer Science, MIT, Cambridge, Mass., Mar. 1984.

[26] W.E. Weihl, "Commutativity-Based Concurrency Control for Abstract Data Types," *IEEE Trans. Computers*, Vol. 37, No. 12, Dec. 1988, pp. 1488-1505.

[27] W.E. Weihl, "Local Atomicity Properties: Modular Concurrency Control for Abstract Data Types," *ACM Trans. Programming Languages and Systems*, Vol. 11, No. 2, Apr. 1989, pp. 249-282.

Replicated Data Management in Distributed Systems

D istributed computing systems have become common-place in all types of organizations. Computers (or *nodes*) in such systems collectively have large amounts of computational and storage resources. These resources can be exploited to build highly available systems. For example, by a file being replicated at nodes that have independent failure modes, a user can be allowed to access the data in the file even when some of the nodes that store copies of the file have failed. Although increased availability is a major benefit of data replication, it also provides the opportunity to share the load generated by user requests between the nodes that have copies. An access to a file requires reading of data from a disk, processing, and possibly writing the data back to the disk (after the data have been modified). If data are not replicated, all user requests that access a file must wait at a single node for the data to be read or written. When the data are replicated, the load generated by the requests can be shared by nodes having the copies; hence, the response time for the requests can be improved.

Data replication increases the probability that there is an operational (that is, nonfailed) node that has a copy of the data when a request is made; however, it may not be sufficient to just locate one such node and read or write the copy stored at that node. Such a copy may be outdated, because the node storing it may have failed when the data were last updated. Thus, it is necessary to use algorithms that implement rules for accessing the copies, so that correctness is ensured (see the next section, entitled "Correctness criteria"). These rules may disallow access to data, even when copies of the data exist at operational nodes, when it is not possible to determine if the copies at the operational nodes are up-to-date.

The algorithms that control access to replicated data are called *replica control protocols*. A *replica* refers to a single copy of the data in a system that employs replication. A large number of replica control protocols have been developed. In this paper, we present many of these protocols, explain their workings, and relate them by showing that most of the replica control protocols belong to a small number of protocol families. We also discuss both the performance enhancements made possible by the replica control

Mustaque Ahamad,

Mostafa H. Ammar, and

Shun Yan Cheung

protocols and the costs that are incurred when they are used. The two main performance measures we are concerned with are *data availability* and *response time*. Data availability is defined as the probability that there are enough functioning (or available) resources in the distributed system (that is, in the nodes storing data and in the communication network) so that an arriving request can be satisfied. Response time is defined as the time required for an access request to complete. Thus, response time depends not only on the failure characteristics of the system but also on the load and the I/O, processing, and communication capacities in the system.

This paper is organized into seven sections. In the first section, we precisely define the correctness criteria that must be met when data are replicated. The second section introduces the concept of replica control. We have categorized the protocols into three basic types, the operations of which are described in detail in the third, fourth, and fifth sections. The sixth section presents a number of methods that are improvements of the basic protocols described in earlier sections. The seventh section concludes the paper with a description of possible future directions.

Correctness criteria

In a replicated data system, although there exist multiple copies of a data item that can be accessed by users, it is desirable to maintain the view that there is logically a single copy of the data item. A replica control protocol is a synchronization layer imposed by a distributed system to hide the fact that data are replicated and to present to the users the illusion that there is only a single copy of the data item. It provides for a set of rules to regulate reading and writing of the replicas and to determine the actual value of the data, thus allowing replication of data to be *transparent* to users. Hence, users are not burdened with the task of implementing procedures that control access to the replicas and can exploit the benefits of high availability and improved response time, without being aware of the fact that the data are replicated. Since there are correctness criteria that must be satisfied by a set of data items, even when there is a single copy of each item, the same correctness criteria must also be met when the data are replicated. Thus, correctness criteria for a replicated data system are defined using correctness criteria of data when the data are not replicated.

Much of the work in replicated data systems has been done in the context of distributed databases. Access requests to data in a database are modeled as *transactions*. A transaction consists of a number of related operations that read and possibly update the state of the database. When a single transaction at a time is executed by the system, its execution transforms the database from one *consistent* state into another consistent state. Thus, serial execution of a set of transactions (that is, one at a time) by a database that is initially in a consistent state preserves the correctness of the database and leaves it in a consistent state.

Transactions can be executed concurrently to improve performance and system utilization. When transactions do not access common data items, they do not interfere with each other and the effect of executing them concurrently is equivalent to a serial execution in an arbitrary order. However, when transactions read and write common data items, they must synchronize access to the shared items. Otherwise, the database state may become *inconsistent* and the execution of the transactions may be incorrect.

For example, consider the transactions T_1 and T_2, where T_1 and T_2 deposit $10 and $20, respectively, to an account with an initial balance of $$x$. The transactions first read the value of x, increase it by the proper amount, and write the result back to x. Suppose that initially $x = \$100$; then, the execution orderings $T_1 T_2$ and $T_2 T_1$ will result in $x = \$130$. Both execution orderings produce the same final result. However, in an uncontrolled concurrent execution of T_1 and T_2, the read and write operations (R and W, respectively) can be interleaved in the following manner: $T_1 : R(x = \$100)$, $T_2 : R(x = \$100)$, $T_1 : W(x = \$110)$ and $T_2 : W(x = \$120)$. The final value of x is $120, which does not conform with the

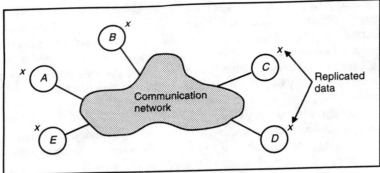

Figure 1. A distributed system with replicas of x.

effect produced by any serial execution of T_1 and T_2. Data inconsistency may result from concurrent executions of transactions that use common data items.

An accepted notion of correctness for concurrently executing transactions is *serializability*. An interleaved execution of transactions $T_1, T_2, \ldots, T_n$ is *serializable* if the effect of the execution is the same as some serial execution of the transactions. Thus, the execution of the transactions T_1 and T_2 given above is not serializable, because the effect of the execution is not the same as any possible serial execution of T_1 and T_2. Synchronization schemes such as two-phase locking, time stamp ordering, and optimistic concurrency control [BHG87] ensure that the effect of concurrent execution of transactions is equivalent to that of some serial execution order; that is, the execution is serializable. Serializability can be ensured by a synchronization protocol if it guarantees that if a data item is modified by the operations of a transaction T, it should not be read or written by operations of other transactions until T completes.

Since the goal of a replicated database system is to improve data availability and enhance response time for transactions, such a system must also allow concurrent execution of transactions, but the consistency of the data should not be compromised. In other words, the system must ensure *single-copy serializability*, which means that transactions execute as if there were a single copy of the database and the transactions appear to execute in some serial order. The replica control protocols that we discuss in the following sections all satisfy this correctness criterion for replicated data.

Replica control protocols

In order to understand the subtleties involved in designing a replica control protocol, consider the following naive protocol for accessing the replicated data item x in the system shown in Figure 1:

"Read from and write to the local replica"

Transactions T_c and T_D executing concurrently at nodes C and D, respectively, each wish to read x, add 1 to the value read, and write the result back. If the above protocol is used, the final value of x is only 1 larger than the original value at nodes C and D and it is not changed at other nodes. The result would be the same, even if T_c and T_D were executed serially (that is, at different times). The problem with this protocol is that it does not make the replicas behave as a single copy and fails to maintain data consistency because any future transaction will read an incorrect value.

remove x from its up-list. If node x was maintaining the primary copy, the next node in the up-list becomes the new maintainer.

Link failures can cause network partitioning. The nodes that are in the same partition as node i, which maintains the primary copy, will continue to recognize node i as the one holding the primary copy. But nodes that are separated from i will think that i has failed and will choose a different primary-copy node. There will then be multiple primary copies, and each one will accept different update requests. The content of the database will become inconsistent, because update operations in different partitions will not be aware of each other's executions. To avoid this situation, the primary copy is allowed to exist only if a majority of all replicas of the item are accessible within the partition. Since there can be at most only one partition with a majority of replicas, this guarantees that two or more primary copies do not exist at the same time. If the network cannot partition, the primary-copy scheme can allow read and write operations to access the data if at least one replica is available.

Performance issues

The primary-copy method was designed with the idea that the database was fragmented in such a way that most accesses made to the data originate from users at the node having the primary copy. Thus, local read and write requests can be satisfied by the primary copy, without having to involve remote nodes in their processing. Although the changes must be propagated to the other replicas, the local transaction can finish as soon as the changes are made to the primary copy.

The primary copy becomes a bottleneck in a large system, because read requests from transactions at nodes that do not store a replica and all write requests are sent to it. Although read requests can be processed in parallel by nodes with replicas, the processing of write requests is done by a single node.

Quorum consensus method

In quorum consensus protocols, an operation can be allowed to proceed to completion if it can get permission from a group of nodes. A group with the minimal number of nodes that can allow an operation to proceed is called a *quorum group* and the collection of all such groups is called a *quorum set*. An operation (for example, read or write) can proceed only if it can obtain permission from all members of a quorum group. The system requirements determine which groups are in the quorum set. For instance, operations requiring mutually exclusive access can be executed when permission is obtained from a group consisting of a majority of nodes.

The concept of quorum consensus is simple and lends itself to a wide range of applications. In the maintenance of replicated data, quorum sets are used to determine if operations for accessing the replicas can be executed. Generally, the type of operations allowed are read and write; consequently, two quorum sets are defined: R and W, for read and write operations, respectively. Read operations can be executed concurrently with other read operations, but write operations must be performed in a mutually exclusive manner.

Quorum sets are used not only to synchronize conflicting operations, but also to present the single-copy view to the users of the replicated data system. Because of this, the following conditions must be satisfied:

(1) The quorum groups that allow read and write operations to execute must have at least one common node that has a replica, and such a node should not allow the replica to be accessed by concurrent operations that are conflicting. This ensures that read operations will return the value installed by the last write operation and that any write operation concurrent with the read operations is properly synchronized.

(2) The quorum groups that allow write operations must have a common member. This ensures

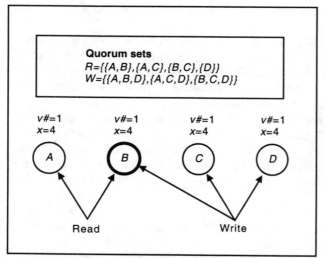

Figure 5. Example of a read and write quorum set pair.

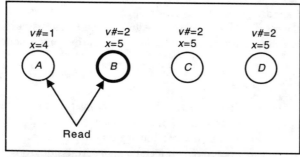

Figure 6. Reading in the quorum consensus protocol.

that write operations are not executed concurrently.

Figure 5 shows a pair of read and write quorum sets R and W that are used to regulate reading and writing of the replicated data item x. Initially, the version number and value are $v\# = 1$ and $x = 4$, respectively, at all replicas. Notice in Figure 5 that any group in R and any group in W intersect and any two groups in W intersect. If read and write operations use read and write quorum groups $\{A, B\}$ and $\{B, C, D\}$, respectively (see Figure 5), node B will detect the conflict and will allow only one of them to proceed. If the write operation is allowed to proceed before the read operation and it updates the value to $x = 5$ at the replicas in its quorum group $\{B, C, D\}$, then a subsequent read operation can detect the update using the version number. For instance, the read operation in Figure 6 that uses $\{A, B\}$ as the quorum group will find that the replica at node B has the highest version number and will return the value associated with that version number as the value of x.

Voting

In general, a quorum set is specified by listing its quorum groups. However, the number of groups in a quorum set can be exponential. For instance, the number of majority groups formed with N nodes is

$$\binom{N}{\left\lceil \frac{N+1}{2} \right\rceil}$$

The order of this binomial expression is exponential in N. A simple way to represent a quorum set is the use of *weighted voting* [Gif79], in which each node i is assigned a positive integral number of votes v_i, for $i = 1, 2, \ldots, N$, and a quorum q is defined. A group of nodes G is a quorum group if the nodes in G collectively have at least q votes and if removing any node from G results in a group with less than q votes. Quorum sets that can be defined by the use of a vote-and-quorum assignment are called *vote assignable*. For example, consider the vote assignment to four nodes where nodes A, B, C, and D receive votes 1, 1, 1, and 2, respectively. We denote this vote assignment by the vector

$\underline{v} = (1, 1, 1, 2)$. Let the quorum assignment q be 2 and consider the group $\{A, B\}$. The number of votes assigned to nodes in the group is q (where $q = 2$) and removal of either A or B will result in a group with less than q votes. Hence, $\{A, B\}$ is a quorum group of q votes. The collection of all quorum groups of q votes is $\{\{A, B\}, \{A, C\}, \{B, C\}, \{D\}\}$, which is the quorum set defined by the vote-and-quorum assignment $(\underline{v}, q)$. Let r and w be the read and write quorums, respectively. The read and write quorum groups R and W in Figure 5 can be defined using vote assignment $\underline{v}$ and the read and write quorums $r = 2$ and $w = 4$, respectively. In fact, a pair of vote-and-quorum assignments $(\underline{v}, q)$ uniquely defines a quorum set, but the same quorum set can be defined by many vote-and-quorum combinations. For instance, the quorum set $\{\{A, B\}, \{A, C\}, \{B, C\}, \{D\}\}$ can also be defined using $\underline{v}' = (2, 2, 2, 3)$ and $q' = 3$.

The synchronization requirement that each read and write quorum group and two different write quorum groups must have nonempty intersections is satisfied if the following two conditions are met:

$$r + w > L, \text{ where } L = \sum_{i=1}^{N} v_i$$

$$2w > L$$

Satisfying the first condition guarantees that a read quorum group will intersect with any write quorum group, because the total votes in two nonintersecting groups are at most L, where $r + w > L$. Similarly, satisfying the second condition guarantees nonempty intersections of any two write groups.

Voting is highly flexible and can be adapted for many types of systems. Consider a system with three replicas of data item x using a voting-based replica control protocol and in which all replicas are assigned one vote each. In systems where most operations are read, the quorum assignment used should be $(r = 1, w = 3)$; that is, it should be read-one/write-all. In contrast, systems that require high write availability should use $(r = 2, w = 2)$, the read-majority/write-majority setting. Thus, read and write quorums can be chosen so that high data availability can be provided for both types of operations.

Weighted voting is not as powerful as the general quorum consensus method. In [GB85], it was demonstrated that there exist quorum sets that cannot be defined using voting. For instance, it was shown in [GB85] that the quorum set $Q = \{\{A, B\}, \{A, C, D\}, \{A, C, E\}, \{A, D, F\}, \{A, E, F\}, \{B, C, F\}, \{B, D, E\}\}$ cannot be defined by any vote assignment.

Multidimensional voting

The *multidimensional-voting (MD-voting)* technique, presented in [AAC91], can be used to represent all quorum sets. In MD voting, the vote value $\underline{v}_i$ assigned to a node and the quorum are *vectors* of nonnegative integers. The number of dimensions is denoted by k, and the votes assigned in the various dimensions are independent of each other. The quorum assignment $\underline{q}_k$ is a k-dimensional vector $(q_1, q_2, \ldots, q_k)$, where q_j is the quorum requirement in dimension j, for $j = 1, 2, \ldots, k$. The vote vectors are added per dimension and compared to the quorum in the corresponding dimension. In addition, a number l — where $1 \le l \le k$ — is defined, which is the number of dimensions of vote assignments for which the quorum must be satisfied. We denote MD voting with a quorum requirement in l of k dimensions as MD(l, k) voting, and the term *single-dimensional voting (SD voting)* refers to the standard weighted-voting method described in [Gif79]. In fact, MD(1, 1) voting is the same as SD voting.

$$y_A = \begin{pmatrix} 2 \\ 0 \\ 2 \\ 2 \end{pmatrix} \quad y_B = \begin{pmatrix} 3 \\ 1 \\ 0 \\ 0 \end{pmatrix} \quad y_C = \begin{pmatrix} 0 \\ 1 \\ 0 \\ 2 \end{pmatrix} \quad y_D = \begin{pmatrix} 1 \\ 0 \\ 1 \\ 1 \end{pmatrix} \quad y_E = \begin{pmatrix} 1 \\ 0 \\ 1 \\ 1 \end{pmatrix} \quad y_F = \begin{pmatrix} 0 \\ 1 \\ 2 \\ 0 \end{pmatrix} \quad \text{and} \quad q = \begin{pmatrix} 5 \\ 3 \\ 5 \\ 5 \end{pmatrix}$$

Figure 7. An MD(1, 4) vote-and-quorum assignment for Q = {{A, B}, {A, C, D}, {A, C, E}, {A, D, F}, {A, E, F}, {B, C, F}, {B, D, E}}.

An MD(l, k) vote-and-quorum assignment defines a unique quorum set in a manner similar to that used in standard voting. A group of nodes G is a quorum group in MD(l, k) voting if the total votes of the nodes in G collectively satisfy quorum requirements in at least l dimensions and if removing any node from G results in a group that satisfies quorum requirements in strictly less than l dimensions. The same quorum set can be defined by different vote-and-quorum assignment with possibly different l and k. The nonvote-assignable quorum set Q given previously can be defined by MD(1, 4) voting using the MD vote-and-quorum assignments given in Figure 7.

Performance issues

The main drawback of quorum consensus schemes is the relatively high overhead incurred in the execution of the read operations. Reading requires participation of nodes in a read quorum group that usually consists of more than one node. In contrast, reading using the primary-copy method requires access to only one replica; this is also the case in the available-copies method, which is discussed in the next section. With the use of quorum consensus, read and write operations can succeed only when a sufficiently large number of replicas are available. In contrast, the primary-copy method may be able to operate as long as one replica is available for updating. To achieve the same high level of data availability, the system must use a higher degree of replication in quorum consensus methods. A major benefit of quorum-consensus-based schemes is that arbitrary communication link failures, including those that partition the network, require no special attention. In the case of network partitioning, write operations can be processed by at most one partition. In contrast, the primary-copy scheme relies on the majority quorum consensus method for determining if a primary copy can be established.

The system behavior depends on the pair of read and write quorum sets used. For instance, a system using the read-one/write-all quorum will have good performance for read operations, but write operations will incur high costs and experience low data availability. At the other end of the spectrum, using the read-majority/write-majority quorum will provide high data availability for both types of operations, but also will incur a high cost of reading. The optimum read and write quorum setting depends on the mix of transactions and the performance measure in question. It was found in [AA89] that when the read-one/write-all quorum is used, data availability will decrease after a certain level of replication. This is due to the fact that write operations must update all replicas. The likelihood of the successful completion of a write operation decreases when the number of replicas is increased; this is not the case with the read-majority/write-majority quorum, because data availability always increases for both read and write operations when the degree of replication is increased.

Determining the best read and write quorum set pair or vote-and-quorum assignment for a given performance measure is difficult because of the complex relationship between system behavior and the quorum sets. However, when the quorum sets are fixed, performance can be easily determined through analytical methods or simulation techniques. The best quorum set pair can be found through a search in the complete set of all quorum sets. In [GB85], an enumeration method was presented that generates a subset of the quorum sets used for synchronizing operations that require mutual exclusion. Each group of the quorum set must intersect with every group in the set to guarantee mutual exclusion; such sets are called *coteries*. In [CAA89], an enumeration algorithm was presented to obtain all read and write quorum sets that are defined by SD voting.

Available-copies method

The easiest way to handle node failures is to ignore them. In the basic available-copies method, updates are applied to replicas at nodes that are operational and a read operation can use any

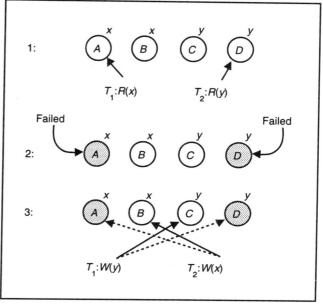

Figure 8. An incorrect execution using a naive read-one/write-all available-copies protocol.

available replica. It was shown in [BHG87] that this basic method does not guarantee data consistency. Consider a system that replicates the value of x at nodes A and B and the value of y at nodes C and D. A transaction T_1 first reads x and then writes y and a transaction T_2 first reads y and then writes x. Figure 8 shows a sequence of events that will cause data inconsistency. Transactions T_1 and T_2 read x at node A and y at node D, respectively. After the read operations are completed, the nodes A and D fail. Then T_1 and T_2 proceed to update all available copies of y and x, respectively. Since nodes A and D have failed, T_1 and T_2 will update the copies only at nodes B and C. Neither transaction is aware of the read operation of the other, and the execution will lead to data inconsistency. The result is not a one-copy serializable execution.

This inconsistency is caused by the failures of nodes A and D where transactions T_1 and T_2 have read the values of x and y, respectively. If nodes A and D had not failed, both transactions T_1 and T_2 would not be able to update y and x, respectively (read locks are placed on behalf of the transactions when they read data at a node). Because of node failures, transactions T_1 and T_2 can no longer synchronize themselves, because their read locks are lost.

The correct available-copies scheme [BHG87] operates as follows: Read operations can be directed to any node holding the latest value of the data, and write operations will succeed only if at least one replica records the update. A transaction can terminate successfully only when it is able to execute the following two-step validation process:

(1) *Missing-writes validation*: The transaction makes sure that all replicas that did not receive its updates are still unavailable.
(2) *Access validation*: The transaction makes sure that all replicas that it read from and wrote to are still available.

The directory-oriented available-copies method

The basic available-copies scheme does not allow dynamic assignment of replicas to nodes and requires that transactions attempt to update replicas at all nodes (even when some nodes have failed). The *directory-oriented* available-copies method [BHG87] uses directory information to direct operations to replicas only on nodes that are believed to be operational. This scheme can also be used to dynamically add and remove replicas.

For each data item x, there is a directory listing $d(x)$ of the nodes that have replicas. The directory $d(x)$ can itself be replicated and stored at different nodes. The directory for x at node M, $d_M(x)$, also contains a list of directory copies for x that node M believes are available. Directories are updated by the following two special transactions:

- Include(x_A), for creating a new replica of x at node A, and
- Exclude(x_A), for destroying the replica at A.

To process a read operation of x, the system first reads a copy of the directory — for example, $d_M(x)$ — and uses the information to find an available copy. A write operation must update all replicas that are listed in the directory entry. Because of node failures, some copies may not be available for updating, and the transaction is aborted. The system then runs an Exclude transaction to update the directories, and the transaction is restarted.

Performance issues

An attractive feature of the available-copies method is the fact that read operations need to access only one copy of the data. Also, the available-copies method provides very high data availability. Both read and write operations can be performed, as long as there is one operational node with a replica. However, the available-copies scheme is not tolerant of network partition failures. When the network can partition, the available-copies method presented above will fail to preserve data consistency. For example, when the system in Figure 8 is separated in the way given in Figure 9, transactions that read and write x and y in the two partitions will not be able to synchronize with each other. To handle network partitions, the available-copies method must be extended to ensure that write operations can be executed in only one partition.

Extensions and hybrid schemes

The basic replica control protocols reviewed in the previous sections can be extended with additional provisions to further enhance the data availability provided by these protocols or to improve other performance measures. Similarly, two of the basic schemes can be combined to exploit the advantages of both. In particular, the weighted-voting method has proven to be very robust and versatile, and many dynamic-voting methods have been derived [Her87], [ET86], [JM90]. The voting method is also used to augment the available-copies scheme to achieve the capability to tolerate network failures. In this section, we review the following protocols that are extensions to or hybrids of the basic replica control protocols: dynamic quorum adjustment, virtual partition, dynamic voting, voting with witnesses, voting with ghosts, and regeneration.

Dynamic quorum adjustment

Dynamic methods can enhance performance by adjusting the rules of a replica control protocol according to the current state of the system. In systems where read operations are predominant, the dynamic quorum adjustment method [Her87] can improve performance by allowing the system to operate with a read quorum set consisting of groups with a small number of nodes. The corresponding write quorum set has large groups, and write operations can complete only when a large number of nodes are operational. Because of failures, a transaction may not be able to find a write quorum, and the protocol can switch to another, more favorable pair of read and write quorum sets. The new write quorum set will have smaller groups, but the groups in the corresponding read quorum set are larger. This

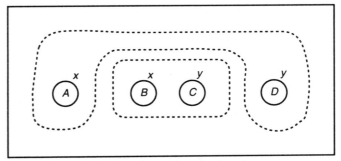

Figure 9. A partitioned network.

technique is called *quorum inflation*. A complementary technique called *quorum deflation* is used to reduce the size of read quorum groups when nodes recover. Hence, the size of read and write quorum groups increases and decreases, respectively, when the number of failures increases.

Let $(R_1 = \{\{A\}, \{B\}, \{C\}\}, W_1 = \{\{A, B, C\}\})$ and $(R_2 = \{\{A, B\}, \{A, C\}, \{B, C\}\}, W_2 = \{\{A, B\}, \{A, C\}, \{B, C\}\})$ be two pairs of read and write quorum sets. Notice that a group in W_2 is a subset of a group in W_1. Thus, a group of nodes that constitute a write quorum group in W_1 is also a write quorum group in W_2; therefore, W_2 is a more favorable quorum set for writing. Correspondingly, the read quorum set R_2 is less favorable for reading because it contains larger quorum groups than R_1. If one of the nodes fails (making the data unavailable for writing using W_1), the quorum inflation technique, which increases the size of read quorum groups while decreasing the size of write groups, is used to switch the system from the quorum set (R_1, W_1) to (R_2, W_2) in case of a failure.

In the dynamic quorum adjustment method, the system can operate at a number of levels, and each level has associated read and write quorum sets (in the above example, two levels are shown). Transactions are also assigned a level number, and the ones operating at the same level synchronize with each other using the read and write quorum sets defined for the level. Transactions operating at different levels are synchronized by additional read/write rules that ensure lower level transactions are completed before higher level ones. A transaction restarts by choosing a higher level number.

Virtual partition

The dynamic scheme presented in [ET86] allows a node to make use of its view about the state of the system (that is, to make use of its information about operational nodes) and to adjust the replica control protocol accordingly. The *view* maintained by each node i is a set that contains nodes with which i can communicate. The view need not accurately reflect connectivity of the nodes. Each view is associated with a unique view identifier and two nodes are in the same view, if they have the same view identifier. Provisions are made to allow nodes to change their views according to changes in the system.

Each replica of a data item x is assigned one vote, and read and write accessibility thresholds $r[x]$ and $w[x]$ are defined. The data item x is read and write accessible by nodes in a view only if $r[x]$ and $w[x]$ votes, respectively, are available at nodes in the same view. The accessibility thresholds $r[x]$ and $w[x]$ satisfy the following constraints:

$$r[x] + w[x] > N[x]$$

$$2w[x] > N[x]$$

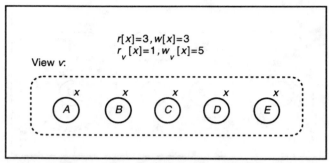

$r[x]=3, w[x]=3$
$r_v[x]=1, w_v[x]=5$

View v:

Figure 10. Virtual partition scheme: no-failures operation.

where $N[x]$ is the total number of replicas of x in the system. These requirements are similar to those used in the basic quorum consensus protocol to ensure intersection of a read quorum group and a write quorum group and the intersection of two write quorum groups. However, $r[x]$ and $w[x]$ are not the read and write quorums.

When a view v is established, the nodes in the view determine if the data are read and write accessible. In the case that the data are accessible, a read quorum and a write quorum $r_v[x]$ and $w_v[x]$, respectively, are chosen that may be different from $r[x]$ and $w[x]$. The quorums $r_v[x]$ and $w_v[x]$ must satisfy the following constraints:

$$r_v[x] + w_v[x] > N[x]$$

$$w_v[x] \geq w[x]$$

These constraints ensure that

- A write quorum group in a view v intersects with all read quorum groups in the same view; thus, read operations will be able to determine the current value.
- All write quorum groups intersect with each other; thus, write operations cannot execute concurrently in two different views.

For example, consider a five-node system using $r[x] = 3$ and $w[x] = 3$. Figure 10 shows the system in the no-failures state where all nodes have the same view v and the read and write quorums are $r_v[x] = 1$ and $w_v[x] = 5$, respectively, to provide high performance for read operations. Alternately, the system can use the quorum assignments $(r_v[x] = 2, w_v[x] = 4)$ or $(r_v[x] = 3, w_v[x] = 3)$ in view v. Suppose nodes D and E are separated from the other nodes as shown in Figure 11; the nodes A, B, and C will change their views to v'. The data are read and write accessible in the $\{A, B, C\}$ partition and, in this case, the only read and write quorum assignments allowed are $r_v[x] = 3$ and $w_v[x] = 3$. Thus, in a failure state, the system has fewer choices for quorum settings. The use of quorum assignment in conjunction with accessibility thresholds allows the system to improve performance by using a favorable pair of read and write quorum sets when it is in a no-failures state. In failure states, the system can switch to use other, less favorable quorum assignments, and the data remain available.

Dynamic voting

The basic dynamic-voting method [JM90] assigns one vote to each replica and maintains — in addition to a version number — the update node cardinality U, which is the number of replicas updated by the last transaction that updated the data item. The version number is used to determine both the current value and the update node cardinality. Reading and writing use the majority quorum with respect to the current update cardinality, and an update is performed on replicas at all operational nodes.

The operation of the dynamic-voting method is best illustrated by an example. Consider the system in Figure 12, where the data item x is replicated at five nodes. Initially, all nodes contain the same information. The version number $v\#$, the update node cardinality U, and the value of x are 1, 5, and 4, respectively. A transaction T_1 that wants to access the data item x first determines that the last update operation has written to five replicas and that the current version number $v\# = 1$. If T_1 can obtain permission from three (a majority of five) nodes with replicas that contain the current version number $v\# = 1$, it is allowed to proceed. Otherwise, T_1 must wait or abort.

Assume that nodes D and E fail, and a transaction T_2 wants to increment x by 1. T_2 will determine from information at nodes A, B, and C that $U = 5$ and $v\# = 1$. Since the group $\{A, B, C\}$ is a majority group with respect to the current update cardinality U, T_2 can access the data item $x = 4$, add 1 to x, and update the replicas at nodes A, B, and C. The resulting state is given in Figure 13; notice that the update node cardinality recorded is 3.

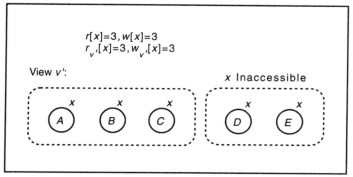

$r[x]=3, w[x]=3$
$r_{v'}[x]=3, w_{v'}[x]=3$

View v':

x Inaccessible

Figure 11. Virtual partition scheme: failure operation.

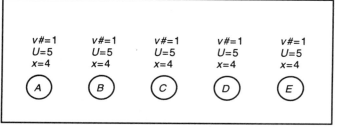

$v\#=1$ $v\#=1$ $v\#=1$ $v\#=1$ $v\#=1$
$U=5$ $U=5$ $U=5$ $U=5$ $U=5$
$x=4$ $x=4$ $x=4$ $x=4$ $x=4$

Figure 12. Dynamic voting: no-failures operation.

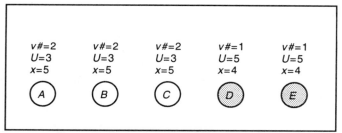

$v\#=2$ $v\#=2$ $v\#=2$ $v\#=1$ $v\#=1$
$U=3$ $U=3$ $U=3$ $U=5$ $U=5$
$x=5$ $x=5$ $x=5$ $x=4$ $x=4$

Figure 13. Dynamic voting: failure operation.

Suppose that node A also fails, and another transaction T_3 wants to increment x by 1. T_3 now determines that $v\# = 2$, $U = 3$, and $x = 5$. Since the current update node cardinality $U = 3$, the group of operational nodes $\{B, C\}$ is a valid majority quorum. Notice that $\{B, C\}$ is not a majority group in the initial state where the update node cardinality is 5. Transaction T_3 can be allowed to access x and record the updates at nodes B and C. The update node cardinality is now equal to 2. The resulting state is given in Figure 14.

The dynamic-voting method can thus allow the system to adapt its quorum requirement to changes in the system state. Notice in Figure 14 that a minority of the replicas contain the most recent value. It is thus possible that a majority of the replicas are operational and that none of these operational replicas are holding the current value. For example, if nodes B and C fail, and nodes A, D, and E recover simultaneously, we will have the state given in Figure 15, where a majority of the nodes with replicas are operational, but none have the current value of x. The dynamic-voting protocol will disallow access to out-of-date values. A transaction T_4 that wants to access x will determine that

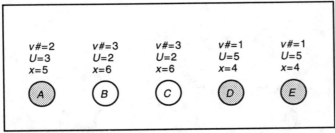

Figure 14. Dynamic voting: failure operation, continued.

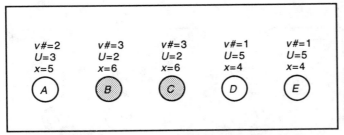

Figure 15. Dynamic voting: failure operation, continued.

$v\# = 2$ and $U = 3$, but only one node (namely, A) has the most recent value. Nodes D and E, which have out-of-date version numbers, cannot be included in the quorum. T_4 will not be able to obtain a valid quorum and must wait or abort.

The hybrid dynamic-voting [JM90] method operates in a manner similar to that of the basic dynamic-voting scheme. It uses the basic dynamic-voting method when the update node cardinality is at least three nodes. When less than three nodes with replicas are operational, the hybrid scheme will use static majority voting as the replica control method. It was shown in [JM90] that the hybrid scheme provides better data availability than the basic dynamic-voting protocol.

Voting with witnesses

The replicas in the basic weighted-voting scheme store a version number and the value of the data item. The voting-with-witnesses method [Pâr86] replaces some of the replicas by *witnesses*, which are copies that contain only the version number, but no data. The witnesses are assigned votes and will cast them when they receive voting requests from transactions. They provide the transactions with their version numbers, which are used to identify the current value of the data item. Although the witnesses do not maintain data, they can testify about the validity of the value provided by some other replica. Because of the fact that witnesses do not contain the data item itself, the read and write operations on witnesses are implemented as follows:

- When a witness is a member of a read quorum, it provides the requester with its version number. It cannot provide the value of the data item.
- When a witness is a member of a write quorum, it records the version number provided in the write request. The value of the data item is ignored.

Consider the system in Figure 16 with two full replicas of x and one witness, where initially all version numbers are 1 and $x = 4$. The state of a full replica and a witness can be represented by the tuples (*version number, value*) and (*version number, -*), respectively. The state of the system in Figure 16 can be represented by the triplet of tuples $((1, 4), (1, 4), (1, -))$, where the first, second, and third tuples represent the state of the item stored at nodes A, B, and C, respectively. A replica and witness are assigned one vote each and the replica control method used is read-majority/write-majority. Thus, a majority can be two full replicas, or one full replica and one witness.

If a transaction T updates $x = 5$ using the replica at node B and the witness at node C as the write quorum group, the state of the system becomes $((1, 4), (2, 5), (2, -))$. Notice that the value is not stored at C, but its version number reflects the fact that the replica at node A does not contain the current value. When a read operation uses nodes A and C as a quorum group, the version number returned by the witness will testify that the value at node A is out-of-date. It is thus possible for a read operation to obtain permission from a read quorum group and not find the current value of the data item. An analysis in [Pâr86] showed that the data availability in a system with

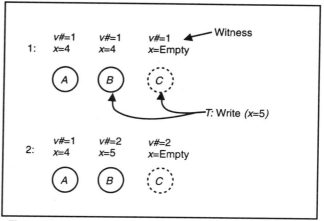

Figure 16. Voting with witnesses using two full replicas and one witness.

two full replicas and one witness is slightly lower than that in a system with three full replicas. The voting-with-witnesses scheme can effectively raise the data availability without having to replicate the data item.

Voting with ghosts

A system that uses the voting-with-ghosts method [vRT87] is assumed to consist of a number of network segments, and the nodes located in the same segment cannot be separated from one another. A network segment can fail, and the nodes in that segment will not be able to communicate. This model can be used to represent the operation of Ethernet segments interconnected through gateways where gateway failures can partition the network, but nodes on the same segment can communicate as long as the segment is operational.

The voting-with-ghosts protocol uses weighted voting as its basic replica control scheme and extends it with the notion of *ghosts* to increase the availability of write operations. A ghost is a process without any storage space and its task is to testify to the fact that a node with a replica has failed. The ghost for a failed node holding a replica is started on the same segment of the network where the failed node is located. Hence, when a ghost responds to a request, a transaction can safely assume that the network is not partitioned and that the node with the replica has failed.

Like a witness in [Pâr86], a ghost is assigned votes equal in number to that given to the replica at the failed node. A ghost, unlike a witness, does not participate in a read quorum. This difference between a ghost and a witness is caused by the fact that a ghost does not maintain any information on the data item, while a witness can know the latest version number. A ghost can be a member of a write quorum group and, like a witness, it will ignore the value in the write operation. Furthermore, the version number in the write operation will be ignored as well. The ghost will only return its vote in response to a write request.

Consider the system in Figure 17 with N replicas of a data item x, where all replicas are assigned one vote each. Assume that the read quorum is 1; then, the corresponding write quorum must be N, and a failure of any node with a replica will make the system unavailable for writing using the basic voting scheme. In voting with ghosts, the failure of a node with a replica will trigger the creation of a ghost process, and the ghost will reply on behalf of the failed node. The ghost will not respond to read requests, so that a read operation will be processed only by a node holding a replica of x. When a write request is sent to all nodes with replicas, the ghost will respond on behalf of the failed node and the transaction will be able to obtain a write quorum and complete the write operation. Note that

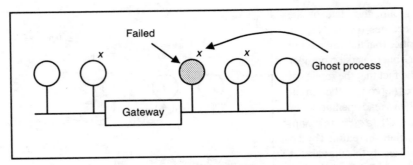

Figure 17. Voting with ghosts.

all available replicas are part of a write quorum and will be updated. When a node recovers from failure, it must obtain the latest value of the data item before it can participate in a read quorum. Thus, a subsequent read operation will obtain the current value. In fact, the voting-with-ghosts protocol using the read-one/write-all quorum assignment and the basic available-copies method operate in a similar manner when the network cannot partition. Both methods will read from one replica and update all available replicas. But the voting-with-ghosts method is not restricted to the use of the read-one/write-all assignment and can use an arbitrary vote-and/or-quorum assignment.

Regeneration

The regeneration scheme [PNP88], which was implemented in the Eden distributed system at the University of Washington, attempts to maintain exactly *N* available replicas at all times. When a node storing a replica fails, the system will try to boost the availability of the data by regenerating a new replica on another operational node. Directories that store the location of the replicas are modified accordingly to direct transactions to read and write the newly generated copies. The replicas stored at failed nodes will not be accessible through directories and effectively become garbage when the nodes recover from failures. A garbage-collection subsystem is used to reclaim the space occupied by such replicas.

The basic regeneration scheme is *read-one/write-N*. Read operations will succeed as long as there is at least one available replica. Write operations succeed only if *N* replicas can be written. When there are fewer than *N* replicas available for update, the system will regenerate a number of replicas to supplement up to a total of *N* replicas. Write operations will fail if the system cannot regenerate replicas (because of shortage of disk space). The basic regeneration method is similar to the directory-oriented available-copies method, but uses a policy to include additional replicas when the system detects that fewer than *N* replicas are available.

An extension to the basic regeneration scheme is to use the available-copies scheme when the system has exhausted the disk space for regenerating replicas. As long as the system has more space available, write operations will update exactly *N* replicas. In the event that no more space is available, write operations will update only the available copies. Read operations will access one replica in either case.

Future directions

High-speed networking and the falling costs of hardware will make it possible for resources to be shared in distributed systems that span hundreds or thousands of nodes. Although the reliability of the nodes and network components may be high in these systems, the need for data replication will still exist. Data replication can ensure that data can be found locally or close to the nodes where requests for the data are made; thus, network latency costs can be avoided. Many of the replica control protocols presented in this paper have not been evaluated for such environments, and it may be that they do not perform well. Discussed below are some of the issues that must be addressed in the design and evaluation of replica control protocols that will be suitable for large distributed systems.

(1)   The major goal of many of the replica control protocols has been to maximize the availability of data. However, when nodes are highly reliable, a very high level of data availability can be achieved with a small degree of replication [AA89]. Clearly, the small number of nodes that store replicas can become bottlenecks in a large distributed system. Thus, a high degree of replication may be desirable to ensure that a replica can be found close to the node where a request arrives and also that the load generated by the requests is shared between a large number of nodes. More work needs to be done to develop replica control protocols that exploit the load-sharing benefits of replicated data.

(2)   The communication and processing overhead of replica control protocols is high because these protocols ensure single-copy serializability. Although this type of correctness may be necessary in some applications, there exist many application domains where a weaker correctness condition is acceptable. An example of such a domain may be file systems where users can tolerate occasional inconsistencies to get high data availability at low cost. It is necessary to develop precise characterizations of weaker consistency of data and to exploit this weakening in developing efficient replica control protocols.

(3)   There is strong evidence that the network environment has a considerable impact on the effective use of replication. An understanding of the interaction of replication and the networking environment remains to be achieved. For example, a replica control protocol based on voting can use broadcast or multicast communication to reach the nodes that have been assigned votes. Such protocols may not be suitable in networks where broadcast or multicast communication is expensive or not feasible. It may be possible to attain better performance by using a replica control protocol that exploits the mechanisms of the underlying network. It may also be that replication can be used to overcome the effect of poor-quality communication links.

(4)   The performance of a large number of protocols has been studied both analytically and using simulation studies. Unfortunately, there are few actual implementations of these protocols in real systems. It is necessary to build these protocols and experimentally evaluate their performance in realistic application domains. Perhaps the lack of experimental research is the reason for the limited impact that data replication has had in the design and implementation of distributed systems.

Data replication in distributed systems is still an active research area, and many of the above issues should be resolved in the coming years. The results of this research, along with the results already obtained, hold the promise for exploiting the potential of distributed systems in building highly available and powerful systems.

Acknowledgments

This work was supported in part by NSF grants NCR-8604850 and CCR-8806358 and by the University Research Committee of Emory University, Atlanta, Georgia.

References

[AA89] M. Ahamad and M.H. Ammar, "Performance Characterization of Quorum-Consensus Algorithms for Replicated Data," *IEEE Trans. Software Eng.*, Vol. SE-15, No. 4, Apr. 1989, pp. 492-496.

[AAC91] M. Ahamad, M.H. Ammar, and S.Y. Cheung, "Multidimensional Voting," *ACM Trans. Computer Systems,*Vol. 9, No. 4, Nov. 1991, pp. 399-431.

[BHG87] P.A. Bernstein, V. Hadzilacos, and N. Goodman, *Concurrency Control and Recovery in Database Systems*, Addison-Wesley, Reading, Mass., 1987.

[CAA89] S.Y. Cheung, M. Ahamad, and M.H. Ammar, "Optimizing Vote and Quorum Assignments for Reading and Writing," *IEEE Trans. Knowledge and Data Eng.*, Vol. 1, No. 3, Sept. 1989, pp. 387-397.

[ET86] A. El Abbadi and S. Toueg, "Maintaining Availability in Partitioned Replicated Databases," *Proc. Symp. Principles Database Systems (PODS)*, ACM Press, New York, N.Y., 1986, pp. 340-351.

[GB85] H. Garcia-Molina and D. Barbara, "How to Assign Votes in a Distributed System," *J. ACM*, Vol. 32, No. 4, Oct. 1985, pp. 841-860.

[Gif79] H. Gifford, "Weighted Voting for Replicated Data," *Proc. Seventh Symp. Operating Systems*, ACM Press, New York, N.Y., 1979, pp. 150-162.

[Her87] M. Herlihy, "Dynamic Quorum Adjustment for Partitioned Data," *ACM Trans. Database Systems*, Vol. 12, No. 2, June 1987, pp. 170-194.

[JM90] S. Jajodia and D. Mutchler, "Dynamic Voting Algorithms for Maintaining the Consistency of a Replicated Database," *ACM Trans. Database Systems*, Vol. 15, No. 2, June 1990, pp. 230-280.

[Pâr86] J.-F. Pâris, "Voting with Witnesses: A Consistency Scheme for Replicated Files," *Proc. Sixth Int'l Conf. Distributed Computing Systems*, IEEE Computer Soc. Press, Los Alamitos, Calif., 1986, pp. 606-612.

[PNP88] C. Pu, J.D. Noe, and A. Proudfoot, "Regeneration of Replicated Objects: A Technique and Its Eden Implementation," *IEEE Trans. Software Eng.*, Vol. SE-14, No. 7, July 1988, pp. 936-945.

[Sto79] M. Stonebraker, "Concurrency Control and Consistency of Multiple Copies of Data in Distributed INGRES," *IEEE Trans. Software Eng.*, Vol. SE-5, No. 3, May 1979, pp. 188-194.

[vRT87] R. van Renesse and A.S. Tanenbaum, "Voting with Ghosts," *Proc. Eighth Int'l Conf. Distributed Computing Systems*, IEEE Computer Soc. Press, Los Alamitos, Calif., 1988, pp. 456-462.

Additional reading

In addition to those works listed in the references above, other important works in the area of data replication are listed below.

D. Agrawal and A. El Abbadi, "Reducing Storage for Quorum Consensus Algorithms," *Proc. Int'l Conf. Very Large Data Bases*, 1988, pp. 419-430.

D. Agrawal and A. El Abbadi, "An Efficient Solution to the Distributed Mutual Exclusion Problem," *Proc. Principles Distributed Computing*, 1989, pp. 193-200.

D. Barbara, H. Garcia-Molina, and A. Spauster, "Protocols for Dynamic Vote Reassignment," *Proc. Principles Distributed Computing*, ACM Press, New York, N.Y., 1986, pp. 195-205.

D. Barbara and H. Garcia-Molina, "The Reliability of Voting Mechanisms," *IEEE Trans. Computers*, Vol. C-36, No. 10, Oct. 1987, pp. 1197-1208.

P.A. Bernstein and N. Goodman, "An Algorithm for Concurrency Control and Recovery in Replicated Distributed Databases," *ACM Trans. Database Systems*, Vol. 9, No. 4, Dec. 1984, pp. 596-615.

S.Y. Cheung, M.H. Ammar, and M. Ahamad, "On the Optimality of Voting," Tech. Report GIT-ICS-90/30, Georgia Inst. Technology, Atlanta, Ga., 1990.

S.Y. Cheung, M.H. Ammar, and M. Ahamad, "The Grid Protocol: A High Performance Scheme for Maintaining Replicated Data," *Proc. Sixth Int'l Conf. Data Eng.*, IEEE Computer Soc. Press, Los Alamitos, Calif., 1990, pp. 438-445.

S.B. Davidson, H. Garcia-Molina, and D. Skeen, "Consistency in Partitioned Networks," *ACM Computing Surveys*, Vol. 17, No. 3, Sept. 1985, pp. 341-370.

D.L. Eager and K.C. Sevcik, "Achieving Robustness in Distributed Database Systems," *ACM Trans. Database Systems*, Vol. 4, No. 1, Sept. 1983, pp. 354-381.

M. Herlihy, "A Quorum-Consensus Replication Method for Abstract Data Types," *ACM Trans. Computer Systems*, Vol. 4, No. 1, Feb. 1986, pp. 32-53.

T.A. Joseph and K.P. Birman, "Low Cost Management of Replicated Data in Fault-Tolerant Distributed Systems," *ACM Trans. Computer Systems*, Vol. 4, No. 1, Feb. 1986, pp. 54-70.

A. Kumar, "Performance Analysis of a Hierarchical Quorum Consensus Algorithm for Replicated Objects," *Proc. 10th Int'l Conf. Distributed Computing Systems*, IEEE Computer Soc. Press, Los Alamitos, Calif., 1990, pp. 378-385.

D.D.E. Long, J.L. Carroll, and K. Stewart, "The Reliability of Regeneration-Based Replica Control Protocols," *Proc. Ninth Int'l Conf. Distributed Computing Systems*, IEEE Computer Soc. Press, Los Alamitos, Calif., 1989, pp. 465-473.

M. Obradovic and P. Berman, "Voting as the Optimal Static Pessimistic Scheme for Managing Replicated Data," *Proc. Ninth Symp. Reliable Distributed Systems*, IEEE Computer Soc. Press, Los Alamitos, Calif., 1990, pp. 126-135.

J.-F. Pâris and F.D. Berman, "How to Make Your Votes Count," Tech. Report UH-CS-99-16, Dept. of Computer Science, Univ. of Houston, Houston, Texas, 1988.

J.-F. Pâris and D.D.E. Long, "The Performance of Available Copy Protocols for the Management of Replicated Data," *Performance Evaluation*, Vol. 11, 1990, pp. 9-30.

Proc. Workshop Management Replicated Data, IEEE Computer Soc. Press, Los Alamitos, Calif., 1990.

J. Tang and N. Natarajan, "A Scheme for Maintaining Consistency and Availability of Replicated Files in a Partitioned Distributed System," *Proc. Fifth Int'l Conf. Data Eng.*, IEEE Computer Soc. Press, Los Alamitos, Calif., 1989, pp. 530-537.

Z. Tong and R.Y. Kain, "Vote Assignments in Weighted Voting Mechanisms," *Proc. Seventh Symp. Reliable Distributed Systems*, IEEE Computer Soc. Press, Los Alamitos, Calif., 1988, pp. 138-143.

Scheduling Transactions for Distributed Time-Critical Applications

Database systems in which transactions have timing constraints such as *deadlines* are called *real-time database systems* (RTDBSs). The correctness of the system depends not only on the logical results, but also on the time within which the results are produced. In RTDBSs, transactions must be scheduled in such a way that they can be completed before their corresponding deadlines expire. For example, both the update and the query on the tracking data for a missile must be processed within given deadlines.

RTDBSs are becoming increasingly important in a wide range of applications, including aerospace and weapon systems, computer-integrated manufacturing, robotics, nuclear power plants, and traffic control systems. In recent real-time computing workshops — for example, the IEEE Workshop on Real-Time Operating Systems and Software [IEEE90] and the Office of Naval Research (ONR) Workshop on Foundations of Real-Time Computing [ONR90], both held in 1990 — researchers pointed to the need for basic research in database systems that satisfy timing constraints in collecting, updating, and retrieving shared data, because traditional data models and databases are not adequate for time-critical applications. Very few conventional database systems allow users to specify or ensure timing constraints. Interest in the time-critical-application domain is growing in the database community also. Recently, a number of research results appeared in the literature [Abbo92], [ACM88], [Buch89], [Kort90], [Lin89], [Lin90], [Sha88], [Sha91], [Son90c].

It is useful to categorize transactions in RTDBSs into *hard transactions* and *soft transactions* [ACM88]. We define hard real-time transactions as those transactions whose timing constraints must be guaranteed. Missing deadlines of this type of transaction may result in catastrophic consequences. In contrast, soft real-time transactions have timing constraints, but there may still be some justification in completing the transactions after the deadline. Catastrophic consequences do not result if soft real-time transactions miss their deadlines. Soft real-time transactions are scheduled taking into account their timing requirements, but they are not guaranteed to make their deadlines. There are many real-time systems that need database support for both types of transactions.

Sang H. Son and

Seog Park

Because it is very difficult to guarantee hard real-time deadlines with unpredictable data requirements, we deal only with soft real-time RTDBSs in this paper.

Conventional database systems are typically not used in real-time applications because of two inadequacies: poor performance and lack of predictability. In conventional database systems, transaction processing requires access to a database stored on secondary storage; thus, transaction response time is limited by disk access delays, which can be in the order of milliseconds. Still, these databases are fast enough for traditional applications in which a response time of a few seconds is often acceptable to human users. However, these systems may not be able to provide a response fast enough for high-performance real-time applications. One approach to achieving high performance is to replace slow devices (for example, a disk) by a high-speed version (for example, a large RAM). Another alternative is to use application-specific knowledge to increase the degree of concurrency. For example, by exploiting the semantic information associated with transactions and data, we may use a notion of correctness different from serializability. As observed by Bernstein [Bern87], serializability may be too strong as a correctness criterion for concurrency control in database systems with timing constraints, because of the limitation on concurrency. If necessary, data consistency might be compromised to satisfy timing constraints.

In terms of predictability, current database systems do not schedule transactions to meet response-time requirements and they commonly lock data to assure consistency. Time-driven scheduling and locks are basically incompatible. Low-priority transactions may block higher priority transactions, leading to timing-requirement failures. Consequently, the requirements and design objectives of RTDBSs differ widely from those of conventional database systems. New techniques are necessary to manage database consistency. They should be compatible with time-driven scheduling and meet the system response times and temporal-consistency requirements. It is natural to ask how a conventional database system must be modified so that its performance and predictability can be acceptable for real-time applications.

In addition to timing constraints of a transaction, such as a deadline, *criticality* that represents the importance of a transaction should be considered in calculating the priority of the transaction. Therefore, proper management of priorities and conflict resolution in real-time transaction scheduling are essential for responsiveness and predictability of RTDBSs.

While the theories of concurrency control in database systems and real-time task scheduling have both advanced, little attention has been paid to the interaction between concurrency control protocols and real-time scheduling algorithms [Stan88]. In database concurrency control, meeting the deadline is typically not addressed. The objective is to provide a high degree of concurrency and thus faster average response time without violating data consistency. In real-time scheduling, on the other hand, it is customary to assume that tasks are independent, or that the time spent synchronizing their access to shared data is negligible compared with execution time. The objective here is to maximize resources, such as CPU utilization, subject to meeting timing constraints. As in serializability, data consistency is not a consideration in real-time scheduling; hence, the problem of guaranteeing the consistency of shared data is ignored. In addition, conventional real-time systems assume advance knowledge of the resource and data requirements of tasks.

One of the challenges of RTDBSs is the creation of a theory for real-time scheduling and concurrency control protocols that maximizes both concurrency and resource utilization, subject to three constraints: data consistency, transaction correctness, and transaction deadlines [Stan88]. Several recent projects have investigated the issue of adding real-time constraints into database systems to facilitate efficient and correct management of timing constraints in RTDBSs [ACM88], [Buch89], [Son90c]. There are several difficulties in achieving this goal. A database access operation, for example, takes a highly variable amount of time, depending on whether or not disk I/O, logging, and buffering, for instance, are required. Furthermore, concurrency control may cause aborts or delays of indeterminate length.

The advent of an RTDBS presents many new and challenging problems, including the following:

- What is an appropriate model for real-time transactions and data?
- What are the language constructs that can be used to specify real-time constraints?
- What mechanisms are needed for describing and evaluating triggers?
- What are the measures of system predictability?
- How are transactions scheduled?
- What is the effect of real-time constraints on concurrency control?

This paper addresses the last two issues, which are associated with transaction scheduling and concurrency control, and presents an integrated scheduler using the *optimistic approach* for concurrency control of RTDBSs.

Scheduling and concurrency control

Conventional real-time systems take into account timing constraints of individual tasks but ignore data consistency problems. Also, they typically deal with simple tasks that have predictable data requirements. In real-time task scheduling, it is usually assumed that all tasks are preemptable. But preempting a task that uses a file resource in the exclusive mode of writing may result in subsequent tasks reading inconsistent information [Zhao87]. In contrast to real-time systems, conventional database systems do not emphasize the notion of timing constraints or deadlines for transactions. The performance goal is to reduce response times of transactions by using a *serialization order* among conflicting transactions. Thus, when a decision of database scheduling is made, individual timing constraints are ignored. For example, the most commonly used *two-phase locking* (2PL) protocol [Bern87] synchronizes concurrent data access of transactions by blocking and rollback and, thus, might violate timing constraints of transactions.

The goal of scheduling in RTDBSs is twofold: to meet timing constraints and to enforce data consistency. Real-time task-scheduling methods can be extended to real-time transaction scheduling, yet concurrency control protocols are still needed for operation scheduling to maintain data consistency. However, the integration of the two mechanisms in RTDBSs is not straightforward. The general approach is to utilize existing concurrency control protocols, especially 2PL, and to apply time-critical transaction-scheduling methods that favor more urgent transactions [Abbo92], [Sha88], [Son89]. Such approaches have the inherent disadvantage of being limited by the concurrency control protocol upon which they depend, because all existing concurrency control methods synchronize concurrent data access of transactions by the combination of two measures: *blocking* and *rollbacks* of transactions. Both are barriers to meeting time-critical schedules.

We summarize characteristics of real-time systems, database systems, and real-time database systems in Table 1.

Concurrency control protocols induce a serialization order among conflicting transactions. In nonreal-time concurrency control protocols, timing constraints are not a factor in the construction of this order. This is obviously a drawback for RTDBSs. For example, with the 2PL protocol, the serialization order is dynamically constructed and corresponds to the order in which conflicting transactions access shared data. In other words, the serialization order is bound to the past execution history, with no flexibility. When a transaction T_H with a higher priority requests an exclusive lock that is being held by another transaction T_L with a lower priority, the only choices are either aborting T_L or letting T_H wait for T_L. Neither choice is satisfactory. The conservative 2PL uses blocking; however, in RTDBSs, blocking may cause *priority inversion*. Priority inversion is said to occur when a high-priority transaction is blocked by lower priority transactions [Sha88]. The alternative is to abort low-priority transactions when a priority inversion occurs. This wastes the work done by the aborted

Table 1. Characteristics of real-time systems, database systems, and real-time database systems.

Criteria / Systems	Correctness constraints	Predictability for resources	Performance goal	Scheduling
Real-time systems	Time (deadline)	Predictable data requirement and execution time	Maximize time-related performance metric (meeting deadlines)	CPU-oriented
Database systems	Data consistency	Unpredictable data requirement	Minimize response time	I/O-oriented
Real-time database systems (RTDBSs)	Time and data consistency	Predictable CPU and unpredictable data requirement	Compromise benefits of criticality and deadline with data consistency	Considers both CPU and I/O

transactions and, in turn, may have a negative effect on time-critical scheduling. Various scheduling policies with lock-based concurrency control mechanisms for real-time transactions have been investigated [Abbo92]. Also, a time-stamp-based concurrency control mechanism was studied for avoiding priority inversions [Baba90].

The priority ceiling protocol, which was initially developed as a task-scheduling protocol for real-time operating systems, has been extended to RTDBSs [Sha88]. It is based on 2PL and employs only blocking, but not rollback, to solve conflicts. This is a conservative approach. For conventional database systems, it has been shown that optimal performance may be achieved by compromising blocking and rollback [Yu90]. For RTDBSs, we may expect similar results. Aborting a few low-priority transactions and restarting them later may allow high-priority transactions to meet their deadlines, resulting in improved system performance. A drawback of the priority ceiling protocol is that it requires knowledge of all transactions that will be executed in the future. This is too harsh a condition for most database systems to satisfy.

For a concurrency control protocol to accommodate the timeliness of transactions, the serialization order it produces should reflect the priority of transactions. An optimistic method [Boks87], [Kung81] is a possible way to achieve this goal. Because of its validation phase conflict resolution, it can be ensured that eventually discarded transactions do not abort other transactions and transaction priorities are considered. Several concurrency control protocols based on the optimistic approach have been proposed [Hari90a], [Hari90b], [Son90b], [Lin90]. The key component of optimistic concurrency control protocols is the validation phase, in which a transaction's destiny is determined. Few of them (for example, the Opt-Wait protocol [Hari90a]) incorporate priority-based conflict-resolution mechanisms, such as *priority wait*, that make low-priority transactions wait for conflicting high-priority transactions to complete. However, this approach of detecting conflicts during the validation phase degrades system predictability, because it may be too late to restart the transaction and meet the deadline. An integrated scheduler may solve this problem if a lock-based concurrency control protocol supports a mechanism to dynamically adjust the serialization order of active transactions. One integrated scheduler is proposed in the next section (entitled "Integrated scheduler") that integrates a priority-based locking with an optimistic approach.

Another important problem that needs further study is a different notion of "correct execution" in transaction processing. Based on the argument that timing constraints may be more important than data consistency in RTDBSs, attempts have been made to satisfy timing constraints by temporarily sacrificing database consistency to some degree [Lin89], [Vrbs88]. These attempts are based on a new consistency model of real-time databases, in which maintaining *external data consistency* (wherein values of data objects represent correct values of the external world outside the database) has priority over maintaining *internal data consistency* (wherein no data violate consistency constraints). Although in some applications weaker consistency is acceptable [Garc83], a general-purpose consistency criterion that is less stringent than serializability has not yet been proposed. The problem is that temporary inconsistencies may affect active transactions, and so the commitment of these transactions may still need to be delayed until the inconsistencies are removed; otherwise, even committed transactions may need to be rolled back. However, in real-time systems, some actions are not reversible.

The use of semantic information in transaction scheduling and multiversion data is often proposed for RTDBS applications [Liu88], [Son88], [Son90a], [Song90]. Multiple versions are useful in situations that require the monitoring of data values as they change with time. In such situations, the trends exhibited by these data values can be used to initiate proper actions [Kort90]. Examples include falling values in stock market trading and the rising temperature of a furnace in a nuclear reactor. Two of the objectives of using multiple versions are to increase the degree of concurrency and to reduce the possibility of transaction rejection by providing a succession of views of data. There are several problems that must be solved in order to use multiple versions effectively. For example, the selection of old versions for a transaction must ensure the required consistency of the state seen by the transaction.

Integrated scheduler

Time-critical scheduling in real-time databases consists of two scheduling mechanisms: *transaction scheduling* and *operation scheduling*. To find new concurrency control methods, we will focus on solutions to the operation-scheduling aspect of time-critical scheduling.

By delaying the write operations of transactions, the past transaction execution based on the serialization order can be relaxed. This allows the serialization order among transactions to be dynamically adjusted in compliance with the timeliness and criticality of transactions. In order to dynamically adjust the serialization order of active transactions, we introduce the priority-dependent locking protocol. This protocol makes it possible for transactions with higher priorities to be executed first; therefore, higher priority transactions are never blocked by uncommitted lower priority transactions, while lower priority transactions may not have to be aborted even in the face of conflicting operations.

For example, $T2$ and $T1$ are two transactions, with $T2$ having a higher priority. $T1$ writes a data object x before $T2$ reads it. If there is a conflict over x in 2PL, even in the absence of any other conflicting operations between these two transactions, $T2$ has either to abort $T1$ or to be blocked until $T1$ releases the write lock. This is because the serialization order $T1 \rightarrow T2$ has already been determined by the past execution history. $T2$ can never precede $T1$ in the serialization order. By the priority-dependent locking protocol, when such conflict occurs, the serialization order of the two transactions will be adjusted in favor of $T2$ (that is, $T2 \rightarrow T1$) and, in this example, neither is $T2$ blocked nor is $T1$ aborted.

Priority-dependent locking protocol

We assume that the operating environment of an RTDBS is a single processor with randomly arriving transactions. (We extend the protocol to distributed systems in the section entitled "Extension to Distributed Systems.") When each transaction is submitted to the system, it is assigned an *initial priority* and a *start-time-stamp*. The initial priority can be based on the deadline and the criticality of the transaction. The criticality of a transaction represents its relative importance, compared with other transactions. The start-time-stamp is appended to the initial priority to form the *actual priority* that is used in scheduling. When we refer to the priority of a transaction, we always mean the actual priority, with the start-time-stamp appended. Because the start-time-stamp is unique, so is the priority of each transaction. The priorities of transactions with the same initial priority are distinguished by their start-time-stamps. An aborted transaction is assigned a new priority only on a restart.

All transactions that can be scheduled are placed into a *ready queue*. Only transactions in a ready queue are scheduled for execution. When a transaction is *blocked*, it is removed from a ready queue. When a transaction is *unblocked*, it is inserted into a ready queue again but may still be waiting to be assigned a CPU. A transaction is said to be *suspended* when it is not executing but is still in a ready queue. When a transaction is doing an I/O operation, it is blocked; once it completes, it is usually unblocked. When a transaction is waiting for its lock request to be granted, it is also blocked.

The execution of each transaction is divided into three phases: the *read phase*, the *wait phase*, and the *write phase*. This is similar to the optimistic methods. During the read phase, a transaction reads from the database and writes to its local workspace. After it completes, it waits for its chance to commit in the wait phase. If it is committed, it switches into the write phase, during which all of its updates are made permanent in the database. A transaction in any of the three phases is called *active*. If an active transaction is in the write phase, then it is committed and writing into the database. This approach is based on an approach of integrated schedulers in that it uses 2PL for read-write conflicts and the Thomas' Write Rule (TWR) for write-write conflicts. The TWR allows ignoring the write request that has arrived too late, instead of rejecting it [Bern87]. The following is the outline of a transaction:

transaction = {*t*begin();
        read phase;
        wait phase;
        write phase;
        }.

In this approach, there are various data structures that need to be read and updated in a consistent manner. Therefore, we assume the existence of critical sections to guarantee that only one process at a time updates these data structures. We assume critical sections to group the various data structures to allow maximum concurrency.

Read phase

The read phase is the normal execution of the transaction, except that write operations are performed on the private data copies in the local workspace of the transaction, instead of on the data objects in the database. We call such write operations *prewrite operations*. One advantage of this prewrite operation is that when a transaction is aborted, all that has to be done for recovery is to simply discard the data in its local workspace. No rollback is needed, because no changes have been made in the database. We use the notations $r_T[x]$, $w_T[x]$, and $pw_T[x]$ to denote that a transaction T reads, writes, and prewrites, respectively, a data object x.

The read-prewrite or prewrite-read conflicts among active transactions are synchronized in the read phase by a *priority-based locking protocol*. Before a transaction can perform a read operation on a data object, it must obtain the read lock on that data object first; likewise, before a transaction can perform a prewrite operation on a data object, it must obtain the write lock on that data object first. If a transaction reads a data object that has been written by itself, it gets the private copy in its own workspace immediately, and no read lock is needed.

Each lock contains the priority of the transaction holding the lock, as well as other usual information such as the lock-holding transaction identifier and the lock type. The locking protocol is based on the principle that higher priority transactions should complete before lower priority transactions. This means that if two transactions conflict, the higher priority transaction should precede the lower priority transaction in the serialization order. With the CPU scheduling policy, which takes into account the priorities of transactions first, a high-priority transaction is scheduled to commit before a low-priority transaction, except when a low-priority transaction has already committed and is in the write phase. If a low-priority transaction does complete before a high-priority transaction, it is required to wait until it is sure that its commitment will not cause the abortion of a higher priority transaction. Since transactions do not write into the database during the read phase, write-write conflicts need not be considered in our protocol.

Suppose that active transaction $T1$ has lower priority than active transaction $T2$. We have the following four cases of conflict and the transaction dependencies they set in the serialization order:

Case 1	$r_{T2}[x], pw_{T1}[x]$	$\Rightarrow$	$T2 \rightarrow T1$
Case 2	$pw_{T2}[x], r_{T1}[x]$	$\Rightarrow$	$T2 \rightarrow T1$
			(delayed reading)
			or
			$T1 \rightarrow T2$
			(immediate reading)
Case 3	$r_{T1}[x], pw_{T2}[x]$	$\Rightarrow$	$T1 \rightarrow T2$
Case 4	$pw_{T1}[x], r_{T2}[x]$	$\Rightarrow$	$T2 \rightarrow T1$
			(immediate reading)
			or
			$T1 \rightarrow T2$
			(delayed reading)

Case 1 meets the principle of completing high-priority transactions before low-priority ones. In Case 2, following our principle, we should choose delayed reading; that is, $T1$ should not read x until $T2$ has committed and has written x in the database. So, $T1 \rightarrow T2$ (immediate reading) is excluded. Case 3 violates our principle. In this case, unless it is already committed, $T1$ is usually aborted, because otherwise $T1$ must commit before $T2$ and thus will block $T2$. However, if $T1$ has already finished its work—that is, if it is in the wait phase—we should avoid aborting it, because aborting a transaction that has completed its work imposes a considerable penalty on system performance. In the meantime, we still do not want $T2$ to be blocked by $T1$. Therefore, when such a conflict occurs and $T1$ is in the wait phase, we do not abort $T1$ until $T2$ is committed, hoping that $T1$ may get a chance to commit before $T2$ commits. In Case 4, if $T1$ is already committed and in the write phase, we should delay $T2$ so that it reads x after $T1$ writes it. This blocking is not a serious problem for $T2$, because $T1$ is already in the write phase and is expected to finish writing x soon. $T2$ can read x as soon as $T1$ finishes writing x in the database, not necessarily after $T1$ completes the whole write phase. Therefore, $T2$ will not be blocked for a long time. Otherwise, if $T1$ is not committed yet—that is, if it is in either the read phase or the wait phase—$T2$ should read x immediately from a database, because that is in accordance with the principle that high-priority transactions execute before lower priority transactions.

As transactions are being executed and conflicting operations occur, all the information about the induced dependencies in the serialization order needs to be retained. To do this, we associate with each transaction two sets — *before-trans-set* and *after-trans-set* — and a count — *before-count*. The set before-trans-set contains all the active lower priority transactions that must precede this transaction in the serialization order; the set after-trans-set contains all the active lower priority transactions that must come after this transaction in the serialization order. Before-count is the number of the higher priority transactions that precede this transaction in the serialization order. When a conflict occurs between two transactions, their dependency is determined, and their values of before-trans-set, after-trans-set, and before-count will be changed correspondingly.

In summarizing what we discuss above, we define the priority-dependent *locking protocol* (LP) as follows:

LP1. A transaction T requests a read lock on a data object x.

> *for* each transaction t holding a write lock on x (that is, the holder) *do*
> > *if* the priority of the holder (t) is > the requester (T) or
> > > the holder is in write phase,
> >
> > *then*   deny the lock and exit;
> > *endif*
>
> *enddo*
> *for* each transaction t holding a write lock on x *do*
> > *if* the holder is a member of before-trans-set of the requester
> > *then*   abort the holder
> > *else*
> > > *if* the holder is not a member of after-trans-set of the requester
> > > *then*   add the holder to after-trans-set of the requester and
> > >   increase before-count of the holder by one
> > > *endif*
> >
> > *endif*
>
> *enddo*
> grant the read lock

LP2. A transaction T requests a write lock on a data object x.

> *for* each transaction t holding a read lock on x *do*
> > *if* the priority of the holder (t) is > the requester (T)
> > *then*
> > > *if* the requester is not a member of after-trans-set of the holder
> > > *then*   add the requester to after-trans-set of the holder and
> > >   increase before-count of the requester by one
> > > *endif*
> >
> > *else*
> > > *if* the holder is in wait phase
> > > *then*
> > > > *if* the holder is a member of after-trans-set of the requester
> > > > *then*   abort the holder
> > > > *else*   add the holder to before-trans-set of the requester
> > > > *endif*
> > >
> > > *else*
> > > > *if* the holder is in read phase
> > > > *then*   abort the holder
> > > > *endif*
> > >
> > > *endif*
> >
> > *endif*
>
> *enddo*
> grant the write lock

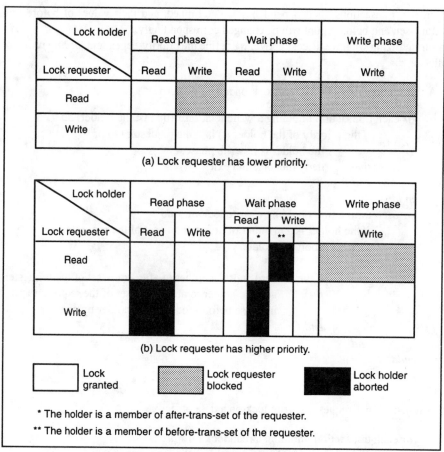

(a) Lock requester has lower priority.

(b) Lock requester has higher priority.

| | Lock granted | | Lock requester blocked | | Lock holder aborted |

* The holder is a member of after-trans-set of the requester.

** The holder is a member of before-trans-set of the requester.

Figure 1a. Lock compatibility table.

LP1 and LP2 are actually two procedures of the lock manager that are executed when a lock is requested. When a lock is denied because of a conflicting lock, the request is suspended until that conflicting lock is released. Then, the locking protocol is invoked once again from the very beginning in order to decide if the lock can then be granted. Figure 1a shows the lock compatibility tables in which the compatibilities are expressed by possible actions taken when conflicts occur. The compatibility depends on the priorities of the transactions holding and requesting the lock and the phase of the lock holder, as well as the lock types. Even with the same lock types, different actions may be taken, depending on the priorities of the lock holder and the lock requester. Therefore, a table entry may have more than one block reflecting the different possible actions.

Note that with our locking protocol, as shown in Figure 1a, a data object may be both read locked and write locked simultaneously by several transactions. Unlike in 2PL, locks are not classified simply as *shared locks* and *exclusive locks*. Figure 1b summarizes the lock compatibility of 2PL with the *high-priority scheme;* in this scheme, high-priority transactions never block for a lock held by a low-priority transaction [Abbo92]. Comparison of Figures 1a and 1b makes it obvious that our locking protocol is much more flexible and thus incurs less blocking and abort. Note that in Figure 1, the abort of lower priority transactions in the wait phase is included. In our locking protocol, a high-priority transaction is not blocked or aborted because of a conflict with an uncommitted lower priority transaction. Under identical conditions, the number of cases in which a lower priority transaction is aborted should be less than that in 2PL.

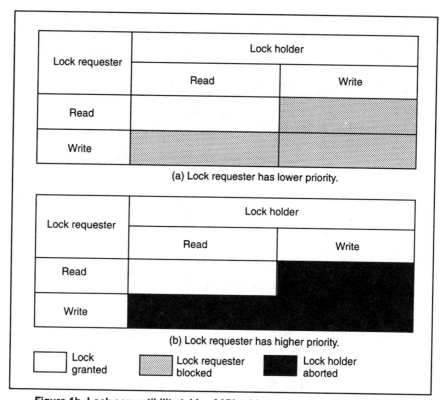

Figure 1b. Lock compatibility table of 2PL with the high-priority scheme.

Transactions are released for execution as soon as they arrive. First, the transaction is in the read phase. When it tries to read or prewrite a data object, it requests the lock. The lock may be granted or not granted, according to the locking protocol. Transactions may be aborted when lock requests are processed. To abort a transaction, the procedure is as follows:

abort = (
        release all locks;
        for each transaction *t* of after-trans-set of *T do*
                decrease before-count of *t* by one;
                if before-count of *t* is equal to zero and is in the wait phase,
                then   unblock it;
                endif
        enddo
        delete an aborted transaction (*T*) from the phase it belongs to;
        remove reference to *T* from before-trans-set and after-trans-set of others;
).

Wait phase

The wait phase allows a transaction to wait until it can commit. A transaction *T* can commit only if all transactions with higher priorities that must precede it in the serialization order are either committed or aborted. Because the before-count of T is the number of such transactions, T can commit only if its before-count becomes zero. Once a transaction in the wait phase gets its chance to commit—that is, once its before-count goes to zero—it switches into the write phase and releases all its read locks. A final time stamp is assigned to it, which is the absolute serialization order. The procedure is as follows:

```
wait = (
          waiting := TRUE;
          while (waiting) do
                  if T can be committed (before-count = 0),
                  then    switch T into the write phase and
                          attach a final time stamp to T using the system time stamp;
                          for each transaction t of before-trans-set of T do
                                  if t is in the read or wait phase,
                                  then    abort t;
                                  endif
                          enddo
                          waiting := FALSE;
                  else let T be blocked;
                  endif
          enddo
  release all read locks;
          for each transaction t of after-trans-set of T do
                  if t is in the read or wait phase,
                  then    decrease before-count by one;
                          if before-count is equal to zero and is in the wait phase,
                          then unblock t;
                          endif
                  endif
          enddo
  ).
```

There are two reasons for which a transaction T in the wait phase may be aborted. First, by the locking protocol, T may be aborted because of a conflicting lock request by a higher priority transaction, because T is not committed yet and is still holding all the locks. (See Example 1, below.) Second, T may be aborted because of the commitment of a higher priority transaction that must follow T in the serialization order. (See Example 2, below.) When such a transaction commits, if T is found in its before-trans-set, then T is aborted.

Example 1. Suppose that active transaction $T1$ has lower priority than active transaction $T2$. Transactions are released for execution as soon as they arrive. Let $T1$ be $pw_{T1}[y] \, r_{T1}[x]$ and $T2$ be $r_{T2}[y] \, pw_{T2}[x]$. The two execution sequences that follow are considered.
The first execution sequence is

$$H1 = pw_{T1}[y] \, r_{T2}[y] \, r_{T1}[x] \, pw_{T2}[x]$$

The first write-read conflict on y belongs to Case 4. Thus, the transaction dependency between them in the serialization order is assumed to be $T2 \rightarrow T1$ (immediate reading). Then, $T1$ is included in the after-trans-set of $T2$, and the before-count of $T1$ is set to one. After that, a read lock on y is granted to $T2$. The second read-write conflict belongs to Case 3. After $r_{T1}[x]$, $T1$ is in the wait phase. Then, the new transaction dependency should be $T1 \rightarrow T2$, according to Case 3. This order is contradictory with the previous order $T2 \rightarrow T1$. Since $T1$ is a member of the after-trans-set of $T2$, $T1$ is aborted.

The second execution sequence is

$$H2 = r_{T1}[x] \, pw_{T2}[x] \, pw_{T1}[y] \, r_{T2}[y]$$

The first read-write conflict on x belongs to Case 3. Thus, the transaction dependency $T1 \rightarrow T2$ is assumed. Since $T1$ is in the read phase, $T1$ is aborted. If we modify the order of write operations to $pw_{T1}[y] \, pw_{T2}[x]$, instead of $pw_{T2}[x] \, pw_{T1}[y]$, then $T1$ would be in the wait phase, and the before-trans-set of $T2$ will include $T1$ and a write lock on x will be granted to $T2$. Next, the conflict $pw_{T1}[y] \, r_{T2}[y]$ belongs to Case 4. Then, the new transaction dependency $T2 \rightarrow T1$ should be considered. But, since $T1$ is a member of the before-trans-set of $T2$, $T1$ is aborted.

Therefore, whenever any sequence of two active transactions contains $H1$ or $H2$, only the higher priority transaction is executed, and the lower priority transaction is aborted.

Example 2. Suppose that there are three active transactions, $T1$, $T2$, and $T3$, in which $T3$ has the highest priority and $T1$ has the lowest. Also, transactions are released for execution as soon as they arrive. Let $T1$ be $r_{T1}[x]$, $T2$ be $pw_{T2}[x] \, r_{T2}[y]$, and $T3$ be $pw_{T3}[y]$. The execution sequence that follows is considered. We assume that $T1$ and $T2$ are in the wait phase after $r_{T1}[x]$ and $r_{T2}[y]$, respectively. Then, we proceed to $T3$.

$$H3 = r_{T1}[x] \, pw_{T2}[x] \, r_{T2}[y] \, pw_{T3}[y]$$

In $H3$, there are two read-write conflicts belonging to Case 3. At the first conflict, transaction dependency $T1 \rightarrow T2$ is assumed. After $r_{T1}[x]$, $T1$ is in the wait phase and $T1$ is added to the before-trans-set of $T2$. Then, a write lock on x is granted to $T2$. The second conflict, $T2 \rightarrow T3$, is similarly handled. After $r_{T2}[y]$, $T2$ is in the wait phase and $T2$ is added to the before-trans-set of $T3$. Then, a write lock on y is granted.

If $T3$ is committed after $pw_{T3}[y]$, then $T2$ should be aborted, because $T2$ is in the before-trans-set of $T3$, as we show above in Example 1. Next, $T1$ could be committed. Otherwise, if $T3$ is aborted, then $T2$ could be committed and $T1$ should be aborted.

Therefore, $T1$ or $T2$ can be committed, depending on whether or not $T3$ is committed. The reason is that lower priority transactions, which have already finished their work, wait for a chance to commit, even in the face of conflicts with higher priority transactions. In general, if an execution sequence of transactions contains a series of read-write conflicts, like $H3$, half of the transactions in front of the last transaction (for example, $T3$ in $H3$) could be committed. This is a significant performance improvement by the integrated priority-based locking protocol over traditional locking protocols.

Assume that we use the 2PL protocol in this example. When a high-priority transaction requests a lock that is held by a low-priority transaction, we either let the high-priority transaction wait or abort the low-priority transaction. If we choose the first alternative, $T2$ would be blocked by $T1$, because $T1$ holds a read lock on x. If we choose the second alternative, $T1$ will be aborted by $T2$ when $T2$ prewrites x, and then $T2$ will be aborted by $T3$ when $T3$ prewrites y. This example clearly illustrates the advantage of using the integrated priority-based locking protocol.

Write phase

Once a transaction is in the write phase, it is considered to be committed. All committed transactions can be serialized by the final time stamp order. In the write phase, the only work of a transaction is making all its updates permanent in the database. Data items are copied from the local workspace into the database. After each write operation, the corresponding write lock is released. The TWR is applied here.

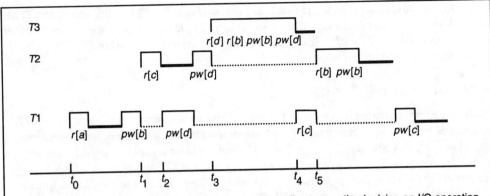

Note: A solid line at a low level indicates that the corresponding transaction is doing an I/O operation because of a *page fault* or is in the write phase. A dotted line at a low level indicates that the corresponding transaction is either suspended or blocked and is not doing any I/O operation. A line raised to a higher level indicates that the transaction is executing. The absence of a line indicates that the transaction has not yet arrived or has already completed.

Figure 2. An example.

The write requests of each transaction are sent to the data manager, which carries out the write operations in the database. Transactions submit write requests along with their final time stamps.

For each data object, write requests are sent to the data manager only in ascending time stamp order. After a write request on data object x with time stamp n has been issued to the data manager, no other write request on x with a time stamp smaller than n will be sent. The write requests are buffered by the data manager. The data manager can work with the first-come, first-served policy or can always select the write request with the highest priority to process. When a new request arrives, if there is another buffered write request on the same data object, the request with the smaller time stamp is discarded. Therefore, for each data object, there is at most one write request in the buffer. This guarantees the TWR.

Example 3. As shown in Figure 2, there are three transactions in Example 3: $T1$, $T2$, and $T3$. $T3$ has the highest priority and $T1$ has the lowest. $T1$ arrives at time t_0 and reads data object a. This causes a page fault. After an I/O operation, $T1$ prewrites b. Then $T2$ comes in at time t_1 and preempts $T1$. At time t_2, it reads c and causes another page fault. So, $T2$ is blocked for an I/O operation and $T1$ resumes execution. After $T1$ has prewritten d, $T2$ finishes I/O and preempts $T1$ again. It prewrites d, which is only write locked by $T1$. At time t_3, $T3$ arrives and preempts $T2$. $T3$ first reads d, which is write locked by both $T2$ and $T1$. Therefore, the after-trans-set of $T3$ becomes $\{T2, T1\}$ and both the before-count of $T2$ and the before-count of $T1$ become one. Then, $T3$ reads b, which is write locked by $T1$. Since $T1$ is already in the after-trans-set of $T3$, nothing is changed. Then $T3$ prewrites b and prewrites d. Since these two data objects are not read locked by any other transactions, the write locks are granted to $T3$ directly. At time t_4, $T3$ switches into the write phase. Both the before-count of $T2$ and the before-count of $T1$ go back to zero. Then, $T2$ should be executed, but it needs to read b, which is being write locked by $T3$; hence, $T1$ is executed instead. It reads c, which is read locked by $T2$. At time t_5, $T3$ finishes writing b and releases the write lock so that $T2$ can preempt $T1$ to continue its work. It reads b, which is write locked by $T1$. Then, the after-trans-set of $T2$ becomes $\{T1\}$ and the before-count of $T1$ becomes one. After $T2$ has prewritten b, it switches into the write phase and the before-count of $T1$ becomes zero again. Then, $T1$ executes and also switches into write phase after prewriting c.

In this example, $T3$, which is supposed to be the most urgent transaction, finishes first, although it is the last to arrive. $T1$, which is supposed to be the least urgent one, is the last one to commit. None of the three transactions need to be aborted. Assume that we use 2PL in the above example. Suppose that when a conflict occurs, we let the high-priority transaction wait; then, both T2 and T3 would be blocked by T1, because T1 holds a write lock on d. If we abort the low-priority transaction at the conflict, T1 will be aborted by T2 when T2 prewrites d, and then T2 will be aborted by T3 when T3 reads d. This example again illustrates the advantage of the integrated protocol over 2PL.

It is surprising that for RTDBSs, it appears that optimistic approaches outperform lock-based pessimistic approaches over a wide range of system loads and resource availabilities, since performance studies of concurrency control protocols for conventional database systems [Agra87] have concluded that locking protocols tend to perform better than optimistic techniques when resources are limited [Hari90a]. More theoretical, as well as experimental, studies are necessary in this area before we can draw definitive conclusions.

While our priority-based locking protocol integrates a priority-based locking with an optimistic approach by delaying write operations and dynamically adjusting the serialization order of conflict transactions, there are other approaches to use optimistic concurrency control for RTDBSs. For example, the Wait-50 protocol [Hari90a] incorporates priority information based on deadlines into an optimistic concurrency control algorithm intended for use in RTDBSs. It features a wait control mechanism, which monitors transaction conflict states and dynamically decides when, and for how long, a low-priority transaction should be made to wait.

The priority-based locking protocol analyzes read-write conflicts among transactions as early as possible and resolves conflicts by giving preference to the higher priority transaction; however, in Wait-50, conflict resolution is performed only in the validation phase. A transaction is made to wait only when a conflict is detected and when the percentage of conflicting higher priority transactions compared to the transaction's total conflict size is greater than or equal to 50. Actually, Wait-50 is an extension of Opt-Wait [Hari90a], which always waits for a *conflict high-priority transaction*. Because of this late detection of conflicts, Wait-50 causes late restarts and increases the number of conflicting transactions, resulting in more restarts.

In the priority-based locking protocol, when a read-write conflict occurs between two transactions, a serialization order is assumed in favor of the higher priority transaction. If another conflict occurs between the same two transactions, a new serialization order will be determined. If the new serialization order is not coincident with the old one, the lower priority transaction should be aborted, because these two transactions cannot be committed together, regardless of which serialization order is taken. This is shown in Example 1. If we can change the serialization (commit) order of two transactions, and both can be committed, then we block the lower priority transaction, as shown below in Example 4.

Therefore, the priority-dependent locking protocol deals with read-write conflicts efficiently by giving preference to higher priority transactions. In addition, write-write conflicts are resolved by the TWR. With preferential treatment and the TWR, the scheduler can dynamically adjust the serialization order. However, there remains the problem of *wasted sacrifices*, in which a transaction is sacrificed on behalf of another transaction that will be later discarded.

Example 4. Suppose that there are three active transactions, T1, T2, and T3, in which T3 has the highest priority and T1 has the lowest. Transactions are released for execution as soon as they arrive. Let T1 be $pw_{T1}[x]$, T2 be $r_{T2}[x] \, pw_{T2}[y]$, and T3 be $r_{T3}[y]$. The execution sequence that follows is considered. We assume that T1 and T2 are in the wait phase before T3 is committed or aborted.

$$H4 = pw_{T1}[x] \, r_{T2}[x] \, pw_{T2}[y] \, r_{T3}[y]$$

In H4, there are two write-read conflicts belonging to Case 4. At the first conflict, transaction dependency $T2 \rightarrow T1$ is assumed, and the after-trans-set of T2 becomes T1 and the before-count of

$T1$ is increased by one. Then, a read lock on x is granted to $T2$. Similarly, at the second conflict, $T3 \rightarrow T2$ is assumed, and the after-trans-set of $T3$ becomes $T2$ and the before-count of $T2$ is increased by one. Then, if $T3$ is committed or aborted, $T2$ can be committed and $T1$ can be committed. Therefore, no abort of $T1$ and $T2$ occurs, which is similar to the situation in Opt-Wait. This example illustrates that a conflict high-priority transaction commit does not necessarily imply that the waiting transaction has to be restarted. However, data conflicts will be increased because of $T1$ and $T2$ in the wait phase, which are holding all the locks.

Priority inversion, which occurs when a lower priority transaction delays the execution of a higher priority one, causes transactions not to execute in a timely manner and creates some difficulties for scheduling in RTDBSs. The priority-based locking protocol is intended to decrease priority inversions and to increase the number of transactions executed before their deadlines. Babaoglu, Marzullo, and Schneider [Baba90] introduced new protocols for preventing priority inversions; in these protocols, the problem of priority inversion is formalized using wait-for relations to represent requester-holder relationships for resources and priority relations among transactions.

Performance evaluation

Because the integrated real-time locking protocol assumes that the data requirement or execution time of each transaction is not known, we should compare the protocol with other protocols with the same assumption. The results obtained through a simulation study indicate the behavior of the real-time locking protocol in comparison to 2PL.

The performance of the real-time locking protocol was studied using a prototyping environment for database systems [Son90c]. Figure 3 is a high-level block diagram of the system. In our simulation model, the system consists of a single processor and indefinitely many I/O processors for fully parallel disk access.

Transactions are generated and put into the *start-up queue*. When a transaction has started, it leaves the start-up queue and enters the *ready queue*. Transactions in the ready queue are ordered from the highest to the lowest priority. The transaction with the highest priority is always selected to run. The current running transaction sends requests to the *concurrency controller (CC) scheduler*. The transaction may be blocked and placed into the *block queue*. Also, it may be aborted and restarted; in such a case, it is first delayed for a certain amount of time and then put into the ready queue again. When a transaction in the block queue is unblocked, it leaves the block queue and is placed into the ready queue again. Whenever a transaction enters the ready queue and its priority is higher than the current running transaction, it preempts the current running transaction.

When a transaction enters the start-up queue, it has the *arrival time*, the *deadline*, the *priority*, the *read se*t (the set of data objects to read), and the *write set* (the set of data objects to write) associated with it. The *transaction interarrival time* (the time between two arrivals) is a random variable with exponential distribution. The deadline and the priority are computed by the following equations:

$$deadline_T = arrival_T + (slack)(time_T)$$
$$priority_T = 1/deadline_T$$

where: $deadline_T$ = deadline time of transaction T
$arrival_T$ = arrival time of transaction T
$slack$ = slack factor
$time_T$ = service time of transaction T
$priority_T$ = priority of transaction T

The *slack factor* is a random variable with a value between three and five with uniform distribution.

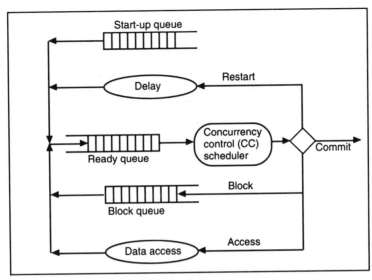

Figure 3. Simulator diagram.

The *service time* is the total time that the transaction needs for its data processing; this includes the CPU time and the I/O time. The deadline equation is designed to ensure that all transactions, independent of their service requirement, have the same chance of making their deadline. The transaction-priority-assignment policy is *earliest deadline*: Transactions with earlier deadlines have higher priority than transactions with later deadlines. A greater priority value means higher priority. The data objects in the read set and the write set are uniformly distributed across the entire database. A transaction consists of a sequence of read and write operations. A read operation involves a concurrency control request to get access permission, followed by a disk I/O to read the data object, followed by a period of CPU usage for processing the data object. Write operations are handled similarly, except for their disk I/O. Because it is assumed that transactions maintain deferred update lists in buffers in the main memory, disk activity of write access is deferred until the transaction has committed and switched into the write phase. A transaction can be discarded at any time if its deadline is missed. Therefore, our model employs a hard-deadline policy.

To ensure significance of our comparison, the classical two-phase locking needs to be augmented with a priority scheme to ensure that higher priority transactions are not delayed by lower priority transactions. We used the high-priority scheme [Abbo92], in which all data conflicts are resolved in favor of the transaction with higher priority. When a transaction requests a lock on a data object held by other transactions in an incompatible mode, if the requester's priority is higher than that of all the lock holders, the holders are restarted and the requester is granted the lock; if the requester's priority is lower, it waits for the lock holders to release the lock. This scheme has the advantage of deadlock prevention.

Because of space considerations, we cannot present all our results but rather have selected for presentation here the graphs that best illustrate the performance difference of the protocols. For example, we have omitted the results of an experiment that varied the size of the database and thus the number of conflicts.

For each experiment, we collected performance statistics and averaged over 10 runs. We used *transaction size* (the number of data objects that a transaction needs to access) as one of the key variables in the experiments; this varied from a small fraction to a relatively large portion (15 percent) of the database, so that conflicts would occur frequently. High conflict rate allows concurrency

Table 2. Simulation model parameters.

Parameter	Meaning	Default value
cpu_cost	CPU time per data object	3 ms
IO_cost	I/O time per data object	10 ms
abort_cost	Transaction abort CPU time	9 ms
db_size	Database size	100
num_trans	Number of transactions	50
trans_size	Number of transaction data access operations	8
write_percent	Percentage of write operations	50 percent
mean	Mean transaction interarrival time	70 ms
slack	Slack factor in deadline formula	4 (3 to 5)

control protocols to play a significant role in system performance. We chose the average arrival rate so that protocols were tested in a heavily loaded, rather than a lightly loaded, system. This choice was made because, for designing real-time systems, one must consider high-load situations. Even though high-load situations may not arise frequently, one would like to have a system that misses as few deadlines as possible when the system is under stress [Abbo92].

The primary performance metric used in analyzing the experimental results was the *miss percentage* of the system, defined as the percentage of transactions that do not complete before their deadline. Miss percentage values in the range of zero to 20 can be taken to represent system performance under "normal" loadings, while miss percentage values in the range of 20 to 100 can be taken to represent system performance under "heavy" loading [Hari90a]. A secondary performance metric used was *restarts*, which is the number of restarts for a fixed number of transactions. We chose this metric because it provides insight into system behavior. The advantage of the real-time locking protocol is that while high-priority transactions are not blocked by low-priority transactions, low-priority transactions need not be restarted most of the time; we can verify this by using restarts as a performance metric.

Table 2 summarizes the key parameters of the simulation model and their default values. *Trans_size* is the total number of data access operations of each transaction. Among all the data access operations of a transaction, the percentage of write operations is specified by *write_percent*. *Mean* is the mean transaction interarrival time; by changing this, we were able to study system performance under normal load and heavy load. Figure 4 shows that the real-time locking protocol performed better than 2PL under both normal load and heavy load. If we consider a miss percentage under 20

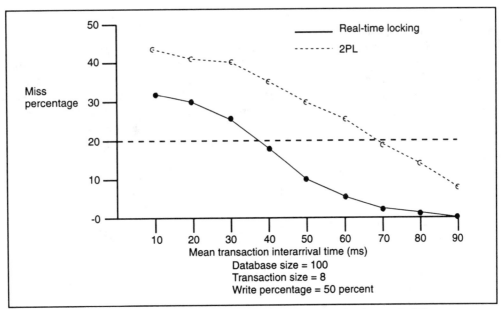

Figure 4. Sensitivity of miss percentage to mean transaction interarrival time.

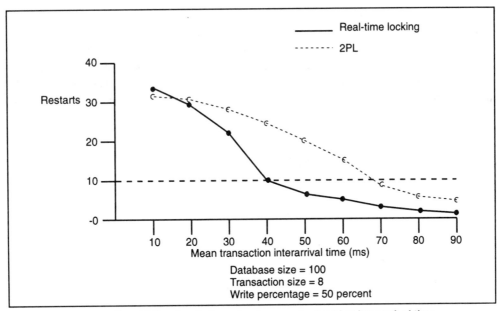

Figure 5. Sensitivity of restart number to mean transaction interarrival time.

as "normal," the real-time locking protocol can keep the system operating satisfactorily when the mean transaction interarrival time is as small as 40 milliseconds (ms); with 2PL, on the other hand, the system can maintain a normal load only when the mean transaction interarrival time is 70 ms or greater. Another interesting result is that under normal load, the restart number for each protocol was less than 10, as shown in Figure 5. A restart number greater than 10 indicates a degraded system performance for both protocols. However, if the arrival rate is gradually increased, 2PL reaches this critical point much earlier than the real-time locking protocol. Therefore, the real-time locking protocol has a wider operation range.

The cause for the better performance of the real-time locking protocol is its lower number of restarts, as shown in Figure 5. With the same mean transaction interarrival time, and thus the same data-contention level, the real-time locking protocol allows greater lock compatibility and aborts less low-priority transactions for restart. In Figure 5, when the mean transaction interarrival time was either very large or very small, the restart numbers of the two protocols were almost identical. However, as shown in Figure 4, the miss percentage of the real-time locking protocol was lower than that for 2PL in both of these extreme cases. This is due to less "useless restarts" in the real-time locking protocol. In 2PL, a transaction can generate restarts at any time during its execution. Therefore, even a transaction that is later discarded can cause restarts. However, in the real-time locking protocol, most transactions are restarted by committing transactions.

We can obtain different levels of data contention and system load by varying the transaction size while the mean transaction interarrival time, the slack factor, and the database size are fixed. In Figures 6 and 7, we observe results similar to those of the previous experiment. When the transaction size was either very large or very small, the performance of the two protocols was almost indistinguishable. However, with "normal" transaction size, the real-time locking protocol outperformed 2PL, just as we expected.

Figures 8 and 9 show system behavior when the percentage of write operations in each transaction was varied. The results indicate that 2PL is much more sensitive to the write percentage than the real-time locking protocol. In Figures 8 and 9, when the write percentage was low, both protocols performed well. As the write percentage was increased, the performance of 2PL was significantly degraded, while with the real-time locking protocol, the system performed even better when the write percentage was very high. The reason for the great difference in the behavior of the two protocols is obvious. In 2PL, write locks are exclusive locks. More write locks mean more data contention. In the real-time locking protocol, write locks can be shared. Locks of different types may be incompatible only under certain circumstances. Therefore, higher write percentage does not mean higher data-contention level. If the write percentage is 100, the restart number will become zero, because all the write locks can be shared. This is just the same as if the write percentage were zero.

Extension to distributed systems

We have extended our integrated scheduler to distributed database systems. (We do not consider recovery protocols for site or communication link failures in this paper.) We assume that the execution of a distributed transaction T involves several sites and that there is an *agent* (process) for T at all sites where T accesses data items. Each agent receives read and write requests from the home site of T, performs the operations, and sends the results back to the home site. For a write request, the agent writes to the local workspace, as in a centralized system. Similar to in a centralized system, each agent maintains its local before-trans-set, after-trans-set, and before-count for the transaction T it represents. Each site maintains its local read phase, wait phase, and write phase.

Suppose that each site has a unique site number. To produce unique priority for transactions originating at different sites, the home site number, as well as the start-time-stamp, is appended to the initial priority of a transaction. To compare the priorities of two transactions, their initial priorities are compared first. If these are equivalent, we compare their start-time-stamps. If they are started at two different sites, their time stamps may be the same. In this case, we compare their home site numbers; they must be different. If discrimination among different sites is not problematic, we can simply append the home site number to the initial priority of each transaction to produce a unique priority.

When a site receives the first read or write request of a transaction from its home site, a new agent for it is created and is released for execution. The locking protocol works in the same way as a

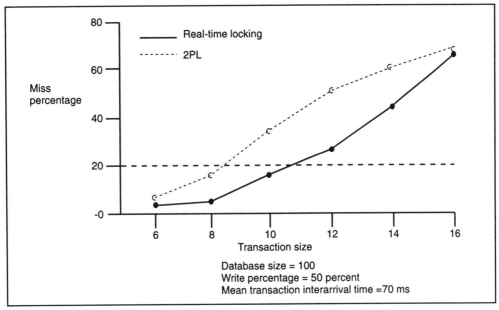

Figure 6. Sensitivity of miss percentage to transaction size.

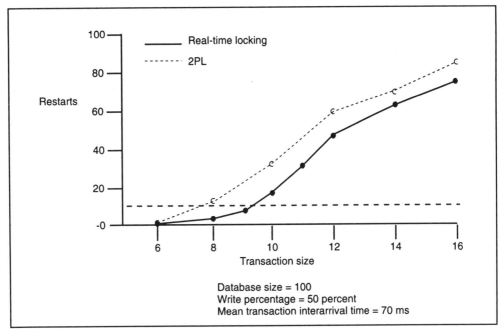

Figure 7. Sensitivity of restart number to transaction size.

centralized system using the local information at the site. To detect transactions that are doomed to be aborted, the local before-trans-set and the local after-trans-set of each agent are sent back to the home agent when they are changed. Such information can be sent with the reply messages for read or write requests to reduce the communication overhead. The home agent of each transaction changes its before-trans-set and its after-trans-set according to its local information and information sent back

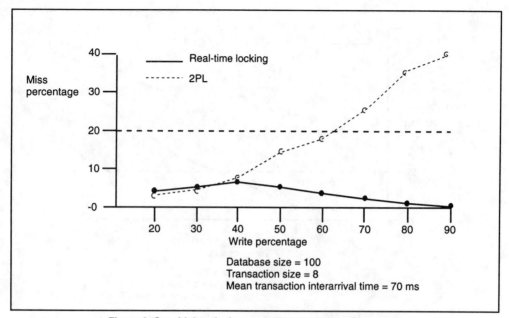

Figure 8. Sensitivity of miss percentage to write percentage.

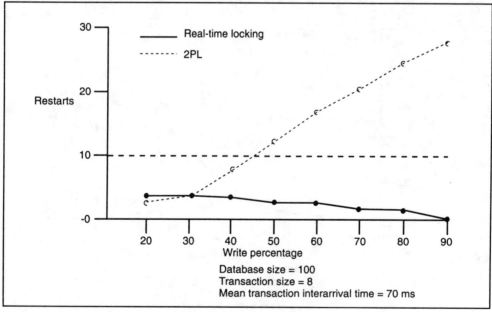

Figure 9. Sensitivity of restart number to write percentage.

from other sites. In this way, transactions that are in both the before-trans-set and the after-trans-set of a transaction can be detected and aborted. The home agents of these aborted transactions may be at different sites. The *common sites* of two transactions are the sites at which both transactions access some data. For one transaction to send an abort command to another transaction, it has to send the command to only one of their common sites. A common site must know the home site of the aborted transaction. Each agent can also send its local before-trans-set and after-trans-set after a certain number of changes in order to reduce the number of messages. There is a trade-off between communication cost and resource contention, because it is desirable to abort a failed transaction as soon as possible without much overhead.

A transaction in a distributed database system is a logically atomic operation: It must be processed at all sites or at none of them. Thus, a commit or abort operation of a transaction must be processed at all sites where the transaction is executed to ensure a consistent termination.

Atomic commit attempt

In a centralized system, a transaction in the wait phase is committed when its before-count becomes zero. In a distributed system, a transaction can be committed if its before-count goes to zero at all sites where it has an agent. This is not simple, because the local before-count of a transaction can be incremented by other high-priority transactions at any time. If we freeze the before-count for transactions in the wait phase, high-priority transactions may be blocked by low-priority transactions that are in the wait phase. This is obviously unacceptable. Also, if we allow the before-count to be changed all the time, a transaction can never be committed, because the home agent may never be certain that the local before-counts of the transaction at all sites are zero. Our solution to this problem is a compromise: a short-term freeze. A transaction in the wait phase can be switched into the *semicommitted* state, in which its before-count is frozen for a short period of time so that its before-count can only be decreased, but not increased. High-priority transactions may have to be blocked during this short period.

When a transaction has finished its read phase, the home agent sends a read-phase-termination message to all participating agents. This message also contains the site addresses of all agents that will participate in the termination protocol. Upon receiving this message, each agent switches into the wait phase and sends back an acknowledgment along with the local before-count. After receiving acknowledgments from all agents, the home agent then waits until the before-counts of all agents are zero in order to initiate an attempt to commit. During this waiting period, each agent reports to the home site whenever its before-count switches from one to zero or from zero to one. Each *commit attempt* (*CA*) is a variant of the *two-phase commit* (*2PC*) protocol. If the before-counts of all agents, including the home agent, are zero, then the home agent initiates a CA by sending a Try-Commit message to all agents. If an agent finds its before-count to be zero, it switches into the semicommitted state and sends back a reply to the home agent. Only when all agents are in the semicommitted state can the home agent decide to commit the transaction. Then, the home agent sends a Commit message to all agents. The CA will fail if at least one agent finds its before-count to be greater than zero. If it fails, then the failed agent sends an Attempt-Fail message to all other agents, which takes them back to the wait phase. Then, the home agent has to wait for the next chance to initiate another CA. This process goes on until either a CA succeeds or the transaction is aborted by a high-priority transaction.

Only the transactions in the wait phase can be switched into the semicommitted state. A transaction in the semicommitted state is different from one that is only in the wait phase in the following two respects:

(1)   When an agent is in the semicommitted state, agents in the read phase for other transactions cannot increase its before-count. The only time when its before-count could be increased is when another agent with higher priority requests a read lock on a data object that is being write locked by this agent (compare to LP1). However, when this transaction is in the semicommitted state, the higher priority transaction will be blocked on the read lock request, as if this transaction were in the write phase. If the CA fails, then this agent is changed back from the semicommitted state to the wait phase, and the higher priority transaction is unblocked and the locking protocol is invoked

again to decide if the lock is available then. In this way, high-priority transactions may be blocked by uncommitted low-priority transactions only for their CA periods. Then, the locking protocol LP1 should be modified to produce the following:

DLP1. A transaction T requests a read lock on a data object x.

> *for* each transaction t holding a write lock on x (that is, the holder) *do*
> > *if*   the priority of the holder (t) is > the requester (T) or
> > the holder is in write phase or
> > the holder is in the semicommitted state,
> > *then*   deny the lock and exit;
> > *endif*
> *enddo*
> *for* each transaction t holding a write lock on x *do*
> > if the holder is a member of before-trans-set of the requester
> > *then*   abort the holder
> > *else*
> > > *if* the holder is not a member of after-trans-set of the requester
> > > *then*   add the holder to after-trans-set of the requester and
> > > increase before-count of the holder by one
> > > *endif*
> > *endif*
> *enddo*
> grant the read lock

(2)   A transaction in the semicommitted state cannot be aborted. This may require high-priority transactions to delay commit operations. The only reason to cause a transaction to be aborted in the semicommitted state is the commitment of another higher priority transaction whose before-trans-set contains this transaction. When a transaction $T2$ tries to switch into the semicommitted state, if in its before-trans-set there is a transaction $T1$ that is already in the semicommitted state, $T2$ has to wait until $T1$ is not in the semicommitted state — that is, either $T1$ is committed or its CA has failed. Otherwise (that is, if $T2$ does not wait), commitment of $T2$ will cause the abort of $T1$, which is in the semicommitted state. This is also a short-term blocking of a high-priority transaction by a low-priority transaction.

Next, we consider the assignment of a correct final time stamp. First, we need serial commitment of conflicting transactions. If two transactions, $T1$ and $T2$, have a read-write or a write-read conflict at a common site, they should not be allowed to commit concurrently. Suppose that $T2$ has a higher priority. $T1$ must be either in $T2$'s before-trans-set or in $T2$'s after-trans-set. For the latter case, the before-count of $T1$ effectively prevents $T1$ from committing before $T2$. For the former case, $T1$ can begin its CA process before $T2$. If $T1$ is in the CA process, $T2$ should not begin its CA process until $T1$ either commits or exits its CA process because of a failure. Since $T2$ knows that $T1$ is in its before-trans-set, $T2$ can check this case without any difficulty. On the other hand, if $T2$ is in the semicommitted state, $T2$ should prevent $T1$ from committing until either $T2$ commits and aborts $T1$ or $T2$ exits the CA process. To do this, each transaction must also retain another count: an *after-count*. If a transaction switches into the semicommitted state (that is, if it initiates a CA), then the following procedure is performed: Check its before-trans-set to see whether or not it is empty. If it is not empty, then for each transaction in its before-trans-set, increase that transaction's after-count, which is the number of high-priority transactions that follow that transaction in the serialization order. If a transaction commits or it fails its CA (that is, it goes back to the wait phase), then for each transaction in its before-trans-set, decrease that transaction's after-count by one if it had been increased by the transaction that committed or failed. A transaction cannot switch into the semicommitted state if its after-count is not zero.

To commit a transaction, the home agent sends the commit command and a final time stamp to all agents. With serial commitment of conflicting transactions, a correct time-stamp-assignment policy has to ensure only that at each site, if transaction $T1$ commits and is assigned a final time stamp before another transaction $T2$, the final time stamp of $T2$ will be greater than that of $T1$. Each site should maintain the largest final time stamp, max_ts, ever assigned to a committed transaction on that site. When an agent switches into the semicommitted state, it sends this max_ts to the home agent. The home agent assigns a final time stamp that is greater than any max_ts of the agents. This time stamp can always be made unique by appending either the transaction identifier or home site number to it. For two transactions that have only write-write conflicts (actually, they are not conflicts in our algorithm), they must have the same serialization order at their common sites, because the agents of a transaction get the same final time stamp assigned by the home site. Therefore, the final time stamp assignment described above is correct.

In a distributed system, a transaction with a smaller final time stamp may switch into the write phase after a transaction with a greater final time stamp due to a communication delay. Therefore, we have to associate with each data object the time stamp of its latest write operation for some reasonable period. The write procedure is simpler than that in a centralized system. It is just the direct application of the TWR. The cost we pay is the overhead of the time stamp management for all data objects. This overhead can be reduced by efficient time-stamp-management techniques [Bern87].

The CA protocol is summarized as follows:

(1)　When the local before-count of an agent changes from one to zero or from zero to one, it reports the change to the home agent.

(2)　When the home agent knows that the local before-counts of all agents are zero, it sends a Try-Commit message to all agents, along with the site addresses of all participating agents.

(3)　Upon receiving Try-Commit, an agent does the following:

If the local before-count or after-count is not zero, the agent sends Attempt-Fail to the home agent and to all other agents and terminates the CA process.

If the local before-count and after-count are zero, but at least one transaction in the before-trans-set is in the semicommitted state, the agent waits until no transaction in the before-trans-set is in the semicommitted state. While it is waiting, if its before-count or its after-count is increased, the agent immediately sends Attempt-Fail to the home agent as well as all to other agents and terminates this CA process.

If the local before-count and after-count are zero, and no transaction in the before-trans-set is in the semicommitted phase, the agent switches into the semicommitted state, increases the after-count of all the transactions in the before-trans-set, if they are neither committed nor aborted, and sends Ready and max_ts back to the home agent.

(4)　As soon as an agent receives Attempt-Fail from any other agent, the CA process is terminated, and it switches out of the semicommitted state to wait for the next Try-Commit message.

(5)　Upon receiving Attempt-Fail, the home agent stops the CA process and keeps on waiting for the next chance to initiate the CA process.

(6)　If the home agent receives Ready from all agents, it sends Commit and the unique final time stamp to all of them. The time stamp is greater than the max_ts of any agent.

(7)　Upon receiving Commit and the final time stamp, an agent switches into the write phase and changes its max_ts if its max_ts is less than its final time stamp.

(8)   Whenever an agent gets out of the semicommitted state, it decreases the after-count of the active transactions in its before-trans-set if they have been increased by this agent. (The agent may exit the CA process after incrementing only some of the after-count when it finds a transaction in its before-trans-set to be in the semicommitted state.)

Note that the home agent does all the work of a normal agent besides its coordinating work.

Messages may be delayed and not arrive in the order in which they are sent. This may cause serious problems. For example, an agent may receive an ATTEMPT-FAIL message of an earlier CA invocation after it sends out the READY message for this invocation. It then mistakenly exits the semicommitted state before it receives the COMMIT message of this invocation from the home agent. In order to avoid such a problem, the home agent assigns the number n to the nth invocation of the CA protocol. All messages of that CA process contain this invocation number, so that the message receiver can always know if the message is the right one. Whenever a message with a new invocation number is received, the agent switches to the new CA process immediately.

Conclusions and further work

In this paper, we describe characteristics of real-time database systems such as correctness constraints, predictability, and performance goals. We address the issues associated with transaction scheduling and concurrency control for real-time database systems. We focus on the operation-scheduling aspect of time-critical scheduling and introduce an integrated scheduler for conflict resolution that integrates a priority-based locking with an optimistic approach. This integrated scheduler is a priority-based concurrency control mechanism for real-time database systems. In the integrated scheduler, the execution of a transaction is divided into read, wait, and write phases, in a way similar to that used in optimistic concurrency control mechanisms. By delaying write operations of transactions, the restrictions imposed by past execution sequences on the serialization order can be relaxed. We introduce the priority-dependent locking protocol, which dynamically adjusts the serialization order of active transactions. We assume that the priority of a transaction reflects its timing constraints such as deadline and criticality. The 2PL protocol is used for read-write conflicts and the TWR is used for write-write conflicts. The integrated scheduler makes it possible for transactions with high priorities to be executed first, so that higher priority transactions are never blocked by uncommitted lower priority ones. That is, a high-priority transaction is scheduled to commit before a low-priority transaction, except when a low-priority transaction has already committed and is in the write phase.

Also, this integrated scheduler incurs less blocking and aborts than the 2PL protocol with the high-priority scheme [Abbo92]. It can reduce the number of late restarts and the number of conflicting transactions compared to the Wait-50 protocol [Hari90a], because it analyzes read-write conflicts among transactions as early as possible and resolves them by giving preference to higher priority transactions without unnecessarily delaying conflict resolution. It features the ability to allow transactions to meet their timing constraints as much as possible, without reducing the concurrency level of the system. It works in applications that require handling of unpredictable data.

Using a detailed simulation model of an RTDBS, we studied the performance of the real-time locking protocol over a wide range of workloads and data access patterns. We showed that system performance can be significantly improved with the real-time locking protocol, in conjunction with a time-critical transaction-scheduling policy.

The protocol has been extended to distributed database systems. We are currently working on the performance evaluation of the distributed protocol using a database-prototyping system. We intend to look into issues to improve the integrated scheduler, such as the problems arising from dynamic priority assignment, the overhead of aborting a transaction in the read phase, and time-critical CPU scheduling with predictable execution time.

Acknowledgments

This work was supported in part by the Office of Naval Research under grant N00014-88-K-0245, in part by CIT contract CIT-INF-90-011, and in part by IBM Federal Systems Division.

References

[Abbo92] R. Abbott and H. Garcia-Molina, "Scheduling Real-Time Transactions: A Performance Evaluation," *ACM Trans. Database Systems*, Vol. 17, No. 3, Sept. 1992, pp. 513-560.

[ACM88] *ACM SIGMOD Record*, Vol. 17, No. 1, Mar. 1988 (special issue on real-time database systems).

[Agra87] R. Argrawal et al., "Concurrency Control Performance Modeling: Alternatives and Implications," *ACM Trans. Database Systems*, Vol. 12, No. 4, Dec. 1987, pp. 609-654.

[Baba90] O. Babaoglu, K. Marzullo, and F. Schneider, "Priority Inversion and Its Prevention," tech. report, Dept. of Computer Science, Cornell Univ., Ithaca, N.Y., 1990.

[Bern87] P. Bernstein, V. Hadzilacos, and N. Goodman, *Concurrency Control and Recovery in Database Systems*, Addison-Wesley Pub. Co., Reading, Mass., 1987.

[Boks87] C. Boksenbaum et al., "Concurrent Certifications by Intervals of Timestamps in Distributed Database Systems," *IEEE Trans. Software Eng.*, Vol. SE-13, No. 4, Apr. 1987, pp. 409-419.

[Buch89] A.P. Buchmann et al., "Time-Critical Database Scheduling: A Framework for Integrating Real-Time Scheduling and Concurrency Control," *Proc. Fifth Int'l Conf. Data Eng.*, IEEE Computer Soc. Press, Los Alamitos, Calif., 1989, pp. 470-480.

[Garc83] H. Garcia-Molina, "Using Semantic Knowledge for Transaction Processing in a Distributed Database," *ACM Trans. Database Systems*, Vol. 8, No. 2, June 1983, pp. 186-213.

[Hari90a] J.R. Haritsa, M.J. Carey, and M. Livny, "Dynamic Real-Time Optimistic Concurrency Control," *Proc. Real-Time Systems Symp.*, IEEE Computer Soc. Press, Los Alamitos, Calif., 1990, pp. 94-103.

[Hari90b] J. Haritsa, M. Carey, and M. Livny, "On Being Optimistic on Real-Time Constraints," Tech. Report TR 906, Department of Computer Science, Univ. of Wisconsin, Wisc., 1990.

[IEEE90] *Proc. Seventh IEEE Workshop Real-Time Operating Systems and Software*, IEEE Computer Society Press, Los Alamitos, Calif., 1990.

[Kung81] H. Kung and J. Robinson, "On Optimistic Methods for Concurrency Control," *ACM Trans. Database Systems*, Vol. 6, No. 2, June 1981, pp. 213-226.

[Kort90] H. Korth, "Triggered Real-Time Databases with Consistency Constraints," *Proc. Conf. Very Large Data Bases (VLDB)*, 1990.

[Lin89] K.-J. Lin, "Consistency Issues in Real-Time Database Systems," *Proc. 22nd Ann. Hawaii Int'l Conf. System Sciences*, IEEE Computer Soc. Press, Los Alamitos, Calif., 1989, pp. 654-661.

[Lin90] Y. Lin and S.H. Son, "Concurrency Control in Real-Time Databases by Dynamic Adjustment of Serialization Order," *Proc. Real-Time Systems Symp.*, IEEE Computer Soc. Press, Los Alamitos, Calif., 1990, pp. 104-112.

[Liu88] J.W.S. Liu, K.J. Lin, and X. Song, "Scheduling Hard Real-Time Transactions," *Proc. Fifth IEEE Workshop Real-Time Operating Systems and Software*, IEEE Computer Society, Washington, D.C., 1988, pp. 112-260.

[ONR90] *Proc. ONR Workshop Foundations Real-Time Computing*, Office of Naval Research, Washington, D.C., 1990.

[Sha88] L. Sha, R. Rajkumar, and J. Lehoczky, "Concurrency Control for Distributed Real-Time Databases," *ACM SIGMOD Record*, Vol. 17, No. 1, Mar. 1988, pp. 82-98.

[Sha91]   L. Sha et al., "A Real-Time Locking Protocol," *IEEE Trans. Computers*, Vol. 40, No. 7, July 1991, pp. 782-800.

[Son88]   S.H. Son, "Semantic Information and Consistency in Distributed Real-Time Systems," *Information and Software Technology*, Vol. 30, No. 7, Sept. 1988, pp. 443-449.

[Son89]   S.H. Son, "On Priority-Based Synchronization Protocols for Distributed Real-Time Database Systems," *Proc. IFAC/IFIP Workshop Distributed Databases Real-Time Control*, Int'l Federation of Automatic Control, Budapest, Hungary, 1989, pp. 67-72.

[Son90a]   S.H. Son and N. Haghighi, "Performance Evaluation of Multiversion Database Systems," *Proc. Sixth Int'l Conf. Data Eng.*, IEEE Computer Soc. Press, Los Alamitos, Calif., 1990, pp. 129-136.

[Son90b]   S.H. Son and J. Lee, "Scheduling Real-Time Transactions in Distributed Database Systems," *Proc. Seventh IEEE Workshop Real-Time Operating Systems and Software*, IEEE Computer Soc. Press, Los Alamitos, Calif. 1990, pp. 39-43.

[Son90c]   S.H. Son and C.-H. Chang, "Performance Evaluation of Real-Time Locking Protocols Using a Distributed Software Prototyping Environment," *Proc. 10th Int'l Conf. Distributed Computing Systems*, IEEE Computer Soc. Press, Los Alamitos, Calif., 1990, pp. 124-131.

[Song90]   X. Song and J.W.S. Liu, "Performance of Multiversion Concurrency Control Algorithms in Maintaining Temporal Consistency," *Proc. 14th Ann. Int'l Computer Software and Applications Conf. (COMPSAC 90)*, IEEE Computer Soc. Press, Los Alamitos, Calif., 1990, pp. 132-139.

[Stan88]   J.A. Stankovic, "Misconceptions about Real-Time Computing: A Serious Problem for Next-Generation Systems," *Computer*, Vol. 21, No. 10, Oct. 1988, pp. 10-19.

[Vrbs88]   S.V. Vrbsky and K.-J. Lin, "Recovering Imprecise Transactions with Real-Time Constraints," *Proc. Symp. Reliable Distributed Systems*, IEEE Computer Soc. Press, Los Alamitos, Calif., 1988, pp. 185-193.

[Yu90]   P.S. Yu and D.M. Dias, "Concurrency Control Using Locking with Deferred Blocking," *Proc. Sixth Int'l Conf. Data Eng.*, IEEE Computer Soc. Press, Los Alamitos, Calif., 1990, pp. 30-36.

[Zhao87]   W. Zhao, K. Ramamritham, and J.A. Stankovic, "Preemptive Scheduling under Time and Resource Constraints," *IEEE Trans. Computers*, Vol. C-36, No. 8, Aug. 1987, pp. 949-960.

Author Profiles

T homas L. Casavant is an associate professor of electrical and computer engineering at the University of Iowa, where he is also director of the Parallel Processing Laboratory. He is currently on sabbatical at the Swiss Federal Institute of Technology in Zurich. Previously, he was on the faculty at Purdue University, where he was also director of the PASM Parallel Processing Project and the Electrical Engineering School's Parallel Processing Laboratory.

Casavant has published over 50 technical papers on parallel and distributed computing. He is an associate editor for the *Journal of Parallel and Distributed Computing* and has served as a guest editor for *Computer* and the *Journal of Parallel and Distributed Computing*.

His research interests include distributed multiprocessor systems, load-balancing-based scheduling algorithms, parallel computer architecture and systems, programming tools for parallel/distributed computing, graph theory, and distributed algorithm modeling, routing, and task management in parallel systems. He designed and implemented an operating system for a point-to-point network of workstations that behave as a single, integrated, transparent multiprocessor.

Casavant received the BS degree in computer science and the MS and PhD degrees in electrical and computer engineering from the University of Iowa in 1982, 1983, and 1986, respectively. He is a member of the IEEE Computer Society and the Association for Computing Machinery.

M ukesh Singhal is an associate professor of computer and information science at Ohio State University. He has published in *Computer, IEEE Transactions on Computers, IEEE Transactions on Software Engineering, IEEE Transactions on Knowledge and Data Engineering, IEEE Transactions on Parallel and Distributed Systems, Journal of Parallel and Distributed Computing, Performance Evaluation, Information Processing Letters, Information Science,* and *Distributed Computing*. He coauthored a book entitled *Advanced Concepts in Operating Systems*, published by McGraw-Hill.

His research interests include distributed systems, operating systems, databases, and performance modeling.

Singhal received the BE degree in electronics and communication engineering from the University of Roorkee, India, in 1980 and the PhD degree in computer science from the University of Maryland, College Park, in 1986. He is a member of the IEEE Computer Society.

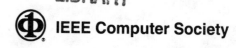

IEEE Computer Society

IEEE Computer Society Press Publications

Monographs: A monograph is an authored book consisting of 100-percent original material.

Tutorials: A tutorial is a collection of original materials prepared by the editors and reprints of the best articles published in a subject area. Tutorials must contain at least five percent of original material (although we recommend 15 to 20 percent of original material).

Reprint collections: A reprint collection contains reprints (divided into sections) with a preface, table of contents, and section introductions discussing the reprints and why they were selected. Collections contain less than five percent of original material.

Technology series: Each technology series is a brief reprint collection — approximately 126-136 pages and containing 12 to 13 papers, each paper focusing on a subset of a specific discipline, such as networks, architecture, software, or robotics.

Submission of proposals: For guidelines on preparing CS Press books, write the Managing Editor, IEEE Computer Society Press, PO Box 3014, 10662 Los Vaqueros Circle, Los Alamitos, CA 90720-1264, or telephone (714) 821-8380.

Purpose

The IEEE Computer Society advances the theory and practice of computer science and engineering, promotes the exchange of technical information among 100,000 members worldwide, and provides a wide range of services to members and nonmembers.

Membership

All members receive the acclaimed monthly magazine *Computer*, discounts, and opportunities to serve (all activities are led by volunteer members). Membership is open to all IEEE members, affiliate society members, and others seriously interested in the computer field.

Publications and Activities

Computer **magazine:** An authoritative, easy-to-read magazine containing tutorials and in-depth articles on topics across the computer field, plus news, conference reports, book reviews, calendars, calls for papers, interviews, and new products.

Periodicals: The society publishes six magazines and five research transactions. For more details, refer to our membership application or request information as noted above.

Conference proceedings, tutorial texts, and standards documents: The IEEE Computer Society Press publishes more than 100 titles every year.

Standards working groups: Over 100 of these groups produce IEEE standards used throughout the industrial world.

Technical committees: Over 30 TCs publish newsletters, provide interaction with peers in specialty areas, and directly influence standards, conferences, and education.

Conferences/Education: The society holds about 100 conferences each year and sponsors many educational activities, including computing science accreditation.

Chapters: Regular and student chapters worldwide provide the opportunity to interact with colleagues, hear technical experts, and serve the local professional community.